IMAGES
of America

PROVINCETOWN
VOLUME II

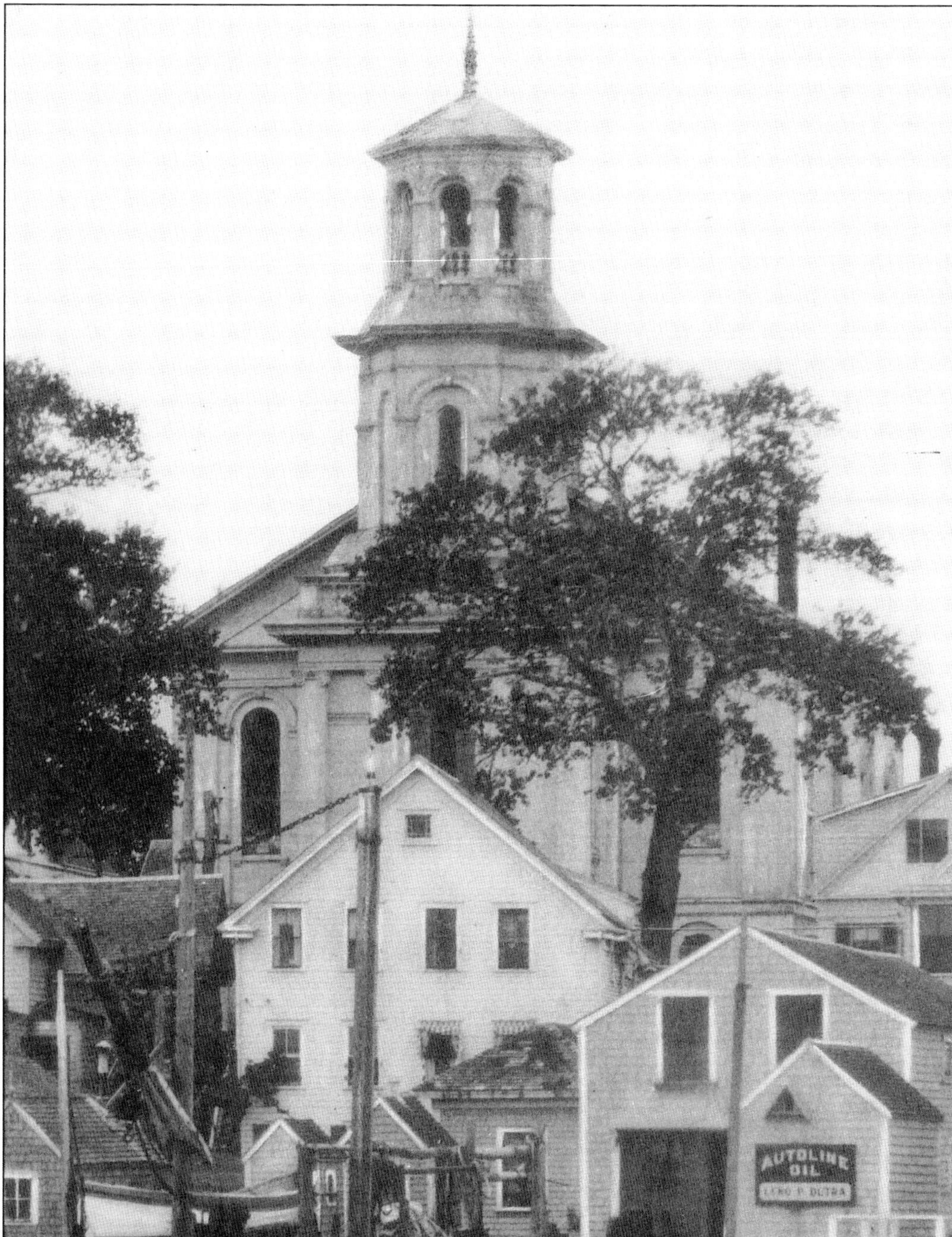

A Bit of Provincetown (c. 1935 postcard published by The Town Crier Shop, Provincetown). Even without the full complement of its 162-foot steeple—taken down after the horrific Portland Gale of 1898—the Classical-style former Center Methodist Episcopal Church (built in 1860, now the Provincetown Heritage Museum) has stood sentry as a landmark over the densely built residences, restaurants, stores, and boat and fishing shacks along busy Commercial Street near the center of town.

IMAGES
of America

PROVINCETOWN
VOLUME II

John Hardy Wright

ARCADIA
PUBLISHING

ISBN 978-0-7385-9027-1

Published by Arcadia Publishing
Charleston, South Carolina

Printed in the United States of America

Library of Congress Catalog Card Number: 98-85879

For all general information contact Arcadia Publishing at:
Telephone 843-853-2070
Fax 843-853-0044
E-mail sales@arcadiapublishing.com
For customer service and orders:
Toll-Free 1-888-313-2665

Visit us on the Internet at www.arcadiapublishing.com

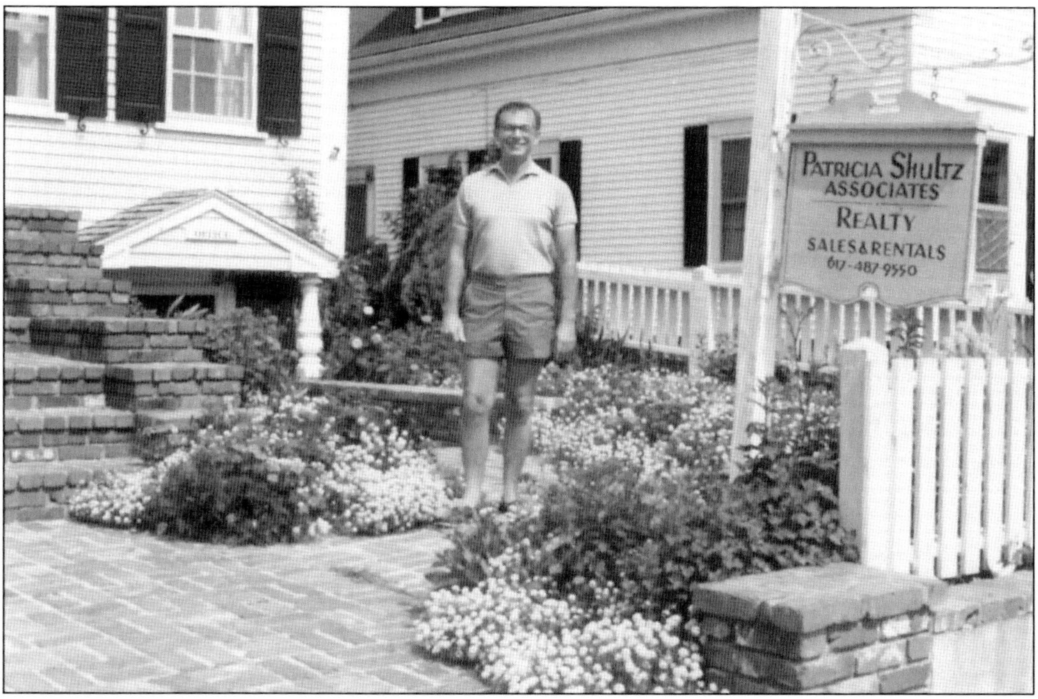

This book is dedicated to the memory of Ed Dugas, an interior designer from Baton Rouge, Louisiana, who visited Provincetown once during the summer of 1982 with Oklahoman cousins Sandra Maxwell and Max Lee, and who fell in love with the town as did the author more than 30 summers ago.

Contents

Acknowledgments

People who live in Provincetown now, or who were past residents, and who know the town more intimately than the author, and others who have helped in one tremendous way or another, are Jack Barnett, James A. Bayard, Laurie Greenbaum Beitch, Robert Belletzkie (whose commentary was most helpful), Gabriel Brooke, Howard M. Bushnell, Jamie (Curci) Carter, Peter Coes, Ken Conrad, James Cote, Dan DePalma, Charles P. Duffy, Leona Rust Egan, Ann Lindenmuth Fisk, Frank W. Ford, F. Ronald Fowler, Robert F. Gilbert, Samuel H. Graybill Jr., Kenneth Gregory, Arthur Griffin, Elena Curtis Hall, Frederick Hemley, Jack Hofflander, Donald Howie, Peter B. Little, George Littrell, Michael Lussier, Norman Mailer, Bryan McMullin, JoAnn S. Mooy, Len Paoletti, Joseph A. Peters, Eugenia A. Rogers, Francis E. and Irene Santos, Stephen J. Schier, Al Stilson, Daniel Towler, Napi Vandereck, Emery K. Warner, Thelma E. Wiley, and Michael Young. Local historian Bonnie Steele McGhee's ongoing research and future publication on the evolution of the town's wharves proved most helpful in determining what was located where and for how long. People who are employed by institutions or who are their own bosses also deserve to be mentioned for their assistance, and they are Mary-Jo Avellar (*Provincetown Advocate*), Ronald Bourgeault and Dennis Radulski (Northeast Auctions, Hampton, NH), William Burke (park historian, National Park Service, Cape Cod National Seashore, So. Wellfleet, MA), Jay Caldwell (The Caldwell Gallery, Manlius, NY), Stephen Campbell Management (Beverly Hills, CA), James Crawford (curator, Canajoharie Library and Art Gallery, Canajoharie, NY), Debra deJonker-Berry, Lu Hetlyn, and Beverly Whitbeck (director, assistant director, and children's librarian, Provincetown Public Library), Annette Fern (research and reference librarian, The Harvard Theatre Collection, The Houghton Library, Harvard University, Cambridge, MA), William Fitzpatrick (West End Antiques, Provincetown), Kathy M. Flynn (photography department, Peabody Essex Museum, Salem, MA), David H. Hall (Boston, MA), Julie Heller (Julie Heller Gallery, Provincetown), D. Roger Howlett and Judith Ocker Schulze (Childs Gallery, Boston, MA), Patricia Kane (curator, American Decorative Arts, Yale University Art Gallery, New Haven, CT), Robert E. Landry and Peter L. Combs (Landry Antiques, Essex, MA), Jeffory Morris (curator, Pilgrim Monument & Provincetown Museum), John K. Roderick (president, Seamen's Bank, Provincetown), Kenneth C. Turino (director, Lynn Historical Society, Lynn, MA), Abbot W. and Robert C. Vose III (Vose Galleries of Boston, Inc.), and Robyn Watson and James Zimmerman (director and photography archivist, Provincetown Art Association and Museum).

The indices of books in the "Gay and Lesbian Studies" section of major bookstores make little or no reference to Provincetown. Information for the chapters on "Entertainers" and "Alternative Lifestyles" in this book has been garnered from oral history interviews with people who have resided in Provincetown during the period under consideration. This book could <u>not</u> have been written without the various anecdotes of many aforementioned individuals. Very special thanks to Mr. and Mrs. H.H. ("Skip" and Arpina E.) Stanton, whose collection of personally autographed studio photographs of entertainers is a reflection of their past rapport and fondness for them, almost all of whom are, sadly, no longer alive.

Introduction

Every year, the gay and the free flock here [Provincetown] for a vacation. They flutter about the shore like sea gulls. They join the art classes. They pose for reporters and their pictures appear in the write-ups of "Quaint Provincetown." They fly away early. The Artists and the Natives go on undiscovered.

—Nancy W. Paine Smith, *A Book About the Artists*, 1927.

As early as 1856 a contributor to *Gleason's Pictorial Drawing-Room Companion* wrote that Provincetown "has become during the summer the resort of a great many strangers, for the purposes of fishing and inhaling the invigorating sea breezes." Fishing and whaling did sustain the inhabitants over the first centuries of the town's history. Provincetown, which is still part of the Province Lands, was founded in 1727, but the artists Mrs. Smith mentioned did not arrive in town until the late 19th century. Before 1900 the first of several successive art schools had been established. Singularly, or in groups of varying sizes, artists appeared on the beaches in summer to paint the colorful Portuguese fishermen and dock workers, their families, and their fishing vessels, or models seated under polychrome beach umbrellas. Playwrights and authors followed the great migration of artists to the tip of Cape Cod before World War I shattered the world's peace. During the late 19th century tourism began increasingly to supplant fishing as an economic base for the picturesque town. Today tourism is the mainstay as there are less than two dozen active fishing vessels with local connections. Tourists include many day-trippers who, more often than not, arrive by ferry from Boston for a frenzied three-hour visit. A reporter for the *Boston Herald* wrote an article on the town in August 1941, the title and by-line of which read as follows: "Provincetown is Famous For Art, Fishing, Sand Dunes. Hasty Visitors Find Only Carnival, Those Who Linger, Town of Charm." The carnival aspect, however, is part of the town's character, and can be attributed to the influx of artistic types, Bohemians, hippies, bikers, gays, and Lesbians, and others in search of personal or creative freedom. Each group has added to the town's flavor for good or bad, according to those whose families have resided there for generations. Over the decades men and women who have espoused alternative lifestyles—frequently with a spouse of the same sex—have melded with the descendants of the white Anglo-Saxon Protestants, the Irish Catholics, and the Latin cultures of the Portuguese and Cape Verdeans. And almost everybody loves to watch a parade, which is what downtown Commercial Street becomes during many happenings, scheduled and impromptu, all year.

Provincetown is certainly a special, atypical Cape Cod community, one that is very trendy and alive and yet still possesses a strong link to its historic and cultural roots.

Author's Note: The architecture and related aspects of Provincetown's history appear in *Provincetown Volume I*, published in 1997. In this sequel the contents of the first three chapters are arranged for the most part from left to right—from the West to the East End of town—for the benefit of townspeople and tourists alike.

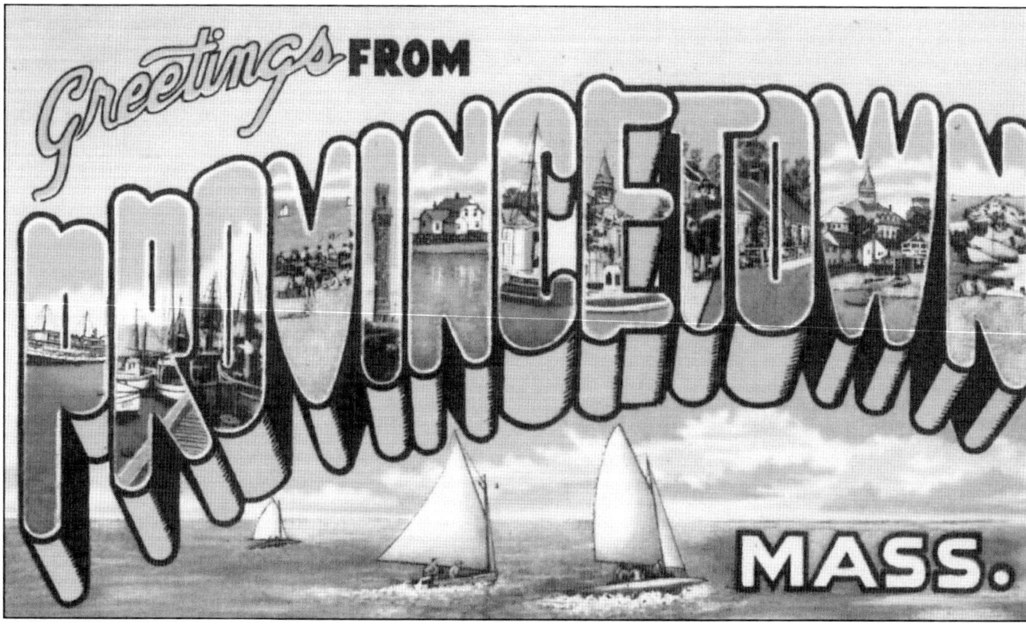

Greetings from Provincetown, Mass. (c. 1940 postcard published by Genuine Curteich, Chicago, IL). Twelve mini-vignettes of local sites or activities appear in the three-dimensional rounded letters of this polychrome postcard with a "linen" surface. While visiting in June, the correspondent wrote to friends, "Here we are in Provincetown & it is so beautiful. . . . We watched the fishing fleet go out today & went up in the Pilgrim Monument. We have a beautiful cabin with a private beach right on Provincetown Harbor."

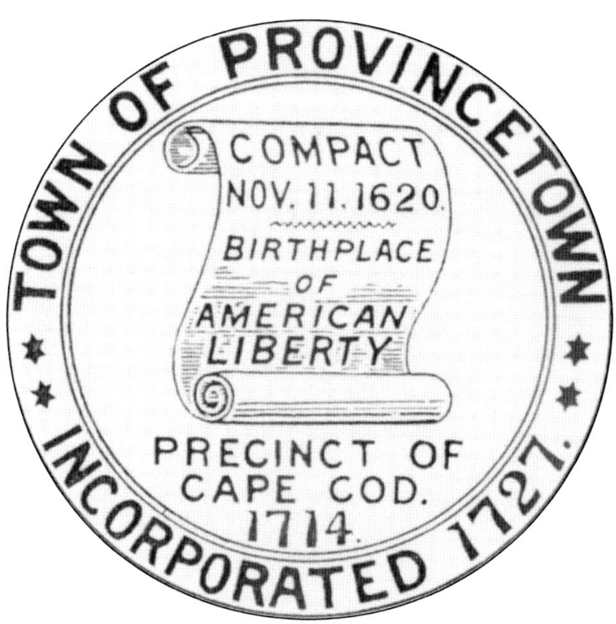

One

Shore and Harbor Views

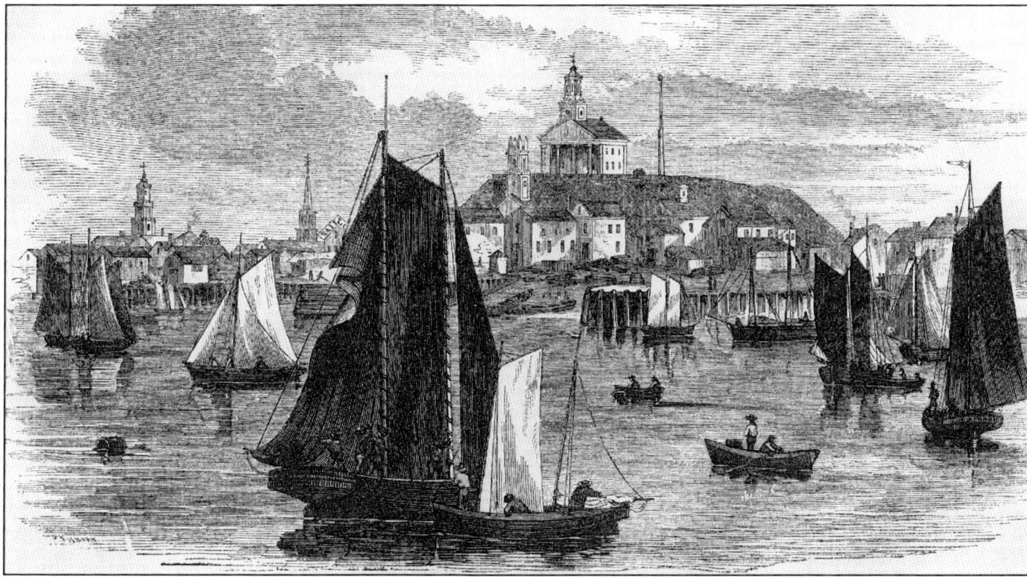

View of Provincetown (1856 wood engraving in *Gleason's Pictorial Drawing-Room Companion*). Provincetown has long been associated with the image of a scenic waterfront town and bustling harbor. During the mid- to late 19th century the first Town Hall—erected on High Pole Hill (now Monument Hill), one of seven hills in town—presided over the residences, stores, and fishing-related structures of the inhabitants, most of whom attended the three Protestant churches on Commercial Street. The Universalist church (far left) was built in 1847, and is now the oldest surviving religious edifice in town. The Congregational church (middle) was constructed in 1843; deconsecrated and without its steeple, it is located to the left of the second and present Town Hall. Infrequently depicted is the Gothic steeple of the Methodist church (right), also built in 1847. The Greek Revival Town Hall was constructed in 1853—this was probably the impetus for the engraving—but was destroyed by fire in 1877. The site was later chosen by the Cape Cod Pilgrim Memorial Association for the all-granite Pilgrim Memorial Monument, which was dedicated in 1910. A windmill for grinding corn was on this hill at one time, and shown to the right of the building is a tall mast from which warning flags were displayed for vessels at sea. (Courtesy Stephen J. Schier.)

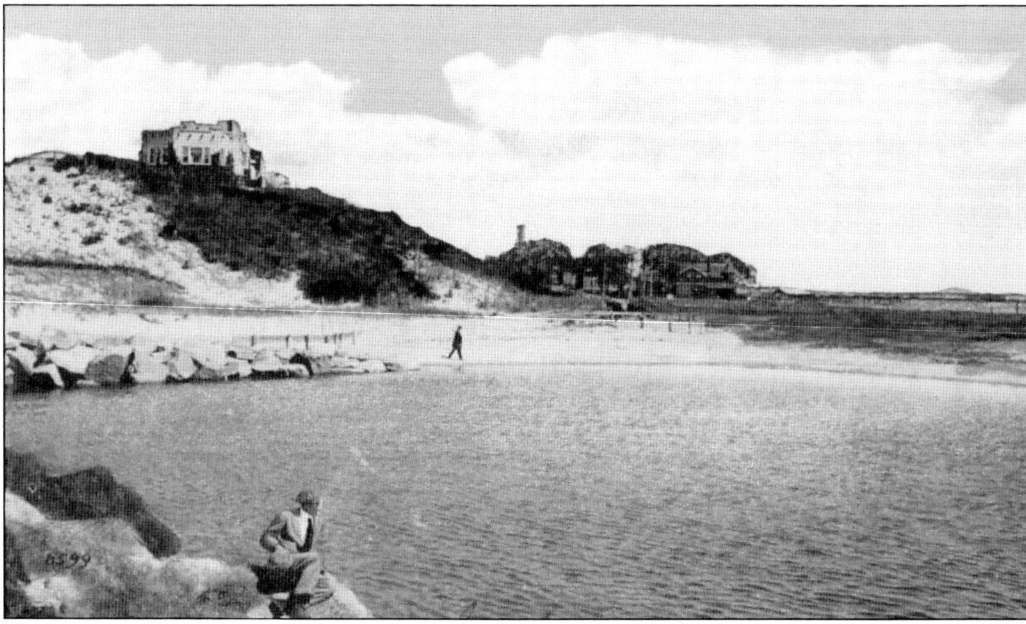

View from New Breakwater (c. 1925 postcard published by The New England News Co., Boston, MA). In 1911 the federal government paid to have the protective granite breakwater built at Land's End, the traditional "Landing Place of the Pilgrims" at the beginning of Commercial Street in the far West End. A leisurely walk over the irregular, juxtaposed granite blocks brings present-day "Pilgrims" to the outer arm of Cape Cod near Wood End Light, the middle lighthouse of three that guide navigators to Provincetown Harbor.

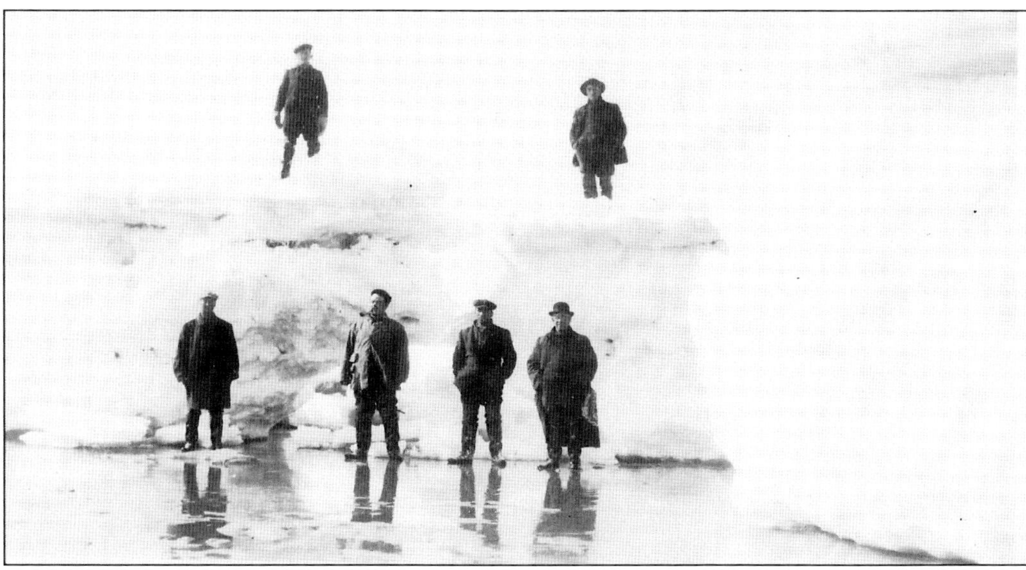

Icebergs in the West End (early-20th-century photocard; publisher unknown). Local men stand by or on "icebergs"—some have been up to 20 feet high by 8 feet thick—near the breakwater during one of many memorable Provincetown winters, such as that which occurred in 1902. Sunsets are usually magnificent in the winter; there is relatively little snow now, and often mild weather. (Courtesy Elena Curtis Hall.)

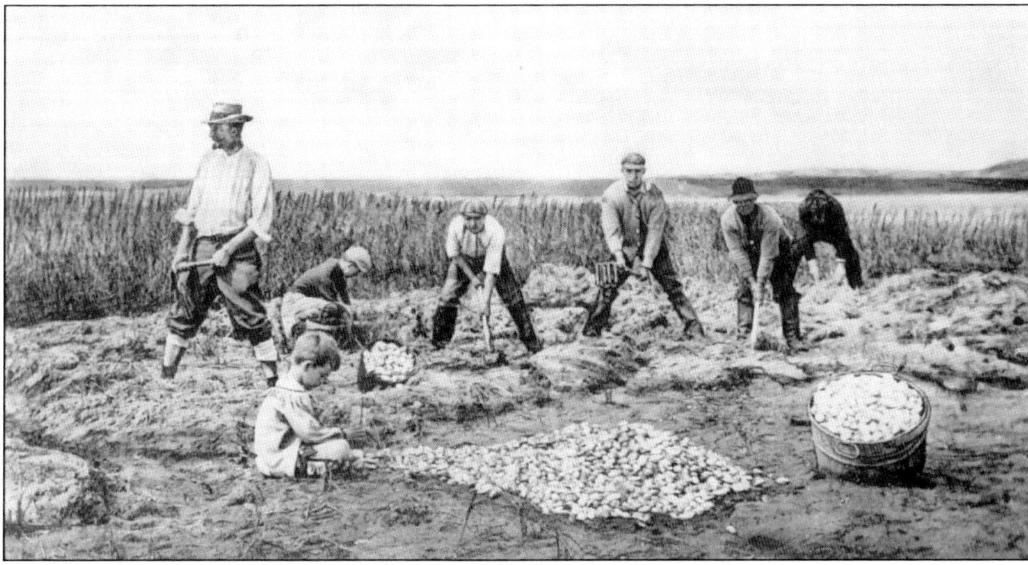

Clam Diggers (early-20th-century postcard published by the *Provincetown Advocate*, hereinafter referred to as the *Advocate*). Clamming in the West End by the breakwater was a small industry which employed young men before the advent of World War II. Around 1943 a clammer could harvest 20 buckets of the bivalve mollusks in a 24-square-foot area, but three years later two clams couldn't be found after an hour of scouring the clam flats. At Hatches Harbor (between Race Point and Herring Cove Beach), "One could pick the finest clams on this earth," recalled an elderly former clammer.

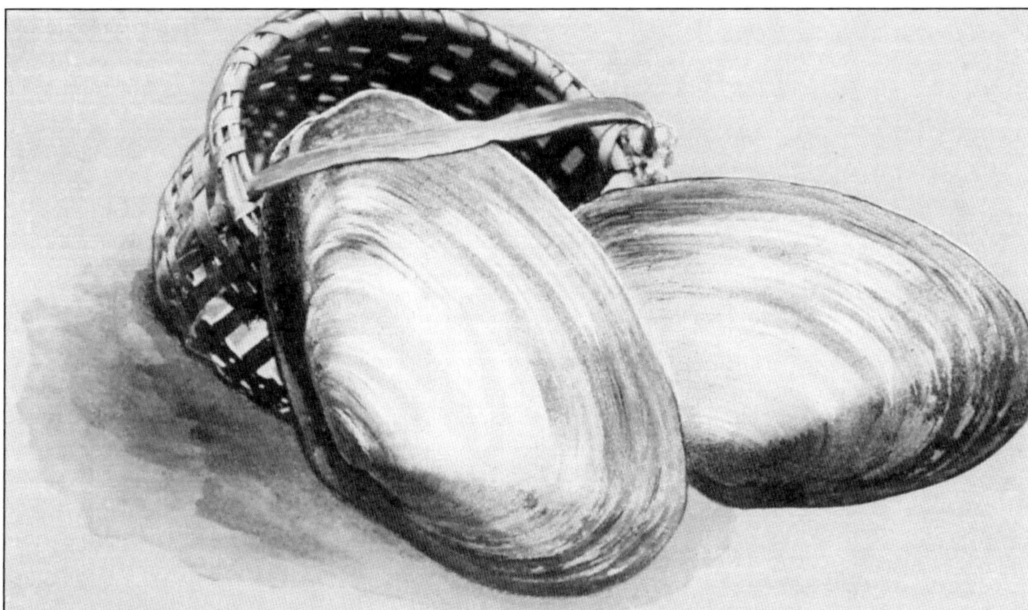

Cape Cod Fruit (c. 1920 postcard published by H.A. Dickerman & Son, Taunton, MA). This generic postcard was sent to a Provincetown visitor's friend in Maine, who was probably unaware of the local nickname for clams. "Dear Joe," wrote the correspondent, "This is the clam to use. Six at 5 cents apiece. 1/2 doz—makes a pie large enough to serve 6 people, and a clam pie is a good thing. I'd like to send you some—perhaps I can when the weather gets cool."

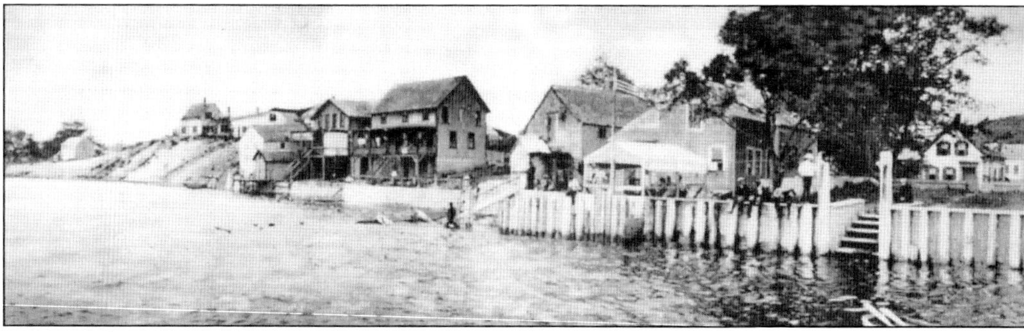

West End Cottages (early-20th-century postcard published by the *Advocate*). People who lived in or tourists who stayed in these small West End cottages could bathe off the floats or swim at low tide at nearby Ellis Bathing Beach. Chip Hill, an area near the center of Tremont Street, received its nickname from the pile of hardened chips at Nathaniel Hopkins' shipyard.

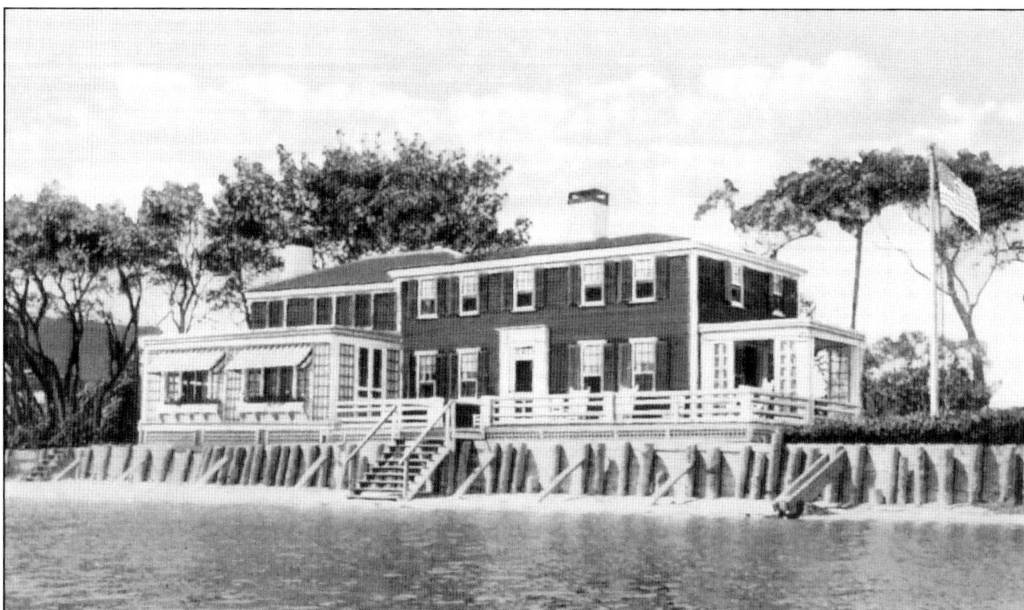

The Red Inn, 15 Commercial Street (c. 1920 postcard published by H.A. Dickerman & Son). Built in 1805 and remodeled in 1915, the Red Inn has remained a popular hostelry with a breathtaking panoramic view of the harbor looking toward the center of town, Truro, and beyond. Gull Hill, located "Way-Up-Along" (the far West End of town) on the land side of Commercial Street, was evidently named for the various types of seagulls that have inhabited the area at different times of the year. Great Black-backed, Herring (abundant in winter), Northern Gannet, and Sooty Shearwater still leave their mark in Provincetown.

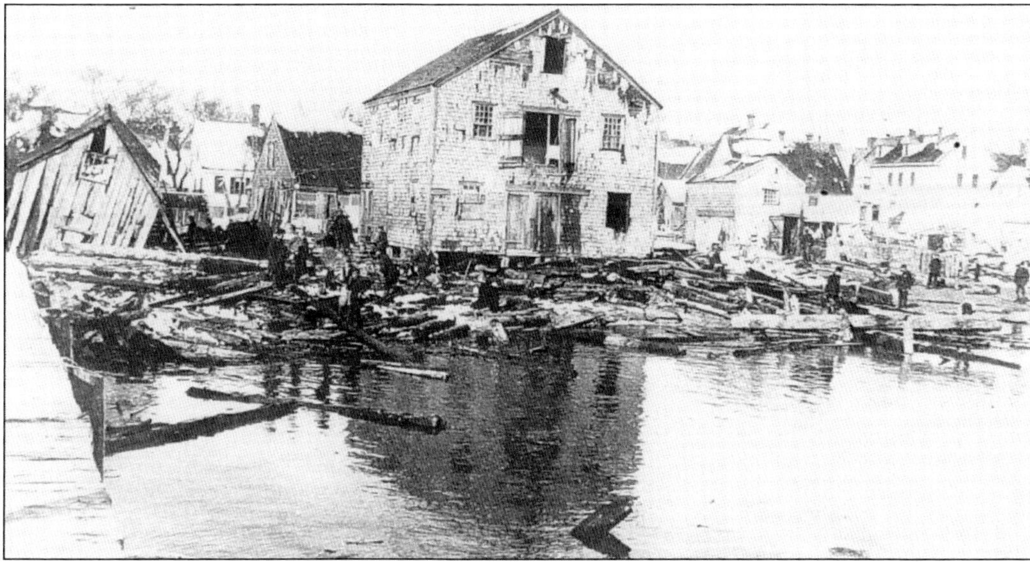

After the Portland Gale (1898 photocard; publisher unknown). A report by the U.S. Coast Guard the following year stated that the Portland Gale of November 27, 1898, was "a Cyclonic tempest, raging with unprecedented violence for twenty-four hours with gradually abating force for 12 hours longer." The gale, which turned into a blizzard, was named for the *Portland*, a side-wheel steamer that was en route from Boston to Portland, Maine, when she sank about 25 miles north of Race Point along with about 175 passengers and crew members. (Courtesy of the Cape Cod Pilgrim Memorial Association.)

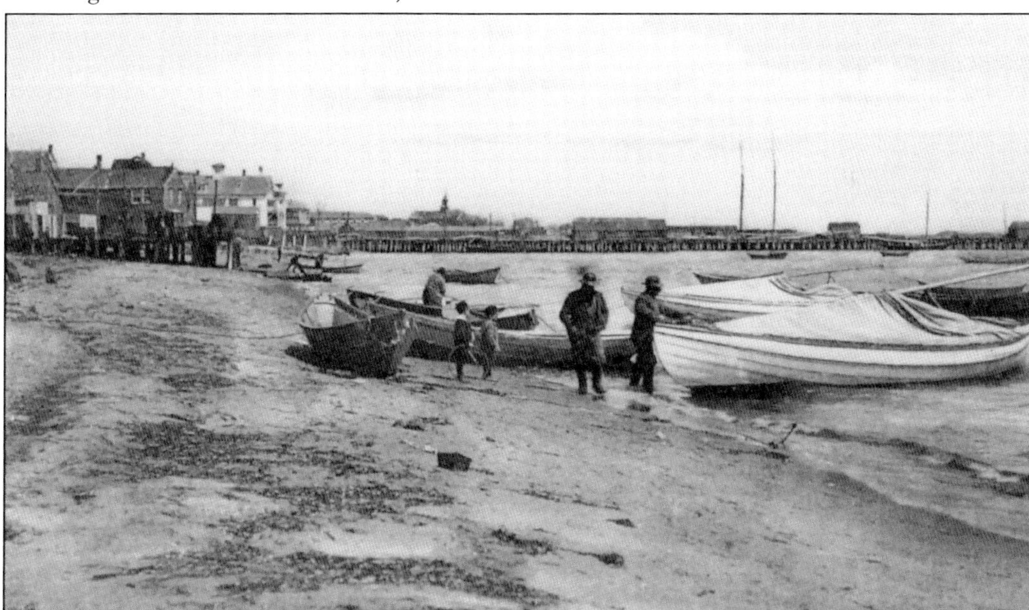

Gasolene Dones [*sic*] (early-20th-century postcard published by the *Advocate*). Two children, one with a hoop and stick (a popular 19th-century game), inspect gasolene dories along a beach. These "one-lunger" dories were used for fishing close to shore during the winter months; Portuguese fishermen called them "steamers." Many of the 29-to-42-foot dories were built in Amesbury, Massachusetts, along the Merrimack River adjacent to Newburyport.

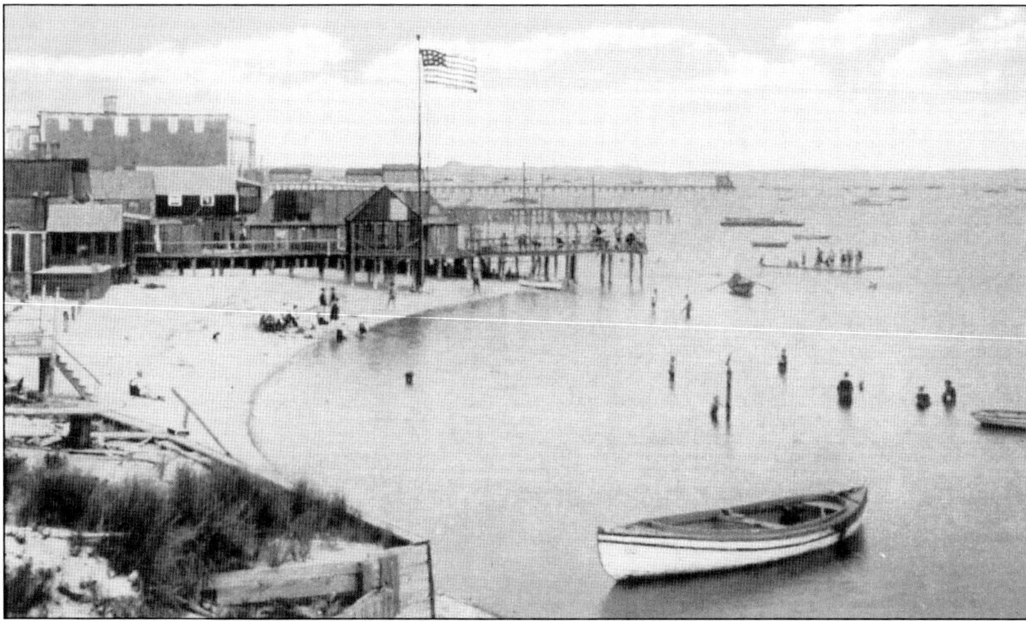

Shore View, West End (c. 1915 postcard published by E.D. West Co., South Yarmouth, Cape Cod). Bathers enjoy a tranquil dip along the crescent-shaped beach near the large, shingled Cape Cod Cold Storage plant. Before 1850 more than 70 salt works (which processed sea salt for the fishing industry) and their windmills were also strategically located along the shore, with many being in the West End.

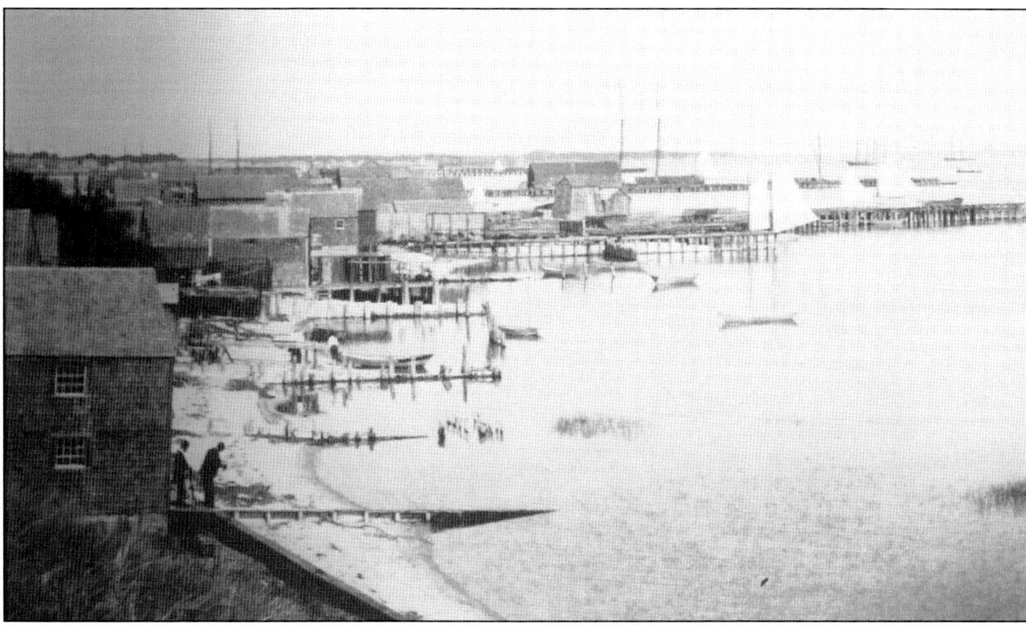

Shore Scene (c. 1916 postcard published by F.H. Dearborn, Provincetown). Union Wharf (1831), in the background at 99–101 Commercial Street, was the second wharf built in town. It was over 1,000 feet in length, and had a marine railway added to it in 1852. Around the turn of the century Andrew T. Williams operated a ship chandlery there which was called the West End Market. In the 1930s the structure was known as Furtado's Wharf.

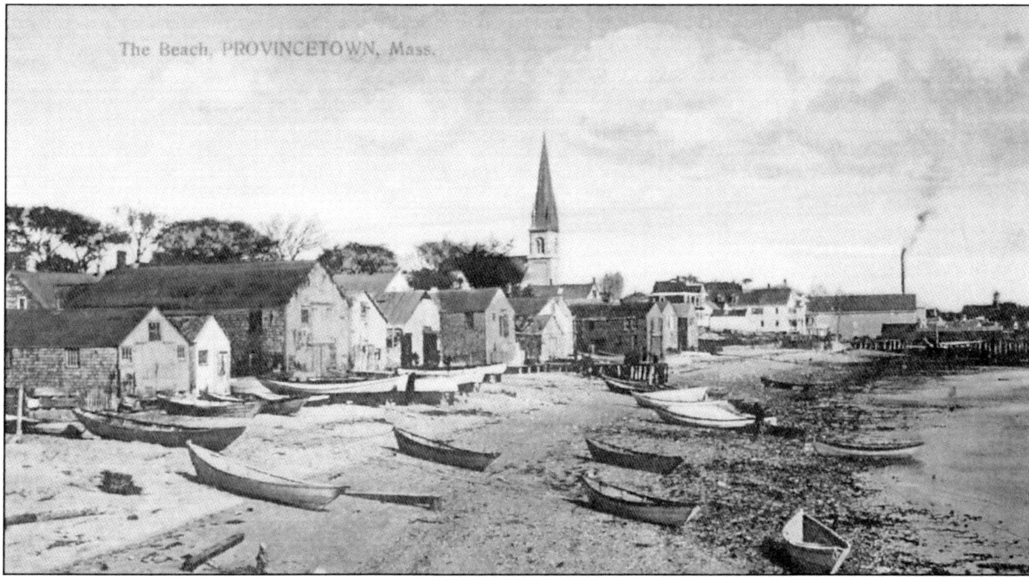

The Beach (c. 1905 postcard published by A.M.S.). Beached dories, both covered and opened, sit immobilized along with wooden debris at low tide. Most of Provincetown's 50-odd wharves were damaged or destroyed during the Portland Gale, and about 30 large vessels were beached or sunk in the harbor, causing financial devastation to the town. Shingled fishing shacks and shanties are lined up with their gable ends facing the harbor, as is the facade of the Centenary M.E. Church, built in 1866 at 170 Commercial Street, and toppled by fire in 1908.

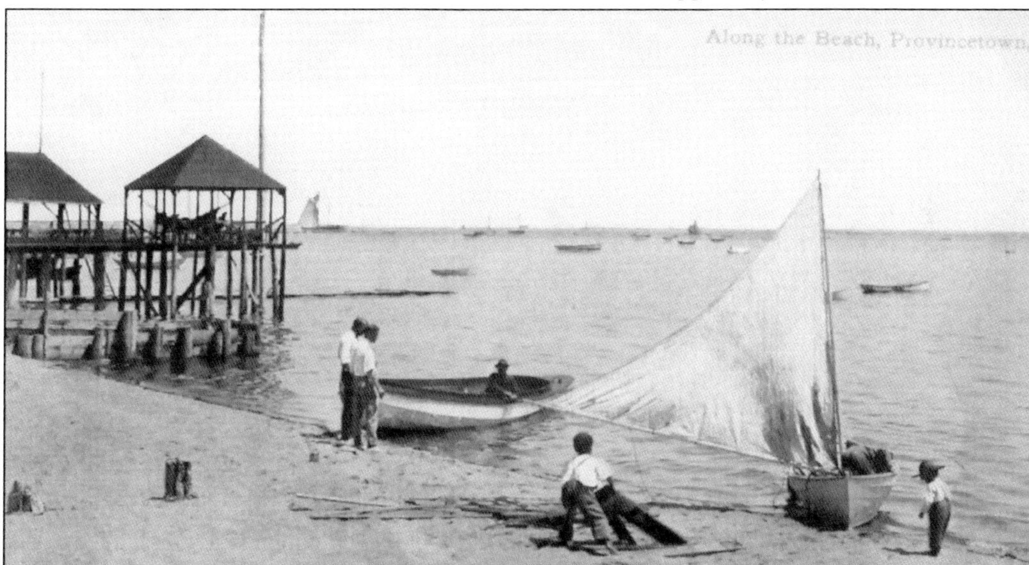

Along the Beach (early-20th-century postcard published by The Valentine & Sons Pub. Co., Inc., New York and Boston). These pavilions on high poles in the West End were a delight for those who wanted to view the shoreline or horizon in the shade or out of the rain. In 1871 during the month of August, the *Provincetown Advocate* related the following quaint tale: "a young man who went bathing last Saturday evening, lost his shirt with valuable studs attached. He no longer believes in virtuous Provincetowners, and after this proposes taking his clothing into the water with him."

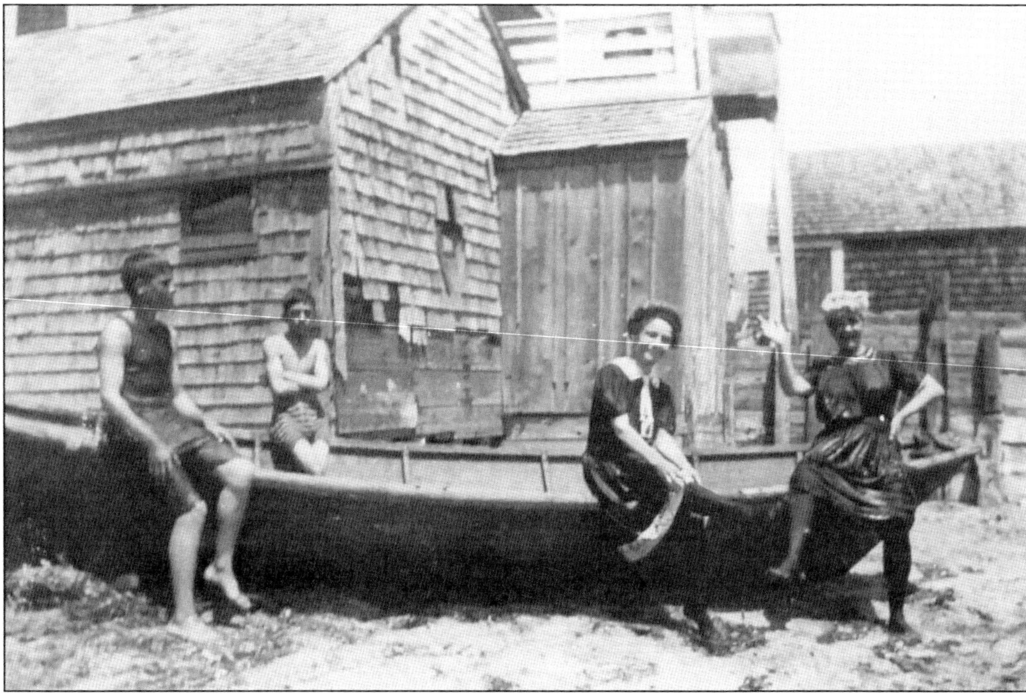

Peaches Found in Provincetown (1911 photograph). Waving while clowning around for the photographer, Annie Whitney McKennon (right) and her friend, Grace Armstrong, seem oblivious to the young men who also share the dory's sides as a perch. Miss McKennon was the great-aunt of Eugenia Ruth Atkins Rogers, who with her husband, Francis, ran the historic Norse Wall Guest House at the corner of Cottage and Tremont Streets. (Courtesy Eugenia A. Rogers.)

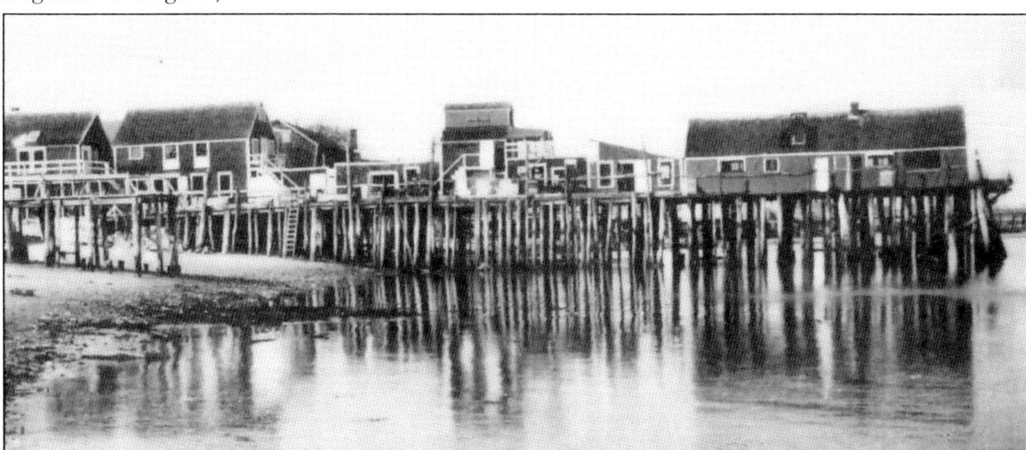

"Studios on the Sea," Capt. Jack's Wharf, 73 Commercial Street (early-20th-century postcard published by Miller & Co., Provincetown). Capt. Jack's Wharf near the foot of Nickerson Street is the most colorful surviving wharf in town with its 15 or so various added-on buildings and shacks. Local fisherman Jackson R. Williams built a 100-foot wharf in 1897, and then added another hundred feet to it a few years later. "This old citadel of fishing lore," according to the postcard caption, "delights the guest who wishes to enjoy modern comforts in the sea-going atmosphere of olden days."

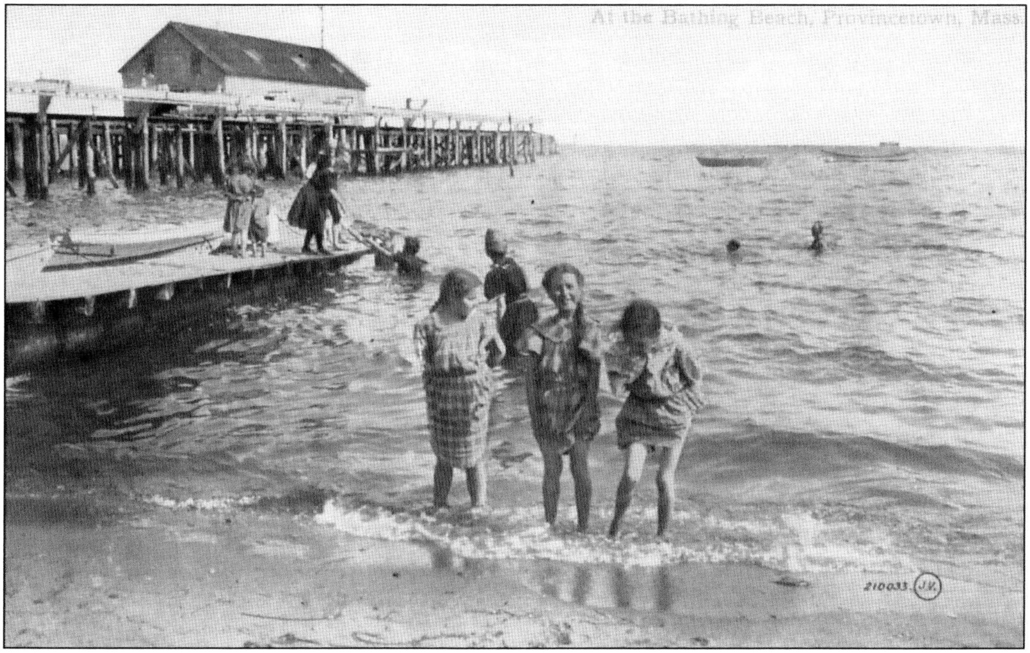

At the Bathing Beach (c. 1915 postcard published by The Valentine & Sons Co., Inc.). These three young girls playfully test the waters at Brown's Bathing Beach, perhaps at the beginning of the summer season. The beach had changing rooms, and was located near the architecturally delightful Delight Cottage (Vol. I, p. 107) at 113 Commercial Street, by the L-shaped bend at the present U.S. Coast Guard Station.

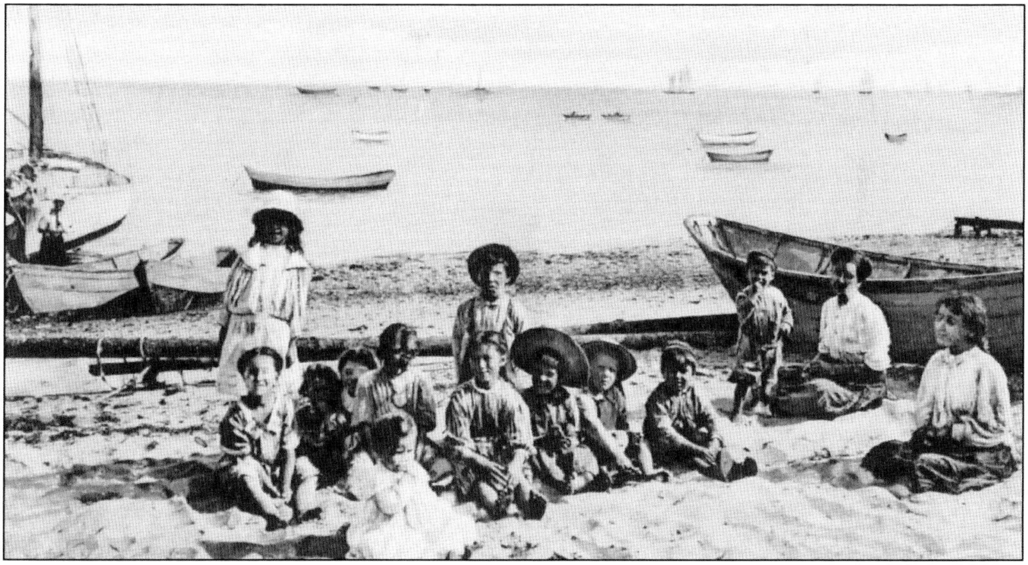

Children on the Beach (c. 1915 postcard published by The Valentine & Sons Pub. Co., Ltd.). Gleeful children gladly pose for the photographer who, then as now, may have smiled and admonished them to "Say cheese!" In her 1942 book *Time and the Town*, Mary Heaton Vorse (1874–1966) wrote that "In front of my house [in the East End] the children of the neighborhood come to swim. These children, both Portuguese and Yankee, are a different breed from the summer children who join them—so hard and so well muscled are they."

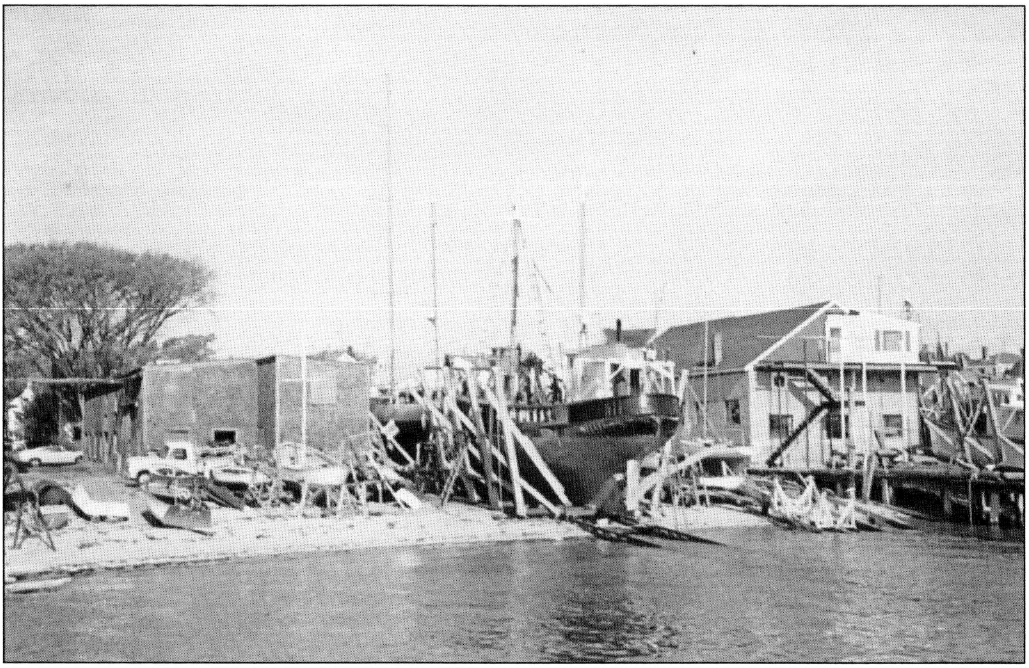

Fishing Trawler and Yachts on Marine Railways (1975 postcard published by Dexter Press, West Nyack, NY). The Cape Cod Cold Storage plant was located on the site of the aforementioned Coast Guard station, and Flyer's Boat Shop (the building at the right) is at the foot of Good Templar Place. Francis "Flyer" Santos opened his boat shop in November of 1952, and it has been the scene of much maritime activity during the following decades. Summer jobs at the cold storage plant netted workers about $10 a week in the 1950s.

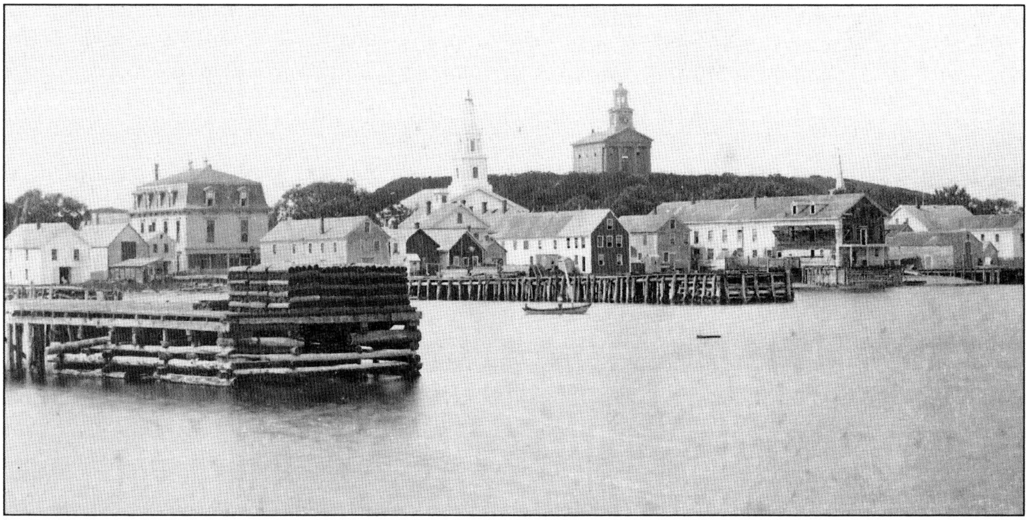

Provincetown Steamboat Wharf (c. 1875 stereopticon view photographed by George H. Nickerson). Three distinctive public buildings are silhouetted against the skyline in this early view published by one of the town's most prolific photographers. From left to right are the Second Empire Masonic Hall at 224 Commercial Street (built in 1870, it remained a three-story structure until 1973, when it was lowered one story); the Universalist church; and the first Town Hall with a clock in its tower.

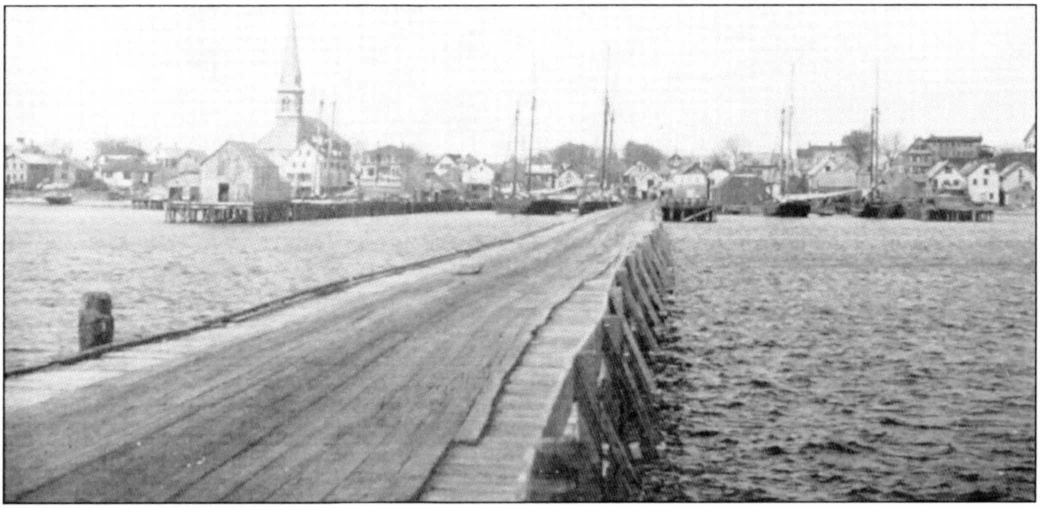

View from the Harbor (1898 photograph by The Perry Pictures Co., Malden and Boston, MA and New York). The first wharf to be built in Provincetown's noteworthy deep harbor may have been that owned by Thomas Lothrop in 1826. Steamboat Wharf (above) had been erected in 1849 as Bowley's Wharf, and by the turn of the century was also known as Matheson's Wharf for then-owner William Matheson. Located at the foot of Court Street, Steamboat Wharf accommodated early steamers and ferryboats, as has Railroad Wharf (now MacMillan Wharf) ever since.

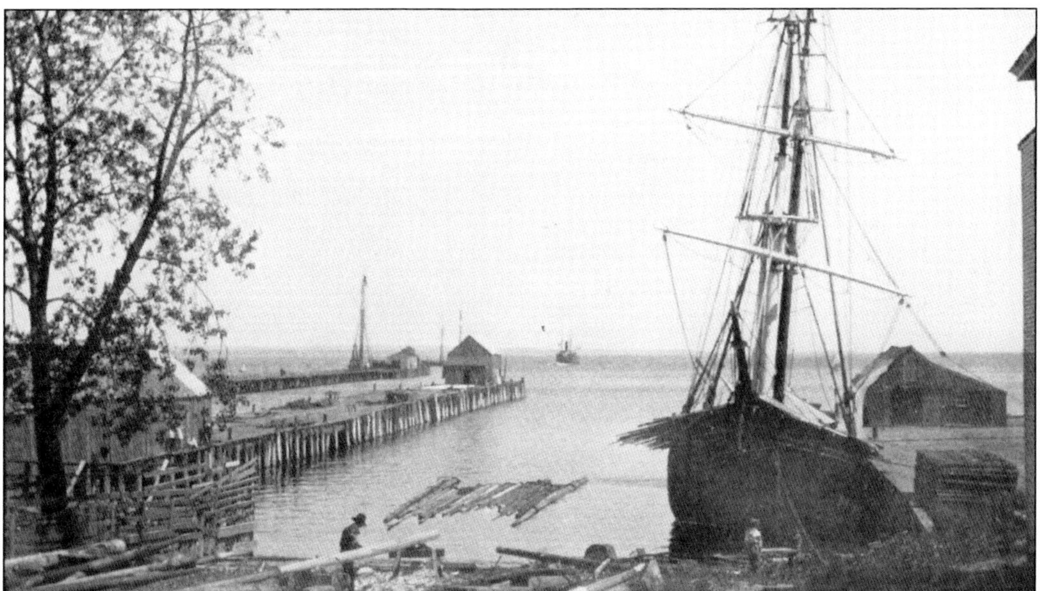

Steamboat *Longfellow* Approaching the Wharf (1898 photograph by The Perry Pictures Co.). Between 1883 and 1902 the *Longfellow* ferried passengers between Boston and Provincetown; she is shown in the distance sailing toward Steamboat Wharf at the far left. Joseph Manta's Wharf is in the center, and B.H. Dyer's Wharf (formerly D.A. Smalls' Wharf) is at the right with an old fishing vessel or whaling schooner berthed alongside. The *Baltic*, the town's last whaling vessel, was roofed over and used for storage purposes, and, as noted by an observer, "will probably never sail again."

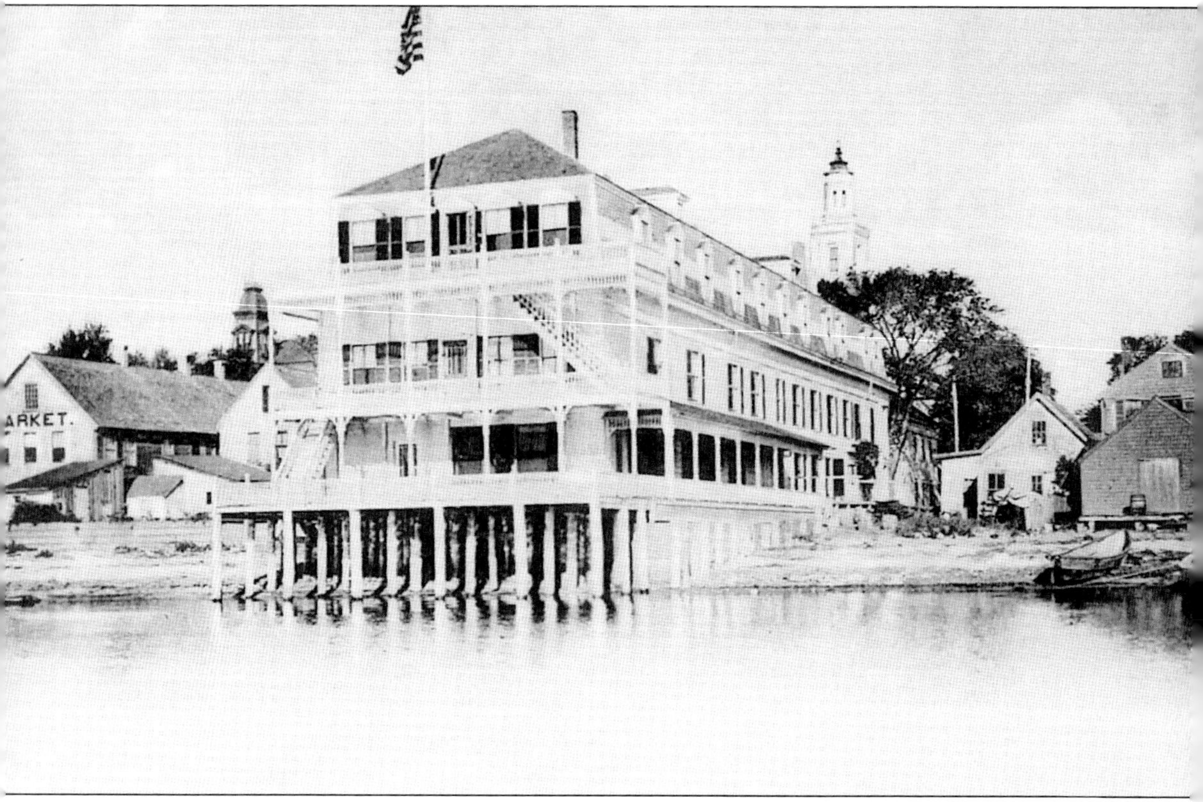

New Central House, 247 Commercial Street (c. 1915 postcard published by The Metropolitan News Co., Boston, MA). A French Second Empire mansard roof changed the appearance of the Central House (remodeled c. 1903) from its original Greek Revival look. The structure was originally built during the mid-19th century, sometime around 1847, when the Universalist church was constructed across the street. Patrons could enjoy the harbor view from the three balconies, and those who chose to wade or swim near the pilings could do so. Benjamin Lancy's fine Victorian mansion at 230 Commercial Street, the tower of which is visible between the roof of the market and the hotel, was built in 1874. On February 10, 1998, the rear half of the massive hotel (known as the Crown & Anchor Motor Inn) with a later L-shaped addition and two adjacent structures—a mid-19th-century house containing a jewelry shop called The Handcrafter, and the former movie theater with its 1919 brick facade, known for many years as Whaler's Wharf, featuring artists and craftsmen—were unfortunately destroyed in a spectacular evening blaze.

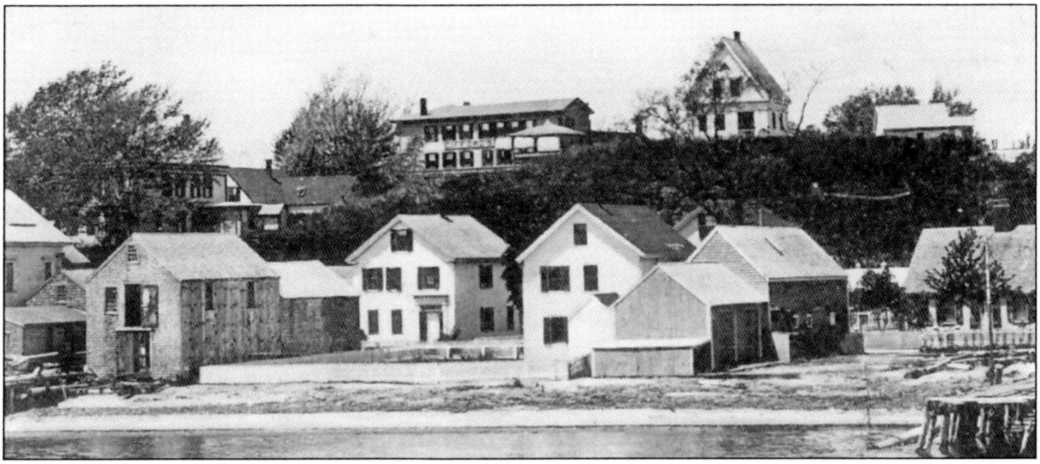

Gifford and Annex, Corner of Bradford and Carver Streets (*c.* 1908 postcard published by the *Advocate*). The steeply pitched "lightning-splitter" roof of the annex to the Gifford House is as much a landmark today as when it was built in the 1850s. Somewhat similar gable-end-to-the-street dwellings and warehouses on Commercial Street, however, have been greatly altered or razed. A newspaper notice stated that in 1869 James Gifford, Esq., one of the harbor commissioners, bought Mr. M.L. Adams' house, "which he intends remodeling in order to accommodate a few boarders during the summer season."

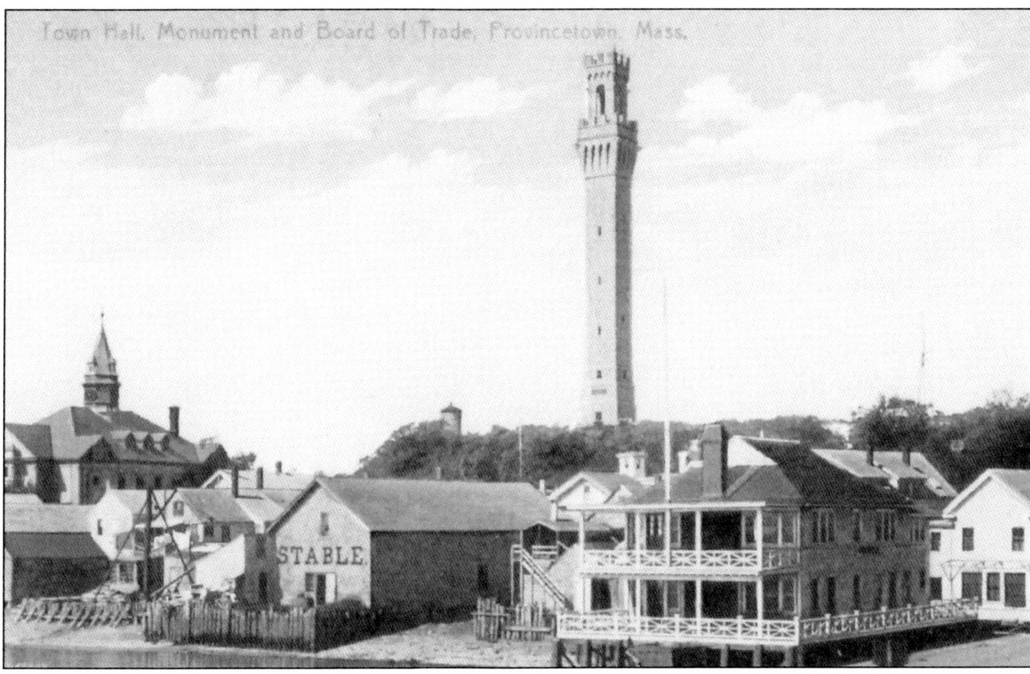

Town Hall, Monument and Board of Trade (*c.* 1915 postcard published by Irving L. Rosenthal, Provincetown). The Pilgrim Memorial Monument—modeled on the Torre del Mangia in Siena, Italy—towers over all other structures in Provincetown, no matter the view. A copper-clad steeple is the distinctive feature on the high Victorian Town Hall, built in 1886 on the corner of Commercial and Ryder Streets. The Provincetown Board of Trade building (a businessmen's club) served a similar function as today's chamber of commerce; it was located near the beginning of MacMillan Wharf in what later became Lopes Square.

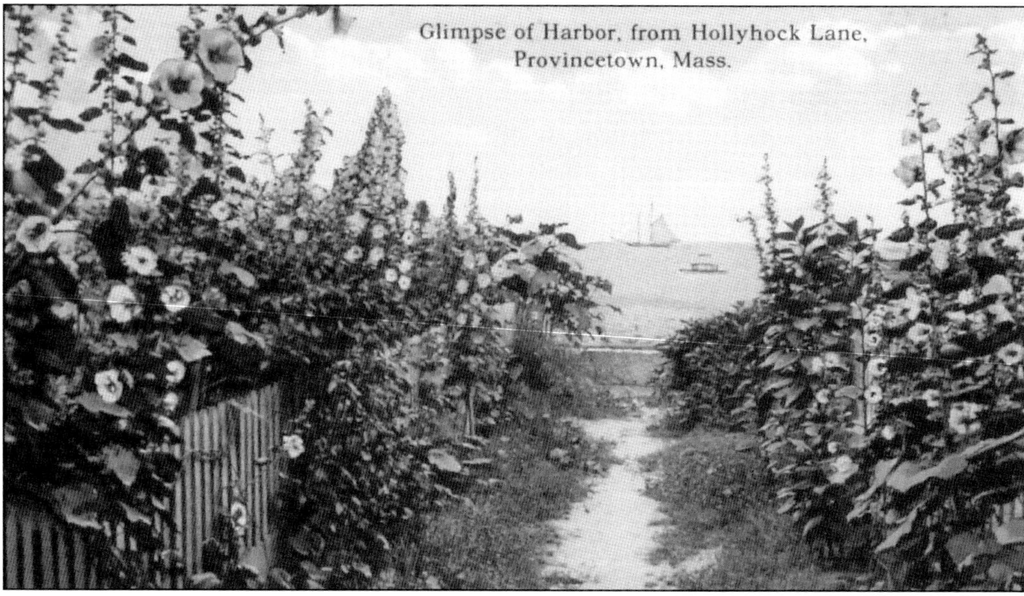

Glimpse of Harbor, from Hollyhock Lane (early-20th-century postcard published by C.T. Photochrom, Chicago, IL). This most photogenic spot along the shore was once an open passageway across from the Town Hall (see frontispiece, Vol. I); the lush summer scene was the subject of at least 32 different postcards! Adjacent abutters Rosetta L. Cook and Louise C. Paine both cared for the colorful hollyhocks and other vegetation.

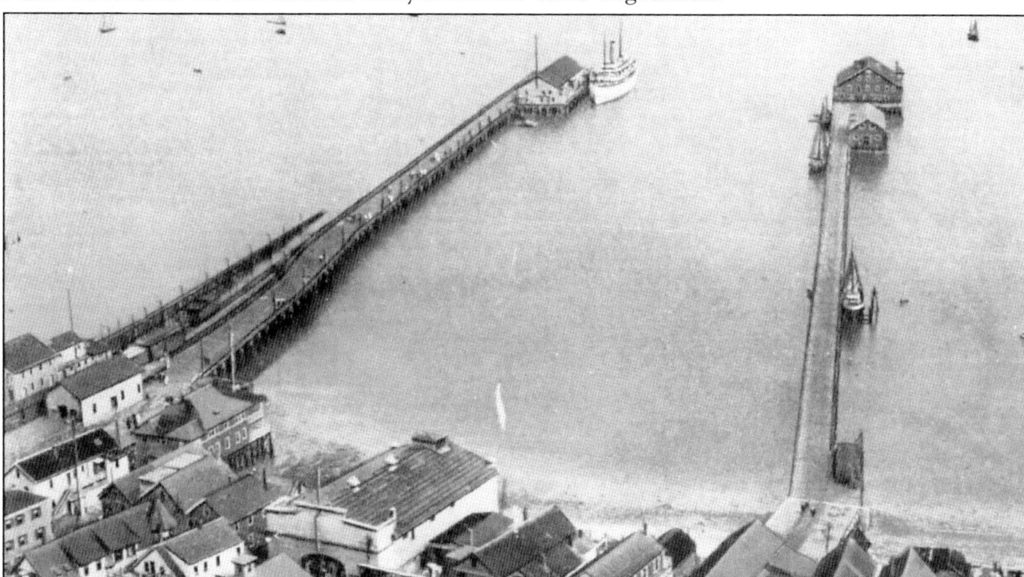

View from Pilgrim Memorial Monument (early-20th-century postcard published by H.A. Dickerman & Son). Railroad Wharf (with the docked ferryboat) and Monument Wharf—later Sklaroff's Wharf as established by S. Sklaroff & Sons in 1892—appear almost equal in length in this tranquil harbor view. A snowstorm in March of 1960 removed the large storage building from Sklaroff's Wharf, and two years later in January, a fire destroyed the main wharf building, causing the wharf itself to decay until it was acquired in 1969 by the Fisherman's Cooperative, and rebuilt as a marina.

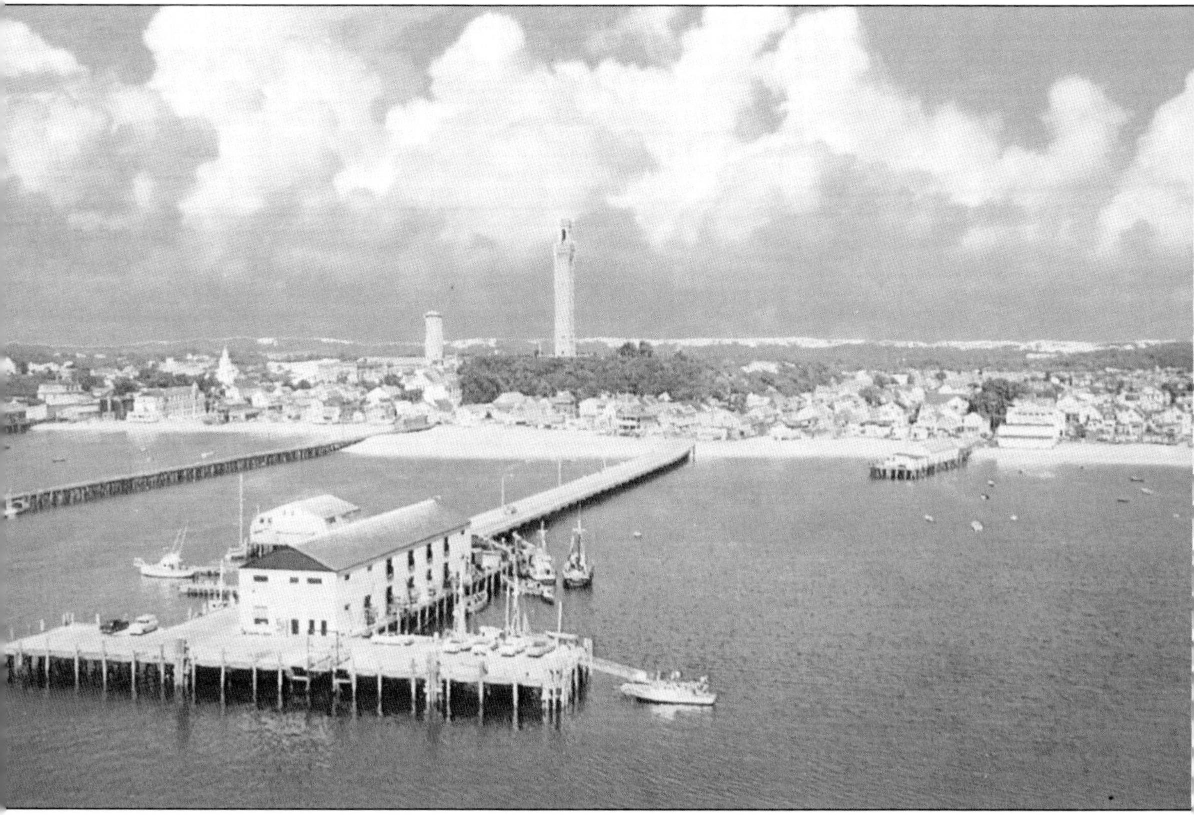

Bird's-eye View of the Town Pier (c. 1960 postcard published by The Mayflower Sales Co., Provincetown). Most of the town's fishing and pleasure vessels were out to sea on this cloud-filled day. The large, two-story concrete building used by fishermen at the end of the pier was razed in the 1980s. Sklaroff's, now Fisherman's Wharf, is at the left, and the truncated wharf at the right is Macara's Wharf at the foot of Freeman Street. Many of the early wharves began to be constructed in Provincetown during the decade when the County Road—Front, later Commercial Street—was extended through the town (1835), and when the wood-plank sidewalk was laid down on the land side of that street (1838).

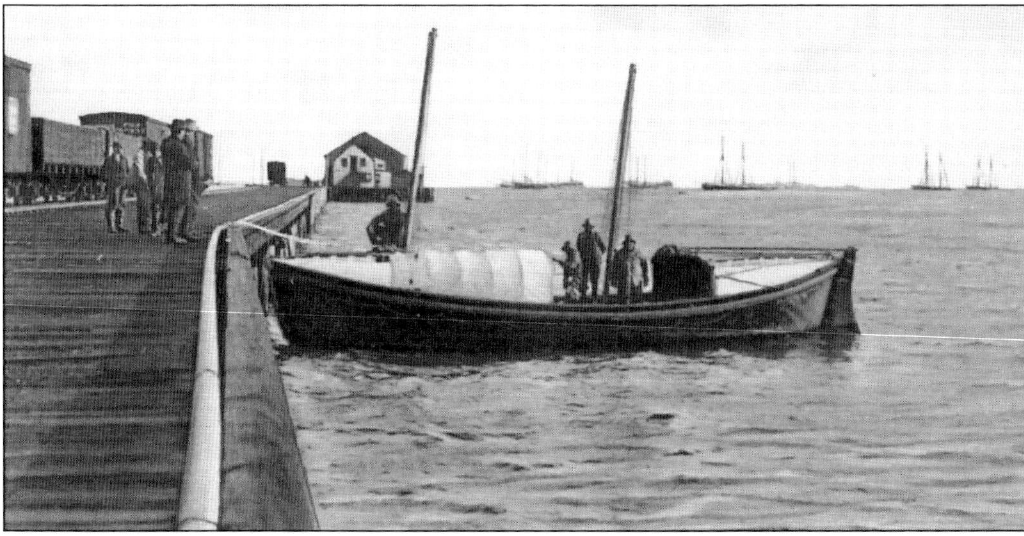

New Life Saving Boat, *Victory*, of the Wood End Station (early-20th-century postcard published by the *Advocate*). Men wearing foul-weather gear pose in the new vessel acquired for use at the Wood End Life Saving Station across the harbor on Long Point. After it was discovered that flat-bottomed boats were not swift in emergencies at sea, lifeboats were built both narrow and deep with sharp bows and sterns and airtight compartments. Smaller than whale boats, many in local service, were built by William W. Smith, usually within the period of a week.

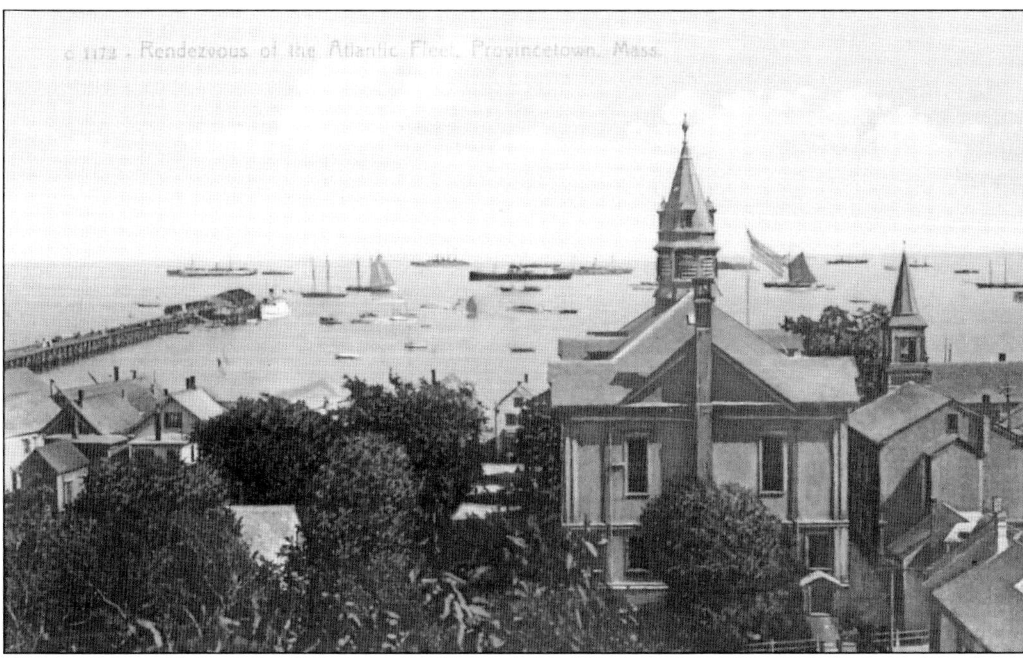

Rendezvous of the Atlantic Fleet (early-20th-century postcard published by the *Advocate*). Until around 1939, the U.S. Atlantic Fleet often visited Provincetown, where they would meet in the vastness of the harbor and then perform naval maneuvers in nearby waters. The photographer was standing on Monument Hill overlooking the Town Hall and Railroad Wharf. A 2,500-foot granite breakwater was constructed in the inner harbor in 1972.

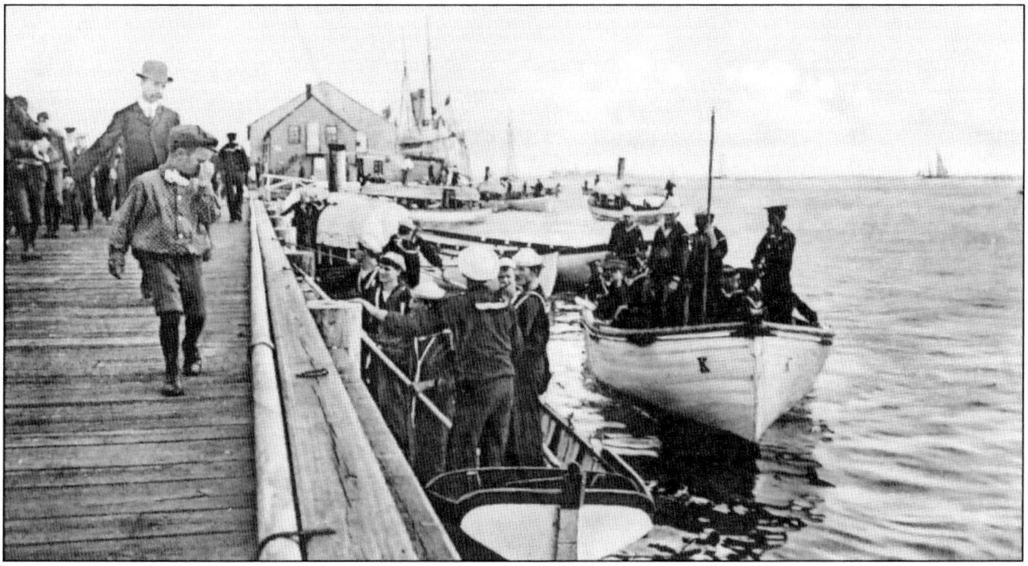

Sailors from Atlantic Fleet Landing at Railroad Wharf (c. 1910 postcard published by the *Advocate*). A camera-shy youngster wearing a polka-dot shirt and white bow tie walks along the wharf as sailors, arriving from one of the naval vessels in the harbor, share a joke in a nearby launch. The pipe that ran along the wharf's edge supplied fresh water to the end of the wharf.

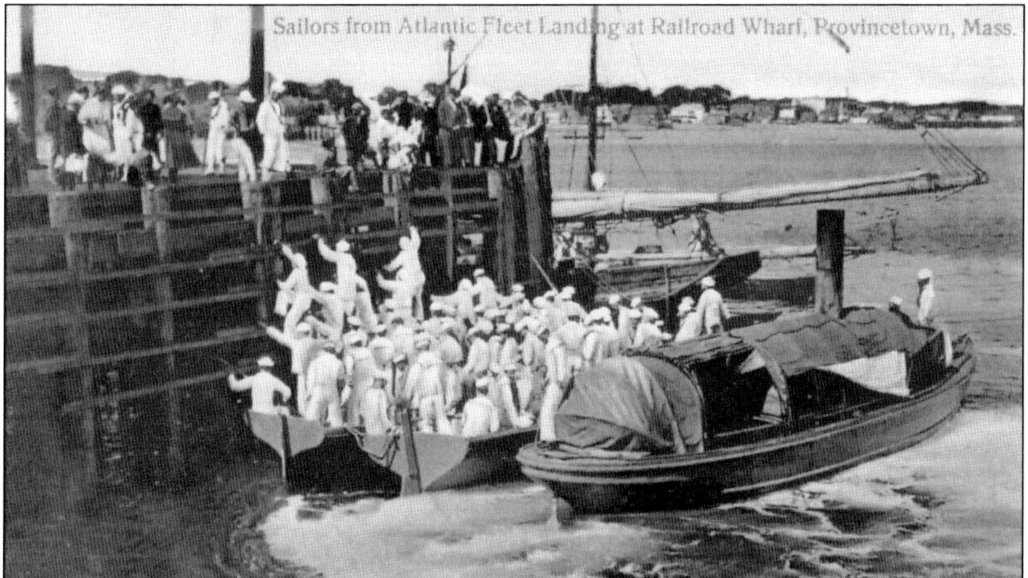

Sailors from Atlantic Fleet Landing at Railroad Wharf (c. 1910 postcard published by the *Advocate*). Sailors from three launches scramble past each other and up the sides of the wharf for a day ashore. Eating and drinking will be followed by taking in the sights and hopefully meeting some nice young women to impress in their freshly pressed "whites." Quite possibly they are either arriving in August of 1907 or 1910 to serve as escorts for Presidents Theodore Roosevelt or William Howard Taft at the respective laying of the cornerstone or dedication of the Pilgrim Memorial Monument.

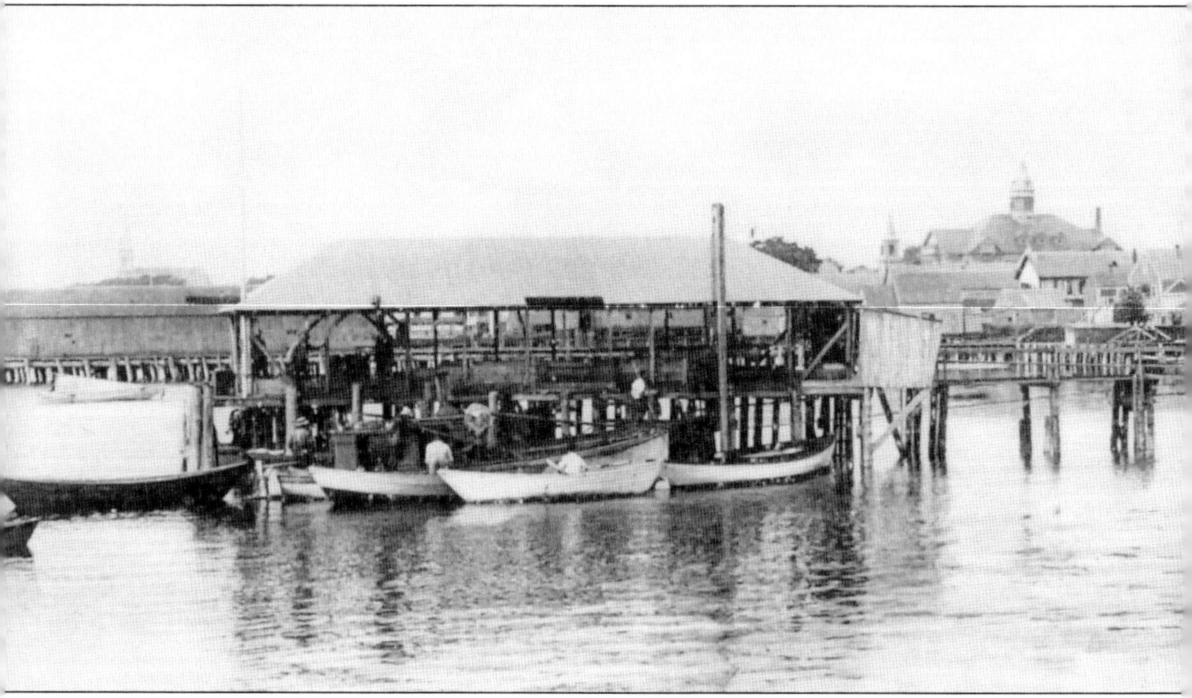

Panorama of Water Front & East End (early-20th-century postcard published by the *Advocate*). A hipped-roof pavilion, wharves, and pilings dominate this elongated harbor view between the Town Wharf and the shadow of the Center M.E. Church. Some waterfront businesses, such as Duncan Matheson's dry goods store at 186 Commercial Street and a nearby sail loft, were well patronized.

Alma Martin's affinity for the town at the tip of Cape Cod is revealed in her poem, "The Heavenly Town," included in Nancy W. Paine Smith's *The Provincetown Book* (1922):

"A heavenly town is Provincetown.
Its streets go winding up and down,
Way-down-along, way-up-along,
With laughter, mirthful jest and song.
Dark Portuguese
From far-off seas
Their ships in bay
Pass time of day
With friends who wander up and down
The pleasant streets of Provincetown.

"Hello!" the friendly children call
To high and low, to great and small.
Bright blossoms gaily nod their heads,
Strong zinnias, yellow, purples, reds,
Gay marigolds and hollyhocks
Whose hues are matched by artists' smocks.
Dark laughing boys,

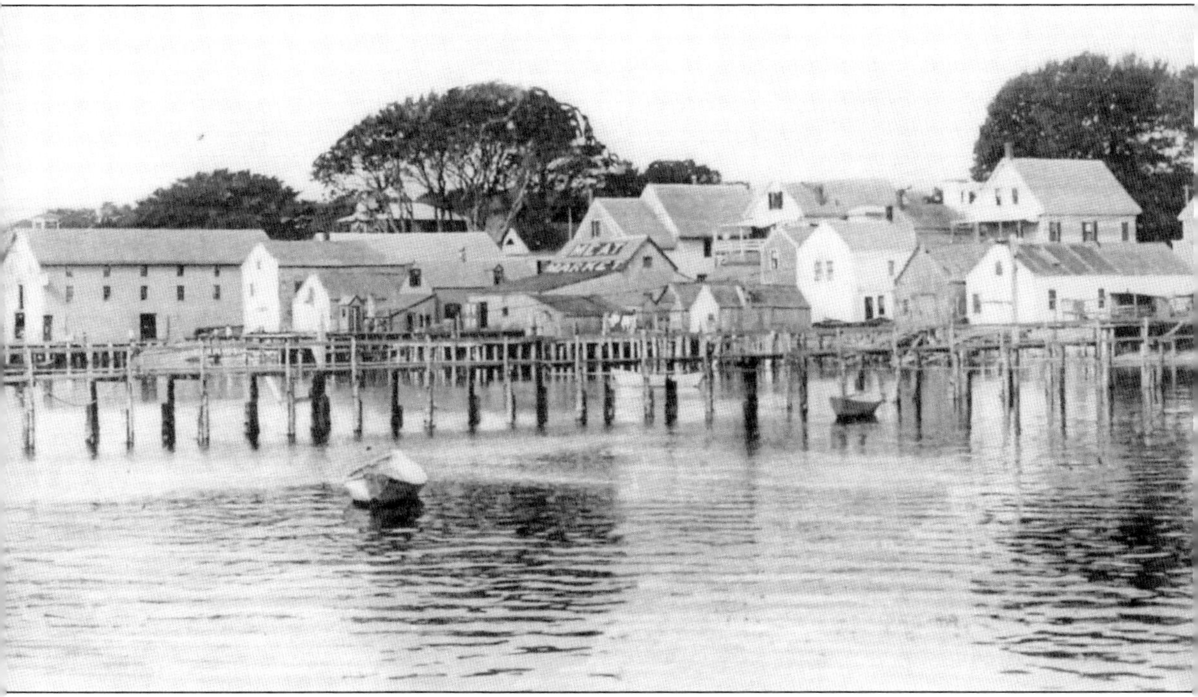

Dark smiling girls,
With here and there a native son,
With blue eyes full of Yankee fun,
Go up and down the village street;
Gay words for every one they meet,
And fill the summer air with song,
Way-up-along, way-down-along.

The air is crisp with briny smells,
The time is told by chime of bells,
The painters sketch each little nook,
In colors like a children's book.
Yellow shutters, windows pink,
Purple shingles, trees of ink.
Front street, Back street,
Narrow winding lanes,
Many colored fishing boats,
Sails and nets and seines,
East End, West End,
High sandy dunes,
Wonderful by moonlight
Or in shining noons.
Oh, a heavenly town is Provincetown
Whose streets go winding up and down."

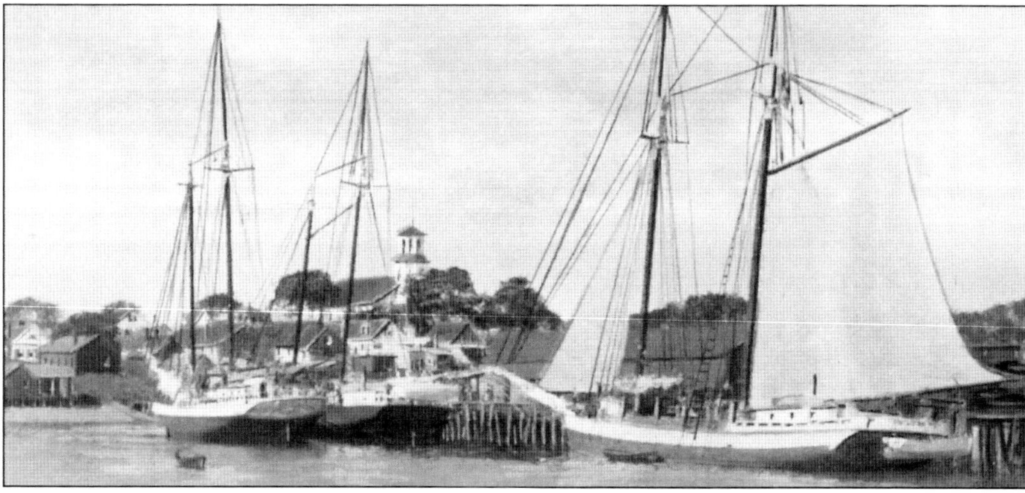

Lumber Schooners at Hilliard's Wharf (early-20th-century photograph). Three two-masted lumber schooners, probably from Maine, are docked alongside Hilliard's, later Higgins' Wharf, at the foot of Freeman Street. Thomas Hilliard, the wharf's earlier owner, was a merchant and trader who wore a tall black beaver hat. During the early part of the 20th century, "Jake" Smith and Joe "Garlalia" Souza were employed to unload lumber from the schooners. (Courtesy Seamen's Bank.)

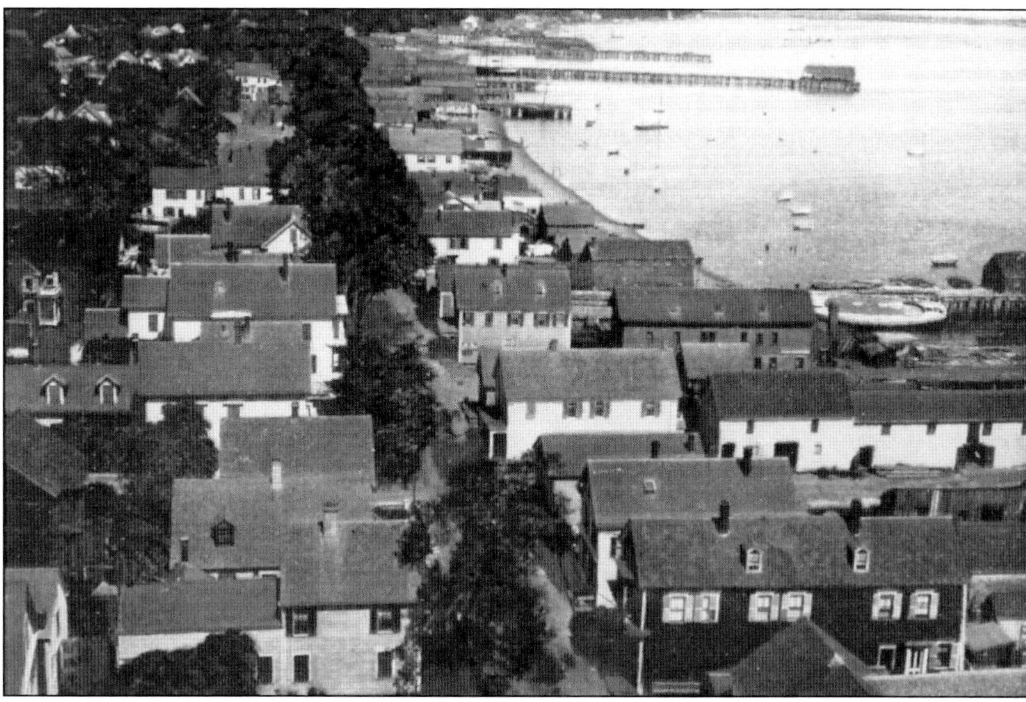

East End (c. 1900 postcard published by Hugh C. Leighton Co., Portland, ME). Houses and wharf-related structures crowd each other in this bird's-eye view taken from the steeple of the Center M.E. Church shortly after the Portland Gale. Four years following the Civil War, in 1869, the Commonwealth of Massachusetts paid to have a protective granite dike built in this section of the town. The long wharf in the background was probably that behind the Consolidated Cold Storage (now the Ice House Condominiums) at the foot of Howland Street.

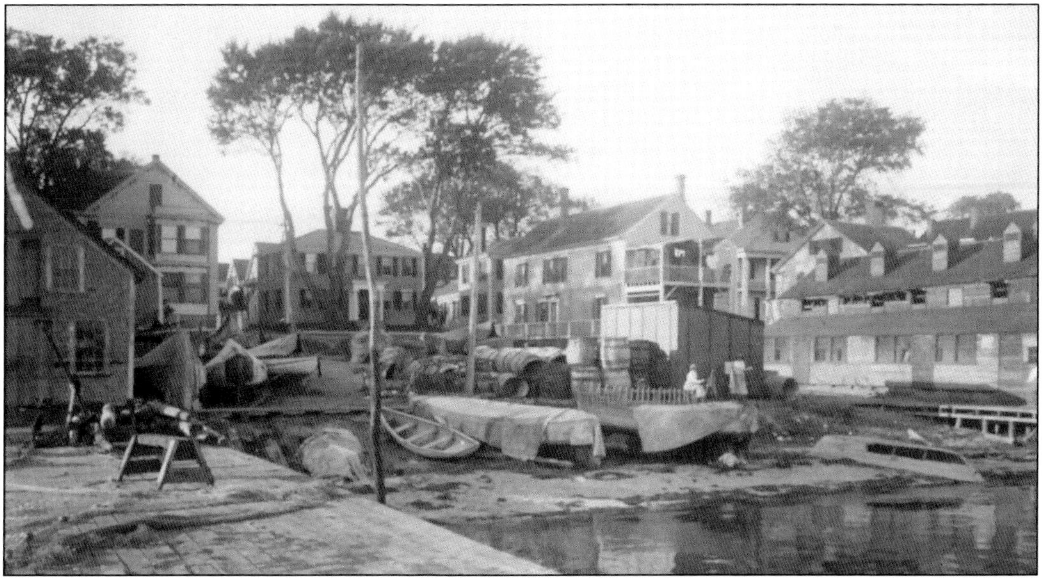

The Law Street Beach (c. 1910 postcard published by the *Advocate*). Two women artists have found a very picturesque spot amongst burlap-covered dories, large barrels, and fishing nets on the beach between Law and Washington Streets. David Conwell's (a.k.a. Cannery) Wharf at the left had a tar pit on the premises, and the smokehouse at the right, with its row of dormers for ventilating smoked fish, was located on Small's Wharf. The hipped-roof Colonial house in the background at 396 Commercial Street has the date "1789" lettered on the chimney, and it features a later Greek Revival porch with Ionic capitals. (Courtesy Seamen's Bank.)

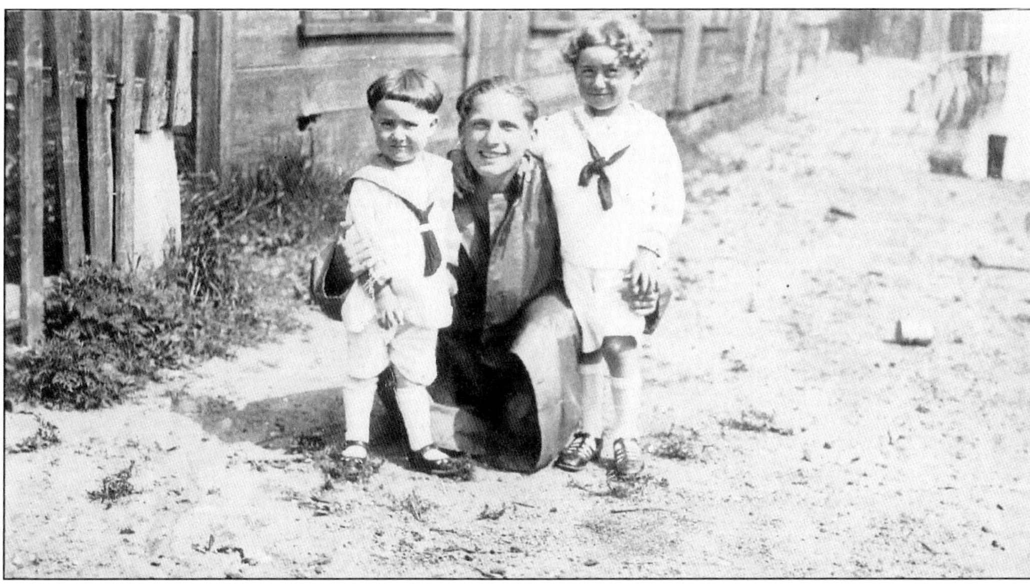

Sailor Boys with a Friend (c. 1924 photograph). An unidentified young man, either a visiting relative or a friend of the family, poses with young sailors Lucien (left) and Arthur Cross, children of Primo and Lucy (da Cruz) Cross, who resided at 401 Commercial Street. The smokehouse in the background on Small's Wharf was located behind their home, which has been in the family for several generations. (Courtesy Hall Collection.)

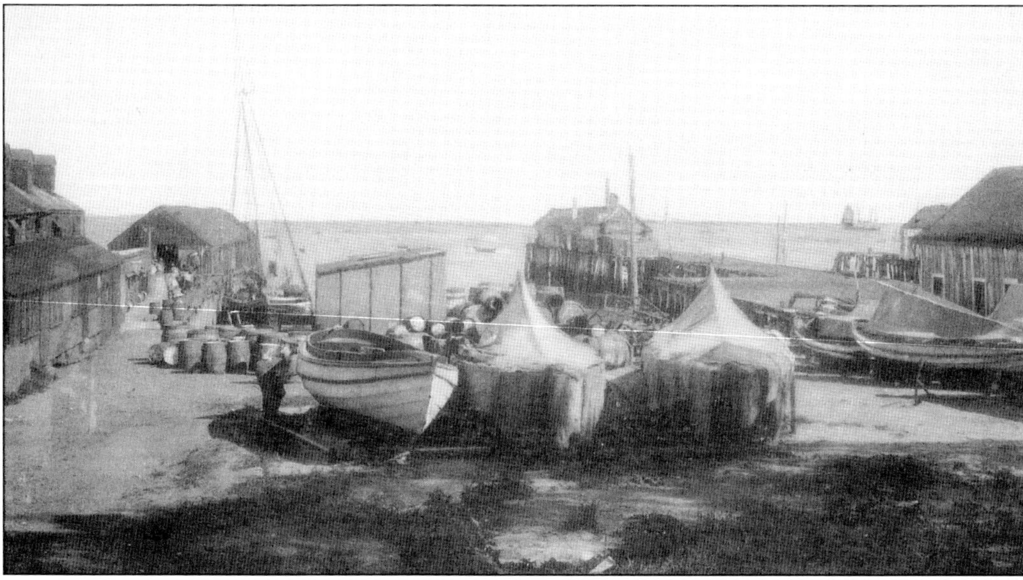

Fisherman's Dories (c. 1920 postcard published by The Town Crier Shop). A trio of beached "gasolener" dories was the focus of this scene. The smokehouse at left is in front of Small's Wharf, and Conwell's Wharf is at right, with the Pickert fish plant at wharf's end.

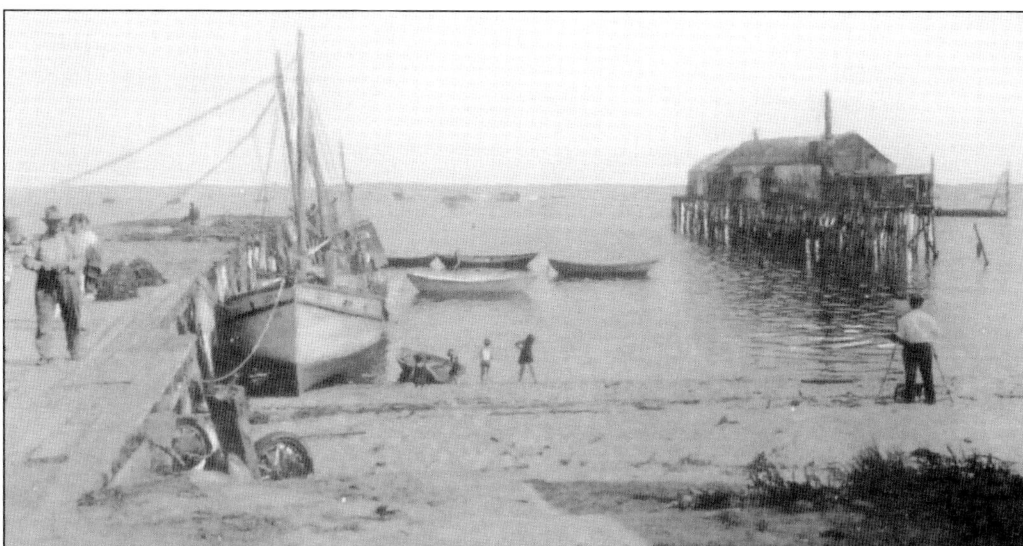

Wharf Scene (c. 1928 postcard published by American Art Post Card Co., Brookline, MA). People walk along Small's Wharf, where recently the warehouse was located, and an artist paints the Pickert fish plant, the wharf on which it was built no longer reaching the shore. On November 16, 1926, the Coast Guard cutter *Morrill*'s anchors failed to hold during a southeast gale, and she damaged both wharves. Twelve years later on September 21, 1938, a hurricane affected Provincetown and "caused excessive tides on the mainland shores of Nantucket Sound, Narragansett and Buzzards Bays."

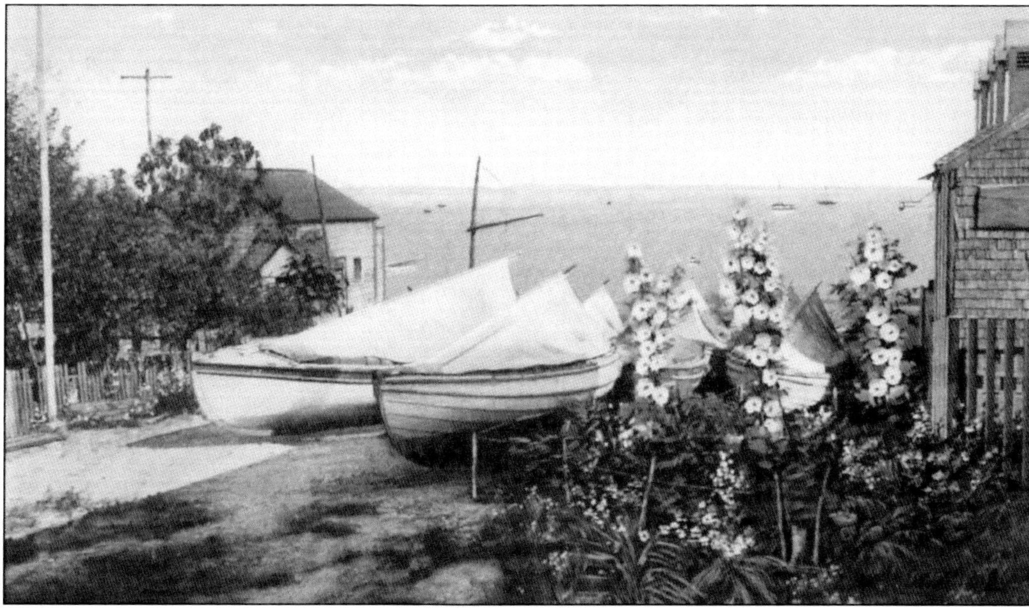

"Off Duty" Fishing Boats (early-20th-century postcard published by H.A. Dickerman & Son). Thousands of tourists purchased this attractive postcard of burlap-covered dories and colorful hollyhocks adjacent to the smokehouse on Small's Wharf. The small building at the left is on a shortened wharf and was known as "Jason's Cottage."

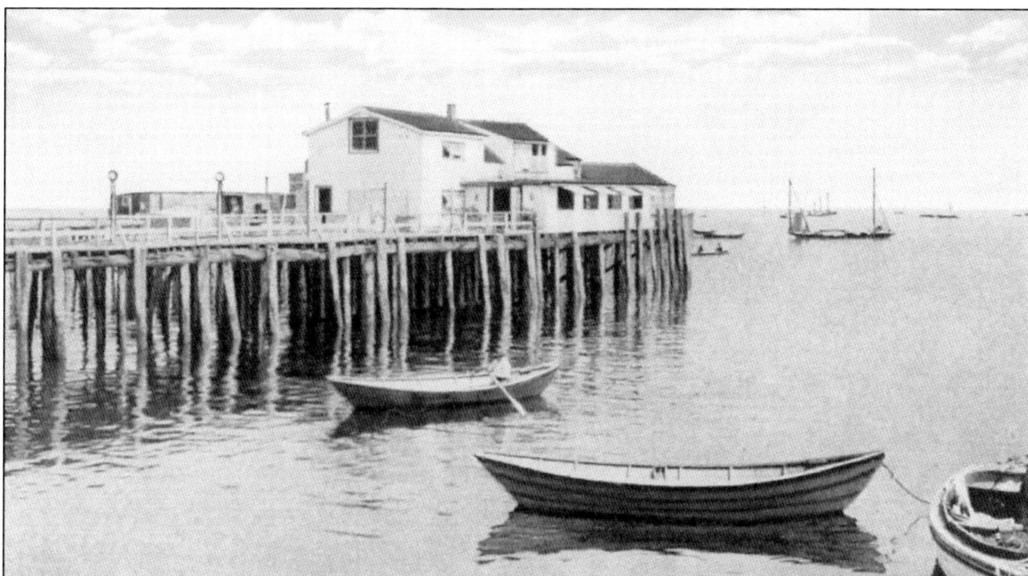

Casino (c. 1935 postcard published by E.D. West Co.). With the repeal of Prohibition in 1933, cafés, bars, taverns, and nightclubs opened to a thirsty and hungry crowd who wanted to have a good time. The Casino was a relatively large structure thought to have been located at the end of Knowles' Wharf at the foot of Pearl Street. It was one of the first combination restaurant/nightclubs in town; The Ship was another early nightclub, run by Inez Hogan, an illustrator of children's books. The Flagship, the Lobster Pot, and the White Whale also became well-patronized establishments.

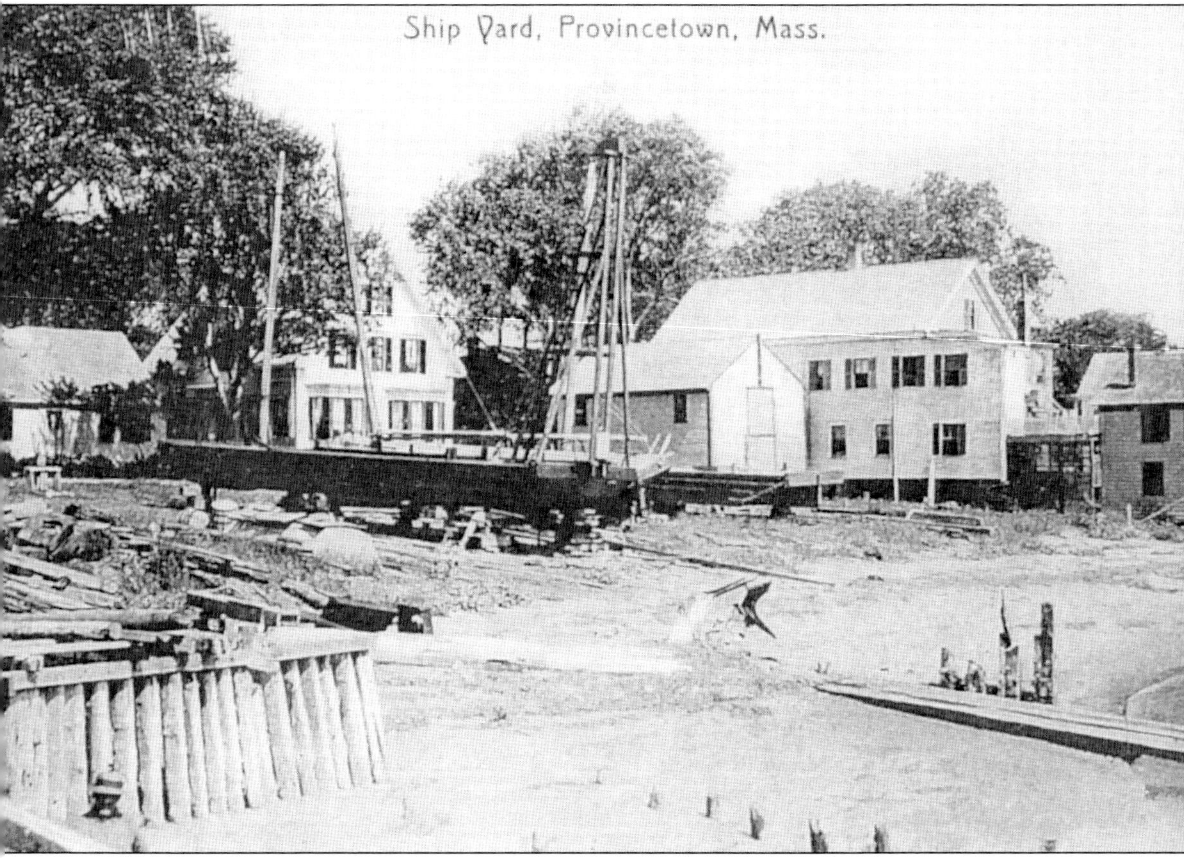

Ship Yard, Commercial Street, between Bangs and Cook Streets (early-20th-century panoramic postcard published by the *Advocate*). This shipyard in the East End, once owned by John G. Whitcomb—and the scene of much maritime activity—is bordered by houses of noteworthy Provincetown inhabitants of the past. The Cape Cod cottage at the left (466 Commercial Street) was built around 1795 by Ephraim Cook, the fishing father of fishing son, Kibbe Cook, and it was acquired in 1907 by longtime resident, author, and war correspondent Mary Heaton Vorse. The "lightning-splitter" Greek Revival house (468 Commercial Street)

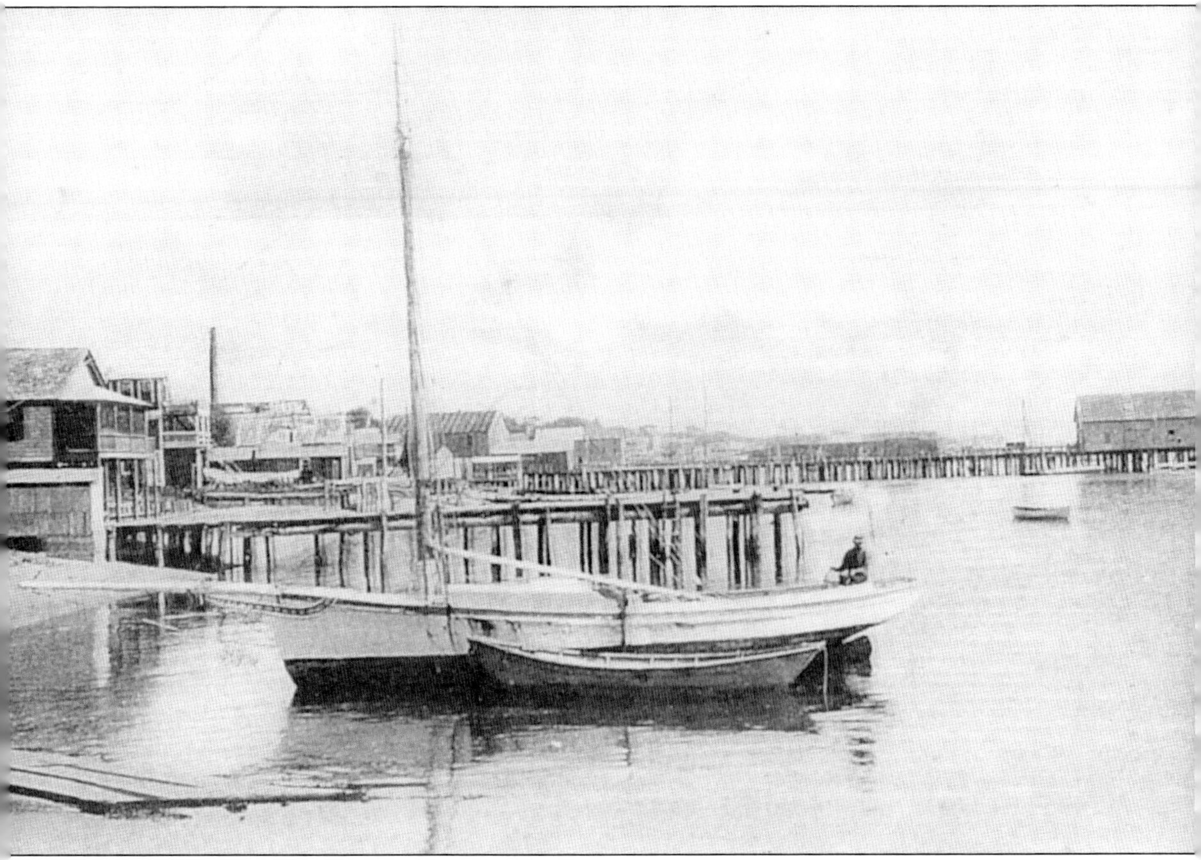

next door to Vorse's residence was the home of other members of the Cook family. Rear Admiral Donald B. and Mrs. MacMillan lived in the large dwelling across the street (473). The Arctic explorer (1874–1970), who is regarded as Provincetown's most illustrious son, reached the North Pole with Admiral Robert E. Peary in 1909. The structure on the short wharf behind the MacMillan house may have been a barracks on Long Point before the Civil War, and the long wharf in the background was probably the Consolidated Cold Storage Wharf. (Courtesy West End Antiques.)

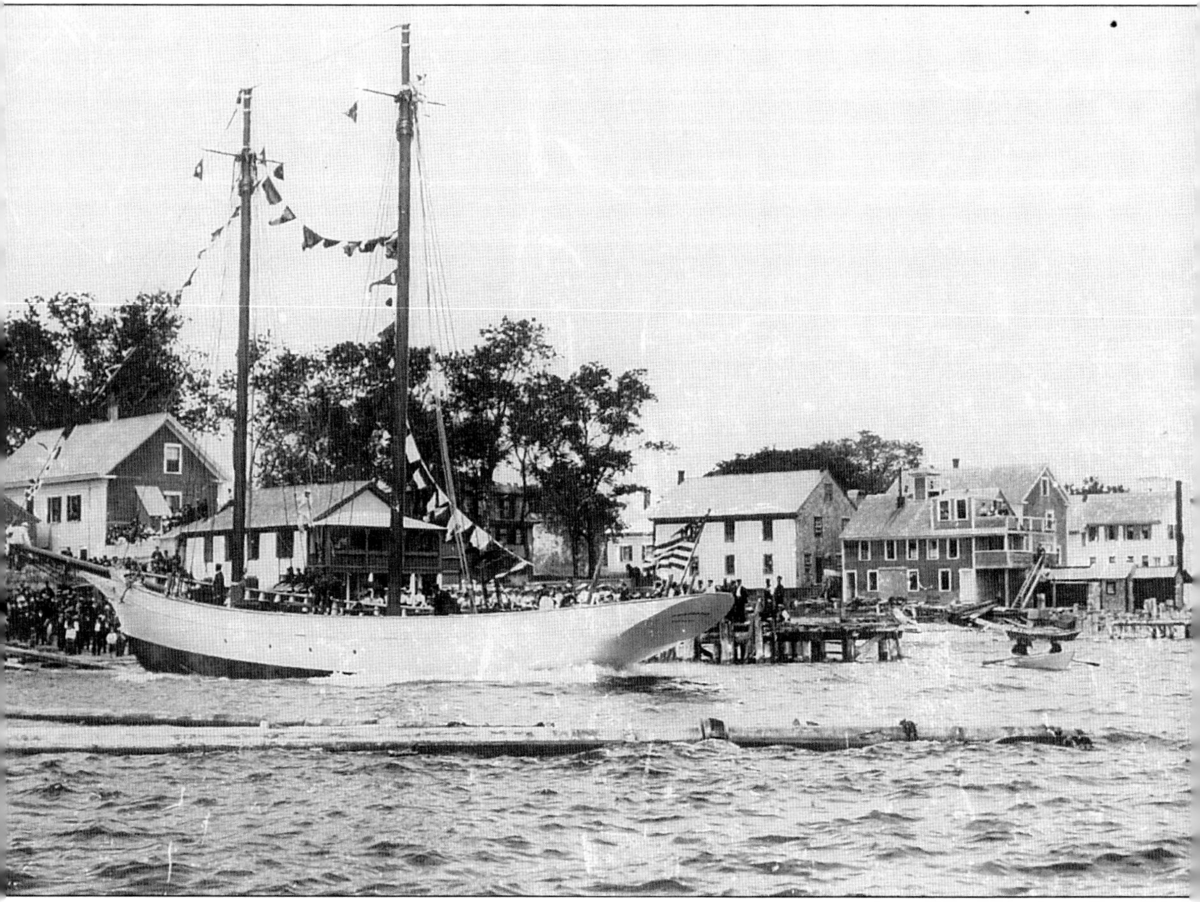

Launching of the *Charlotte* (June 18, 1901, photograph). After being christened with sparkling champagne by the wife of Chicago owner James A. Lawrence, the 88-foot schooner/yacht *Charlotte* slid fully rigged into Provincetown Harbor. The launching was the last of its kind in local maritime history for a vessel of her size. Townspeople watched as the yacht was being constructed, and on the historic summer's day John G. Whitcomb's shipyard and the surrounding areas were filled with well-wishers and schoolchildren who witnessed the exciting event. (Courtesy of the Cape Cod Pilgrim Memorial Association.)

Two

Whaling and Fishing

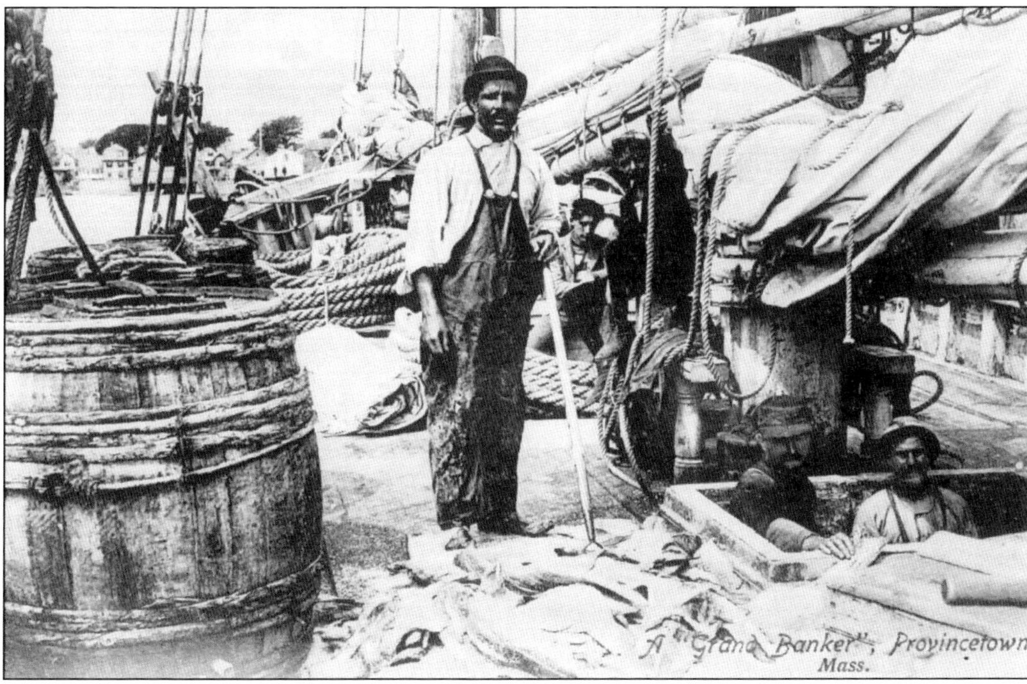

A Grand Banker (early-20th-century postcard published by the *Advocate*). Although the Province Lands were recognized as a fishing reserve as early as 1654, it was not until around 1825 that Provincetown fishermen began traveling to the Grand Banks (southeast of Newfoundland) for larger quantities of fish. By the mid- to late 19th century, hundreds of "Grand Bankers" and Georges Banks (located 180 miles east of Cape Cod) fishing schooners and a large mackerel fleet comprised the Provincetown fishing fleet. Grand Bankers usually left port during the month of April on a voyage that often lasted five months. One of the town's well-known Grand Bankers had the fascinating name *Virgin Rock David*. The Portuguese fishermen in the picture have returned from such an expedition on a three-masted schooner, the size of which can be determined by the masts, the loosely wrapped sails, the thick roping, and the large wooden hogsheads containing salt to "dress down" the catch. While two men peer from the hold to catch a whiff of fresh air, their friend stands with a pitchfork, wearing overalls and a Derby hat—often favored by first-generation Portuguese men, who adapted their personal taste to American fashion.

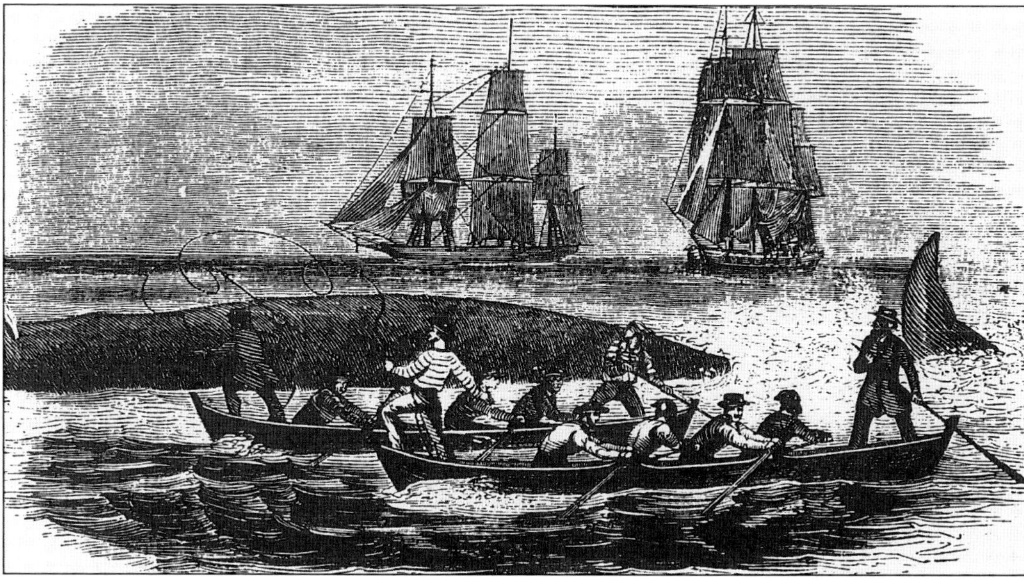

Exploit of an American Harpooner (mid-19th-century wood engraving). Between 1737—when 12 Provincetown whalers sailed for the Davis Straits (between Baffin Island, Canada, and West Greenland)—and 1921—the last year a single whaler left the port—Provincetown maintained a distinguished record in this now illegal industry. By the 1840s the industry was profiting local businessmen who had invested in the ventures, and by 1863, Provincetown had become the second largest whaling port in the United States, after New Bedford, Massachusetts. (Courtesy Lynn Historical Society, Lynn, Massachusetts.)

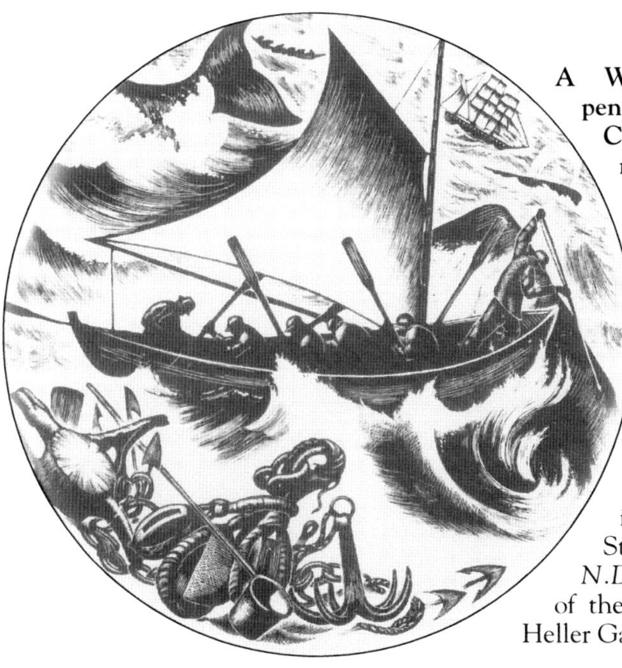

A Whaling Scene (mid-20th-century pen-and-ink drawing by Englishwoman Claire Leighton, who summered in nearby Wellfleet). This dramatic rondo design was one of several used by Wedgwood of Etruria & Barlaston, England, for black-and-white commemorative plates in their collectible "New England Industries" series. The initial chase, harpooning, and then messy dissection of the whale—every part was used—was a dangerous occupation for crew members aboard a whaler or in a dory. Some local men involved in the industry were Captain Stephen A. Ryder, master of the bark *N.D. Chase*, and Captain Samuel Soper of the *Ardent*. (Photograph courtesy Julie Heller Gallery, Provincetown.)

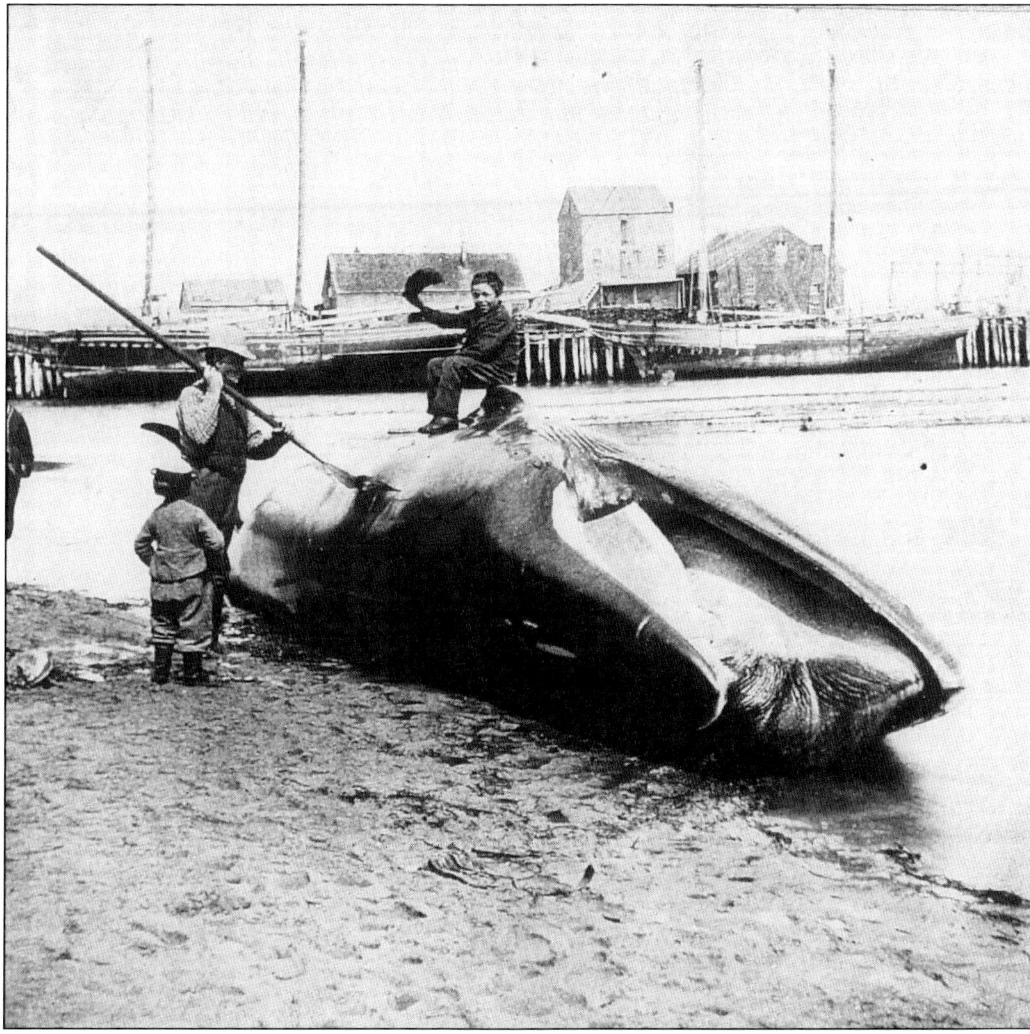

Finback Whale (c. 1908 stereopticon view taken by George H. Nickerson). A cheerful young boy doffs his cap to the photographer while seated on the side of a beached finback whale. The vested man prods the mammal with a whaling spade, or blubber flenser, as another child with arms akimbo has a closer look. Fishing schooners are tied up alongside a nearby wharf. Restaurateur and Provincetown art collector Napi Vandereck recalls that whale-watching as a form of entertainment and education began locally around 1960. A prime area to see these creatures of the deep is the Stellwagen Bank National Marine Sanctuary (designated in 1992), which is roughly between Cape Ann and Cape Cod. (Courtesy of the Cape Cod Pilgrim Memorial Association.)

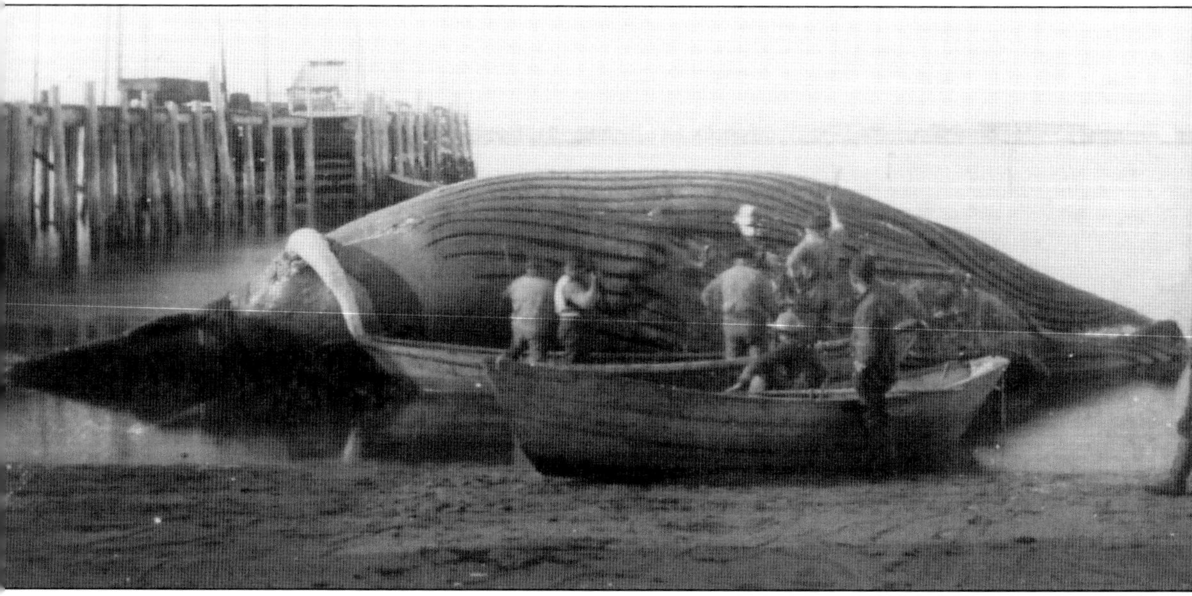

The Long Point Oil Works (c. 1880s photograph). David C. Stull (1844–1926), a Provincetown native, was known as the "Ambergris King" for the wealth he accumulated by selling the gray waxy substance found only in the intestines of diseased sperm whales. After exposure to air, the ambergris hardened and became an earthly fragrant solid that was favored in France for the manufacture of perfumes. The "king's" office and refinery of clock and watch oil was on Commercial Street next to Bryant's Market, and he resided on the corner of Commercial and Cook Streets. (Courtesy Michael Young.)

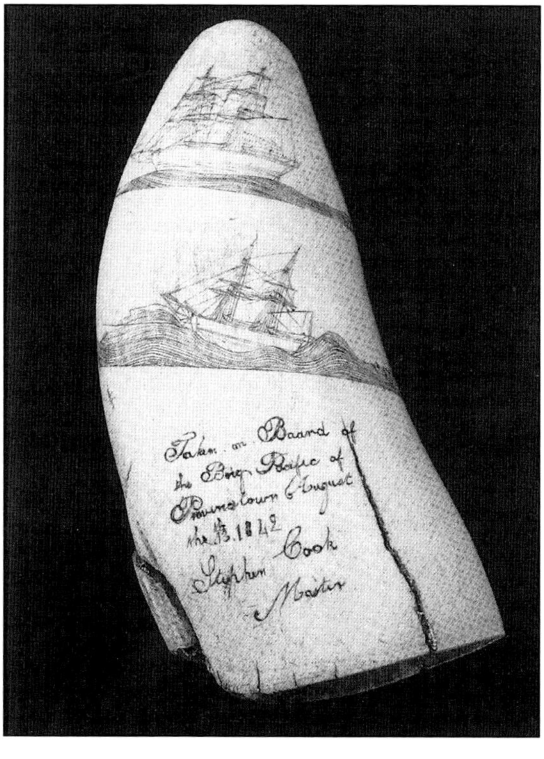

Commemorative Scrimshaw Whale's Tooth (mid-20th-century postcard published by Coastal Photo Scenics, Southwest Harbor, ME). "Scrimshaw pieces such as this engraved sperm whale tooth were made on board whaling vessels to pass the time. The brig *Pacific* . . . was built in 1842 and left Provincetown April 12 of the same year for the Atlantic whaling ground. It returned June 26, 1843 with 235 barrels of sperm oil and 50 barrels of whale oil." The *Charles W. Morgan* (berthed at Mystic Seaport, Inc., Mystic, Connecticut) was the last Provincetown-owned and registered whaling ship. Her final voyage occurred in 1921. (Courtesy Ken Conrad.)

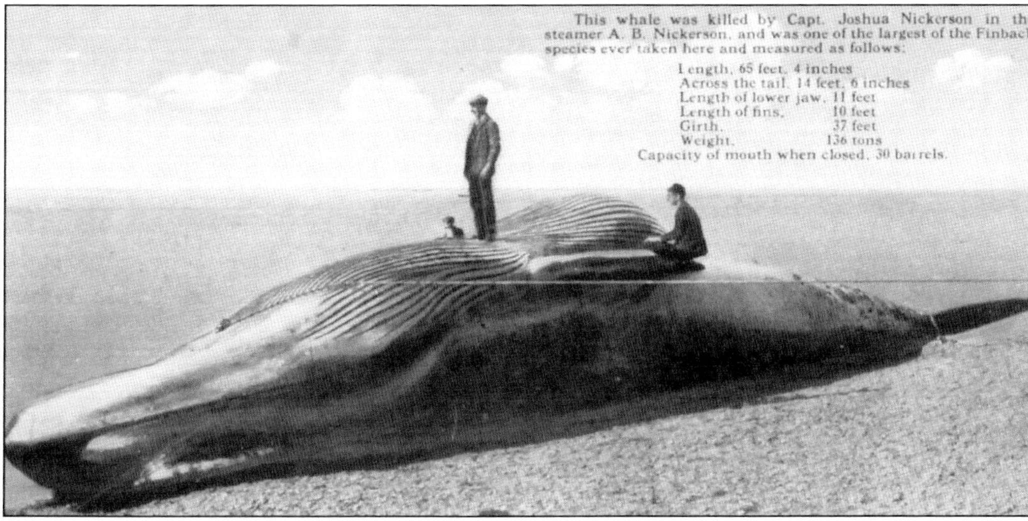

Whale Ashore on Beach (early-20th-century postcard published by H.A. Dickerman & Son). On May 11, 1843, the largest whale caught was captured southeast of Chatham by Ebenezer Cook of Provincetown in the little, pink-sterned schooner *Cordelia*. The second-largest leviathan, according to local lore, was caught by Captain Joshua Nickerson aboard the steamer *A.B. Nickerson* around 1889. This enormous whale was sold to a Chicago syndicate for exhibition purposes, and was accompanied by another captain, Newton P. West, on specially adapted railroad cars with the captain delivering factual lectures along the way.

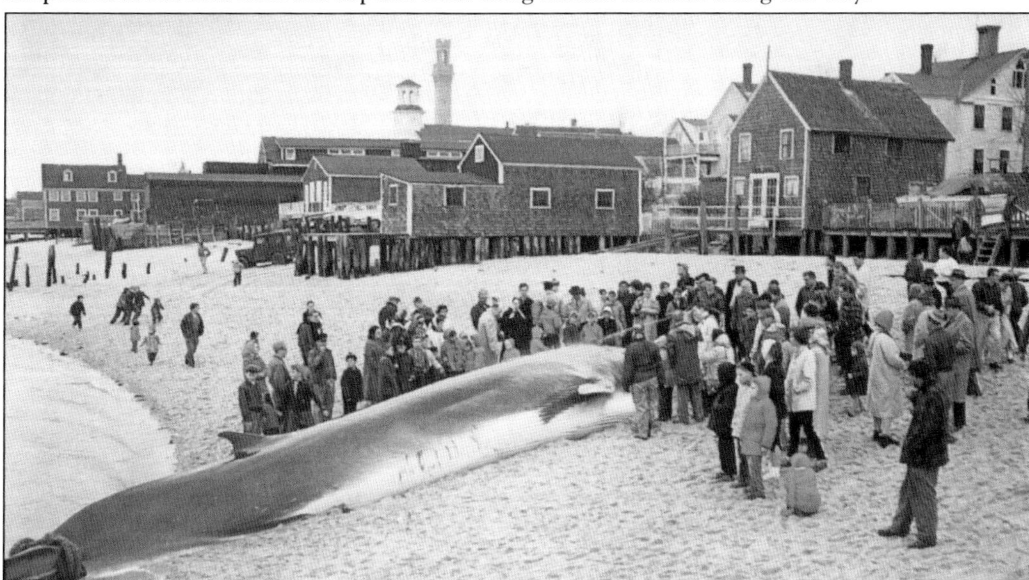

Beached Finback Whale (c. 1960 postcard published by Cape Cod Photos, Orleans, MA). This beached whale became the subject of the children's book *When the Whale Came to My Town*, written in 1974 by Jim Young (who was living in Provincetown in 1959), with photographs by Daniel Bernstein. According to the puzzled young male narrator in the story, the whale apparently chose to die and slipped away several times from Coast Guardsmen who tried unsuccessfully to haul it back into the harbor. It finally died in early December of 1959 in the vicinity of Washington Avenue in the East End of town.

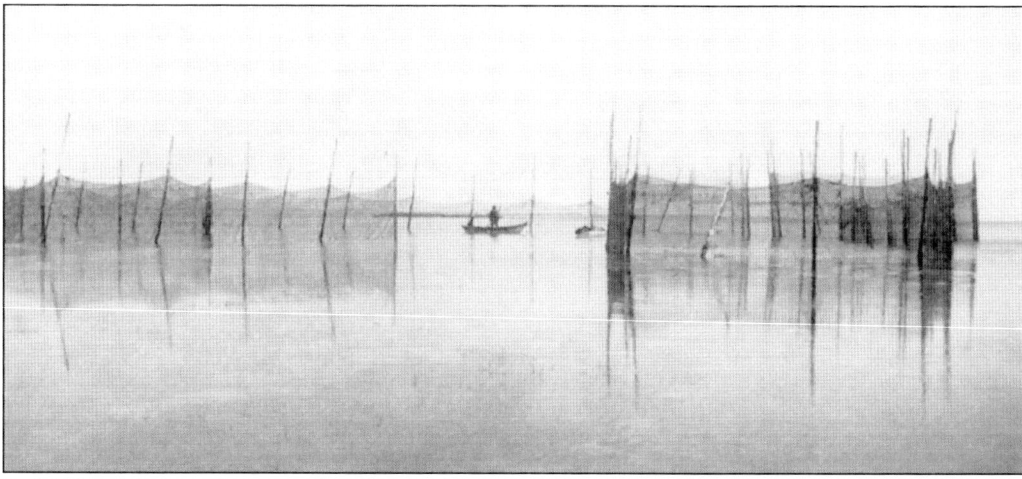

Fish Weirs (1898 photograph published by The Perry Pictures Co.). In 1869 a large fish weir was built in the East End by two men from Orleans and by John Young and Ephraim Ryder of Provincetown. Many weir-trap boats were unloaded at Railroad Wharf after its construction in 1873; trap boats (large dories with live fish wells) were unloaded in the morning, and draggers (fishing vessels with dragnets) in the afternoon. Portuguese fisherman Louis Cordeiro owned the last trap boat in town, the *Charlotte* (on display at the Provincetown Heritage Museum), when the era ended in 1975.

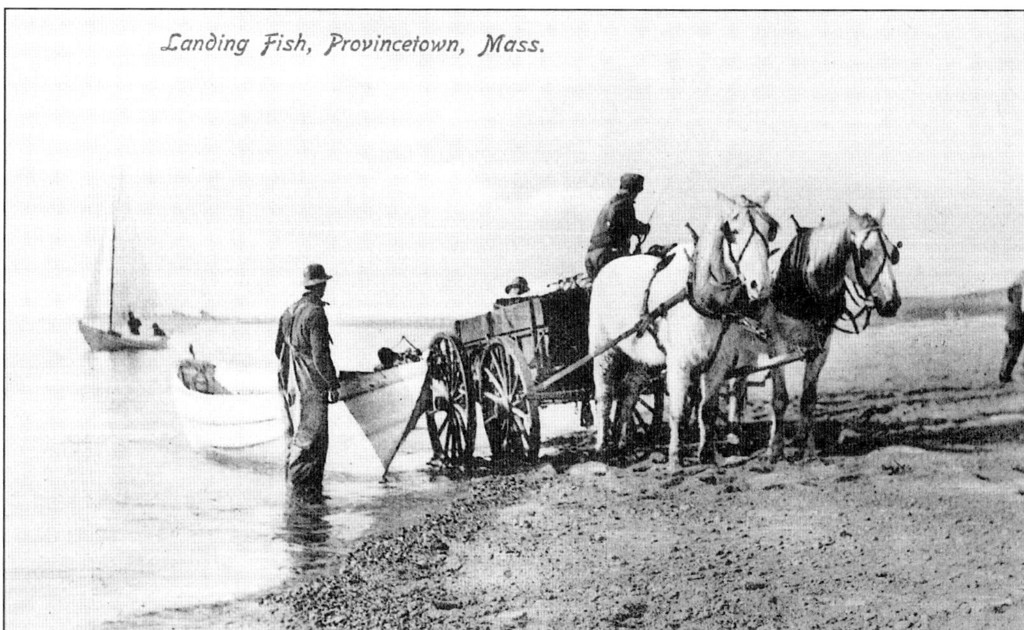

Landing Fish (early-20th-century postcard published by the *Advocate*). Fish caught by "McCart" Tavers are being pitchforked by William "Bushy Bill" Prada onto his wagon while "Dick" and "Baby" wait patiently along the shore of "Helltown." Helltown was located between Herring Cove Beach—named for the herring run there—and Hatches Harbor. About 125 hard-working, resourceful fishermen and their families lived there at one time in approximately 35 shacks. Transient fishermen have harvested the waters off Provincetown for centuries.

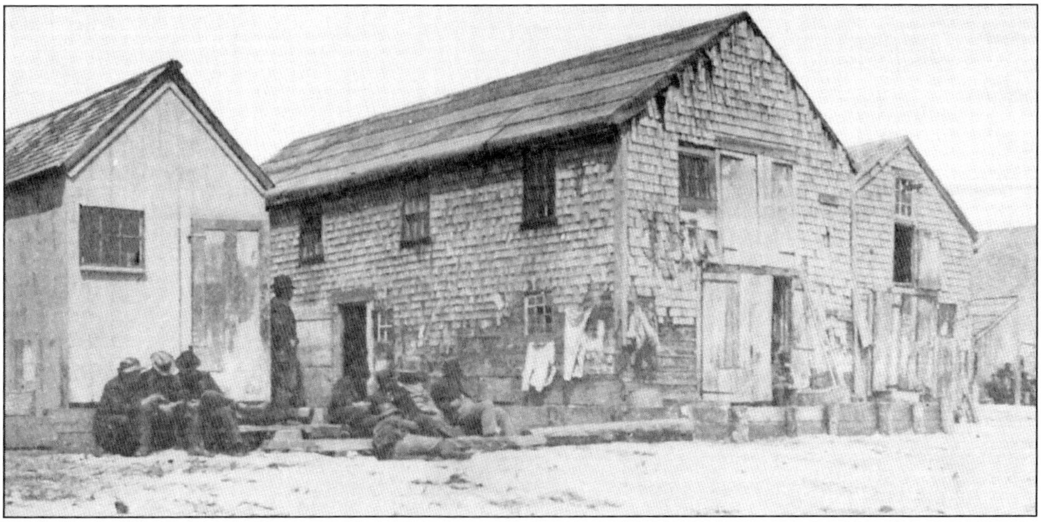

Fishermen Quarters (early-20th-century postcard issued by an unidentified publisher). Old salts exchange yarns by the shingled and board-sided fishermen's shacks and stores along the shore. Nineteenth-century structures such as these were either converted to shops, artists' studios, homes, or restaurants in the early 20th century, or else disappeared through fire, storm, or natural attrition. The traditional construction date of the first shack of this type on the Provincetown shore is 1680. During the mid-19th century, Joshua E. Bowley was a well-known ship chandler and grocer in town.

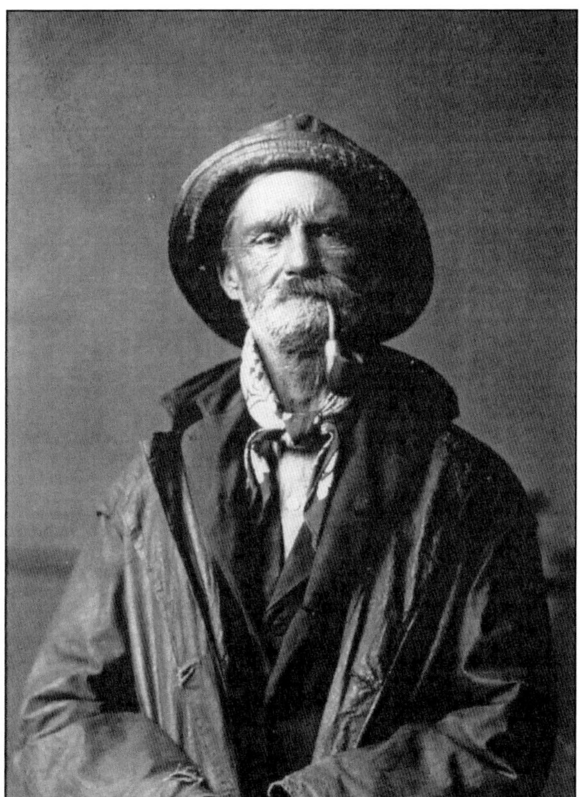

George Washington Ready (c. 1900 photograph). Weather-beaten G.W. Ready was wearing foul-weather gear when he sat for this photograph. Ready was known nationally as the man who spotted a "monstrous big sea serpent . . . which had three red eyes to port, and three green eyes to starboard" off Herring Cove in 1886. As the town crier, Mr. Ready wore everyday clothing with a colorful neck scarf (Vol. I, p. 37). Town criers did not don "Colonial" or "Pilgrim" costumes until around the 1920s. (Courtesy Provincetown Art Association and Museum.)

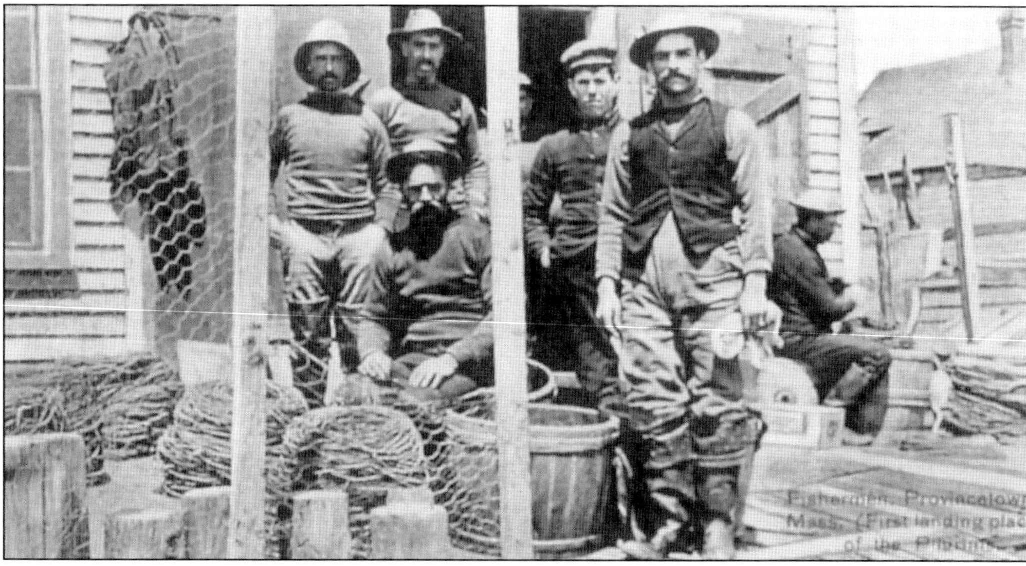

Fishermen (early-20th-century postcard published by the *Advocate*). Tawny-skinned fishermen stand on the deck of a warehouse with some of the tools of their trade. Varieties of fish caught and processed most often in Provincetown included bass, cod, flounder, haddock, mackerel, swordfish, and whiting. Mary Heaton Vorse wrote that "Men who fish for a living must have an easy courage. A good seaman cannot spend his time doubting himself. . . . A man who can make his living from the sea, and has the arrogance caused by having mastered the water from the time he can walk, is of necessity a good animal."

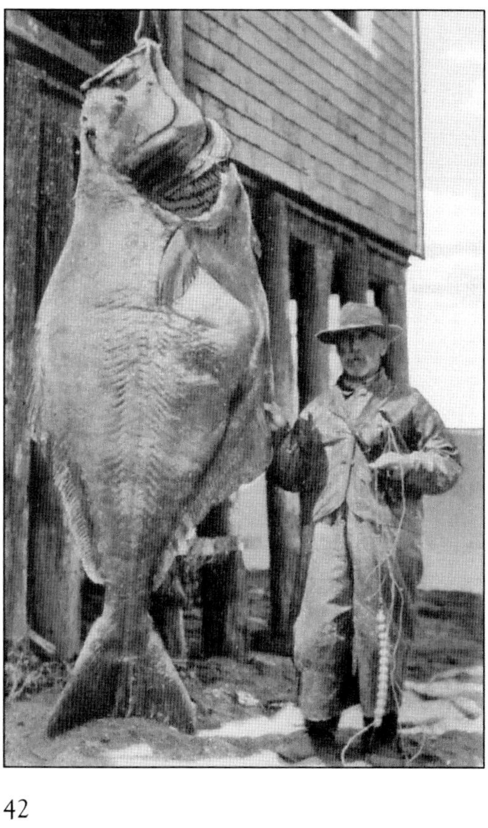

A 270-pound Halibut Caught at Provincetown (c. 1910 postcard published by H.A. Dickerman & Son). This honest-to-goodness "fish tale" of a postcard proved to be quite popular with tourists for almost a quarter century. Frank Cook, a lone fisherman, caught the gigantic halibut off Wood End around 1910, and by some unimaginable feat of strength loaded it into his dory and rowed back to a town pier, a distance of more than 5 miles. Cook's outstretched arms were not long enough to later show inquiring people the length of his once-in-a-lifetime amazing catch.

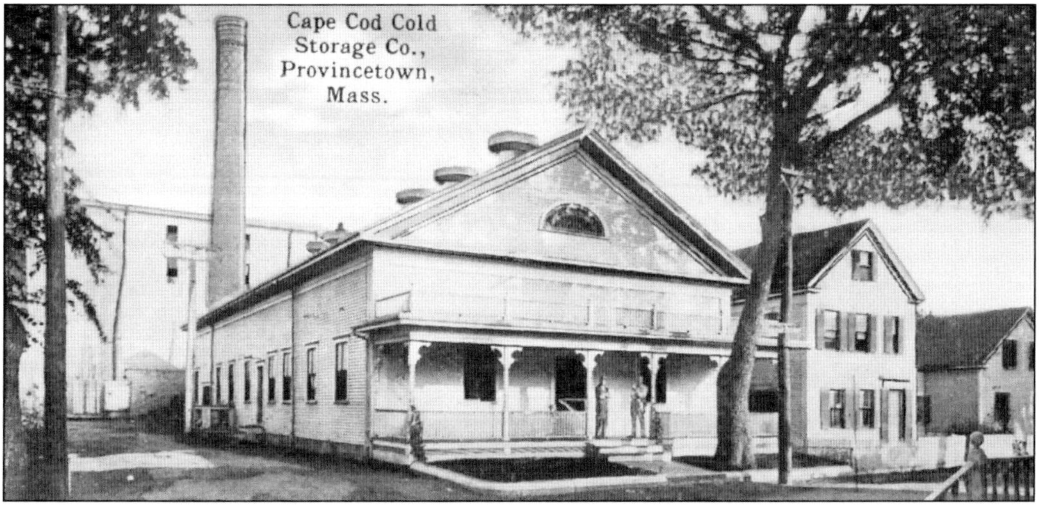

Cape Cod Cold Storage Co., 125–129 Commercial Street (early-20th-century postcard published by The Advocate Gift Shop). Two employees of the company—located on the present site of the U.S. Coast Guard Station where Commercial Street turns left—take a cigarette break during a quiet time of the day. During the early 20th century, seven oversized and architecturally out-of-scale fish processing and cold storage facilities were situated along the shore. Each had a tall brick chimney that vomited smoke. A four-story, plain concrete addition is in contrast to this clapboard-sided structure with its porch, balcony, and decorative fan-shaped glass window.

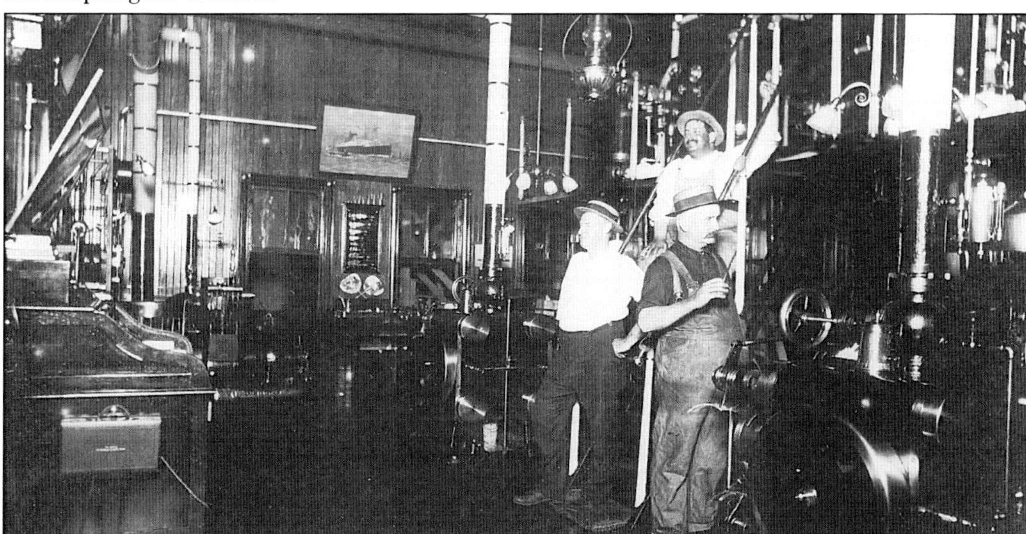

Interior of the Fisherman's Cold Storage, Foot of Court Street (early-20th-century photograph). The introduction of cold storage plants in Provincetown followed the abandoning of the salt works along the shore in the mid- to late 19th century, along with the advent of electric refrigeration. The first cold storage plant to be built in town was the Provincetown Cold Storage, constructed in 1893 by Dan Frank Small at the foot of Johnson Street; "Fat" Alves was the engineer at the plant in the 1930s. Compressed anhydrous ammonia in pipes maintained at a mean temperature of zero kept fish and bait frozen until transported or used in town. (Courtesy of the Cape Cod Pilgrim Memorial Association.)

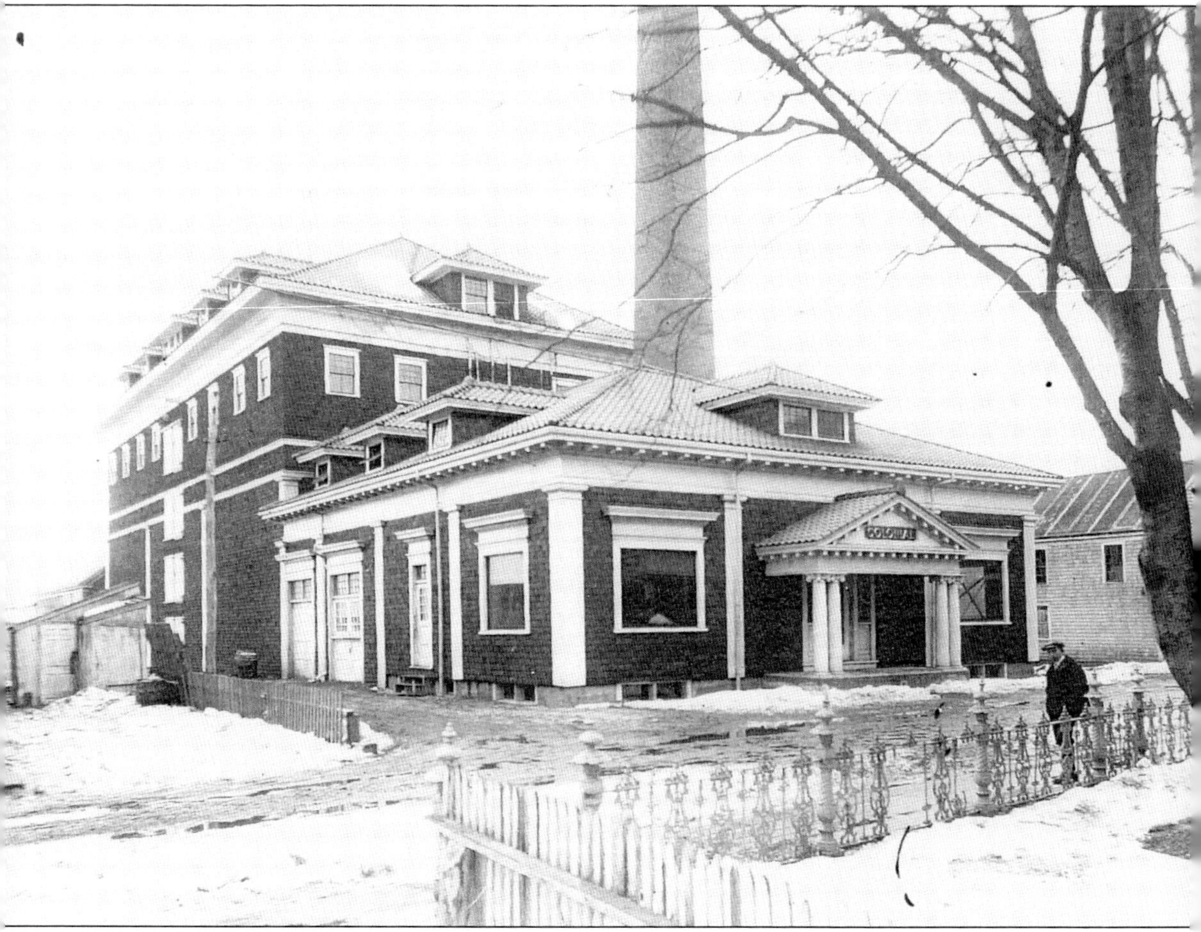

The Colonial Cold Storage Co., 229 Commercial Street (early-20th-century photograph). Atypical (to Cape Cod architecture) terra-cotta roof tiles protect and embellish hipped roofs, dormer windows, and the projecting front porch with its paired columns featuring Ionic capitals. The two four-square buildings—with the power house in front and the freezer in back—were joined together and had interior parking spaces for the fish-transporting vehicles. The front building is still a distinctive landmark across from Masonic Place. Some of the wharves behind the cold storage plants had railroad tracks for moving the fish-filled containers from the vessels tied alongside. Most of the structures (built at an average cost of $100,000) were later abandoned or destroyed; the Consolidated Cold Storage at 505 Commercial Street in the East End of town was recycled into living quarters now known as the Ice House Condominiums. (Private Collection.)

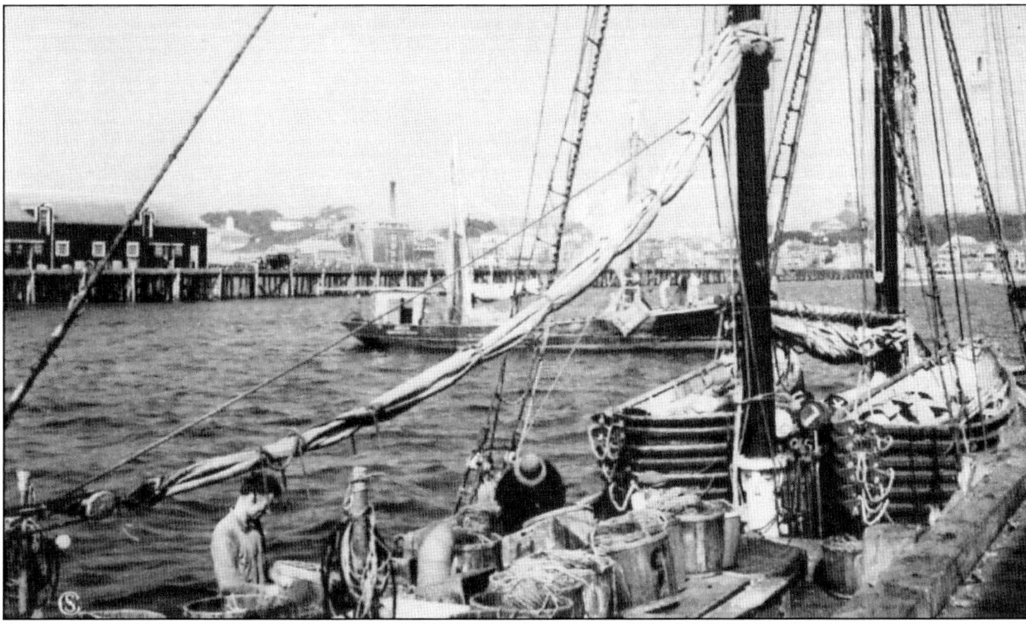

Fishing Boats (c. 1940 postcard published by The American Scene, New Haven, CT). Marblehead, Massachusetts, artist, photographer, and gourmand Samuel Chamberlain (1895–1975) took this well-composed photograph of fishing vessels with the town as a backdrop. Many local fishermen belonged to the Sandbar Club, which was located across the street from "The Oldest House" in the West End. During the Great Depression of 1929 the market for fresh fish fell drastically, and a decade later the *Mary P. Goulart* was one of the last great fishing schooners to leave the harbor.

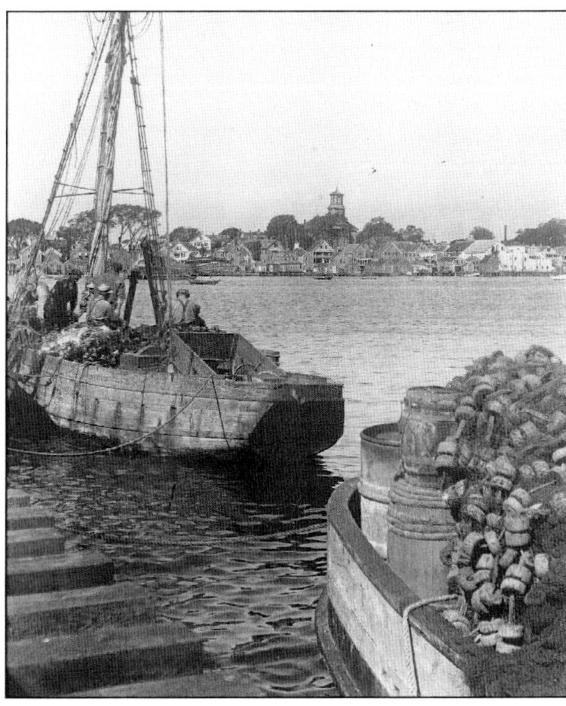

Dockside Fishermen (early-20th-century photograph by George Elmer Browne). Local artist/photographer George Elmer Browne (1871–1946) composed this arresting image of a tilting fishing vessel and its crew juxtaposed with a boatload of cork-net floats and metal and wooden barrels alongside Railroad Wharf. The two-tiered octagonal tower of the Center M.E. Church is visible in the background. (Private Collection.)

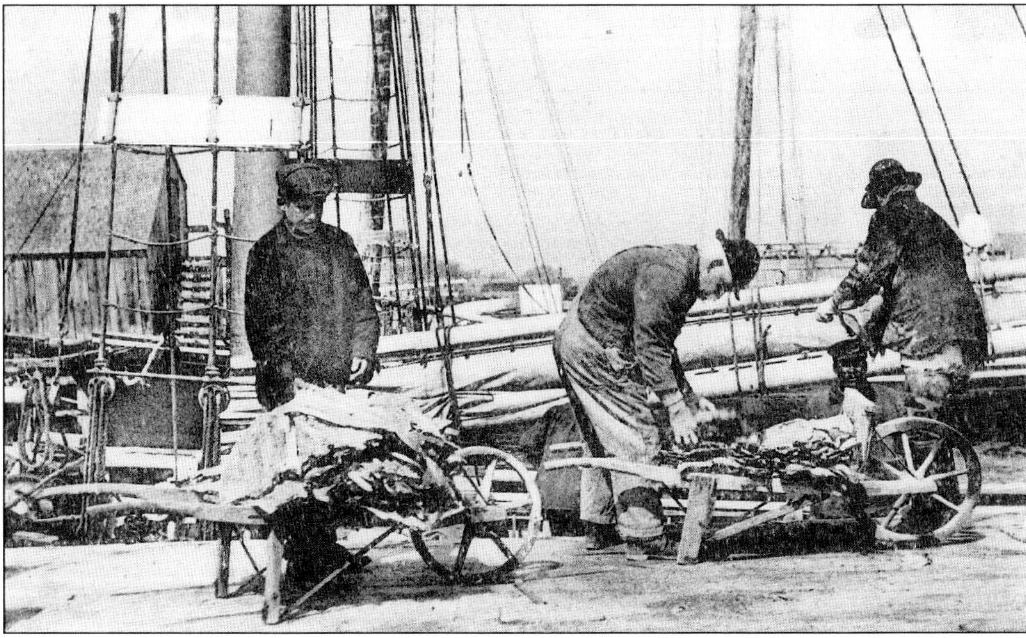

Shipping Fish (c. 1900 postcard published by the *Advocate*). An elderly dock worker bends over to hand dried fish flakes from his wheelbarrow to the man at the right, who is transferring them to the schooner. A much younger fellow worker awaits his turn. The term "fares" pertained to salted fish that was returned as cargo.

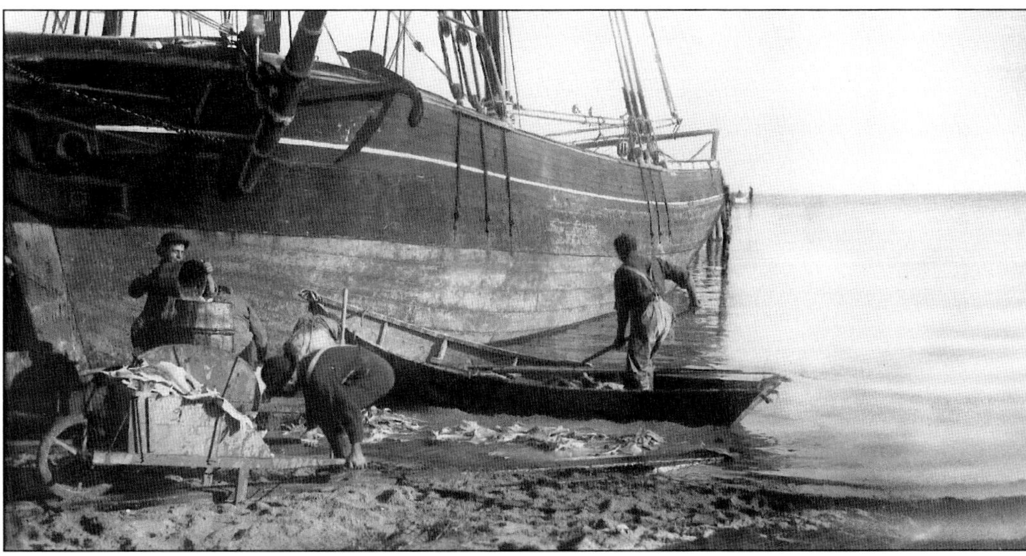

Washing Codfish (late-19th-century photograph). Salted cod from Grand Banks schooners was unloaded at the wharves by being pitchforked from the hold onto wheelbarrows. The split cod was then washed in a seawater-filled boat and packed into pickling barrels for shipment, or taken ashore to the numerous flake yards to be cured in the air and sun. Most fishermen were involved in the cod and mackerel fishery. By the time of the Civil War newer and larger vessels with steel hulls were being built, thus employing more men and boys. The Provincetown cod fishery ranked second only to Gloucester in 1875. (Courtesy Seamen's Bank.)

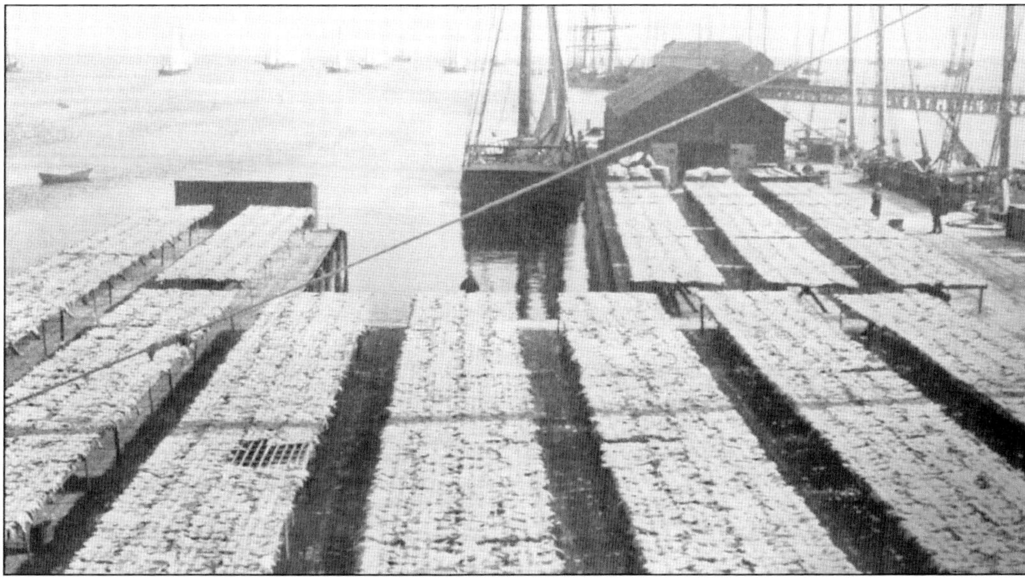

Drying Codfish (1898 photograph by The Perry Pictures Co.). Halved codfish—with their fleshy sides exposed to the air and sun—dry on long rows of "fish flakes" on Freeman's and Hilliard's salt codfish wharves (opposite the library), built during the mid-19th century. The fish house was constructed around 1874, and was destroyed by fire in 1974. Wharves were always changing hands; these later became Macara's Wharf. One of the longest wharves in town, Railroad Wharf, is at the right with fishing schooners tied alongside.

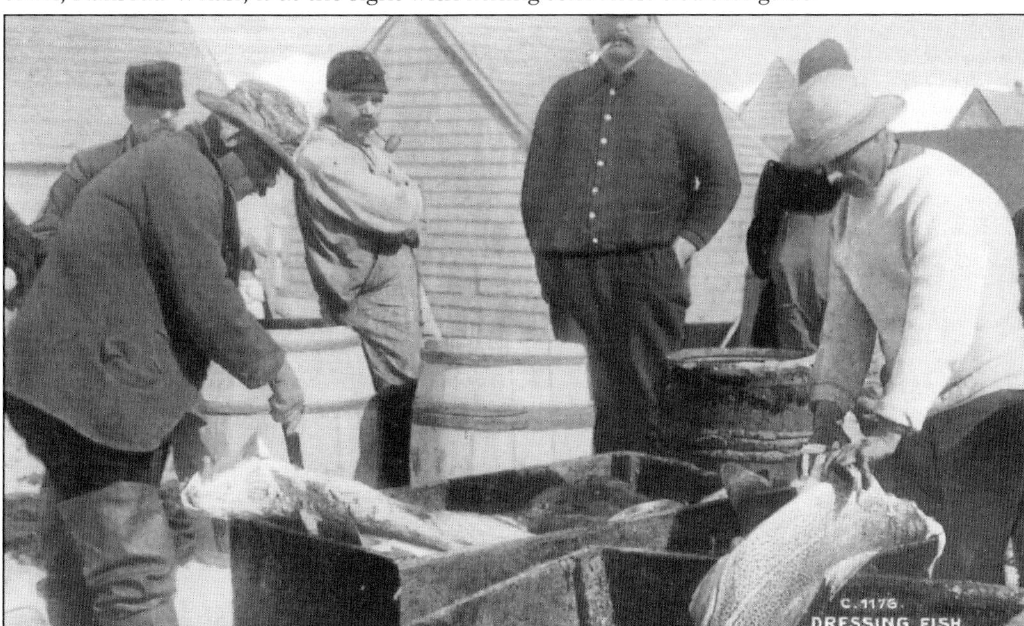

Dressing Fish (early-20th-century postcard published by the *Advocate*). Throaters, gutters, and splitters quickly dressed fish with skillful knives. One of the best all-time fish cutters, or gutters, was Francis N. "Frankie Bottles" Souza, a bachelor, who worked at the profession all his life (he died in 1997). Mr. Souza developed a method for skinning frozen whiting, and being paid for piece-work.

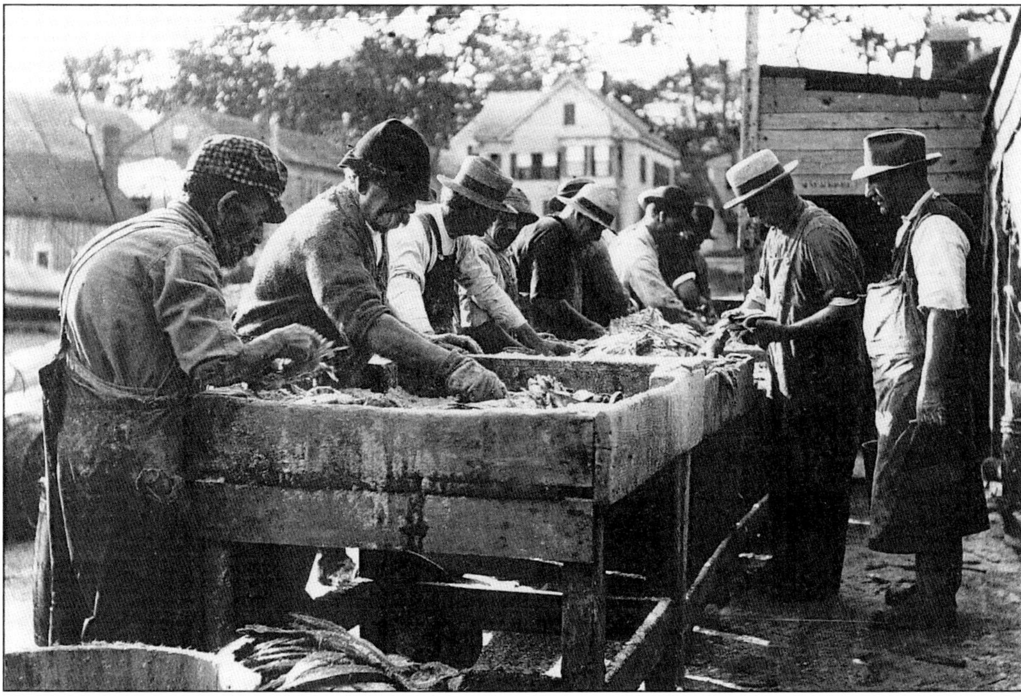

Salting Fish (early-20th-century photograph). Portuguese sailors and fishermen started to arrive in Provincetown around 1840 as extra crewmen on whaling and fishing vessels, and they began to displace the Yankees in the fishing industry. By the last quarter of the 19th century numerous immigrants had come from the Azores, and sent for their families. Most of the fishermen in town were of Portuguese descent by the beginning of the 20th century, often with Anglicized surnames. These "old salts" may have spoken Portuguese only. (Private Collection.)

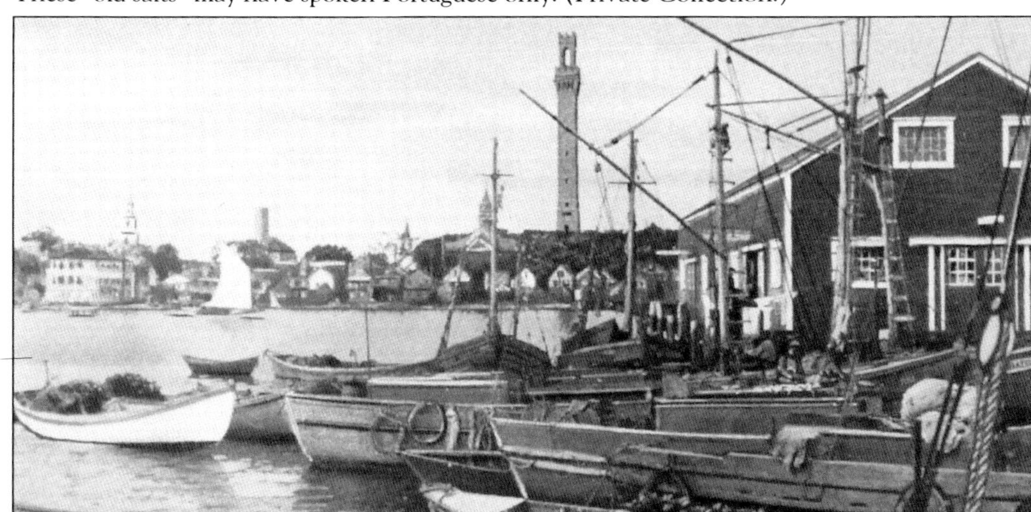

Fishing Boats (c. 1915 postcard published by H.A. Dickerman & Son). The masts and angled rigging of the fishing boats alongside the Town Pier compete for the viewer's attention with the solid granite shaft of the Pilgrim Memorial Monument. At one point in time before Provincetown was incorporated in 1727, it was called "Herrington," after the abundance of fish caught locally.

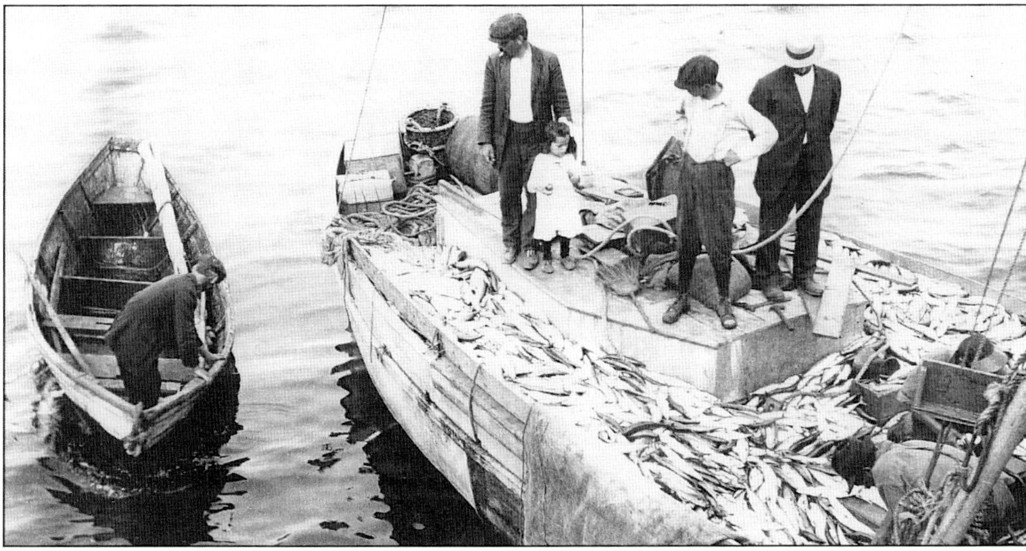

Laden with Mackerel (early-20th-century photograph). The young girl may be experiencing the sights and smells of a relative's fishing vessel for the first time. A whisk broom and a hammer rest helter-skelter on top of the hatchway along with rope and other paraphernalia. Most fresh-fish schooners were approximately 125 feet in length, and they were known for their agility and safety. (Private Collection.)

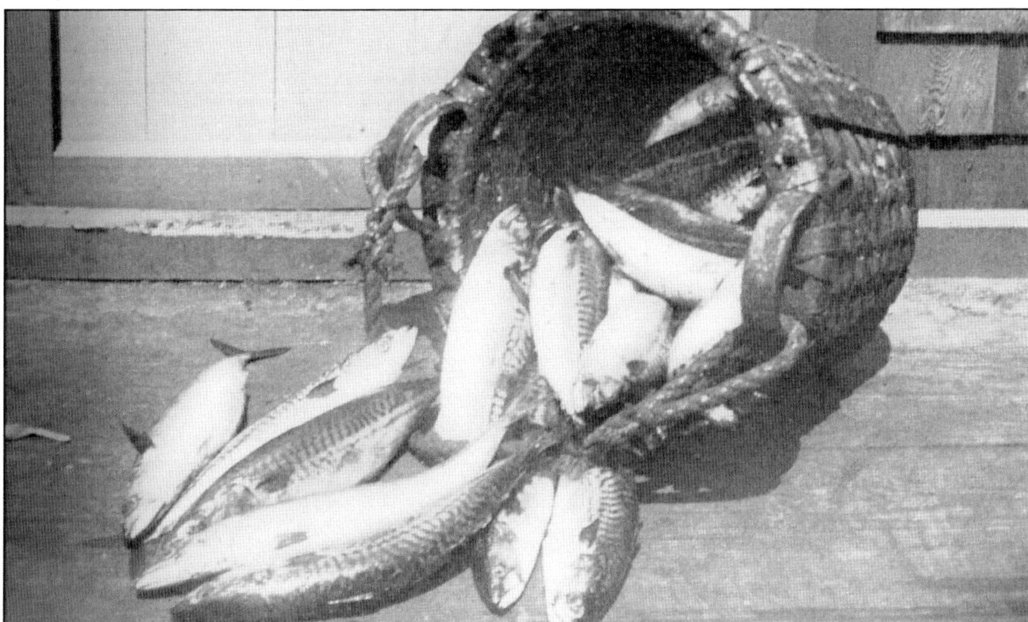

A Catch of Mackerel (1898 photograph by The Perry Pictures Co.). In 1851, 60 Provincetown-owned vessels weighing a total of 4,332 tons were engaged in the mackerel fishery, employing around 688 men and boys. By 1864 a great catch of mackerel resulted in that year being referred to as "The Boon Island Year." However, in May of 1871 it was reported that "the mackerel fishermen got so small a price . . . last week that it scarcely paid to catch them. Wait till we get a railroad [locals said] then we'll not depend upon Boston for a market." The railroad's arrival in Provincetown two years later improved all aspects of the fishing industry.

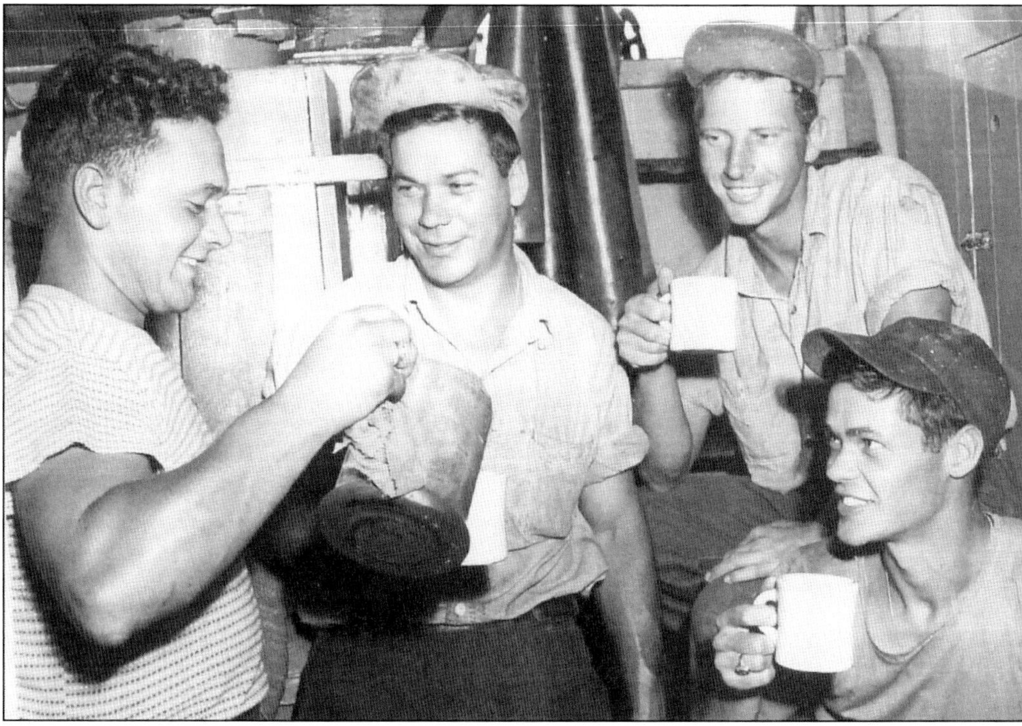

Morning Coffee Break (c. 1946 photograph by George Melnik). These Portuguese fishermen are savoring their early morning mug of coffee aboard the *Frances and Marion*. Pouring the brew for Sylvester Santos, Joe Perry, and Rudy Santos (the youngest fisherman) is "Barshie" Santos. Breakfast any morning might consist of a "malasada," an omelet or pancake; "rabanadas," French toast; or "flippers," fried sweet bread dough served with molasses or maple syrup. After a hard day's work, one of the thirsty fishermen might say to his buddies: "Vamos mas é beber uma cervejola!" (Let's have a beer instead!). (Private Collection.)

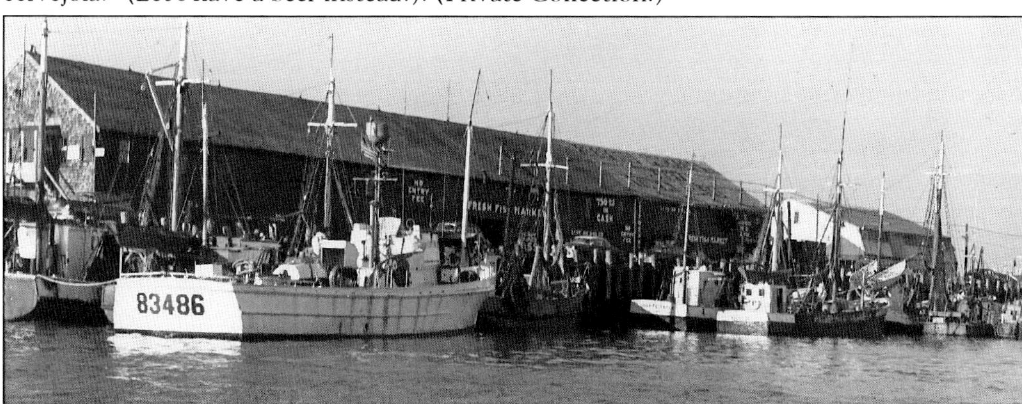

Fishing Fleet at the Town Pier (c. 1950s photograph by Cyril J. Patrick). The *Liberty Belle* (next to the *Noah A.*) was photographed about a quarter century before she sank around 1979; the owners raised and rebuilt the fishing boat shortly thereafter. Some of the signs on the fish storage warehouse state: "We Buy Striped Bass" and "Live Boiled Lobsters." Dragging for fish, a process that involves raking the ocean floor, was introduced by Portuguese fishermen around 1895. (Courtesy Seamen's Bank.)

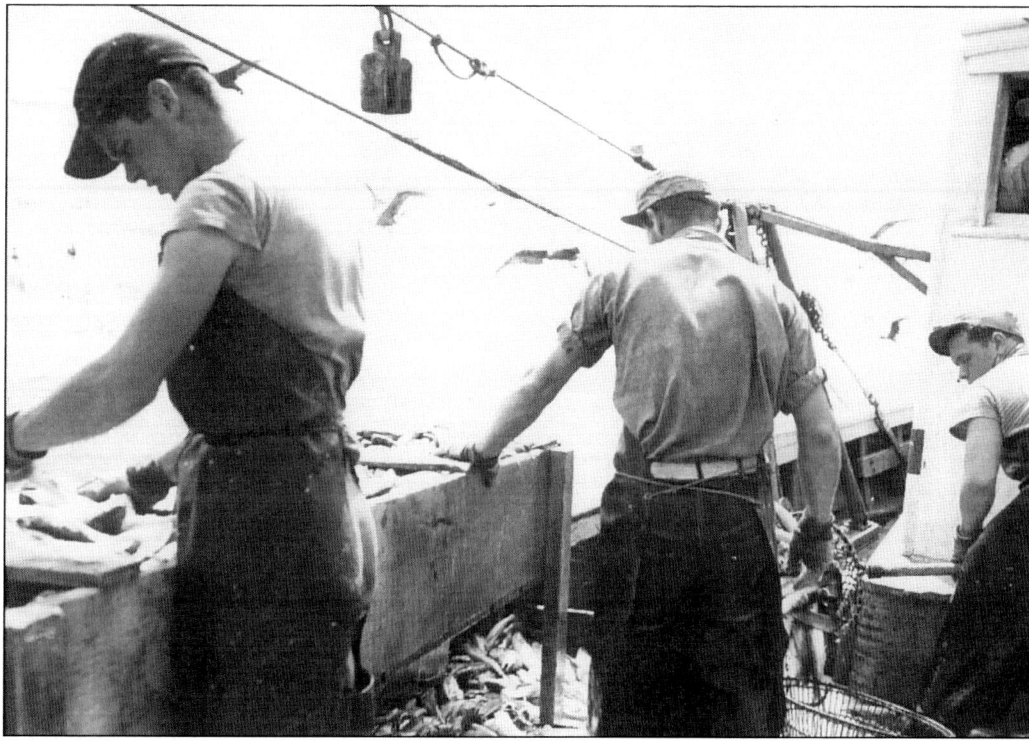

Fishermen's Tasks and Thoughts (c. 1946 photograph by George Melnik). As Sylvester Santos surveys fellow crew members at work, he may be recalling a Portuguese saying he had heard from his father or grandfather: "não se pescam trutas de bragas enxutas" ("dry shoes won't catch fish"). Santos may also be thinking about his supper when the dragger returns to port. That evening the family might enjoy hearty kale soup, "porco empau" (marinated pork cubes), "Skully Joes" (brine-soaked then dried fish), or "chouriço" (spicy sausage) served with "favas" (broad beans) and homemade bread. Blueberry pie from Burch's Bakery would be a fitting dessert, accompanied by "cachaça" (a strong homemade liquor) and equally strong coffee. (Private Collection.)

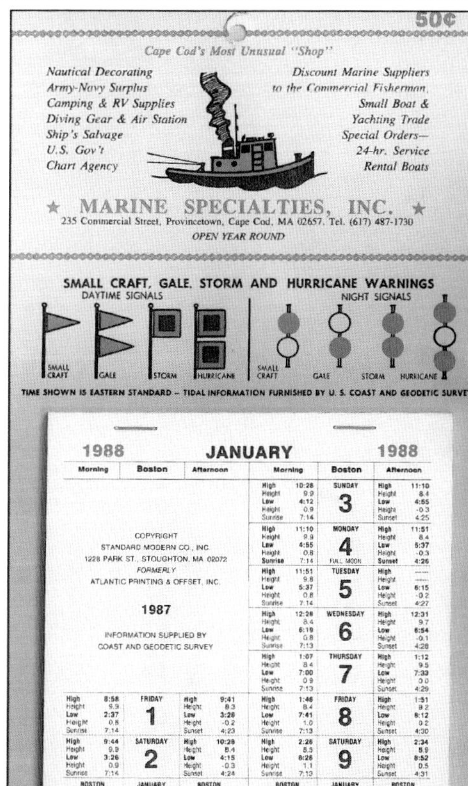

Tidal Information Calendar (1988). Marine Specialties, Inc., at 235 Commercial Street was part of a galvanized trap shed built by Mickey Finkle, and prior to that it was Cabral's Fish Market, run by Frank and Joseph Cabral. Regarded by many tourists as "a very unique and interesting store," it is a genuine army and navy surplus store that specializes in military clothing, boots, leather accouterments, moorings, etc., from many nations. (Courtesy Schier Collection.)

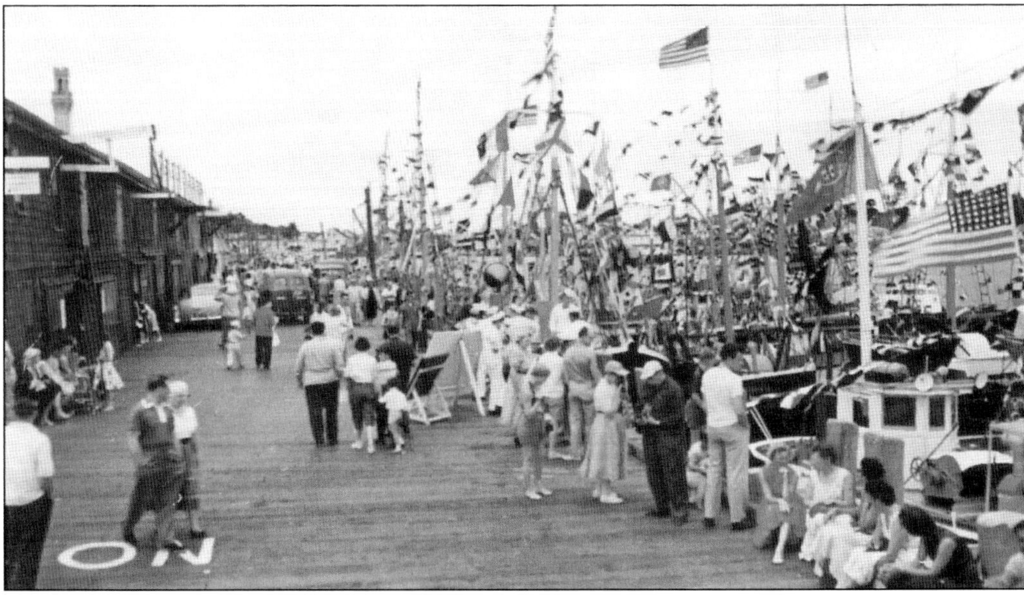

Gala Wharf Scene at Blessing of the Fleet (c. 1965 postcard published by E.D. West Co.). Tourists sit or stroll by docked fishing vessels adorned with multicolored banners and streamers to celebrate the annual Blessing of the Fleet, which occurs on the last Sunday in June. Flying everywhere, in different sizes, is the Portuguese national flag, which has a field of red and green with a red-and-white shield over a circular yellow background. At early Blessings the Linguica Band entertained all with their lively renditions of traditional and popular melodies.

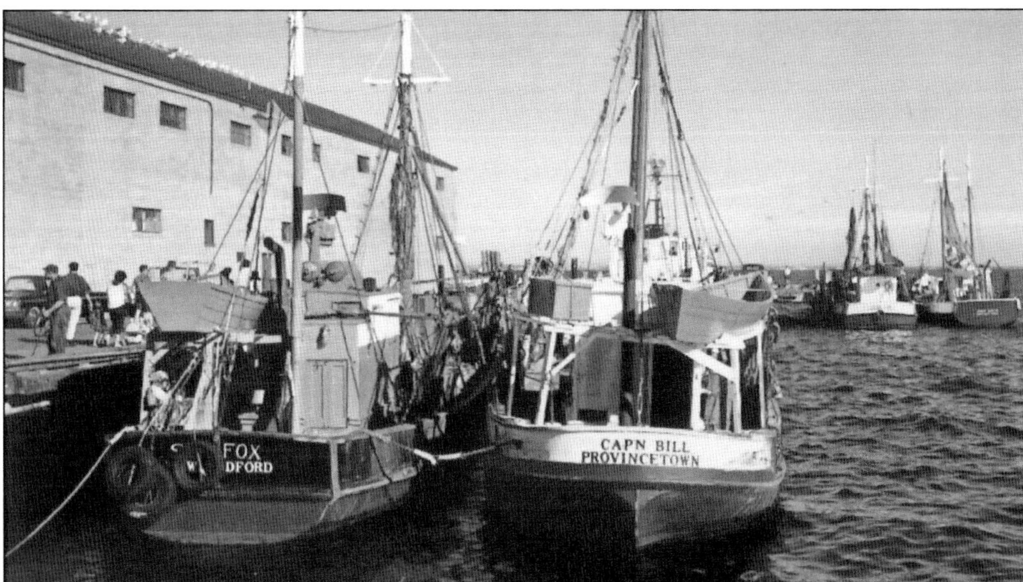

Fishing Boats at the Town Pier (c. 1970 postcard published by Bromley & Co., Boston, MA). On or about February 9, 1978, Ralph Andrews and his crew perished in a boating accident on the dragger *Cap'n Bill.* The *Sea Fox*, then out of New Bedford, was sold to Manuel Henrique little more than a year and a half after Provincetown Captain Manny "Sea Fox" Zora acquired the new dragger in October of 1945.

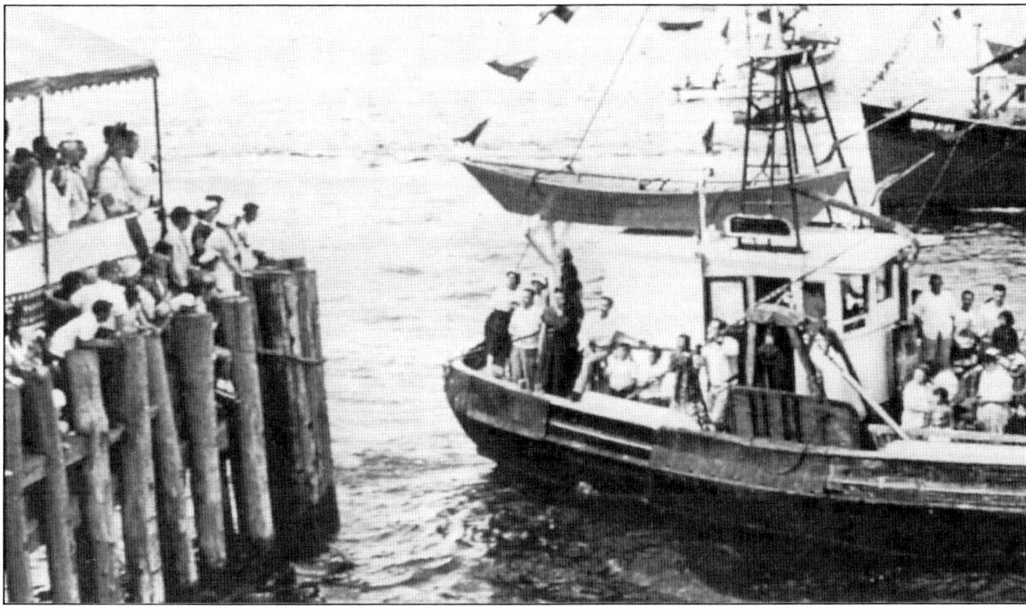

Blessing of the Fleet (mid-20th-century photograph). The fleet's blessing has been a popular tradition and religious celebration in Provincetown since it was first held there in 1947. Arthur Bragg Silva and Domingo "Four-Master" Godinho witnessed the event in Gloucester, Massachusetts, and were members of a committee to bring the celebration to their town. Gaily decorated fishing boats filled with relatives and friends of the owner(s) pass by the end of MacMillan Wharf at noon on the last Sunday in June to be blessed by the officiating prelate to insure a season of safe and profitable fishing. Later the flotilla sets sail for Long Point for partying, swimming, and feasting until twilight. (Courtesy St. Peter the Apostle Church.)

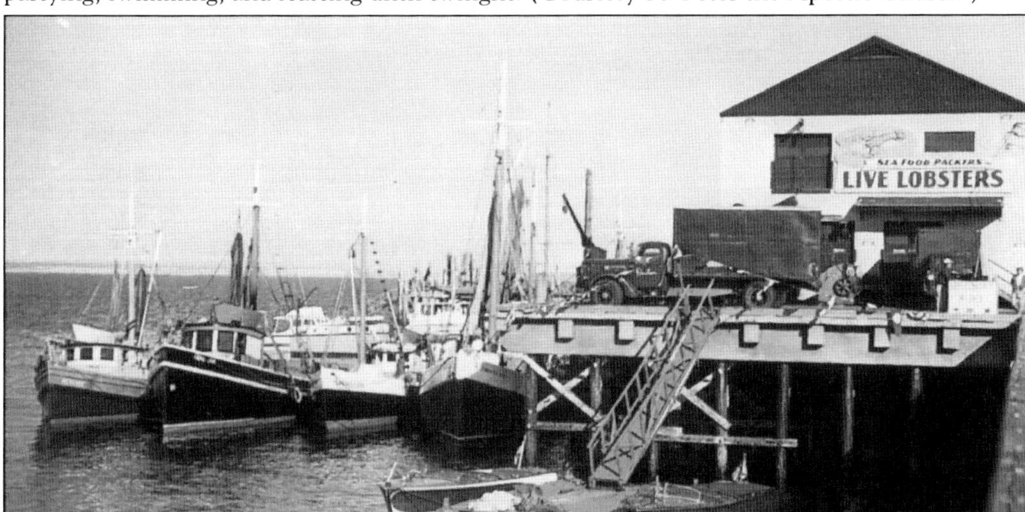

Fishing Boats at the Town Wharf (c. 1970 postcard published by Colourpicture, Inc., Boston, MA). Mickey Finkle owned a lobster pound on the town-owned wharf, but he was not allowed to establish a "tuna empire" there. It is believed that Irish fishermen from Boston introduced trawl fishing to Provincetown around the 1860s. During the first quarter of the 20th century, trawl lines were about a mile in length with about one thousand attached hooks. Local fishermen often trawl for fish in the winter.

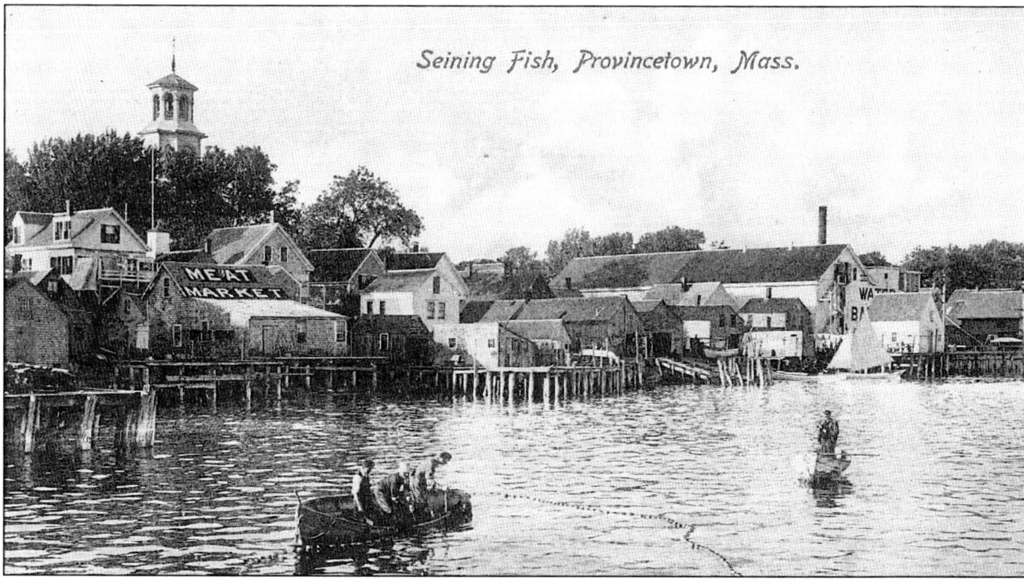

Seining Fish (early-20th-century postcard published by the *Advocate*). These dory fishermen have successfully encircled a school of fish in their purse seine with its cork floats, and are making the circle smaller. Shorefront businesses with predominant signs flanking the Center M.E. Church include that of a meat market and Provincetown Cold Storage—the long, white building with the partially visible "Water and Bait" sign—located at the foot of Johnson Street.

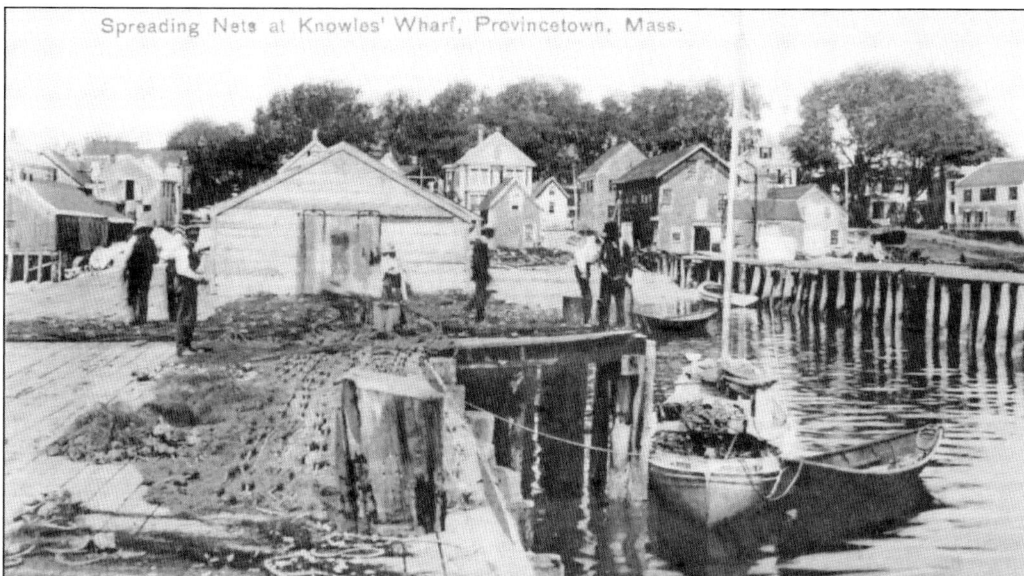

Spreading Nets at Knowles' Wharf (early-20th-century postcard published by the *Advocate*). Frank Knowles's wharf was located opposite Pearl Street in the East End of town. Fish nets were laid out to dry there and then they were tarred in great tar kettles; often they were dried on nearby blueberry bushes in the 19th century. Stephen Cook built the wharf, which was later acquired by Mr. Knowles. Conwell's (a.k.a. Cannery) Wharf at the right also featured a tar pit for keeping fish nets in good condition.

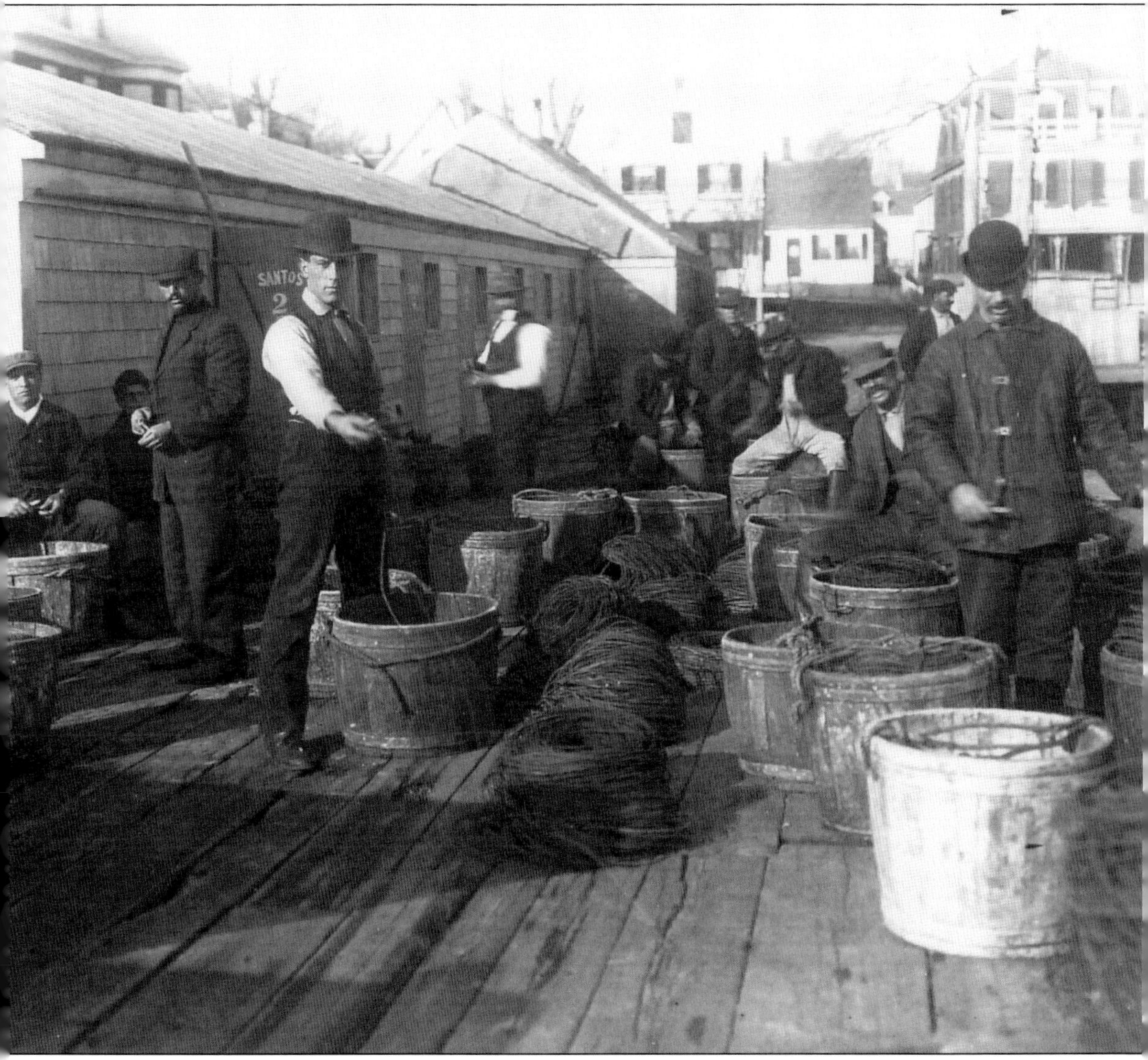

Fishermen at Knowles' Wharf (early-20th-century photograph by George Elmer Browne). Artist/photographer Browne may have used some of the fishermen as models in paintings he produced in Provincetown during the first half of the century. The Santos family name has been connected to the fishing industry in town for generations, as it has in other seaports such as Gloucester and New Bedford. Portuguese fisherman Robert Enos worked as a crew member on the tuna trap boat *Harbor Bar* during the 1960s. He served as a shellfish warden at one time, and would agree with most other fishermen who believe that "fishing is a life more than a business." (Private Collection.)

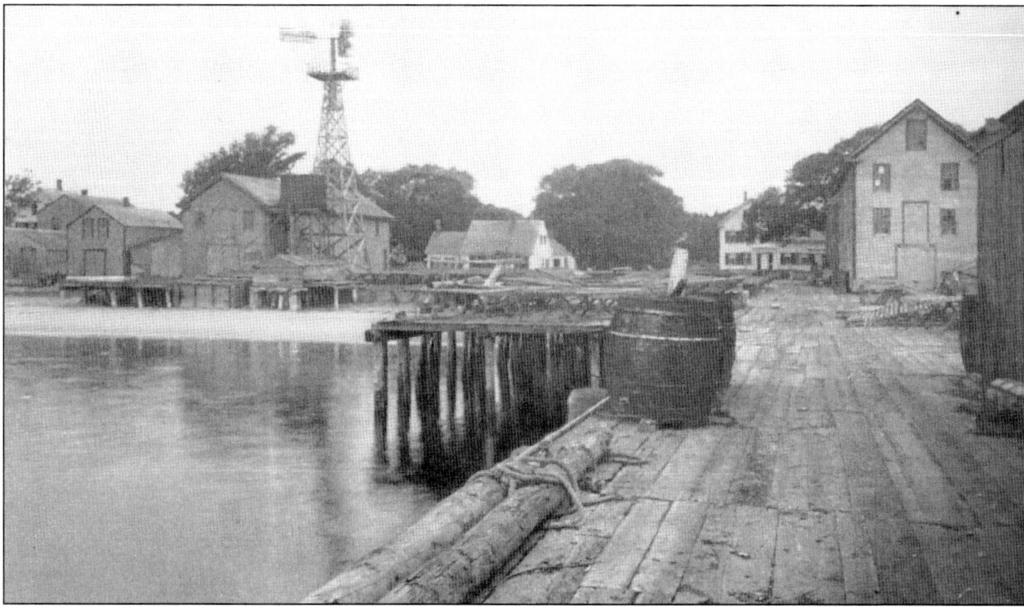

Fish Houses, Fish Flakes, and Wharf (1898 photograph by The Perry Pictures Co.). A windmill catches the viewer's eye in this turn-of-the-century shore image of Philip Whorf's Wharf "Way-Down-Along" before the Portland Gale later that year. During the 1880s Provincetown was the richest town per capita in Massachusetts as a result of the fishing industry's success. Before the aforementioned catastrophic storm, the shoreline was bustling with the related businesses of blacksmiths, chandlers, caulkers, painters, riggers, sailmakers, fitting stores, and at least three marine railways.

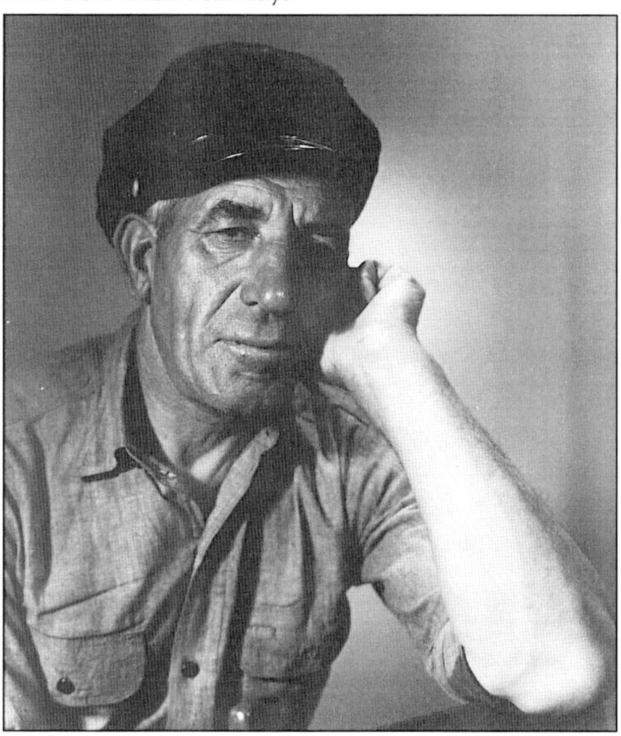

Captain Manuel Zora (c. 1950 photograph by John W. Gregory). The strong features and distinctive appearance of Manny "Sea Fox" Zora have been remarked upon by many who remember the former fisherman, rumrunner (contrabandista), and very popular ladies man, who was raised and retired in Portugal. Zora's exciting life is related in the 1956 novel *The Sea Fox* by Scott Corbett. (Private Collection.)

Three

Back Shore Views and Shipwrecks

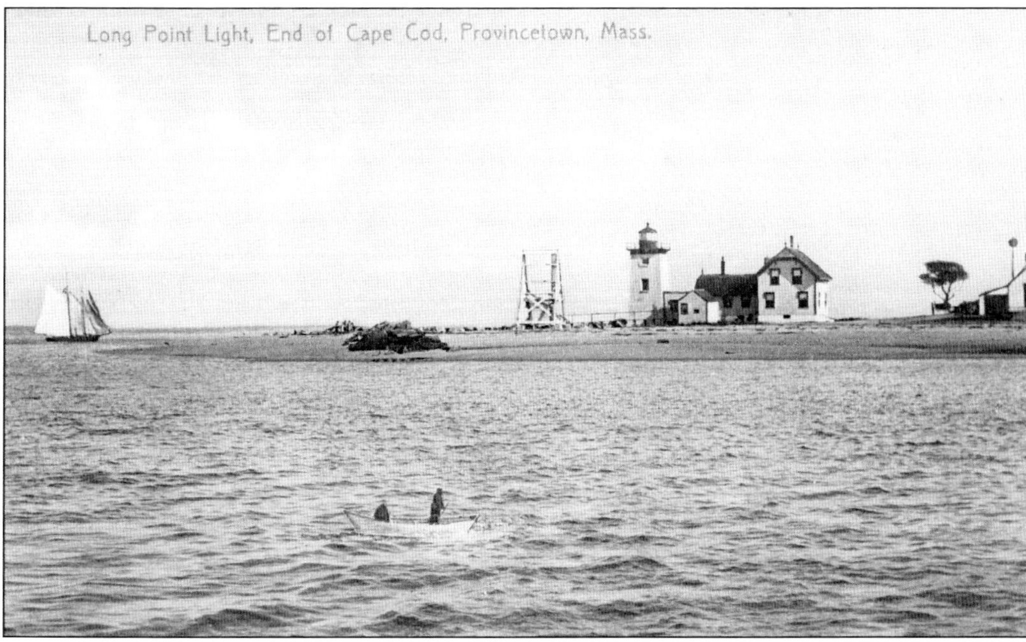

Long Point Light, End of Cape Cod (early-20th-century postcard published by I.L. Rosenthal). The "low-lying grayness of Provincetown" with its 3-mile stretch of similarly gray-and-white buildings is visible from the Atlantic Ocean as one passes the third and last lighthouse on the tip of Cape Cod. Long Point Light was constructed in 1826 and illuminated the following year for the first time. Also known as "Stationary Light," the lighthouse—rebuilt in 1875 and later illuminated by the present automatic system—displays a blinking green light and has a distinctive fog signal. In 1818 the first of about 60 wooden homes was constructed in the area by fishermen who wanted to be close to their work. The community of about two hundred inhabitants prospered there until before the Civil War, when the settlement fell apart. Most of the houses, the schoolhouse (1846), and the bakery (1850) were floated on scows over to the mainland, where most were re-erected in the Gull Hill area. These relocated buildings are identified by blue-and-white enameled plaques depicting a house afloat, which were designed and made by local artist Claude Jensen.

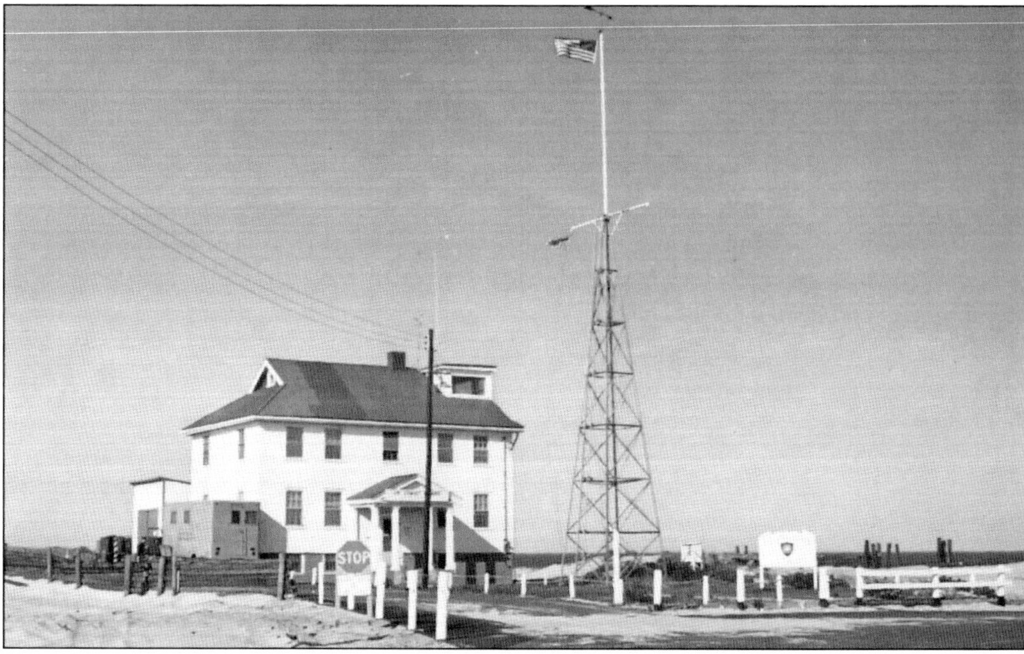

U.S. Coast Guard Station, Race Point (c. 1975 postcard published by Bromley & Co.). The Race Point Coast Guard Station was constructed in 1931 and decommissioned around 1980. Since 1982 it has served as the Race Point Ranger Station for the Cape Cod National Seashore (established by public law on August 7, 1961). The building is located near the site of the Race Point Lifesaving Station, which was built in 1872.

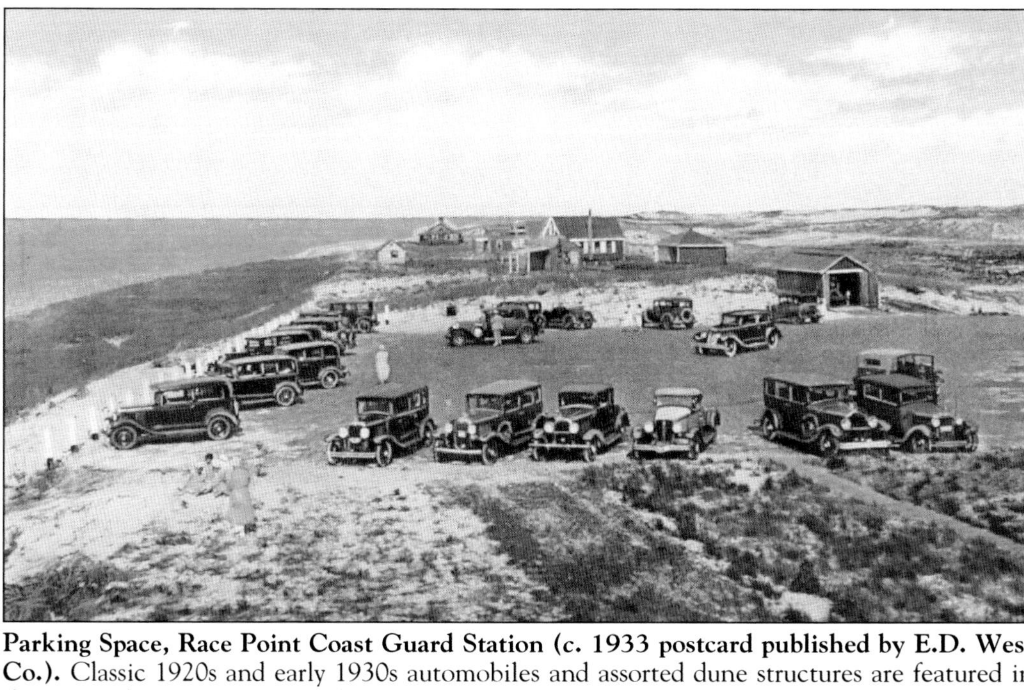

Parking Space, Race Point Coast Guard Station (c. 1933 postcard published by E.D. West Co.). Classic 1920s and early 1930s automobiles and assorted dune structures are featured in this view along Race Point. The Provincetown Municipal Airport and the Old Harbor Life Saving Station are located in this area of awe-inspiring beauty.

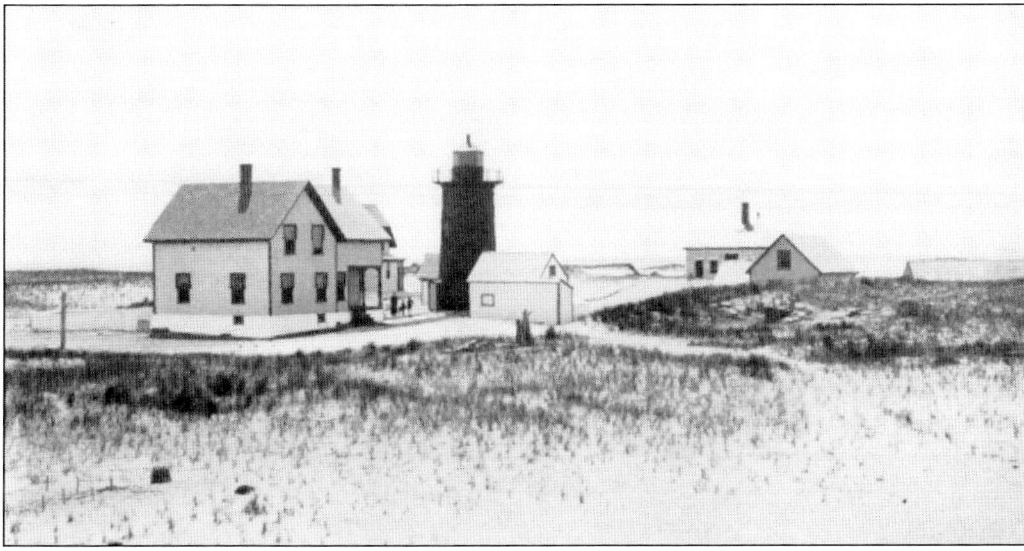

Race Point Light (1898 photograph by The Perry Pictures Co.). The lighthouse at Race Point—at the Cape's "wrist"—is the first one encountered in Provincetown by those who approach the town by vessel from Boston. The 1816 lighthouse was the first of three to be built in the immediate area, and it functioned as such until 1876 (the centennial year), when it was replaced by the present structure. Captain Sam Fisher was in charge of the "guiding light" when debris from several vessels washed ashore during the aftermath of the Portland Gale.

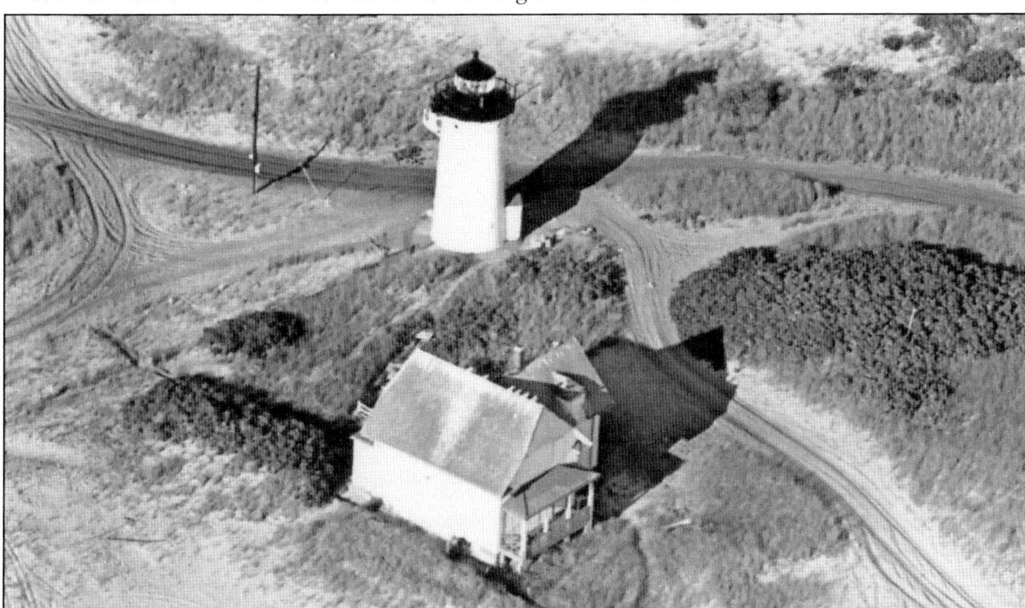

Race Point Lighthouse (c. 1960 postcard published by the Dexter Press). The traditional white tower of most lighthouses, and that of Race Point Light, is 41 feet above water. In the early 1960s the two-family Victorian dwelling was torn down. By 1941 Manuel Henrique had been the officer in charge of the "dangerous surf boat station"—located about 2 miles away along the beach—for 22 years; 10 men were responsible for watching planes and ships which might be in distress.

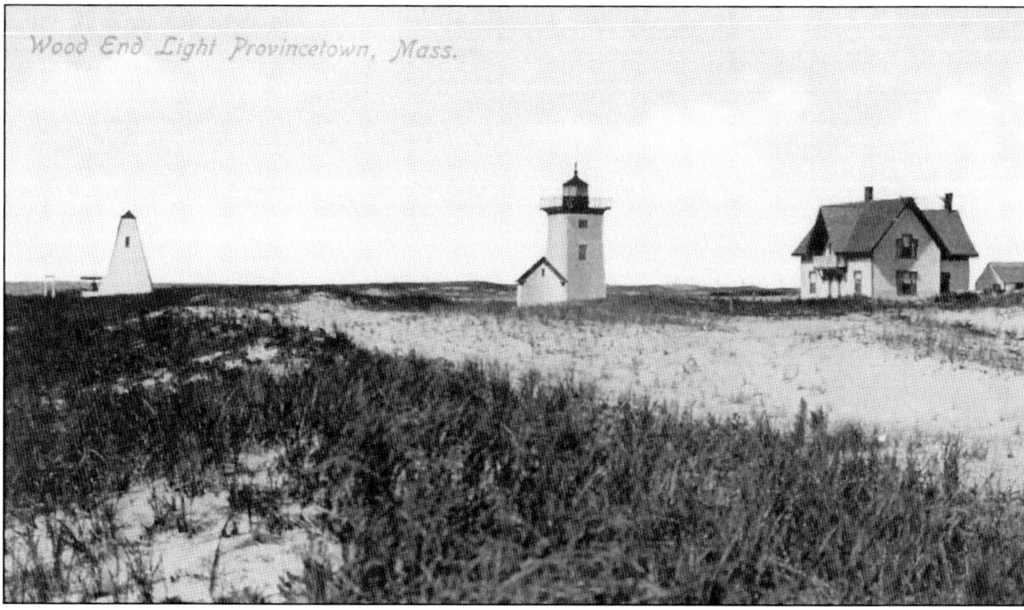

Wood End Light (early-20th-century postcard published by the *Advocate*). Located at the bent "knuckles" of the Cape's arm, Wood End Light is the second lighthouse passed by those who travel from Boston to Provincetown by vessel. The lighthouse was constructed in 1872, and now has a flashing red light powered by solar panels, and, of course, a fog horn signal. On December 17, 1927, the American *S-4* submarine disaster occurred in this area after the vessel had been hit while near the surface during a test run by the Coast Guard destroyer *Paulding*. Anthony Tarvers Sr. was in command of the lighthouse during that unfortunate event when 40 submarine crew members perished.

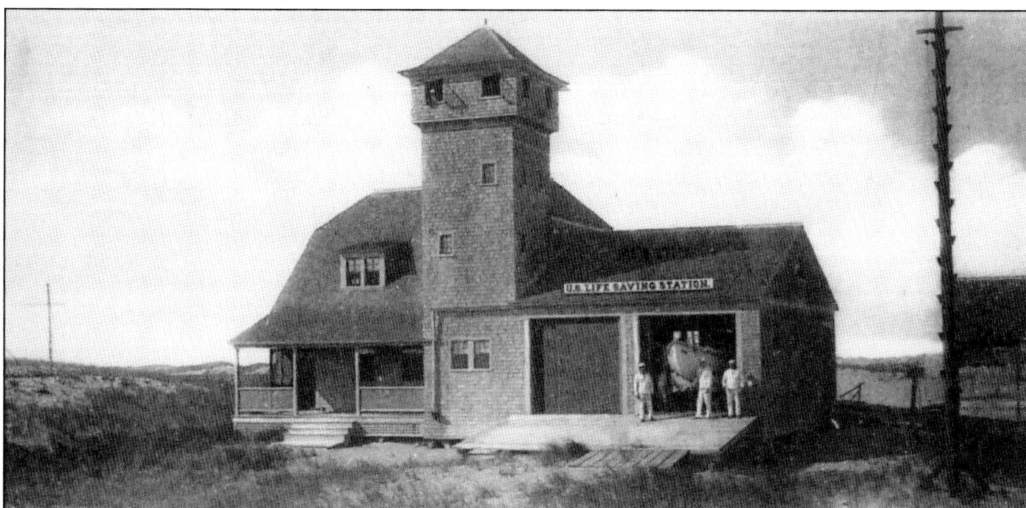

U.S. Life Saving Station, Wood End (1905 postcard published by The Rotograph Co., NY). Congress founded the Life Saving Service in 1872, and in 1915 it was merged with the U.S. Coast Guard. Part of the life-saving crew, dressed in their white uniforms and caps, stand by one of their vessels . . . waiting. Similar in appearance and date is the Old Harbor Life Saving Station, which was moved in two sections from Chatham (where the 40-mile National Seashore leads to Provincetown) to Race Point in 1977.

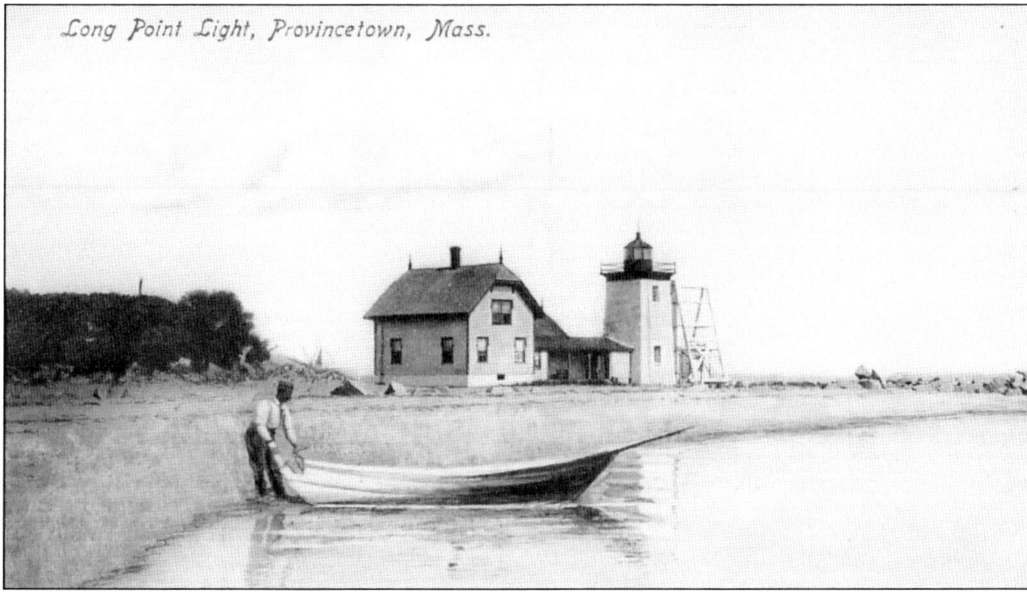

Long Point Light (early-20th-century postcard published by the *Advocate*). A solitary, well-dressed gentleman adjusts the stern of his dory near Long Point Light. He may be going for a sail or "sweetmeating and conker-rinkling," a local term used for catching snails and periwinkles in traps below the low-water mark. The remains of two Civil War sand batteries on Long Point—built in 1864, fully equipped and manned, but obviously never used in a wartime situation—were jocularly referred to as "Fort Useless" and "Fort Ridiculous." In the past, bonfires were a popular Fourth of July treat on Long Point.

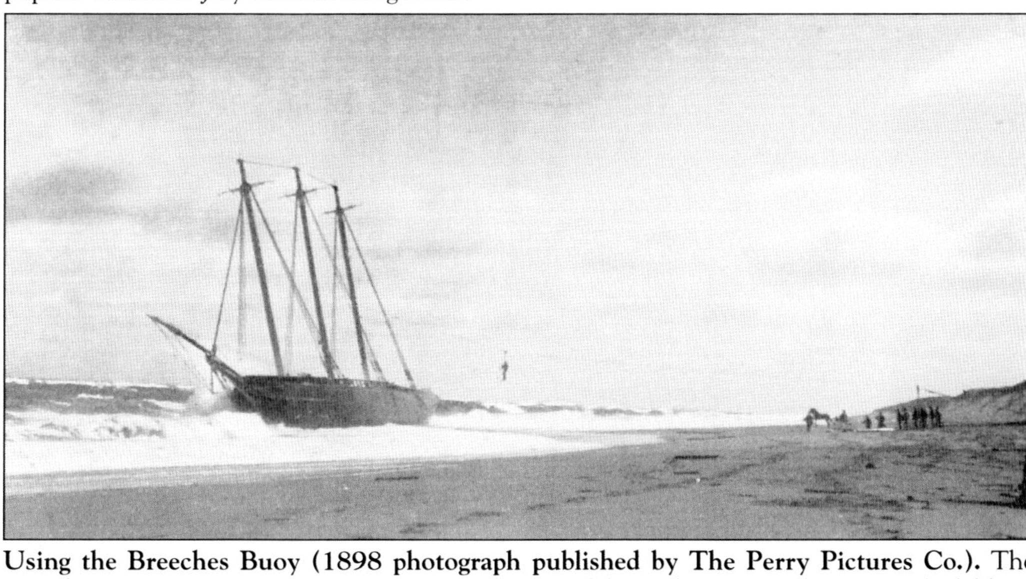

Using the Breeches Buoy (1898 photograph published by The Perry Pictures Co.). The Breeches Buoy came into use during the second half of the 19th century when rescue by lifeboat was impossible. A special type of canon known as the Lyle Gun had a shot-line that was fired into the ship's rigging and then secured to the mast of the distressed vessel. The Breeches Buoy, which was a pair of heavy-duty canvas shorts, was attached to a cork life ring. As soon as a red flag was raised, the person who was positioned in the contraption would be hauled to safety by men on shore.

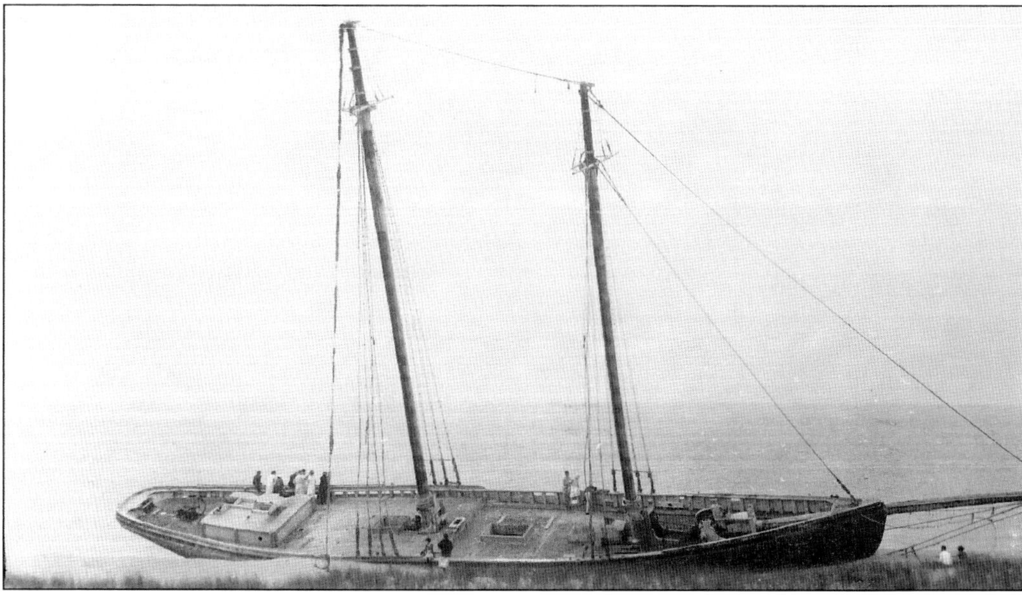

"The Rum Runner" (c. 1924 photocard; publisher unknown). The *Annie L. Spindler*, a Nova Scotian two-masted schooner, was wrecked during a heavy gale at Race Point near the U.S. Coast Guard Station on December 29, 1922. Although referred to as "The Rum Runner," she was actually transporting about eight hundred cases of bootlegged whiskey when she went aground. Officials soon searched the town thoroughly for the jettisoned cases of whiskey. The disintegrating wreck on the beach became a favorite spot for picnickers and painters for many years.

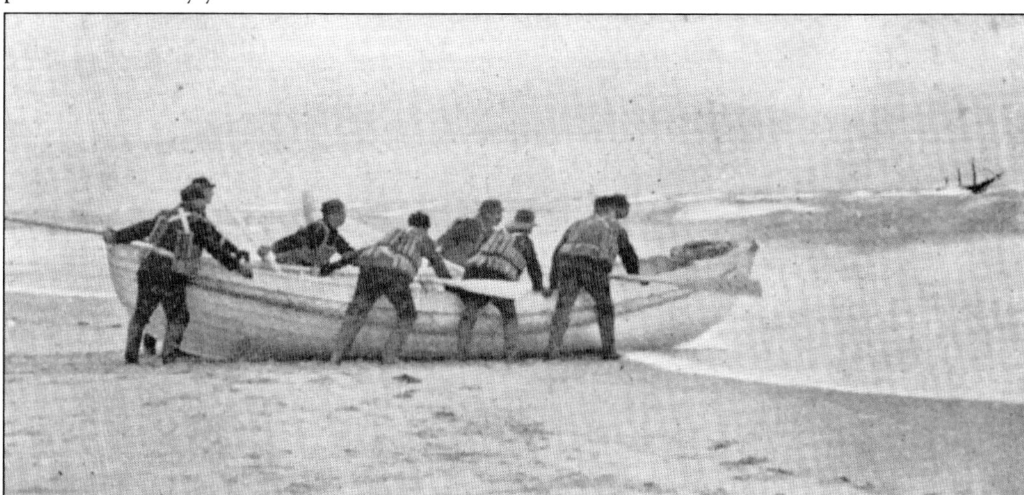

United States Life Saving Station Crew with Life Boat (August 31, 1893, photograph in *Frank Leslie's Weekly*). The Cape Cod coastline is known as the "graveyard of the Atlantic," and the stretch between Peaked Hill Bars to Monomoy (south of Chatham) is the most treacherous. Between 1843 and 1859 there were 500 officially recorded wrecks; between 1880 and 1903, 540 were listed; and for the period between 1910 and 1917 only 156 were known to have occurred. The life-saving crew patrolled the beaches every day and night through inclement weather and blasting sand. Their motto "Semper Paratus" ("Always Ready") unofficially was paraphrased as "You gotta go but you don't have to come back."

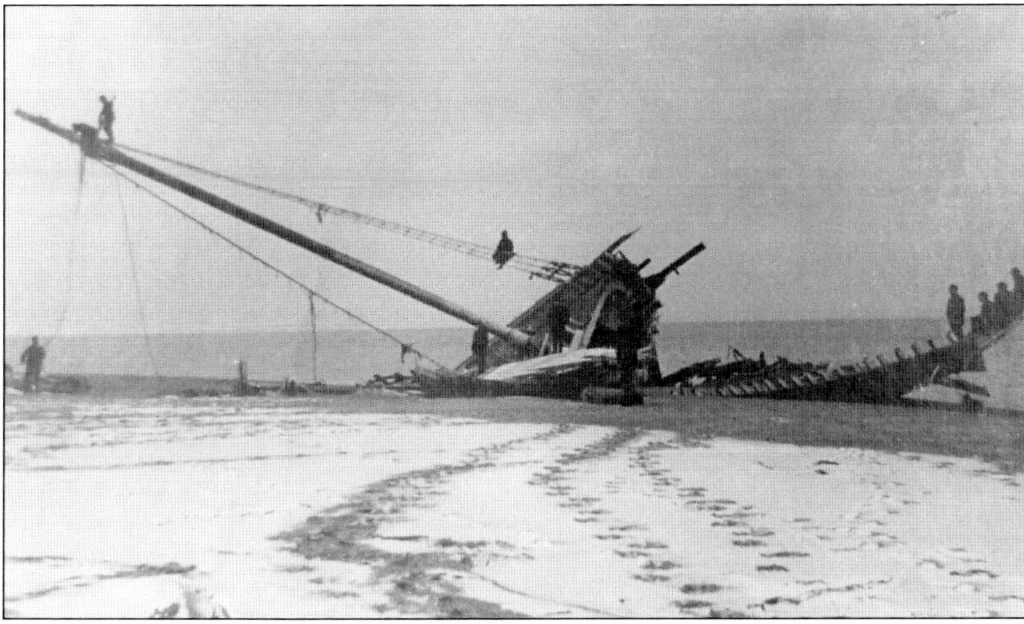

Never to Sail Again (late-19th-century photograph). Men perch precariously for the lensman on the remaining mast, rigging, and vestigial stern of an unidentified schooner that came ashore after being severely damaged. When a vessel is shipwrecked crewmen usually climb up the rigging as a last resort for their safety. (Courtesy Seamen's Bank.)

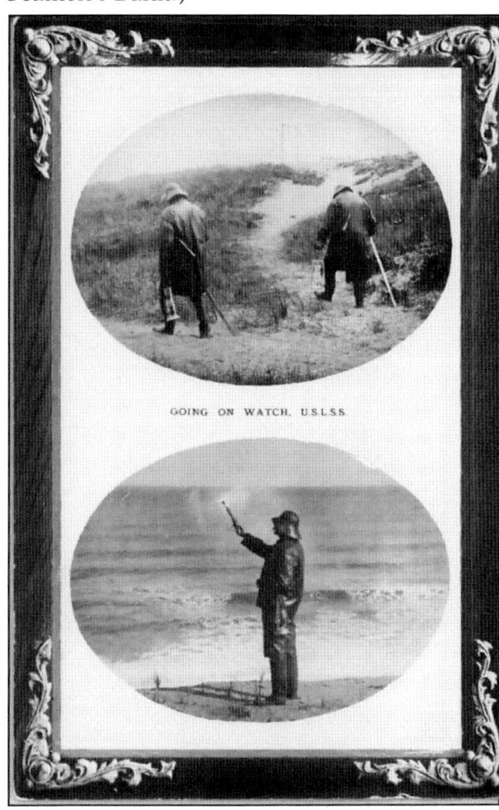

Going on Watch (early-20th-century postcard published by E.I. Nye, Wellfleet, MA). Figures in repoussé, a decorative border, and the subject matter make this an unusual souvenir postcard. During one 25-year period in the early 1900s over a thousand men were rescued from the Peaked Hill Sand Bars area. Beginning at sundown the beach patrol carefully watched their designated areas with two men traveling in opposite directions. (Courtesy Thelma E. Wiley.)

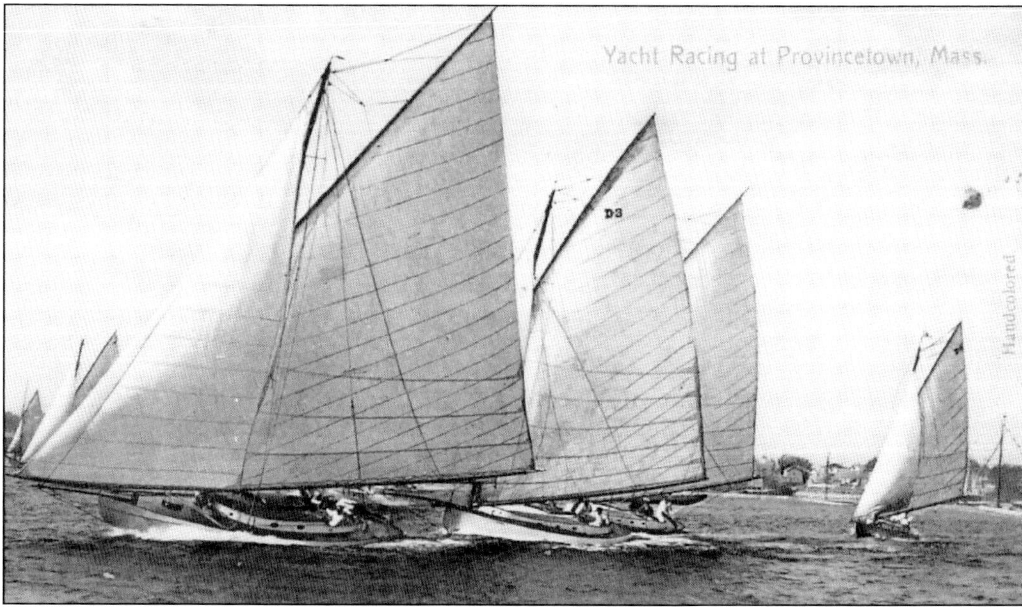

Yacht Racing (c. 1908 postcard published by I.L. Rosenthal). Not as popular as the yachting centers of Marblehead, Massachusetts, and Newport, Rhode Island, the tip of Cape Cod still provided a venue for the gentlemen's sport around the turn of the century. The Provincetown Yacht Club was organized as early as January 5, 1878, but was not incorporated; it was reorganized 50 years later in 1928. In the 1930s the membership consisted of 50 yachting enthusiasts with a fleet of 25 vessels. Since 1952 children have been taught the fundamentals of sailing at the West End Racing Club at 83 Commercial Street.

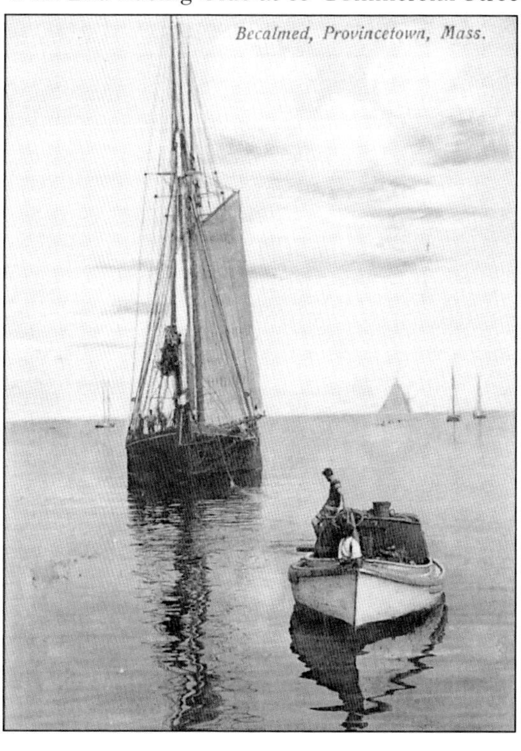

Becalmed (c. 1908 postcard published by the *Advocate*). A man dressed in a swimming suit and his friend watch as a schooner, with most of her sails down, waits for the wind to pick up. The becalmed fishing vessel is in marked contrast to the many others that were wrecked in ferocious storms and washed ashore, or sunk to the depths of the ocean. Many storms and gales come off the Atlantic Ocean; the great gale of November 29, 1945, is still remembered by many townspeople for its path of wrath.

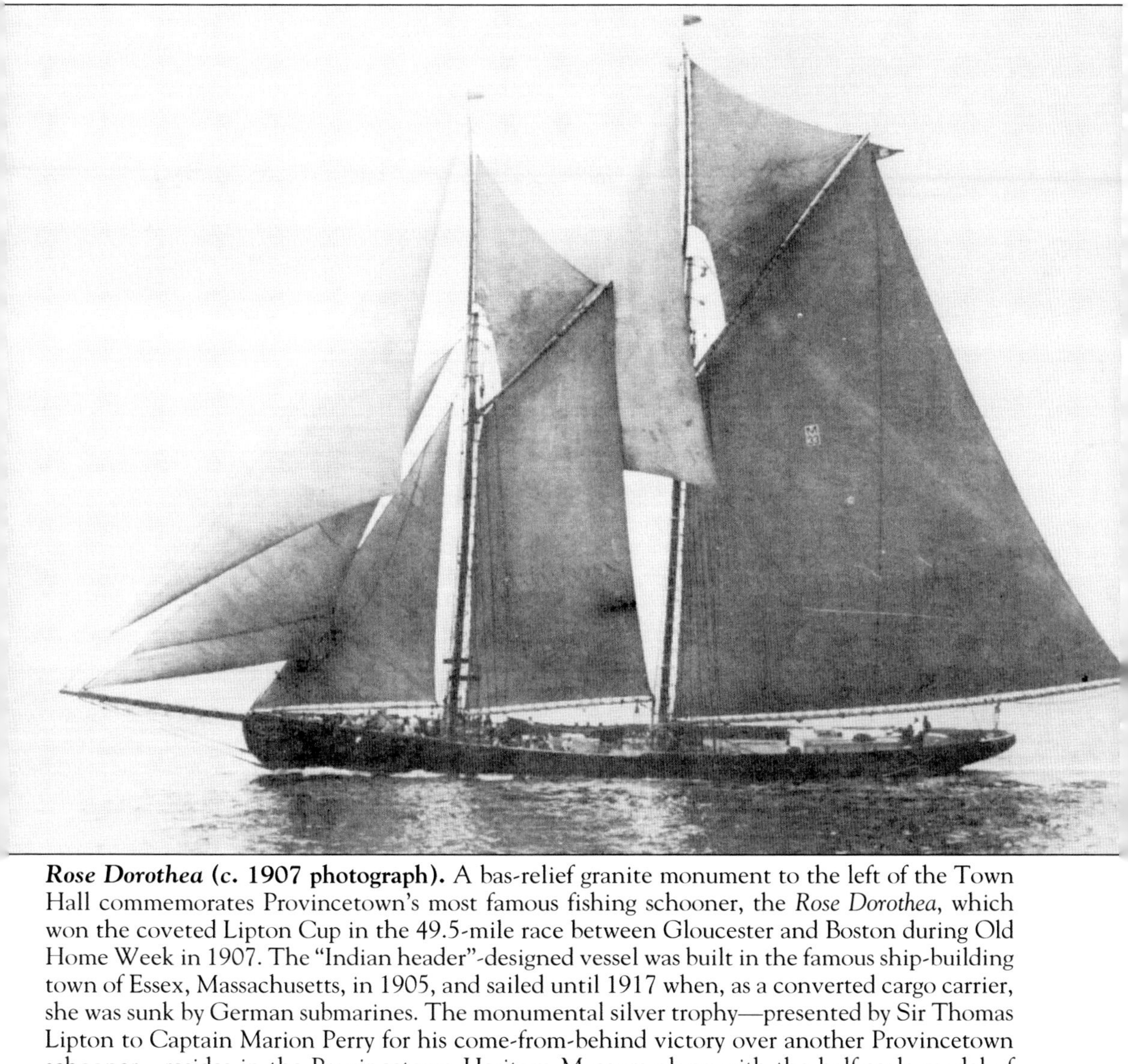

Rose Dorothea (c. 1907 photograph). A bas-relief granite monument to the left of the Town Hall commemorates Provincetown's most famous fishing schooner, the *Rose Dorothea*, which won the coveted Lipton Cup in the 49.5-mile race between Gloucester and Boston during Old Home Week in 1907. The "Indian header"-designed vessel was built in the famous ship-building town of Essex, Massachusetts, in 1905, and sailed until 1917 when, as a converted cargo carrier, she was sunk by German submarines. The monumental silver trophy—presented by Sir Thomas Lipton to Captain Marion Perry for his come-from-behind victory over another Provincetown schooner—resides in the Provincetown Heritage Museum along with the half-scale model of the *Rose Dorothea*. Captain Francis "Flyer" Santos built and shepherded the almost 11-year construction of the replica, which was dedicated on June 25, 1988. Still believed to be the largest indoor scale-model ship in the world, the *Rose Dorothea* makes a grand presence in the second-floor nave of the former Center M.E. Church. (Courtesy Mr. and Mrs. Francis Santos.)

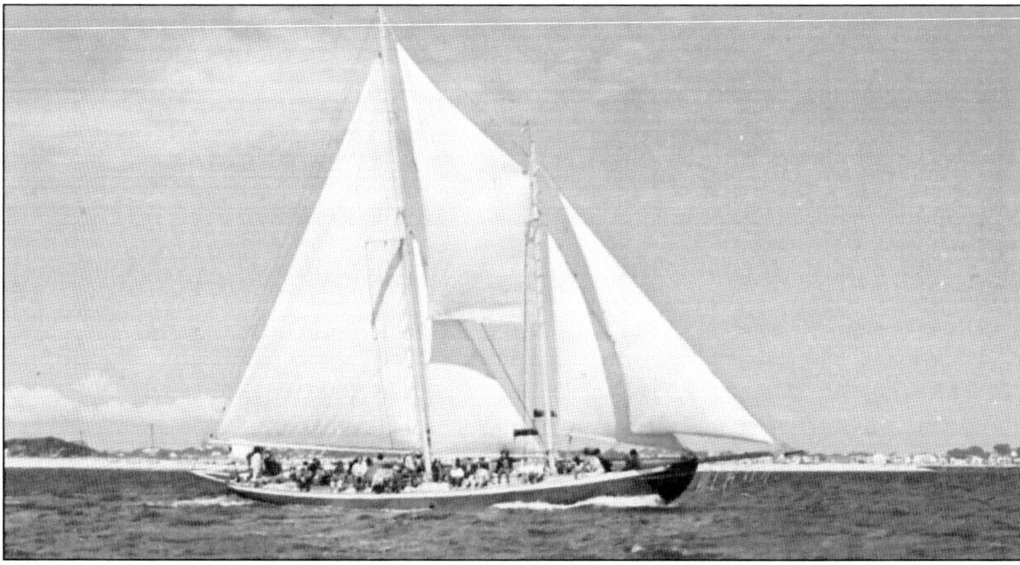

The Schooner *Hindu* (c. 1960 postcard published by Cape Cod Photo & Art, Orleans, MA.). Built in 1925 at East Boothbay Harbor, Maine, the 79-foot wooden schooner currently moored at MacMillan Wharf is a half-scale model of a typical Grand Banks fishing schooner. Captain Justin F. Avellar skippered the *Hindu* for many seasons. During her career she was a private yacht, a cargo ship in the spice trade, a U-boat tracker in World War II, and now, for over four decades, a popular sailing vessel for tourists. (Courtesy Schier Collection.)

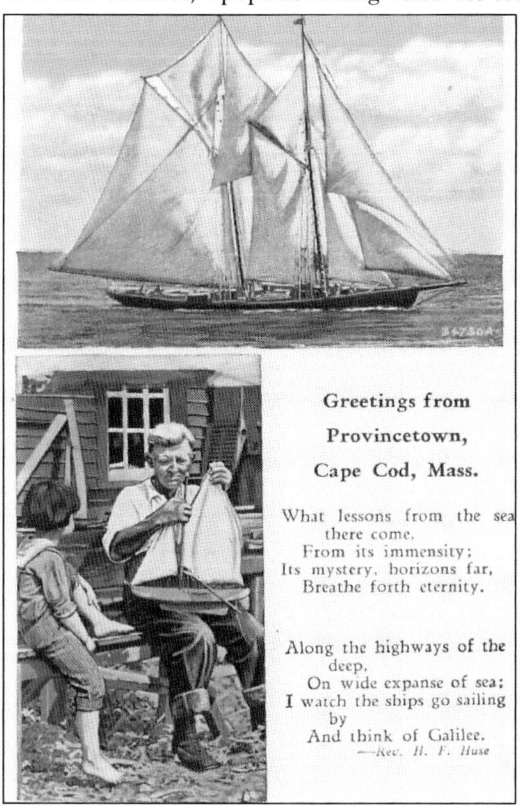

Greetings from Provincetown (early-20th-century postcard; unidentified publisher). In his 1920 book *Chanteys and Ballads*, Harry Kemp included the poem "There's Nothing Like a Ship at Sea," the first stanza of which follows:

There's nothing like a ship at sea with all
her sails full-spread
And the ocean thundering backward 'neath
her mounting figurehead
And the bowsprit plunging starward and
then nosing deep again.
"There's nothing like a ship at sea," sing
ho, ye sailormen.

Four

Art and Artists

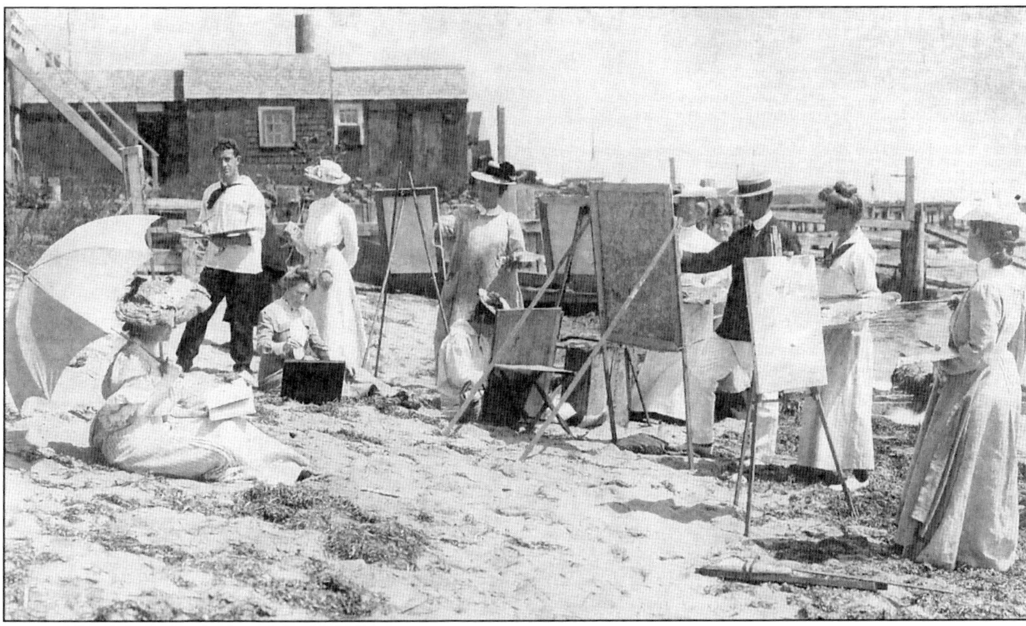

An Early Painting Class along the Shore (c. 1910 photograph). Luminosity, ethnicity, and the freedom to be creative in a special environment were three main drawing cards that drew many artists to Provincetown around the turn of the 20th century, and still do today. The Cape Cod School of Art—established in 1899 by Charles W. Hawthorne (1872–1930), shown assisting a neophyte at the right—was an "en plein air" ("in the open air") school whose students painted mainly along the shore. It had an important impact on artists, as have other summer art schools in town. With the outbreak of World War I, many young artists and their friends arrived in Provincetown in late 1914. These artists followed in the footsteps of those who came in the late 19th century, and they were in turn succeeded by artists of future generations who spent their lives in Provincetown or visited the town seasonally for inspiration in their painting, drawing, and print-making. There was no specific "Provincetown school" of art, but artists from the Boston and New York schools painted there along with local artists who strove for an individual style. Impressionism had become an established art form in America during the early 20th century, but the 1913 International Exhibition of Modern Art, a.k.a. "The Armory Show," in New York City, heralded Modernism. (Courtesy Provincetown Art Association and Museum.)

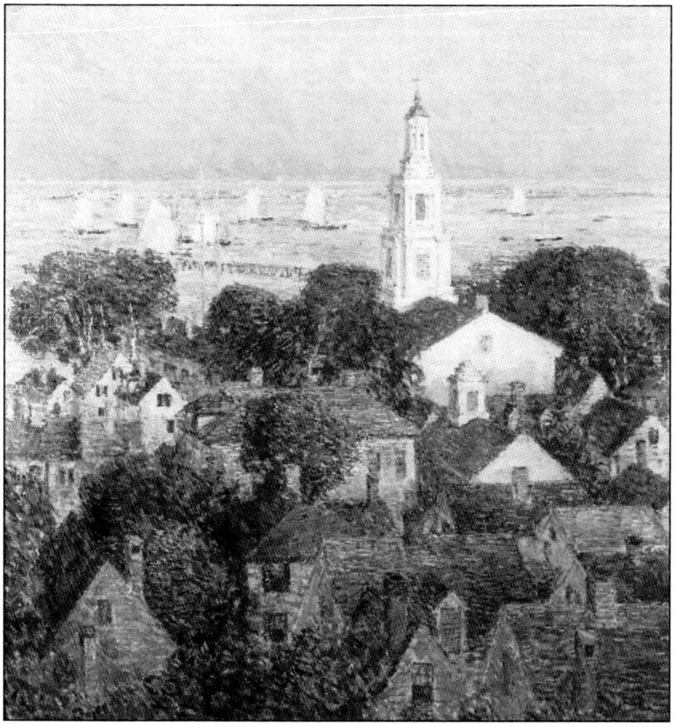

***Provincetown* (1900 oil painting by Frederick Childe Hassam, 1859–1935).** The well-known American impressionist artist was on High Pole Hill when he painted this pleasant picture of a quintessential Cape Cod fishing town with its white-painted cottages nestled around an architecturally significant New England church, in this case the Universalist church. Hassam liked to practice his art within the "lengthy shadows and mellow sunlight" of a summer afternoon, the ideal time for him to apply broken brushstrokes to a canvas. (Courtesy Canajoharie Library and Art Gallery, Canajoharie, New York.)

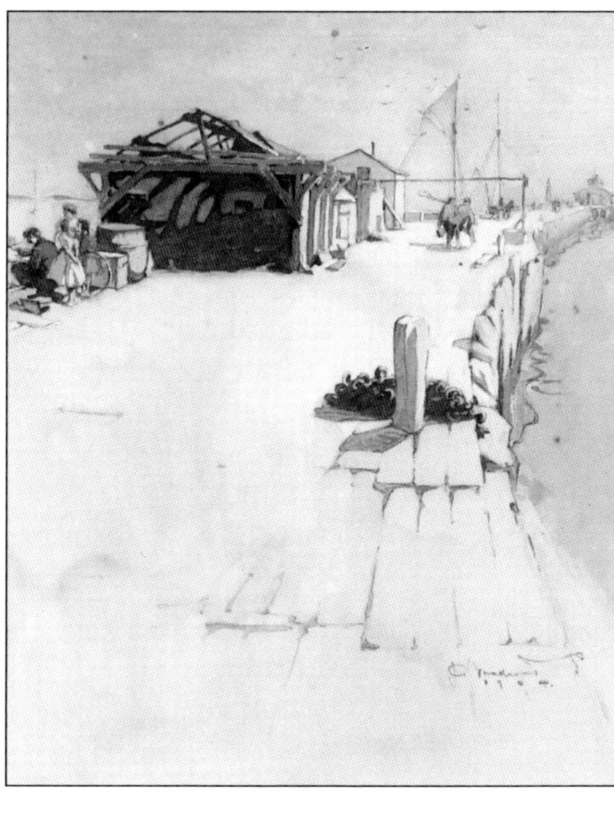

***The Pier in Provincetown* (1904 oil on canvas by John C. Vondrous, b. 1884).** Some artists began arriving along with tourists in Provincetown by train after 1873 when the railroad came to town. The unusual perspective of this wharf scene was chosen by Vondrous, who was born in Bohemia (a region and former province of western Czechoslovakia) and who resided in East Islip, Long Island, New York. (Photograph courtesy Childs Gallery, Boston, Massachusetts.)

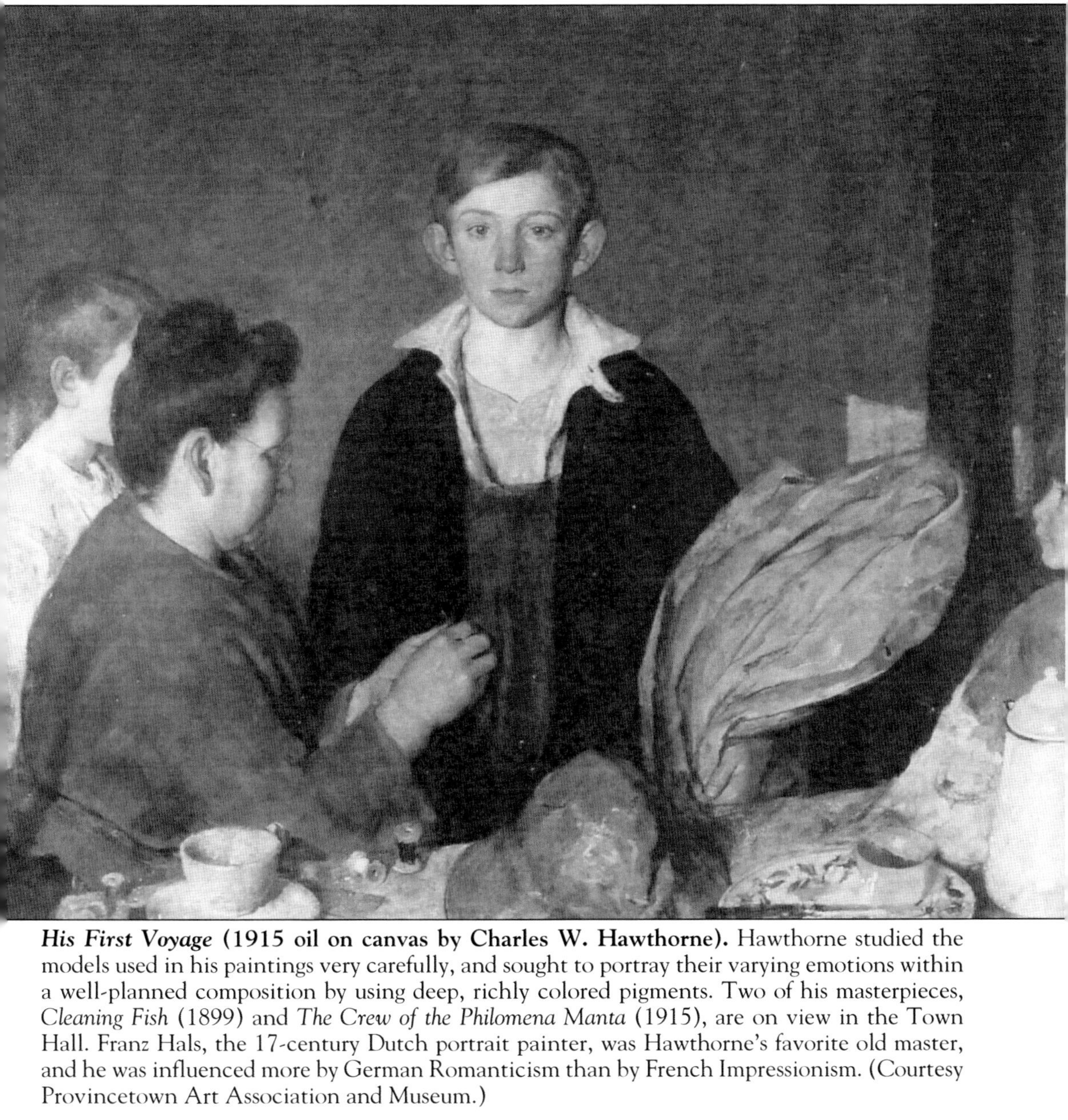

***His First Voyage* (1915 oil on canvas by Charles W. Hawthorne).** Hawthorne studied the models used in his paintings very carefully, and sought to portray their varying emotions within a well-planned composition by using deep, richly colored pigments. Two of his masterpieces, *Cleaning Fish* (1899) and *The Crew of the Philomena Manta* (1915), are on view in the Town Hall. Franz Hals, the 17-century Dutch portrait painter, was Hawthorne's favorite old master, and he was influenced more by German Romanticism than by French Impressionism. (Courtesy Provincetown Art Association and Museum.)

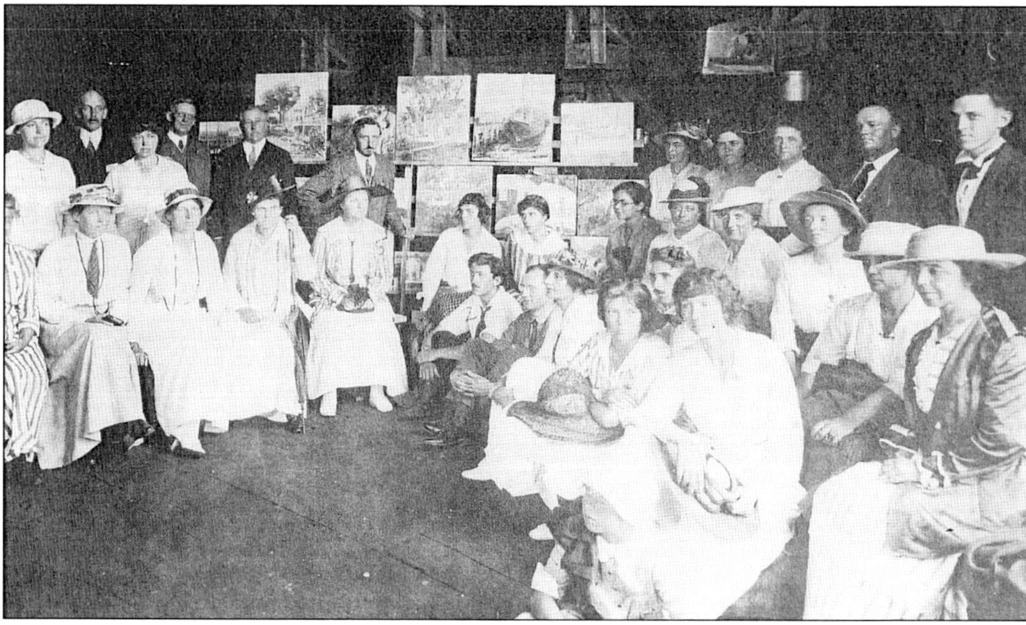

George Elmer Browne's Painting Class (c. 1915 photograph). Well-dressed ladies and gentlemen pose for a group picture in front of some of their recently completed canvases with their instructor standing at the center. Some of the identified artists include Browne's son, Harold Putnam Browne (1894–1931), seated in the first row to the right of his father; Houghton Cranford Smith (1887–1983), seated in front of the woman with a black hatband; and Tod Lindenmuth (1885–1976), standing at the far right. A Modern School of Art had as three of its founders B.J.O. Nordfelt (1878–1955), William Zorach (1887–1966), and Marguerite T. Zorach (1887–1968); the three were also associated with the Provincetown Players, the now famous theatre group formed in the summer of 1915. (Private Collection.)

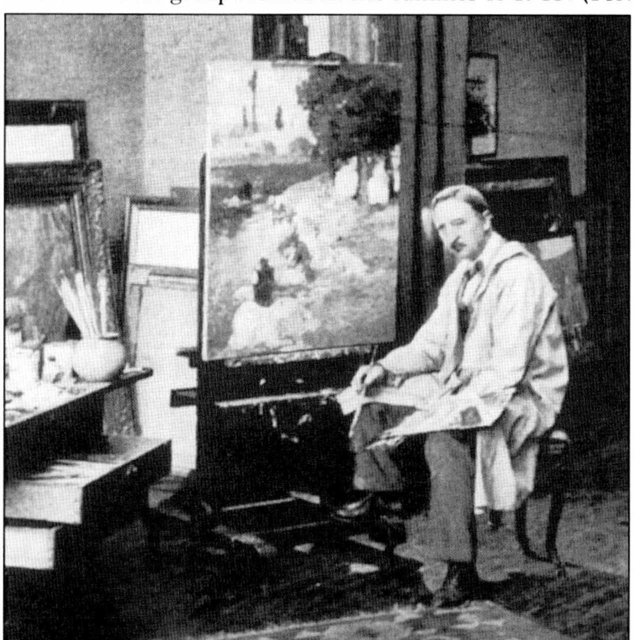

George Elmer Browne in His Studio (c. 1925 photograph). Genial gentleman and popular art teacher George Elmer Browne was born in Gloucester, Massachusetts, of native Provincetowners. Browne opened the West End Art School on a hilltop on Franklin Street, and he stressed the importance of composition in his classes. For several winters he chaperoned some of his young students to European cities to study and paint. Browne resided in Provincetown from the teens until his death. (Private Collection.)

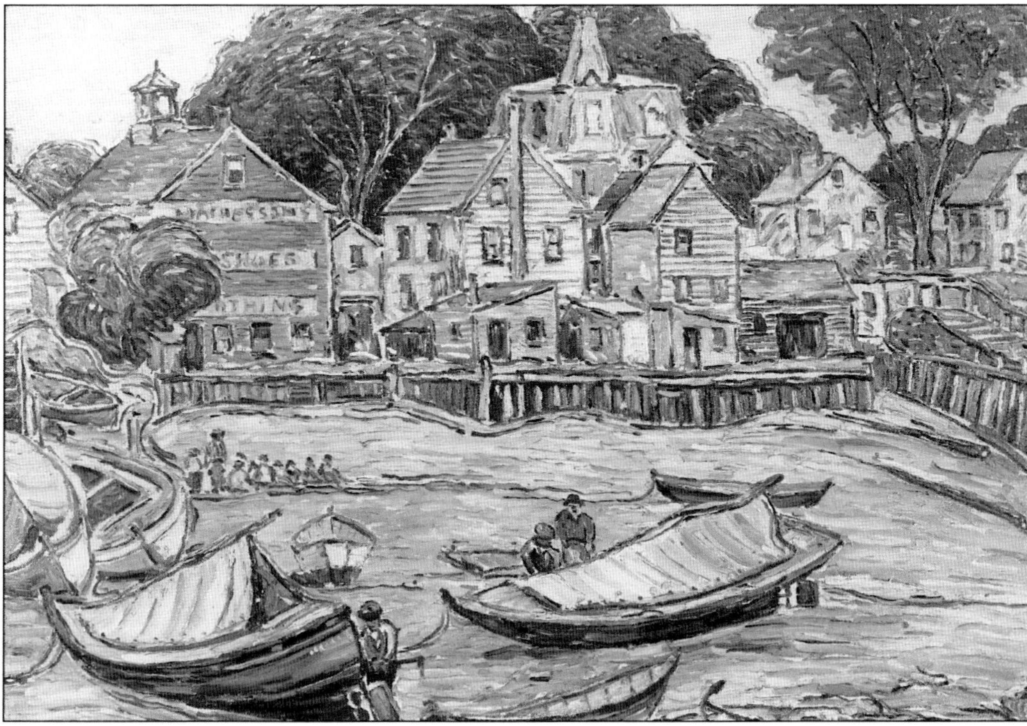

***Provincetown Harbor* (1915 watercolor by Reynolds Beal, 1866–1951).** The high Victorian library at 330 Commercial Street is a visible landmark in this painterly view of waterfront businesses near the center of town. Beal was born in New York City, studied painting on Long Island with William Merritt Chase, and painted at watering holes where the dedicated, financially secure sailor chose to sail his craft and practice his craft of painting. Beal visited Provincetown in 1915, 1916, and in 1920. (Courtesy Vose Galleries of Boston, Inc.; photograph by George M. Cushing.)

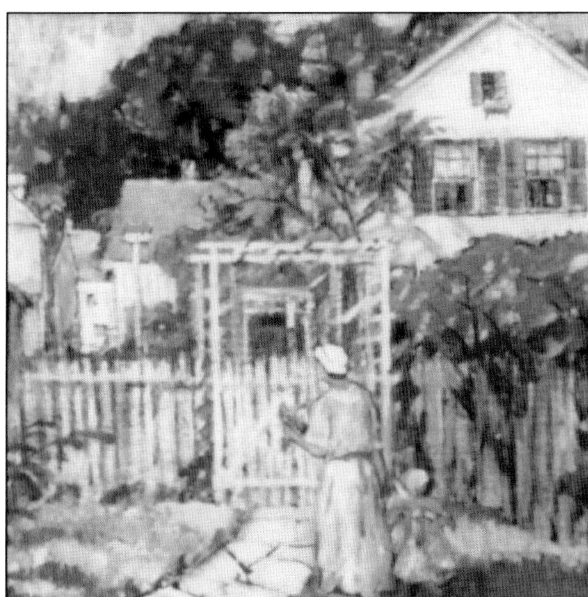

***Woman and Child at Gate* (c. 1915 oil on canvas by Pauline Palmer, 1867–1938).** Born in Illinois, Pauline Palmer resided at 5 Webster Place (off Bradford Street, between Prince and Winslow Streets), and maintained a studio with excellent northern light from about 1910 through the 1930s. Mrs. Palmer was not afraid to use color in her paintings—once she chose to paint the white captain's house at 396 Commercial Street a vivid apple green—and she lectured on art and was a critic as well. (Photograph courtesy The Caldwell Gallery, Manlius, New York).

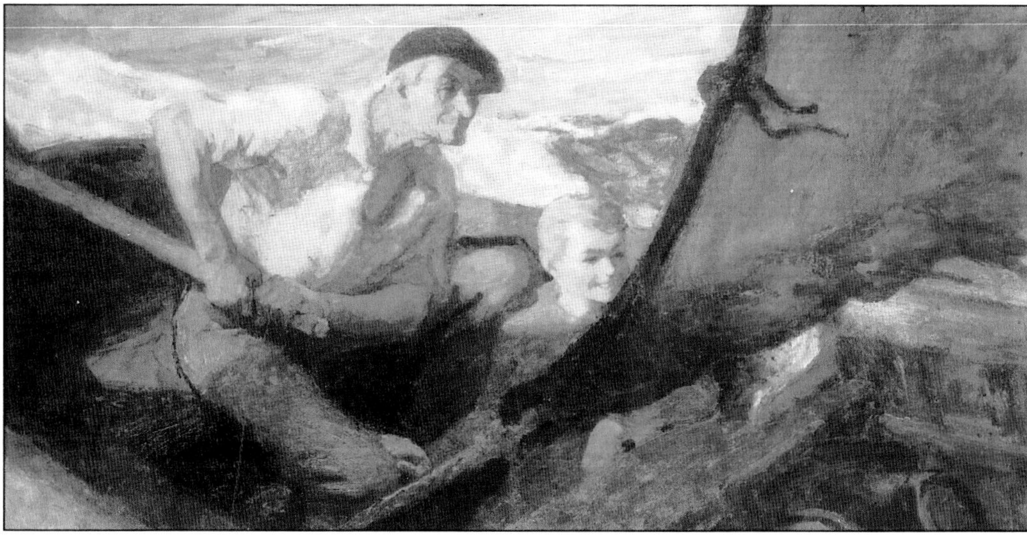

***At Full Sail* (c. 1918 oil on canvas by Max Bohm, 1868–1923).** Of German descent, Max Bohm was born in Cleveland, Ohio, and returned to America from France with his family in 1915 after studying art and painting there. In 1916 the Bohms moved to Provincetown, and three years later they purchased Grand View, an impressive summer cottage built around 1900 on the highest hill in the East End (Vol. I, p. 122). Beachcomber club member Bohm often used a thick impasto technique in his darkly romantic landscapes and portraits. (Photograph courtesy of the Bohm family.)

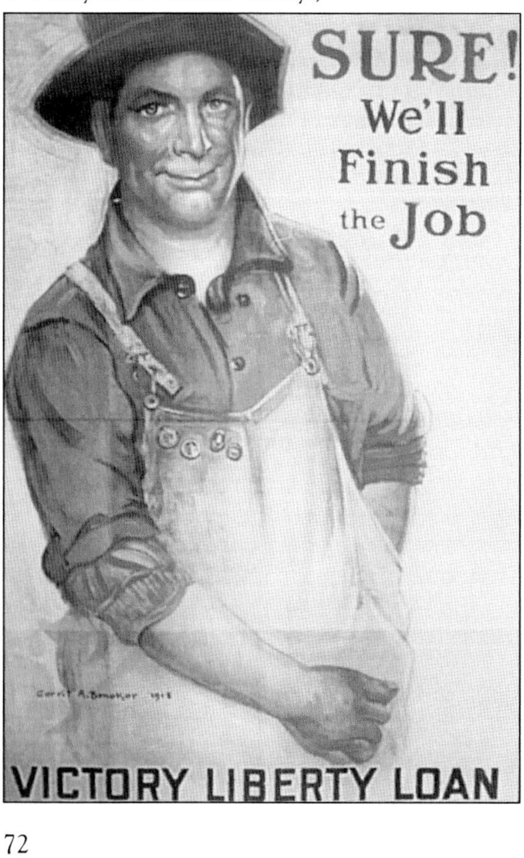

Victory Liberty Loan Poster (1918). Truro painter Gerrit A. Beneker (1882–1932) asked strong-man Anthony Avellar to pose for this portrait, which he then submitted to be used as a poster to help the war effort. Mr. Avellar, of Portuguese descent, and his family must have been thrilled to see the polychrome poster, now quite a collector's item. Along with fellow artists Oscar H. Giebrich, William F. Halsall, Charles W. Hawthorne, and E. Ambrose Webster, Gerrit A. Beneker donated a painting that became part of the nucleus of the town's art collection. (Photograph courtesy Landry Antiques, Essex, Massachusetts.)

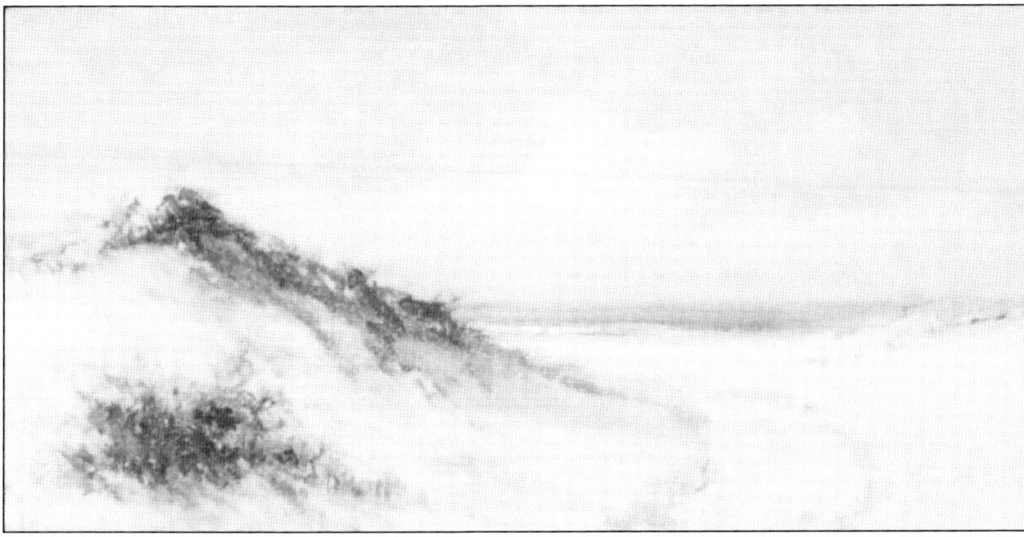

***Dunescape* (c. 1925 oil on canvas by Arthur V. Diehl, 1870–1929).** English-born artist A.V. Diehl has been remembered as a loquacious painter "who belongs to no school. . . . [and who had] a studio and shop on the busiest corner of the busiest street" (Standish and Commercial). He enjoyed painting the Sahara-like "walking" dunes, as did his predecessor, Marcus Waterman (1834–1914), who arrived in Provincetown around 1875. Some florae that thrive in the dunes and in marshy areas are bayberries, beach plums, blueberries, "juicy" pears, and wild cherries. (Photograph courtesy Childs Gallery.)

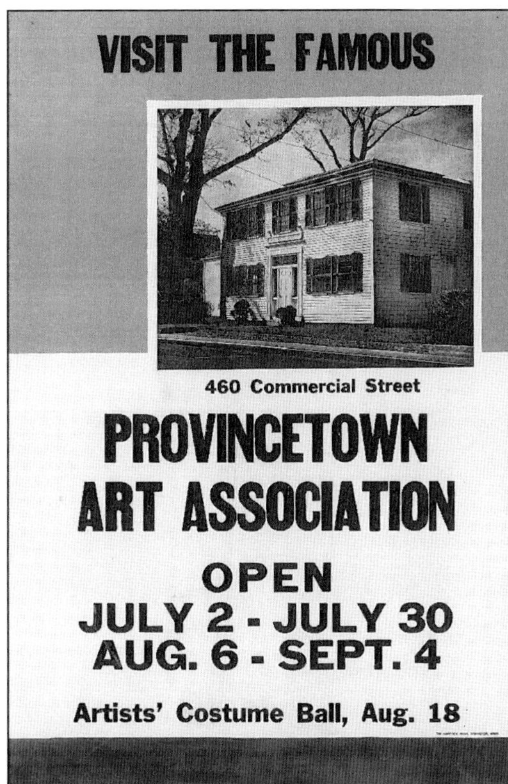

The Provincetown Art Association, 460 Commercial Street (c. 1946 poster). A 1931 advertisement suggested that people should join "not only because it is an association of artists and lovers of art, but also because it offers its members (and often its friends), dances, lectures, music recitals, and a wonderful Costume Ball, which latter will come this year at Town Hall in August." Founded in 1914 and headed by influential members of the community and community of artists, the association grew to include various aspects of the fine and applied arts. (Courtesy Provincetown Art Association and Museum.)

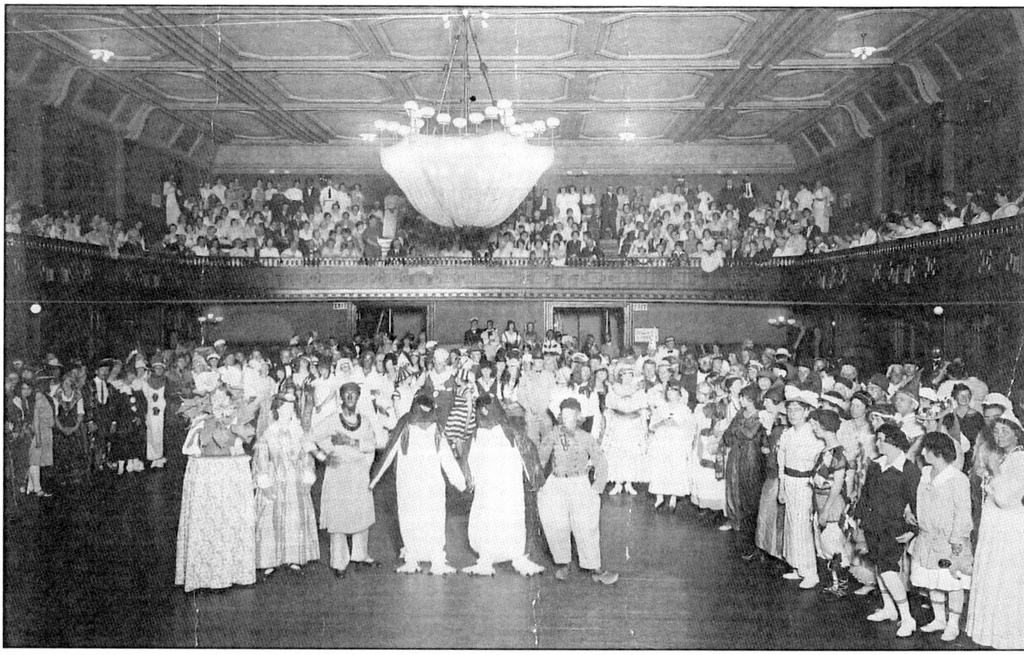

Artists' Costume Ball (1915 photograph). The pair of penguins were undoubtedly prize winners at the first annual artists' ball held in the second-floor auditorium of the Town Hall. Before the art association acquired its headquarters in 1920, the first six annual art exhibitions were held in this large building in a room on the ground floor. Representative art by such painters as the aforementioned Hawthorne, Lena Gurr, Ross Moffett, Pauline Palmer, Henry Steig, and others is on view in the hallways and in some offices of the public building. (Courtesy Provincetown Art Association and Museum.)

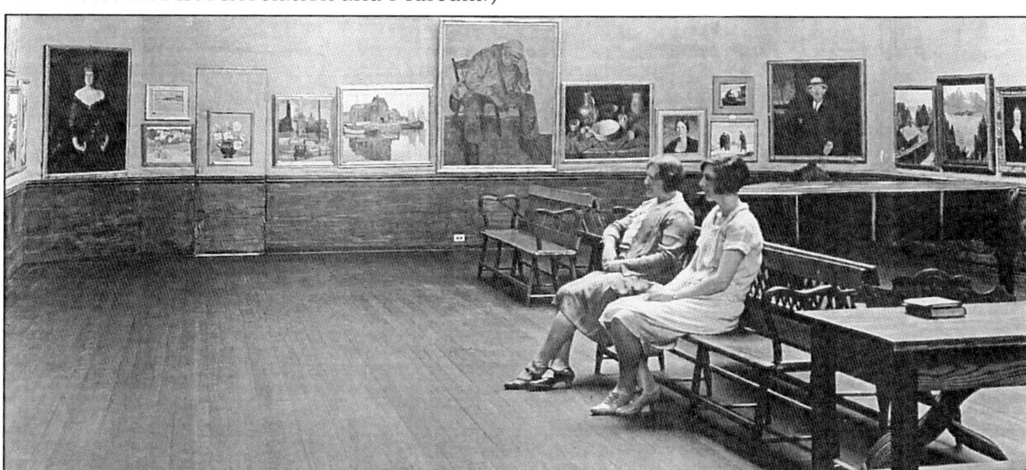

Gallery Exhibition (c. 1930 photograph). Eye-level paintings were arranged side-by-side in a very undramatic way for this early exhibition at the art association's headquarters. William F. Halsall, a "marine painter of the old school," painted a very large canvas in the Puritan Shirt Factory opposite 21 Court Street, but many later artists had studios in their homes. E. Ambrose Webster maintained a studio on a wharf at the foot of Bangs Street; Isaac Henry Caliga painted at his 198 Bradford Street home; and Karl Knaths' residence and studio was at 8 Commercial Street in the far West End. (Courtesy Provincetown Art Association and Museum.)

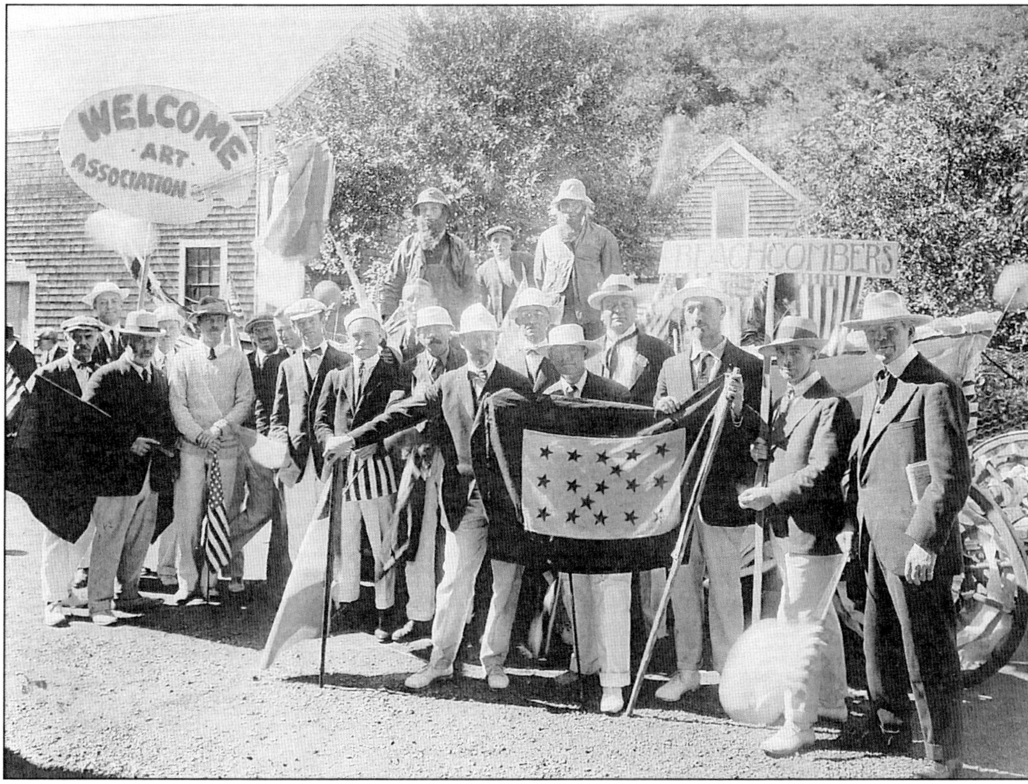

The Beachcomber and Art Association Group at the Provincetown Tercentenary Parade (1920 photograph). From left to right are Melzar Chaffee (wearing a cloth cap); Gerrit A. Beneker; Isaac H. Caliga (holding pennant); W.H.W. Bicknell (always spoken of as "The Etcher"); William L'Engle (wearing a sweater and tie); Ben Katz (wearing a cap); Henry Campbell (sporting a bow tie); Thomas Hanford; Frederick Marvin (with dark mustache); George Elmer Browne (with outstretched arm); Frank Desch; E. Ambrose Webster (behind flag); Max Bohm (wearing a straw hat with black band); Joseph Birren (holding flagpole); S. Chatwood Burton; and John "Wichita Bill" Noble (who always wore a five-gallon Stetson hat and who was the third director of the association from 1920 to 1922). William McGregor Paxton, a society portrait artist and a member of The Guild of Boston Artists, also discovered the many charms of Provincetown around 1916. (Courtesy Provincetown Art Association and Museum.)

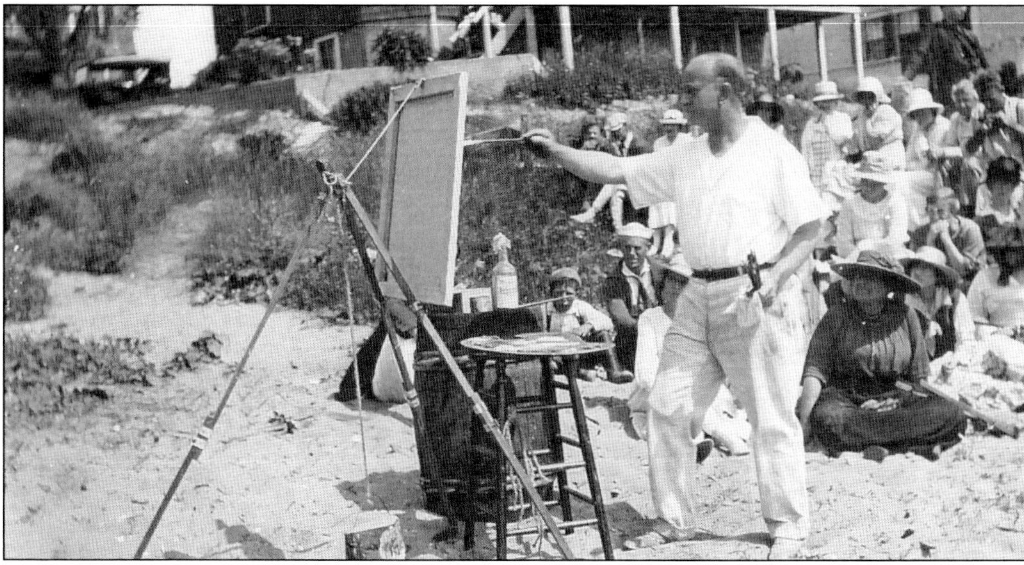

A Master Class in Progress (c. 1925 photograph). The mature Charles W. Hawthorne demonstrates his method of painting "en plein air" to a group of aspiring artists and others who watch the master's every deft brushstroke. His easel, weighted down with a gallon can of paint, adds an amusing touch to the picture. Hawthorne, who often donned white attire, gave weekly outdoor painting demonstrations and Saturday morning critiques at which he stressed the importance of color choices in art. (Courtesy Provincetown Art Association and Museum.)

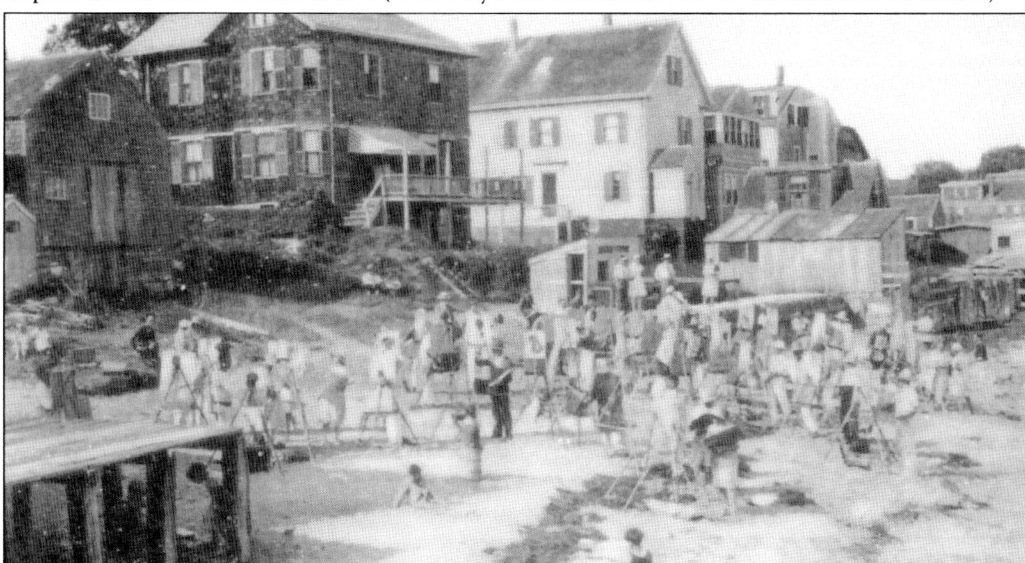

Artist Colony (c. 1925 postcard published by American Art Post Card Co., Boston, MA). With palettes in hand and easels placed almost too close together, a large class of artists on the shore—whose "blocked-in" portraits were kiddingly referred to as "mudheads" by townspeople—focuses on the model, while on-lookers watch their every brushstroke and compare adjacent canvasses. By 1911 artists could rent unheated and unfurnished studio space above Day's Lumberyard at 24 Pearl Street (now the Fine Arts Work Center in Provincetown) for $50 per season.

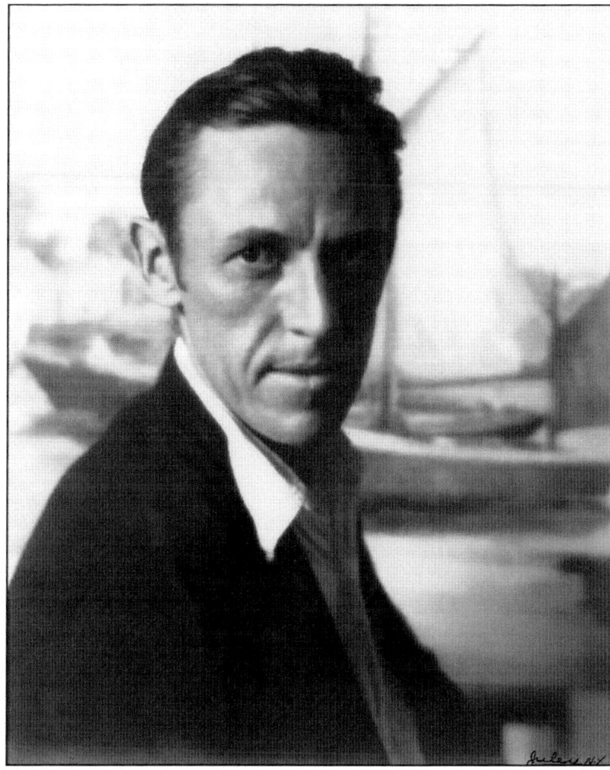

Tod Lindenmuth (c. 1925 photograph). Tod Lindenmuth (1885–1976), a native of Allentown, Pennsylvania, married artist Elizabeth Boardman Warren (1886–1979) in 1925, and they resided at 56 Commercial Street, the front room of which contained their gallery. Lindenmuth and Ross Moffett led artists who banded together as "moderns" in 1926 to be allowed to show their works alongside of those of the "conservatives" at the art association. Not until 1937 was artwork of the two opposing groups exhibited together; for the intermediate 10-year period they had separate gallery spaces in the association's headquarters. (Courtesy Ann Lindenmuth Fisk.)

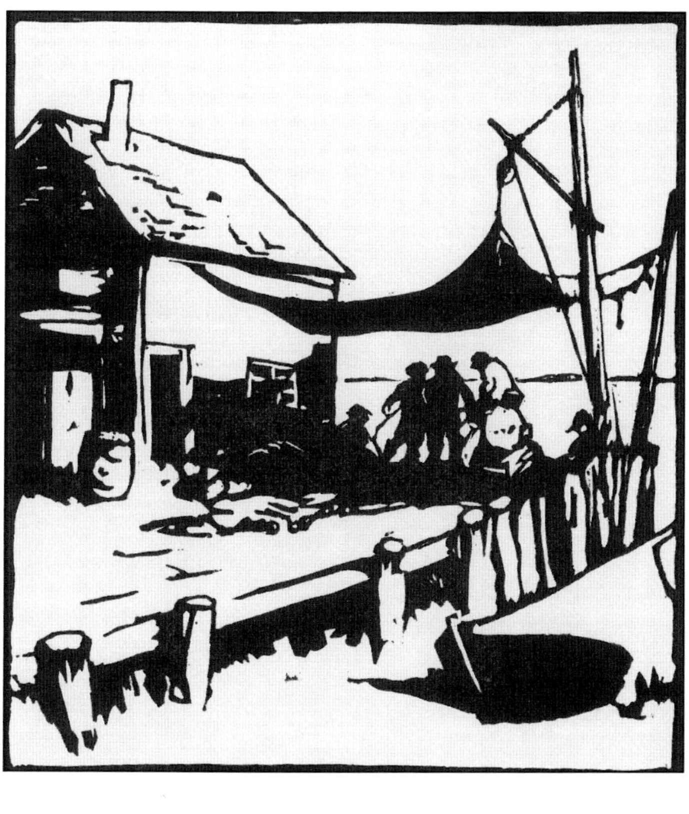

***The Net Menders* (c. 1920 linoleum print by Tod Lindenmuth).** Lindenmuth was attracted to Provincetown in 1913, and during several successive summers he rented a studio in the backyard of artist Harriot B. Newhall's residence. His strong-color linoleum prints, often with an oriental flair, appeared on the covers of the art association's catalogue between 1916 and 1918. In 1933, while still living in Provincetown, the Lindenmuths opened a winter gallery in the artists' colony at St. Augustine, Florida. (Courtesy Fisk Collection.)

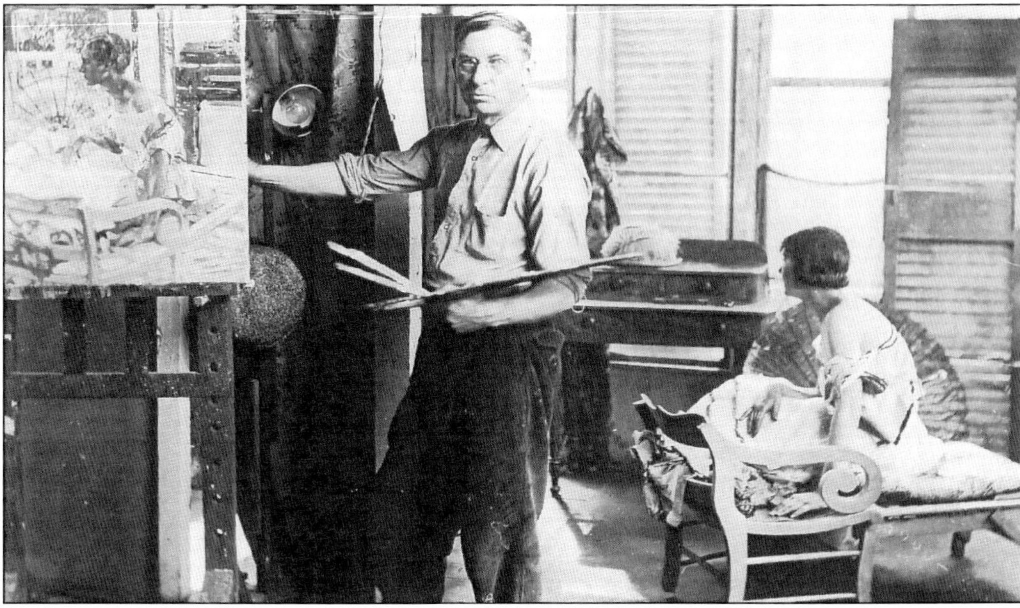

Richard Miller and Model in His Studio (c. 1925 photograph). The serious artist poses at his easel with palette in hand while the seductively clad model maintains her pose in front of the variegated Japanese parasol. Miller (1875–1943) specialized in painting attractive young women in a visually appealing setting with rich colors, patterning, well-thought-out composition, and virtuoso brushwork. The Post-Impressionist artist, who was the director of local WPA art-related projects, lived at one time in a converted barn-studio at 200 Bradford Street. (Photograph courtesy of the Provincetown Art Association and Museum.)

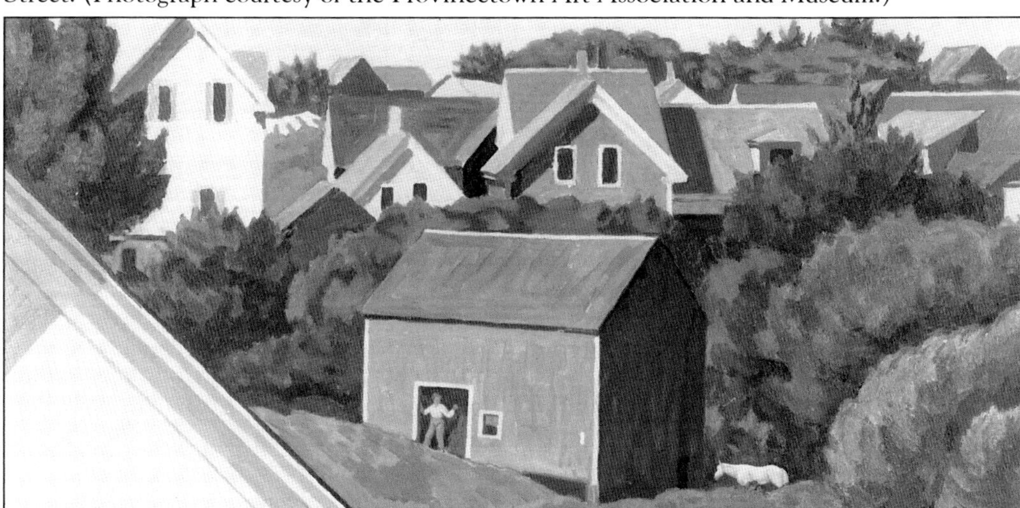

***Provincetown Rooftops* (c. 1927 oil on canvas by Ross Moffett, 1888–1971).** A resident of Provincetown for 58 years, Ross Moffett was an authority on the Native American archaeology of Cape Cod, as well as being a prolific painter—he was a yearly exhibitor at the art association—and the author of *Art in Narrow Streets* (1964), a survey of the artistic history of the first 33 years of the association. Moffett traveled to Abilene, Kansas, to paint murals in the Eisenhower Memorial Museum, and in Provincetown his WPA murals decorated the Town Hall and the high school. (Photograph courtesy Julie Heller Gallery.)

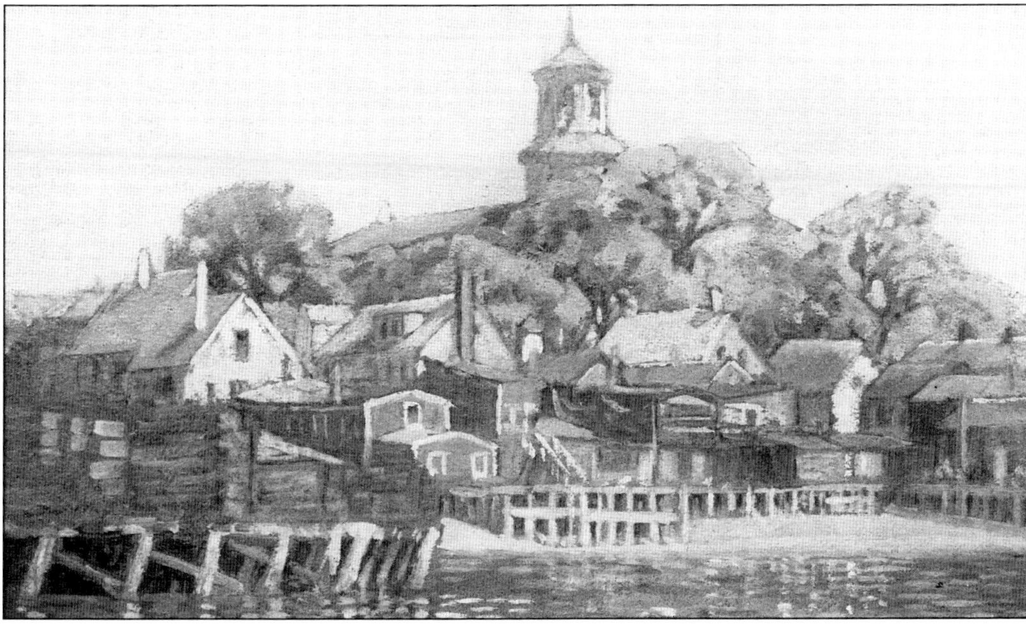

Harbor Scene **(c. 1925 oil on canvas by Mabel M. Woodward, 1877–1945).** Rickety and rigidly truncated wharves along the harbor opposite Center and Johnson Streets support fishing shacks and other structures with the Center M.E. Church in the background. Miss Woodward was born in Providence, Rhode Island, where she was a member of several art clubs. She often summered in Ogunquit, Maine, which also had a thriving seasonal art colony. (Private Collection; photograph courtesy Ronald Bourgeault, Northeast Auctions, Hampton, New Hampshire.)

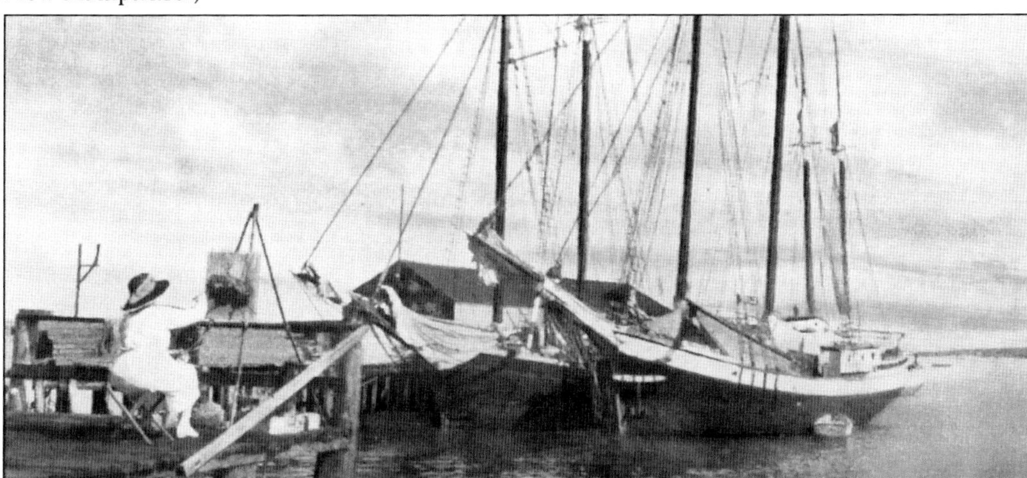

Wharf Scene (early 20th-century postcard published by E.D. West Co.). A generously proportioned woman artist has found a good spot on Higgins' Wharf to paint two schooners, the *Margery Austin* being on the right. The caption states that "Provincetown is one of the quaintest places, not only on the Cape, but in the entire country with its old streets, very narrow at that, and fairly teems with 'local color' which attracts scores of artists every year eager to transfer the odd scenes to canvas. It is entirely unlike any other town . . . and must be seen to be fully appreciated."

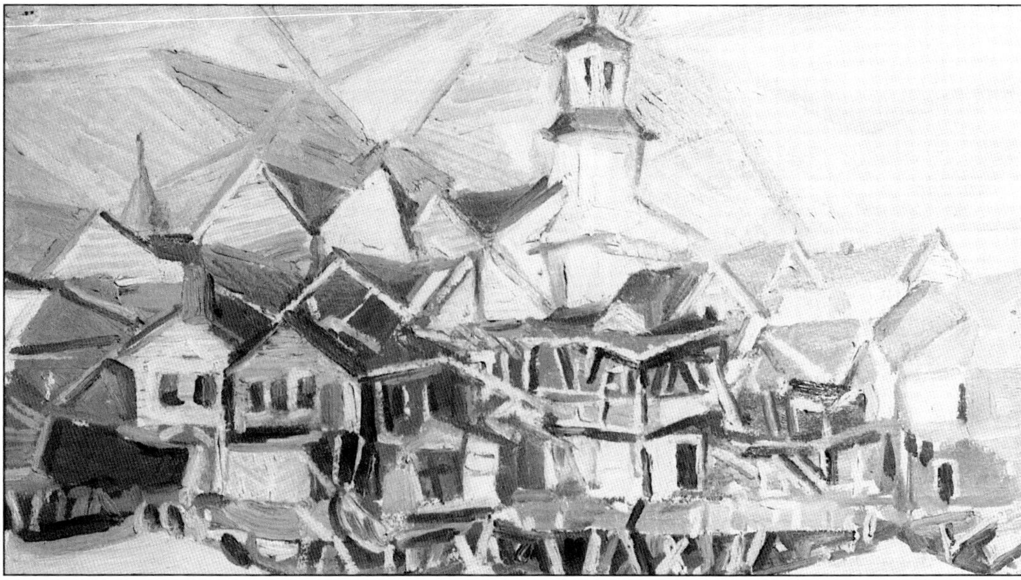

Cubist Town (c. 1948 oil on canvas by Demetri Merinoff, b. 1896). Of several artists who painted the landmark Center M.E. Church in the Cubist style—which was translated into Precisionism by American artists in the 1920s—Marsden Hartley (1877–1943) and Charles Demuth (1883–1935) achieved more prominence in the art world than Merinoff, who painted the dunes during the winter months. Hartley was "a mad and notable painter of triangles and such," and Demuth, who was sickly and died young, was painting "proto-Precisionist" watercolors around 1917. The companion artists roomed together for a few summers in Provincetown. (Photograph courtesy Julie Heller Gallery.)

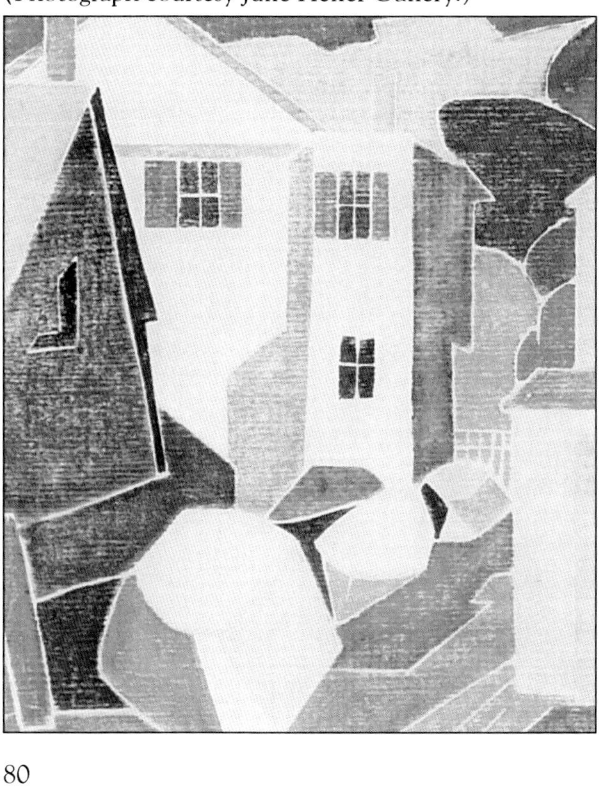

***Beached Boats, Provincetown* (c. 1930 white-line block print by Blanche Lazzell, 1878–1956).** Miss Lazzell is remembered as "a dainty little lady," whose tiny studio at 351A Commercial Street "blooms with boxes of flowers." An early American Cubist artist, she remains the leading female figure who excelled in the innovative medium of white-line block printing. Other women in the group of "Provincetown Printers" (working around 1915 and later) included Edna Boies Hopkins, Ada Gilmore, Mildred McMillen, Juliette Nicholas, Agnes Weinrich, and the Misses Ethel Mars and Maud Squire, who lived and blockprinted together. (Photograph courtesy Julie Heller Gallery.)

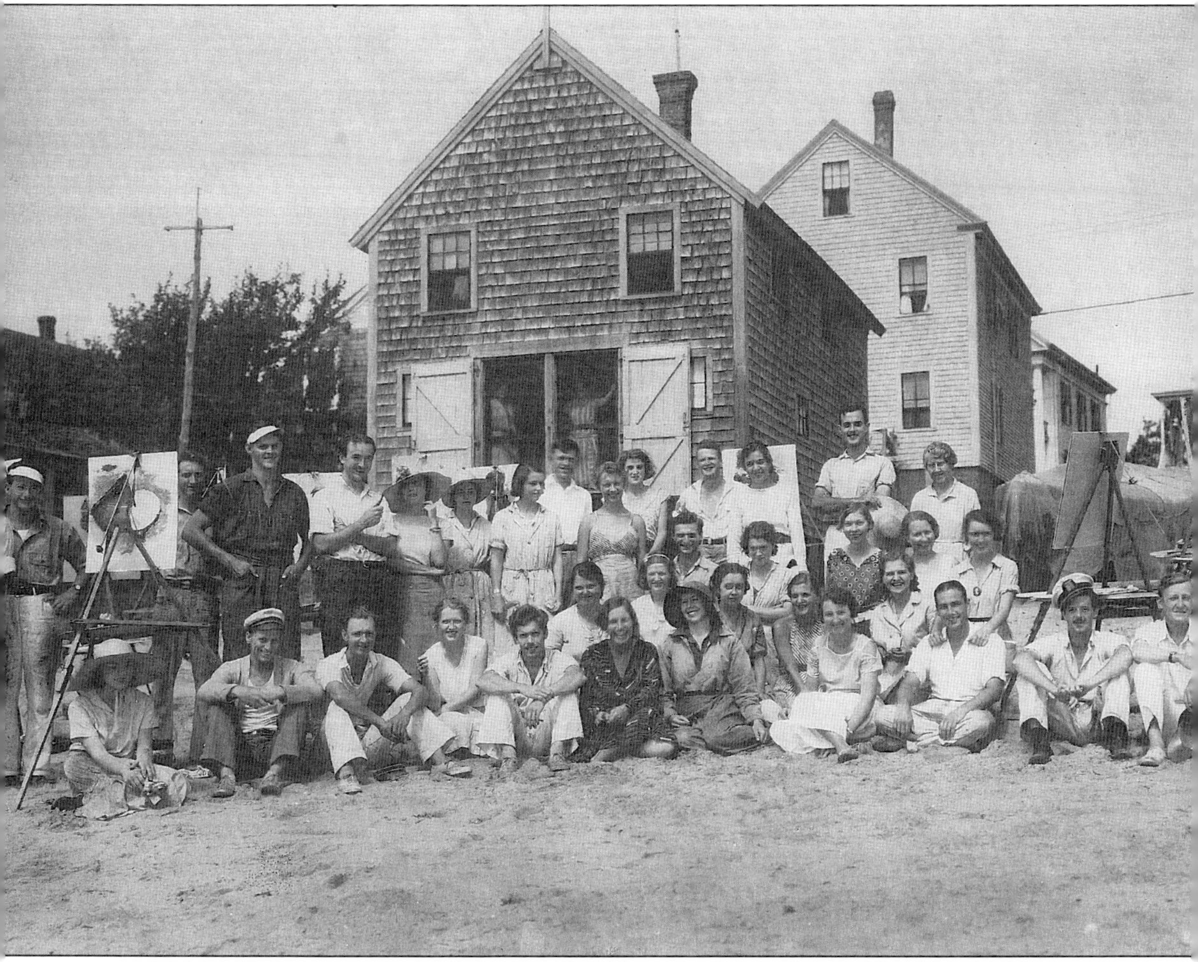

Hawthorne's Former Students (c. 1931 photograph). Some of the famous art teacher's students gathered for this group photograph on the beach at the foot of Washington Street a year or two following his death. Included are Ernie Irmer (behind the easel at the left); George Yater (to his right); Henry Hensche (in front of the double doors—he became Hawthorne's successor in 1930); the Childs sisters (to his left); Kirk Merrick (to the right of the door); Barbara Brown (to his right, later Mrs. Philip Malicoat); Lee Moffett (at the right standing with crossed arms); Paul Burns (seated at far left wearing a sailor's cap); Charles Crawford (next to Burns); Philip Malicoat (seated in the center); Betty Teale (in front of Moffett); Betty Evans (with her hands on Bruce McKain's shoulders); and Johnny Pope (at the far right). (Courtesy Provincetown Art Association and Museum.)

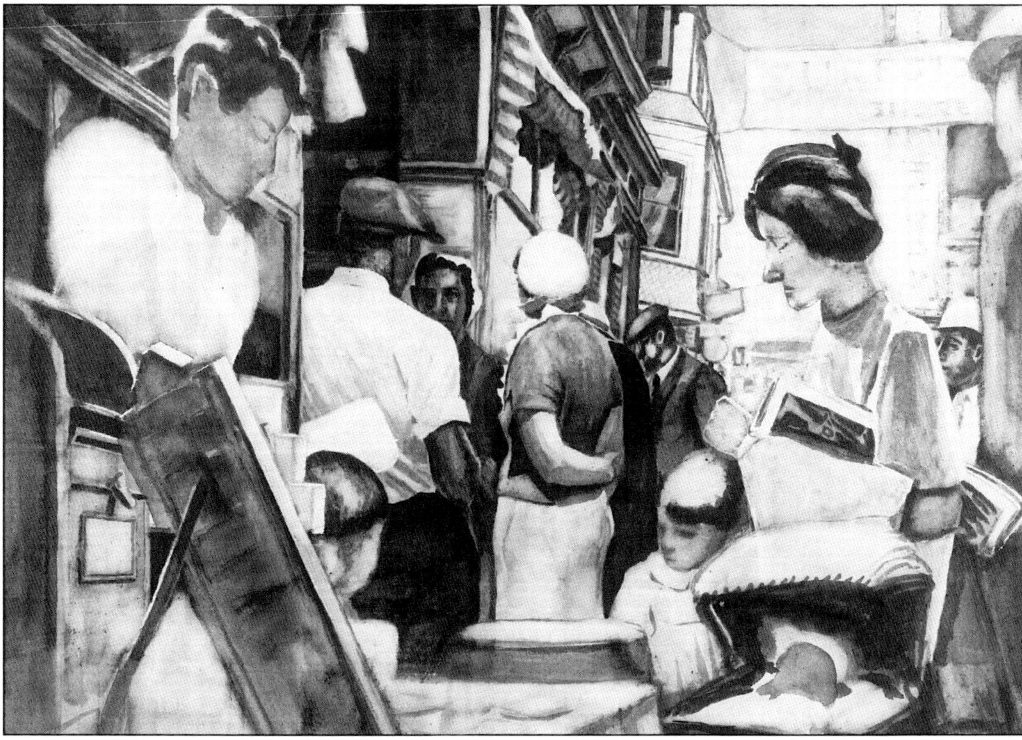

***Afternoon Excursion* (c. 1935 watercolor by LaForce Bailey, 1893–1962).** A native of Urbana, Illinois, LaForce Bailey painted many street and harbor scenes in Provincetown with facile brushwork in the social realism style of the early 20th century. He was an exhibitor at the art association in the late 1920s and early '30s, as were two other Provincetown residents, Philip Malicoat (1908–1981) and John W. Gregory (1903–1992), the artist-photographer. (Photograph courtesy Julie Heller Gallery.)

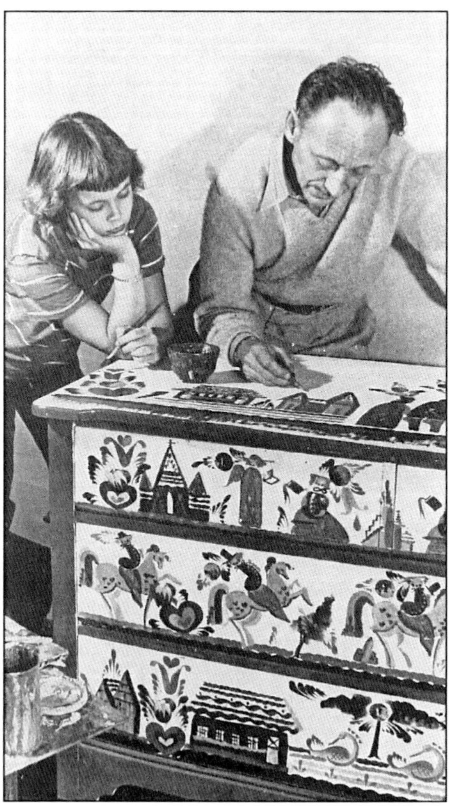

Putting on the Finishing Touches (c. 1942 photograph). The revival of "Old World" decorative painting on furniture and other useful household objects was heralded on Cape Cod by the arrival of Peter Hunt (1898–1969) in Provincetown in 1919. The young admirer (Carol, daughter of artist John Whorf) is watching the former New York City antiques dealer paint whimsical Scandinavian/Pennsylvania Dutch-peasant inspired designs on a plain bureau. Hunt would often add "Ovince" (his Frenchified word for Provincetown) to a completed recreation along with his name and the date. (Courtesy Provincetown Art Association and Museum.)

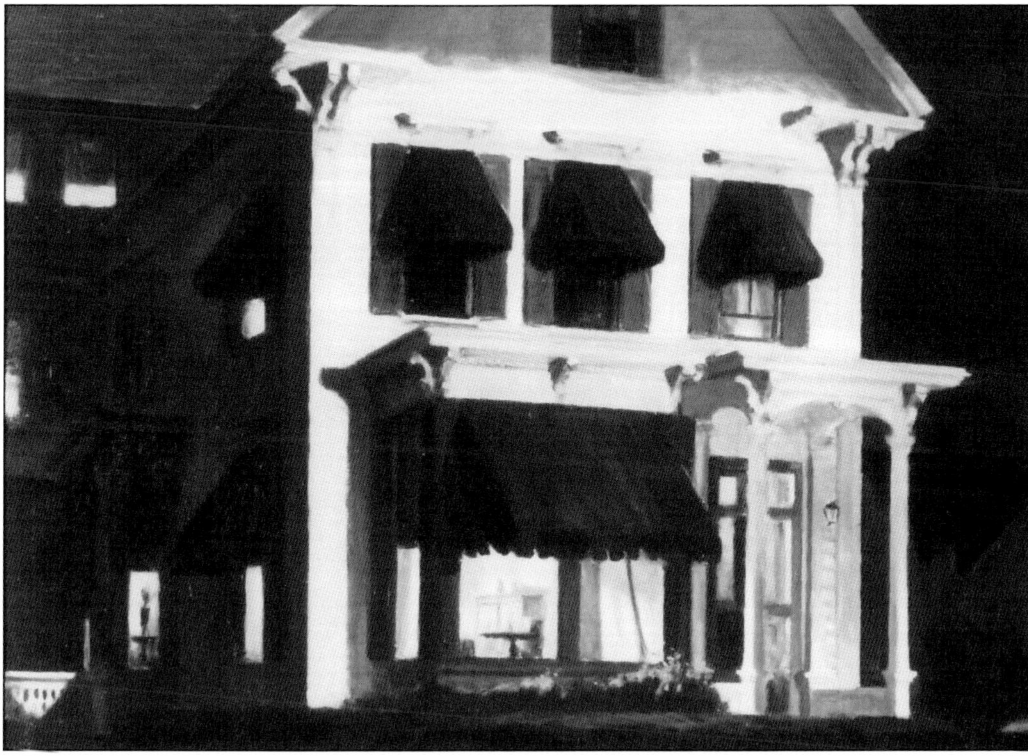

***Rooms for Tourists* (1945 oil on canvas by Edward Hopper, 1882–1967).** In 1930 realist painter Edward Hopper began spending summers in Truro, where he had built an architecturally interesting house and studio. Hopper made a sketch of this Victorian house (now the Sunset Inn at 142 Bradford Street, opposite Center Street) from his car, which was often his modus operandi. Mary Heaton Vorse wrote that large signs advertising "Rooms" became evident by the early 1940s, and that the whole town had become a rooming house. (Courtesy Yale University Art Gallery; Stephen Carlton Clark, B.A., 1903.)

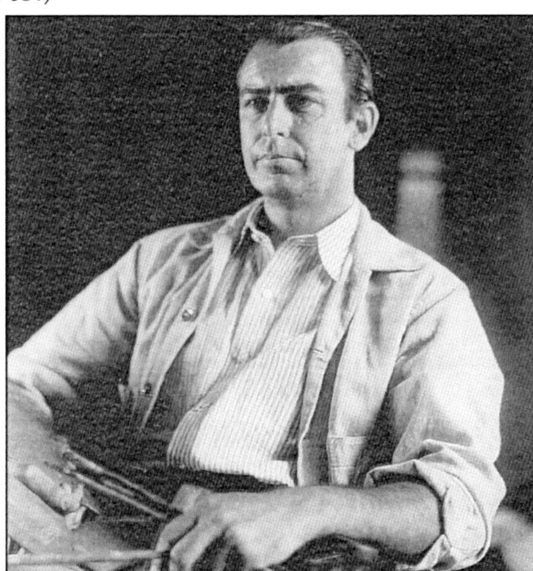

John Whorf (c. 1940 photograph). Hollywood-handsome John Whorf (1903–1959) was a "salty character" who walked with a cane due to a youthful illness. He and his family lived in at least three locations in Provincetown, including, briefly, the Seth Nickerson "Oldest House" at 52 Commercial Street. After 1932 watercolor became Whorf's only medium, and he was nationally recognized for his work. During the 1945 summer season, 9 of his watercolors were sold at the art association, and the following year 16 were sold for a total of $2,225. (Private Collection.)

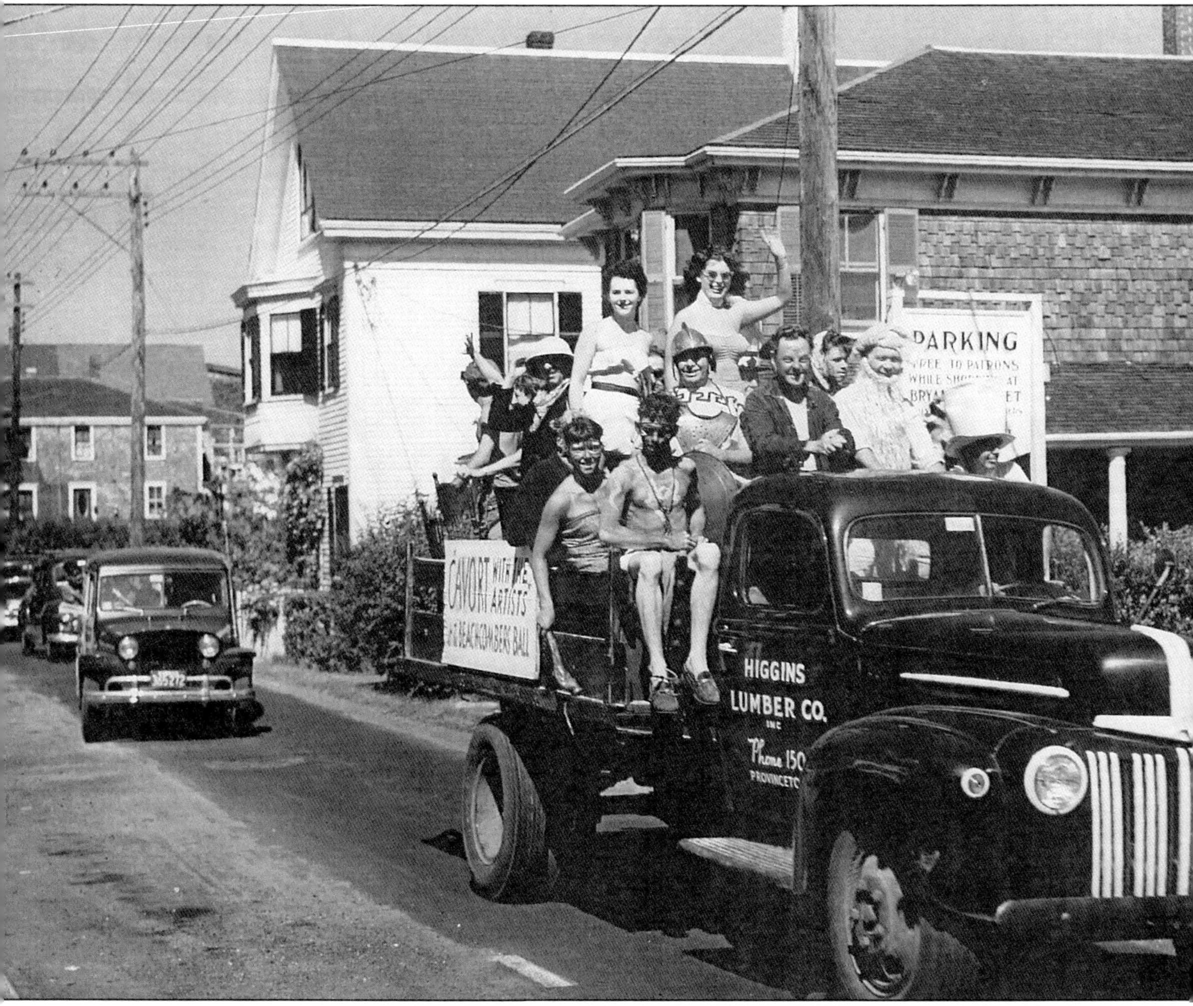

Beachcomber's Ball Float, nearly opposite the Provincetown Art Association and Museum (c. 1949 photograph). This group of costumed artists, or friends of those in the fine arts—Joanne Moore waving to the lensmen; Bruce McKain wearing a Roman-style helmet; and fisherman "Manny" Zora sporting a pith helmet—are having a merry time on an acquaintance's truck advertising the upcoming ball to be sponsored by the Beachcombers. The Saturday night social and dinner club, founded by artists in the teens, met in a fascinating building called the "Hulk," which was attached to the rear of the Flagship Bar & Grill at 463 Commercial Street (Vol. I, p. 115). The non-alcoholic "Sixes-and-Sevens" club was located nearby in the converted Lewis Wharf theatre, which was staffed by a group of fledgling artists. Local author Nancy W. Paine Smith wrote that "The boys could sing and dance, and fiddle and saxophone. They could speak pieces and make faces, and cook a little. . . . They had a good time," until the building and wharf were destroyed, and then "The boys telegraphed home for money." (Courtesy Provincetown Art Association and Museum.)

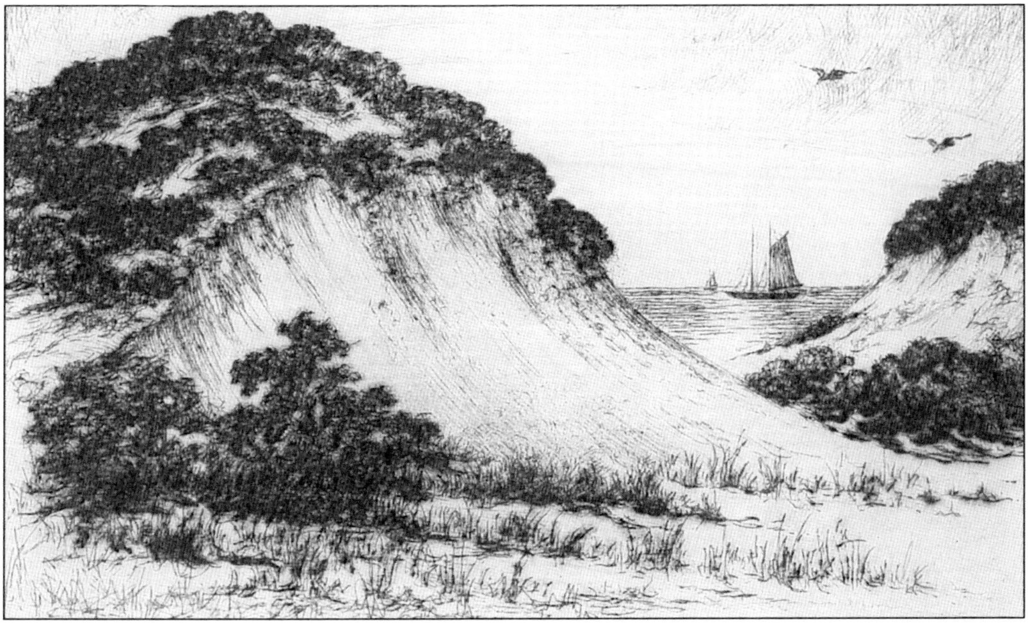

Dune Scene (c. 1935 engraving by Donald F. Witherstine, 1895–1961). Don Witherstine was a respected artist as well as a gallery owner. He resided at 47 Commercial Street in a house that had been floated over from Long Point. The gallery in his home, "Shore Studios," is thought to be the first commercial gallery to be opened in Provincetown (1947). Witherstine was elected director of the Provincetown Art Association and Museum in 1945, and because of his gregarious and businesslike ways, the works of many artist members were sold. (Courtesy Laurie Greenbaum Beitch.)

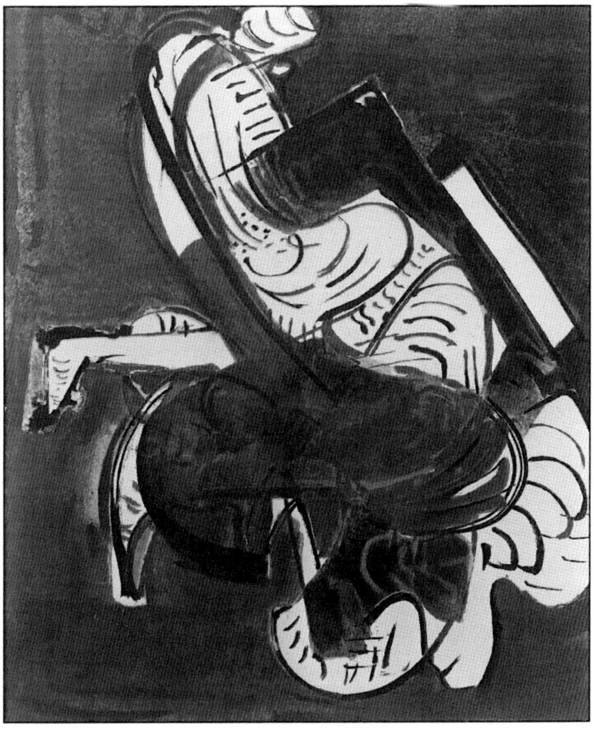

***Composition in Blue* (c. 1950 oil on canvas by Hans Hofmann, 1880–1966).** An artist and teacher until he was 78, Hofmann arrived in Provincetown in the early 1930s and established the Hans Hofmann School of Fine Arts. In 1946, Hofmann, who spoke broken English and was often difficult for his students to understand, acquired with his beloved "Miz" the house at 76 Commercial Street where seascape painter Frederick Judd Waugh (1861–1940) had previously resided. Hawthorne's old studio on Miller Hill Road later became the controversial abstract expressionist's studio. (Photograph courtesy Julie Heller Gallery.)

SHORE STUDIOS

47 Commercial St., Provincetown, Mass.

AND

GALLERY 200

200 Commercial St., Provincetown, Mass.

DONALD F. WITHERSTINE

presents

Oils — Watercolors — Prints

BY THE FOLLOWING NOTED ARTISTS

Sterne
Whorf
Biddle
Hofmann
Farnsworth
Kupferman
Gonzalez
Romano
Sawyer
Zorach
Davidson
Bassford
Sardeau
Gross
Hibbard
Woodward
Gruppe
Dante
Gasser
Hirsch
M. Zorach
Browne
Eastwood
Bye
Cobb
Lazzell
Markow
Heinz
F. Pfeiffer
H. V. Pfeiffer
Schwacha
Harriton
Stillman
Wilson
Colleti
Hodgin
Perkins

Fine
Heintzleman
Moffett
Gregory
Peers
Gottlieb
Lief
Malicoat
McKain
Reichard
Engel
J. Noble, Jr.
Miron
N. Whorf
Press
L. Moffett
Bowman
Gibran
Marantz
C. Waugh
Charles
Hackett
Godal
Leighton
Schucker
Groll
Podorson
Scarlett
Margo
Sheridan
Orr
Mab
L'Engle
Gage
Poole
Warren

Lindenmuth
Ghikas
Thieme
Botkin
Campbell
Bonnar
Bengtz
Bailey
Cox
Hensche
Raynor
Schulein
Corbridge
Littlefield
Myrer
Kees
Walker
M. Hall
Geiberich
Hughes
J. H. Hall
Park
Cohen
Tabak
Coletta
Matta
Fitzgerald
Loeb
Gelb
Jones
Nissen
Kathe
Citron
Bultman
Gibbs
Kamys

Other outstanding artists will be included during the season.

OPEN DAILY - 9 A. M. to 9:30 P. M.

Shore Studios and Gallery 200 Broadside (1949). Although many of the surnames of the artists listed are well known, as are the Christian names to art scholars, it would have been more informative to have included each name in full and to have arranged the list in alphabetical order. Forum '49, with a concurrent exhibit of artists' works, was held at Gallery 200 in the former Ford automobile garage at that number Commercial Street in 1949. The summer-long series of avant-garde programs featured talks on the definition of an artist, Soviet bureaucracy, American jazz, early films, recordings of James Joyce and T.S. Eliot, French art versus United States art, architecture, and psychoanalysis. (Private Collection.)

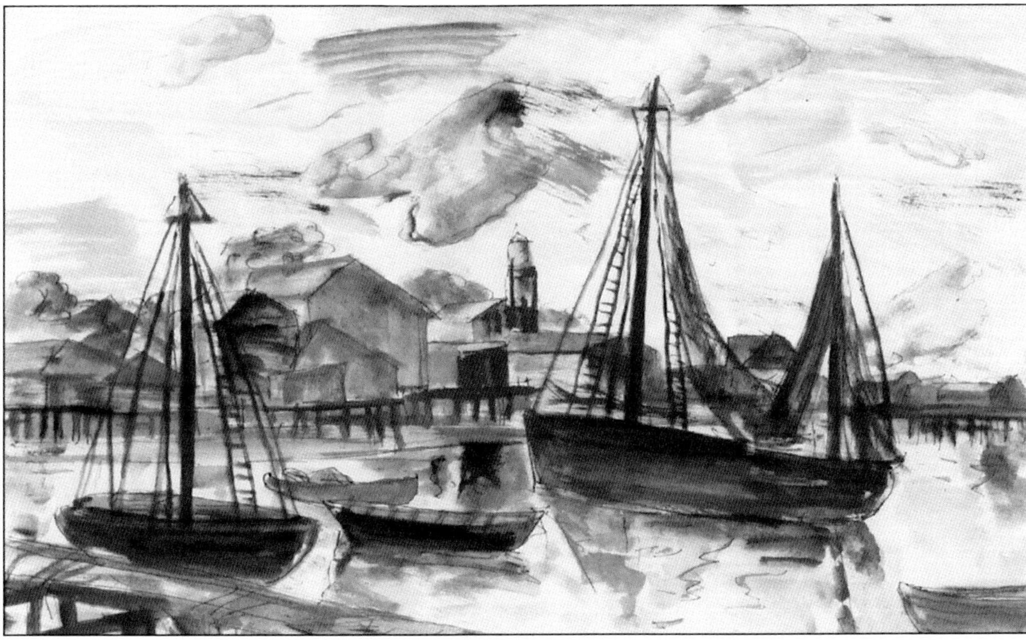

***Harbor Scene* (c. 1955 watercolor by Henry A. Botkin, 1896–1983).** Artist, art organization president, curator, promoter, lecturer, and teacher Henry Botkin became involved in abstraction and collage in the early 1950s, with the latter medium being his only interest from the 1960s until his death. The Boston-born artist and cousin of composer George Gershwin was president of The American Abstract Artists' Group 256 in Provincetown, where he also painted, lectured, and taught privately. (Photograph courtesy Childs Gallery.)

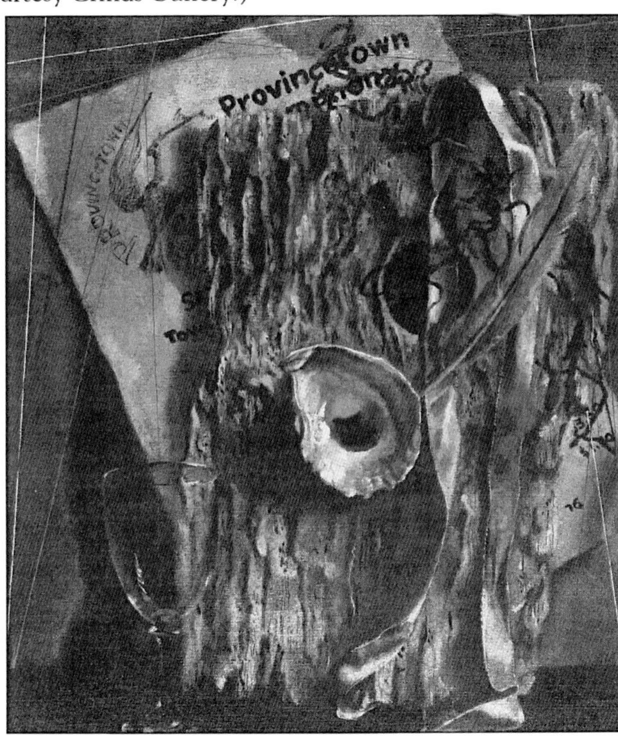

***Driftwood and Ribbon* (mid-20th century oil on canvas by Jerry Farnsworth, 1895–1983).** Georgia native Jerry Farnsworth studied interior decoration at the Parson School of Design in New York City, and met his wife of more than 50 years, Helen Sawyer, at Charles Hawthorne's Cape Cod School of Art. A portraitist whose works appeared several times on the covers of *Time* and *Fortune* magazines, Farnsworth once stated that he "tried to get students to paint still life in the beginning because you learn about using the medium, you learn about color, form, design, and everything." (Courtesy Provincetown Art Association and Museum.)

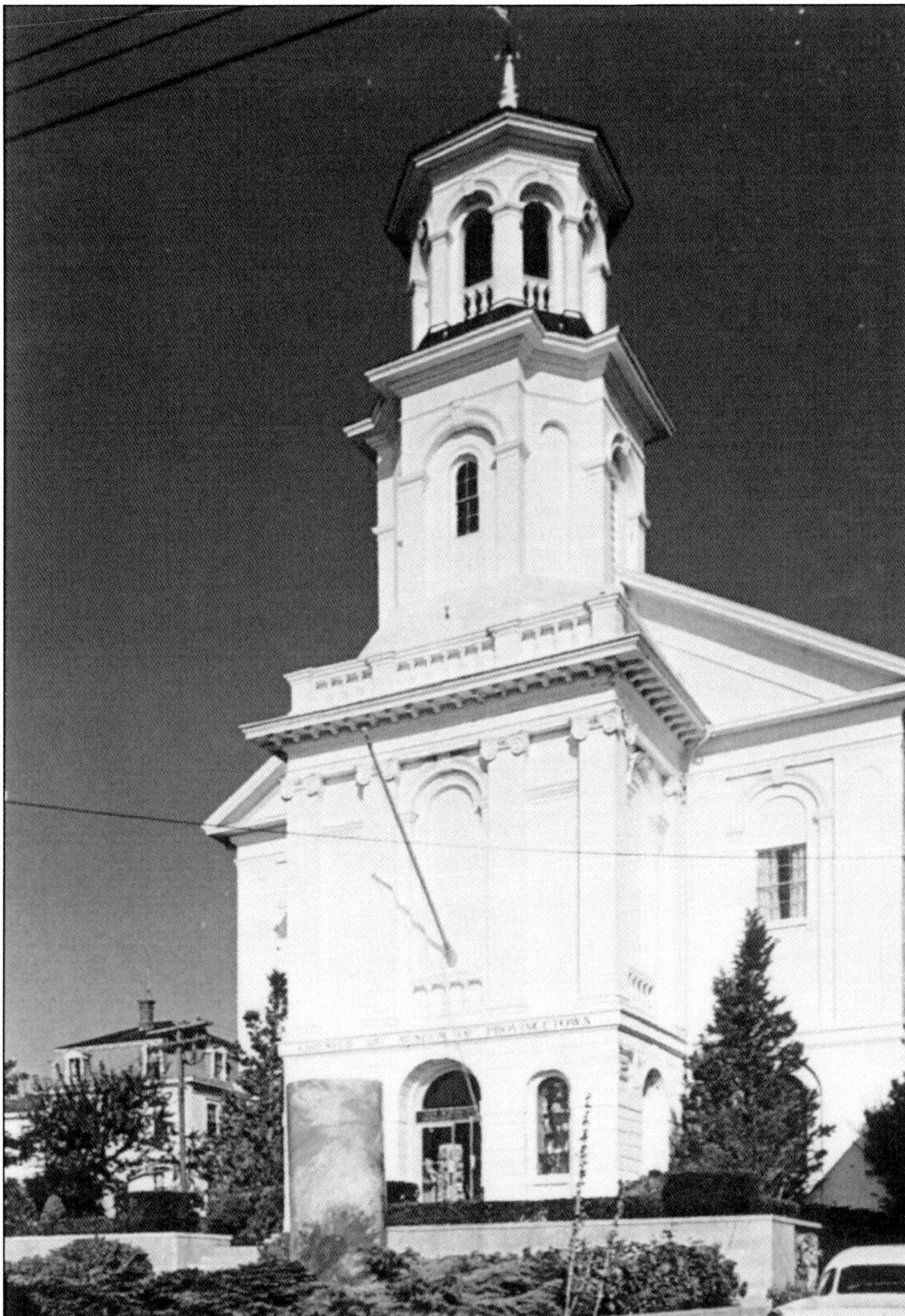

Chrysler Art Museum, 356 Commercial Street (c. 1965 postcard published by Colourpicture, Inc.). After the deconsecration of the Center M.E. Church, millionaire Walter Chrysler Jr. converted the interior of the architectural landmark into a fine arts museum in 1958 with important works from his private collection. In 1971, due to a dispute with the board of selectmen, he transferred the collection to Norfolk, Virginia. Since 1976 the building has been owned by the town and it is known as the Provincetown Heritage Museum.

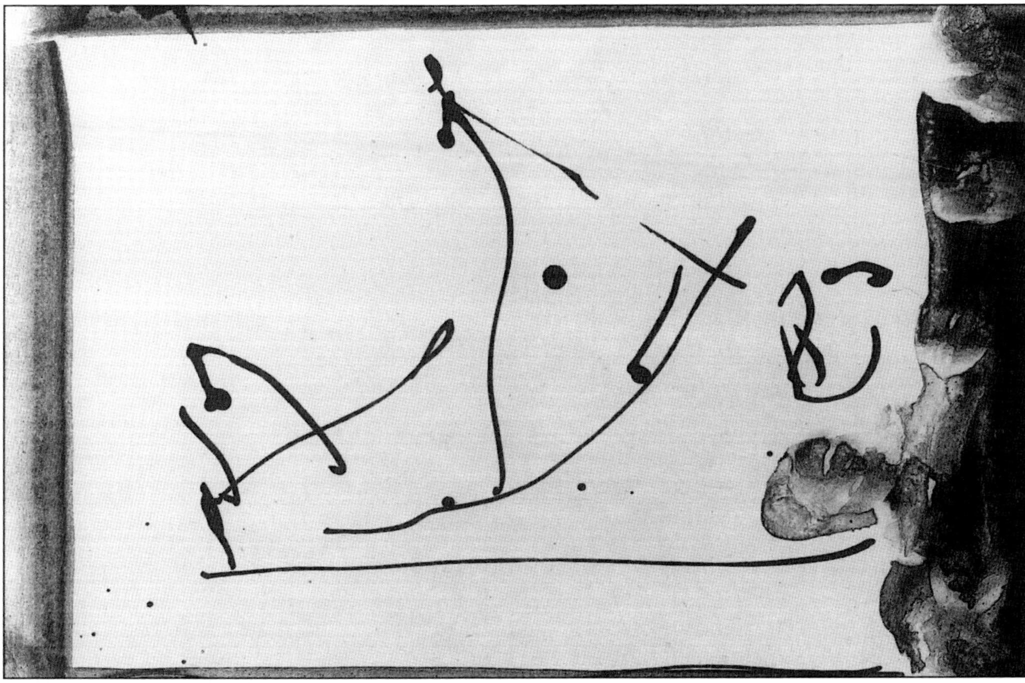

Untitled Abstraction (c. 1965 print by Robert Motherwell, 1915–1992). Provincetown's radiant light was compared to that in Greece by abstract artist Robert Motherwell, who resided at 622 Commercial Street in a late-19th-century structure he named the "Sea Barn." He and his first wife, Helen Frankenthaler (b. 1928), maintained separate studios. The Fine Arts Work Center (FAWC) on Pearl Street was founded in 1968 by Motherwell and other artists. Franz Kline (1910–1962), a bold brushstroke artist, had a studio at 16 Mechanic Street during the mid-20th century. (Photography courtesy Julie Heller Gallery.)

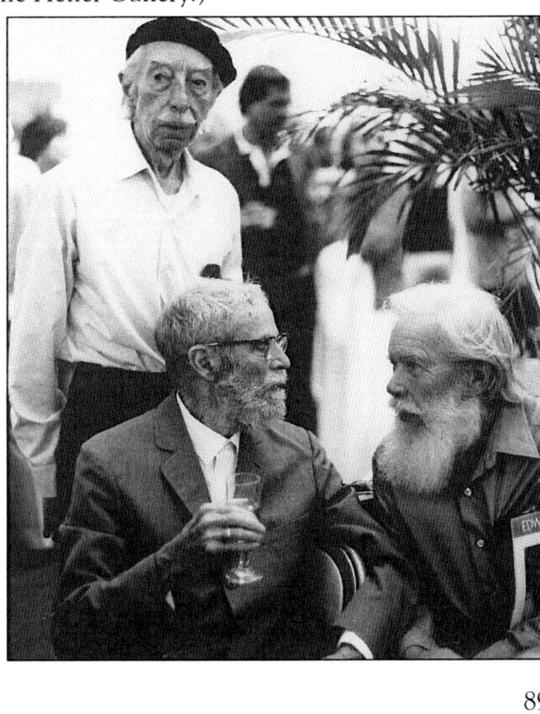

Old Guard Tête-à-Tête (1976 photograph). At the opening of his retrospective, Edwin W. Dickinson (1891–1978) enjoys a libation while engaged in artistic conversation with Philip Malicoat (who holds a catalogue of his friend's exhibition). Third associate Edwin Reeves "Eddy" Euler (1896–1982) is focused on the photographer. The potted palm in the background is in itself an interesting symbol, since, in the past, crossed palm leaves were placed over paintings of recently deceased artist members of the art association. (Courtesy Provincetown Art Association and Museum; photograph by Grace Consoli.)

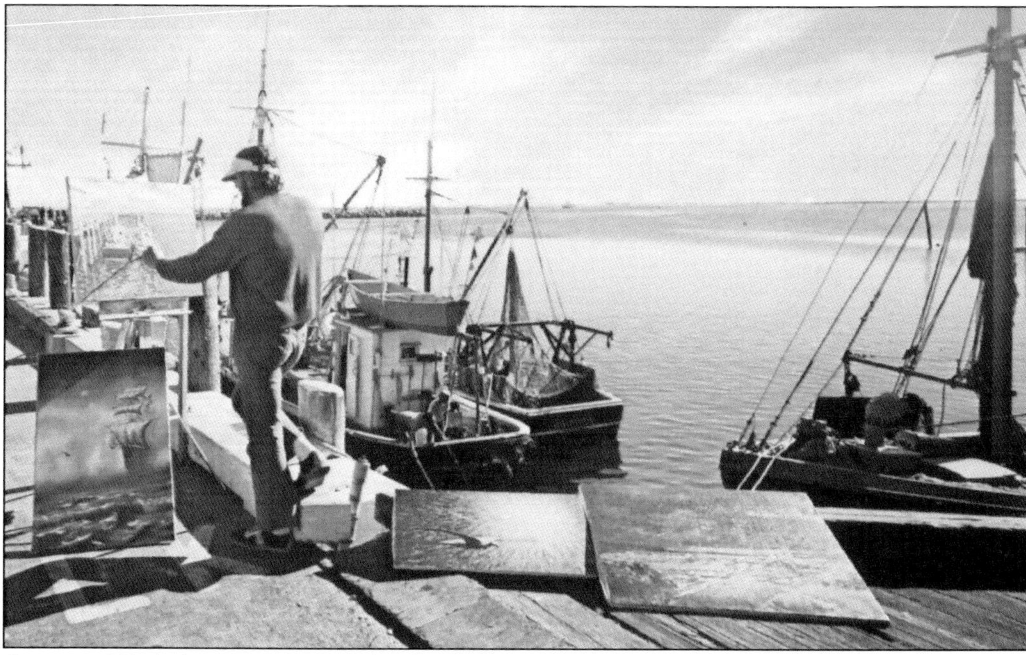

Artist at Work (c. 1980 postcard published by Lazarus Photo, Hyannis, MA). Ever hopeful for a sale, a left-handed artist has found a perfect wharfside location to display recently finished, and still unframed, oil paintings while he works on his current canvas of picturesque fishing boats reflected in the sparkling water.

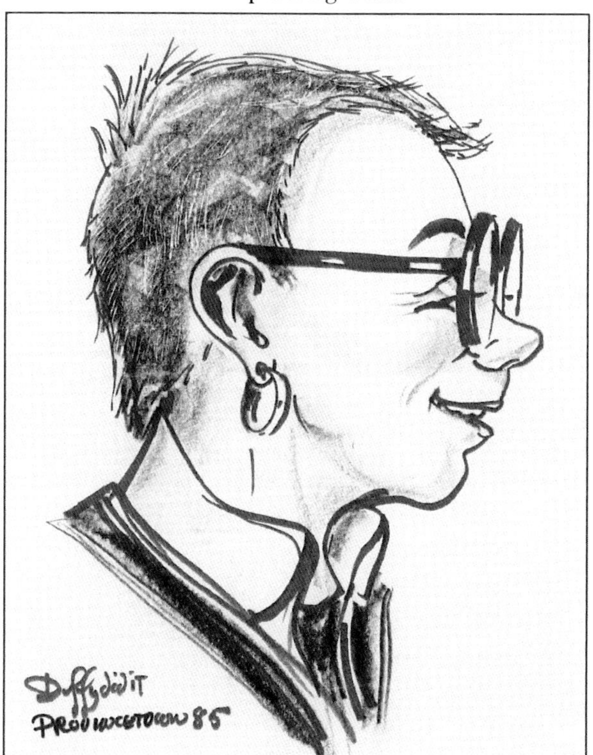

"Duffy did it" (1985 cartoon). Charles P. Duffy has been a cartoonist for four decades, and an "outdoor artist" in Provincetown for 30 of those years, initially at the corner of Small's Court in the town square. Jovial Joyce Battis was employed nearby at the Mayflower Café as a waitress, beginning around 1960, and had "Duffy" draw this five-minute cartoon probably as a memento of the year she is believed to have found other employment. (Courtesy Janoplis family.)

Five

Playwrights, Actors, and Authors

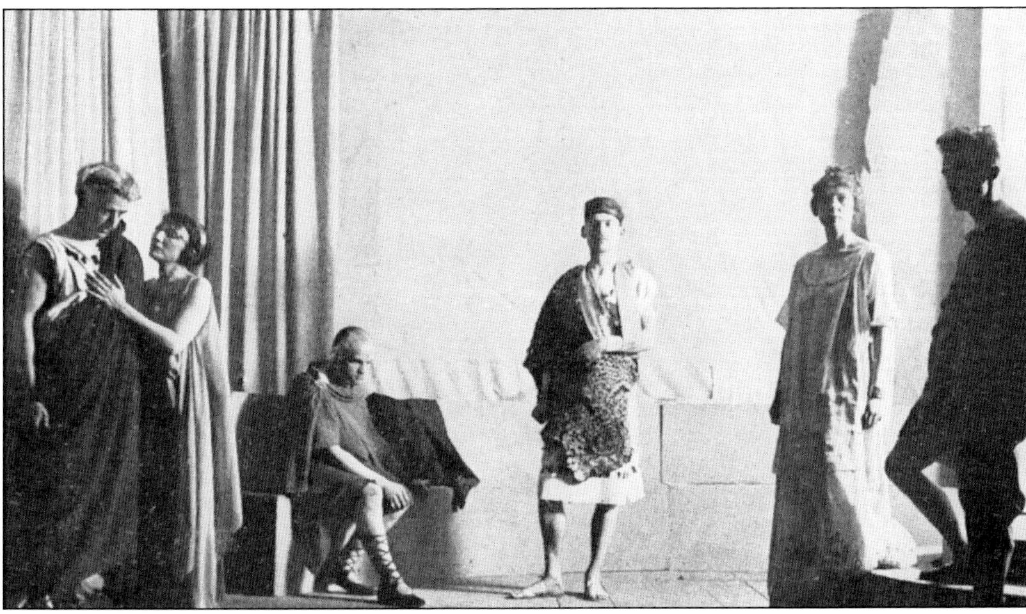

The Athenian Women (1918 photograph). The first full-length play to be presented by the Provincetown Players two years after the nascent company relocated to Greenwich Village in New York City was George Cram Cook's *The Athenian Women*, in April 1918. Thirty characters, including Pericles (the son of Xanthippo, played by Cook) were involved in the three-act, six-scene play which "was the most ambitious offering of this period from the standpoint of production." Dressed in cheesecloth robes the actors valiantly "cloaked their shivers in Periclean dignity," as the building was cold and the stage was crowded. George Cram "Jig" Cook was the founder and first director of the Provincetown Players—so named on September 5, 1916, when most of the sexually liberated Bohemians involved in the theatrical group had returned to Greenwich Village after their first electrically charged summer together in Provincetown. Human relationships and social and political issues of the day were addressed in their amateur productions. The Provincetown Players' life span was relatively brief—one of "high accomplishment and rock bottom failure"—from 1915 to 1922, when Cook left for Greece where he subsequently died, and when "Eugene O'Neill went to Broadway and the world."

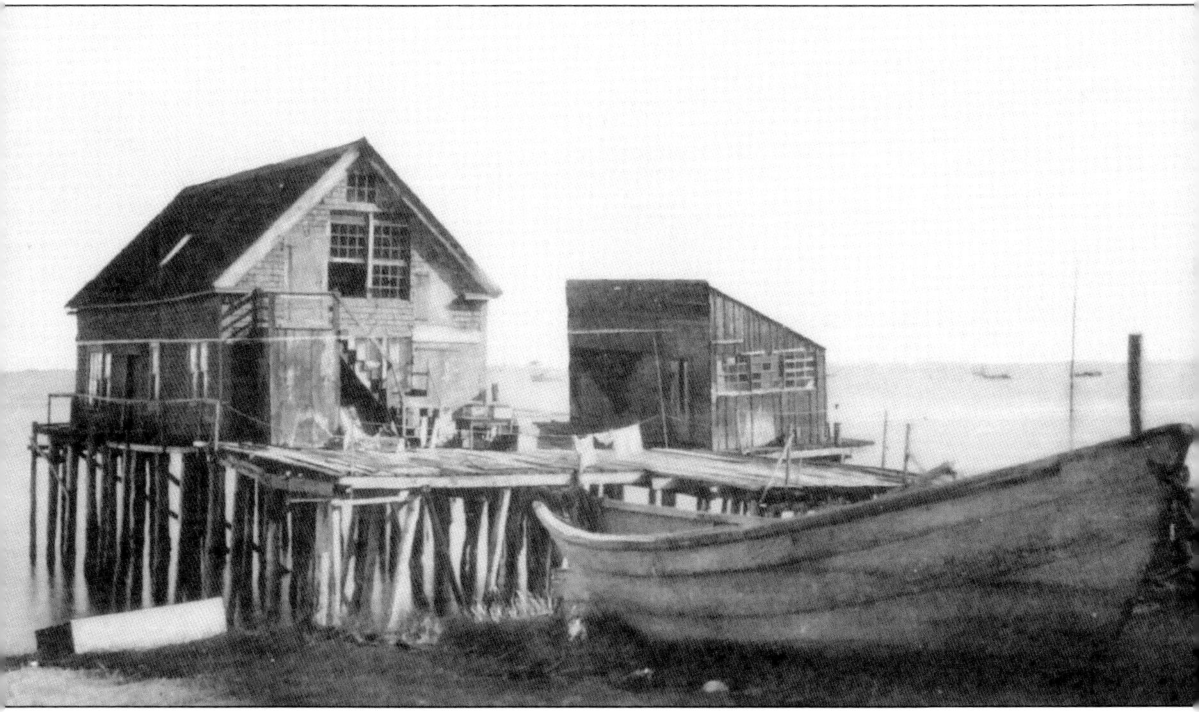

First Playhouse of Provincetown Players, 571 Commercial Street (c. 1920 postcard published by The Town Crier Shop). The former odoriferous fishhouse on Lewis Wharf owned by Mary Heaton Vorse O'Brien became the second location during the summer of 1915 for the Provincetown Players. Two new experimental plays—*Suppressed Desires* by newlyweds Susan Glaspell and George Cram Cook and *Constancy* by Neith and Hutchins Hapgood—were initially performed at the latter's beach cottage at 621 Commercial Street. The fishhouse on the ramshackle wharf, which accommodated Bror Nordfelt's Modern School of Art on the second floor, was "hastily renovated with fish nets and circus benches." The following spring new scripts, electric lights, stationary benches, and improved staging made the interior look more like a little theatre. Nine new one-act plays were performed there in 1916, and the price of admission was 50¢. Lewis Wharf, also known as Mrs. O'Brien's Wharf, was unfortunately destroyed by a noontime high tide in August of 1922.

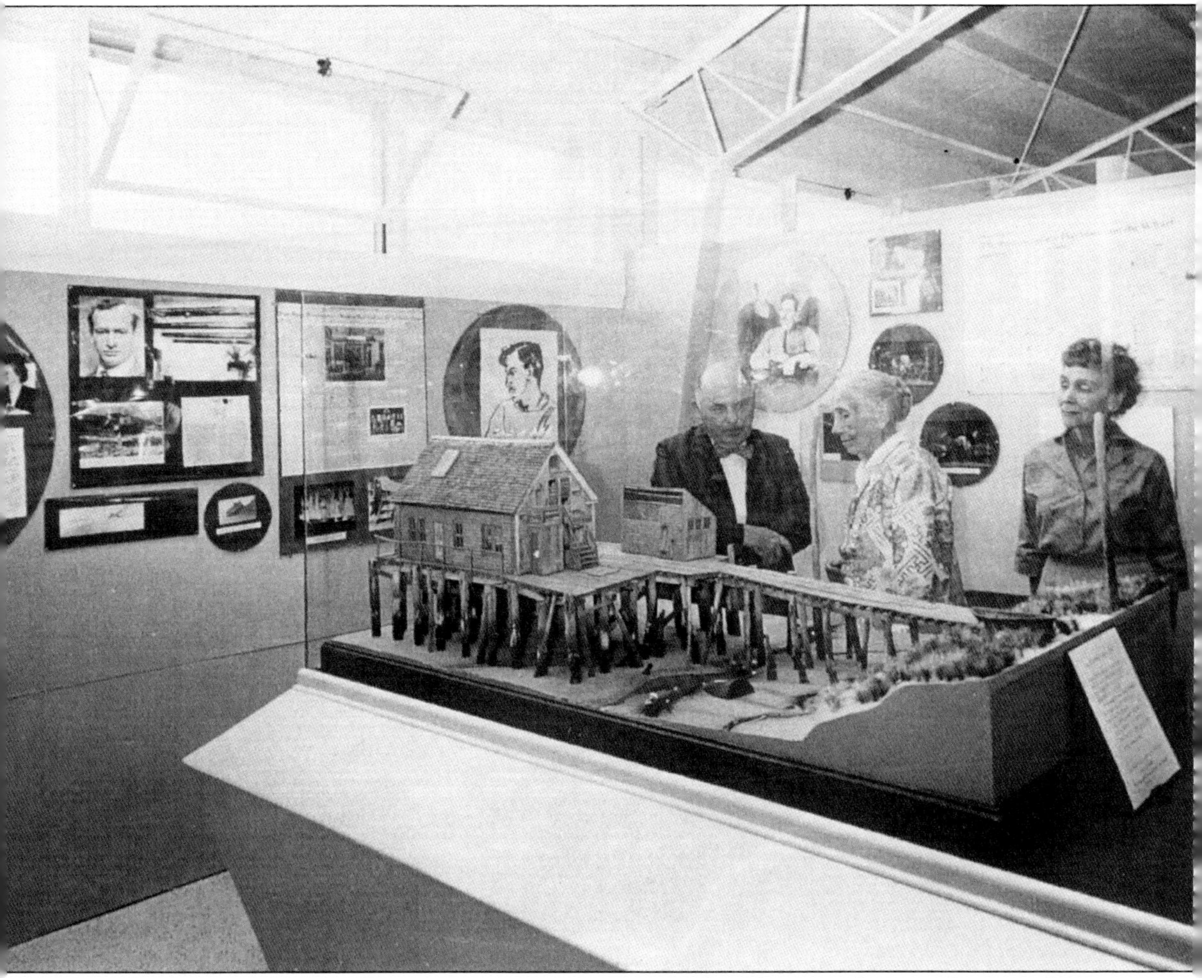

Remembering Lewis Wharf, Provincetown's First "Little Theatre" (1963 photograph). Courtney Allen, one of six art students who ran the "Sixes-and Sevens" coffee shop on Lewis Wharf for a few years, made the detailed model of the famous wharf and playhouse now on display in the Pilgrim Monument & Provincetown Museum. Mr. Allen reminisces with the elderly Mary Heaton Vorse (Mrs. Joseph O'Brien) and Catherine Huntington, one of the founders of the Provincetown Playhouse-on-the-Wharf. In the background of the exhibit at the museum can be seen likenesses of Susan Glaspell (left), "Jig" Cook (center), and a sketch of Eugene O'Neill by William Zorach (above the wharf model). (Courtesy of the Cape Cod Pilgrim Memorial Association.)

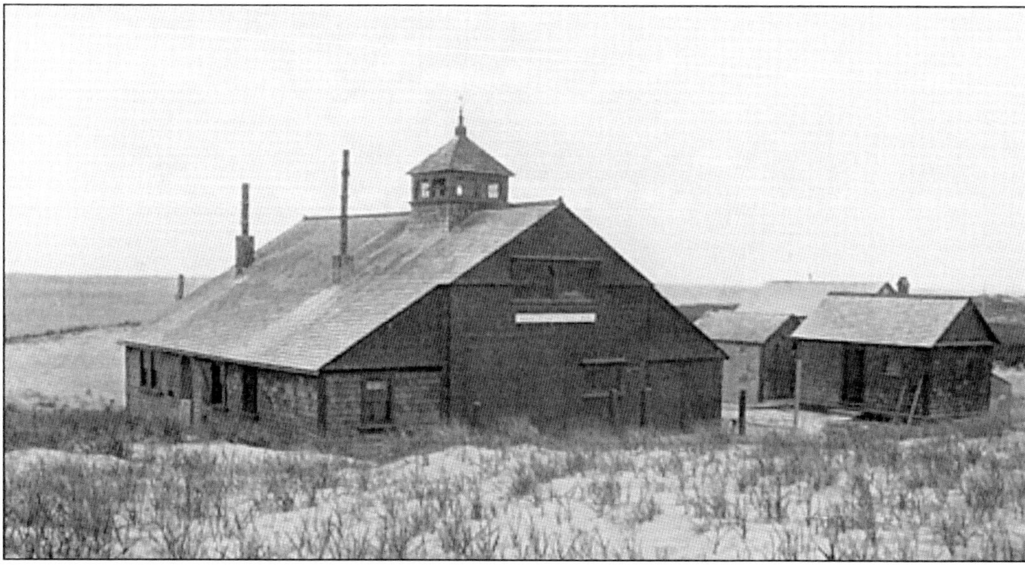

U.S. Life Saving Station (1898 photograph by the Perry Pictures Co.). Only the majestic sand dunes and beach grass (Ammophilia arenaria) remain where the first Peaked Hill Bars Life Saving Station was situated near the Atlantic Ocean off Snail Road. In the spring of 1931 a devastating winter storm washed it into the ocean. The concrete foundation dates to the second structure, which was abandoned after World War II and destroyed by fire in 1958. The O'Neills moved into the shingled structure in April of 1919, and after 1925 Mr. O'Neill rented it to Edmund Wilson. That writer's friends, poet e.e. cummings and author John Dos Passos, were guests there at one time or another.

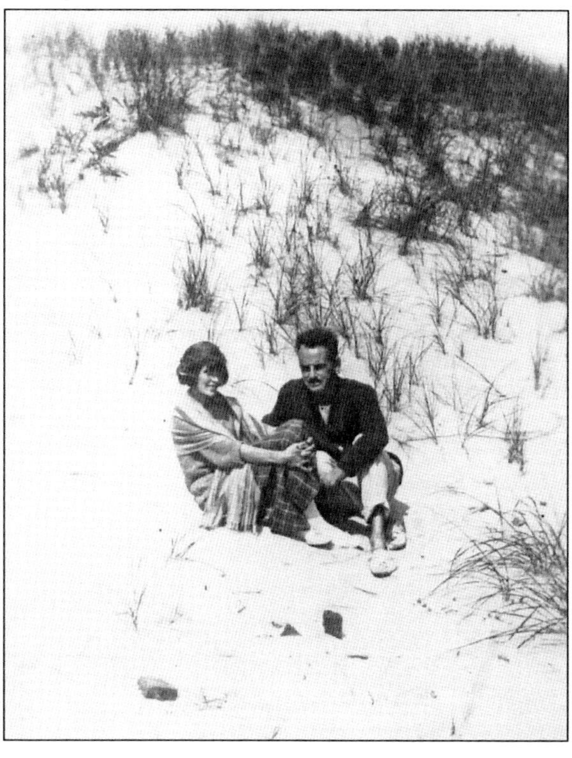

Eugene O'Neill and Agnes Boulton (c. 1918 photograph). The lovers relax in the dunes around the year of their marriage in Provincetown, three years following the propitious summer the Provincetowners met. Remembered as a "shy, dark boy" who had stage fright, O'Neill's first sea play, *Bound East for Cardiff*, was performed to much acclaim on July 28, 1916, at the Lewis Wharf theatre; the sound effects of the harbor waves added extra impact to the presentation. O'Neill won the first of four Pulitzer Prizes in 1920 for his play *Beyond the Horizon*. (Courtesy Provincetown Public Library.)

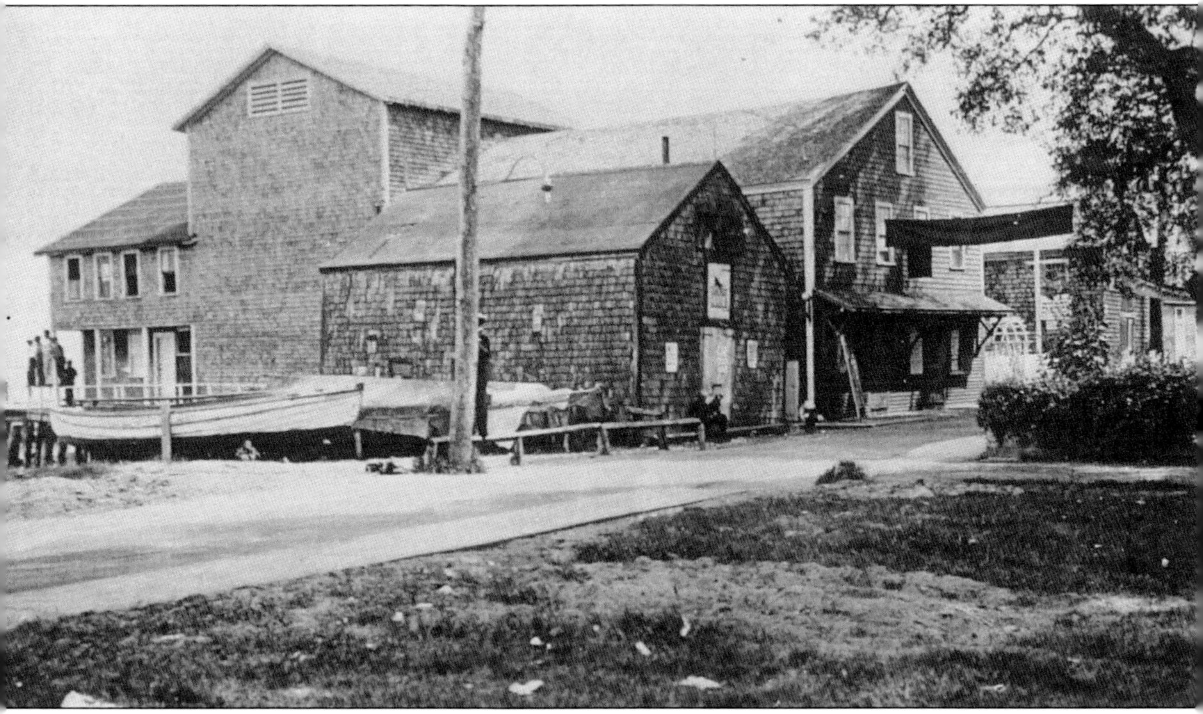

The Wharf Theatre, 83 Commercial Street (c. 1930s photograph). The West End's little theatre was built in 1925 on the remains of a wharf about three streets "Up-along around the Bend" (where Commercial Street makes an L-turn), now the location of the West End Racing Club. Mary Bicknell, actress-wife of the artist William W.H. Bicknell, spearheaded the short-lived theatrical group—financial problems caused it to close in 1927. The management changed hands several times until it was reported in the *Boston Post* on February 15, 1940, that the "historic Wharf Theatre [was] torn apart by last night's gale and with its supporting piling washed away . . . [it] was collapsing into Provincetown Harbor tonight. Bits of wreckage including costumes, scenery and stage effects are being strewn along the shore and the $20,000 structure doomed." Eight years earlier, *Fish for Friday*, Arthur Robinson's "Three-act Portuguese fishing drama in the old Provincetown tradition, with native instruments and vocal sea music" was performed for the summer season. That same year Club Lagoon was the Wharf Players' restaurant "Above the Theatre and Below the Sea." (Courtesy of the Cape Cod Pilgrim Memorial Association.)

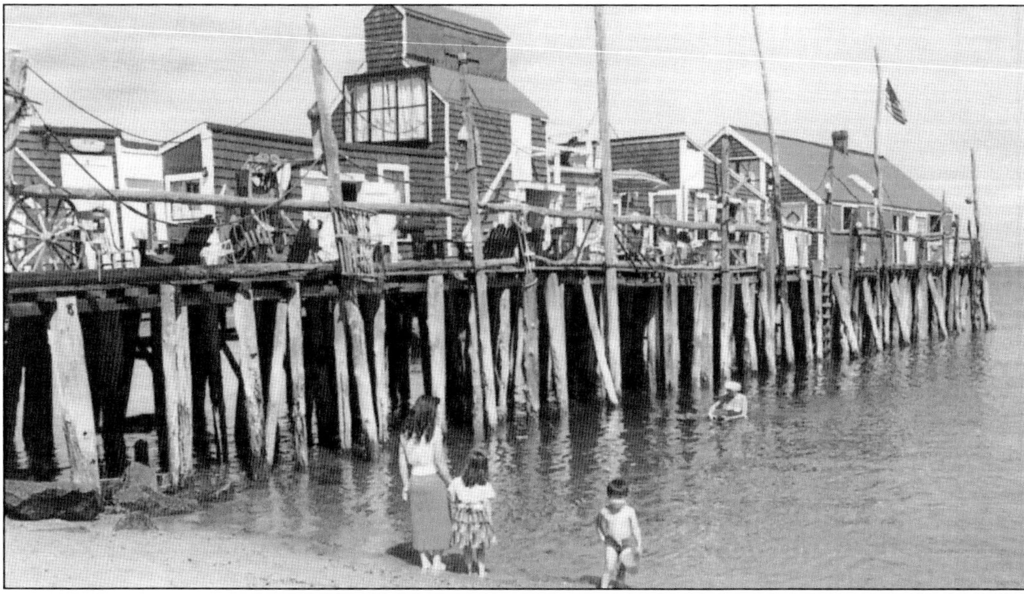

Capt. Jack's Wharf, 73 Commercial Street (c. 1975 postcard published by Colourpicture, Inc.). Thomas Lanier Williams—a.k.a. Tennessee Williams—arrived in town during the summer of 1940, the same year the Provincetown Playhouse-on-the-Wharf presented its first play. The peripatetic and absent-minded young playwright became enamored of Kip Kiernan, a handsome young ballet dancer of Russian descent, and they had a brief affair at Capt. Jack's Wharf. Tennessee Williams dedicated his first collection of short stories, *One Arm and Other Stories*, to the youth who stole his heart. Williams returned to Provincetown at other times and was similarly inspired and intrigued by attractive young men. (Courtesy Schier Collection.)

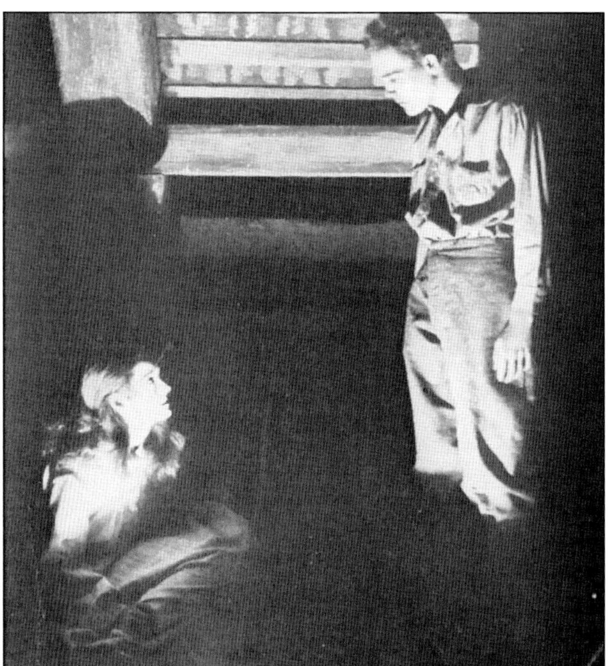

***The Earth Between* (1929 photograph).** Virgil Geddes wrote the two-act, subtly incestuous play that starred the 21-year-old Bette Davis (1908–1989)—"a wraith of a child with true emotional insight"—and William Challee. The players performed the drama as members of the Provincetown Players in Greenwich Village. The always incomparable Miss Davis, her younger sister Barbara (called "Bobby"), and their divorced "classic stage mother, Ruthie" enjoyed the summer of 1924 in Provincetown in the parsonage where the Eugene O'Neills were married.

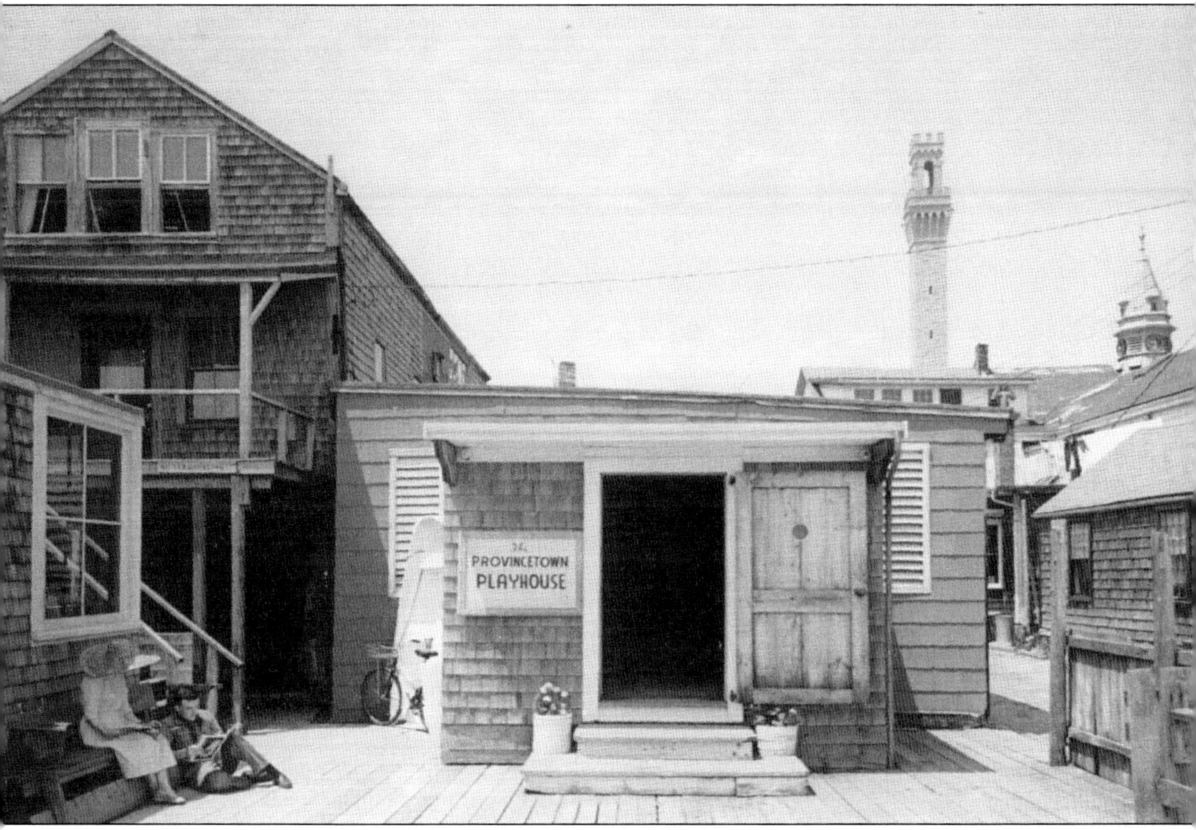

Provincetown Playhouse-on-the-Wharf, Gosnold Street Town Landing (c. 1960 postcard published by The Mayflower Sales Co.). This theatre venture was formed as a repertory company, and it produced many unpublished plays. The audience had a choice of 186 seats, but the actors only had two dressing rooms! Patrons purchased tickets on the sandy walkway side of the former painting school of Ross Moffett and Heinrich Pfeiffer. Ticket prices in 1946 were $1.10, $1.64, and $2.40, and the curtain went up at 8:30 p.m. Eugene O'Neill's play *Diff'rent* was last performed at the playhouse on August 22, 1946. On the 26th of the month, the work of local playwright and town eccentric Harry Kemp—*Boccaccio's Untold Tale*—opened along with the premier performance of Tennessee Williams' *The Unsatisfactory Supper*. Acclaimed actress Gena Rowlands appeared there with Robert Donat in the 1951 play *You Never Can Tell.* Sadly, the theatre was destroyed by arson on March 25, 1977, while Truro resident Adele Heller was the owner and producer.

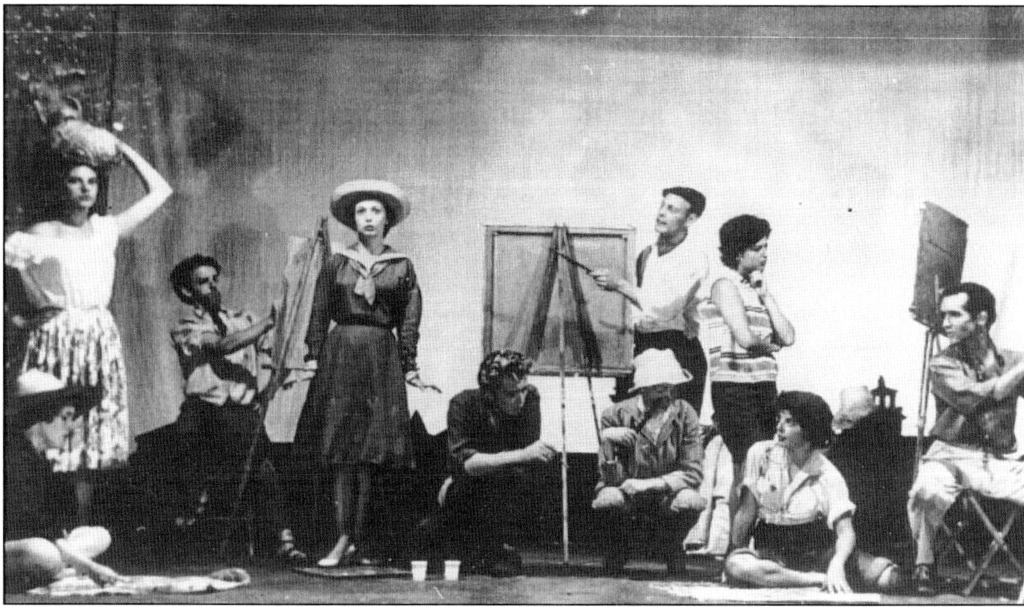

***The Pirates of Provincetown* (1960 photograph).** This production at the Playhouse-on-the-Wharf included, among other aspiring actors and actresses, Billy Clift (third from the left), Montgomery Clift's nephew. During the middle of the same decade, Robert Costa's ACT IV, an avant-garde theatre group, performed new plays by unknown playwrights in the cellar of the Gifford House (77 Bradford Street), which operated as a café theatre until it closed in 1969 for financial reasons. (Courtesy of the Cape Cod Pilgrim Memorial Association.)

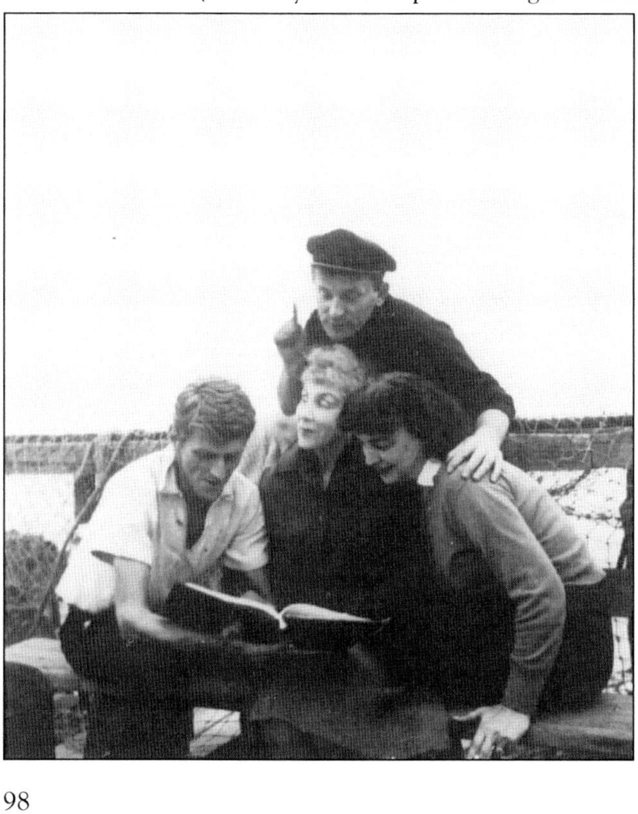

Catherine Huntington with Actor Friends (c. 1950s photograph). Catherine S. Huntington, a financially independent Bostonian, moved to Provincetown around 1940 along with Edwin Burr Pettet and Virginia Thoms. Pettet and Thoms were involved in the New England Repertory Theatre, of which Miss Huntington was the founder. As "Jig" Cook had been the catalyst of the Provincetown Players, so did Catherine Huntington provide the inspiration for the Provincetown Playhouse-on-the-Wharf. Her final curtain was in 1969 when she appeared opposite a young Richard Gere in Tennessee Williams' 1953 play *Camino Real.* (Courtesy Provincetown Public Library.)

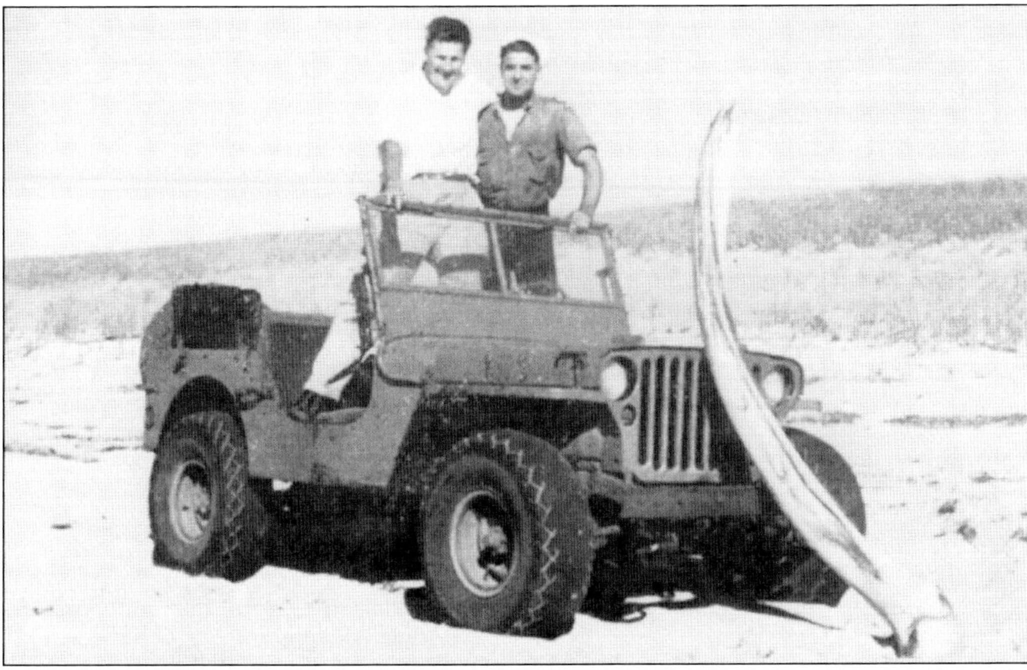

A Jeep at Race Point (c. 1946 photograph). Edward Rowe Snow clasps the shoulder of his driver friend as the two pose with a whale's lower jaw "hood ornament" for a picture that appears in his book, *A Pilgrim Returns to Cape Cod* (1946). Snow, a resident of Marshfield, Massachusetts, may have known fellow novelist John Dos Passos and his wife, Katharine Smith Dos Passos, who lived next door to the site of the Lewis Wharf Theatre at 571 Commercial Street. (Courtesy Schier Collection.)

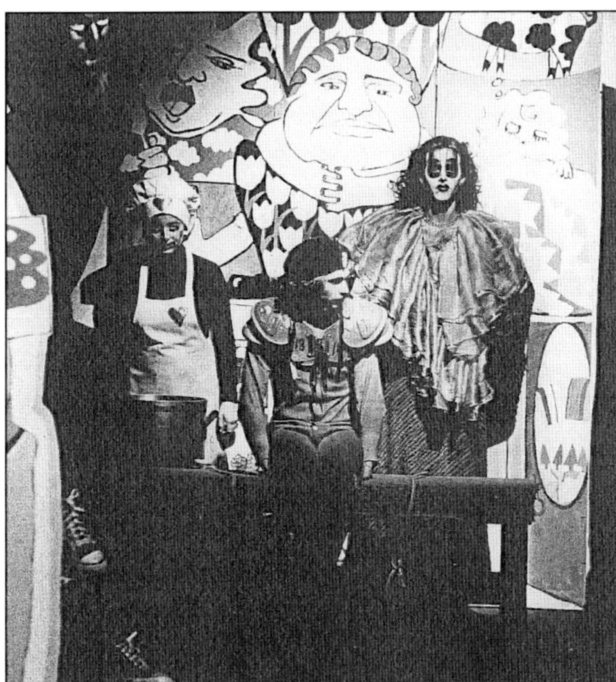

***Alice in Wonderland* (c. 1960s photograph).** Caricatures of Lewis Carroll's whimsical characters set the stage for this performance by the Provincetown Theater Company at the Provincetown Inn at 1 Commercial Street. This recognized acting company performed plays by Shakespeare and by local playwrights. They also held readings, playwriting workshops, and offered year-round performances. (Private Collection.)

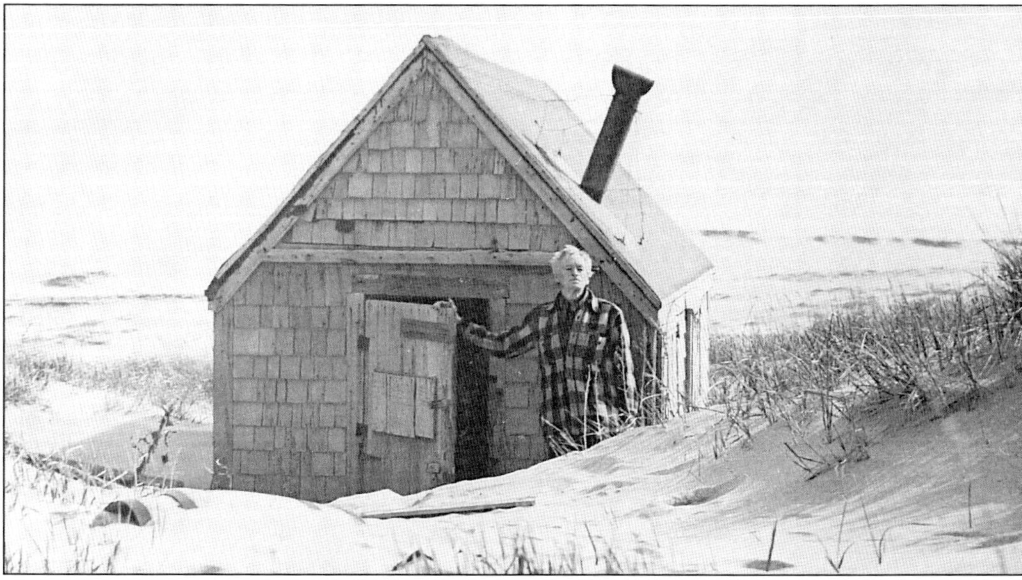

Harry Kemp, "Poet of the Dunes" (c. 1950s photograph). Harry Kemp Way, situated between Conwell and Howland Streets, was named to honor the unconventional poet, activist, and dune-shack dweller who lived near Race Point. Kemp enjoyed dressing up as a "Pilgrim" to advocate Monday—"First Washday"—as a national holiday. He is best known for his book *Tramping on Life*, which was published in 1922. "Euphoria" and "Thalassa," 2 of the approximately 14 remaining dune shacks, were acquired in the 1920s by author Hazel Hawthorne Werner. They have been maintained since 1989 by the Peaked Hill Trust. (Courtesy Provincetown Art Association and Museum.)

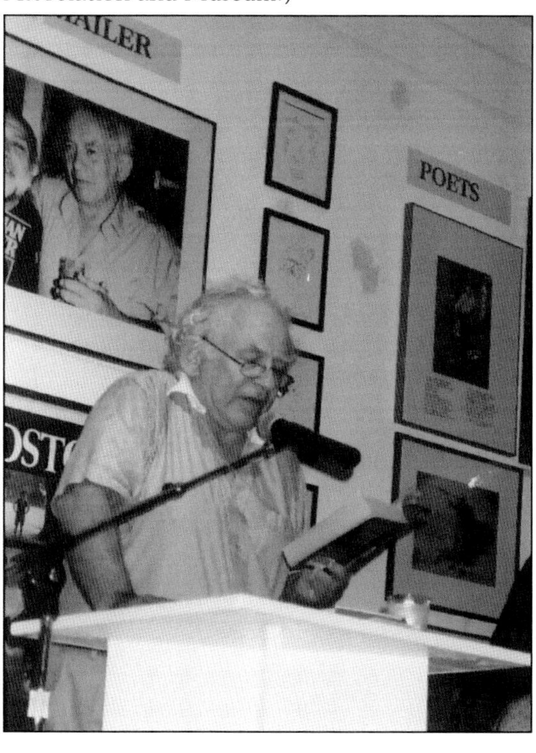

A Reading by Norman Mailer (1990 photograph). Born in 1923 in Long Branch, New Jersey, the prolific author, reporter, and poet grew up in Brooklyn and graduated from Harvard University. In 1987 his novel *Tough Guys Don't Dance*—a convoluted cocaine-related murder mystery set in Provincetown—was made into a film for which he wrote the screenplay and directed actors Ryan O'Neal and Isabella Rossellini. Mailer read from some of his recent works at a champagne reception at the home of his friend, Reginald Cabral, partially shown in the photograph with the distinguished author, who has been visiting Provincetown since 1942.

Six

Entertainers

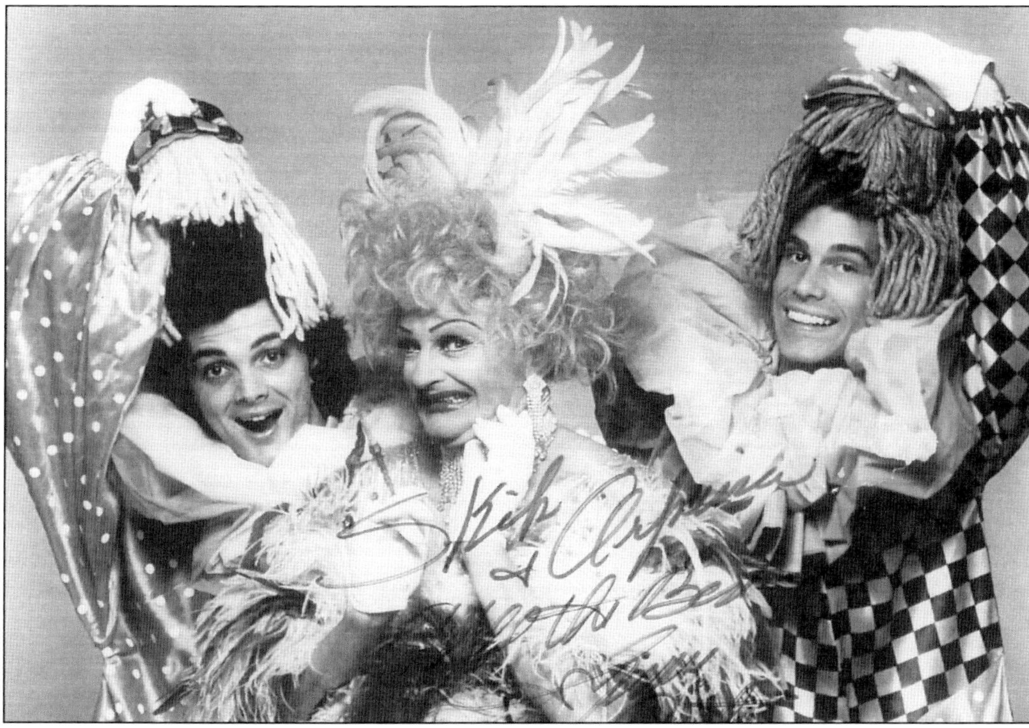

Lynne Carter as Phyllis Diller with Harlequins (c. 1975 photograph). Many famous, and would-be famous, entertainers and personalities have imbued the nightlife of Provincetown with glamour and glitter for decades. Jazz singers and instrumentalists entertained at Reginald "Reggie" Cabral's Atlantic (A-House) House Bar on Masonic Place in the '50s, and during the same period a few female impersonators performed at the Crown & Anchor on Commercial Street. In August of 1950 The Mad Moiselles, "three queens of comedy," appeared in the Surf Room of the latter establishment, then known as the New Central House. These entertainers, and those who began delighting guests at the Pilgrim House's Madeira Club (also on Commercial Street) in the 1970s, added a comedic "bitchy" kind of spice to the avant-garde theatre life of the town. With proper makeup, often flamboyant costumes, and conducive lighting, female impersonators give the illusion that gay-idolized goddesses of the stage and screen live on, either by using their own adaptable voices, by performing to memorable recordings of the entertainers themselves, or by lip-synching. (Courtesy Skip and Arpina Stanton.)

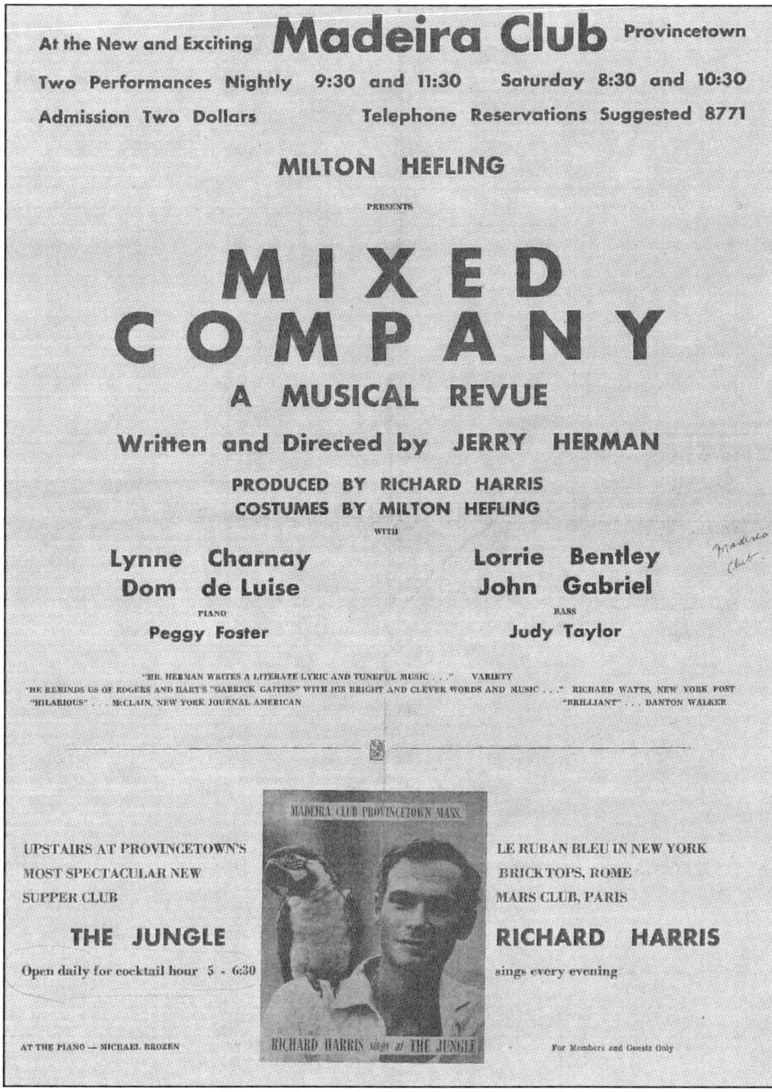

Madeira Club Newspaper Advertisement (the *Advocate*, June 30, 1960). Provincetown's "only real night club," the Madeira Club (formerly the Sea Dragon Club), was the very popular basement lounge of the Pilgrim House, patronized by both straight and gay individuals. After enjoying a late afternoon sing-along at the Moors Restaurant's piano bar, on Bradford Street in the far West End, or at Weathering Heights on Shank Painter Road, people would either dine early in one of the town's trendy restaurants or return to their abodes for rest, then arrive at the Madeira Club for either the first or second evening performance. (Sports coats and ties for gentlemen were de rigueur in local restaurants and bars until around 1964.) The dimly lit basement featured columns, a piano-shaped bar, and a large stage beyond. Songstress Margaret Whiting was one of the last big-name entertainers to perform at the club. Richard Harris was one performer who sang in "The Jungle," when the first floor of the Pilgrim House became a supper club. Those who only wanted to dine on spaghetti and meatballs, such as Elizabeth Taylor and Richard Burton, could do so as the famous Hollywood duo did at least once during the 1960s, at "Mary Spaghetti's" restaurant, a busy after-hours eatery at the corner of Bradford and Nickerson Streets. (Courtesy Stanton Collection.)

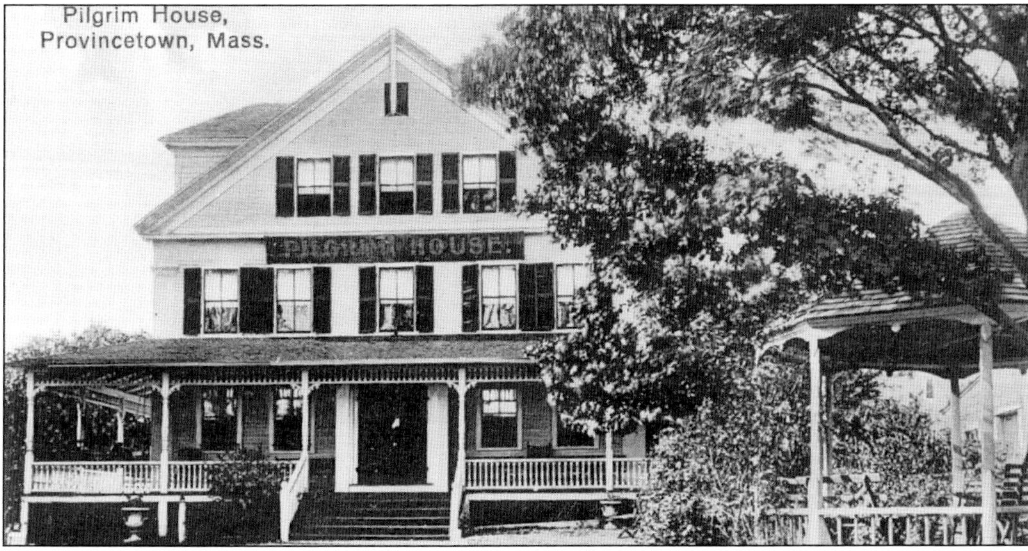

Pilgrim House, 313 Commercial Street (early-20th-century postcard published by H.A. Dickerman & Son). Set back from the "main drag," Provincetown's oldest hotel, the Pilgrim House (built *c.* 1781), retained most of its Greek Revival architectural features up until October of 1990 when it was destroyed by arson. Camp film and stage star Divine received a standing ovation for his performance in *Neon Woman*, featuring Holly Woodlawn, which was presented at the Madeira Club during the 1979 summer season. Transvestite Woodlawn was one of Andy Warhol's early discoveries. Before becoming John Waters' protégé, Harris Glenn Milstead (Divine) once sold antiques and collectibles in Provincetown.

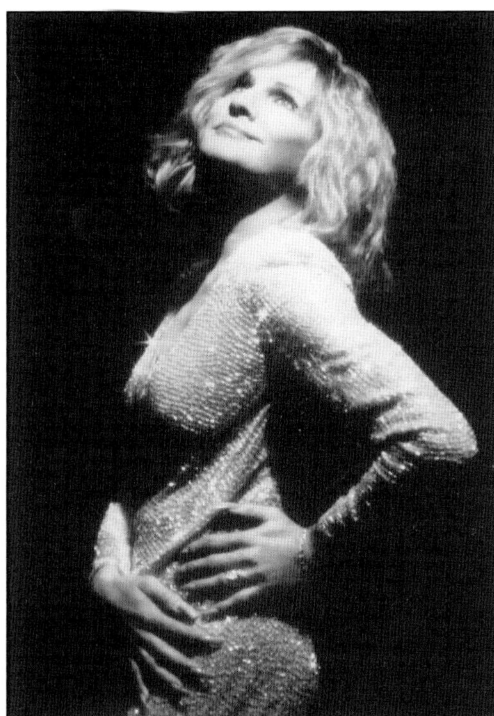

Jim Bailey as Barbra Streisand (c. 1995 photograph). "Master illusionist" Jim Bailey has an operatic background, which he draws upon when appearing in concerts in major American cities and in London—where he has performed at least 20 times. Mr. Bailey has appeared on television on numerous occasions, and in at least four films, including Woody Allen's *Zelig*. An accomplished make-up artist, Bailey once gave a special recreation of the "Somewhere Over the Rainbow" star with her daughter, Liza Minnelli, in their famous Mother and Daughter Concert. (Courtesy Stephen Campbell Management, Beverly Hills, California).

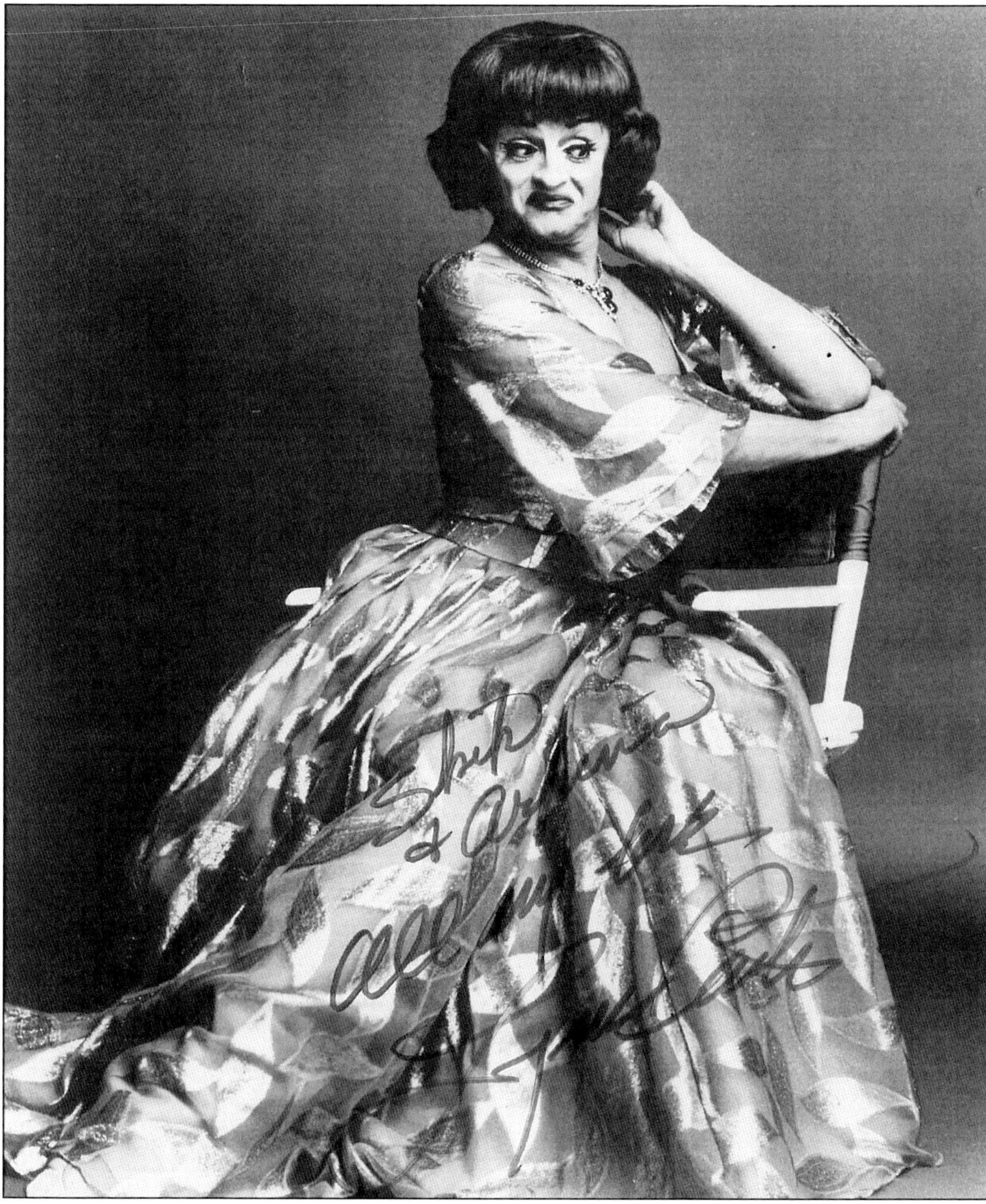

Lynne Carter as Bette Davis (c. 1975 photograph). Humble, gracious, and gregarious are adjectives that described Lynne Carter, who in 1975 purchased the Pilgrim House Hotel from Manuel and Bernadette Brazao. Carter first appeared at the Madeira Club in July of 1966, and he starred there through the early '80s. His campy impersonation of the gay cult's prima donna—over-accentuating Bette Davis's mannered ways with bulging, always moving eyes, angular hip movements, and swinging arms with cigarette in hand—was one of his best and best-loved routines. One day in the mid-'70s when Miss Davis *herself* was driving down Commercial Street in a red Mustang convertible, an ardent admirer of female impersonators dashed over to acknowledge the amazing likeness, whereupon Bette Davis drew herself up and enunciated "No darling, it's the real thing!" (Courtesy Stanton Collection.)

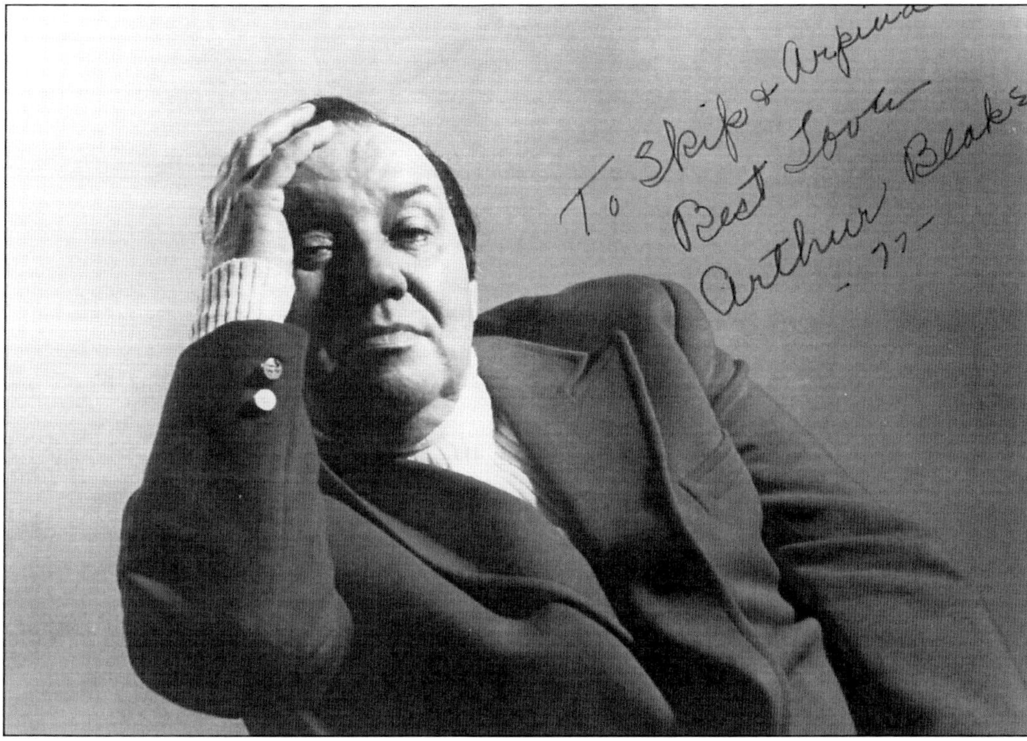

Arthur Blake (1977 photograph). Husky Arthur Blake was under contract with Warner Brothers when he was featured in the 1952 film *Diplomatic Courier*, which starred Tyrone Power. The Altoona, Pennsylvania, native resided in Provincetown for many years, at 9 Arch Street with Irving Cohen, his business manager and lover for more than 50 years. Mr. Blake always opened his show in a tuxedo, and then he would change into a stunning gown for the second act. He first appeared on a Provincetown stage in July of 1953 in "La Salle de Cabaret" at the A-House. (Courtesy Stanton Collection.)

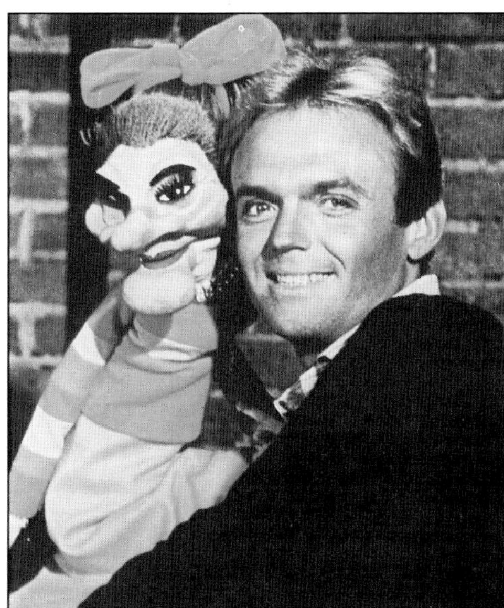

Wayland Flowers and Madame I (c. 1973 photograph). Boyishly handsome Wayland Flowers was in his late twenties when his Hollywood career accelerated. Flowers always escorted his loquacious alter ego (one of the two Madames, or other puppet variations), and he made guest appearances at the Crown & Anchor Motor Inn, the Madeira Club, and the Provincetown Inn. Fellow gay comedian Paul Lynde often visited P-town, but is thought to have never performed on stage. (Courtesy Stanton Collection.)

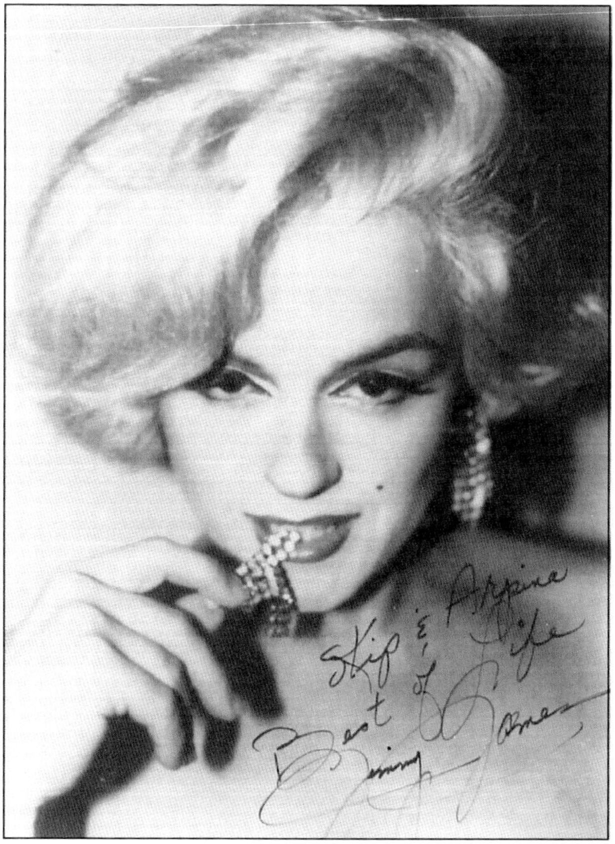

Jimmy James as Marilyn Monroe (c. 1988 photograph). Joey Skilbred took this provocative photograph of the "blonde bombshell" toying with a rhinestone earring. Jimmy James, a native of Laredo, Texas, has been an entertainer since 1984, and he began captivating audiences in Provincetown two years later. His impersonation of Marilyn Monroe is highly regarded, and without missing a note, the remarkable singer can sound like her, Judy Garland, or Bette Davis. (Courtesy Stanton Collection.)

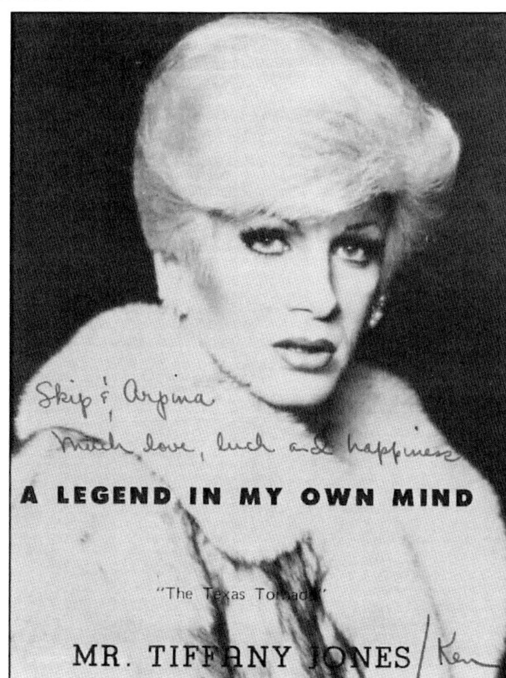

Mr. Tiffany Jones (c. 1983 photograph). "The Texas Tornado" is remembered as a "fabulous person" who was "all male [he always wore a cowboy hat] when out of drag" (DRessed as A Girl). Tiffany (Ken Whitehead) was able to make the most convincing personality switch, and was the most "ultra-feminine female impersonator on stage." His audiences in P-town in the early 1980s roared when he appeared as a flying nun on roller skates. (Courtesy Stanton Collection.)

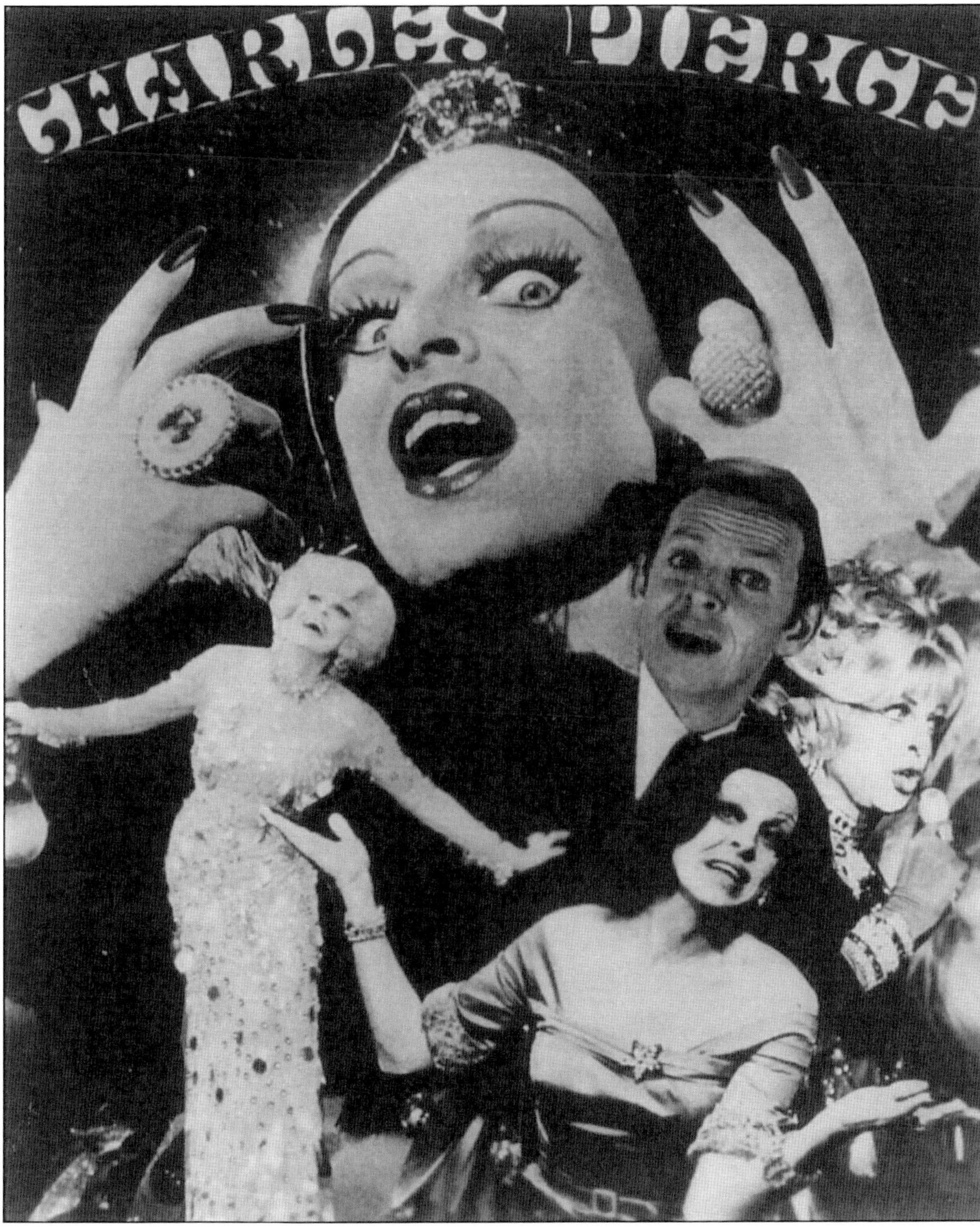

Charles Pierce (c. 1980 photograph). In or out of costume, Charles Pierce's expressive eyes have helped to bring his leading ladies to life. Since the 1950s Pierce has entertained audiences in various locales including Provincetown, where one of his funniest impersonations was that of Eleanor Roosevelt. His imitation of Gloria Swanson in *Sunset Boulevard* (1950), with her bejeweled turban and fingers, always brought gales of laughter from straight couples who enjoy "drag shows" as much as their gay counterparts. Transvestism, or "cross-dressing," as practiced by many straight and gay men, is somewhat related to female impersonation. (Courtesy Stanton Collection.)

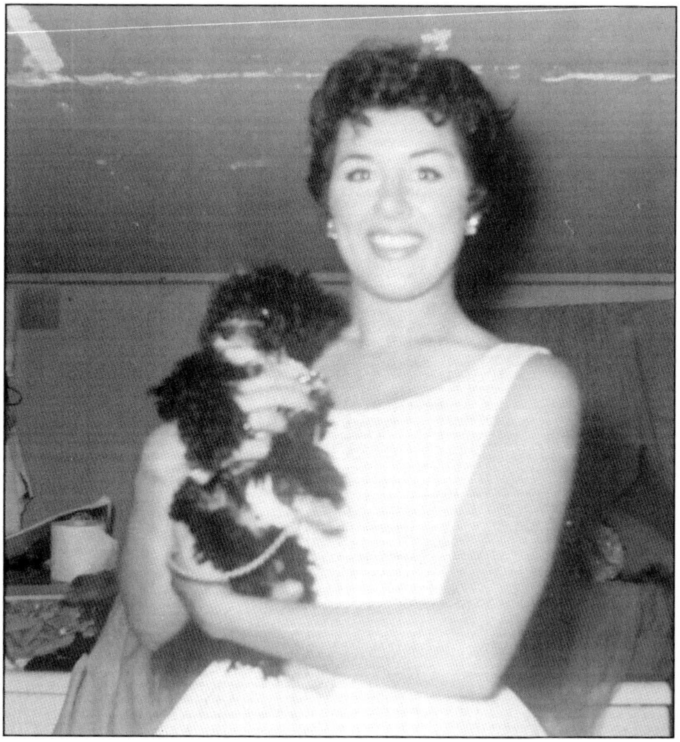

Cindy Lord and Her Pet Dog (1957 photograph). Cute as a button singer Cindy Lord, a greater Boston resident who appeared with Lindy Doherty on TV's "Swan Boat," is shown backstage at the gay-owned nightclub Weathering Heights. During the mid-1940s "Madame Pumpernickle" (Helen Hawkes from Greenwich Village), a diminutive "glorious pianist" who sat on several telephone books, performed in the cocktail lounge of the Moors Restaurant. Roger Kent was another popular piano player there who entertained customers at the sing-along during the 1950s and '60s. (Courtesy Emery Warner.)

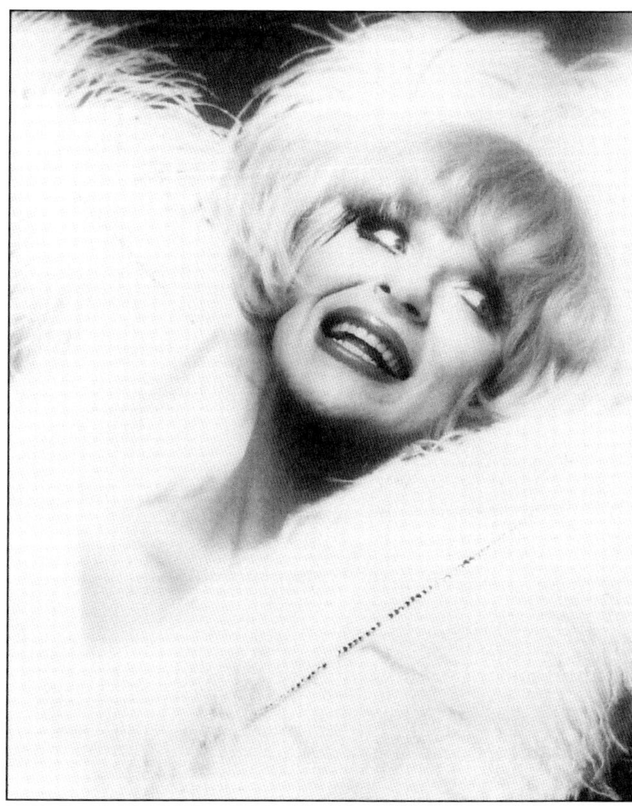

Craig Russell Portraying Carol Channing as Lorelei Lee in *Gentlemen Prefer Blondes* (c. 1980 photograph). Canadian-born Craig Russell was a talented but temperamental individual who appeared, among other places, at Carnegie Hall in New York City, and at the Crown & Anchor and the Madeira Club in Provincetown. Russell starred in the 1977 semi-autobiographical film *Outrageous*—an "off-beat comedy about an unlikely relationship between a [pregnant] schizophrenic and a female impersonator . . . [a story] of courage, hope, and caring"—for which he received the best actor prize at the Berlin Film Festival. (Courtesy Stanton Collection.)

Nina Simone (mid-20th-century photograph). Notes on the back of an album cover state that "Whether it be a folk song, a ballad, or cool jazz, Nina Simone leaves her audience completely captivated. . . . Her brilliant performance is foot stamping, exciting rhythm from first note to last." Miss Simone performed at the A-House Cabaret Room at least once in the 1950s. Drummer Gene Krupa made the joint jump in August of 1955, and Al Martino crooned tunes during the same month of 1951 at the Surf Room in the New Central House. (Courtesy Main Street Art and Antiques, Gloucester, Massachusetts.)

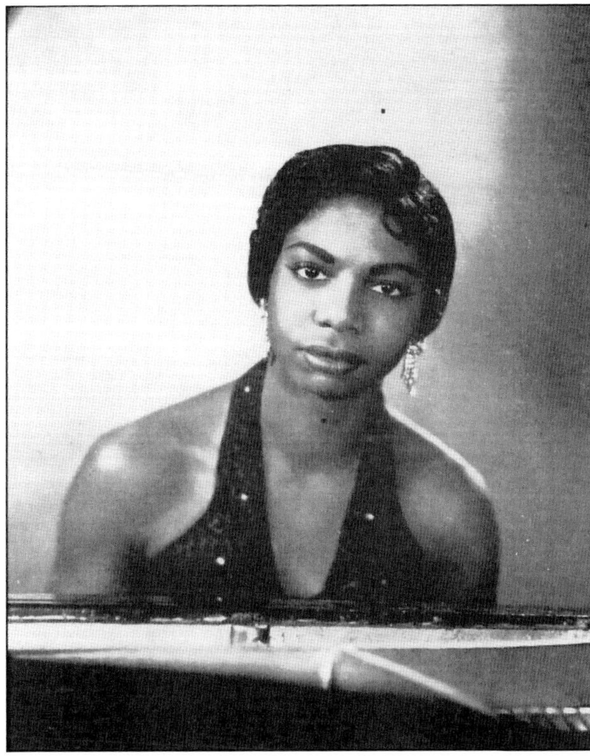

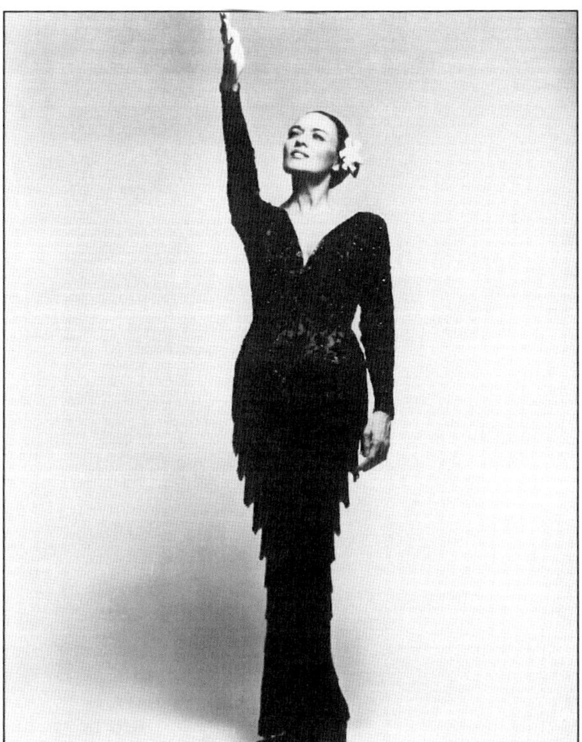

Julie Wilson (c. 1970s photograph). Professional photographer Roy Blakey captured the song stylist in this dramatic pose with her trademark fresh white gardenia gracing her sleek hairstyle. Miss Wilson was a good friend of Arthur Blake and Lynne Carter, and is a close friend of Broadway composer Stephen Sondheim. She appeared as a chanteuse in the 1957 Warner Brothers Cinemascope film *This Could be the Night*, performed at the Madeira Club, and still entertains in New York City nightclubs. (Courtesy Stanton Collection.)

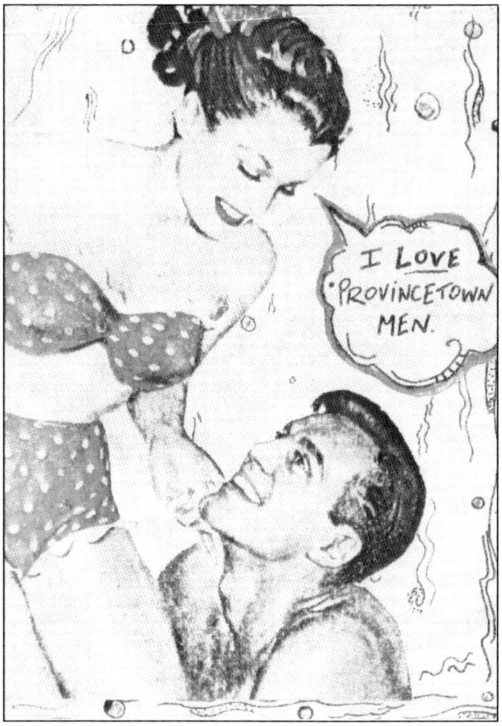

I LOVE PROVINCETOWN MEN (mid-20th-century illustration by an unidentified artist). This young woman has the same distraction as did Joan Crawford's character in the 1947 film *Daisy Kenyon* (thought to have been partially filmed in Provincetown). The movie told the story of a fashion designer who had two men to balance in her life, characters played by Dana Andrews and Henry Fonda. A 1946 photograph in the A-House collection depicts a joyful and slender Marlon Brando wearing a plaid shirt and rolled-up trousers while cavorting on the beach at Race Point with a male and female friend. (Courtesy Schier Collection.)

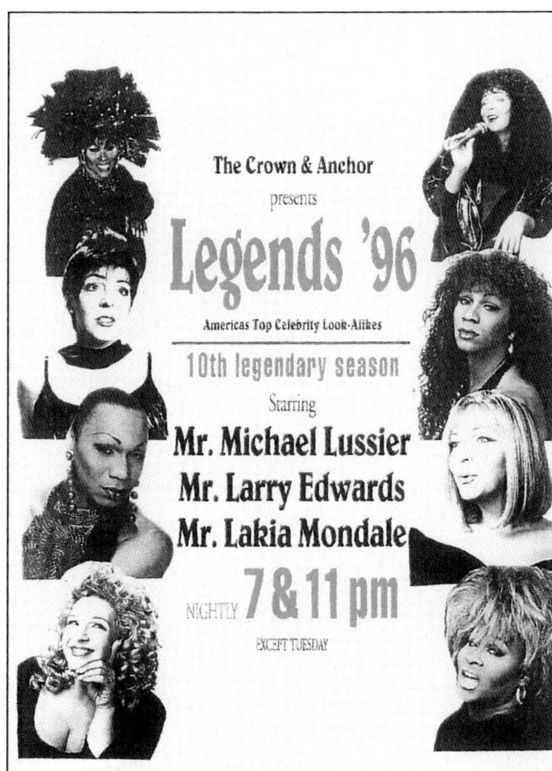

Female Impersonators at the Crown & Anchor (1996 handbill). "America's Top Celebrity Look-Alikes" had been strutting their stuff for over a decade in the lounge of the "Crotch & Ankle" before the fire of 1998. Some "gay-adored" entertainers who performed there in the past were Dorothy Loudon (July 1954), Hildegarde (July 1963), and Odetta (July 1969). Appearing in the past at the Atlantic House Cabaret Room were Billie Holiday and Eartha Kitt (August 1955) and Blossom Dearie (August 1960). Bringing down the Pilgrim House before the fire of 1990 were comediennes Ruth Buzzi (July 1962) and Lily Tomlin (August 1967). During some summers in the 1970s, campy, ribald, and colorfully bewigged "Sylvia Sidney," a towering Boston drag queen, would be heard before being seen as he and his entourage cleared a path down the center of Commercial Street "dishing" those whom he disliked seated on or around the benches in front of the Town Hall.

Seven

Alternative Lifestyles

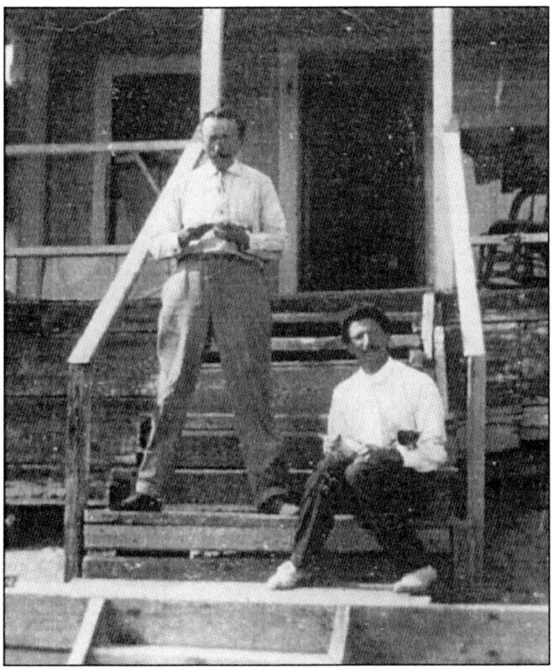

Lifelong Partners (c. 1900 photograph). Italian immigrant Francesco Ronga (seated) and Mary Heaton Vorse's half-brother, Fred Marvin, relax on the stairs of an unidentified Provincetown cottage at the beginning of their nearly 50-year relationship and longtime residence in the town. Marvin met the much younger man in Naples, Italy, and implored him to emigrate to the United States. From 1916 to 1934 "Cesco" ran an Italian restaurant in their comfortable home at 211 Bradford Street, and he eventually became renowned as the "Spaghetti King of Cape Cod," while his companion was a noted local impressionist painter and intellectual. The word "gay" now has a different meaning than it had earlier in the 20th century. In Paul Smith's *A Modern Pilgrim's Guide to Provincetown* (published locally in 1934), the author has a small section on "Night Life," in which he notes that "Your stay in Provincetown will not be complete without a glimpse of the gay life that begins when the sun goes down and easel and brushes are set aside. . . . Call the Wharf Theatre for a report on the weeks [sic] visiting celebrity. Call the night clubs, to find the gayest entertainments, planned and impromptu." Although Cherry Grove on Fire Island off Long Island in the summer and Key West in Florida in the winter have drawn many members of the gay community for decades, it is "P-town" that has been the most popular gay resort on the East Coast all year long. (Courtesy Pat Hallett.)

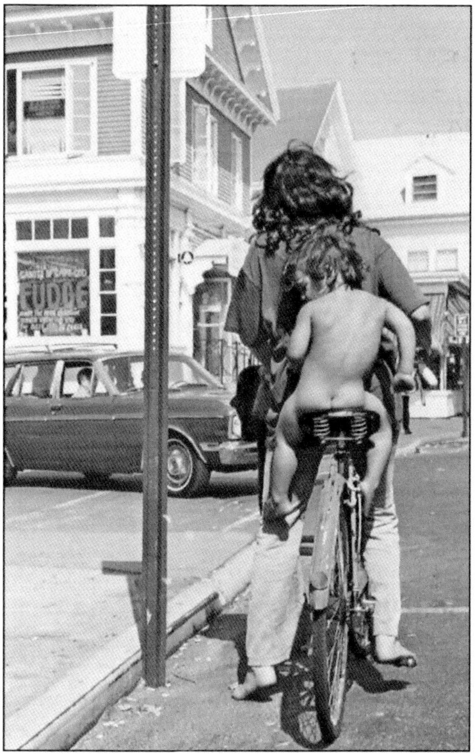

A Different View (c. 1974 postcard published by J. Lazarus). A young barefooted mother wearing jeans and a T-shirt steadies her bicycle at the corner of Commercial and Ryder Streets by the Town Hall. The toddler in its birthday suit may have been the result of "free love," a term associated with the counterculture hippies. Wilbur Daniel Steele's one-act play, *Not Smart* (first performed in Provincetown in 1916), was about *not* getting pregnant; it was a tongue-in-cheek play on the Bohemian lifestyle and the local Portuguese residents. Early birth-control advocate Margaret Sanger visited friends in town around 1915, and fell in love for the summer season.

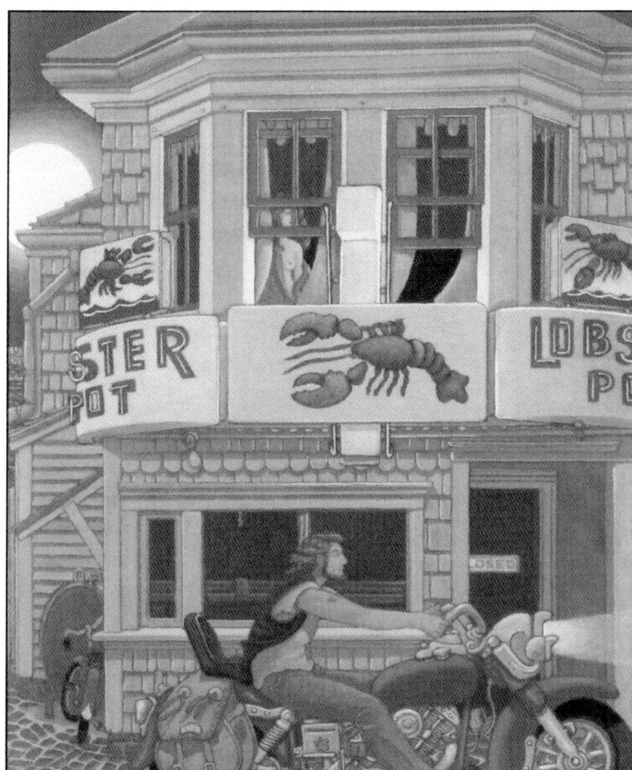

***She Looked Down With Mixed Emotions* (1996 acrylic on panel by Peter Coes, b. 1946).** Hippies dropped out of the mainstream in the 1960s, and their presence in P-town, singularly or in groups, was noticed around that time. "In 1962 Police Chief Francis 'Cheeney' Marshall was picking up hippies and dropping them off down the road on Route 6," recalls a former resident. During that decade and the 1970s large contingents of "bikers" would arrive in town in conjunction with the Blessing of the Fleet weekend. They would hang out at the Old Colony, the Governor Bradford, the Surf Club, and the former Fo'c'sle. (Photograph courtesy Peter Coes.)

I DISCOVERED THE REAL ME IN PROVINCETOWN (c. 1970s broadside; publisher unknown). Five Winslow Street was one of the first gay-owned guest houses in Provincetown, opened to a "mixed" clientele around 1946 by partners Peter Hand and Edward Dammenger. At that time the summer season ended abruptly on Labor Day, with guest-house owners seeking warmer climes and a vacation for themselves. In 1996 there were about 88 alternative-lifestyle guest houses in town catering to men and/or women, and some, when slow, to "straight" singles and couples. (Courtesy Samuel H. Graybill Jr.)

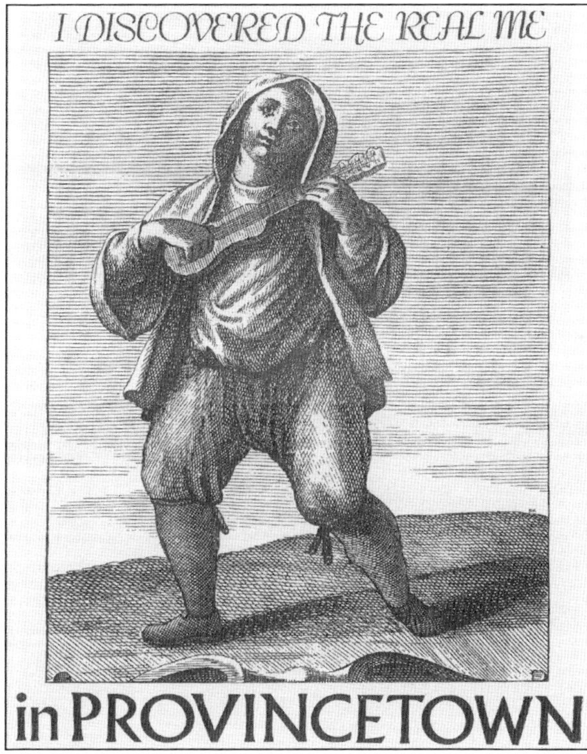

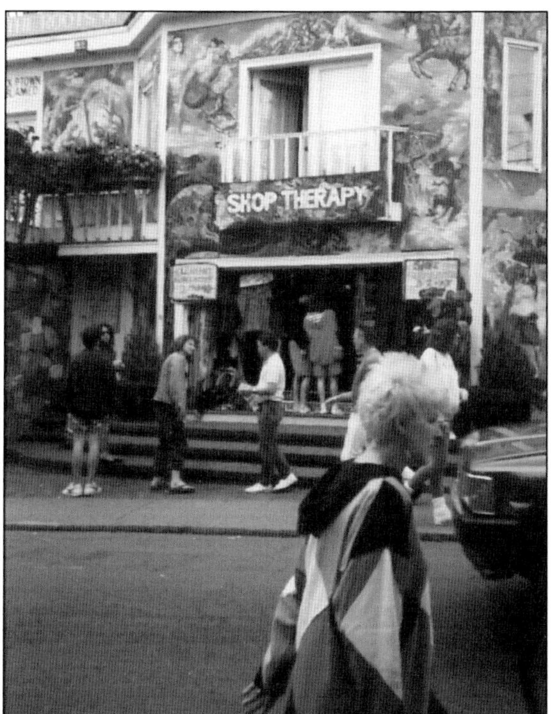

SHOP THERAPY, 346 Commercial Street (1996 photograph). If 19th-century resident Captain Solomon Cook were to return to his home he would neither recognize nor understand the transformation. Hallucinogenic murals and quotations emblazoned in psychedelic colors on the amorphous faux facade—painted by local artist Bob Gasoi, who died in 1997—attract equally colorful passersby for which most businesses remain open in season until 11 p.m. This latter-day "head shop" has "something for everyone . . . retail nirvana for alternative lifestyles," and is known for "keeping it real [as] the long strange trip continues."

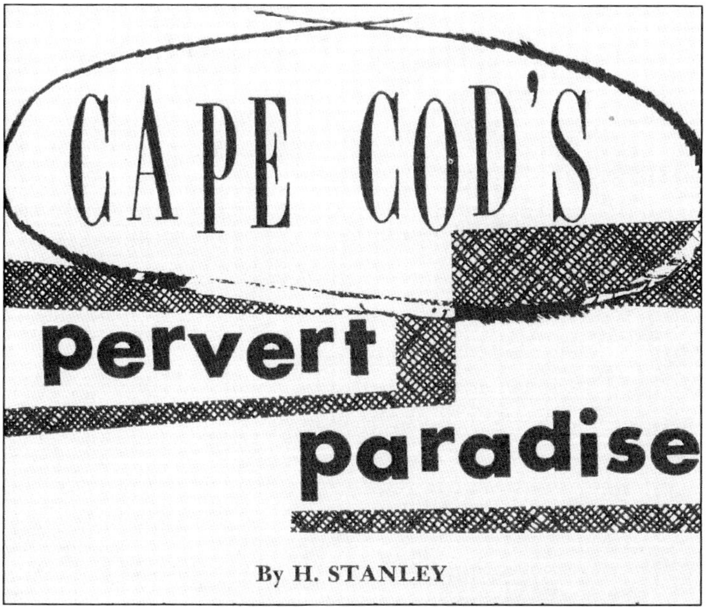

"Cape Cod's pervert paradise" (1955 booklet detail). This 50-page illustrated booklet addresses "sex deviation" invading Provincetown. Interestingly enough, other stories, photographs, and ads are of a strictly prurient nature, geared to "normal" men; bisexuality would have also been anathema to the close-minded author. A traffic sign that caused many a chuckle before it was removed from the intersection of Routes 6 and 6A stated "Provincetown Either Way."

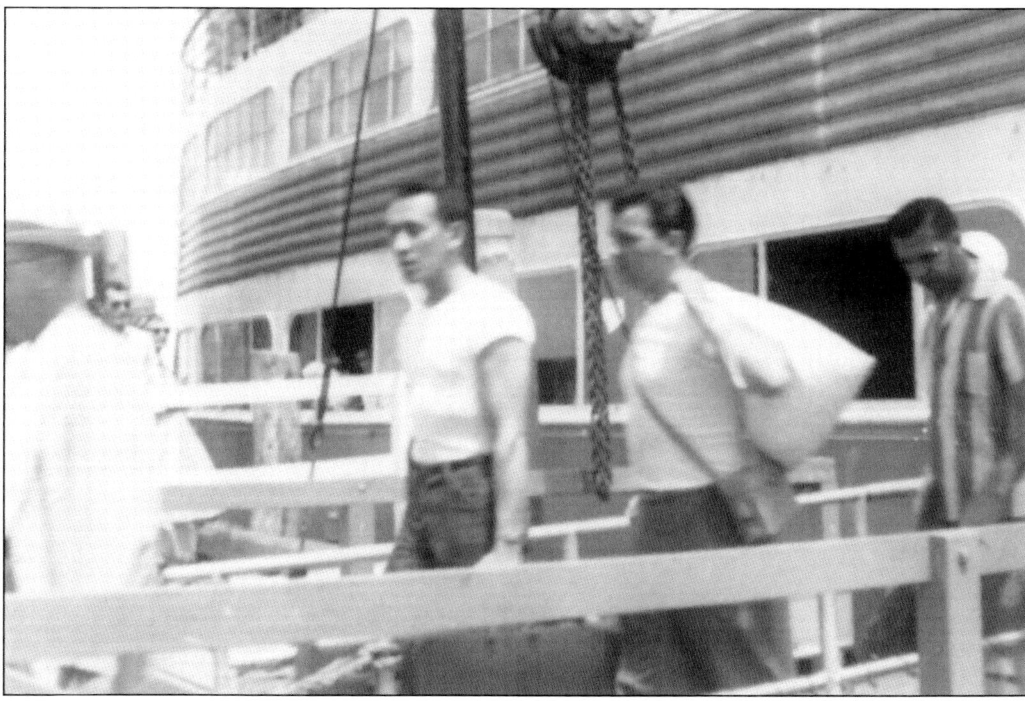

Modern Pilgrims (1961 photograph). Two trim, bachelor friends from a metropolitan city walk down the gangplank of the M.V. *Provincetown*, both in tight-fitting trousers and white T-shirts—often with a pack of cigarettes rolled up under one sleeve—with luggage, indicating that they plan to stay in town and have fun for more than an afternoon. When Henry David Thoreau traveled by stagecoach to Cape Cod in the mid-19th century he commented on his fellow passengers' "free and easy" manner, which describes how most tourists feel when they leave a major port and sail towards a smaller, carefree haven such as Provincetown. (Courtesy Warner Collection.)

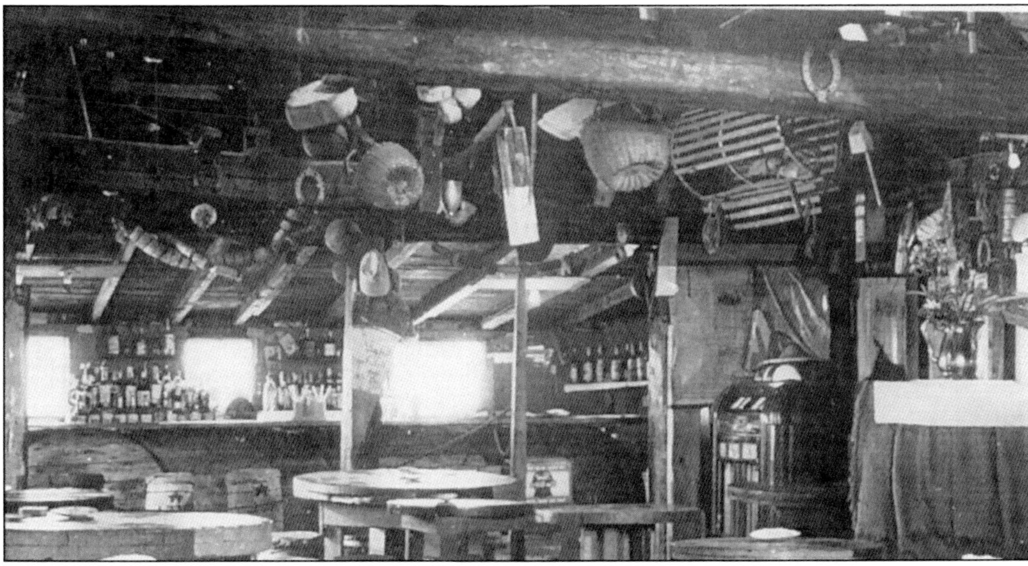

Ace of Spades Club, 193A Commercial Street (c. 1960 postcard published by National Press, Inc., North Chicago, IL). An inviting collection of seaside artifacts, windows overlooking the harbor, fresh flowers, and a jukebox for playing hit tunes of the day made this members-only gay club a popular destination, predominately for Lesbians, from around 1951 until it was destroyed by arson about a decade later. The Pied Piper, also a women's bar, was built on the site. (Private Collection.)

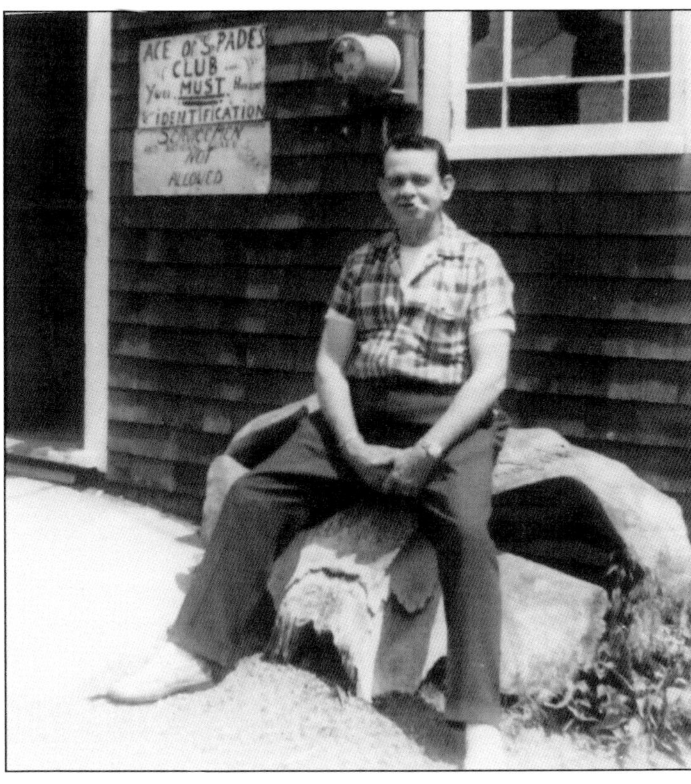

Outside the Ace of Spades Club, 193A Commercial Street (1955 photograph). Servicemen in uniform were not welcome in the club, which was filled to capacity every night. Many who were intrigued by the clientele would change into their civvies and then return, only to discover that the women there were not interested in them. Charlie Randall had his picture taken while perched on a large shark's jaw by the club's entrance. Another photograph of the happy-go-lucky chain smoker depicts him at a 45-degree angle holding up the signpost of the nearby Viking Restaurant. (Courtesy Warner Collection.)

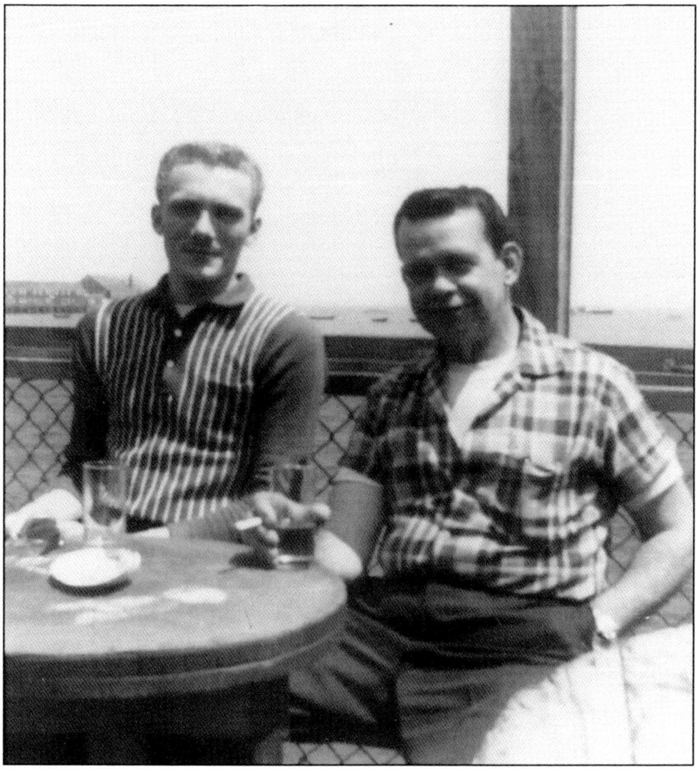

Cocktails at the Ace of Spades Club (1955 photograph). Two buddies from Lynn, Massachusetts, Emery Warner (left) and Charlie Randall, relax on the club's deck with MacMillan Wharf in the background. In between commenting on various aspects of the other patrons, and miscellaneous chit-chat, the friends and their shutterbug associate must decide at what trendy restaurant they will dine later that evening, what they will wear, who they will possibly meet, and what bar they will go to for a nightcap and probably remain at until the house lights signal "last call." (Courtesy Warner Collection.)

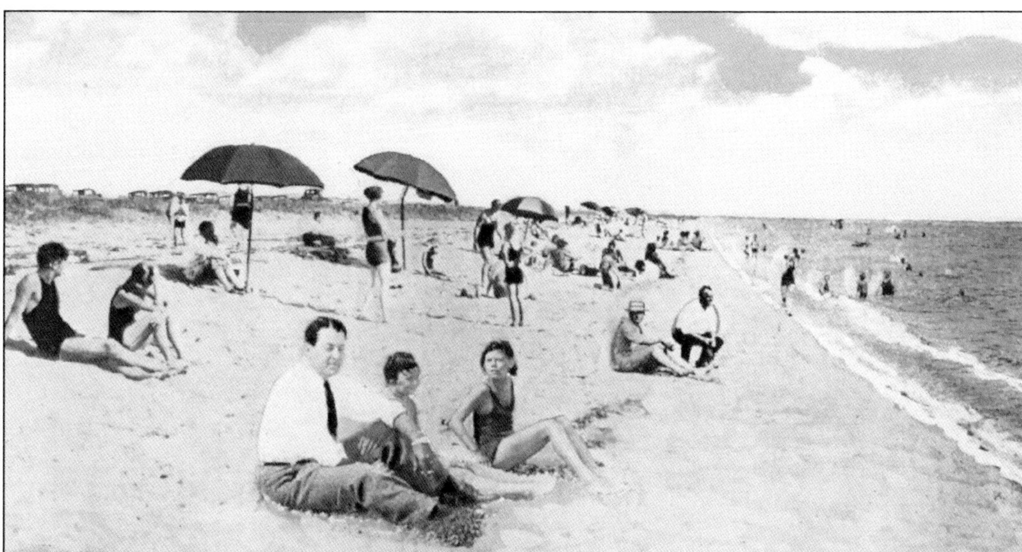

Provincetown Beach on the Dunes Road (c. 1930s postcard by an unidentified publisher). New Beach, now known as Herring Cove Beach, is part of the Province Lands, and it and Race Point Beach are both sandy expanses with strong undertows. Herring Cove Beach is at the end of Route 6A (Bradford Street) across the dunes and to the right where there is a parking lot. Families with children and single or straight couples spread their blankets near the parking space with its beachgoers' amenities, while Lesbians band together a distance to their left. Gay men also prefer their own area, which is beyond that of their female counterparts.

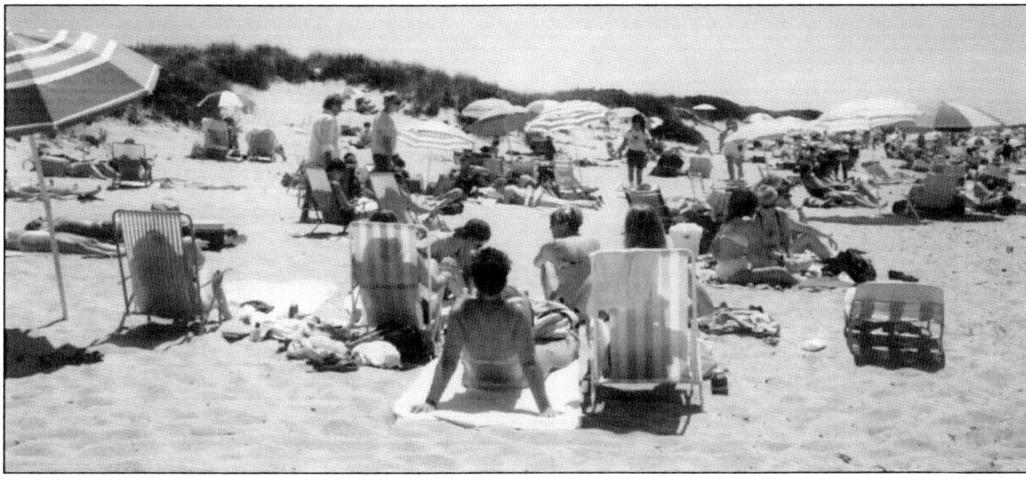

"Women's beach" at Herring Cove (1990 photograph © by JoAnn S. Mooy). Lesbians do not have to walk far beyond the "straight" section of the beautiful beach to enjoy each other's companionship, usually without children, but sometimes with them, either adopted or the issue of a previous heterosexual relationship. "Herring Cove is an energetic, joyous space," states one devotee, "full of the sounds of chatter, laughter, games, and occasional cries of 'Ranger, Ranger,' shouted to alert women who are sunbathing topless, so they can cover up before the rangers arrive." (Courtesy JoAnn S. Mooy.)

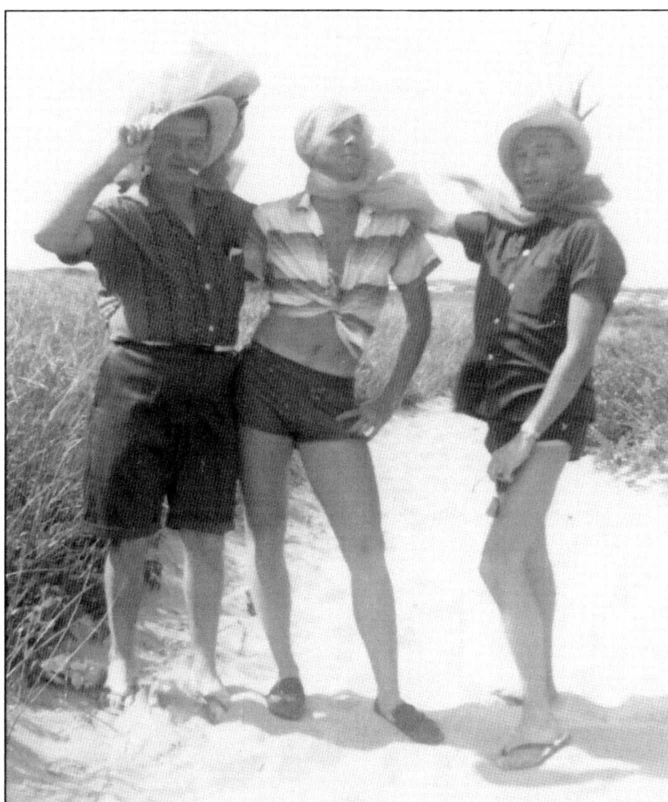

"Camping It Up" (1955 photograph). Having enjoyed a sunny day at New Beach, three "friends of Dorothy" strike attitudinal poses on a much frequented dune path. While sashaying through the sand they enjoyed the flora and fauna and at the same time avoided poison ivy. In the late 1970s another group of gay friends initiated an "Esther Weekend" to honor aquatic movie star Esther Williams. During the weekend (after the Fourth of July) they would don one-piece women's bathing suits and flowery swimming caps to enjoy water sports at the same beach. (Courtesy Warner Collection.)

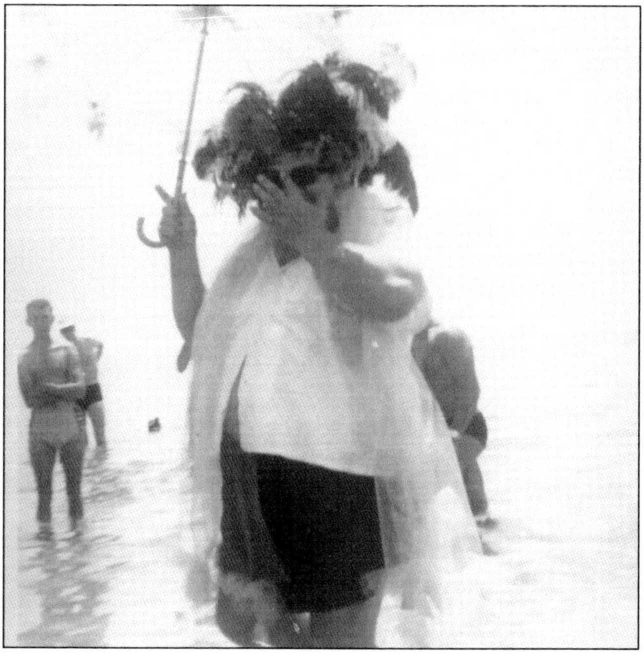

An Ample Water Nymph (1955 photograph). Phil Baiona, owner of Twelve Carver Street, a restaurant and very popular gay bar in Boston's Bay Village, flutters by admirers at New Beach. Each year, on August 15 (the Feast of the Assumption), Phil would traipse to that beach with big jugs to be filled with "holy water." Mr. Bayon (his stage name) first appeared at Weathering Heights (which he later owned) with his Weathering Knights in July of 1951. As a female impersonator, "Bella Baiona" would wear a similar huge picture hat while being lowered from the ceiling on a swing, more often than not insulting much of his audience. (Courtesy Warner Collection.)

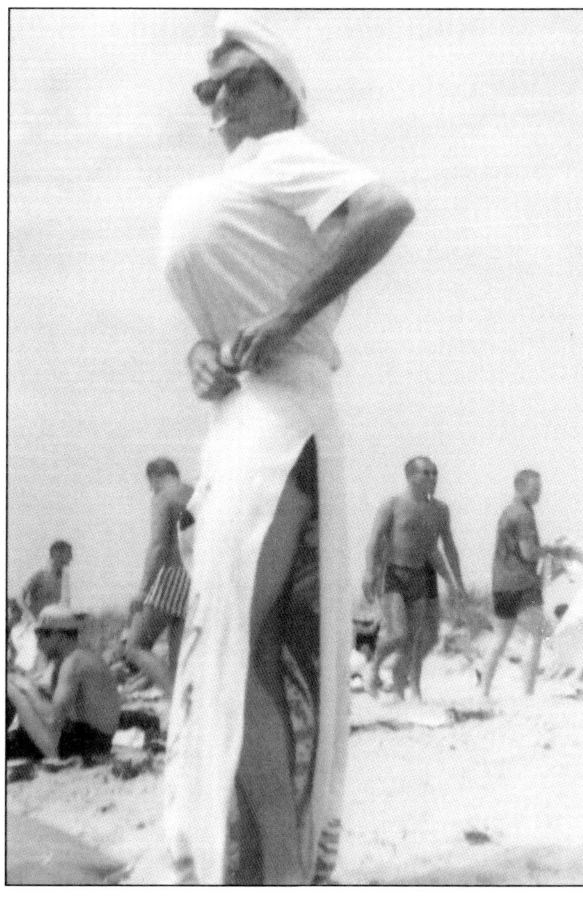

A Busty Beach Beauty (1955 photograph). While adjusting a sarong-like towel, Eddie Bernier, a greater Boston entertainer, displays an enviable bosom "for days." By the early 1940s a number of sarcastic, but funny, epithets or slang phrases had come into use to describe certain types of gay behaviors. Words in Tennessee Williams' everyday vocabulary—according to biographer Lyle Leverich—included "auntie," "butch," "cruise," "flaming belles," "friend," "the poor girl," and the overly used "queen." (Courtesy Warner Collection.)

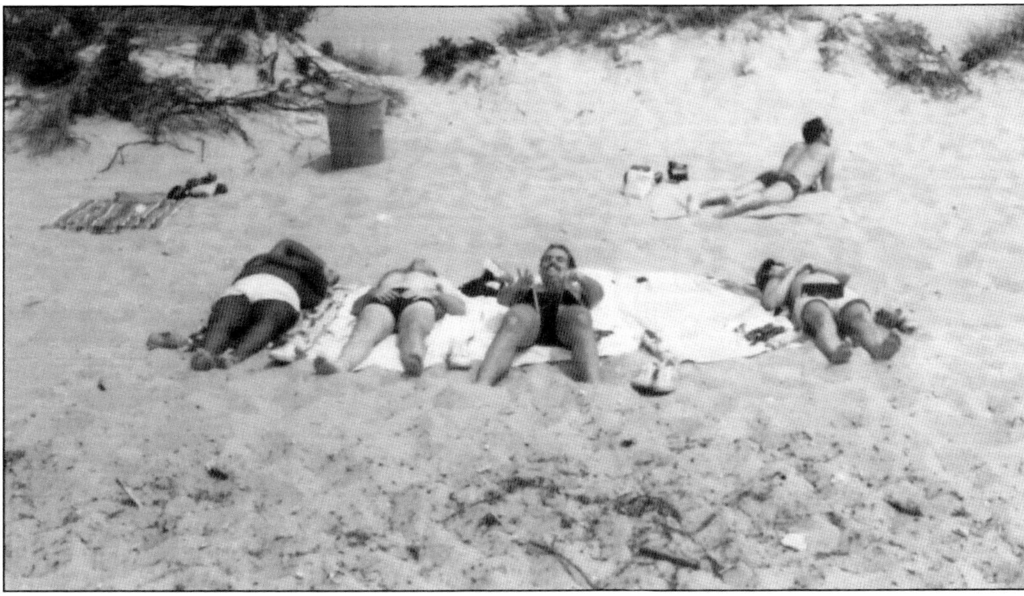

"Where the Boys Are" (1977 photograph). Recumbent beach boys soak in the sun's rays at Herring Cove Beach near a dune's crest. They may have either driven their vehicles, hitched a ride, rented bicycles, or walked to the very sociable gay section of the beach. Most leave around 2:30 p.m. or earlier depending on the sun or their moods. They return to their lodgings to shower and dress in something seductive for the afternoon Tea Dance at The Boatslip and the ensuing evening. (Courtesy Howard Bushnell.)

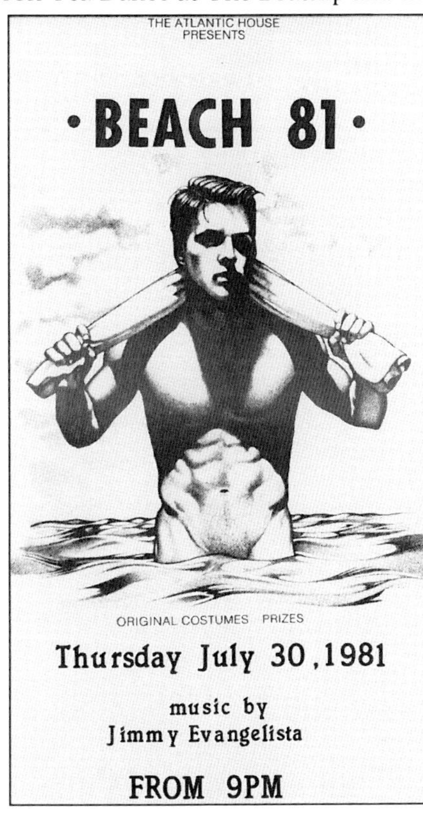

"BEACH 81" (unsigned poster). Artwork of prurient interest, whether straight, or more recently aimed at the gay audience, has been, and always will be, part of our culture, and part of the permissive atmosphere of P-town. (Courtesy Schier Collection.)

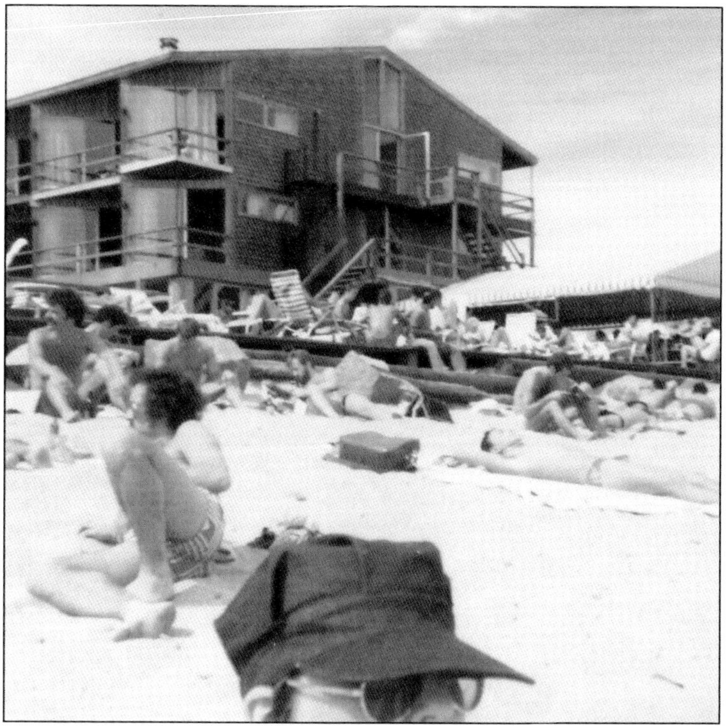

Beach at The Boatslip, 161 Commercial Street (1977 photograph). The practically all-male beach behind The Boatslip was part of Grozier Park, owned by Edwin A. Grozier, a Boston newspaper magnate, whose early Victorian sea captain's mansion with distinctive polygonal cupola is opposite on the land side of the busy street. Most recently the mansion was the residence of Reggie Cabral, who, with his wife, Meara, built The Boatslip as a business venture around 1965. (Courtesy Bushnell Collection.)

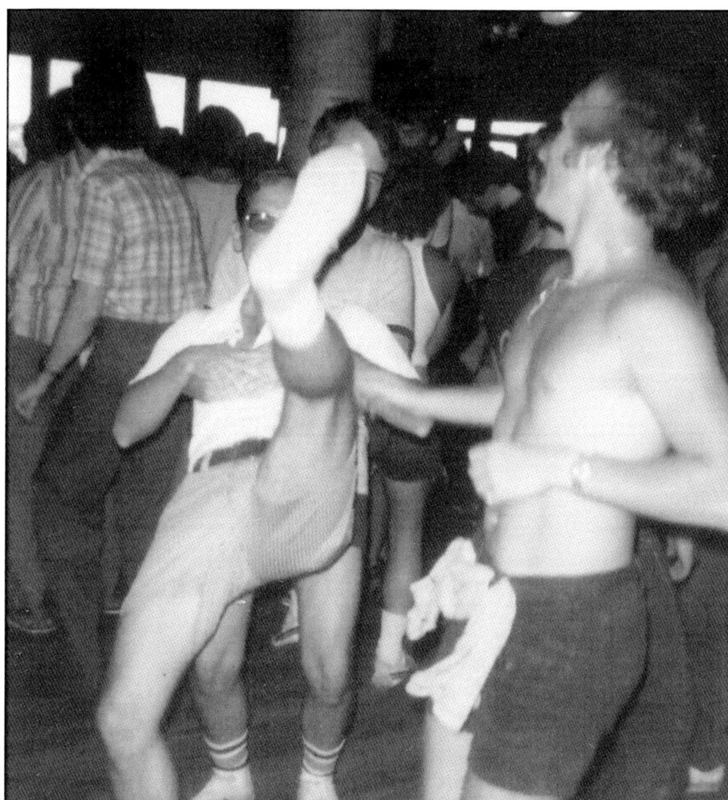

"The Meadowgaze Ballet Troupe" (1977 photograph). Dancers have kicked up their heels to disco and other forms of lively (and loud) music during Tea Dance at The Boatslip since the afternoon tradition was begun there in the late '70s. Now, as then, during the season dancing and socializing take place inside the bars, while "cruising" on the commodious deck overlooking the harbor, by the swimming pool, or on the beach between 3:30 and 6:00 p.m. Men by the hundreds have crowded the complex on holidays and other busy weekends. (Courtesy Bushnell Collection.)

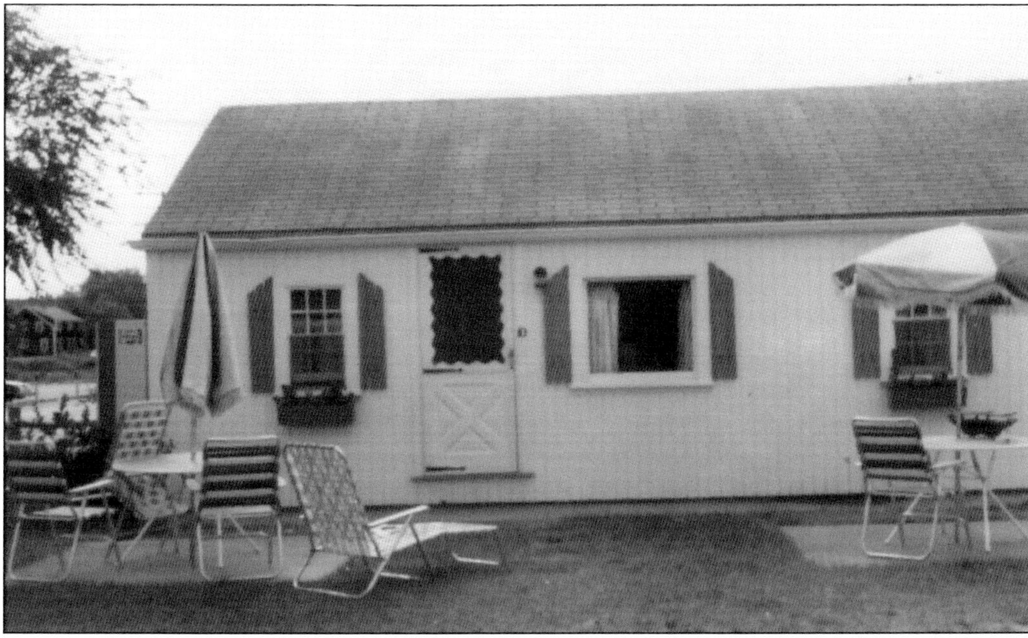

Cottage No. 10, Shamrock Cottages, Shank Painter Road (1977 photograph). Several friends from New Jersey who stayed at this cottage (owned at the time by the Downey family) still talk about the "fabulous chicken liver dish" they enjoyed at The Terrace, formerly located at 133 Bradford Street. This cottage had "two bedrooms, a living room, and a refrigerator and a sink on one side of the living room that could have been used as a kitchen. There was also a separate bathroom. These cottages were TINY, but who cared," remembers one of the guys. "We weren't in them much!" (Courtesy Bushnell Collection.)

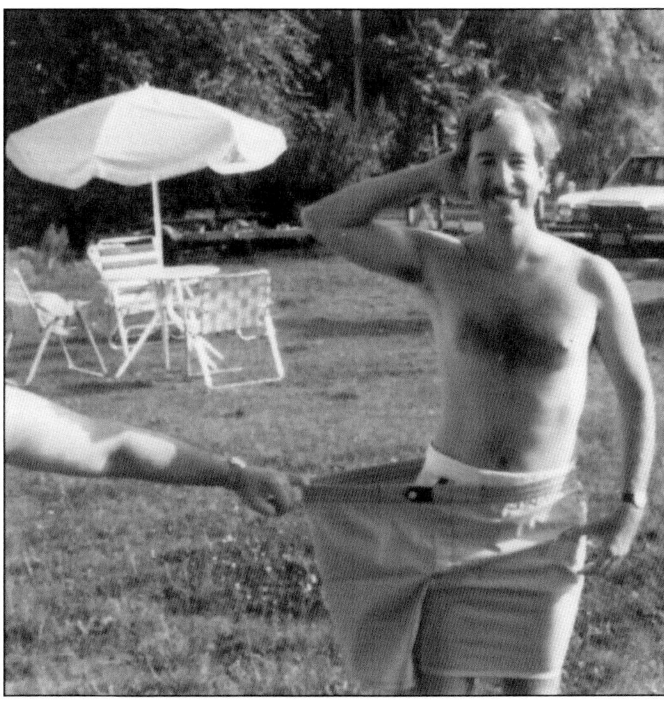

"So Where Did You Have Dinner Last Night?" (1977 photograph). Howard, one of the New Jersey buddies, tries on the shorts he found in Cottage No. 10, much to the amusement of the others. The Cottage, a cozy restaurant at 149 Commercial Street, was a favorite place for breakfast, where over pancakes or eggs, or just a cup of coffee and a cigarette, friends would discuss in great detail, among other trivia, the previous night's conquests or disappointments. (Courtesy Bushnell Collection.)

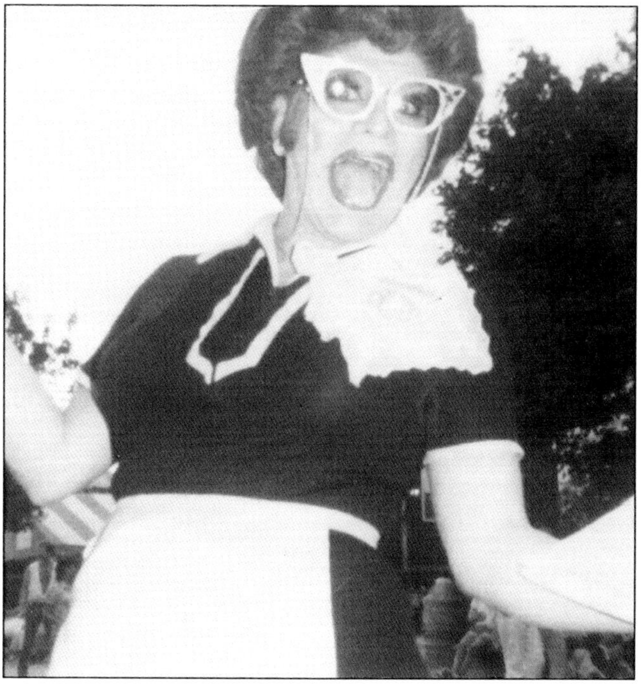

"Coffee, Tea, or Me?" (c. 1979 photograph). On an annual trip to Provincetown with her grandparents, Paul and Angela Nevadonski, Jamie Curci of Rhode Island encountered this colorful character by Café Poyant in the center of town. Dressed as a waitress to advertise entertainment at the Madeira Club, "Gert" gladly posed for this campy snapshot. Like many people whose personalities change when their appearances do, Frank Massey was an introvert until he donned his gay apparel. (Courtesy Jamie [Curci] Carter.)

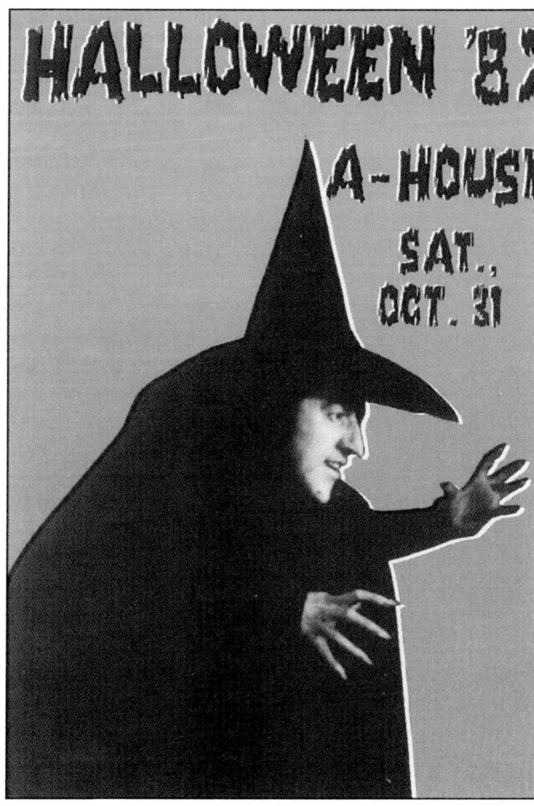

HALLOWEEN '87 Poster. Margaret Hamilton, the unforgettable Wicked Witch of the West in the classic 1939 film *The Wizard of Oz*, is thought to have visited Provincetown once, but not in costume! Unlike a select group of young gay men who befriended a New York City doyenne named Dorothy, the Wicked Witch was definitely "not a friend of Dorothy's." Crazy hats were also worn by the piano player who performed in the second-floor rear lounge of the Bonnie Doone Restaurant at 35 Bradford Street, a popular gay gathering place through the 1950s. (Courtesy Schier Collection.)

Resting in between (1982 photograph). Max Lee, a charismatic and mirthful interior designer, poses in new pajamas while catching up on his reading in the four-poster bed in the Captain's Room of elegant Asheton House at 3 Cook Street. Eleanor Peacock, an earlier decorator from New York City, began renovating the former Cook family home in the 1940s, and partners James Asheton Bayard and Les Schaufler continued the restoration, opening their guest house with its welcoming exterior open-arm staircase in 1977.

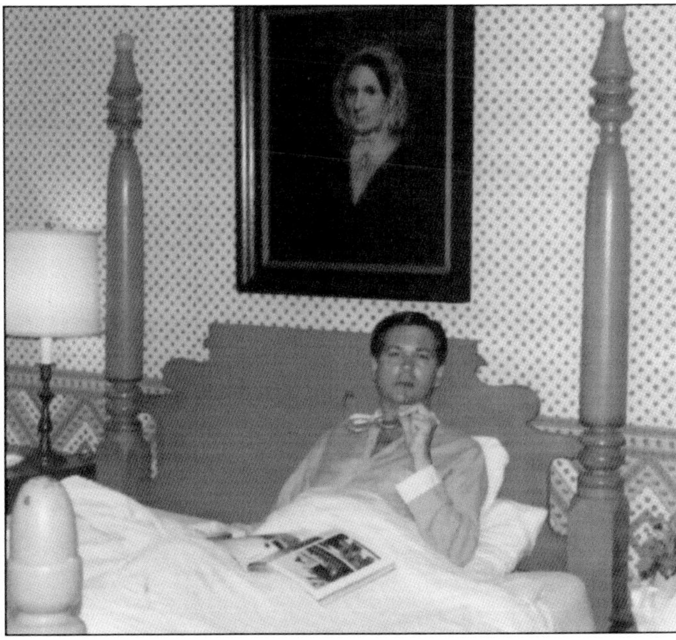

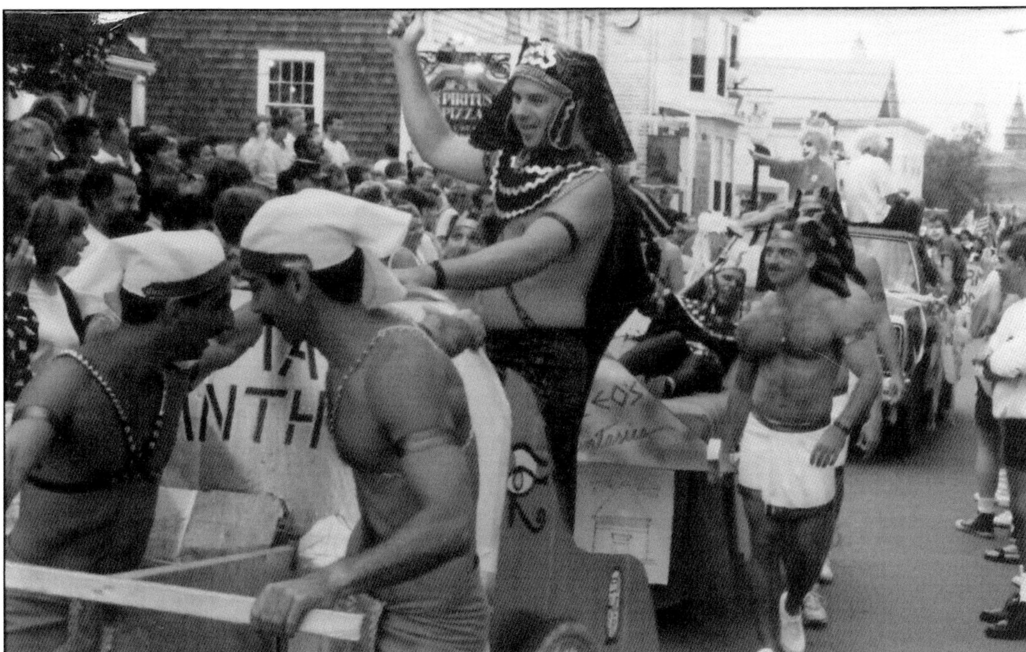

"Cleo's Fantasies" (1991 photograph). Cleopatra and her slaves wend their way along Commercial Street past popular Spirits Pizza in a non-theme Legendary Grand Parade. The first carnival parade in P-town was held in 1977 as planned by three guest house owners who were members of the Provincetown Business Guild—George Littrell of George's Inn (opened in 1965), Skip and Arpina Stanton of The Coat of Arms (opened in 1971), and Al Stilson of The Ranch (opened in 1959). Carnival in August is a week-long happening with varied events, including nightclub performances, cocktail parties, and an impressive parade that gets bigger and better each year. (Courtesy Jack Barnett.)

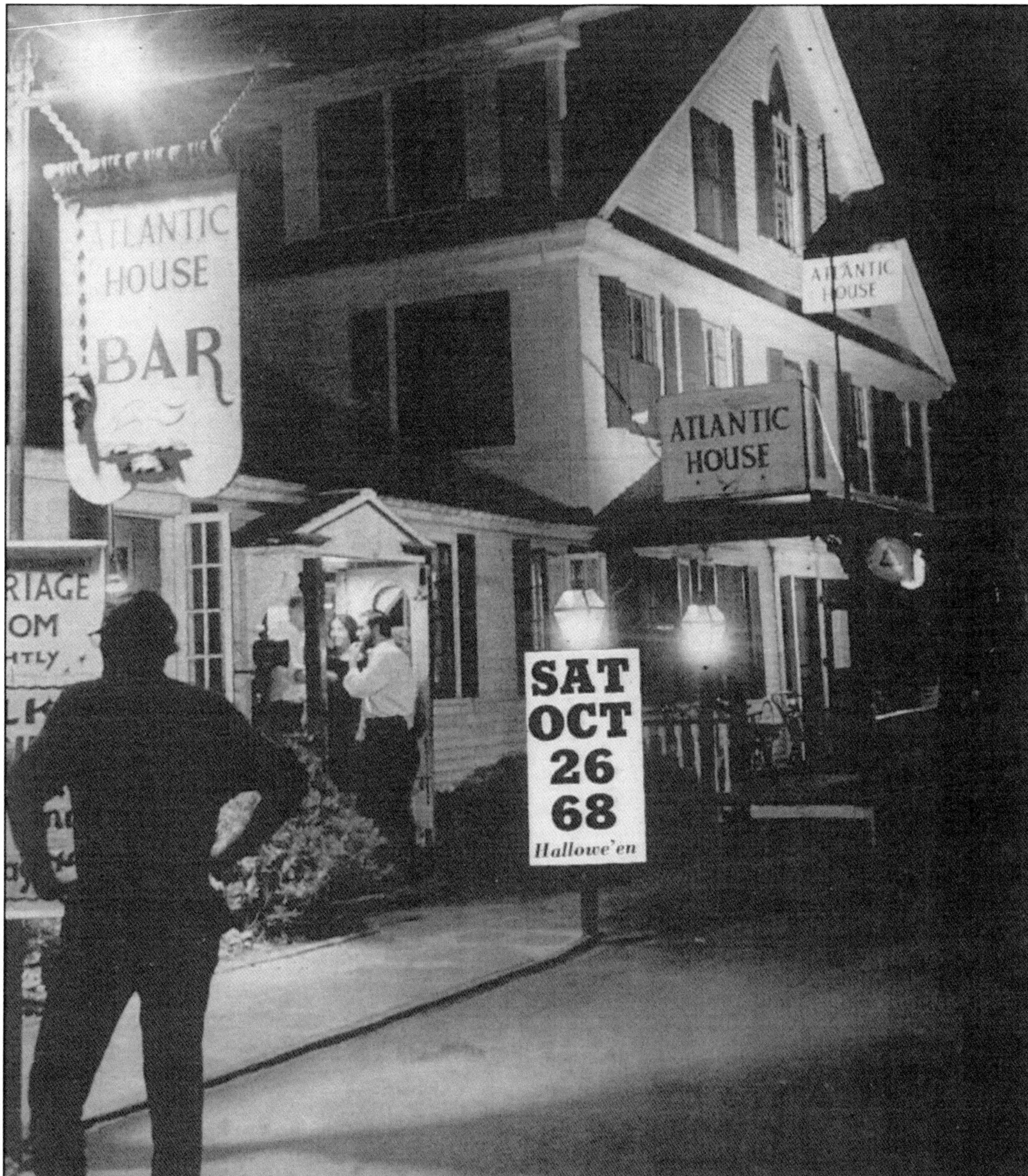

Atlantic House and Atlantic House Bar, 4–6 Masonic Place (1968 poster). Finocchio's in San Francisco is regarded as the first "gay bar" in America, although it started out as a speakeasy (1929) and was legalized after Prohibition (1933). The Atlantic House Bar has been a popular night spot in Provincetown for generations. In 1950 Reginald "Reggie" Cabral and his brother-in-law, Frank Hurst, acquired the business as partners, with Reggie becoming manager around June of the following year, and later sole owner. The "new, amazing Carriage Room" on the second floor of the bar featured a life-size fabricated horse and real carriage when it opened in July of 1954. Foreseeing the wave of the future, entrepreneur and local art collector Cabral made the bar gay-friendly, which it has since been. The dance bar at the A-House has weekly theme parties and special events advertised with eye-catching posters. A leather bar on the second floor over the Little Bar appeals to "macho" men who prefer other men with similar tastes. (Courtesy Stanton Collection.)

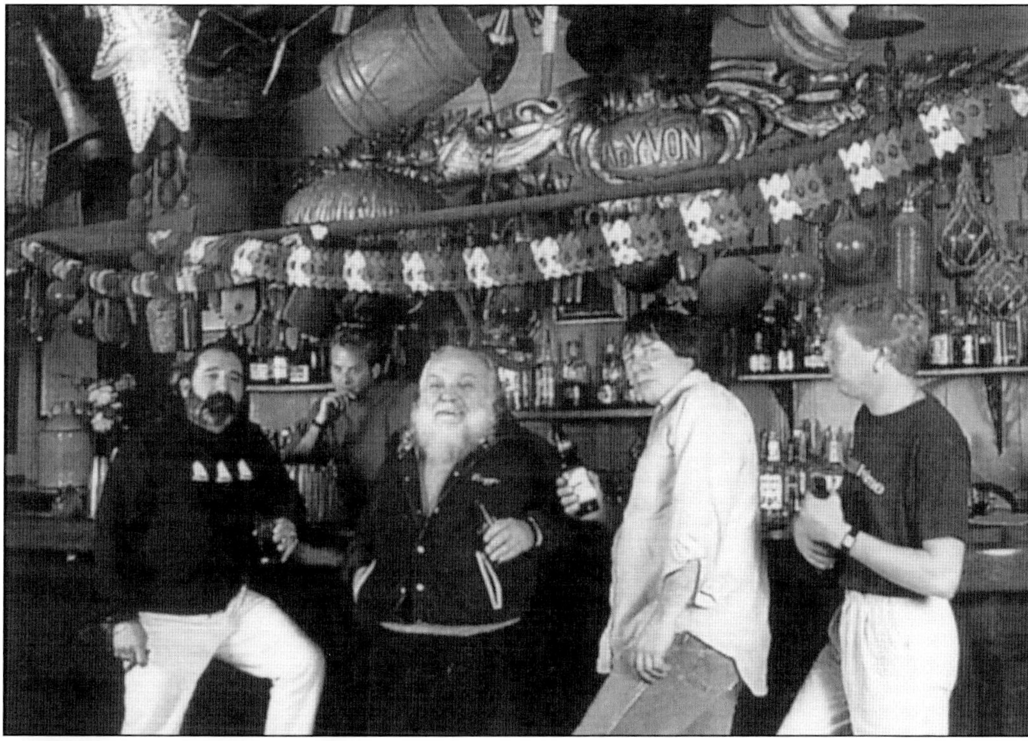

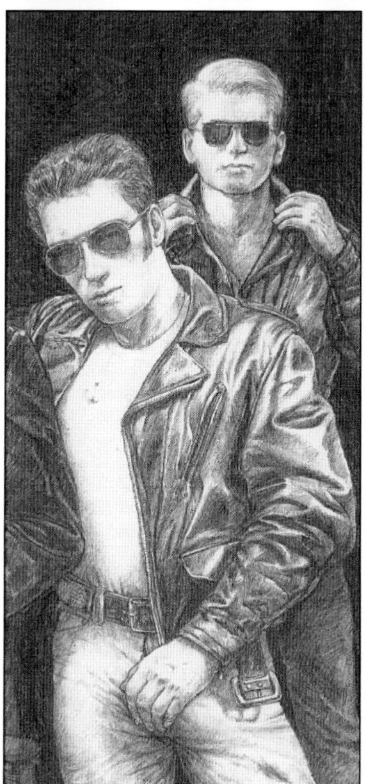

The Little Bar at the A-House (c. 1988 photograph by Ned Manter). Fully bearded in recent years, and quite the jovial chap at times, Reggie Cabral (1923–1996) pauses to enjoy a beer with associate Joe Peters (left) before having dinner with one of his daughters. Others pictured include an unidentified electrician hired for the day, and a patron (far right). Whaling artifacts, fishing accouterments, and other fascinating objects are suspended from the low ceiling of the first-floor room, which has pink overhead lighting and a flagstone floor. On cold afternoons and evenings a bee-line is always made to the far end of the bar, where a welcoming, cheery fireplace warms the exterior before a drink warms the interior. (Courtesy Provincetown Public Library.)

***Leather Jacket* (1996 graphite drawing by F. Ronald Fowler).** These seductively drawn young men may represent "the embodiment of youthful homosexual desire" to other, especially older, individuals of the same persuasion. The artist, who illustrated *The Joy of Gay Sex* (1992), has been a resident of Provincetown since 1980, and recently opened Fowler Gallery at 423 Commercial Street in the East End. (Courtesy Ron Fowler.)

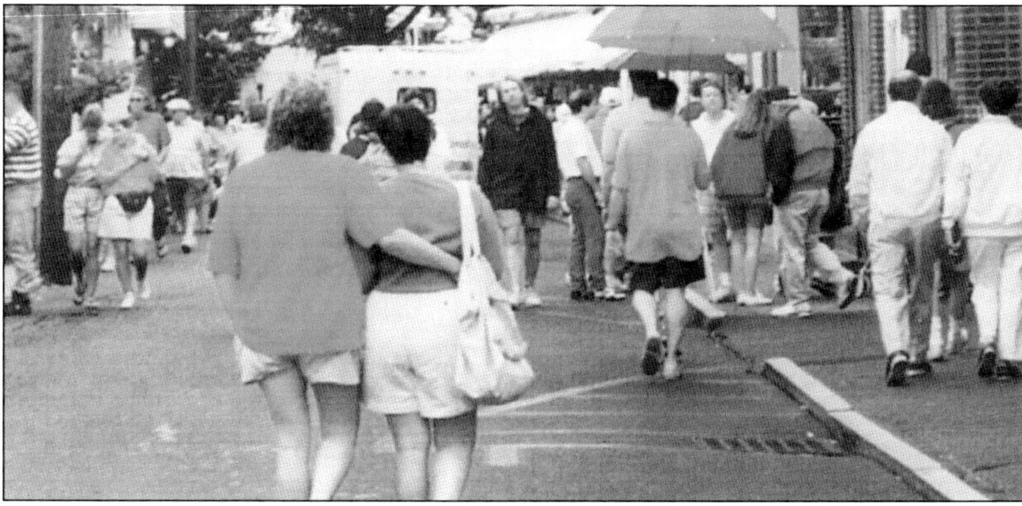

An Embracing Walk on Commercial Street (1995 photograph by Dan DePalma). Around the turn of the 20th century the pejorative term "Boston marriage" became associated with two women who lived together and shared mutual interests without men. Most Lesbians today are "out of the closet," and as couples, they and their male counterparts openly and proudly show affection for each on the streets, in the shops and restaurants, and in other visible places in P-town. (Courtesy Dan DePalma.)

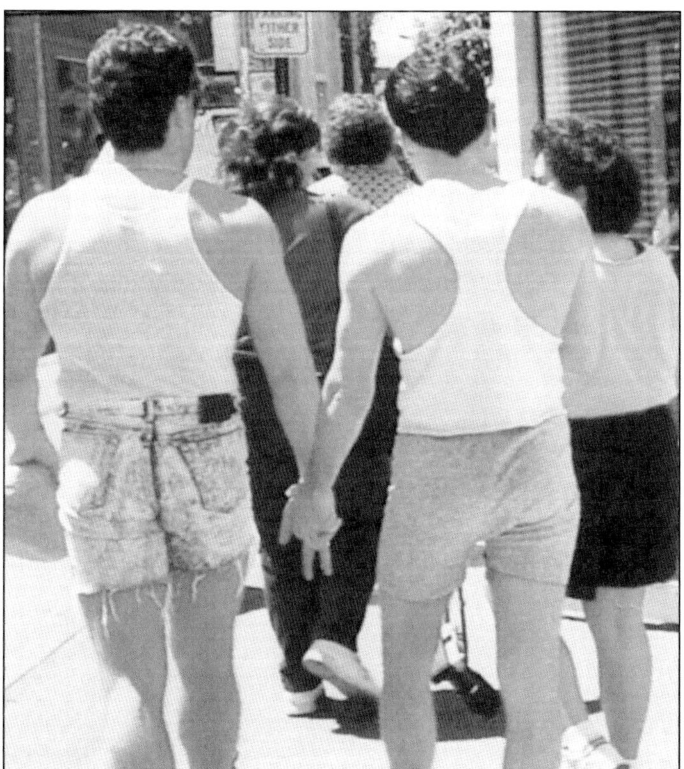

"Only Here" (1995 photograph by Dan DePalma). Form-fitting white tank tops—which turn a shade of lavender under certain lighting effects in bars, and always look good with a well-tanned and muscled body—worn with blue jeans, whether tight-legged or cut-offs with uneven fringes, have been a must for years as body-accentuating summer wear for men and women in P-town. Black leather motorcycle jackets with various chains worn with similar shiny caps, tight chaps over faded and torn jeans, and heavy black leather boots represent another type of outfit seen often around town. (Courtesy Dan DePalma.)

Modeling the *101 Dalmatians* Gown (1995 photograph). Larry Wald, a talented costume designer, fashioned this gown on the Disney film of the same name at a cost of $1,400 for a recent Carnival parade. Jack Barnett, the owner and genial host of the pet-friendly Shire Max Inn on Tremont Street, later purchased the doggish creation for his own amusement. The "GODS" (Gods of Domestic Services), a small guild of domestic service houseboys, formerly met every Wednesday afternoon at different gay guest houses, and they appeared for a few years in early Carnival parades. (Courtesy Barnett Collection.)

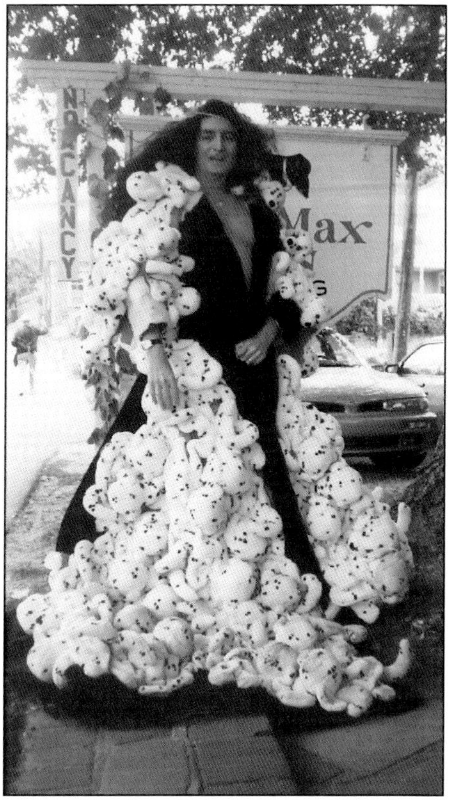

Historic Scenes of Great Renown/In Ye Old Burg of Provincetown (1910 postcard published by C.D. Cahoon). When Tennessee Williams left Provincetown in August of 1940 for New York City, he wistfully wrote what countless others may also experience: "I had an awfully strange feeling as the Boston boat sailed slowly around the lighthouse point and then distantly—austerely—past the new beach and the glittering white sand-dunes. Saw P-town dwindling sort of dream-like behind me. Not real at all. The Pilgrim Monument getting smaller and smaller till it was just a tooth-pick. . . ."

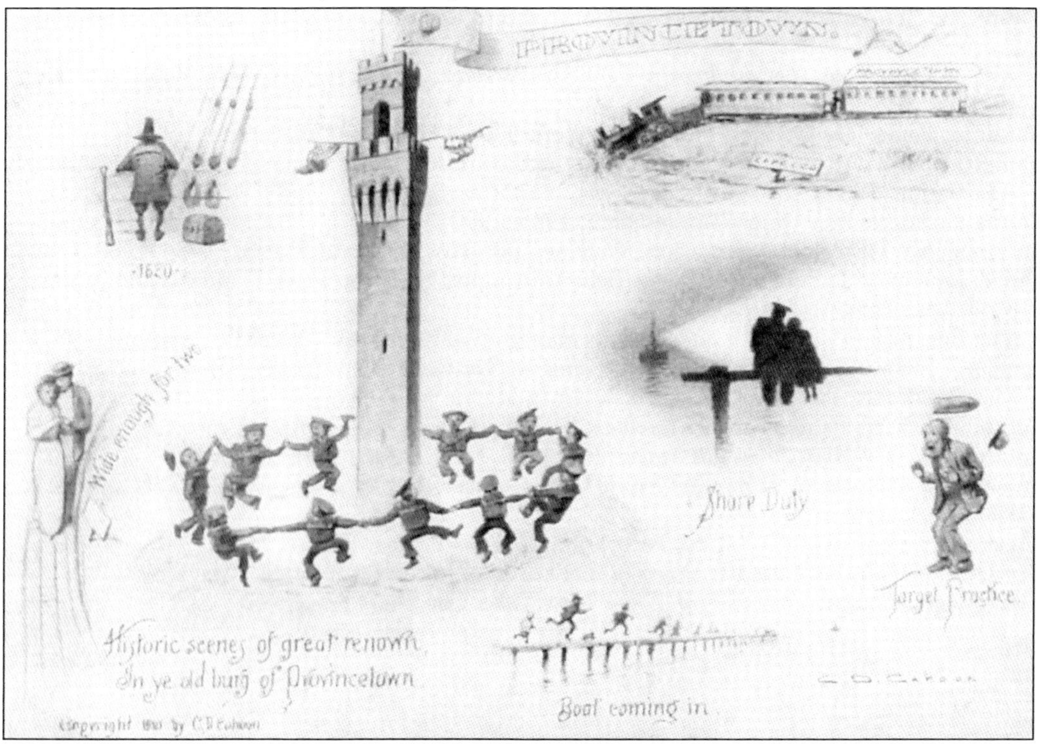

ON THE COVER: KAUL FARM GATHERING. Neighbors, friends, and members of the Kaul family gather at the Kaul farm in 1906. From left to right are (sitting on the ground) William Sudbrink, Fred Kaul (with Lore Kaul on his lap), and William Domann; (standing) Henry Bienlein, Margarethe Kaul, Hilda Anderson, Alvin Mentzel, John Schwengel, Nic Buchholz, and Fred Vocke. At the throttle is the owner of the rig, Fred Shaefer. Also on the engine, from left to right, are Fred Helms, Henry Leissring, and Theo Mentzel. Ernst Klotz Sr. is at the blower. The Kaul farm was at the intersection of Port Washington and Arrowhead Roads. (Courtesy of Arnold Kaul Sr.)

IMAGES
of America

GRAFTON

Debra Krueger and
the Grafton Historical Society

ARCADIA
PUBLISHING

ISBN 978-1-4671-0551-4

Published by Arcadia Publishing
Charleston, South Carolina

Printed in the United States of America

Library of Congress Control Number: 2020934327

For all general information, please contact Arcadia Publishing:
Telephone 843-853-2070
Fax 843-853-0044
E-mail sales@arcadiapublishing.com
For customer service and orders:
Toll-Free 1-888-313-2665

Visit us on the Internet at www.arcadiapublishing.com

To Henry, who is just starting out but already loves history.

Contents

ACKNOWLEDGMENTS

It was quite a wonderful adventure to work on this book. In many ways, it was like solving a series of small mysteries and being excited about the answers that were revealed. It also afforded me the opportunity to meet an incredible group of people, young and old, who all share a love of the history of the area and were willing to share their pictures and their memories. Thanks to the Grafton Historical Society board of directors for their enthusiasm and help when the idea to write this book was first proposed and for their continued support throughout the process. Many thanks go to Nic Schanen, a true son of Grafton, for all his hard work to obtain images for the book and for his unfailing knowledge of and enthusiasm for the history of Grafton. This book would not have been possible without him. Special thanks also go to Colleen Kasper for her great assistance, traveling to obtain images, and sharing her organizational skills.

Many other generous people helped in numerous ways, including Karen Buerosse-Cipressi, Bob Hixon, Allen Buchholz, Lori Ebbert, Gina Studelska, Arnold Kaul Jr., Vivian Scherf Laabs, and Kathy Van Hecke. Thanks to the Ozaukee County Historical Society, Cedarburg Cultural Center, and the Luxembourg American Cultural Center for their willingness to research and share Grafton images from the past and to the other families, too many to mention here, who entrusted their treasured family photographs to us.

Most of all, I would like to thank my family for their advice and support and especially for their optimism in believing that this book would become a reality.

INTRODUCTION

Grafton had its beginnings in the densely wooded lands along the Milwaukee River. The hundreds of Native Americans who had settled there were witness to the first Europeans to venture onto their lands. Fathers Claude-Jean Allouez and Claude Bablon arrived in 1670 from the mission at Green Bay. After that first encounter, they would often stop at the Native American camps on their journey from Green Bay to Milwaukee. It was not until 168 years later, however, that the first European settlers came to Grafton. The first settler was Timothy Wooden, who arrived in 1839, although John Drake was found living in a log and bark shanty in the woods at that time. Wooden claims the title, no doubt because he was the first to purchase land with money he earned from the sale of fish and furs, and he was the first justice of the peace for the area.

Wooden was followed by Irish and German immigrants. The very earliest settlers were farmers who cleared the virgin hardwood forests and began planting the crops they had grown in Europe. It was not long before other enterprising settlers saw a need and an opportunity and came together to build a dam on the Milwaukee River. Beginning in 1841, a dam was built to power a sawmill and gristmill. These early industries were joined by a woolen mill and chair factory. Eventually, there were three dams on the river. Thus were created the beginnings of an industrial Grafton.

A unique and important early industry also lay at the feet of the early settlers in Grafton. Early immigrants took advantage of the vast limestone deposits in the area to create a lime kiln operation in 1846. It grew larger with time, and by 1890, the Milwaukee Falls Lime Company was operating nine kilns there. The products of the lime kilns were exported for profit and also used in home building in the village.

While the farmers were clearing the land, mills and factories were being built, and lime was being mined, Grafton was at the center of governmental changes. It began with the Stone Block Building, erected in 1844–1845, which still stands today. It housed a courthouse and a jail (and a tavern) and provided the facilities that made Grafton a good choice to be the seat of what was then Washington County. In 1853, however, a decision was made to split Washington into two separate counties. This was immediately challenged because the state constitution stipulated that a county could not be smaller than 900 square miles. The battle went to the state supreme court, which ruled that the new county was large enough because its boundaries extended to the middle of Lake Michigan. Thus Ozaukee, or "Yellow Earth," came into being as a county.

At about this same time, Grafton underwent a small identity crisis of its own. In 1840, Jacob Eichler had originally named the area "Hamburg" as a tribute to his German hometown. In 1846, Benjamin Moore changed the name to Grafton after a main street in Dublin, Ireland. In 1857, the name was inexplicably changed to Manchester. In 1862 it was changed back to Grafton, and has remained that since.

By the late 1800s, Grafton was growing significantly. In 1859, it had a population of 400–500. By the beginning of the next century, that number had almost doubled. And with the growth in population came a flurry of businesses to serve the farmers and the waves of immigrants who were arriving to work in the village's industries. In 1880, William Weber, who was also the chief of the volunteer fire department and the first county board member from Grafton, opened his brewery. It joined a creamery, blacksmith shop, carriage and sign-painting business, and a photography studio, among other businesses, in serving the needs of a growing Grafton.

In 1916, Grafton and the music world came together to create something very special—blues recordings. In that year, the Wisconsin Chair Company founded the New York Recording Laboratories and retooled its factory to make records under the Paramount label. Amos and Andy, Bessie Smith, Gene Autry, Charlie Patton, and Skip James, among many others, all traveled to Grafton to record music. The beautiful sounds of country blues, "hokum," good time, "old time," early jazz, and gospel singing wafted out of the old chair factory during nightly recording sessions. Paramount labels indicated that a recording was made in Grafton with a master number beginning with an "L." One of the last recordings was made in 1932, and Paramount Records closed in 1935, a casualty of the Great Depression. But Grafton maintains its unique place in blues history, as it is one of the few sites on the Mississippi Blues Trail outside of the American South.

Grafton prospered during the Roaring Twenties and suffered during the Great Depression, like other villages, cities, and towns in the nation, but it was fortunate that many of its key industries continued to operate.

The years immediately following World War II saw a housing boom in Grafton, with more new houses built per capita than any other community in the state. The population by 1960 had grown to nearly 4,000, a 150-percent increase over the previous decade. There were 28 industries employing more than 1,500 people, with sales of $33 million per year.

As in the past, more residents meant more development. In 1949, Grafton's movie theater opened. In 1954, the parks and recreation department was formed to oversee the 17 parks in the village, and a book drive netted enough volumes to open the village's first library. The multipurpose senior center opened in 1982. Retail growth continued, too.

Today, the village that Timothy Wooden founded so many years ago has grown to a community of nearly 12,000 residents. But some things have not changed—the beauty of the area, the friendliness of the people who live here, the vast potential, and the Milwaukee River, flowing through it all.

One

The Beginnings

At its earliest, the area that would become Grafton was a mid-continental temperate zone wilderness. It was densely forested with hardwood trees. The Milwaukee River ran through the area, providing a source of food, water, and transportation for the earliest peoples here. Native Menomonee, Pottawatomi, Sac, Chippewa, and Fox all camped along the river. By 1800, there was a village of nearly 100 wigwams where Pottawatomi and Menomonee tribes would meet for council. In 1836, Wisconsin was established as a territory by the federal government. Before that, there had already been several attempts at treaty-making with the local tribes. By 1838, their rights to the land had all but been eliminated by a new treaty. The first settlers' deeds were for land between the river and the lakeshore, with the Native Americans having first given up the land east of the river. The tribes remained friendly toward the settlers, and when Timothy Wooden, Grafton's first official resident, arrived, he became a great friend of the Native Americans, enjoying practical jokes with them and recruiting tribe members to cut trees and gather logs to build Grafton's first dam at what was then called Milwaukee Falls. The Native Americans also provided shelter to the very earliest settlers in their large bark wigwams before the settlers could build dwellings of their own. After Wooden, a steady stream of Europeans came to the area. Most of the first were land speculators, but farmers soon followed, and the agricultural phase of Grafton began.

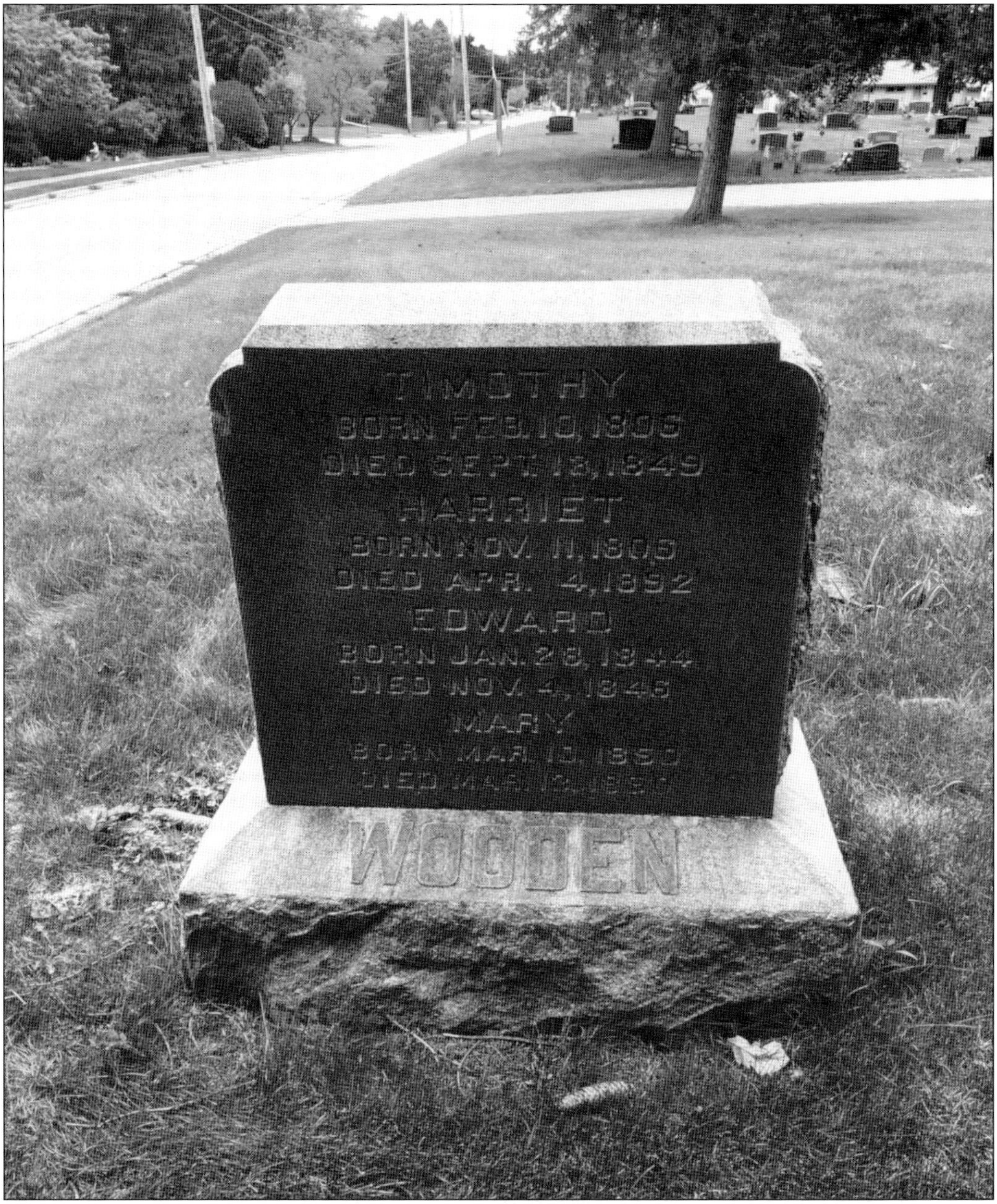

TIMOTHY WOODEN. Regarded as the first citizen of Grafton, Timothy Wooden was born in 1805 and traveled to what would become Grafton. In 1838, he purchased 148 acres of land from the US government. He became Grafton's first justice of the peace. Wooden had a reputation for being quite a local character. One story relates how he often borrowed tools but usually forgot to return them. On one occasion, Wooden borrowed an ax from a friend and promised he would be "a dead man" if he did not return it by a certain date. When the ax was not returned, the friend got together a group of other friends who had also loaned him tools and informed Wooden of his coming wake. Wooden was surprised at the news of his own demise. He happily attended his wake—and returned the ax. Wooden died of cholera in 1849 and is buried in Grafton's Woodlawn Cemetery. (Courtesy of the Grafton Historical Society.)

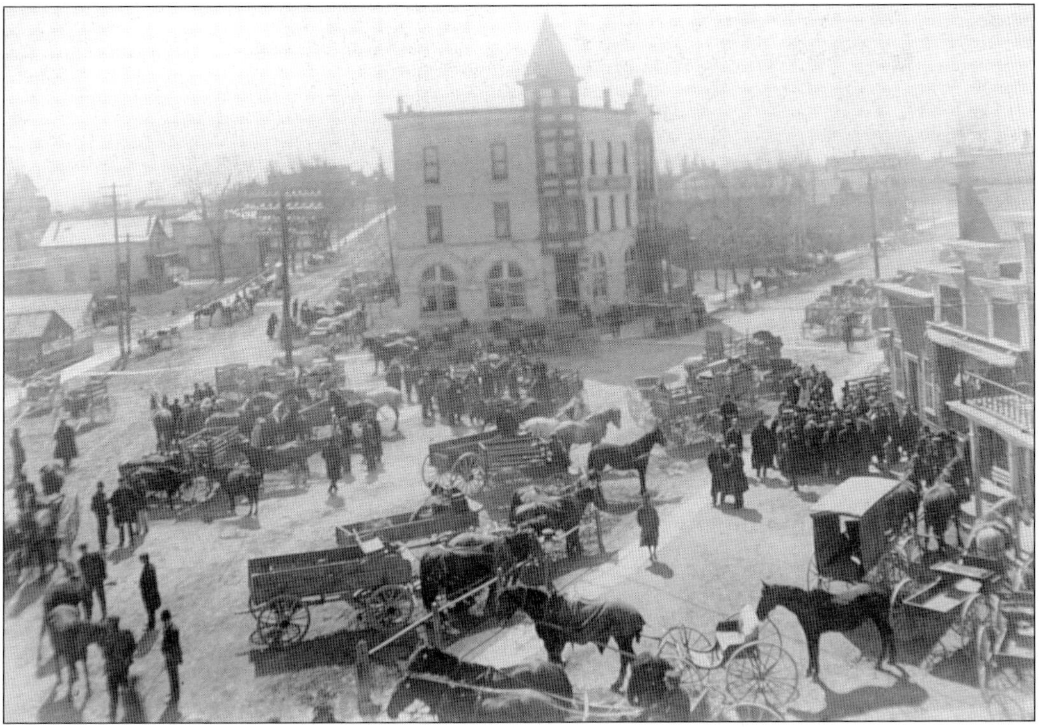

Market Day. Grafton's square was busy on this June 1906 market day. Market day was the first Monday of the month, and in the early days, traders laid planks on sawhorses and set up their wares. Everything from pigs to shoes was sold, largely by barter. Market day ended when people objected to having live animals brought into the downtown area. (Courtesy of the Grafton Historical Society.)

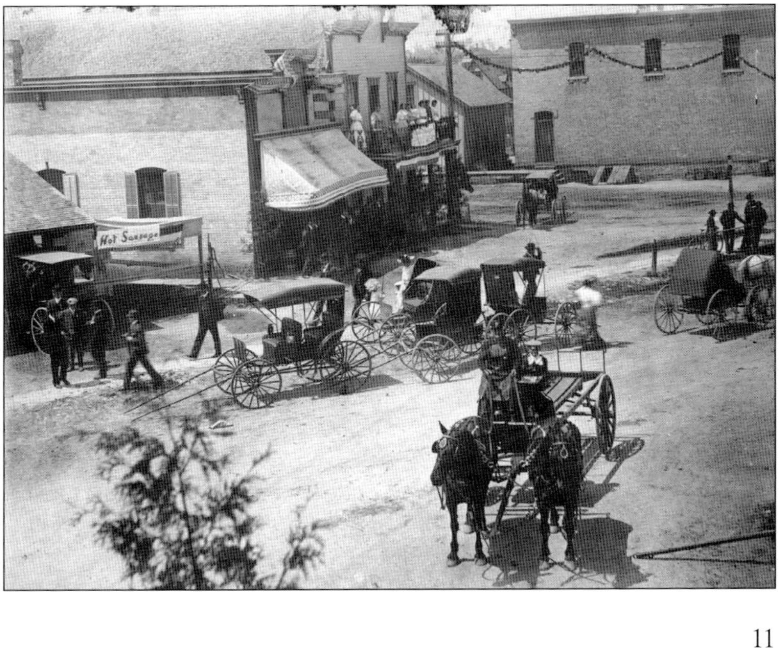

Grafton Square. People begin to gather in Grafton's square in this scene from the early 1900s. The view is looking north on Wisconsin Avenue; the photograph was probably taken from the Hotel Grafton. Note the "Hot Sausage" sign and the people waiting on the balcony at Schanen's Hotel. (Courtesy of the Ozaukee County Historical Society.)

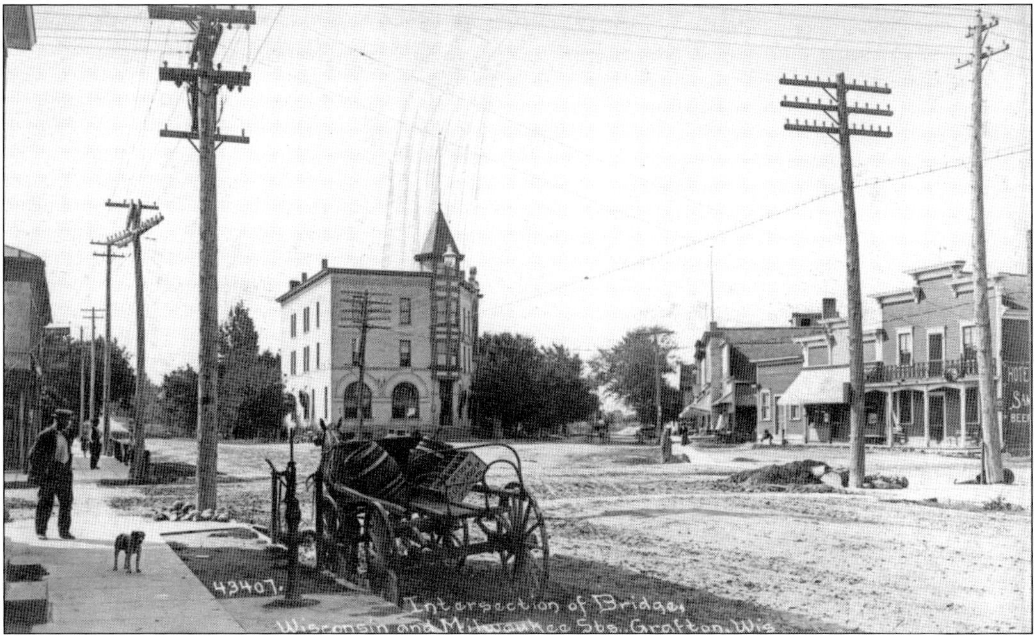

BEER DELIVERY WAGON. A beer delivery wagon takes center stage in this scene from the late 1800s. The view faces south and includes the Hotel Grafton at center and Schanen's Hotel on the right. Note the power lines, the unpaved streets, and the dog happily walking without a leash. (Courtesy of the Sudbrink family.)

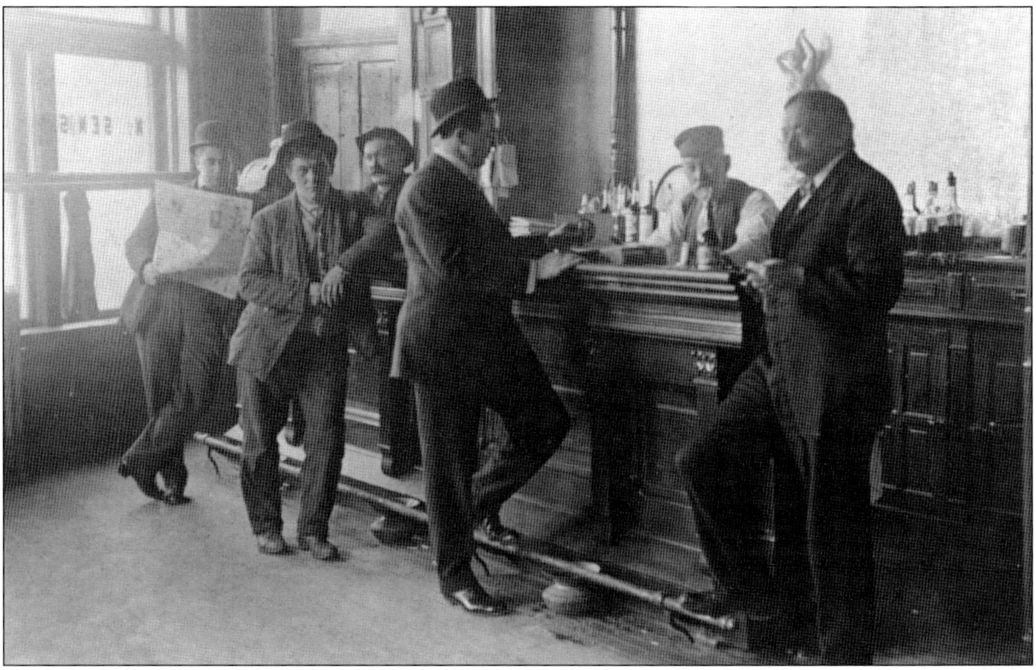

HOTEL NIESEN. In this 1906 scene inside the Hotel Niesen, "Grandpa" Niesen and his son Joseph are behind the bar. Dr. Balkwill is reading the newspaper nearest the window, and John Niesen, who would have been about 26 at the time, is second from the left. The other two men are salesmen. (Courtesy of the Ed Rappold Photograph Collection at the Cedarburg Cultural Center.)

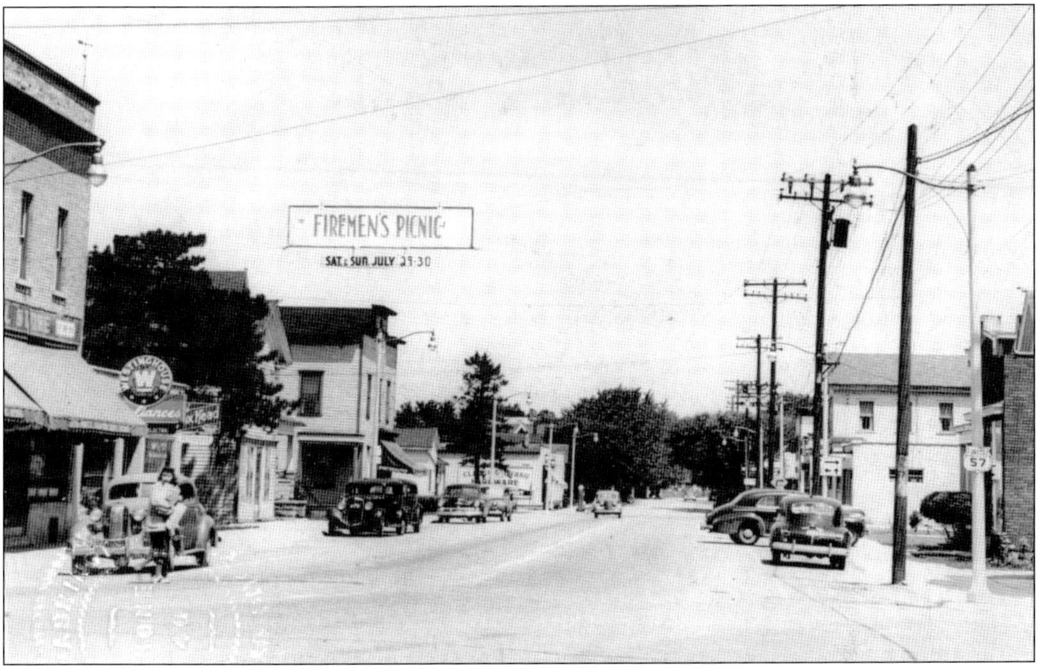

WISCONSIN AVENUE, 1940S. This is a view looking north on Wisconsin Avenue. On the left are Mueller Heuer dry goods and grocery, Liebau hardware, and the photography studio. On the right is the Rilling Tavern and Mueller furniture and funeral home. Note the state highway 57 sign. (Courtesy of Jim Hilgart.)

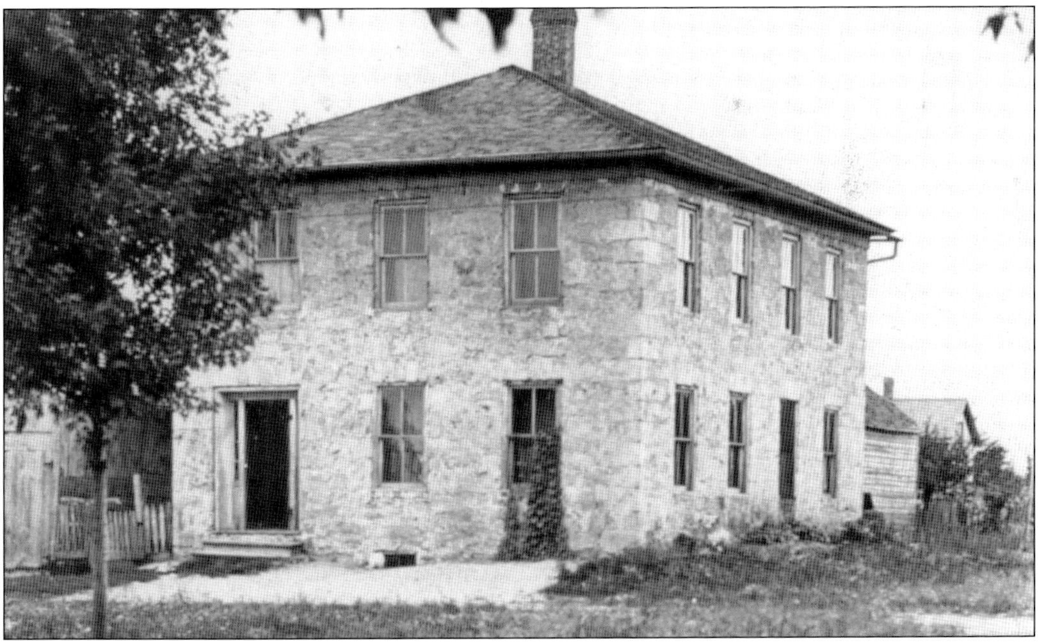

PORT HOME. This stone house at 1105 Eleventh Avenue was built by Michael Port in 1871. He was a Grafton stonemason, and it is thought that he used some of the same stones for this house that were used for St. Paul Church, which he reportedly helped build. (Courtesy of Nic Schanen.)

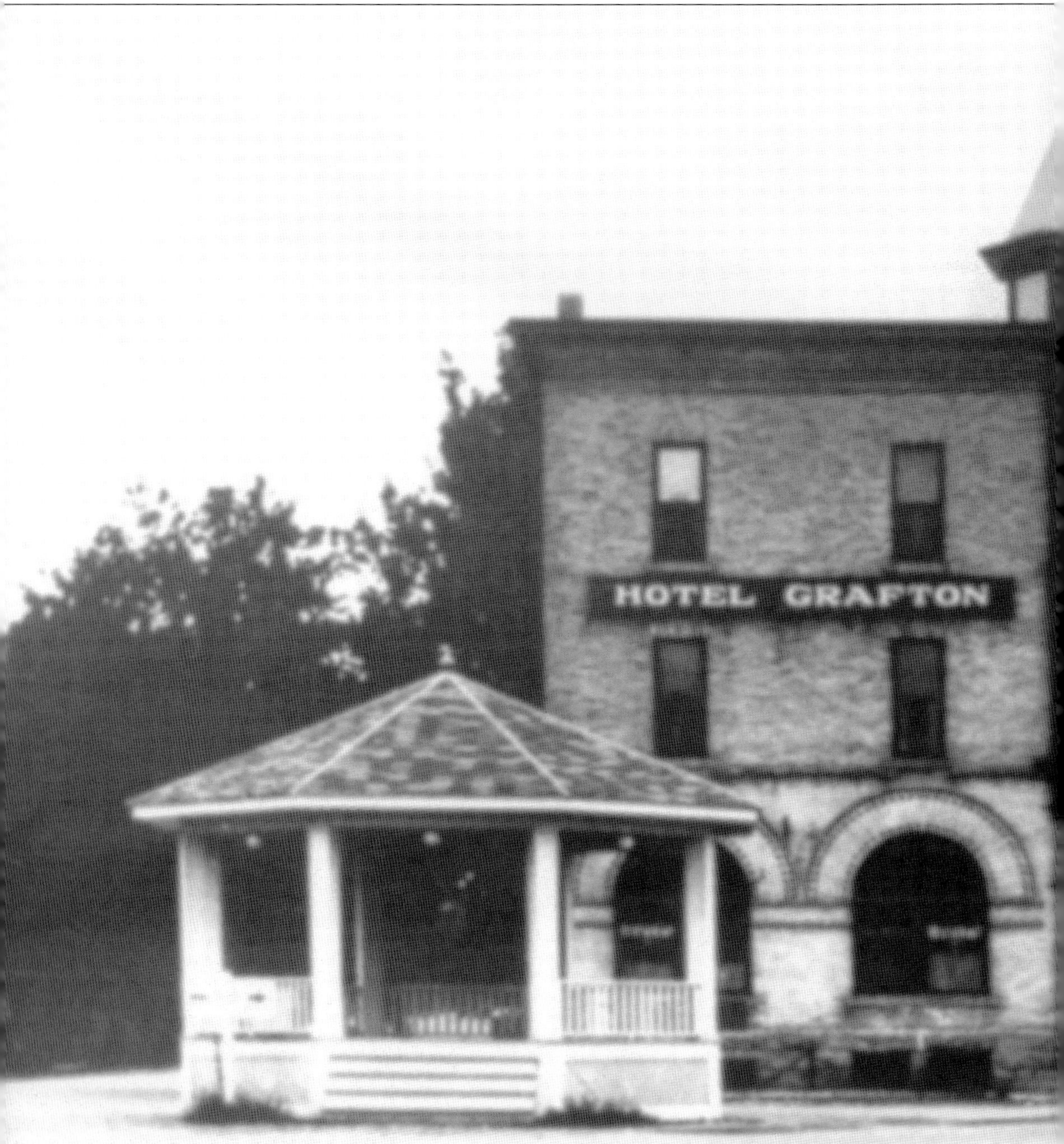

HOTEL GRAFTON. The original hotel in Grafton was the Wisconsin Haus, operated by Valentine and Ursula Jung for many years. It was important to the village for social gatherings and also official ones, as it served as the place where conscription for Civil War soldiers took place. That hotel was razed in 1892, and in 1895, Edward Mueller purchased the property for $4,000. It was first known as Hotel Mueller and then as Hotel Niesen after its purchase by Joseph Niesen in

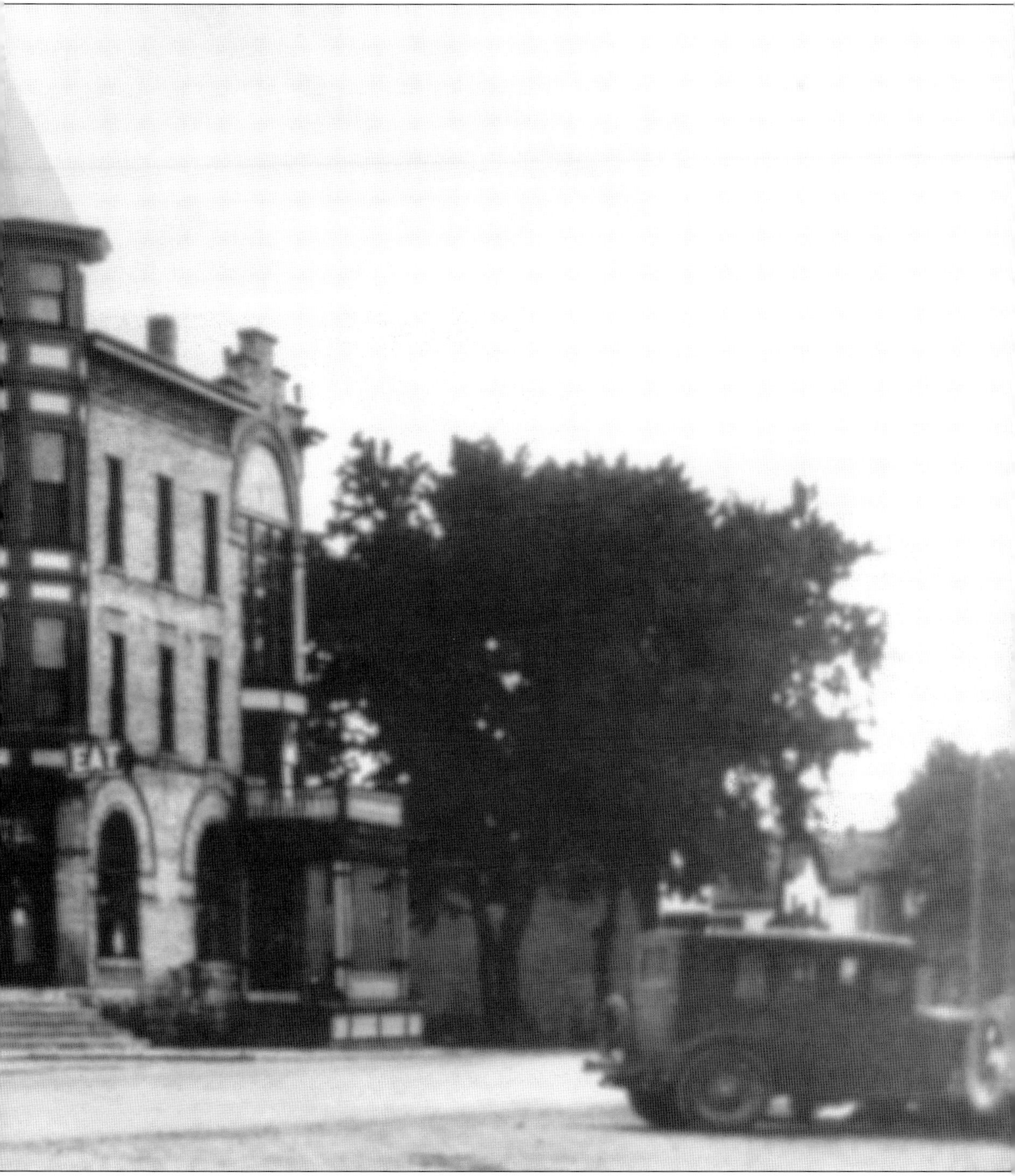

the early 1900s. With three stories that included guest rooms, a saloon, and a barbershop, it was regarded as one of the finest hotels in southeastern Wisconsin. There is a popular story that one guest liked it so much that he never left—a ghost named Freddy. As the story goes, Freddy was waiting for his bride-to-be at the hotel where they were to be married. Unfortunately, she never arrived, and Freddy hanged himself in one of the second-floor rooms. (Courtesy of Paul Rushing.)

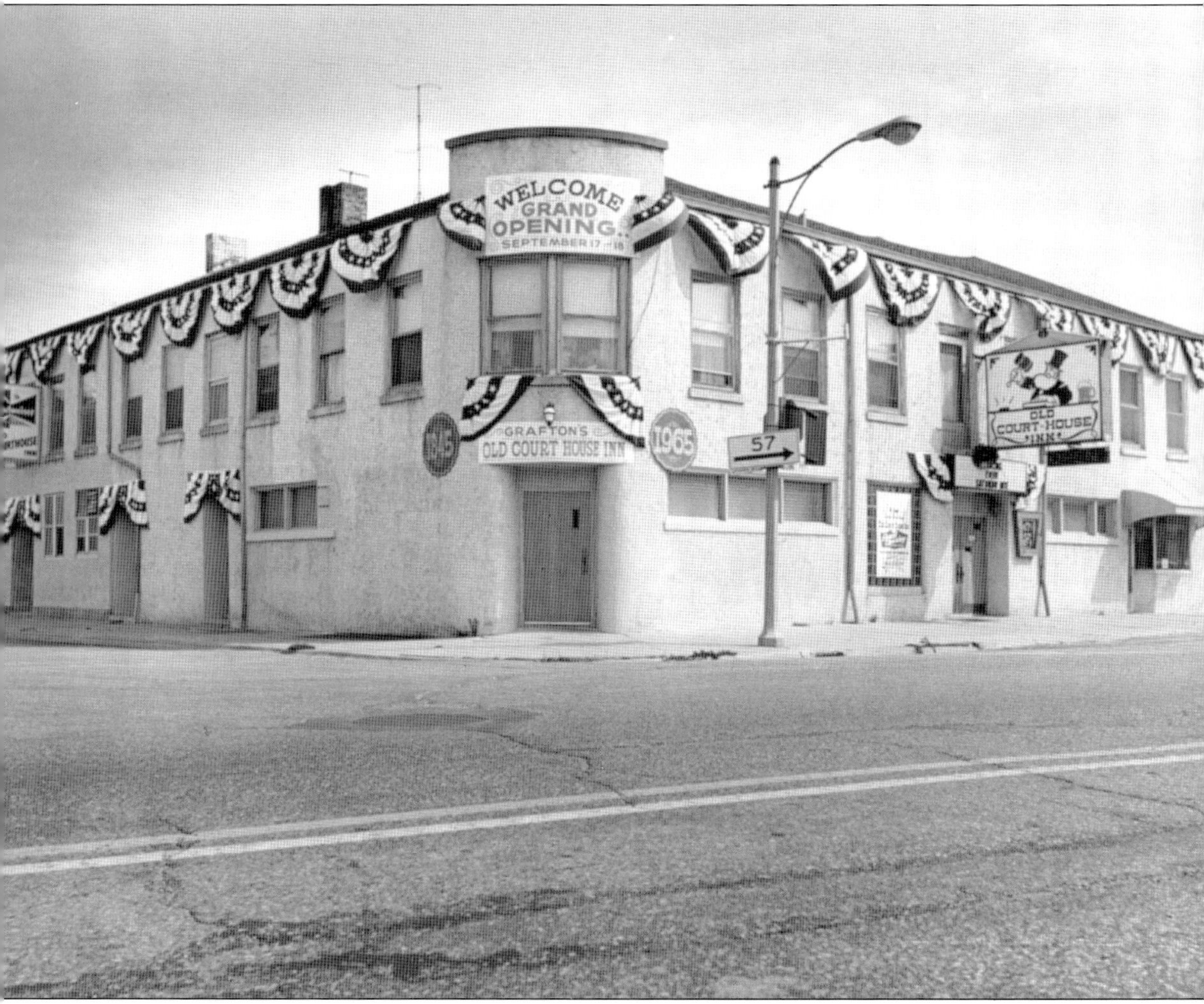

Stone Block Building. Grafton's Stone Block Building, at the southeast corner of Bridge Street and Twelfth Avenue, was one of the first buildings in the village. Built in 1844–1845, it is still in use today. It was constructed by Phineas M. Johnson, Jacob Andreana, and William T. Bonniwell and served as the county courthouse and jail when Grafton was the seat of Washington County, which then included Ozaukee County. The Stone Block Building also served other purposes. From 1853 to 1857, Lutheran church services were held there. By the turn of the 20th century, Andrew Bienlein operated a saloon and hotel rooms in the building. The saloon served Grafton's own Weber Brewery beer. Later, two bowling lanes were added to the building. Over the years, it housed other taverns and restaurants. This photograph is from 1965. (Courtesy of Richard Scheer.)

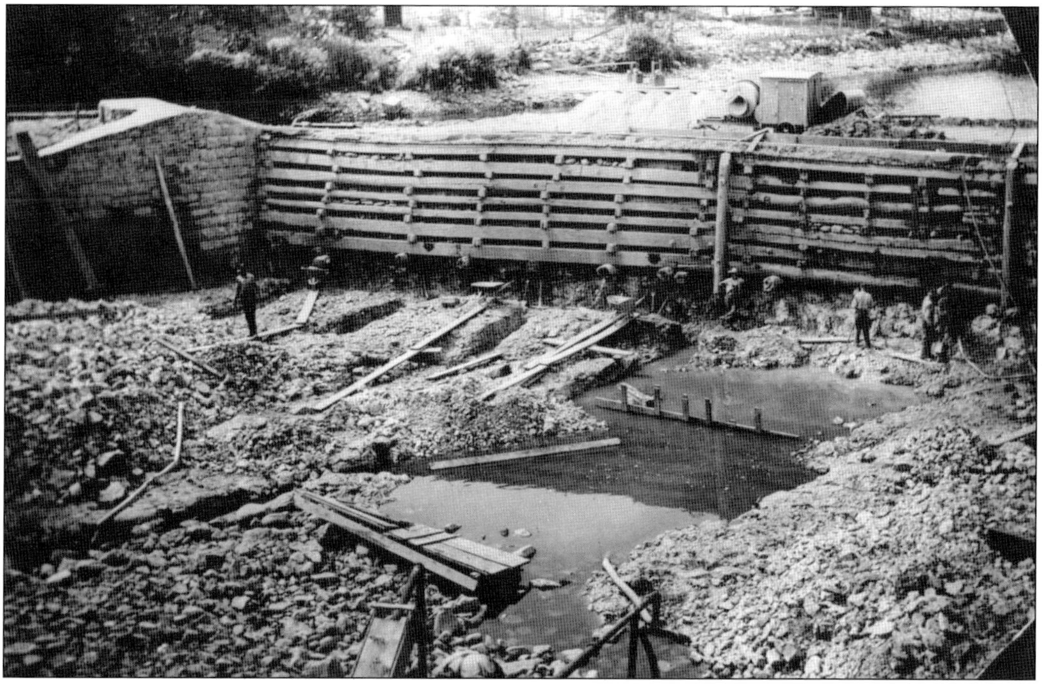

First Wood Dam. Building the first wooden dam in Grafton was a labor-intensive enterprise. First, the gravel and silt were cleared from the river bottom. Logs were then stacked on top of each other across the river, and the spaces between them were filled with large rocks. The layers continued until the dam was high enough that there would be no shallow places in the river behind it. (Courtesy of the Ed Rappold Photograph Collection at the Cedarburg Cultural Center.)

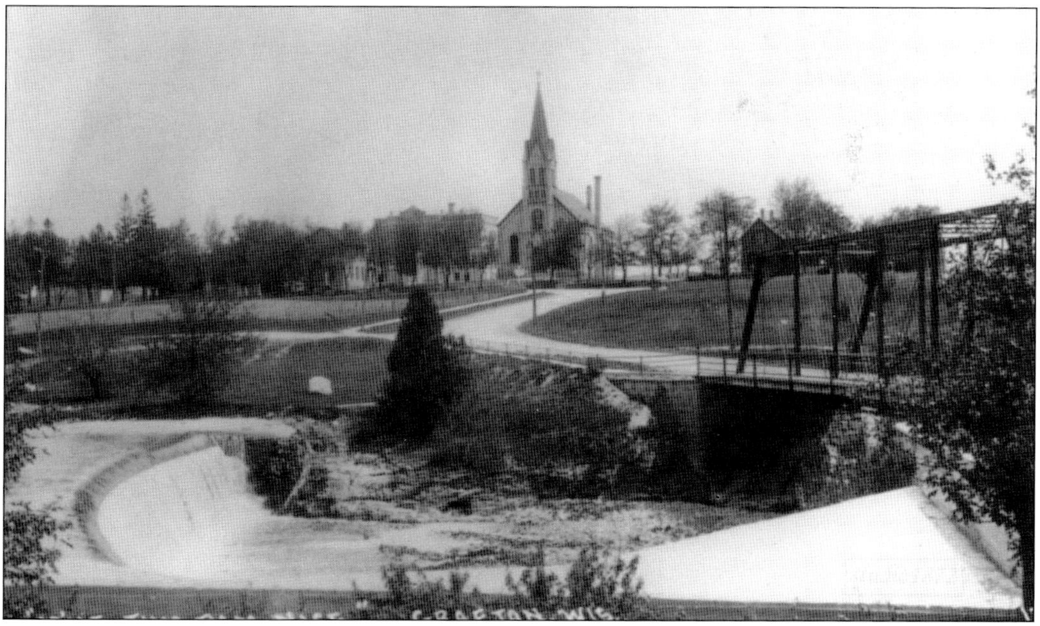

Early Grafton Scene. St. Joseph Catholic Church, school, and rectory are at center. Bridge Street, which had the only bridge in Grafton at the time, is on the right. The iron bridge was only one lane. Also pictured is the Milwaukee River dam. (Courtesy of Nic Schanen.)

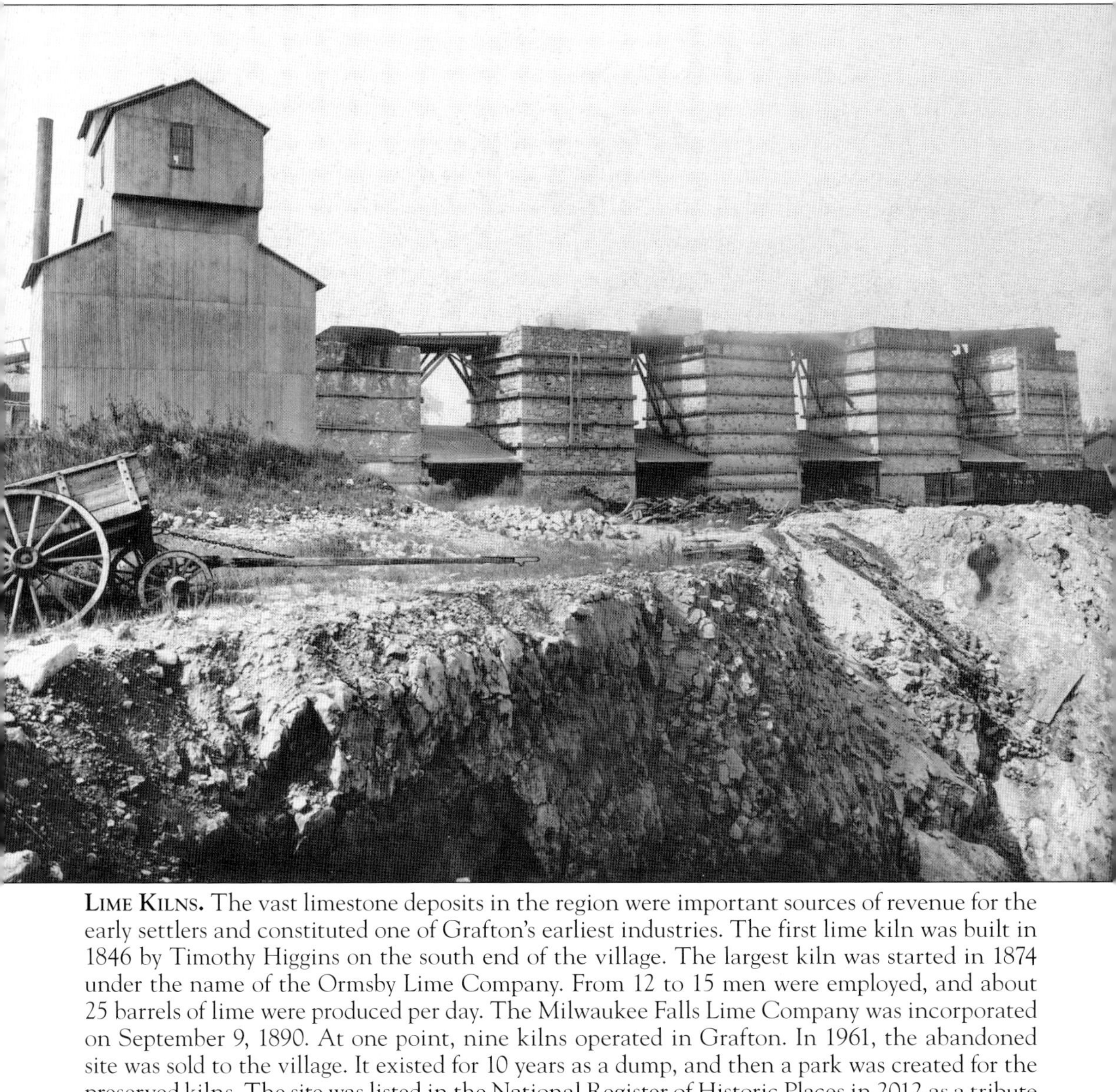

Lime Kilns. The vast limestone deposits in the region were important sources of revenue for the early settlers and constituted one of Grafton's earliest industries. The first lime kiln was built in 1846 by Timothy Higgins on the south end of the village. The largest kiln was started in 1874 under the name of the Ormsby Lime Company. From 12 to 15 men were employed, and about 25 barrels of lime were produced per day. The Milwaukee Falls Lime Company was incorporated on September 9, 1890. At one point, nine kilns operated in Grafton. In 1961, the abandoned site was sold to the village. It existed for 10 years as a dump, and then a park was created for the preserved kilns. The site was listed in the National Register of Historic Places in 2012 as a tribute to the importance of this long-ago industry that was crucial to the development of early Grafton. (Courtesy of the Ozaukee County Historical Society.)

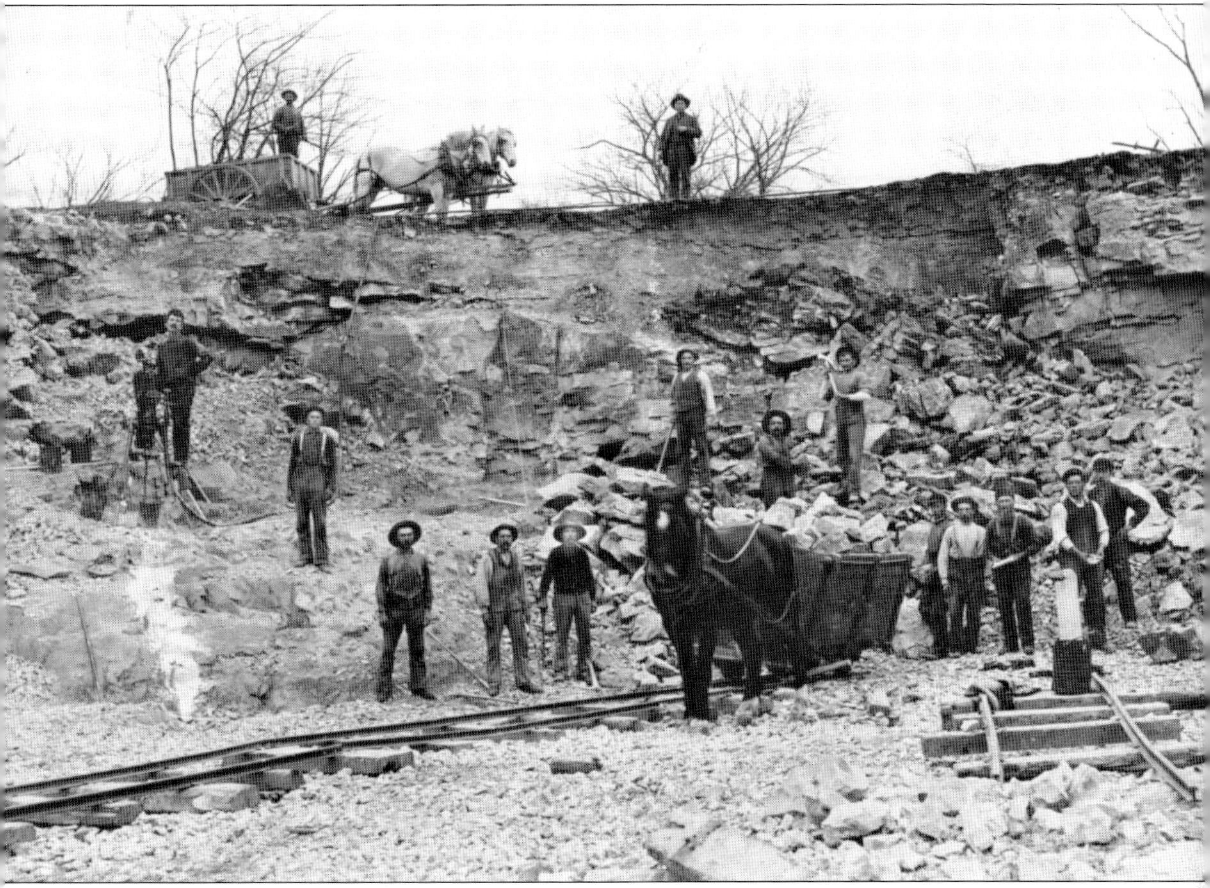

Milwaukee Falls Lime Company. The Milwaukee Falls Lime Company is seen here in operation. It was a leader in lime production for Ozaukee County and was well respected for its efficiency. The president of the company, G.A. Mace, is standing in front of the wagon. Seventeen men worked 60 hours per week and earned $6 at the lime kilns in Grafton. Mules pulled trams of limestone from quarries to the crusher, and then cables pulled them on tracks atop kilns, which were stoked with wood in fireboxes below. The area was heavily forested in those days, so hardwood was easily available. When the limestone was dehydrated, it was pounded into a fine powder, which was used for plaster, mortar, fertilizer, treating animal hides and leather, and for whitewash. A spur line carried the processed lime to the mainline of the Milwaukee & Northern Railway for shipment to Chicago, St. Louis, and Detroit. The company remained in business until 1926. (Courtesy of the Ozaukee County Historical Society.)

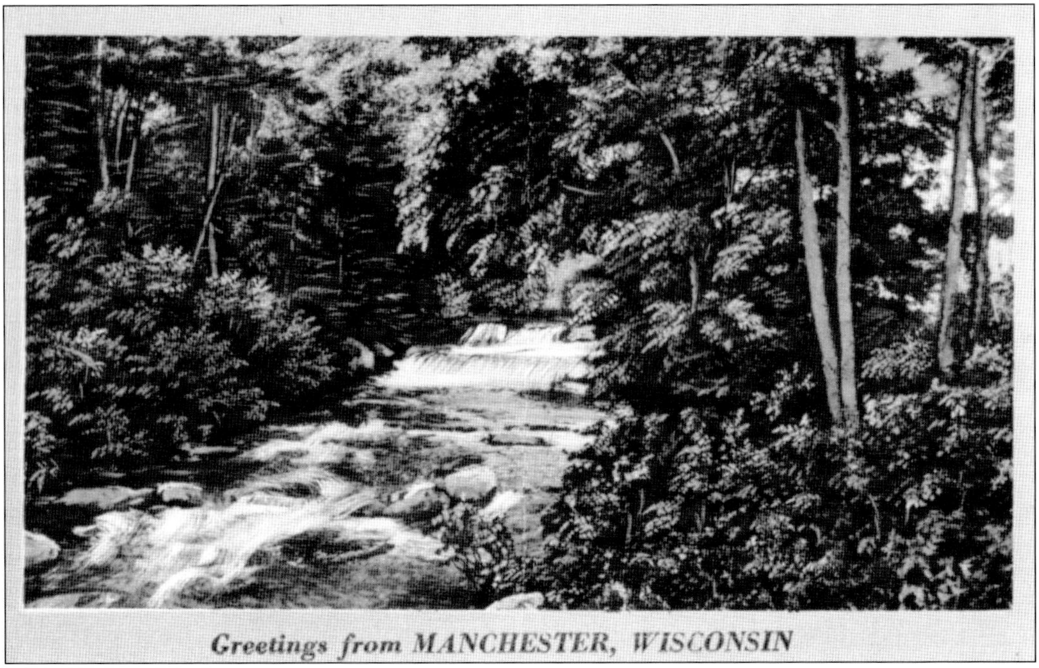

MANCHESTER, WISCONSIN. This postcard shows one of the early names of Grafton. In 1840, Jacob Eichler named the area Hamburg. In 1846, Benjamin Moore changed the name to Grafton, and in 1857, the name was changed to Manchester. In 1862, it was changed back to Grafton. Manchester proved to be a popular name, as there are two others in Wisconsin. (Courtesy of Nic Schanen.)

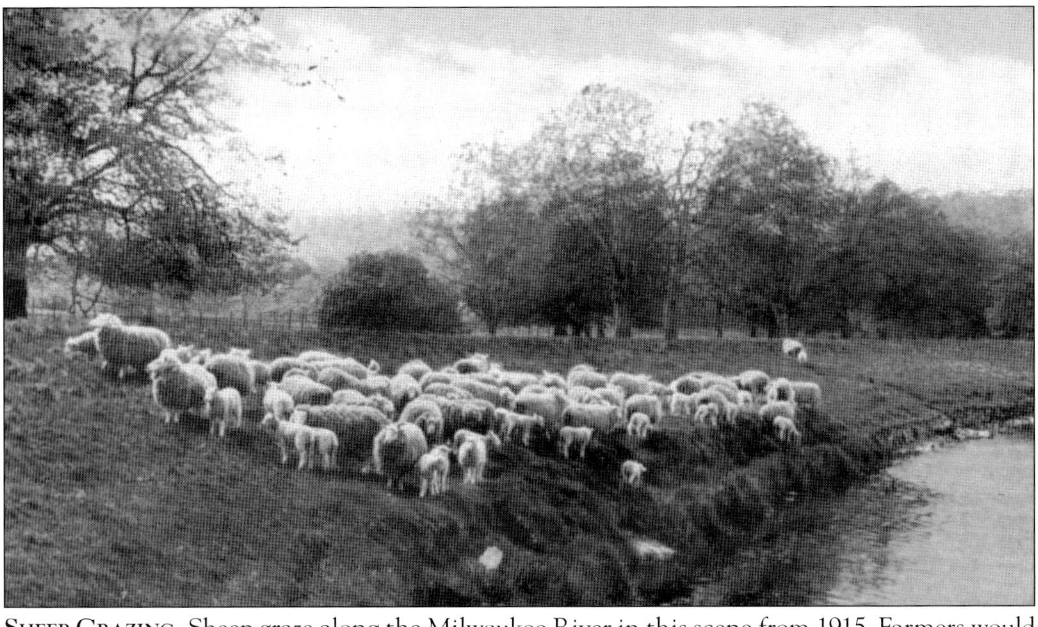

SHEEP GRAZING. Sheep graze along the Milwaukee River in this scene from 1915. Farmers would graze their sheep where the terrain was too rough for cultivation but where there was easy access to water. Around this time, the large-scale raising of sheep moved west to the great plains. (Courtesy of Vivian Scherf Laabs.)

Two

Life on the Farm

Agriculture was crucial to early Grafton. The glaciers had left behind mostly flatlands and rich soil, and the pioneering farmers in the area took advantage of that to raise corn, oats, barley, wheat, and garden crops. They also began to raise horses, cattle, hogs, and sheep as early as 1853. As evidence of the importance of farming, the US Department of Agriculture, for the year 1910, recorded that 94 percent of all the land in Ozaukee County was farmland. The average family farm was nearly 100 acres. Dairy cows numbered 10,000, hogs 12,000, and poultry 100,000. Farming was a $16 million business in those years. For the individual farmer, it could be an exhausting—and sometimes risky—business. The entire family needed to work year-round. While the farmer worked in the fields and the barn, the women cared for the children and tended the vegetable garden and the chickens. They sewed, washed, cooked, milked cows, and often made cheese and butter. It was also their job to dispense medical care to the family. In fall, they canned hundreds of quarts of vegetables, fruits, and berries. Sauerkraut was made and stored in stone crocks. Every winter, it was time for making sausage. Children also had an important role on the farm. They helped weed the family garden plot and worked in the fields during harvest time. Often after a long walk home from school, they would return to the fields and help until it was time for their other chores. In their leisure time, women knitted and quilted. Men often whittled. The family might go for a Sunday drive after church, but rarely left the farm for any length of time. Often, relatives from town would come to the country to visit. As farmers began to prosper in early Grafton, so did those who started the area's early industries.

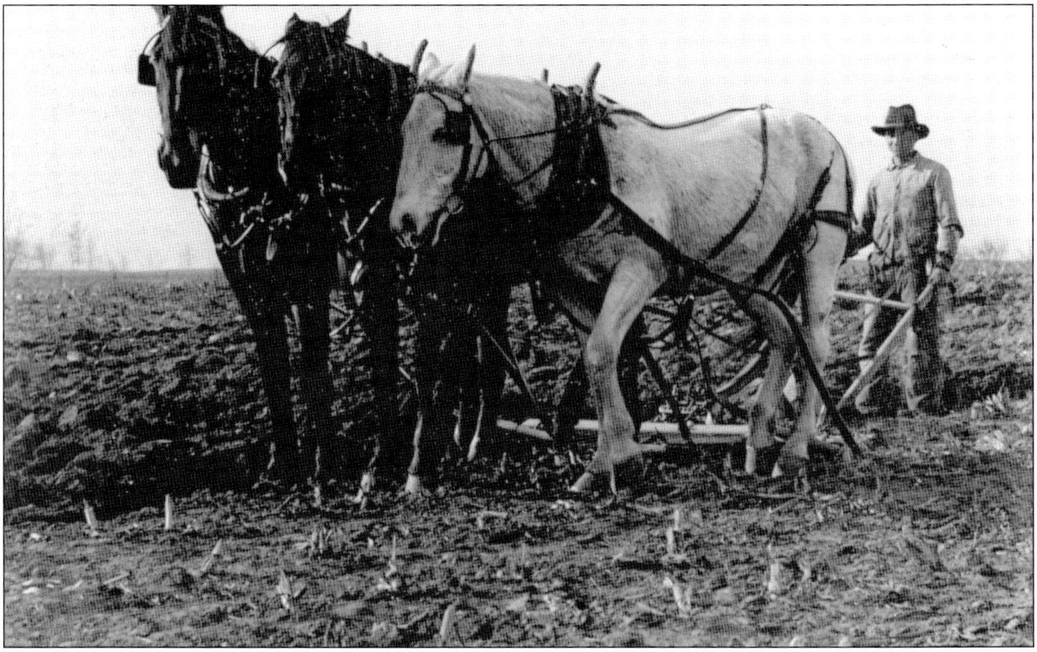

KAUL FARM PLOWING. Each year after the corn was harvested, the cobs and stalks would be blown into the silo for silage. The next step was plowing under the stubble of the corn, as shown here. A third horse was often needed because of the difficulty of pulling the cornstalks from the ground. Arnold Kaul Sr. is shown here with his team. (Courtesy of Arnold Kaul Sr.)

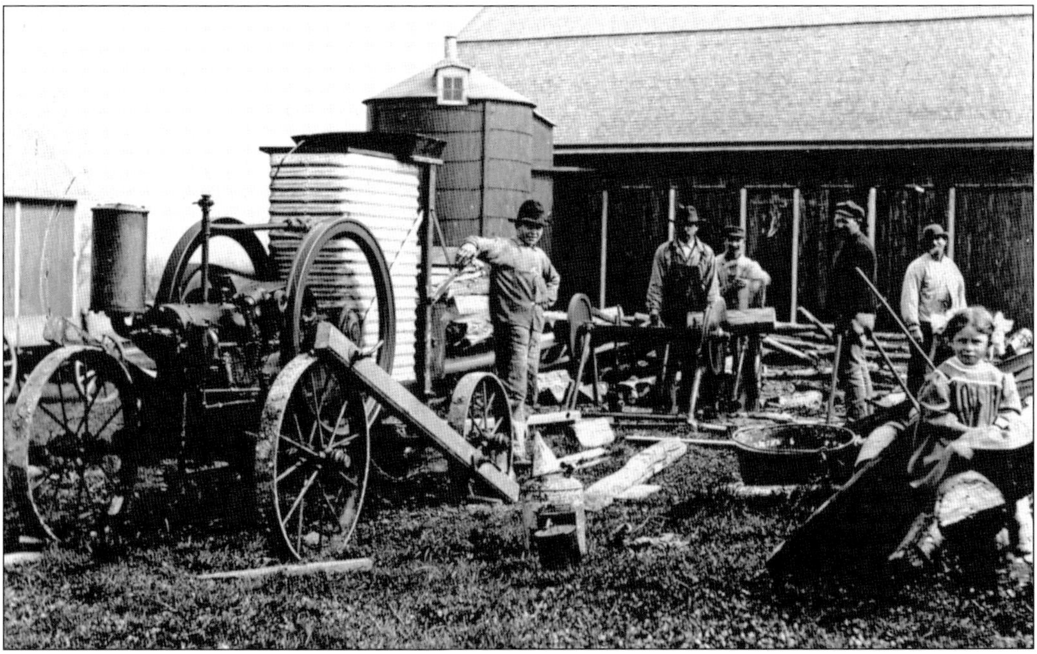

KAUL FARM FIREWOOD MAKING. One of the important jobs on the farm was making firewood to get ready for winter. Shown here from left to right are Arnold Kaul Sr., Fredrich Kaul, and Conrad (a hired hand). The other two men at right are not identified. Lore Kaul is sitting on a log. The engine on the wood splitter is an eight-horsepower 1905 Titan. (Courtesy of Arnold Kaul Sr.)

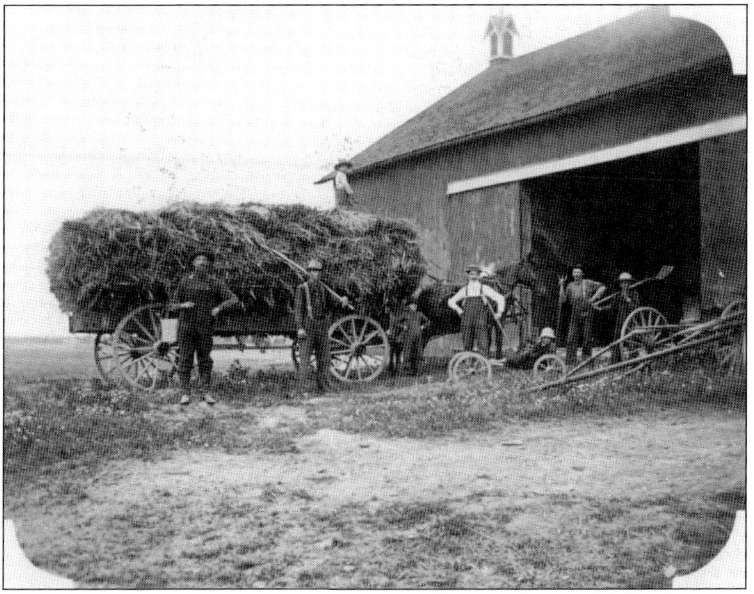

SUDBRINK FARM HAYING. Haying was a farm task usually done three times per year. The hay would be stored in barns or in a haystack. Pictured here at the Sudbrink farm are, from left to right, Ludwig Sudbrink, William Sudbrink, O.R. Mayer, Richard Sudbrink, Louis Sudbrink Jr., and Theodore Sudbrink, with Alex Sudbrink on top of the hay wagon. (Courtesy of the Sudbrink family.)

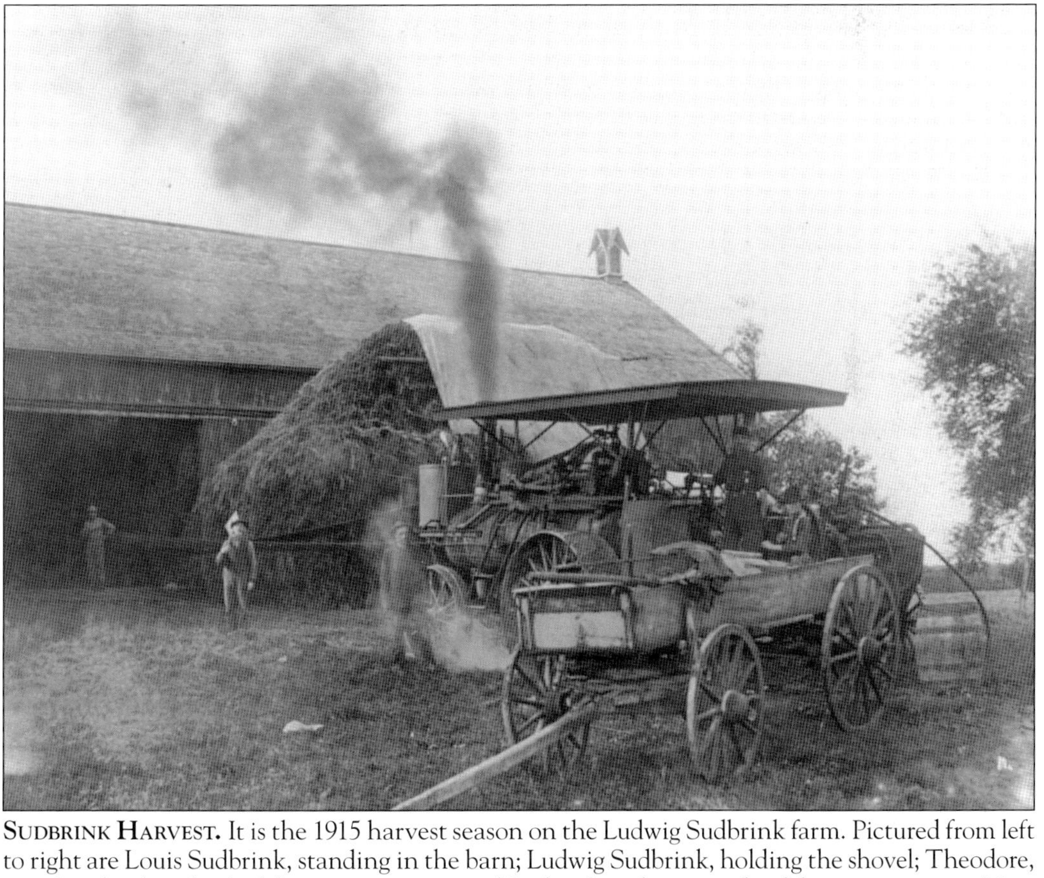

SUDBRINK HARVEST. It is the 1915 harvest season on the Ludwig Sudbrink farm. Pictured from left to right are Louis Sudbrink, standing in the barn; Ludwig Sudbrink, holding the shovel; Theodore, standing by the wheel of the steam engine; and Richard, at the controls of the steam engine. Note the decorative cupola on the barn roof in the background. (Courtesy of the Sudbrink family.)

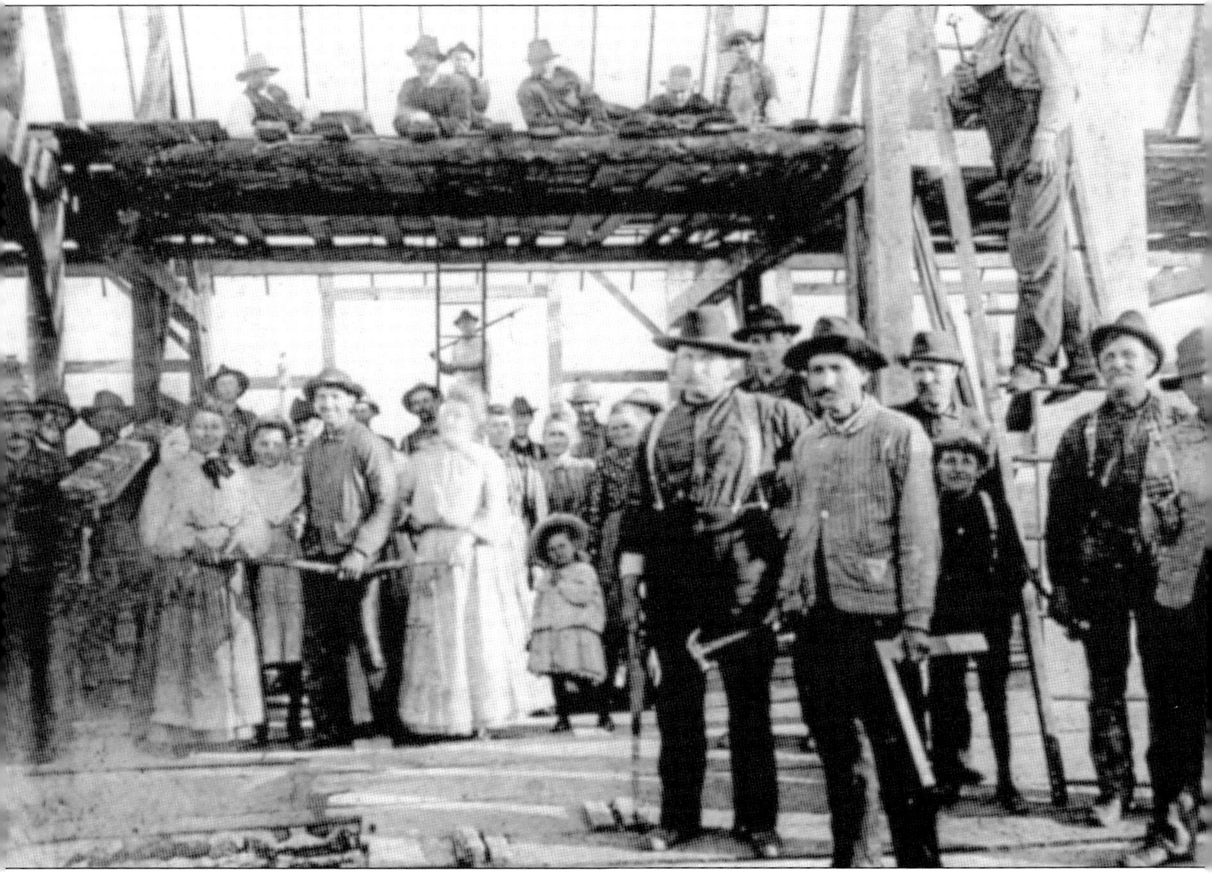

Kaul Farm Barn Building. Barn building at the Kaul farm in 1907 was an exciting community event. Work on the new barn began in the winter when plans were made, land cleared, tradesmen hired, trees cut down to size, and the timbers edged with axes. The timber frames were held together with wooden pegs before being raised into position. The barn "raising" was the process of lifting the large vertical frames that formed the skeleton of the barn. It took a large group of men working together using ropes and poles to erect the heavy wooden structures. Often, a lead man, an expert in barn building who traveled from farm to farm, was hired. Posing amongst the barn-raising workers is Lore Kaul, at center with a hat. Directly behind is her mother, Margarethe Kaul. The other workers are not identified. (Courtesy of Arnold Kaul Sr.)

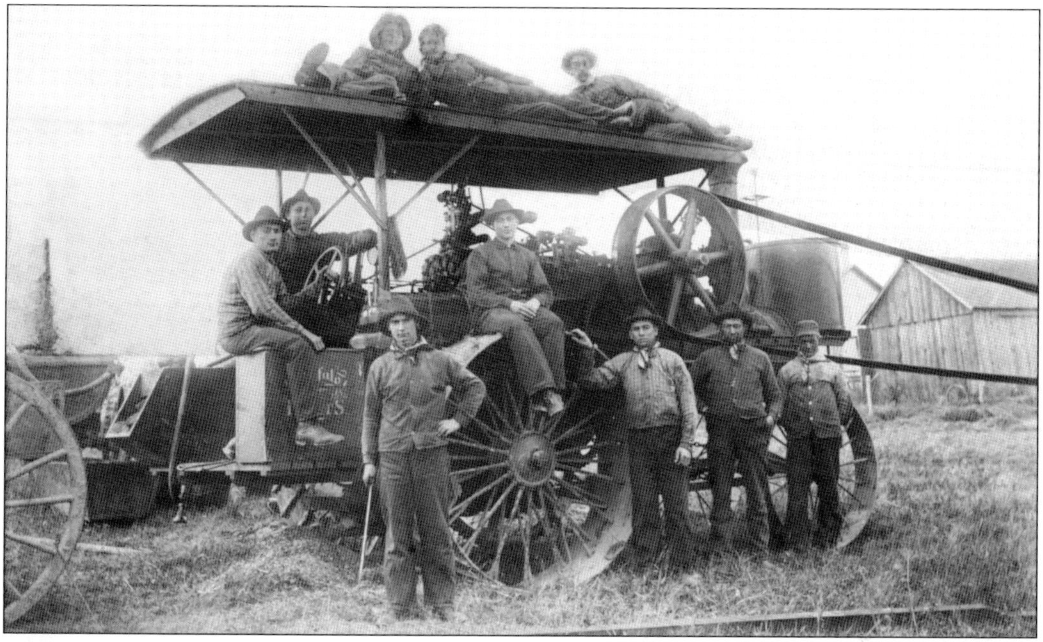

Wegner Farm Steam Tractor. Farmworkers pose proudly around a steam tractor at the Wegner farm on the east side of Seventeenth Avenue. Second from left on the tractor is Charles Wegner. Note the men on the roof of the tractor. Steam tractors made farming more efficient, allowing farmers to pull great amounts of weight. The original Wegner farmhouse is still standing. (Courtesy of Marty Wegner.)

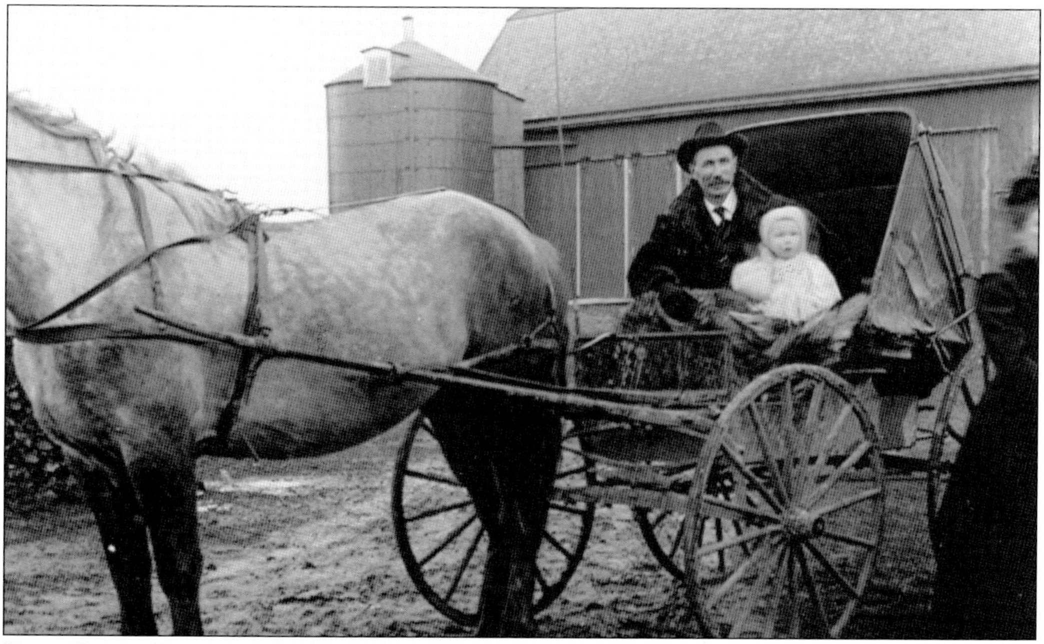

Kaul Family Buggy. In the horse-drawn buggy are Fredrich Kaul and daughter Lore in 1903. The young Friedrich Kaul bought the farm in the fall of 1891, a risky time of year to begin farming in Wisconsin. The farmhouse was already standing when he purchased the farm. (Courtesy of Arnold Kaul Sr.)

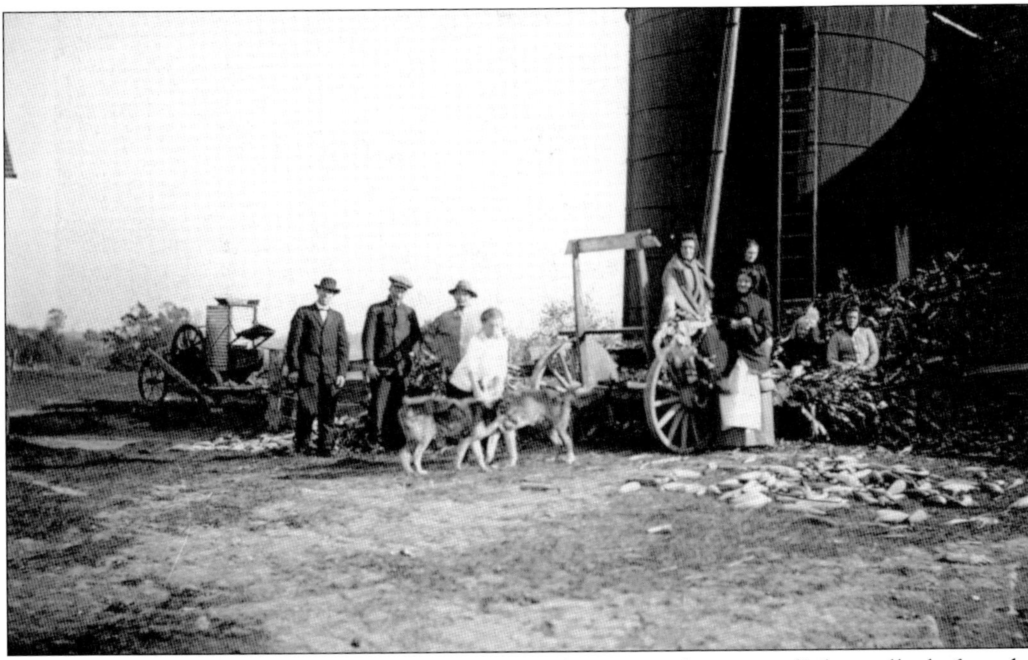

Corn Prep on Kaul Farm. It was the women's job to snap the corn off the stalks before the stalks were chopped and went into the silo. Later, the cobs were husked and put into the corn crib. During the winter, the farmer took the cobs to the feed mill to be ground up for feed for the animals. Lore Kaul is pictured with the farm dogs. (Courtesy of Arnold Kaul Sr.)

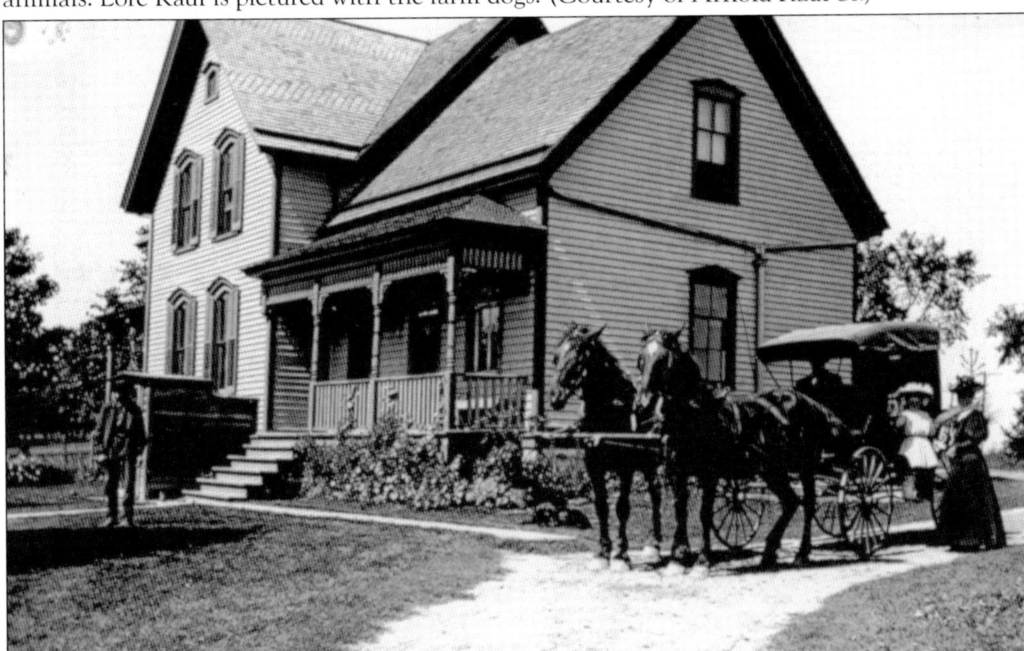

Carriage Ride on Kaul Farm. The Kaul family looks to be coming home from a carriage ride because of the way the carriage is situated in the driveway. From left to right at the carriage are father Fredrich Kaul, daughter Lore, and mother Margarethe; standing at left is Conrad, the family's hired hand. Note the elaborate hats on Lore and her mother. (Courtesy of Arnold Kaul Sr.)

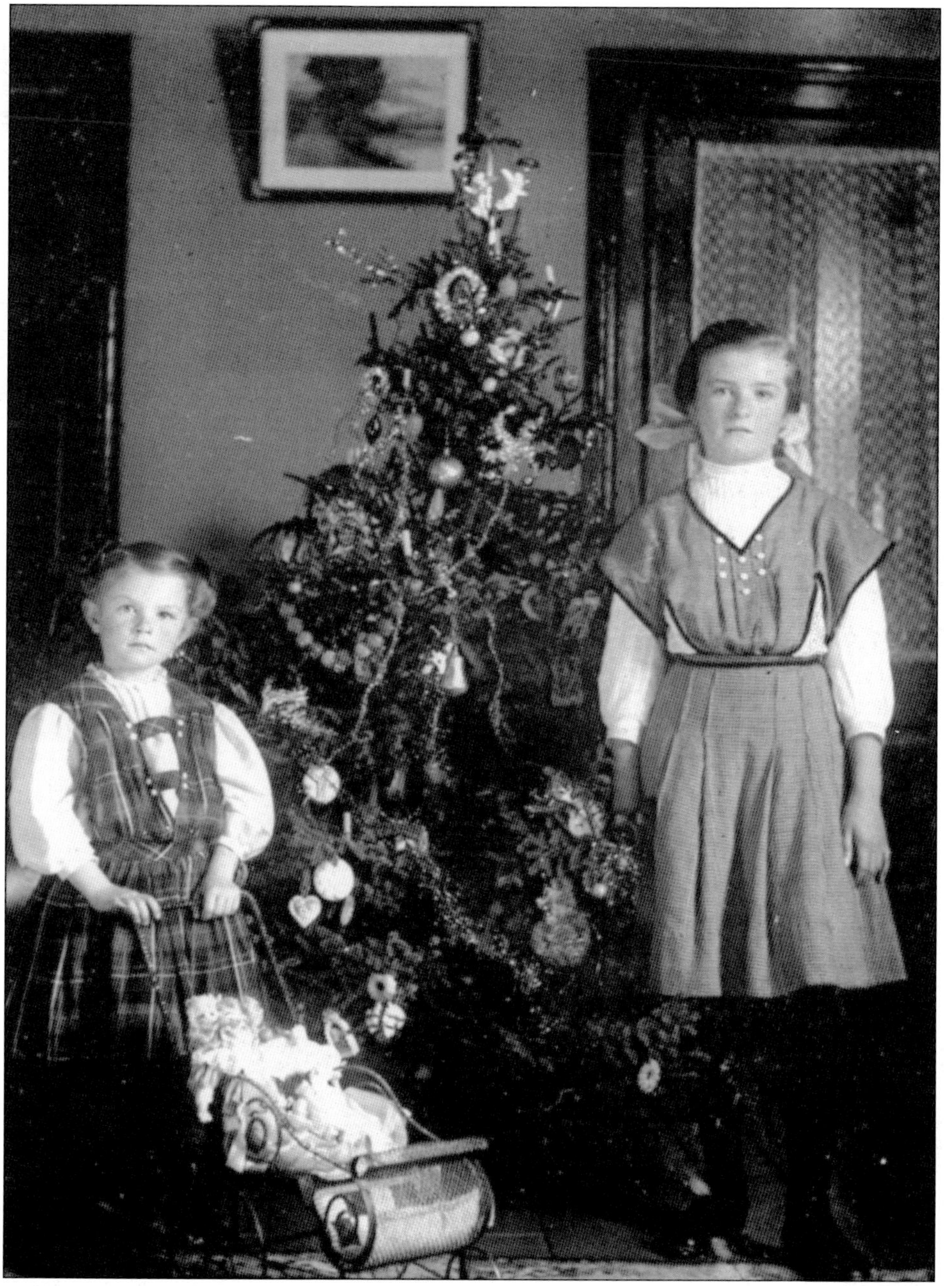

CHRISTMAS AT KAUL FARM. Christmas in Grafton in the early 1900s included many German traditions. Two little girls dressed in their holiday best pose in front of the Christmas tree at the Kaul house in 1909. Those early Christmas trees were often decorated with nuts, strings of popcorn or beads, oranges, lemons, candies, and homemade trinkets and lighted candles. A bucket of water was usually kept next to the tree in case of fire. The first electric Christmas tree lights appeared in the 1880s, thanks to an associate of Thomas Edison, but were too costly for most households. On the farm, Christmas gifts were simple, such as food, wood items, handmade toys, clothing or sewed items, or a pair of work gloves. The children traditionally received one toy, with the rest of the gifts being clothing. (Courtesy of Arnold Kaul Sr.)

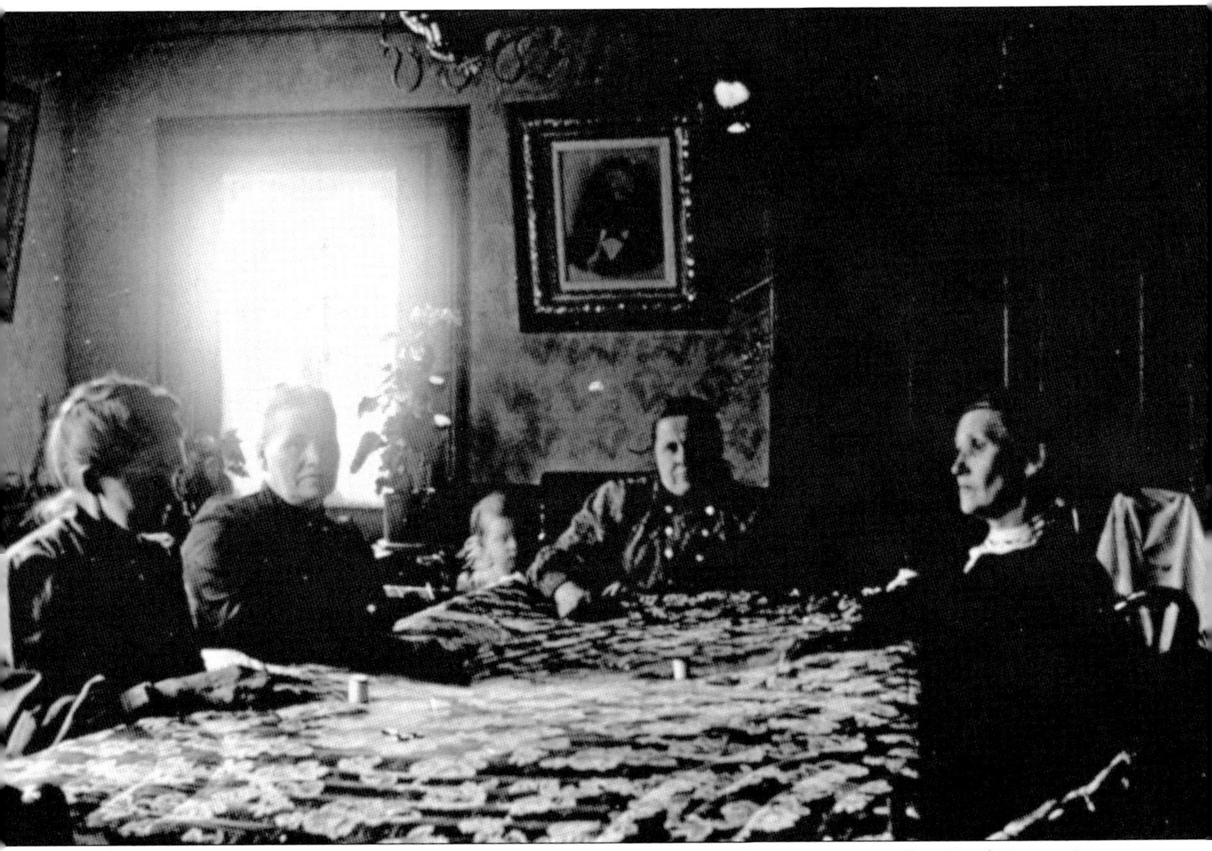

Quilt Making at Kaul Farm. Making quilts was a popular activity at the Kaul Farm. It was often an important social event, bringing together families from miles away. During the long winter months, the women would create the quilt squares and then get together in spring or summer to create the quilt. In the earlier years of quilting, it was a necessity not to waste a scrap of clothing or fabric and to provide warm coverings for the family. As manufactured materials became more available, quilt making evolved from a necessity to an art form. Often, quilts were made to commemorate special events such as weddings and births, and were regarded as heirlooms, prized by families for generations. Note little Lore Kaul watching the ladies sew. (Courtesy of Arnold Kaul Sr.)

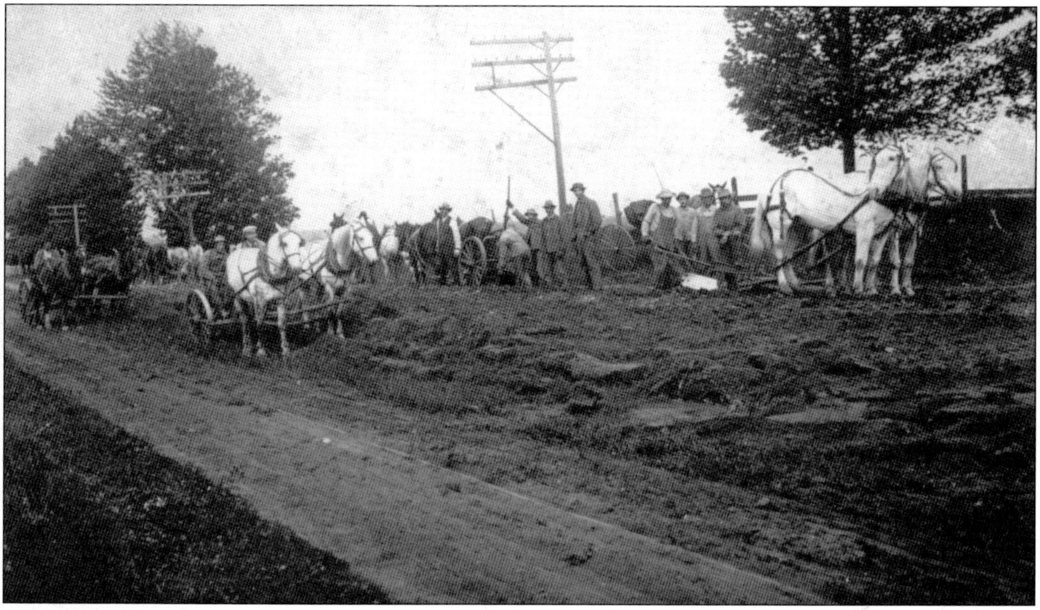

Clearing Land at Wegner Farm. Clearing a farmer's land was also a community event in the early 1900s. In this scene from the Wegner farm, seven neighboring farmers have brought their teams to help remove tree stumps from the land. The Wegner farm was east of Seventeenth Avenue, north of Falls Road. (Courtesy of Marty Wegner.)

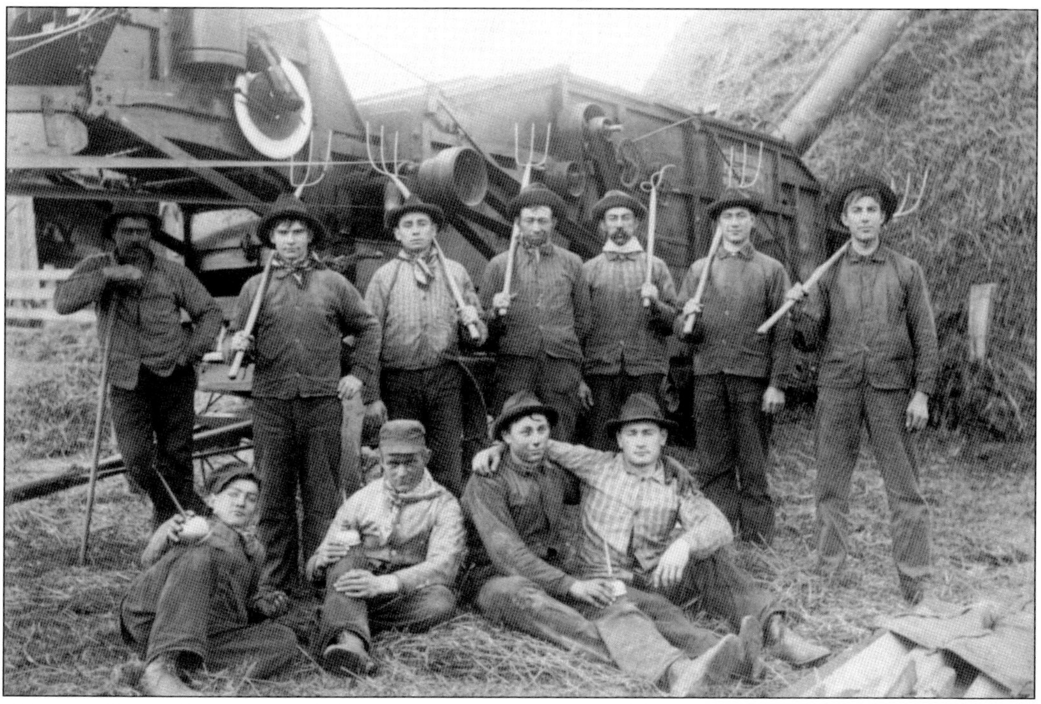

Wegner Farm Threshing Machine. Friends and neighbors pose proudly with the Wegner threshing machine. Charles Wegner is sitting second from the right. The others were neighboring farmers who came to help. Many itinerant farmworkers would travel from farm to farm, working for room and board. (Courtesy of Marty Wegner.)

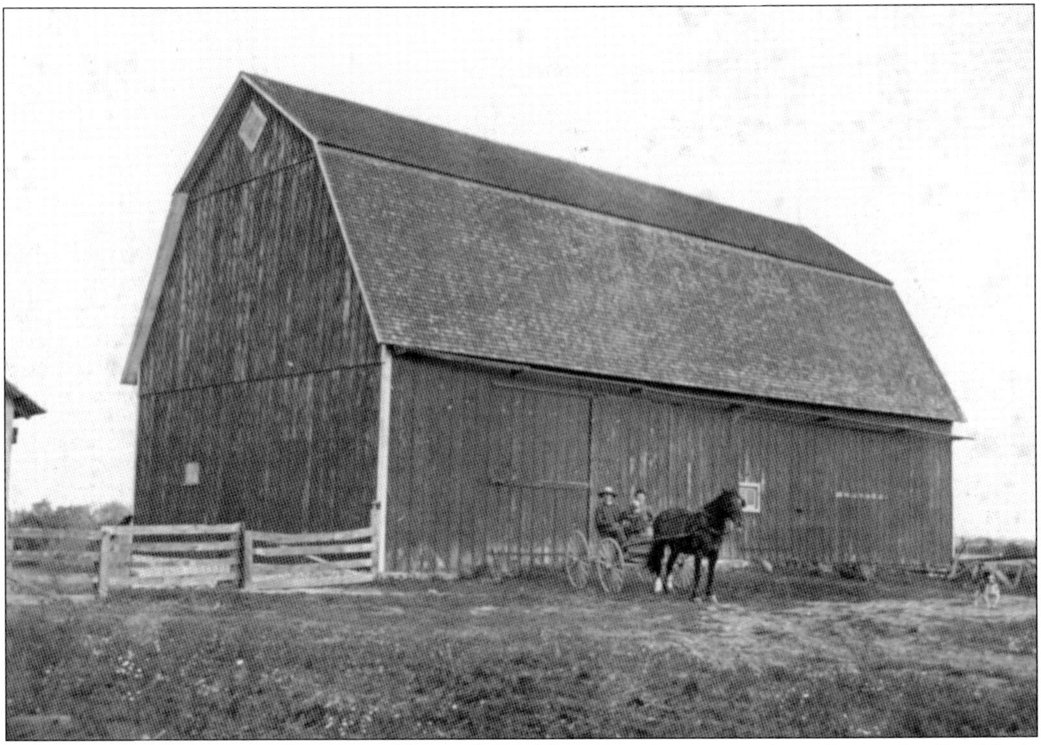

BUCHHOLZ FARM. Nic and Barbara (Oberst) Buchholz are getting ready to leave the Buchholz farm in their buggy. In early times, the barn, rather than the house, was the central focus of the farm. Some farm families actually got running water in the barn before getting indoor plumbing in the house. This farm was on the east side of Port Washington Road, a quarter mile north of Highway 60. (Courtesy of Leone Buchholz.)

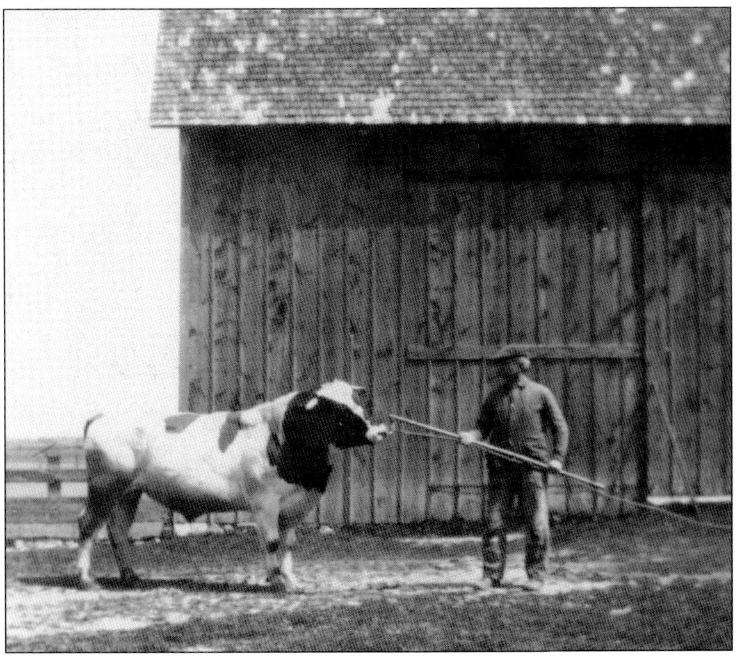

BULL ON BUCHHOLZ FARM. Nic Buchholz leads his bull back to the barn on the Buchholz farm. The bull was often an intimidating animal on the farm. One Grafton farmer recounts, "You couldn't trust a bull. If not for the dog, my dad would have been a goner. The dog grabbed the bull by the tail and held him back from attacking my dad." Note the long pole with the hook on the end that is being used to lead the bull. (Courtesy of Allen Buchholz.)

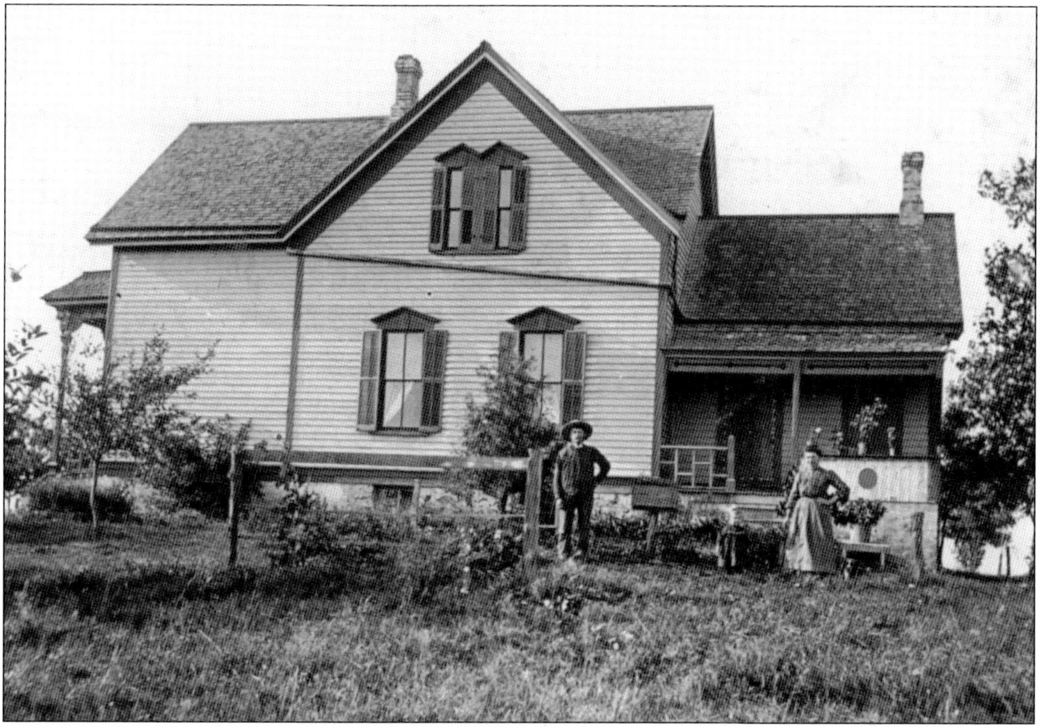

Buchholz Family Scene. Nic and Barbara Buchholz and their daughter Theresa stand in front of their farmhouse in the early 1900s. Their home boasts the classic components of the farmhouses of the time with a covered porch, large door, whitewashed walls, big kitchen, and exposed wood. It was a time when manicured lawns were not a priority on the farm. (Courtesy of Leone Buchholz.)

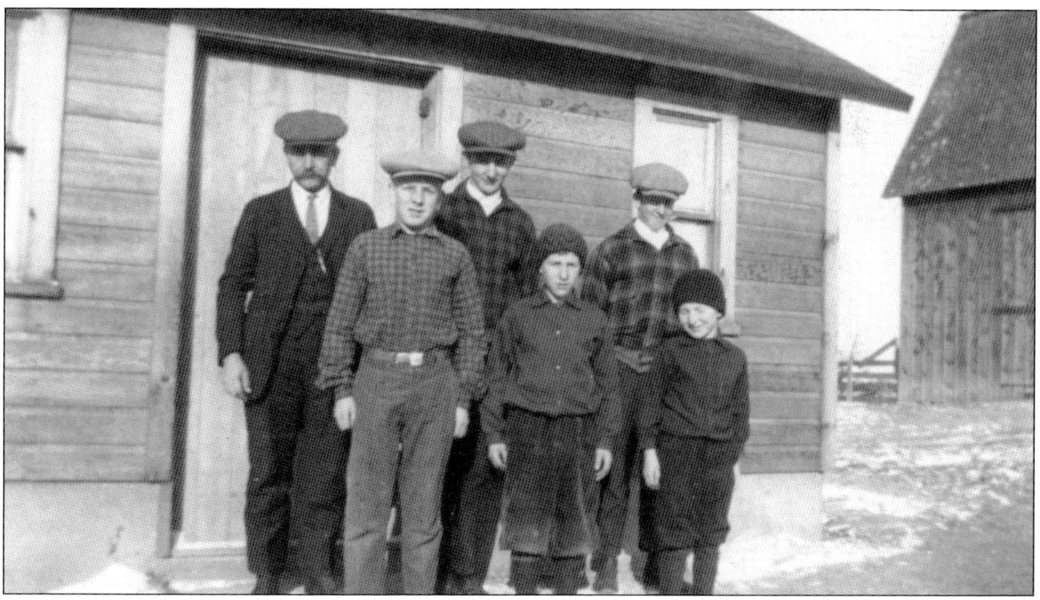

Buchholz and Sons. Nic Buchholz and his sons are seen here on the family farm. From left to right are (first row) Ray, Leo, and Frank; (second row) Nic, Joe, and Clem. Running a farm took the help of the entire family and, often, hired hands. (Courtesy of Leone Buchholz.)

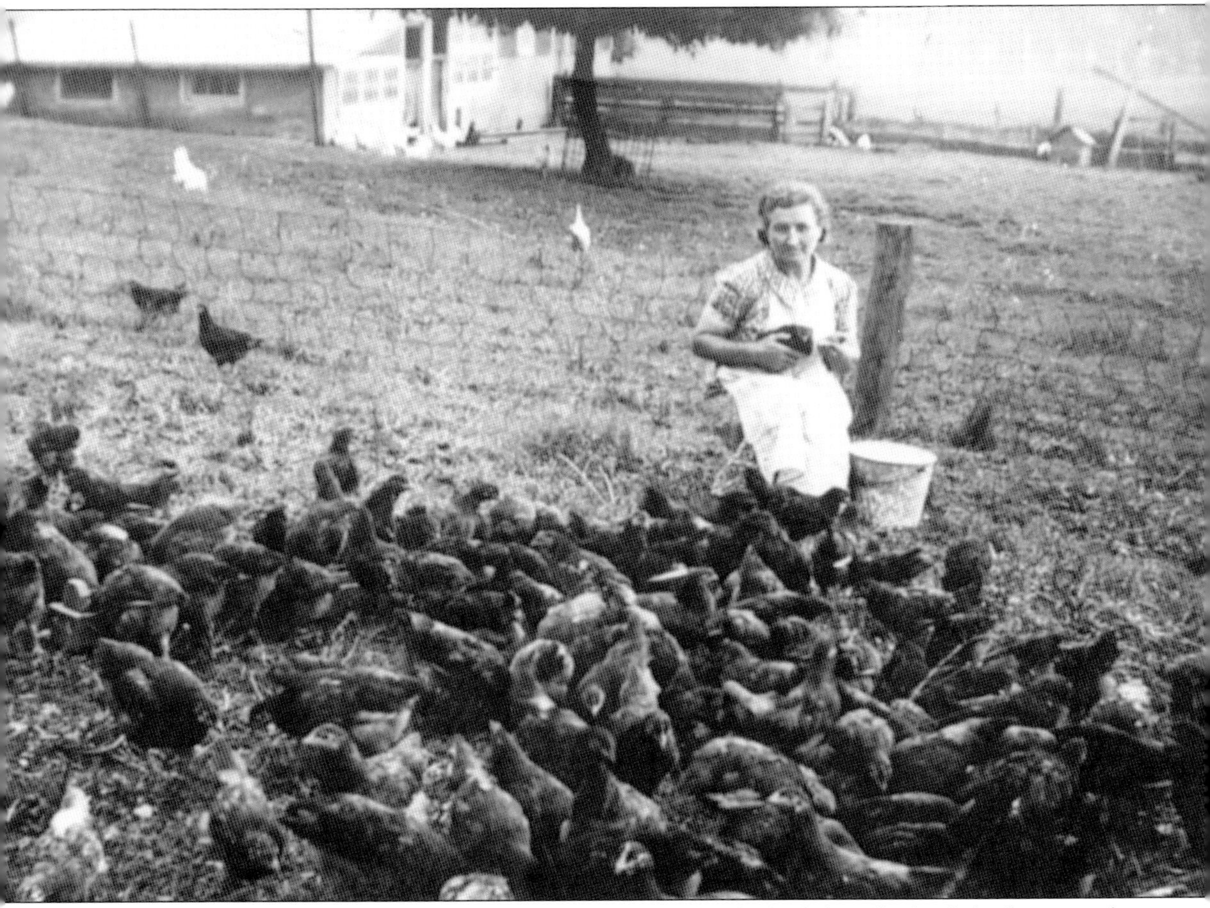

Feeding Chickens on Buchholz Farm. Barbara Buchholz feeds her flock of chickens on the Buchholz farm. Chickens were primarily raised on family farms. They were not raised in large numbers, with a flock of 400 being considered large. Some of the chickens were allowed the run of the yard to help keep insects out of the lawn. At times, however, they fell prey to hawks or owls. Mink were a special threat to chickens in the coop. Families sold the extra eggs as additional income. A chicken dinner was a special event, with the meat considered a delicacy and reserved for holidays and special occasions. The chickens were welcome on the farm, but in April 1907, residents of the village of Grafton asked for a village ordinance to prevent chickens and ducks from walking on public sidewalks, lawns, gardens, and porches. (Courtesy of Leone Buchholz.)

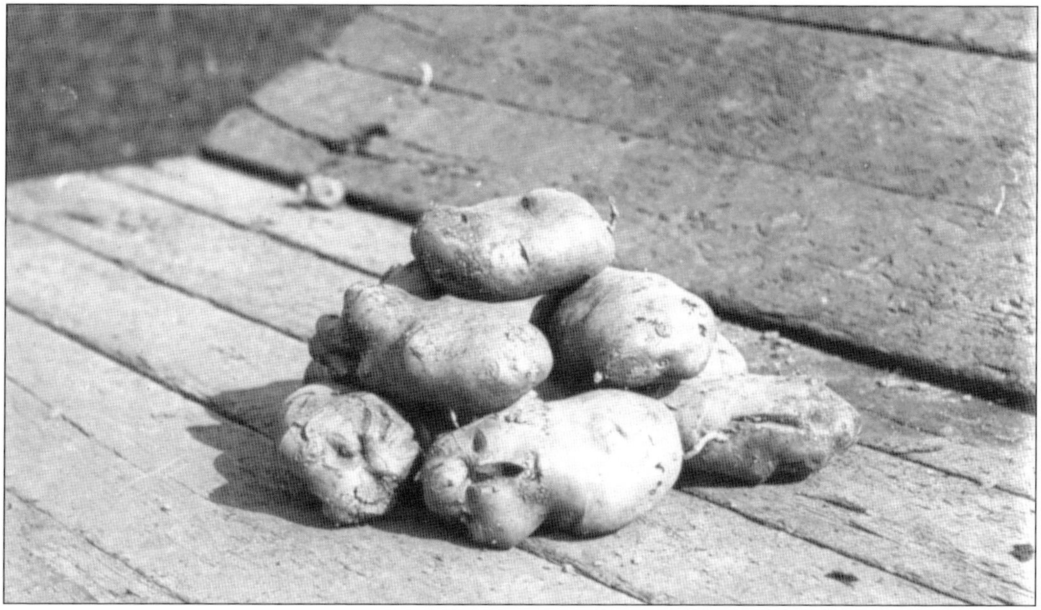

IRISH COBBLER POTATOES. Some farmers in Grafton, like the Kauls, raised Irish cobbler potatoes and took them to Milwaukee to sell to the Irish immigrants living there. The potatoes are thought to have been discovered by an Irish shoemaker in the late 1800s and are today regarded as one of the earliest heirloom potato varieties. (Courtesy of Arnold Kaul Sr.)

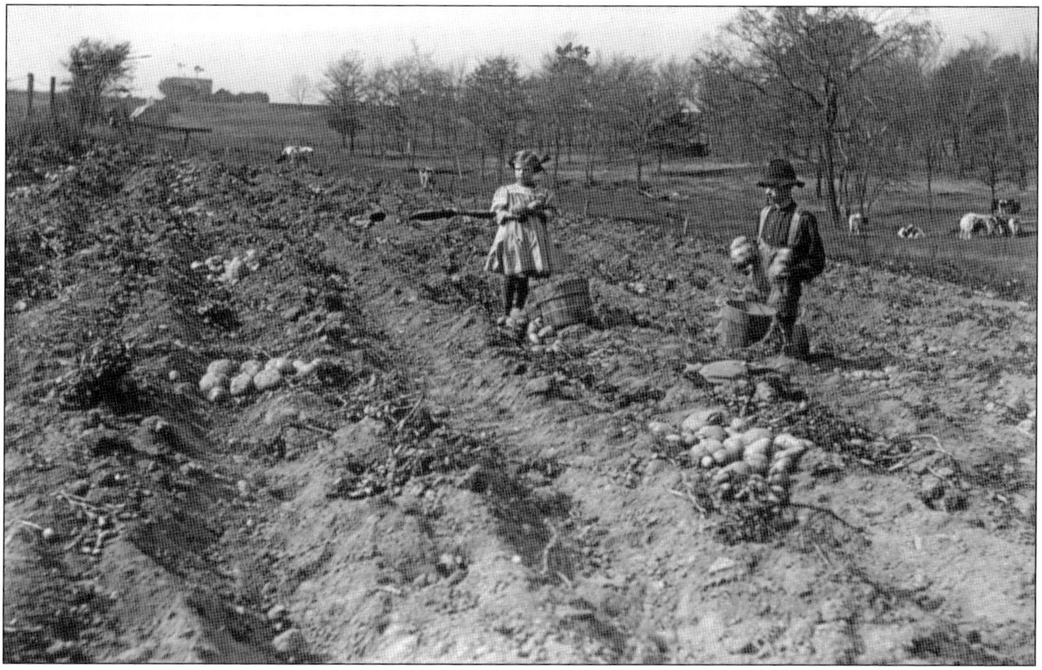

POTATO HARVESTING ON KAUL FARM. It is potato harvesting time on the Kaul farm in 1908, and Lore Kaul is helping her father, Fredrich. This field was at the corner of Arrowhead and North Port Washington Roads, looking west to the Kaul woods. The Ernest Klotz farm buildings are in the distance. There is a running spring behind the shrubbery where butter and milk were kept to keep them from spoiling. (Courtesy of Arnold Kaul Sr.)

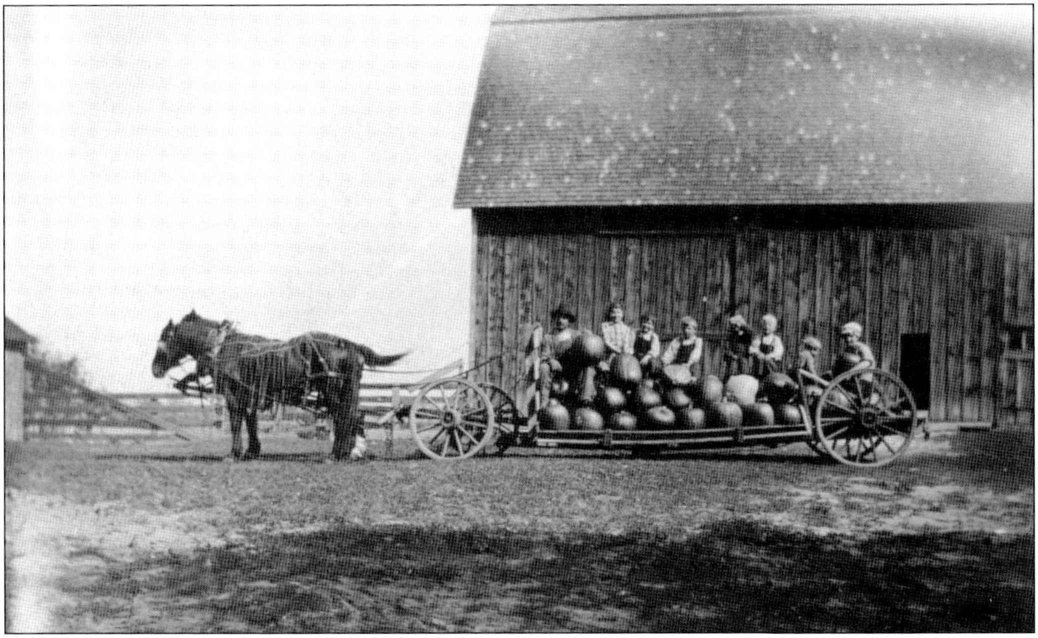

Pumpkins Grown on Buchholz Farm. Nic and Barbara Buchholz, with six of their eight children, load the farm wagon with pumpkins they have grown for sale. This was a favorite activity in the fall for the children. Irish immigrants brought the tradition of carving jack-o-lanterns for Halloween to the United States. (Courtesy of Leone Buchholz.)

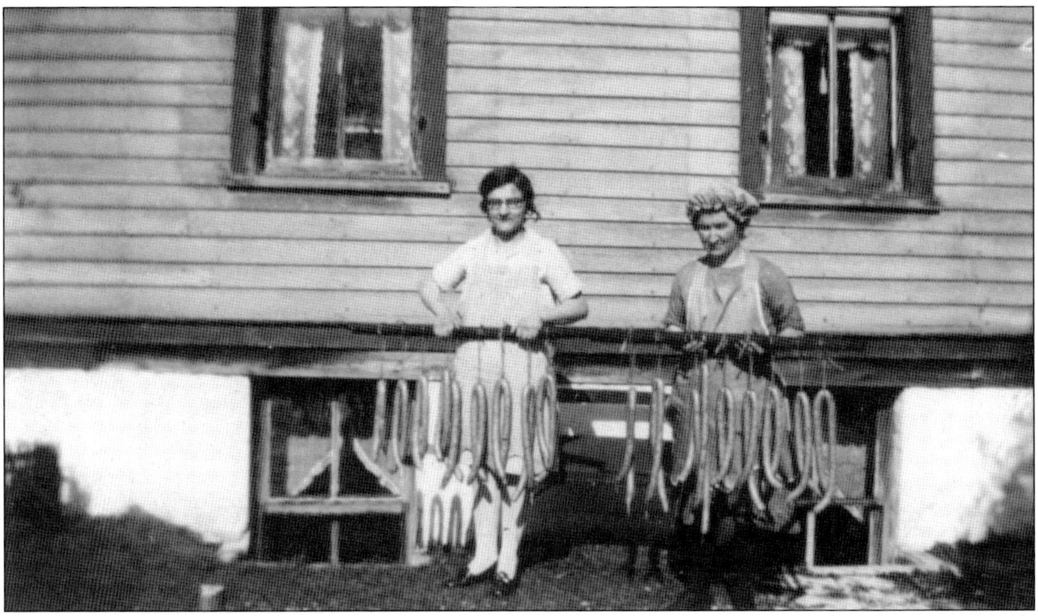

Sausage Making on Buchholz Farm. Eleanore Buchholz Weyker and Barbara Oberst Buchholz make sausage on the Buchholz farm in the 1920s. Every winter on the farm, there was butchering followed by sausage making. The women would cut, grind, mix, season, and sometimes, smoke the meat to get the final tasty product. Among the most popular types of sausage were pork sausage, *mustripen* (Luxembourg blood sausage), liver sausage, head cheese, and *suelz* (a sausage made with pigs' feet). (Courtesy of Leone Buchholz.)

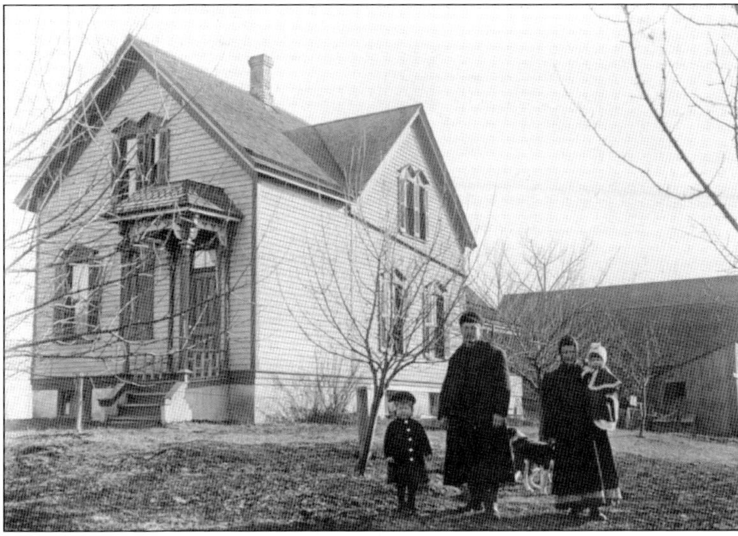

Buchholz Family Home. The Buchholz family is standing in front of their home in 1911. From left to right are Theresa, Nic, Barbara, and Joseph Buchholz. It is thought that little boys wore dresses in earlier days to make potty-training easier, as pants had fasteners and accessories that made them too complicated to take off. (Courtesy of Allen Buchholz.)

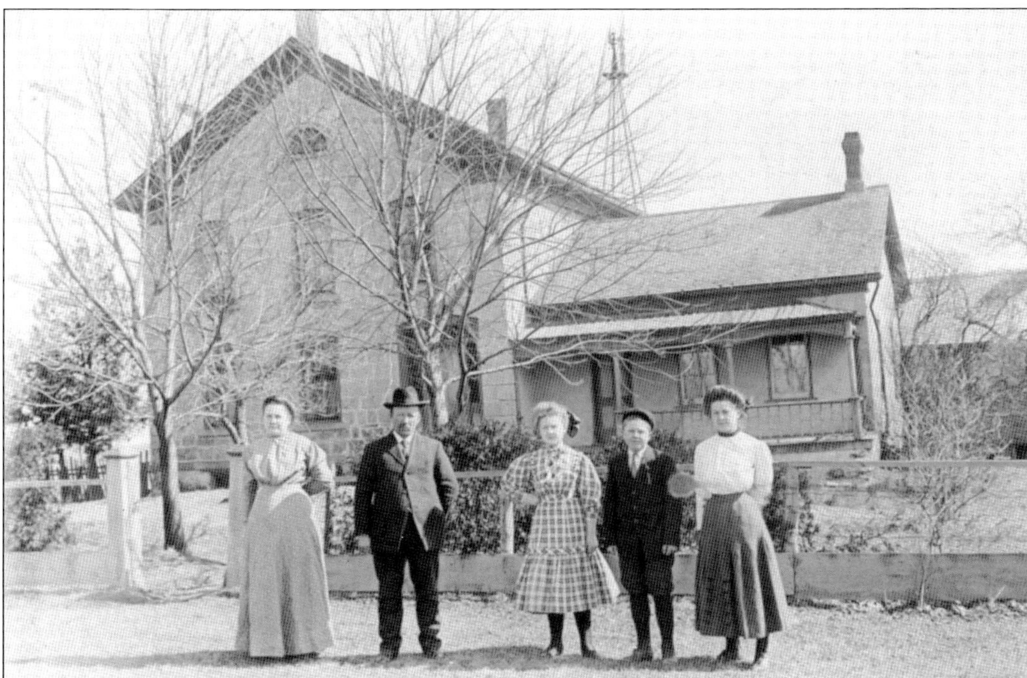

Noltze Family Farm. Pictured here is the Noltze farm in Grafton. The family members are, from left to right, Emma, Julius, Hulda, Alfred, and Flora Noltze. It appears that it is a special occasion because they are wearing their Sunday best. They stand in front of their farmhouse made of limestone, a common construction material in the area. (Courtesy of Bernice Noster.)

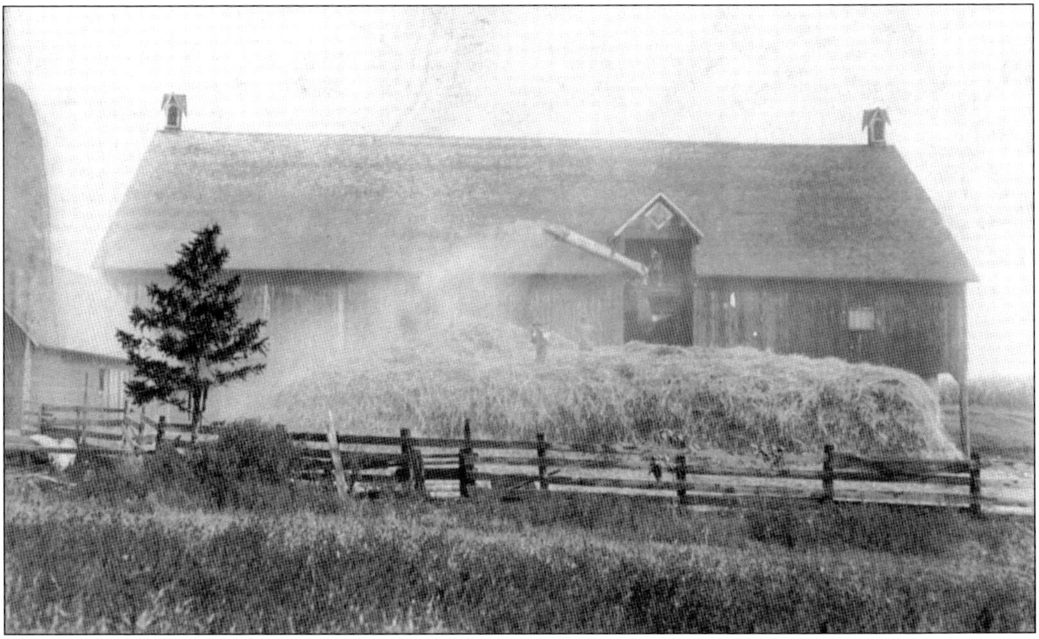

Harvesting on Sudbrink Farm. In general, farmers like the Sudbrinks in early-1900s Grafton tried to harvest hay three times per year, and they stored the hay both in the barns and in haystacks. As farms improved, larger barns were built that could store more than just tools and seed. Large barns, like the one shown here, often held massive amounts of hay stacked in the center (Courtesy of the Sudbrink family.)

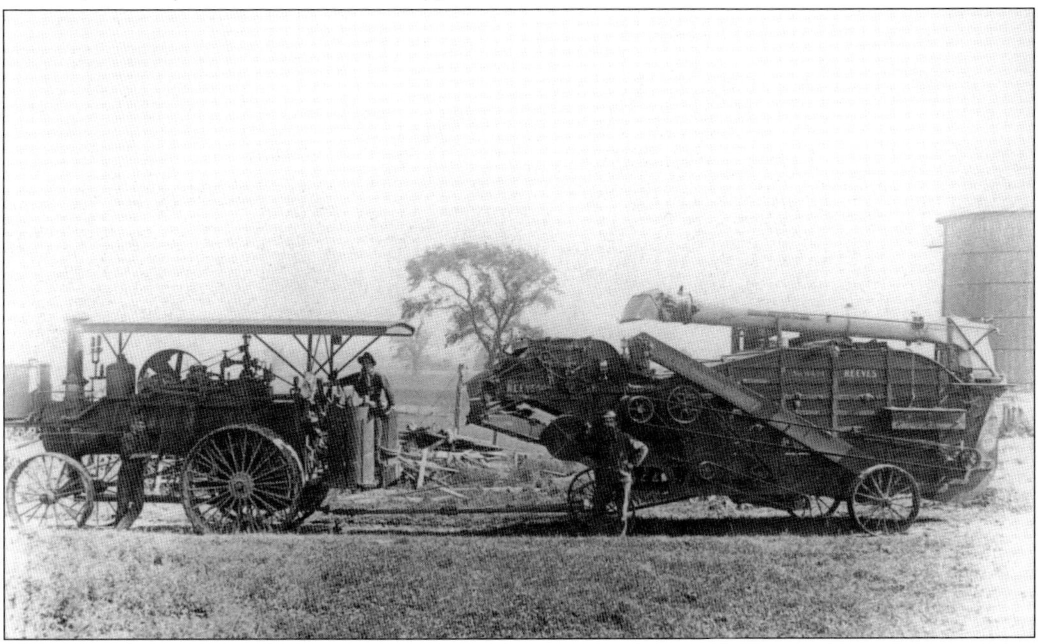

Threshing on the Sudbrink Farm. The Sudbrink brothers are shown here using a steam-engine tractor pulling a Reeves threshing machine. From left to right are Richard, Theodore, and William Sudbrink. A threshing machine removes grain seeds from the stalks and husks. It was a very valuable piece of equipment on the farm. (Courtesy of the Sudbrink family.)

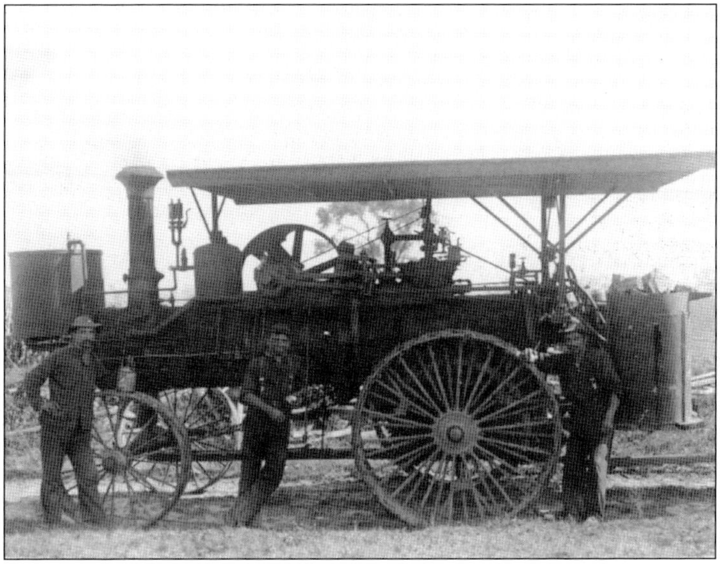

THRESHING ON THE SUDBRINK FARM. It is threshing time on the 160-acre Sudbrink farm. Pictured from left to right are William, Richard, and Theodore Sudbrink. The Sudbrink farm was north of the village of Grafton where the old interurban rail crosses over Interstate 43. In 1909, Ludwig Sudbrink sold the right-of-way through his farm for the interurban. The farm was taken down in the 1970s. (Courtesy of the Sudbrink family.)

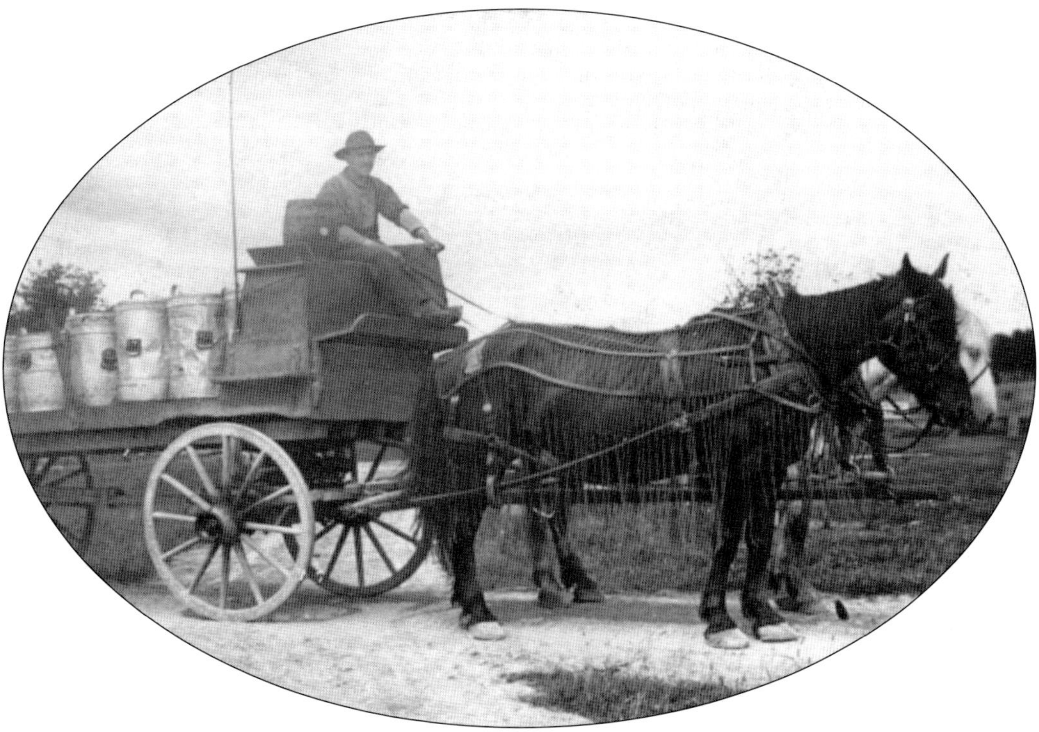

TRIP TO THE CREAMERY. In this 1906 image, Louis Sudbrink Jr. brings milk to the creamery in Grafton. The horse is wearing a leather fly cape, made from small strips of leather that have been cut and braided into a net. Its swinging movements kept flies from settling on and biting the horse. While decorative, they also served an important purpose for farmers because a fly bite could cause the horse to bolt. (Courtesy of the Sudbrink family.)

SUDBRINK WATER WAGON. This scene from the 1914 harvest on the Ludwig Sudbrink farm shows Louis Sudbrink Jr. on the family's water wagon. On many farms, this type of wagon was used to bring water out to the livestock that could not return to the barn through the day. (Courtesy of the Sudbrink family.)

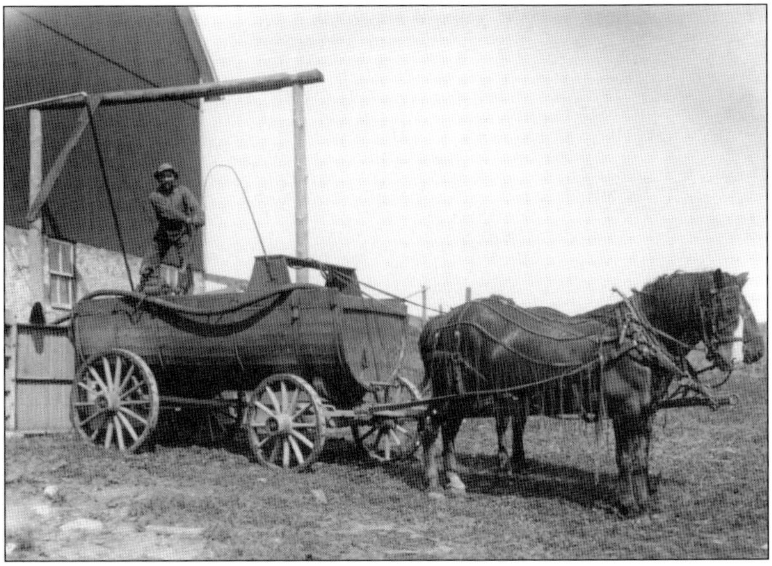

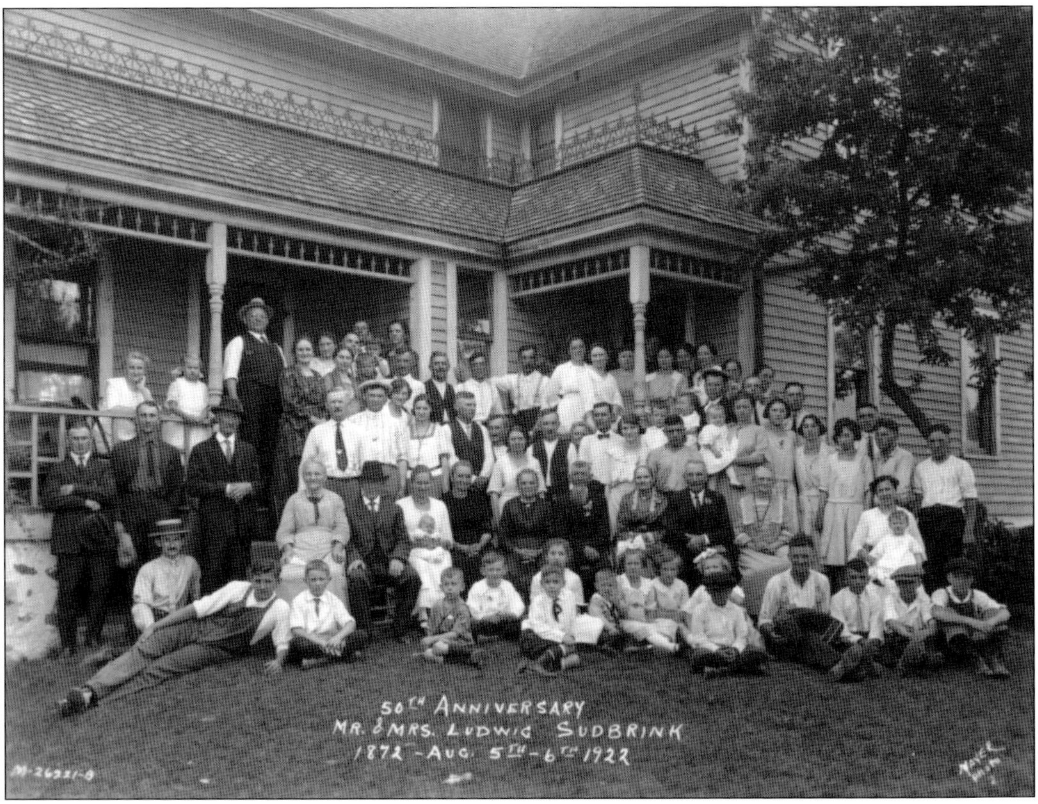

SUDBRINK 50TH ANNIVERSARY. Families often celebrated milestones on the farm. In 1922, many relatives, friends, and neighbors traveled to the farm to help celebrate the 50th anniversary of Ludwig and Augusta Schnabel Sudbrink. At the time, it was quite remarkable for a couple to reach their 50th anniversary. (Courtesy of the Sudbrink family.)

Three

COMMERCE AND INDUSTRY

Industry took center stage in Grafton from its very earliest days. Even before Wisconsin became a state in 1848, the first dam was built to power a gristmill, woolen mill, and sawmill. As the population grew, so did the need for services and products. Local businesses were born, along with Market Day, a monthly local tradition that originated in Ozaukee County. People came to the Square in downtown Grafton to buy and barter animals, tools, food, and clothing. Soon, other businesses sprang up. There were breweries, blacksmith shops, carriage painters, general stores, and a photography studio. What had often operated as a barter economy in Grafton in the past century now was becoming a cash economy in the early 1900s, and the need for a bank arose. In 1906, several businessmen started the Grafton State Bank with an initial capital of $10,000. The bank was a busy place and a boon to villagers and farmers alike, and by the end of its first year, total deposits were $65,000. As the new century began, more industries came to Grafton. The Grafton Foundry was started in 1907, and in 1911, the Jungers Stove and Range Company joined the list of Grafton industries. The Depression years were difficult, but generally, Grafton fared better than other areas of the country, with most of the village's industries surviving the hard times. During the post–World War II boom years, both the population and the number of businesses grew. In the 1950s, the Grafton Industrial Exposition showcased 18 significant industries and businesses. Today, with a population reaching nearly 12,000, Grafton has five large retailers, 17 major employers, and four leading healthcare facilities.

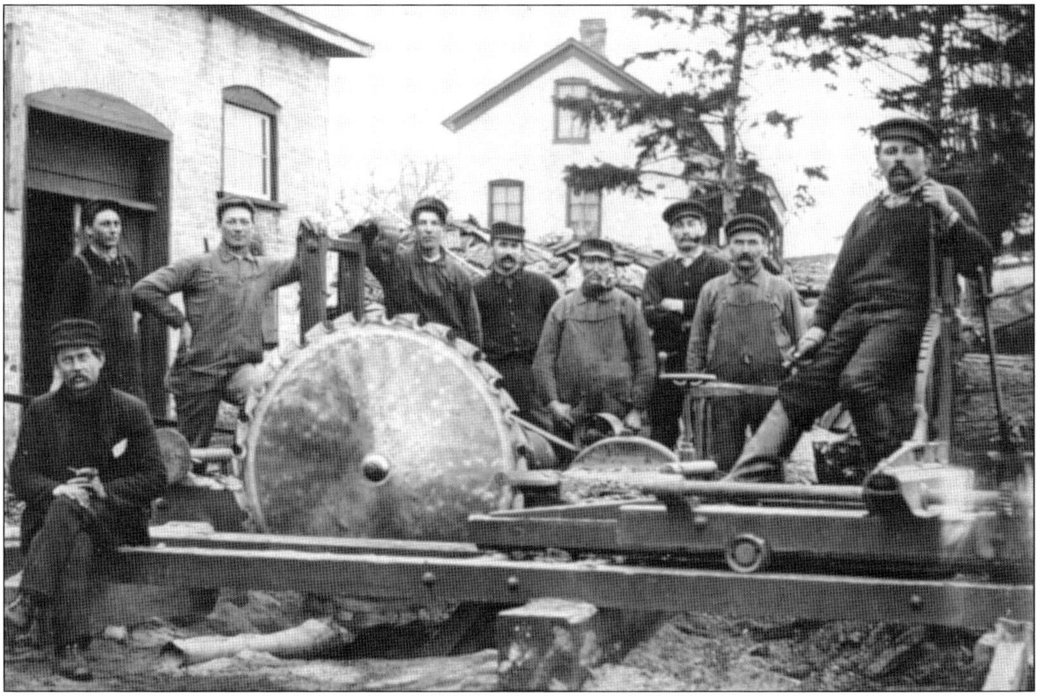

Sawmill. The first dam was built between 1841 and 1844 for the purpose of powering a sawmill on the river. The construction of a sawmill almost always preceded the construction of a gristmill, which was also the case in Grafton. The sawmill was needed to produce timbers and boards from the area's harvested trees. It also produced by-products such as sawdust, bark, and wood chips. Pictured above in 1904 are, from left to right, Lambert Van Langen (sitting), Henry Wegner, Jim Wegner, Herman Wegner, ? Hartman, unidentified (with pipe), William Viesselmann, Joe Spehn Sr., and Nick Hollrith. (Both, courtesy of Jay Van Langen.)

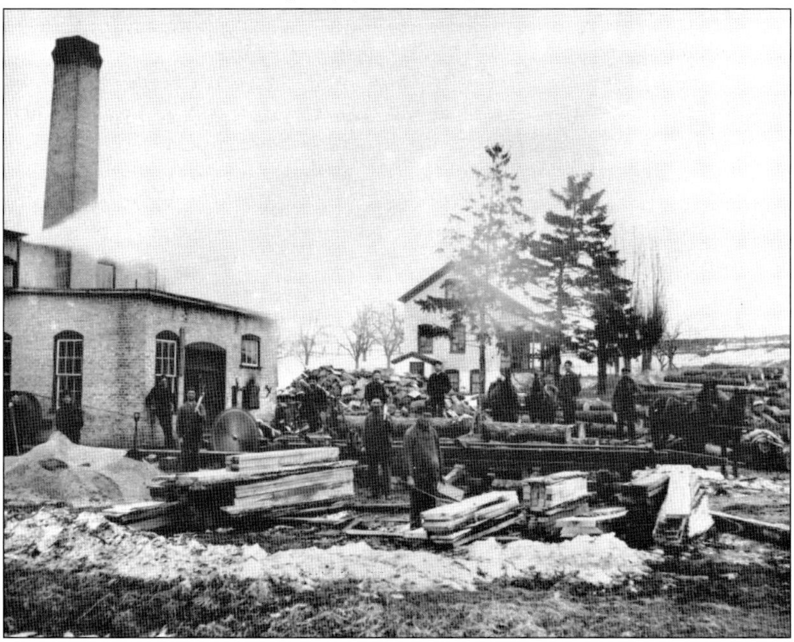

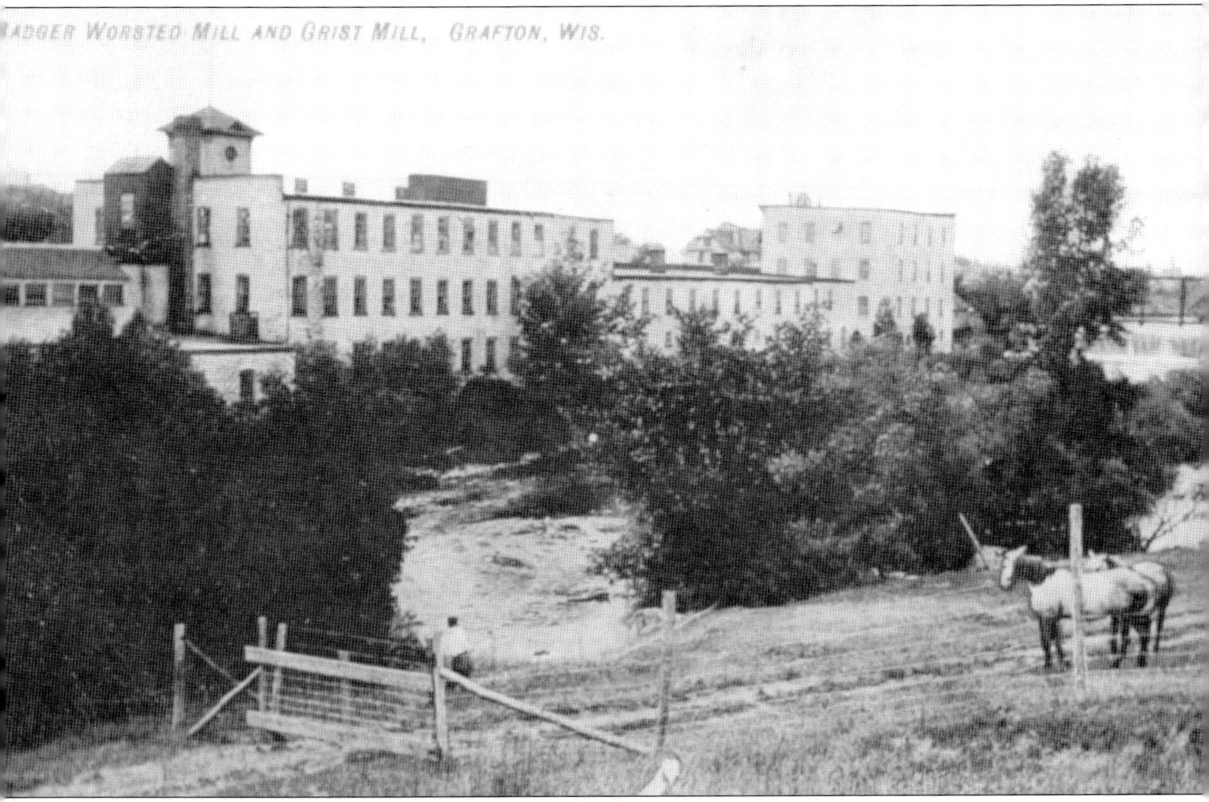

Badger Worsted Mill. Built in 1880, the Badger Worsted Mill was one of the first industries in Grafton. At the height of its production, it employed 100 people making yarns, using equipment imported from England. Its woolen yarn machinery made fuzzy, napped, curly fiber; the more modern worsted, which was smooth; and compact long-fiber yarn. Today, the worsted mill building hosts shops and artist studios. Next door and drawing power from the same dam was the gristmill. The dam was constructed in 1841, and the Grafton Flour Mill began operation in 1855. Five sets of heavy, round, grooved millstones could produce 100 barrels of flour a day, sold in Milwaukee as Lily White flour. In 1884, the flour mill was destroyed by fire. It was rebuilt and became so successful that by 1904, shifts at the company were running around the clock. Flour, however, was not its only important product. There were generators in the basement of the mill that provided the first electricity for Grafton courtesy of a raceway that diverted water from the dam to a water wheel. It was said around town that a dry season meant dim lights. (Courtesy of the Ozaukee County Historical Society.)

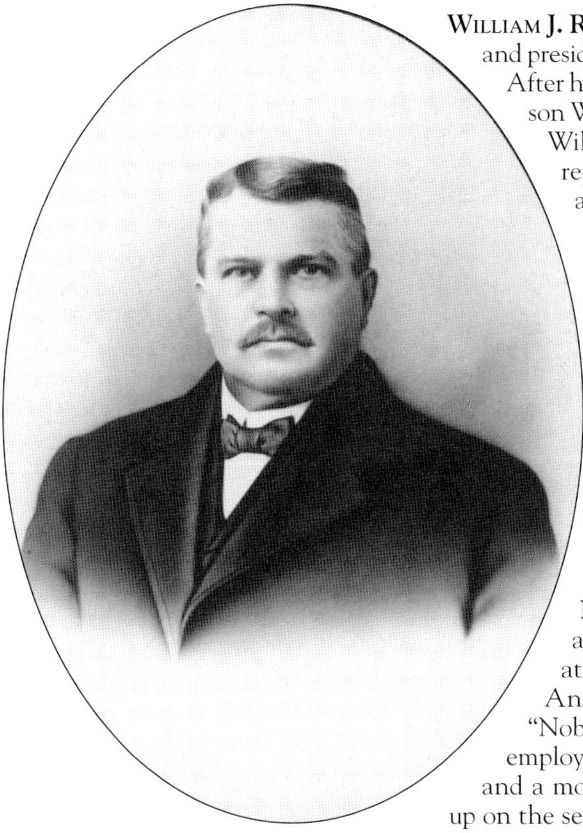

WILLIAM J. ROEBKEN. William J. Roebken was the owner and president of the Badger Worsted Mill in Grafton. After his death, ownership of the mill passed to his son William H. Roebken and grandsons Stanley, William A., Dean, and Howard Roebken. It was reported that the mill operation was always abreast of changes in the textile industry and imported the best machinery available from England. The mill closed in the 1980s. (Courtesy of Nic Schanen.)

BADGER WORSTED MILLS PICNIC. Employees and their families gather for a photograph at the 1916 Badger Worsted Mills picnic. An account from the time proudly stated, "Nobody has been discharged in ten years. Nine employees have been there for over 22 years each and a mother and her two grown daughters work up on the second floor." (Courtesy of Nic Schanen.)

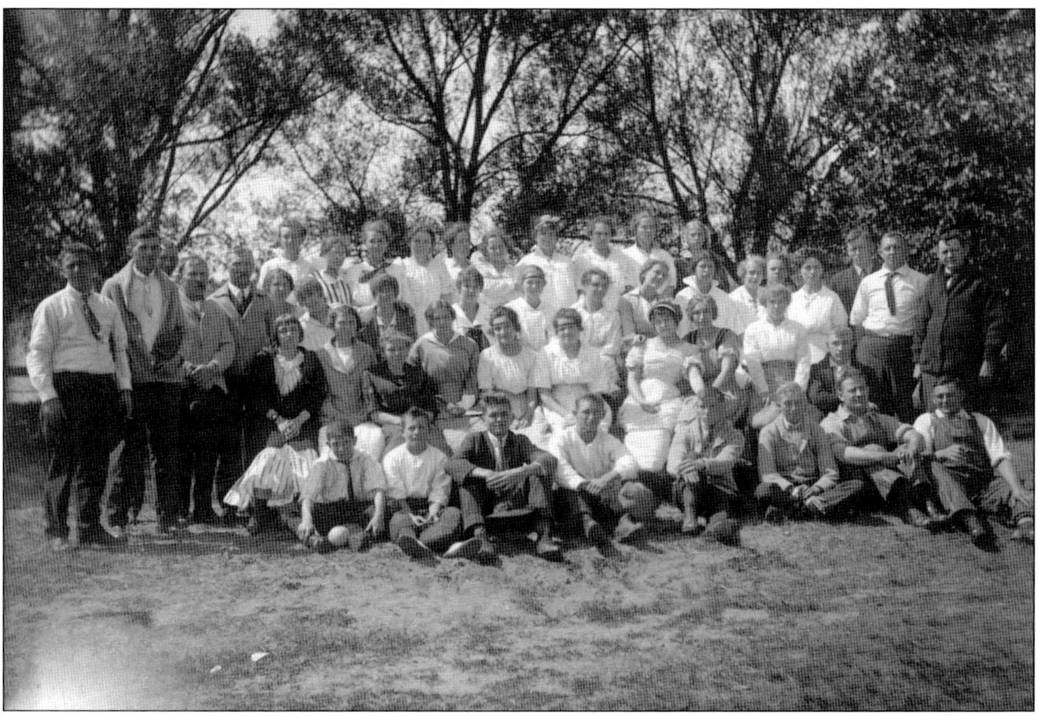

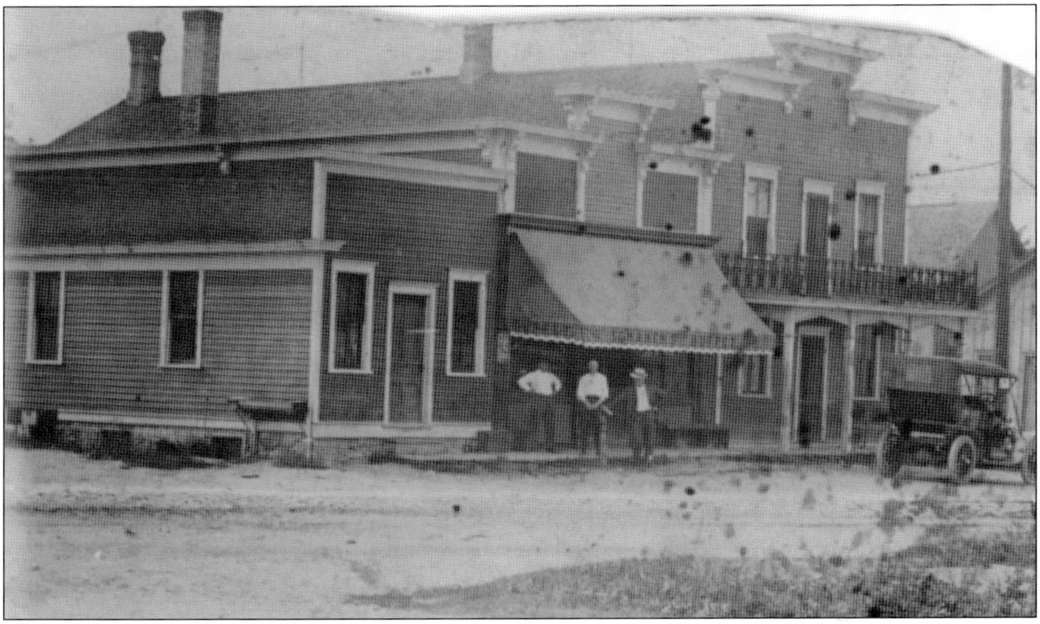

THE SCHANEN HOTEL. The Schanen family purchased this hotel in the early 1900s and ran it for four generations: Nic J. Schanen, Frank and Florence Schanen, Frank Jr. and Jeanne Schanen, and David M. Schanen. The family had their living quarters upstairs in addition to boarding rooms and a banquet hall. The building also contained a restaurant, barbershop, and a bowling alley downstairs. Over time, more alleys were added until there was a total of 12. The hotel provided a beer garden and live music every Saturday night and was a gathering place for many local businesses and for community events. It had its share of excitement too. In the early 1930s, two armed gangsters entered the hotel and stole the slot machines. The Schanen brothers jumped in their car and gave chase, traveling south on Highway 57. When the gangsters pulled into a driveway and fired a few shots, the brothers jumped in their car and headed back to Grafton. (Both, courtesy of the Gramoll family.)

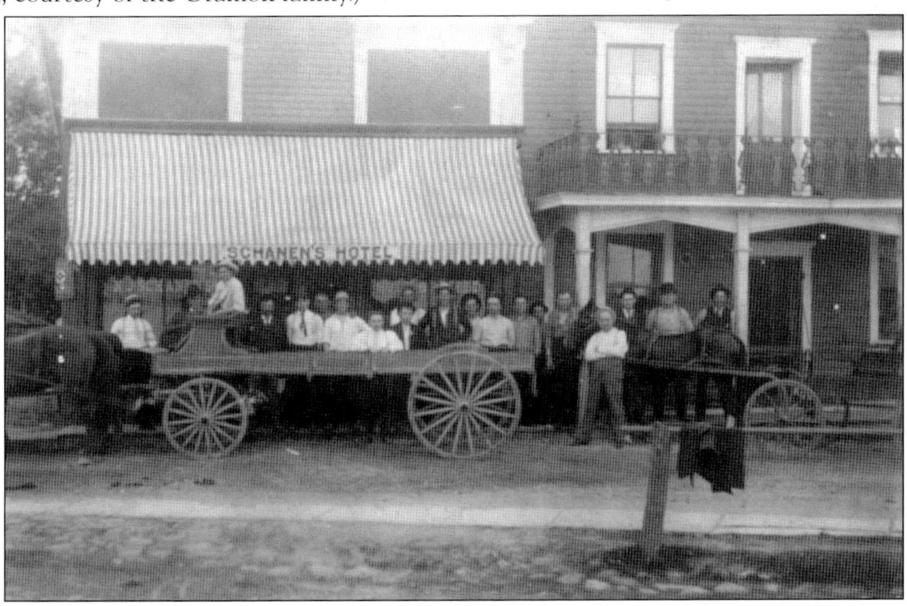

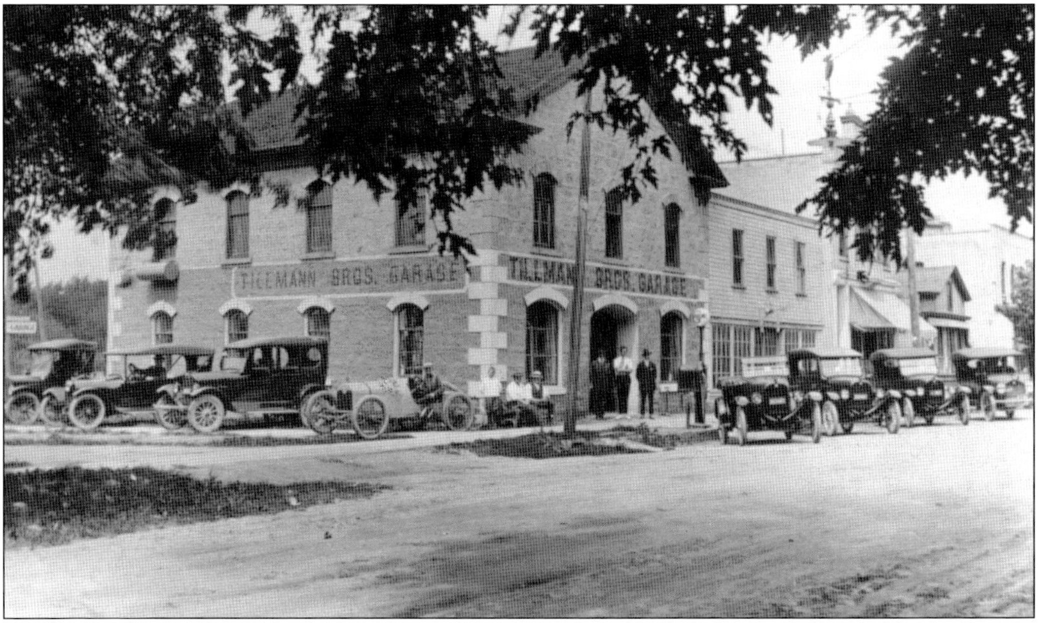

TILLMANN BROTHERS. Tillmann Brothers was an agency for Briscoe automobiles in Ozaukee and Washington Counties in the early 1900s. An ad in a 1916 newspaper advertised a four-cylinder, five-passenger touring car for $725. At the end of the ad is the line, "Get a Briscoe and give us your Horses and Cattle in Exchange." The equipment for the touring car included side curtains, one-man mohair top and dust cover, and a robe rail and footrest. The shop also did auto repairing. (Courtesy of the Grafton Chamber of Commerce.)

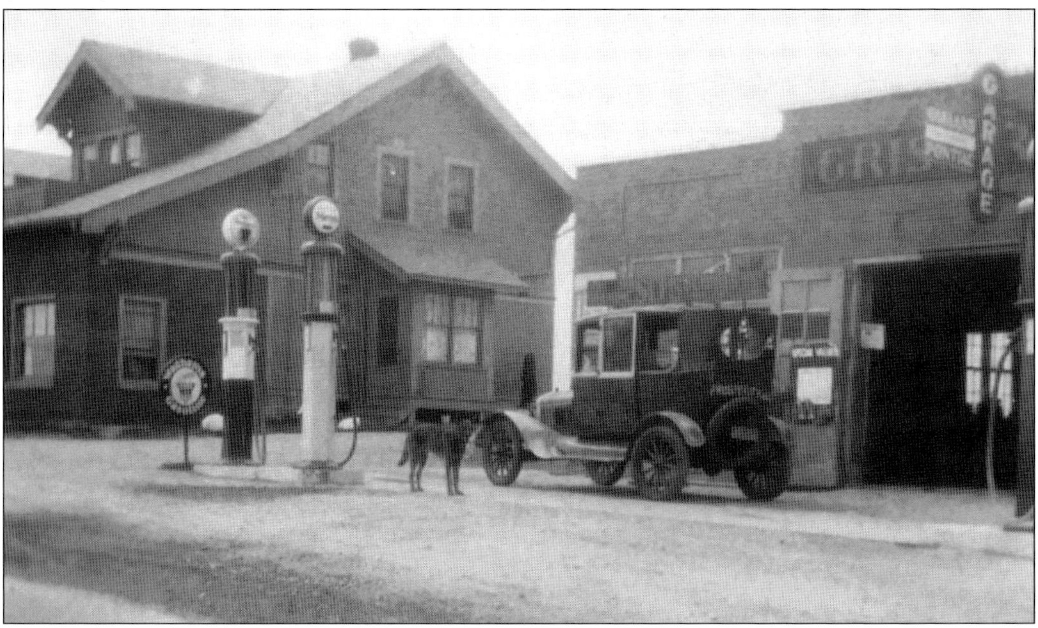

GRISAR GAS STATION. This gas station was operated by Herb and Ed Grisar, on the southwest corner of Highway 60 and Port Washington Road. To the left is the Schmit home. Both buildings have since been torn down, and the gas station's former location is approximately in the middle of the current intersection. (Courtesy of the Grafton Historical Society.)

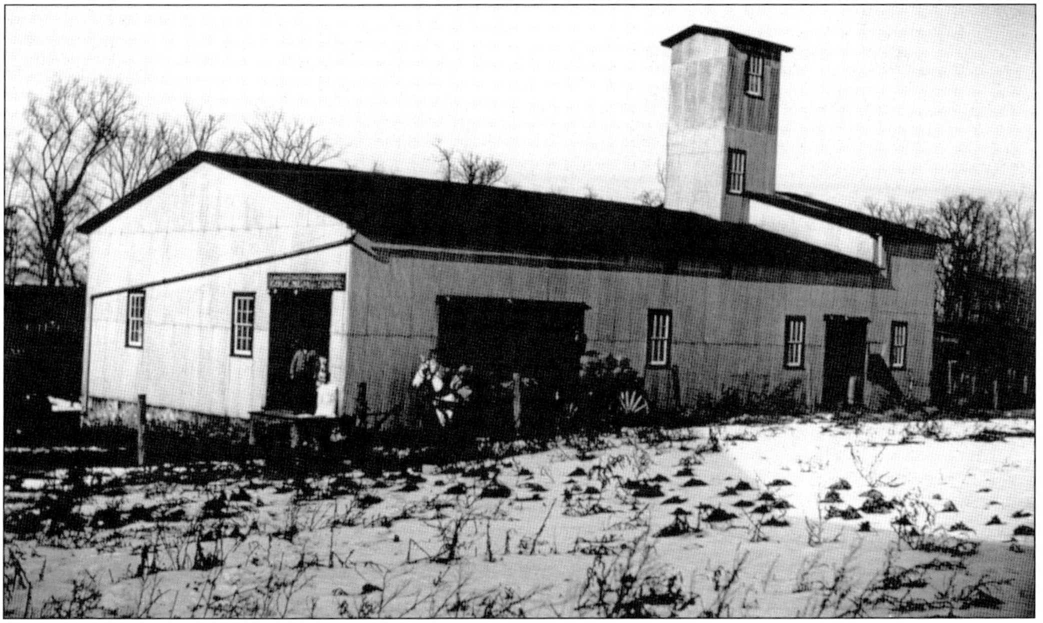

Ulao Coal and Feed. John Hadler stands in the doorway of the Ulao Coal and Feed elevator east of Grafton. The grain elevator was designed to store grain. Before the grain elevator, grain was usually handled in bags rather than in bulk. Note the sign above the door that reads, "Gold Midas Flour." (Courtesy of Arnold Kaul Sr.)

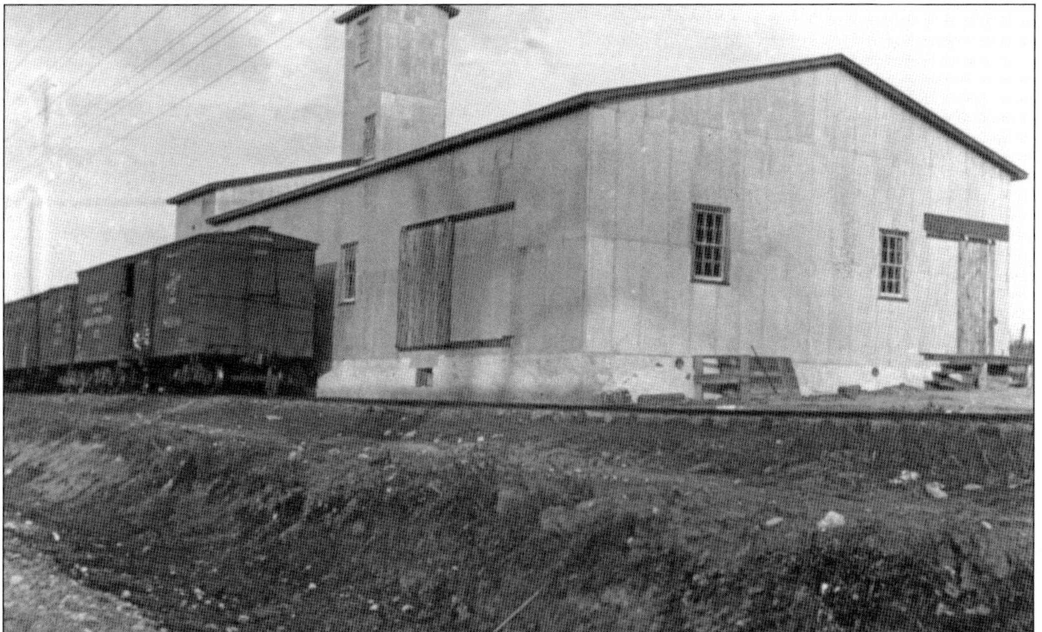

Train at Ulao Depot. A train has pulled up to the grain elevator at the Ulao Coal and Feed depot. The train picked up grain from the grain elevator and brought in goods and products for the farmers. The farmers came to the depot building to buy and receive their merchandise. (Courtesy of Arnold Kaul Sr.)

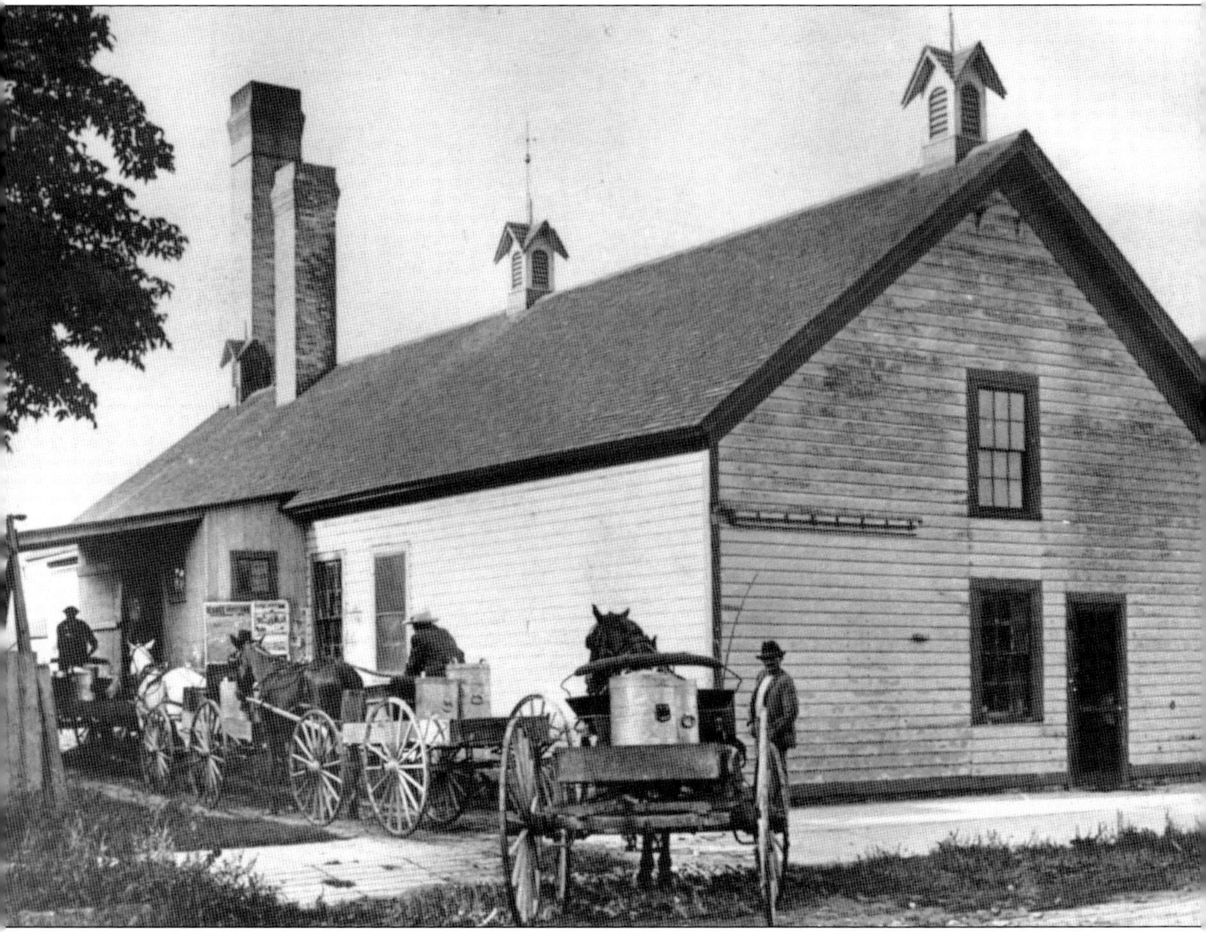

Grafton Creamery. The Grafton Creamery operated in the village for many years beginning in the late 1800s. It was run by the Gerlach family and was located on Bridge Street. Farmers brought milk in 20-gallon cans to be separated. In its heyday, the line of farmers bringing their milk would stretch for blocks. The creamery separated the milk into cream and skimmed milk. The cream was processed into butter by a churn operated by a steam engine and, along with the skimmed milk, was returned back to the farmers. In later years, the creamery may have done a different kind of processing. Legend has it that during Prohibition, it operated as a distillery until federal agents raided the illegal enterprise and closed it down. (Courtesy of the Ozaukee County Historical Society.)

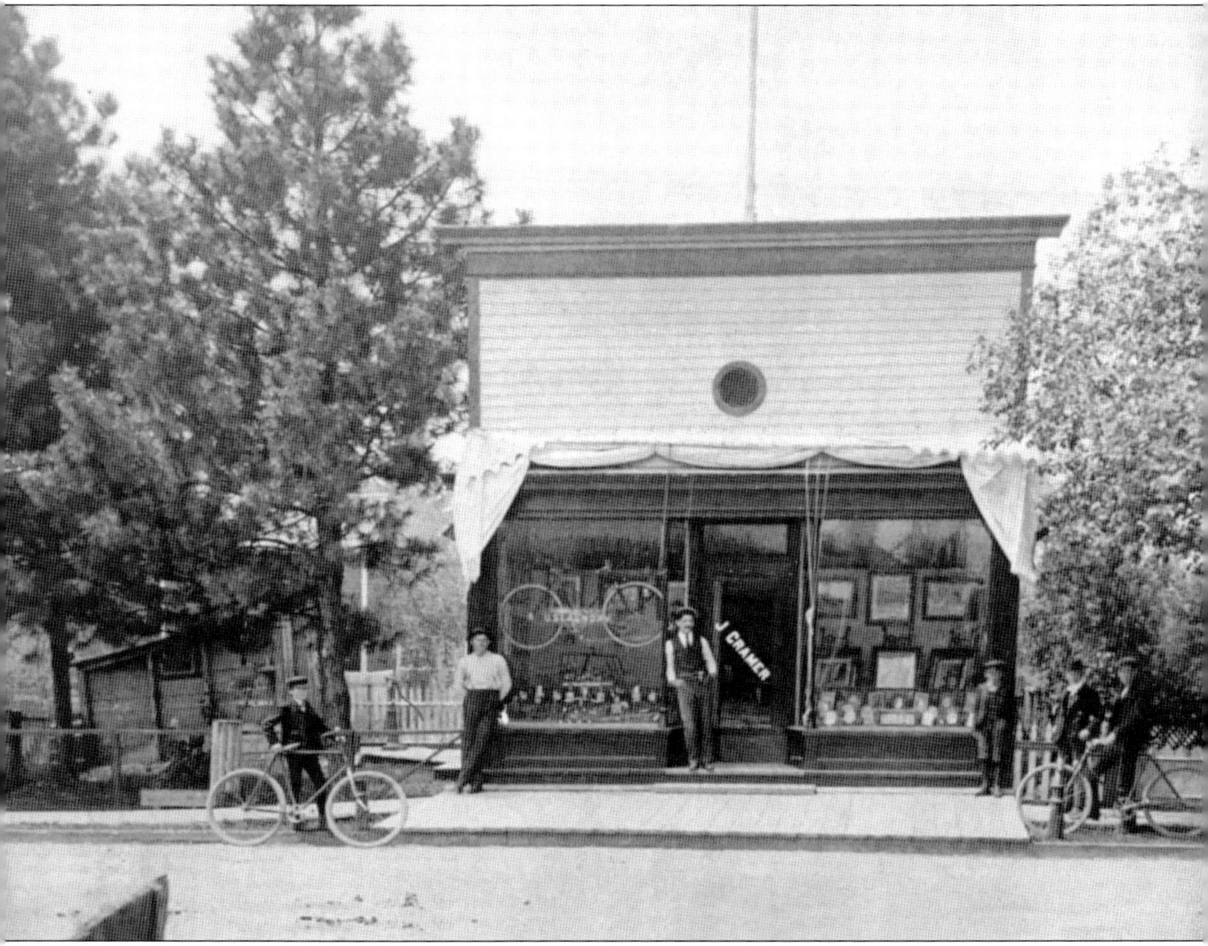

CRAMER PHOTOGRAPHY STUDIO. Following his service in the Civil War, Joseph Cramer started his photography studio in downtown Grafton after purchasing the lot for $11 in 1872. His son John Cramer took over the studio in 1898. It appears from this photograph that it was also a bike shop for a time. Edward Laabs purchased the studio in 1903 and made portraits of Grafton families under the Laabs name. Walter Burhop worked for Laabs as a teenager, took over the studio in 1926, and continued to make photographs under the Laabs name. Michael Matthies carried on the art of photography beginning in 1976 as Photography by Michael, owner of the oldest continuously operating studio in the United States. The building originally had gas lights, a hand pump, and a red glass window in the darkroom. There were also skylights in the roof to provide proper lighting for indoor photography. Note the board sidewalks, dirt road, and hitching posts. (Courtesy of the Grafton Historical Society.)

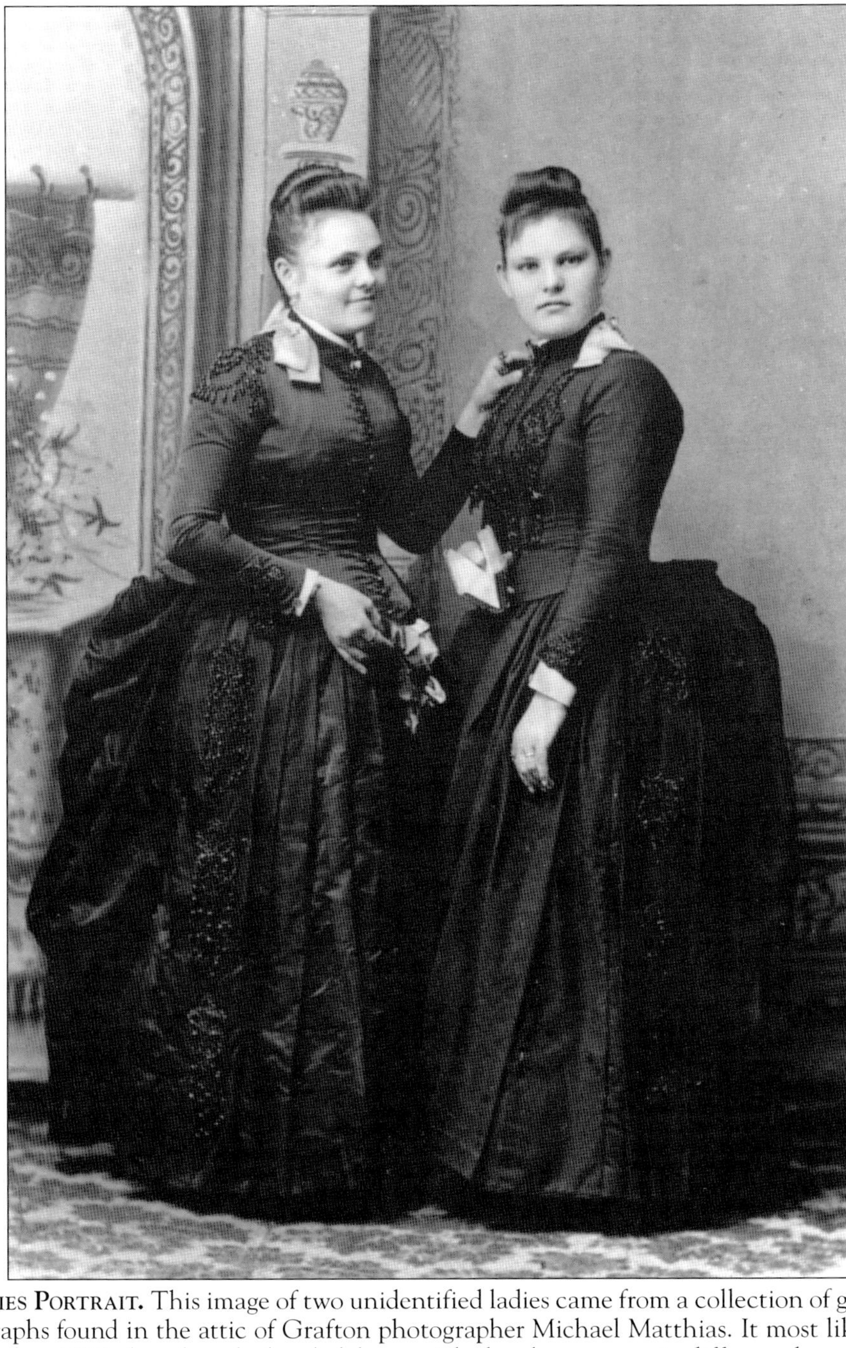

Matthies Portrait. This image of two unidentified ladies came from a collection of glass-plate photographs found in the attic of Grafton photographer Michael Matthias. It most likely dates from the late 1800s, based on the bustled dresses. The bustle was worn in different shapes for most of the 1870s and 1880s, with a short period of non-bustled, flat-backed dresses from 1878 to 1882. In the early stages of the fashion, the fullness to the back of the skirts was carried quite low and often fanned out to create a train. Many of the portrait glass plates were scanned and printed as part of a local Girl Scout troop project. It was a treasure trove of pictures of early Grafton and Ozaukee County residents, but unfortunately, most of the individuals in the pictures could no longer be identified. (Courtesy of Michael Matthies.)

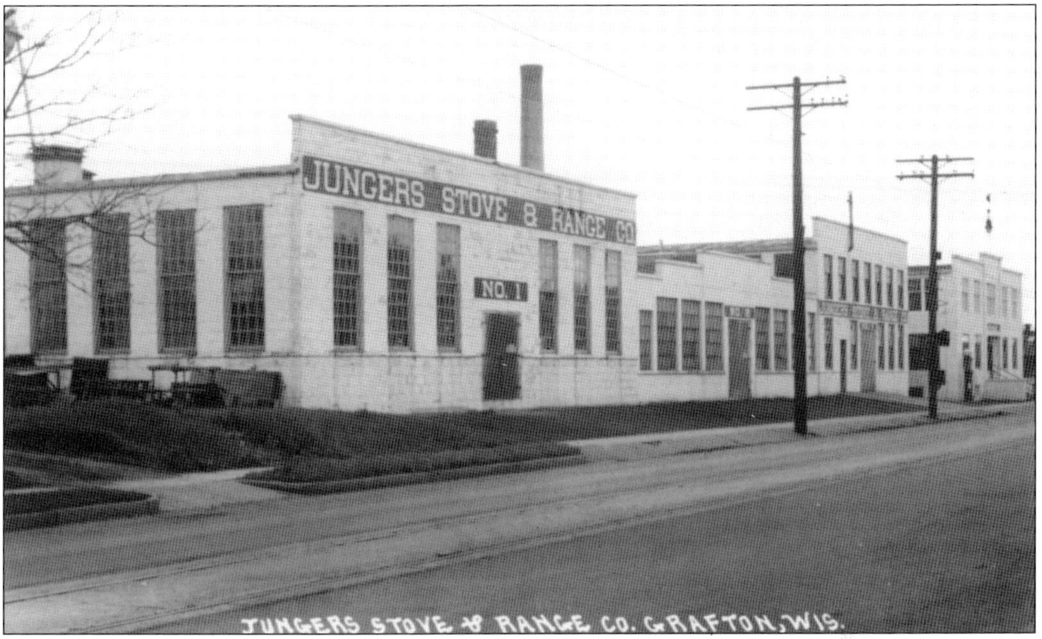

The Jungers Company. The Jungers Company was founded in 1911 by John Jungers. From 1911 until 1933, the company made coal and wood-burning cooking ranges. An ad from 1922 boasted that the Jungers stove had "all nickel platings, rounded seamless corners and a heavy cast iron wall covering the back of the oven." In 1933, manufacture of wickless oil burner units began, and in 1937, the Blufire forced-air, oil-burning units were designed and manufactured. John Jungers also served in the Wisconsin State Assembly in 1927. He died in his home in Grafton as the result of a stroke in 1947. (Above, courtesy of Allen Buchholz; right, courtesy of USS Liberty Memorial Library.)

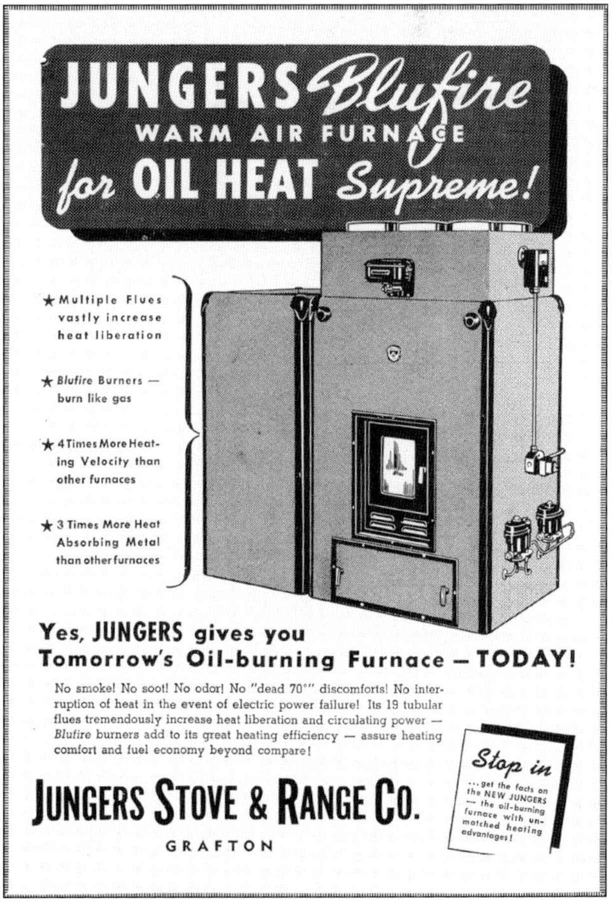

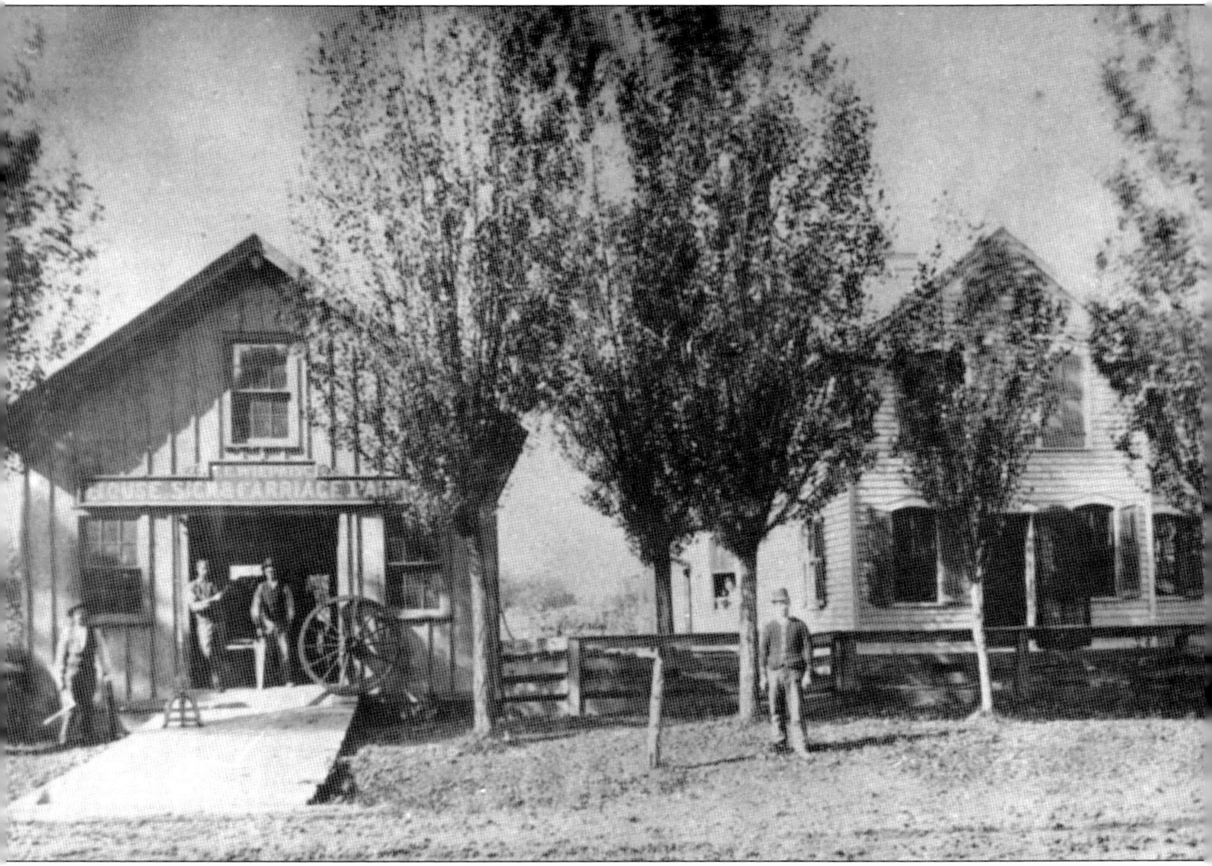

THE WIEPKING HOUSE SIGN AND CARRIAGE PAINTING SHOP. Wiepking House Sign and Carriage Painting Shop was located two blocks north of what is now the Highway 60 and Highway 57 intersection in Grafton. The original method of carriage painting that the shop would have used was the lead color method. Pumice was used along with a pail of clean water, a sponge, a chamois skin, and a water tool. Several coats of paint were applied to the carriage before the finishing coat, which was varnish. Varnishing was a critical part of the process, and a special room was needed. The room had to be controlled for ventilation and heat for the varnish to dry properly. This Grafton carriage painter took great pride in his work, viewing it as true art. (Courtesy of the Grafton Chamber of Commerce.)

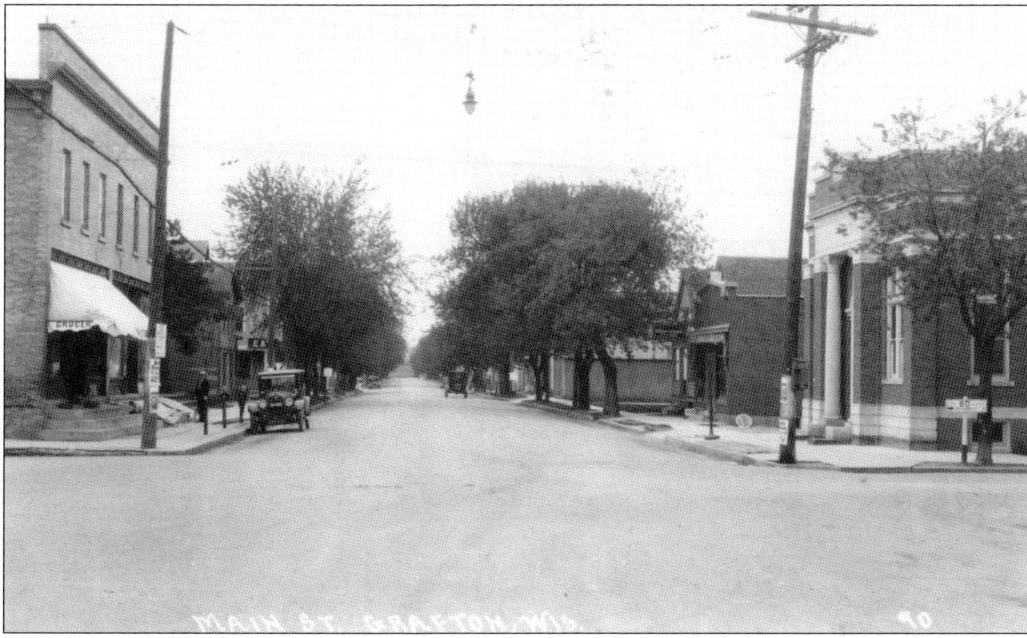

Grafton State Bank. In 1906, the Grafton State Bank was started by William Weber, Frederick C. Mintzlaff, William Horener, and others. They met with Louis Zaun, who had started other banks in Wisconsin and Iowa and began with $6,800 from Zaun himself and $10,000 from 15 local farmers and businessmen who purchased stock for $100 per share. At the end of the first year, the total deposits were $65,000. This is the second Grafton State Bank building erected by Louis Zaun, then president, in 1926. The new bank boasted two impressive limestone columns in the front. The lot, building, furniture, and fixtures cost less than $25,000. It is reported that unlike many other banks, the Grafton State Bank weathered the storm of the Great Depression and prospered. (Above, courtesy of Allen Buchholz; below, courtesy of the Sudbrink family.)

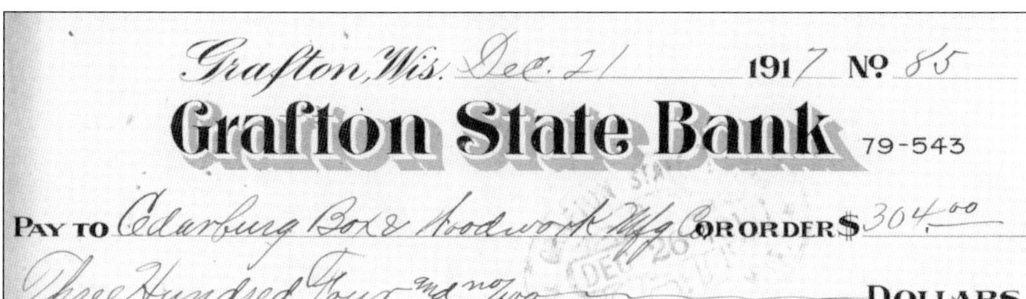
Grafton, Wis. Dec. 21 1917 No. 85

Grafton State Bank 79-543

Pay to Cedarburg Box & Woodwork Mfg Co. or order $304.00

Three Hundred Four and no/100 Dollars

Otto Kohlwey.

RED WING CO.

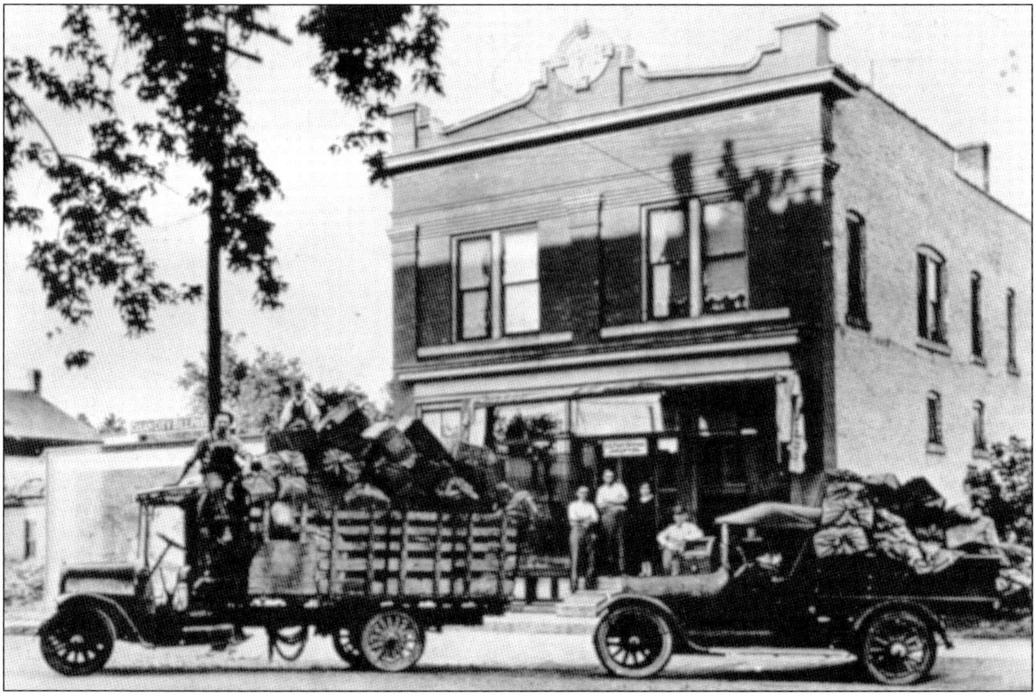

Post Office Records Day. The building at 1316 Twelfth Avenue was built in 1912 and operated as a post office. In later years, it was an IGA grocery store and dime store. Shown here are records produced at the Paramount Record facility awaiting shipment at the Grafton Post Office. (Courtesy of the Grafton Historical Society.)

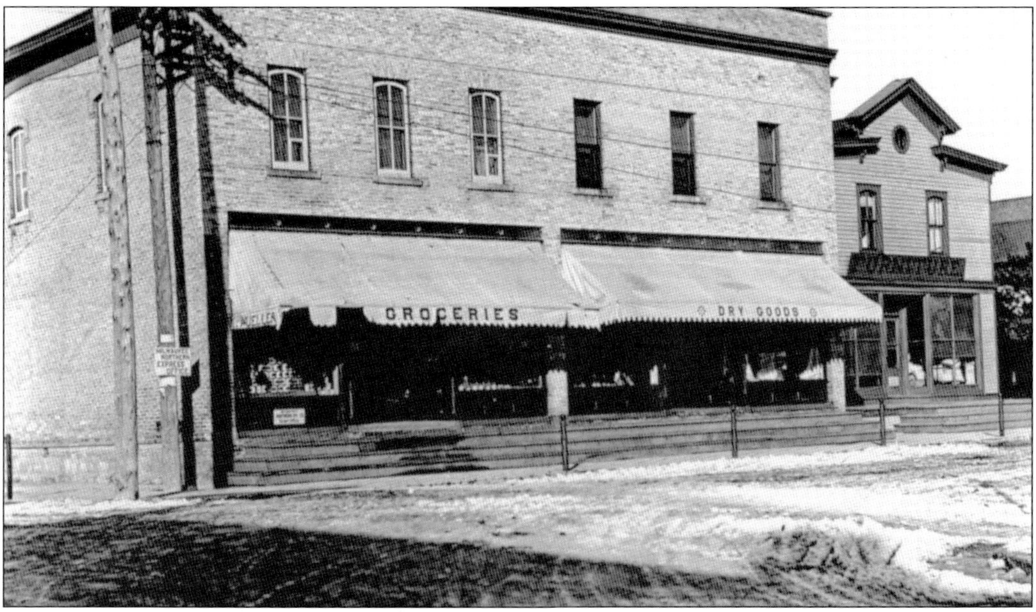

Mueller-Hauer Dry Goods. This building is at the corner of Wisconsin Avenue and Bridge Street. At the time, it was the Mueller-Heuer dry goods and grocery store. Note the Mueller name on the side awning. It was also a location to purchase tickets for the Milwaukee Northern Express. (Courtesy of Arnold Kaul Sr.)

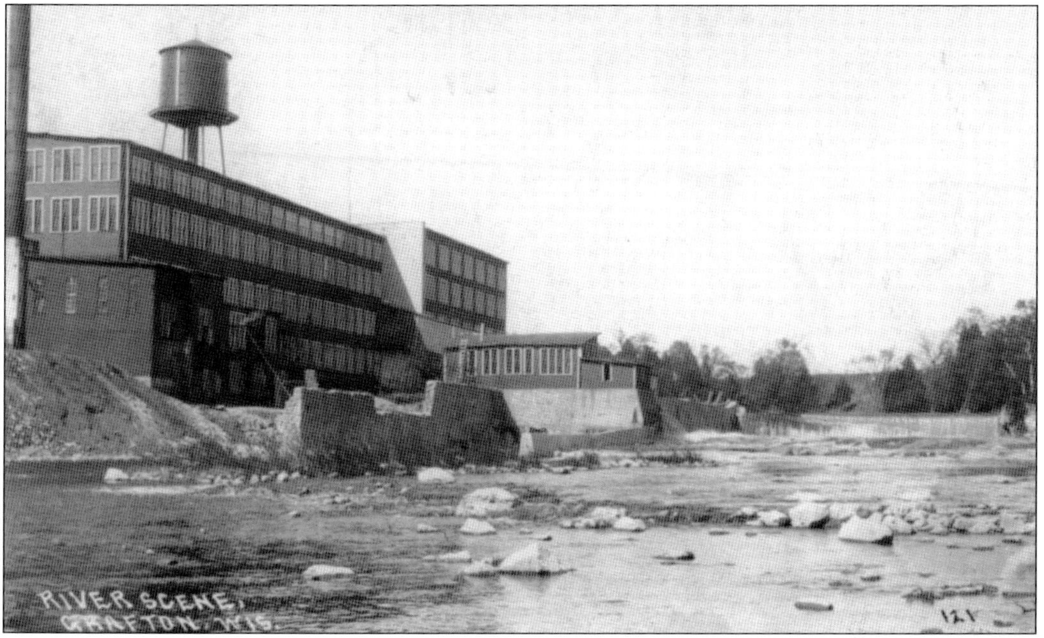

CHAIR FACTORY. The chair factory was one of the early manufacturers attracted to the power provided by the dam on the Milwaukee River. It was built in 1848 to manufacture chairs and bedsteads. It was originally housed in a wooden, four-story building. The factory was known by a variety of names during its existence, including the Milwaukee Chair Company and the Northern Chair Company. (Courtesy of the Grafton Historical Society.)

CHAIR FACTORY INTERIOR. By the early 1900s, the chair factory was turning out more than 40 dozen chairs daily. Several large tenement houses owned by the factory provided living quarters for the workers, many of whom were Slovenian. By 1912, nine Slovenian families and 117 single Slovenian men lived in Grafton. The workers shown here are not identified. (Courtesy of the Grafton Historical Society.)

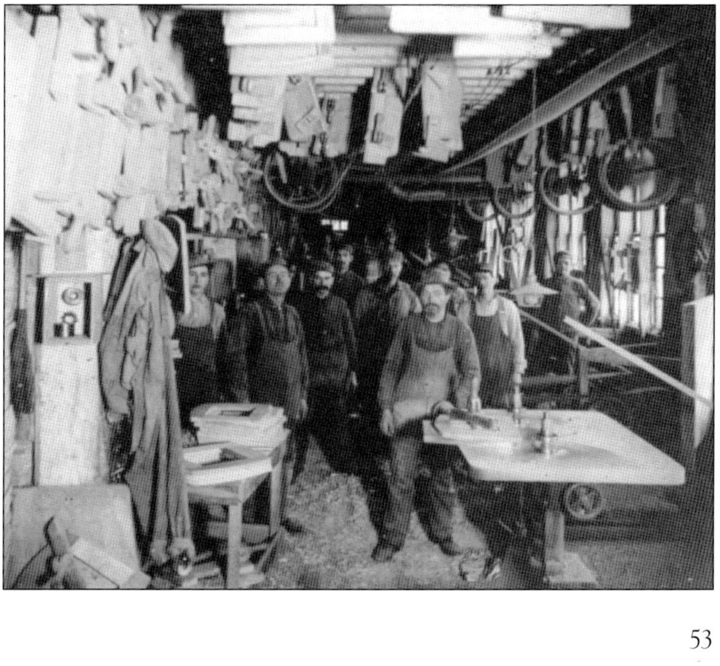

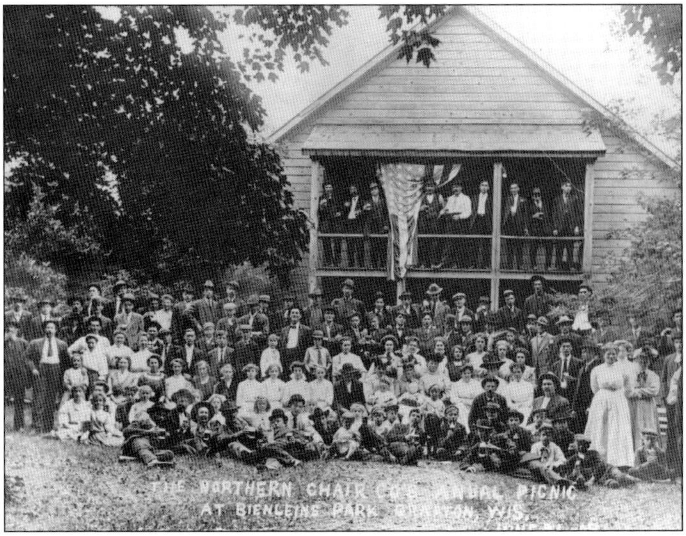

Chair Factory Picnic. Employees of the Grafton Chair factory take a moment from their picnic activities to pose for this picture in Bienlein Park, at Twelfth Avenue and Falls Road adjacent to the chair factory complex. In the early 1900s, it was common for manufacturers to hold summer picnics for employees in local parks. Andrew Beinlein owned and operated the park, which included a dance hall and bar. (Courtesy of the Grafton Historical Society.)

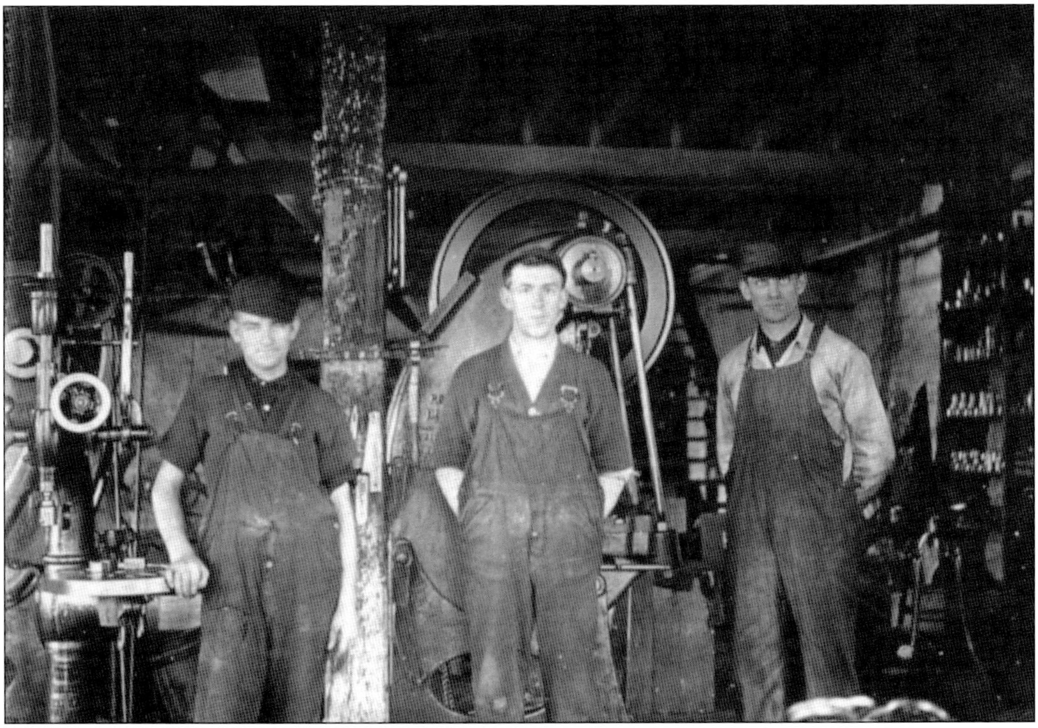

Spaeth Blacksmith Shop. The Spaeth blacksmith shop was on Thirteenth Avenue. Pictured here in 1914 are, from left to right, unidentified, Joe Lorenz, and Bill Hinz. The blacksmith shop was next to their home, and many people remember the hospitality of Mrs. Spaeth. She would often bring out fresh-baked *kuchen* for customers, as they enjoyed her flower garden with its many varieties of gladiolas. (Courtesy of the Grafton Historical Society.)

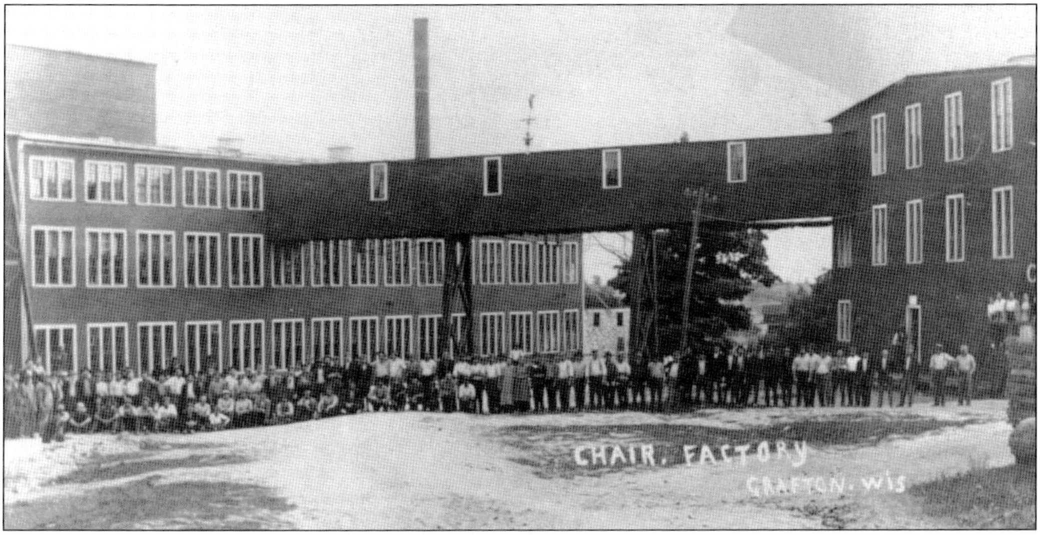

New York Recording Studios. The Wisconsin Chair company founded the New York Recording Laboratories and retooled its factory to make 78-rpm records for use on phonographs. The first record was made from a New York City studio master in June 1917. Wax masters of blues recordings were shipped to Grafton in dry ice from Chicago and New York to prevent them from bubbling when the weather turned warm. Originally, Bill Weiss did most of the hauling with a horse and wagon. Later, Fred Port Sr., who owned a truck line, did the job. The recording studio operated from 1917 to the 1930s with 114 employees. Some of the famous blues artists who traveled to Grafton to record music were Amos and Andy, Bessie Smith, and Gene Autry. Paramount labels were black, with the words "electrically recorded," in capital letters on either side and almost on top of the spindle hole. Grafton recordings show a master number that starts with the letter "L." (Above, courtesy of the Ed Rappold Photograph Collection at the Cedarburg Cultural Center; below, courtesy of Nic Schanen.)

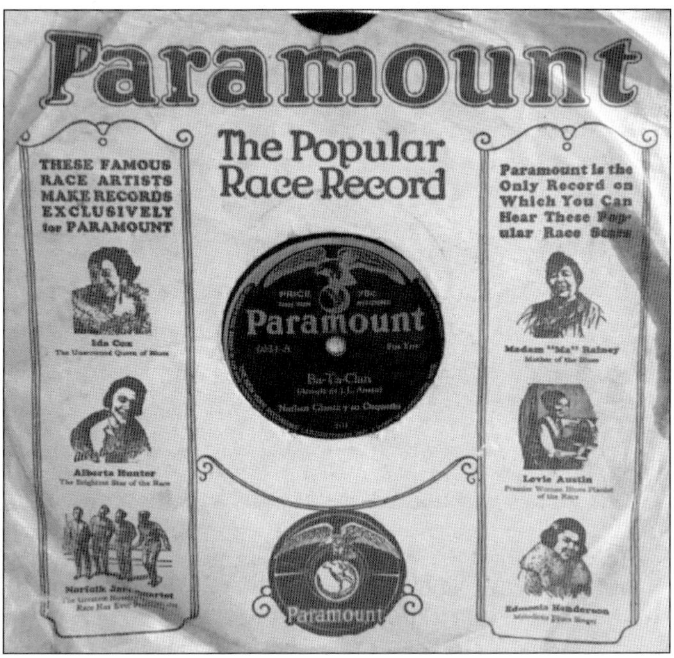

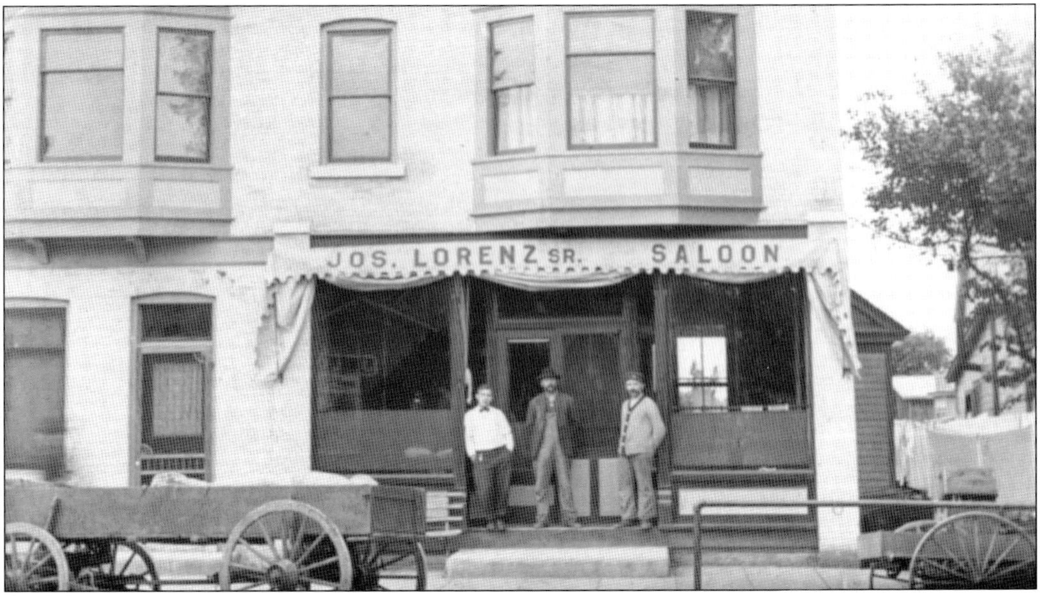

Joseph Lorenz Sr. Saloon. The Joseph Lorenz Sr. Saloon was at 1216–1218 Bridge Street. The building still stands, and most of the upper-story architectural detail remains. It also housed saloons run by John Simon, Joseph Spehn, and Martin Barth before Lorenz bought it in 1907. He removed the old tavern and had a cream-city brick one built on the site, adding a second story in 1911. In this scene from the late 1800s, the barkeep and patrons are not identified. (Courtesy of the Grafton Historical Society.)

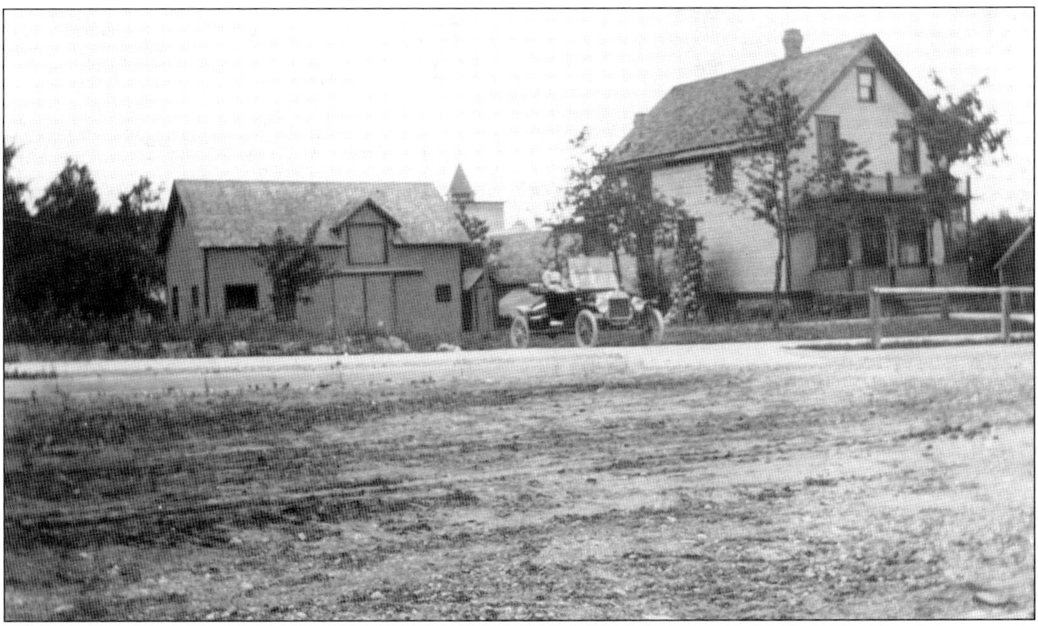

Dr. Joseph Oberst. The home of Grafton veterinarian Dr. Joseph Oberst was at 1327 Thirteenth Avenue, south of Bridge Street. Dr. Oberst was born in Belgium, Wisconsin, and moved to Grafton in 1902, where he began his practice. In 1910, he and his wife, Mary, purchased this property. Dr. Oberst, his wife, and son are pictured in 1920 in their Model T Ford. The house is still standing. (Courtesy of Leone Buchholz.)

Grafton Brewery. There were many trade names for the brewery at 1230 Twelfth Avenue in Grafton. The Grafton Brewery, owned by William Weber, operated from 1890 to 1920. William was the son of Cedarburg brewer John Weber. Beer was sold in both bottles and kegs, and early bottles had the company stamp imprinted into the glass mold. Weber sold lager beer and Weiss (white), which was a champagne-like beer. Near beer was produced during the Prohibition years. William Weber sold the Grafton Brewing Company to George Blessing in 1920. It operated until 1933, when it briefly operated as the Grafton Brewing Company before it became the Wisconsin Cooperative Brewery in 1935. In 1934, production reached 5,367 barrels. Delivery of barrels of beer from the early Grafton Brewing Company is pictured below. William Weber was also the first fire chief in Grafton and served as county board chairman. (Right, courtesy of Vivian Schiff Laabs; below, courtesy of the Grafton Historical Society.)

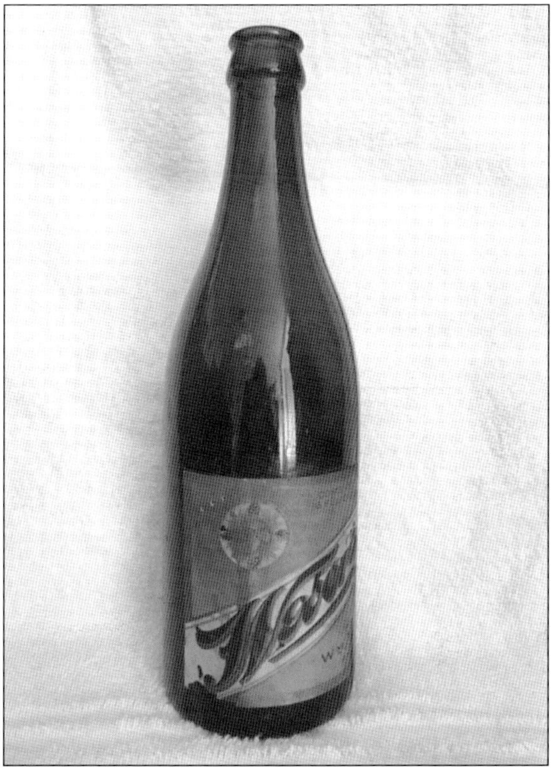

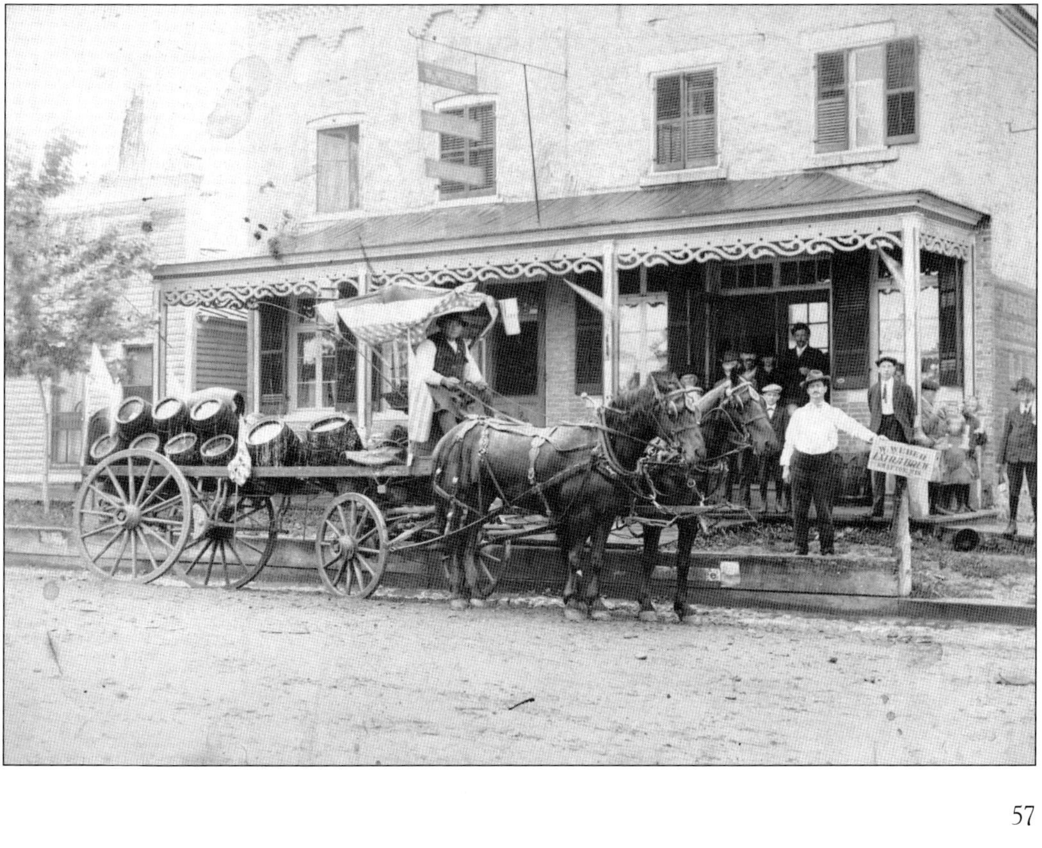

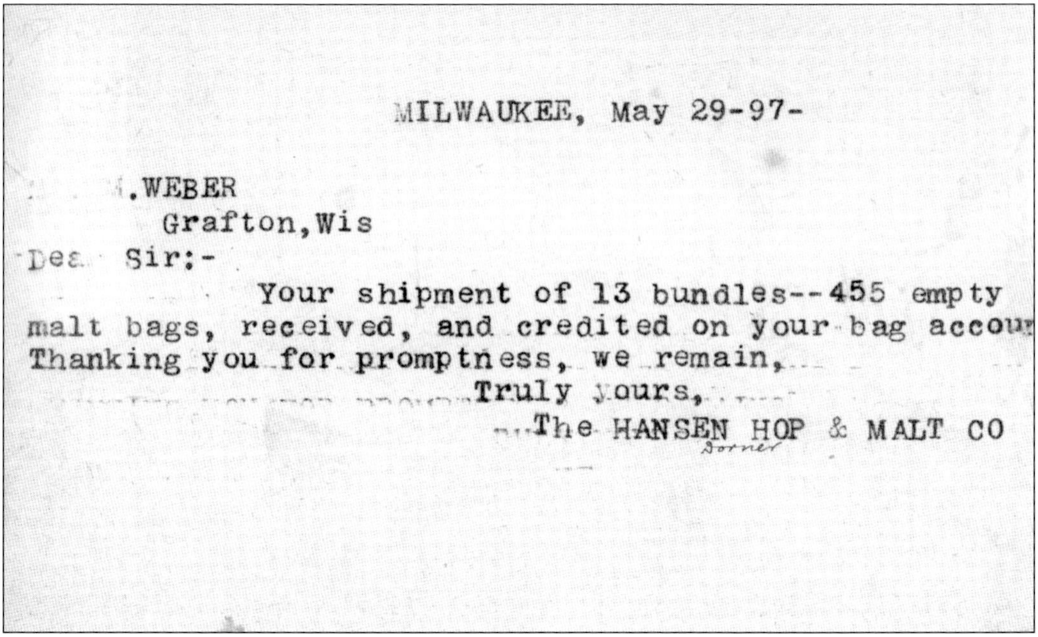

MILWAUKEE, May 29-97-

.WEBER
Grafton,Wis

Dea Sir:-

Your shipment of 13 bundles--455 empty malt bags, received, and credited on your bag accou
Thanking you for promptness, we remain,

Truly yours,
The HANSEN HOP & MALT CO

Weber Postcard. William Weber received this postcard in the spring of 1897 to confirm the receipt of empty malt bags returned to the Hansen Malt and Hop Company for credit. On the front of the postcard, the address was simply, "William Weber, Grafton, Wisconsin," with no street address being necessary. Malt is germinated cereal grain that has been dried, and Weber would have used it in the production of beer and whiskey. (Courtesy of Nic Schanen.)

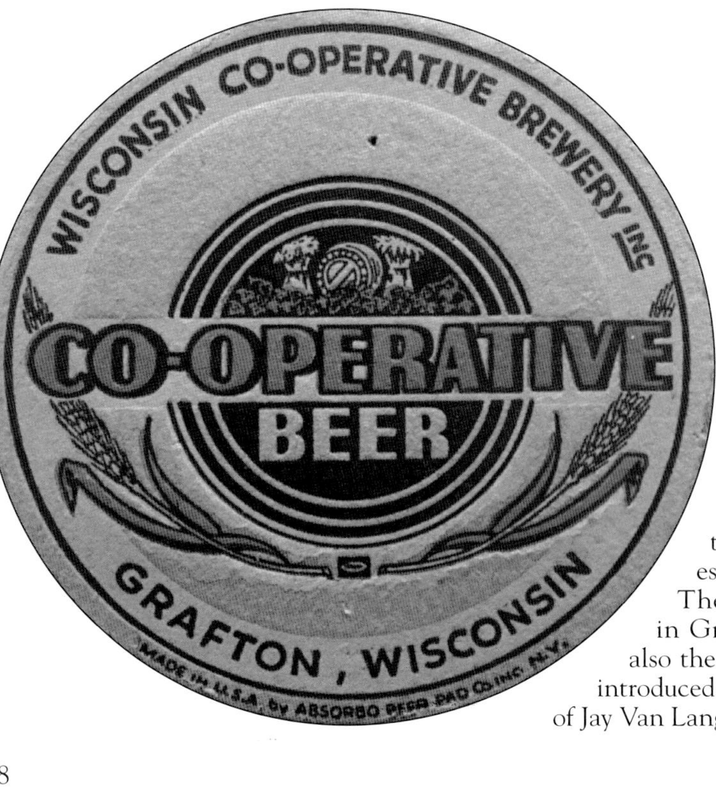

Wisconsin Cooperative Brewery. Wisconsin Cooperative Brewery Inc. opened in 1935 and closed in 1941, operating for six years. It was one of the many breweries that were established after Prohibition. There were three breweries in Grafton at the time. It was also the time when beer cans were introduced by the industry. (Courtesy of Jay Van Langen.)

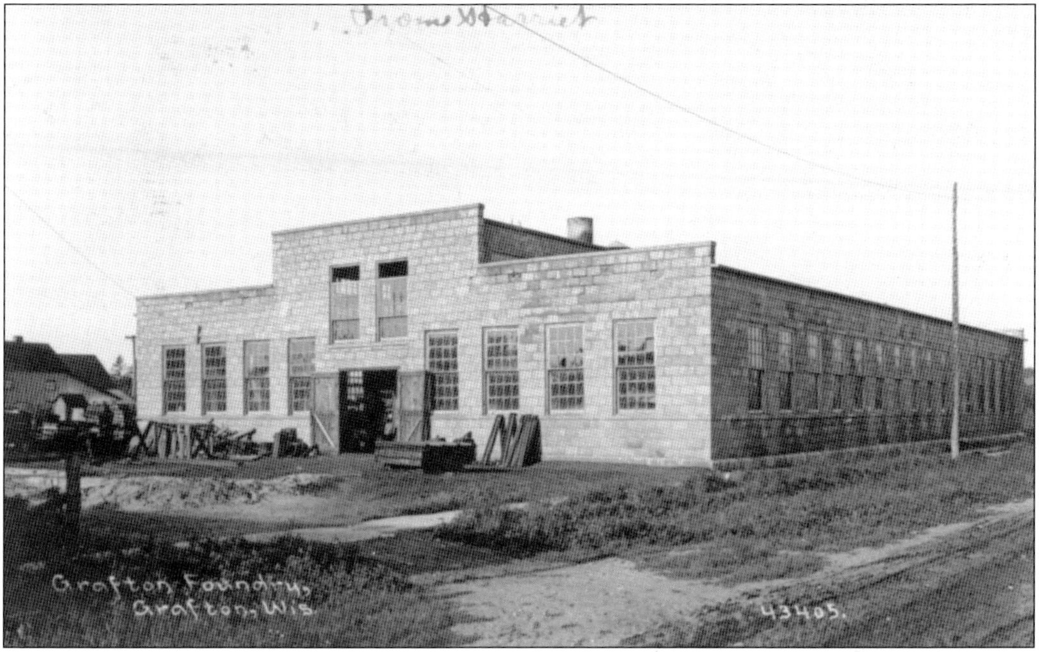

Grafton Foundry. The Grafton Foundry, at 1003 Bridge Street, was built in 1907 with the first casting done in December. Among the businessmen first associated with the foundry were Richard A. Goldberg, Ferdinand Mintzlaff, Louis Zaun, F.W. Mintzlaff, and Henry Kohlwey. Gray iron and alloyed-iron castings were manufactured. (Courtesy of the Sudbrink family.)

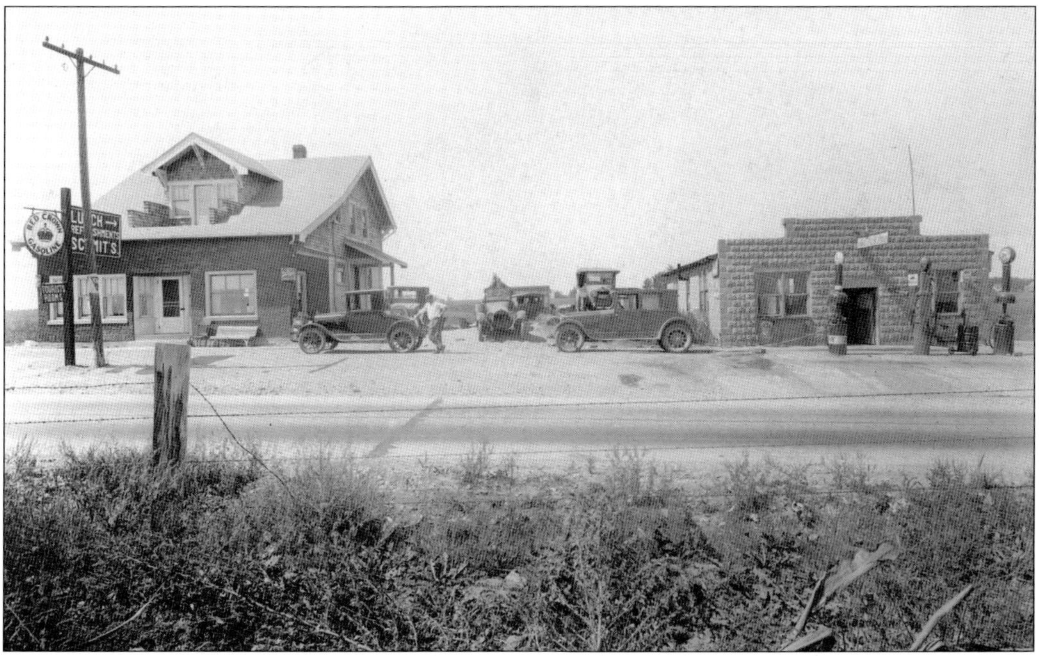

Schmit's Realty and Grisar Garage. Schmit's Realty (left) and Grisar's Garage are shown here. Michael J. Schmit bought the land in 1923 and constructed the Schmit Realty building soon after. It was on the southwest corner of Highway 60 and Port Washington Road. Note the "lunch" sign on the realty building. (Courtesy of Rick Schmit.)

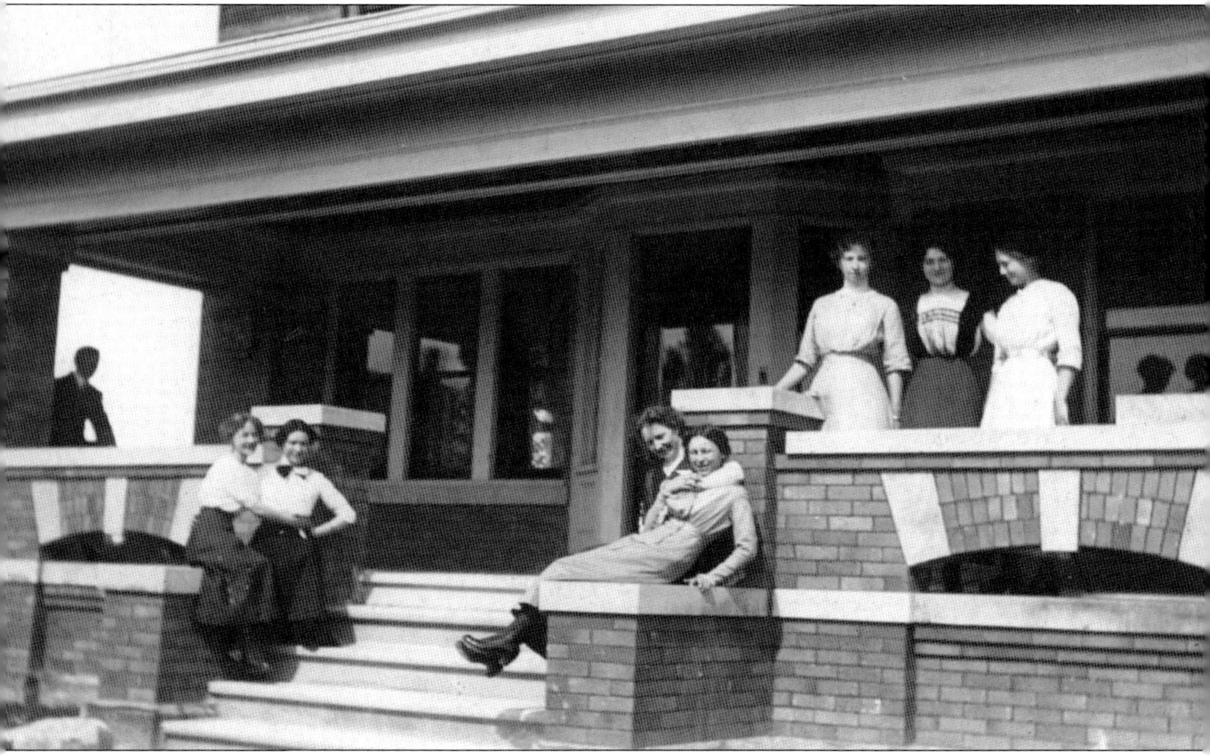

MINTZLAFF HOME. This house at 1646 Twelfth Avenue was the home of Ferdinand C. Mintzlaff. It was built in 1911 and shows the influence of the Prairie School of architecture. Born in Grafton in 1864, Mintzlaff married Emma Kohlwey, whose father and brother operated a blacksmith shop in town. In 1895, Ferdinand Mintzlaff, who was associated with the lime kiln operation, established a lumber business next to the railroad tracks, west of Wisconsin Avenue. A larger building was erected in 1936, when it was known as the Mintzlaff & Behrens Lumber & Coal Co. Ferdinand's son Alfred sold the business to Jerry Kopps in the 1950s, and he continued selling lumber, feed, and oil into the 1970s. Ferdinand was an avid entrepreneur also involved in the start-up of the Grafton Telephone Co., Lincoln Light Co., three gristmills, and a foundry. (Courtesy of Allen Buchholz.)

Grafton Water Tower. This is the first water tower in Grafton. It was on North Street, north of the Ataco Company. The Jungers Stove and Range building is in the background. The water tower was an elevated metal tank, often known as a "tin man"–style tank. It was constructed and put into operation in 1933 as part of the village's new municipal water system. It had a capacity of nearly 143,000 gallons to serve a village population of about 1,100. When the tower was replaced, the city of Pound, Wisconsin, purchased it. (Courtesy of Nic Schanen.)

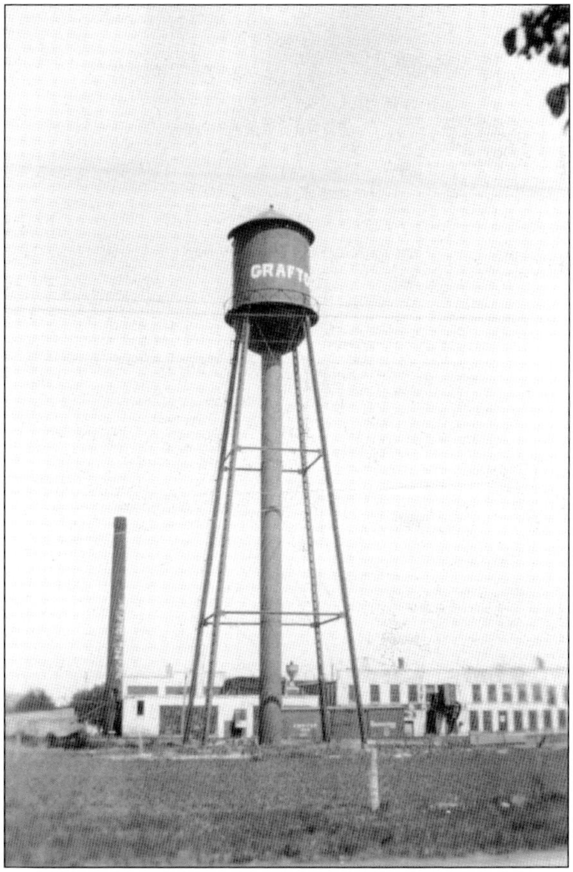

Jim Hilgart at Riebe's Gas Station. Jim Hilgart is looking under the hood of a car at Riebe's gas station in the early 1930s. The car is notable for having a radio (note the makeshift antenna), which was not common at the time. It also had door handles that created what were called "suicide doors"—if the back door opened while the car was moving, the wind would catch it, and passengers could fall out. (Courtesy of Jim Hilgart.)

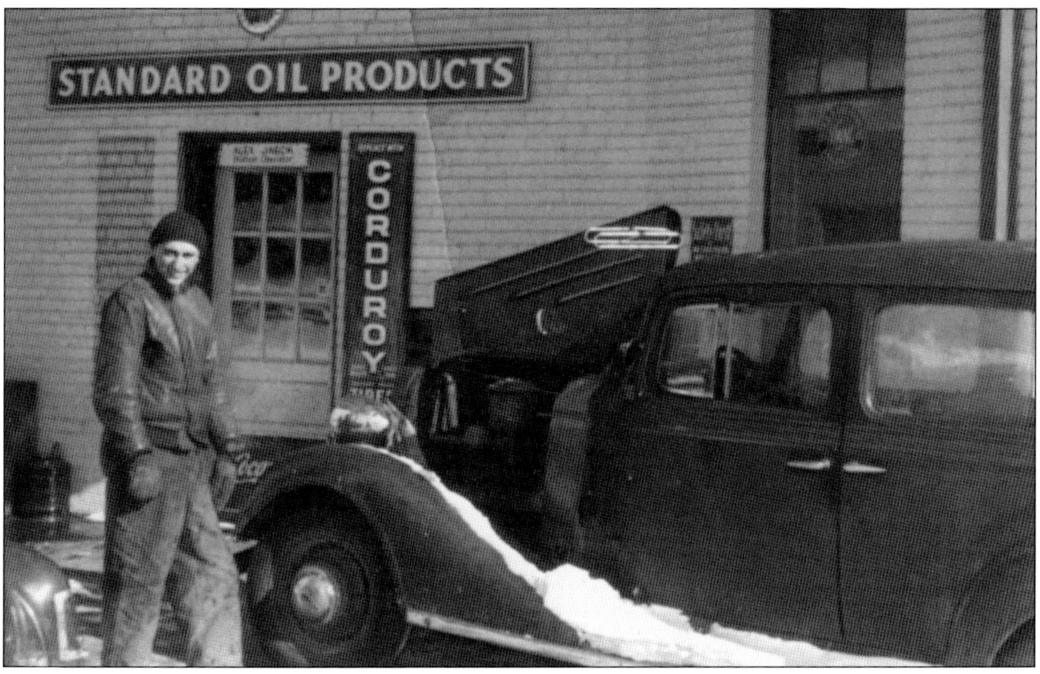

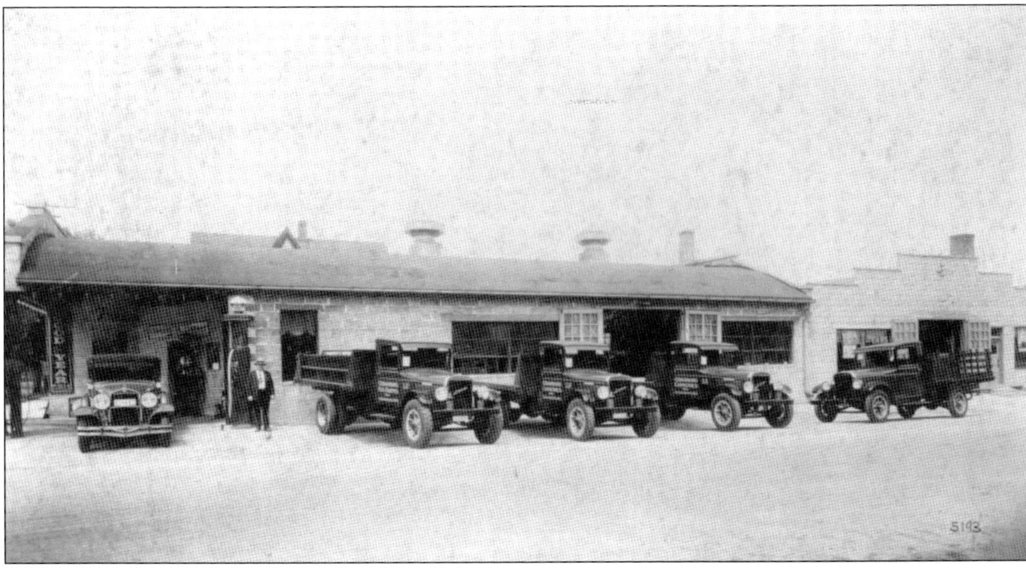

Riebe's Garage. This 1930s view is of the Riebe Garage on Highway 60 and Twelfth Avenue. It boasted an open new-car showroom and an indoor showroom. Riebe's sold new and used automobiles, including Hudsons, as well as trucks. Shown above are brand-new trucks waiting to be delivered to Cedarburg Fox Farms and Cedarburg Canneries. Riebe's also sold Standard Oil products and Goodyear tires. The original owner was Albert, followed by his son Jim, and then Bill Riebe. In the image below, note the man pumping gas and the spire of St. Joseph Church in the background. (Both, courtesy of Bill Riebe.)

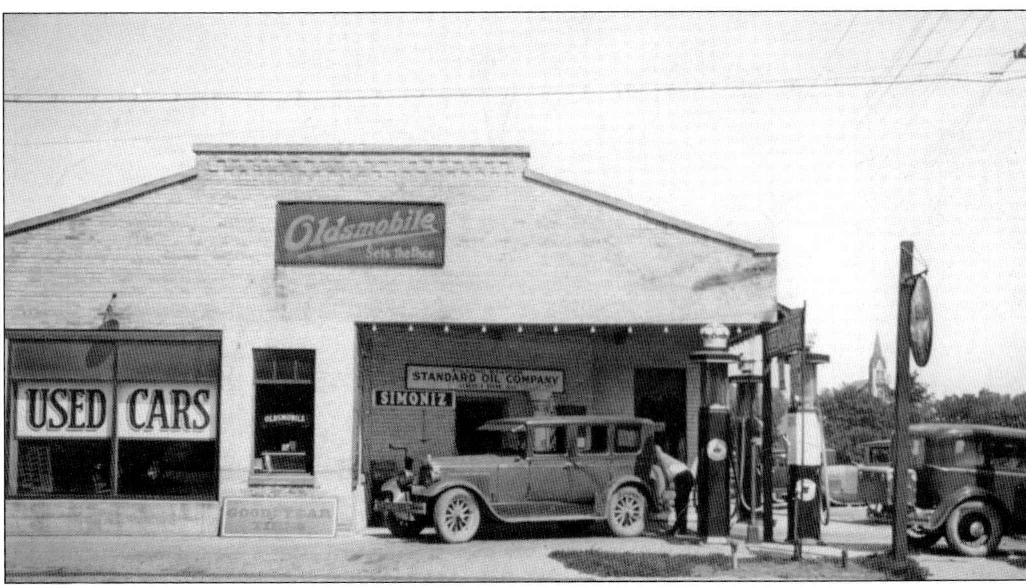

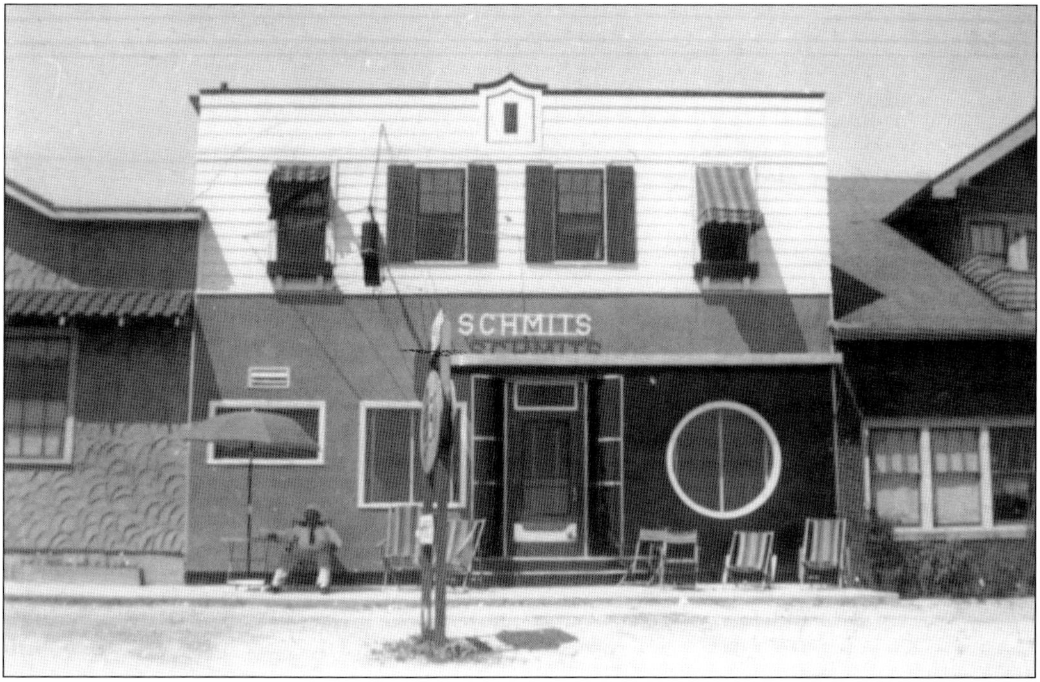

SCHMIT'S REALTY. Schmit's Realty is shown here. Michael J. Schmit bought the land in 1923 and constructed the Schmit Realty building soon after. It was on the southwest corner of Highway 60 and Port Washington Road. The firm, owned by the Schmit family, is still in business today. (Courtesy of the Schmit family.)

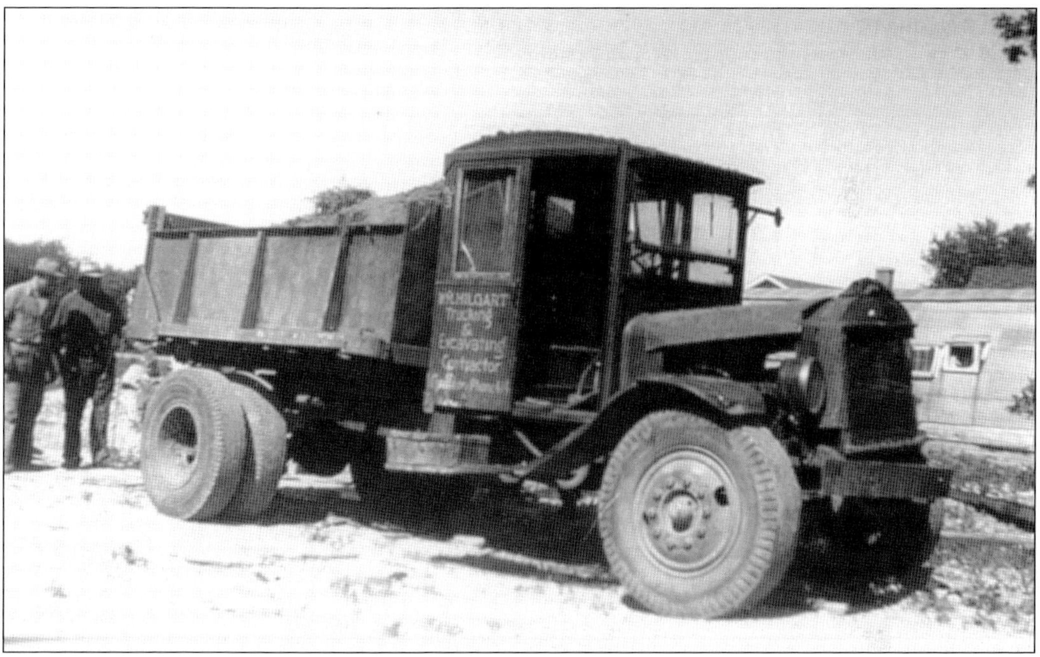

WILLIAM HILGART TRUCKING. Hauling a load of ground was part of the business for William Hilgart Trucking and Excavating, shown here in the 1920s. The men in the photograph are not identified. Note the bald tires on the truck. (Courtesy of Jim Hilgart.)

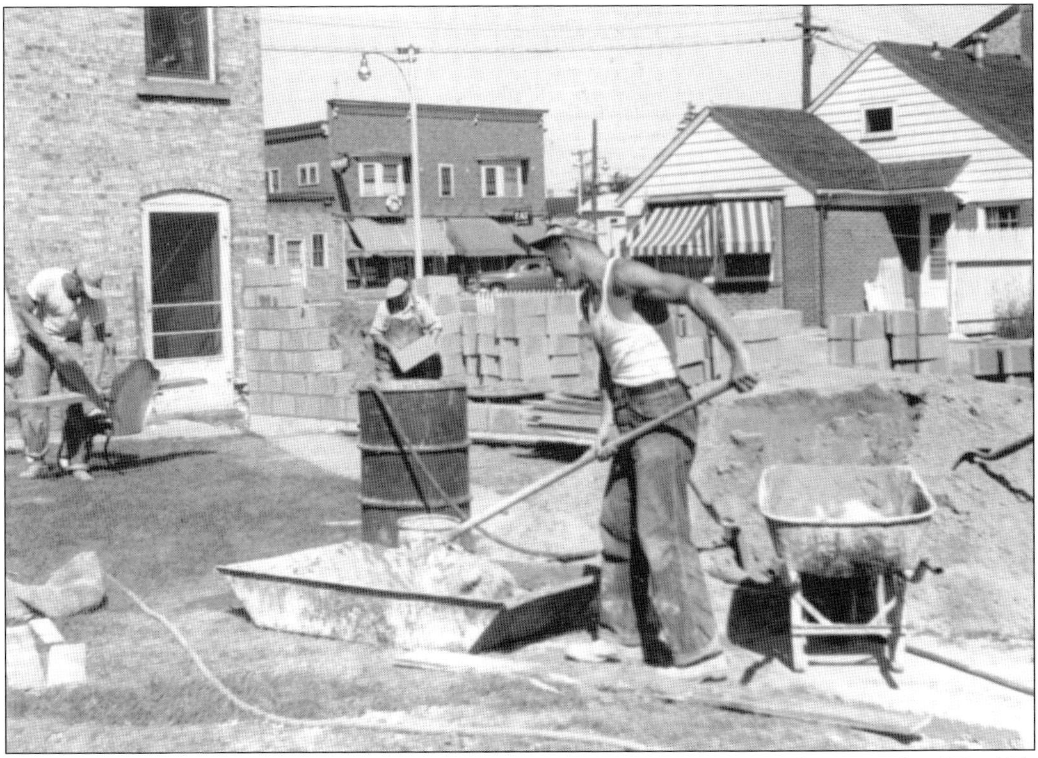

Stern's IGA. This scene shows the construction of Stern's IGA store on the east side of Twelfth Avenue in the 1940s. It was a family-owned and -operated grocery store. The original store, which opened in 1930, was next to it. Peter and Marie were the original owners, followed by Erv Stern. The store moved to Twin City Plaza in the early 1960s, when it became a Sentry Store. (Courtesy of Jim Stern.)

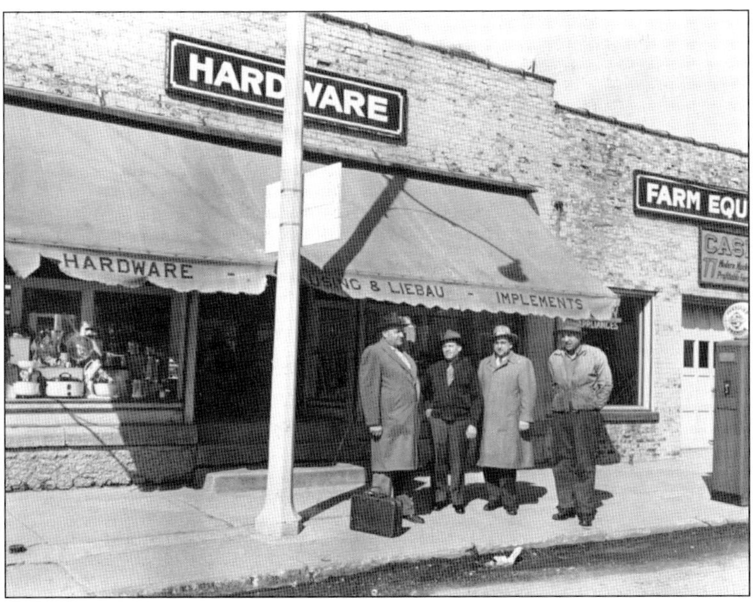

Lauer Hardware. In this scene from 1951, Art Lauer has just purchased the Clausing and Liebau Building to open Lauer Hardware. The hardware store remained at 1145 Twelfth Avenue until moving to Twin City Plaza in 1972, where it remained in business as Lauer Hardware until 1999. Pictured from left to right are Mike Schmit, Albert Clausing, Art Lauer, and Oscar Liebau. (Courtesy of Bob Lauer.)

Four

Churches and Schools

While the clearing of land for crops and the establishment of fledgling industries were crucial to the beginnings of Grafton, so was attending to the religious and educational needs of the community. Almost as soon as they arrived, new settlers met to create parishes. Before they had their own buildings, the Stone Block Building was the very early home of both the Catholic and Lutheran congregations in town. Their own church buildings were soon to come, however. The cornerstone of the first Catholic church was laid in 1849. This stone-and-mortar building stood until 1921. St. Paul Evangelical Lutheran Church erected its first building, a frame structure, in 1857. Even though many early students were not able to attend school on a regular basis, especially in rural areas, belief in the importance of schools was also strong, and Grafton was a leader in the area when it came to education. In 1845, only Grafton and two other townships in the county, Mequon and Germantown, had schools. Grafton had 13 children in attendance. Churches also stepped in to provide education for the children of Grafton. St. Joseph Parish and St. Paul Parish both established early schools, with St. Joseph hiring a lay teacher until the school sisters could come and teach at the parish. Both the churches and schools were central to many community activities such as talent shows, picnics, musical performances, plays, and celebrations of holidays. From those early beginnings, Grafton has now grown to a community of nine churches, six elementary/middle schools, and a high school.

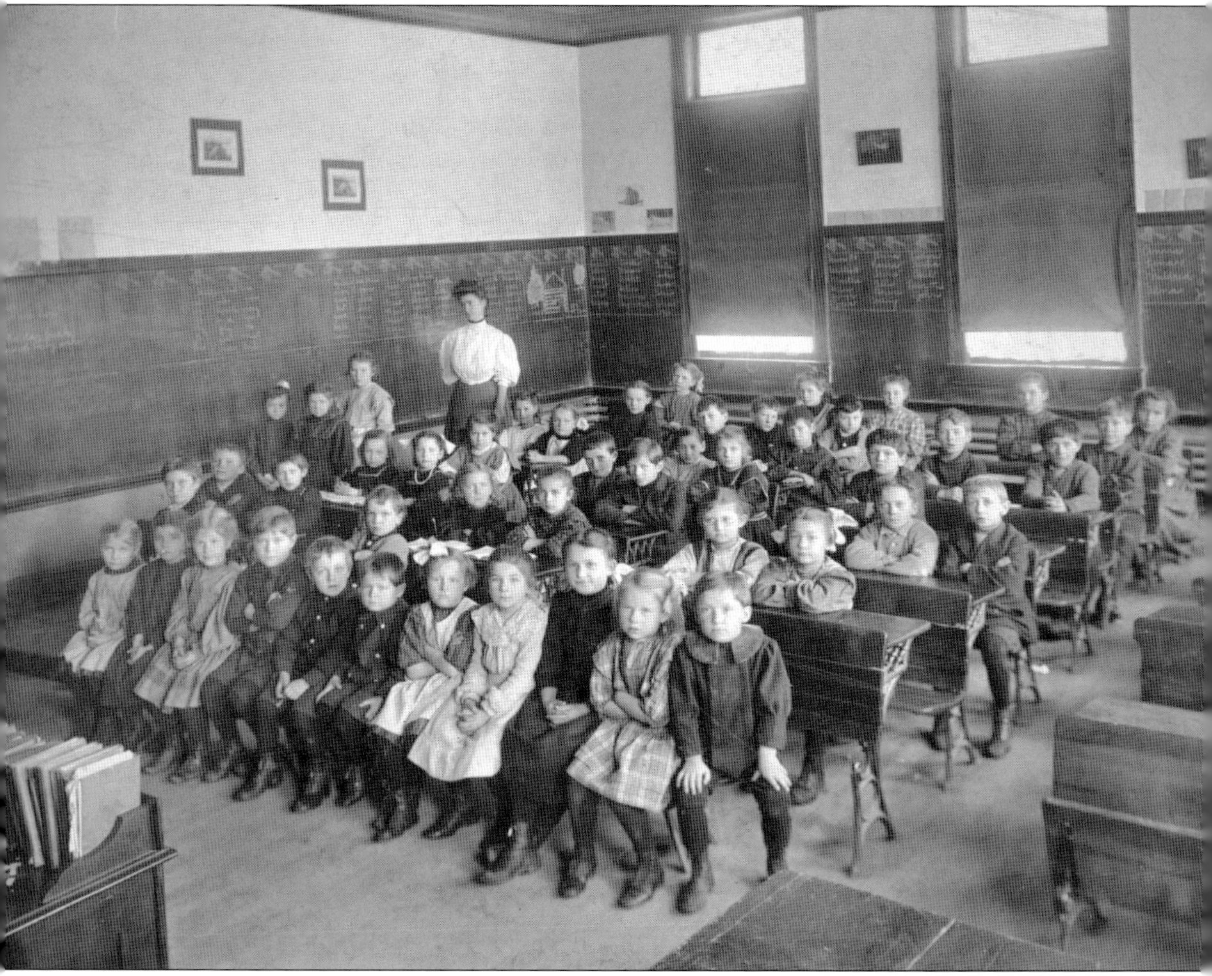

JACKSON SCHOOL, 1906. More than 50 students share a classroom in the Jackson Public School in this 1906 scene. The original school was at a site shared with the firehouse on Thirteenth Avenue. Grafton appears to have been a leader in the early establishment of a school system. Jefferson District 1 existed as early as 1843. By 1845, only Grafton and two other townships in the county, Mequon and Germantown, had schools. Grafton had 13 children in attendance. (Courtesy of the Grafton Historical Society.)

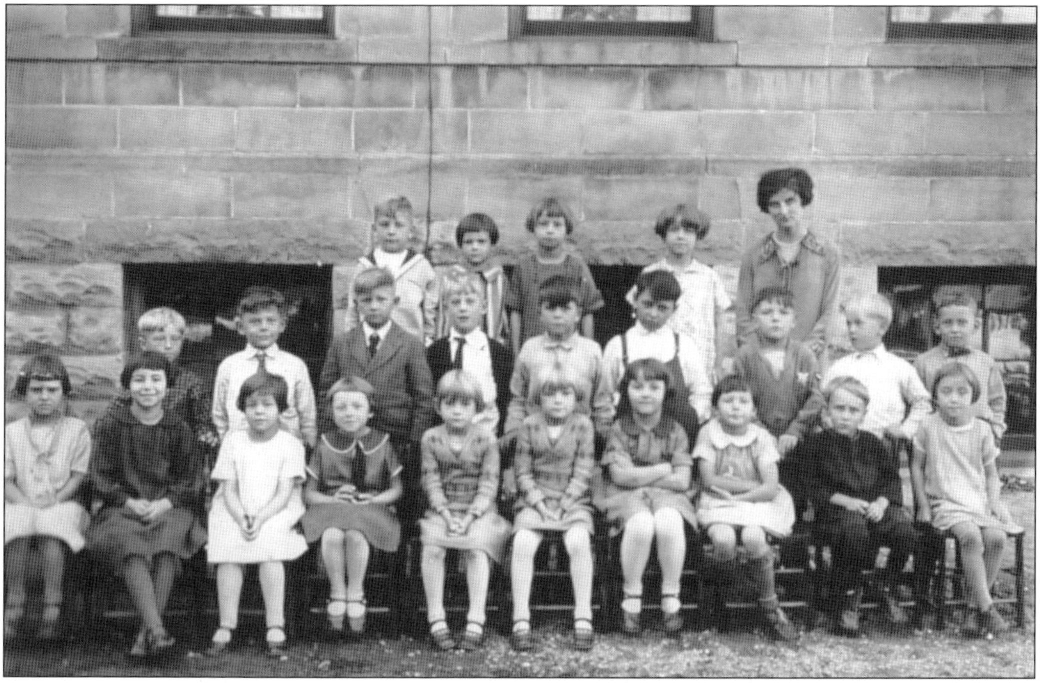

Jackson Public School, 1930s. These Grafton third graders are wearing their "picture day" best as they pose outside the Jackson School in the 1930s. Note the twins in the first row. The Jackson School served as the elementary school for many years and was followed by Grafton Elementary School (later renamed John F. Kennedy School) in 1954, John Long Middle School in 1963, and Woodview Elementary School in 1969. (Courtesy of Nic Schanen.)

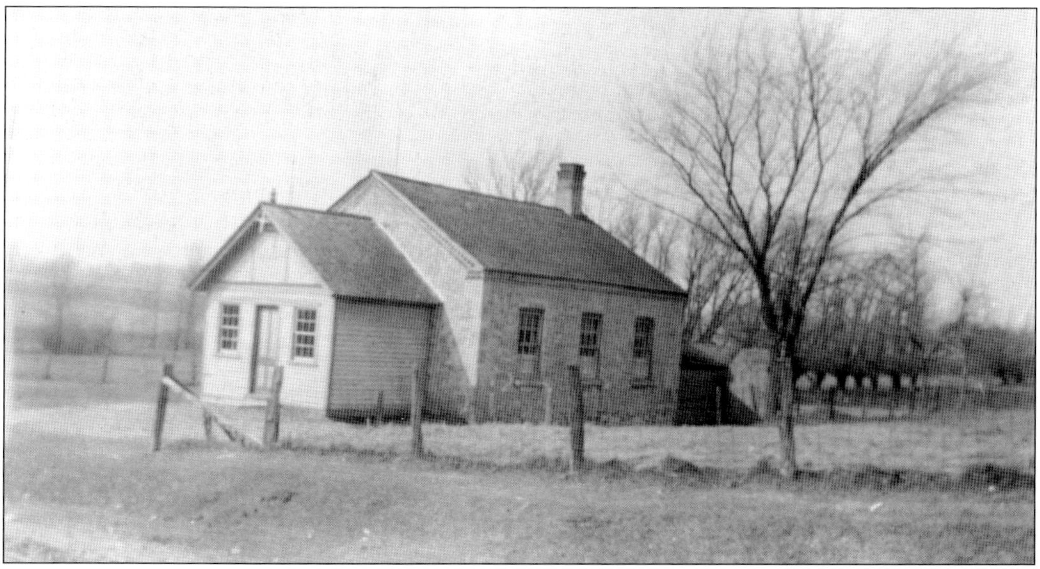

District School at Town Ten. The District School at Town Ten is located in Cedarburg on the north side of Pleasant Valley Road. For many years, it served both Grafton and Cedarburg families. At a time when lay teachers were not available during the late 1800s, the Catholic sisters taught the students. The stone and brick structure is now a private residence. (Courtesy of Allen Buchholz.)

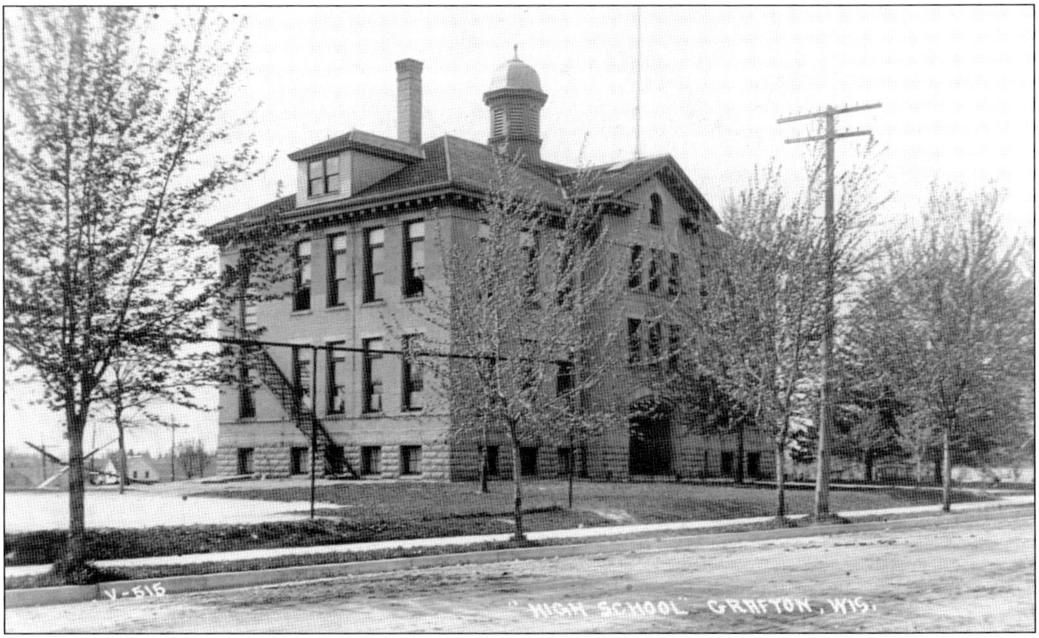

JACKSON SCHOOL. The Andrew Jackson School was built in 1906. It served the village as both a grade school and high school until a new high school was built on the adjacent property. The school then continued to be used as a grade school until 1955. After that, the building was used for storage and as a manual training facility until it was demolished in 1968. (Courtesy of Nic Schanen.)

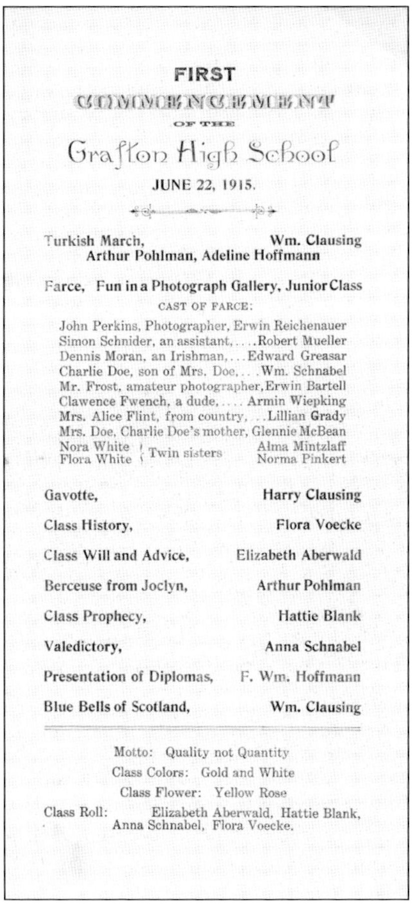

FIRST
COMMENCEMENT
OF THE
Grafton High School
JUNE 22, 1915.

Turkish March, Wm. Clausing
Arthur Pohlman, Adeline Hoffmann

Farce, Fun in a Photograph Gallery, Junior Class

CAST OF FARCE:

John Perkins, Photographer, Erwin Reichenauer
Simon Schnider, an assistant, ...Robert Mueller
Dennis Moran, an Irishman, ...Edward Greasar
Charlie Doe, son of Mrs. Doe, ...Wm. Schnabel
Mr. Frost, amateur photographer, Erwin Bartell
Clawence Fwench, a dude, ... Armin Wiepking
Mrs. Alice Flint, from country, ...Lillian Grady
Mrs. Doe, Charlie Doe's mother, Glennie McBean
Nora White } Twin sisters Alma Mintzlaff
Flora White } Norma Pinkert

Gavotte, Harry Clausing

Class History, Flora Voecke

Class Will and Advice, Elizabeth Aberwald

Berceuse from Joclyn, Arthur Pohlman

Class Prophecy, Hattie Blank

Valedictory, Anna Schnabel

Presentation of Diplomas, F. Wm. Hoffmann

Blue Bells of Scotland, Wm. Clausing

Motto: Quality not Quantity
Class Colors: Gold and White
Class Flower: Yellow Rose
Class Roll: Elizabeth Aberwald, Hattie Blank, Anna Schnabel, Flora Voecke.

GRADUATING CLASS. The first class graduated from Grafton High School on June 22, 1915. Their class motto, "Quality not Quantity," was a fitting one, with only four students in the graduating class. Those students were Flora Vocke, Elizabeth Aberwald, Hattie Blank, and Anna Schnabel. The commencement ceremony included a musical farce called "Fun in a Photograph Gallery." (Courtesy of Nic Schanen.)

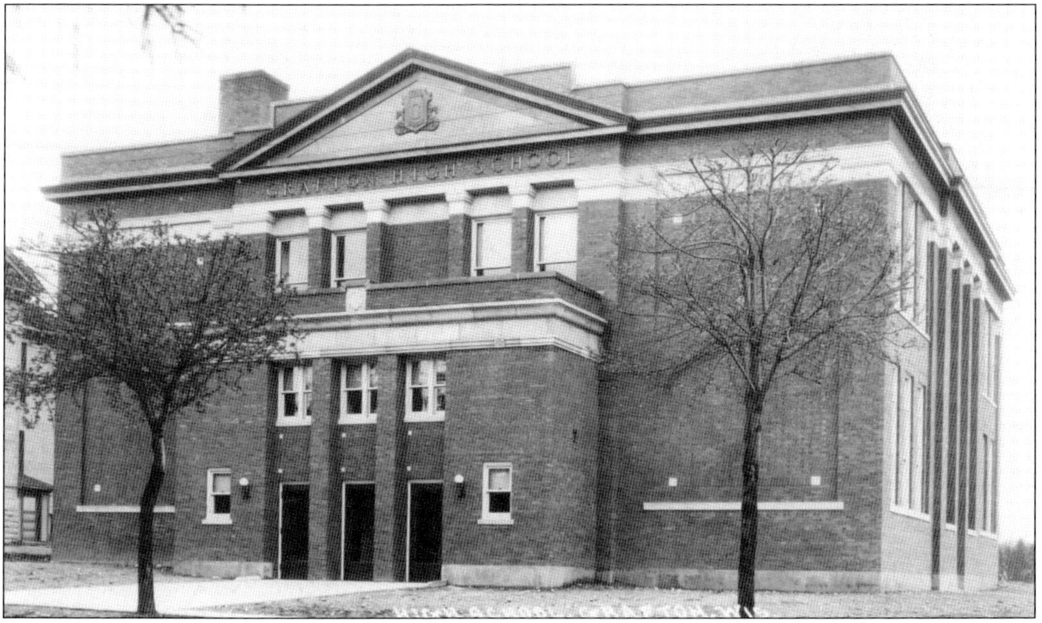

GRAFTON HIGH SCHOOL. In 1927, a new Grafton High School was built on Broad Street between Eleventh and Twelfth Avenues. Prior to this, all students attended the Jackson School, which housed both elementary and high school students. The structure, now named the Timothy Wooden building, is still standing adjacent to the Grafton public library. (Courtesy of the Sudbrink family.)

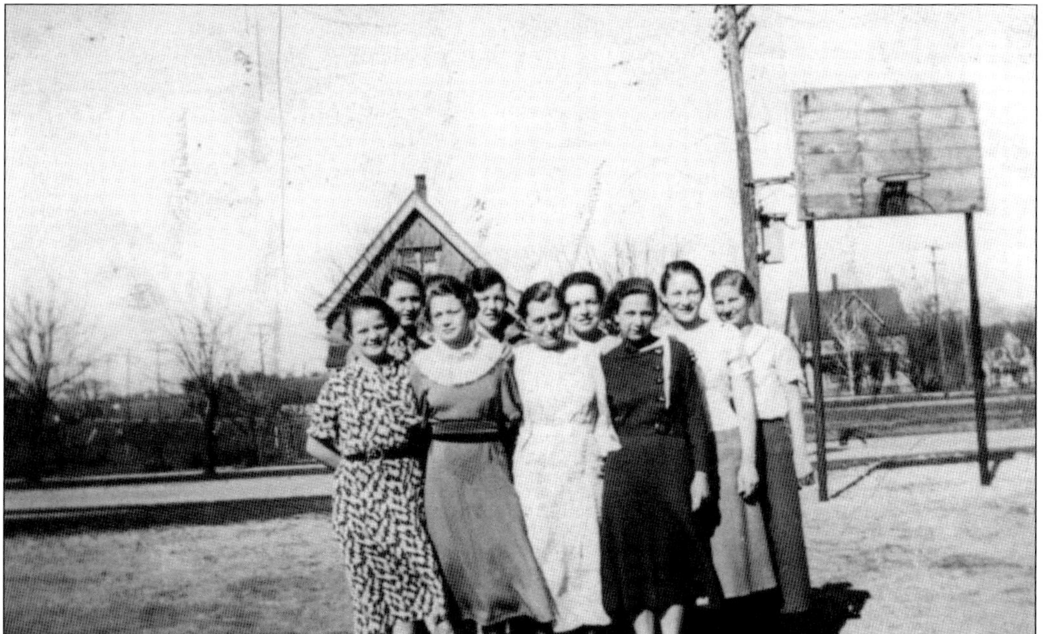

GRAFTON FRESHMAN CLASS. Pictured here is the Grafton High School freshman class of 1935. From left to right are Marion H., Alice Berger, Hilda Schroe, Ruth Bielfo, Eileen Wagner, Anita Blank, Antoinette Wollner, Margueritte Thelen, and Lila Grams. Notice the wooden basketball backboard in the background. (Courtesy of Nic Schanen.)

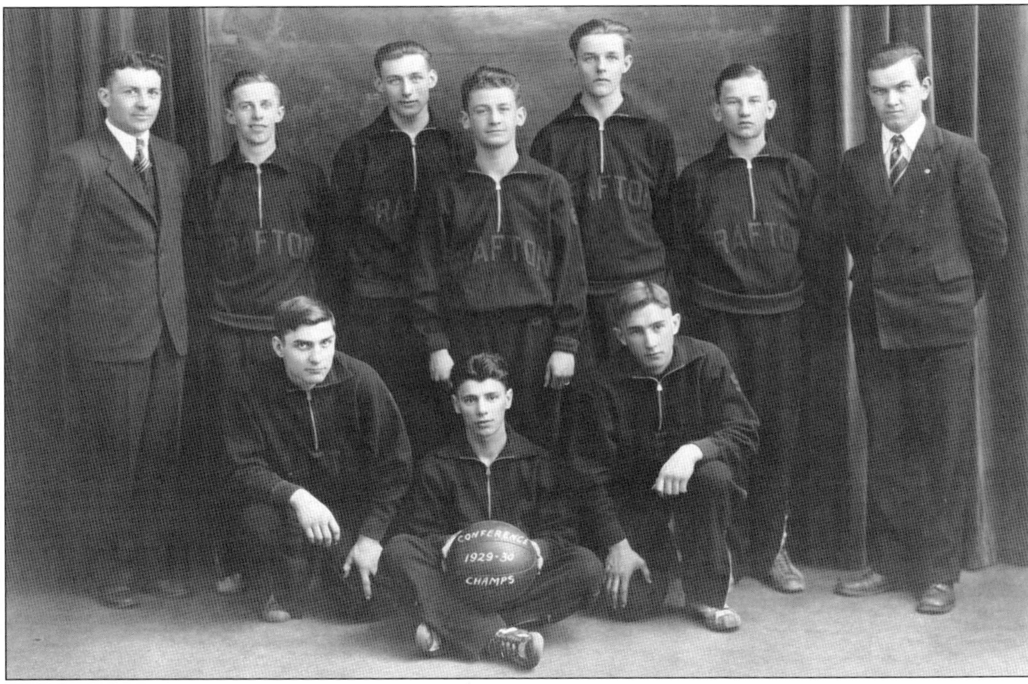

Grafton High School Basketball Team. The Grafton High School basketball team, shown here, took the conference championship for the 1929–1930 season. From left to right are (first row) William Wolf, Jules Shorty Meunier, and Harold Habich; (second row) Orville Maechtle, Wilmer Klotz, Vernel Rief, Tink Rilling, Arnold Rief, Rich Goldberg, and manager Orville Hofmann. (Courtesy of the Gramoll family.)

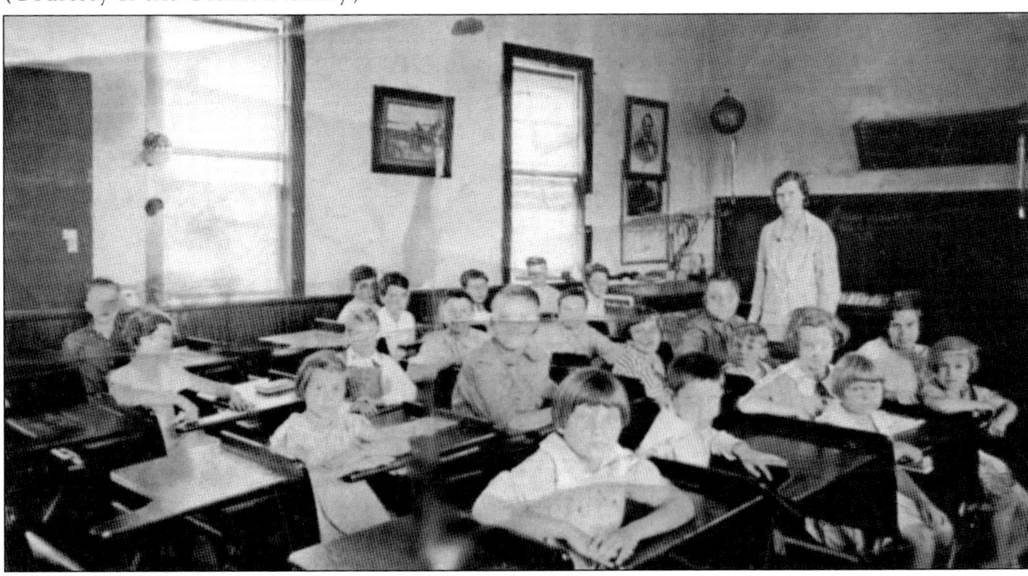

Ulao School. This is a classroom in the Ulao School in Grafton in the 1930s. The school was on the southwest corner of the intersection of Highways C and Q. The wood-frame structure was built in the 1890s and operated as a school until it closed in 1962, when school families joined the Village of Grafton, School District 1. The Ulao School was the last rural school to close. Bernice Oberheu Noster is the little girl at far right. (Courtesy of Bernice Noster.)

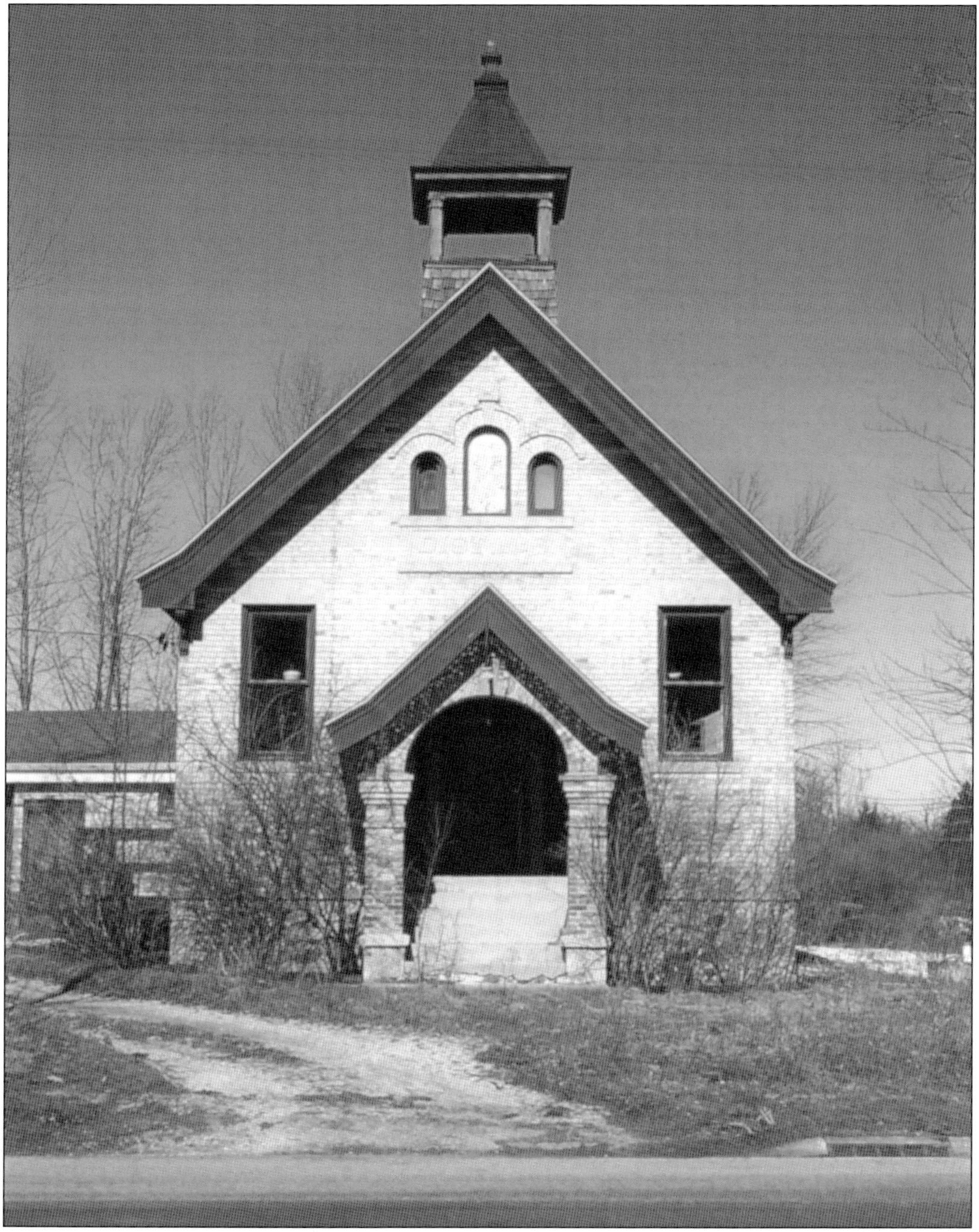

Lakefield Schoolhouse. The Lakefield Schoolhouse was built in 1907 on Port Washington and Lakefield Roads and was part of the system of one-room rural schoolhouses in Ozaukee County. In the early days, Port Washington Road was so dangerous that a pedestrian tunnel was constructed at the corner of Lakefield Road so that students from the east side of the road could cross safely under the highway on their way to school. The tunnel was used until the schoolhouse was closed in 1951. It was left in place and not removed until reconstruction of the intersection. Since the school closed in 1958, the building, which still stands, had been used as a private residence and as a winery. (Courtesy of the Grafton Historical Society.)

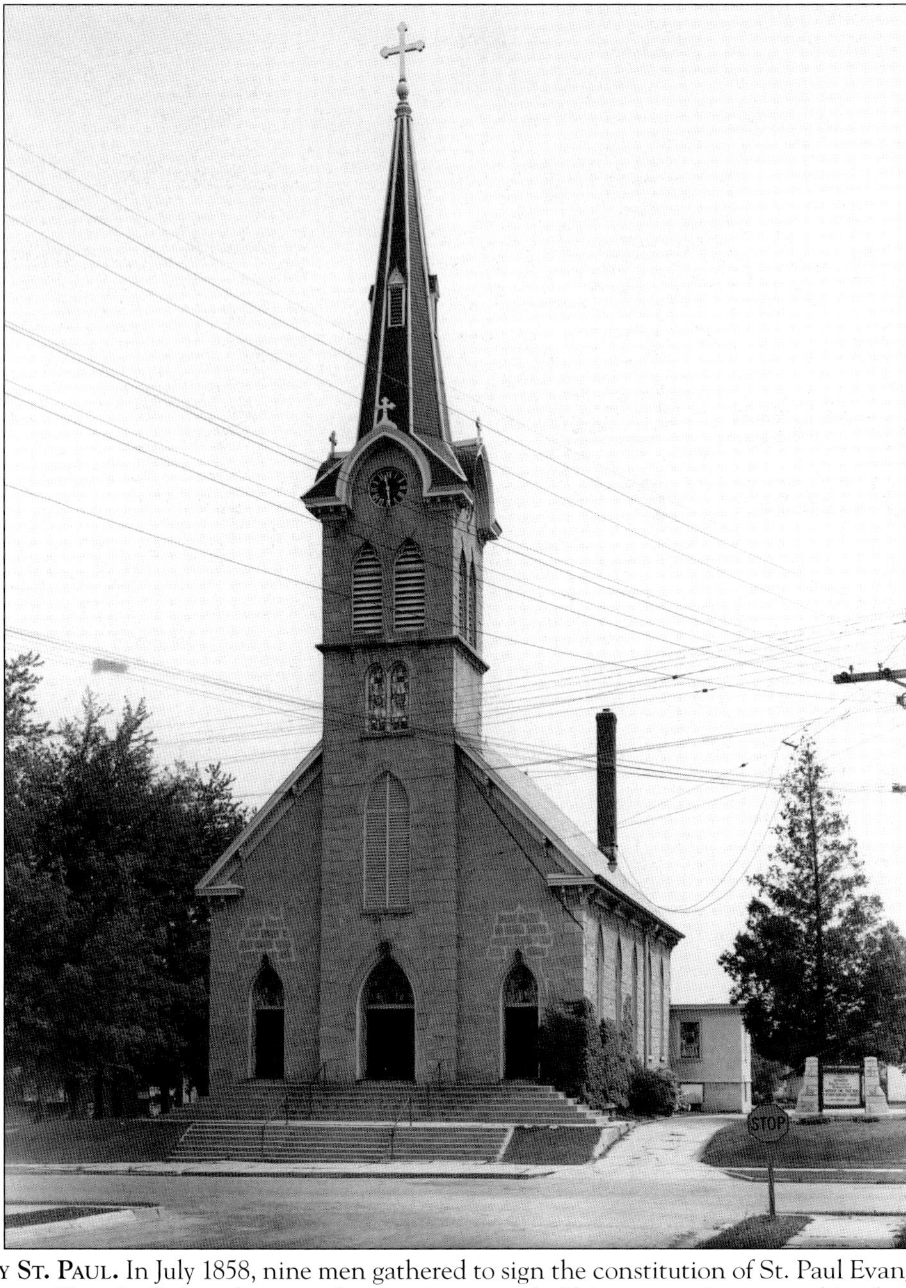

Early St. Paul. In July 1858, nine men gathered to sign the constitution of St. Paul Evangelical Lutheran Church. Before that, worship services were held in private homes and in the Stone Block building, which also served as a courthouse at the time. In 1852, the congregation installed its first pastor, Rev. Johann Boehm, and began construction of a church. That building was completely destroyed in a severe storm before it was completed, and it was not until 1856 that the congregation began construction of a two-story frame structure. The first floor housed the school and the pastor's residence, and the second floor was for services. This limestone church building was completed in 1871 and was used until replaced by a brick building in 1908. All services at St. Paul were conducted in German until 1929, when it was decided that one service a month should be in English. (Courtesy of St. Paul Lutheran Church.)

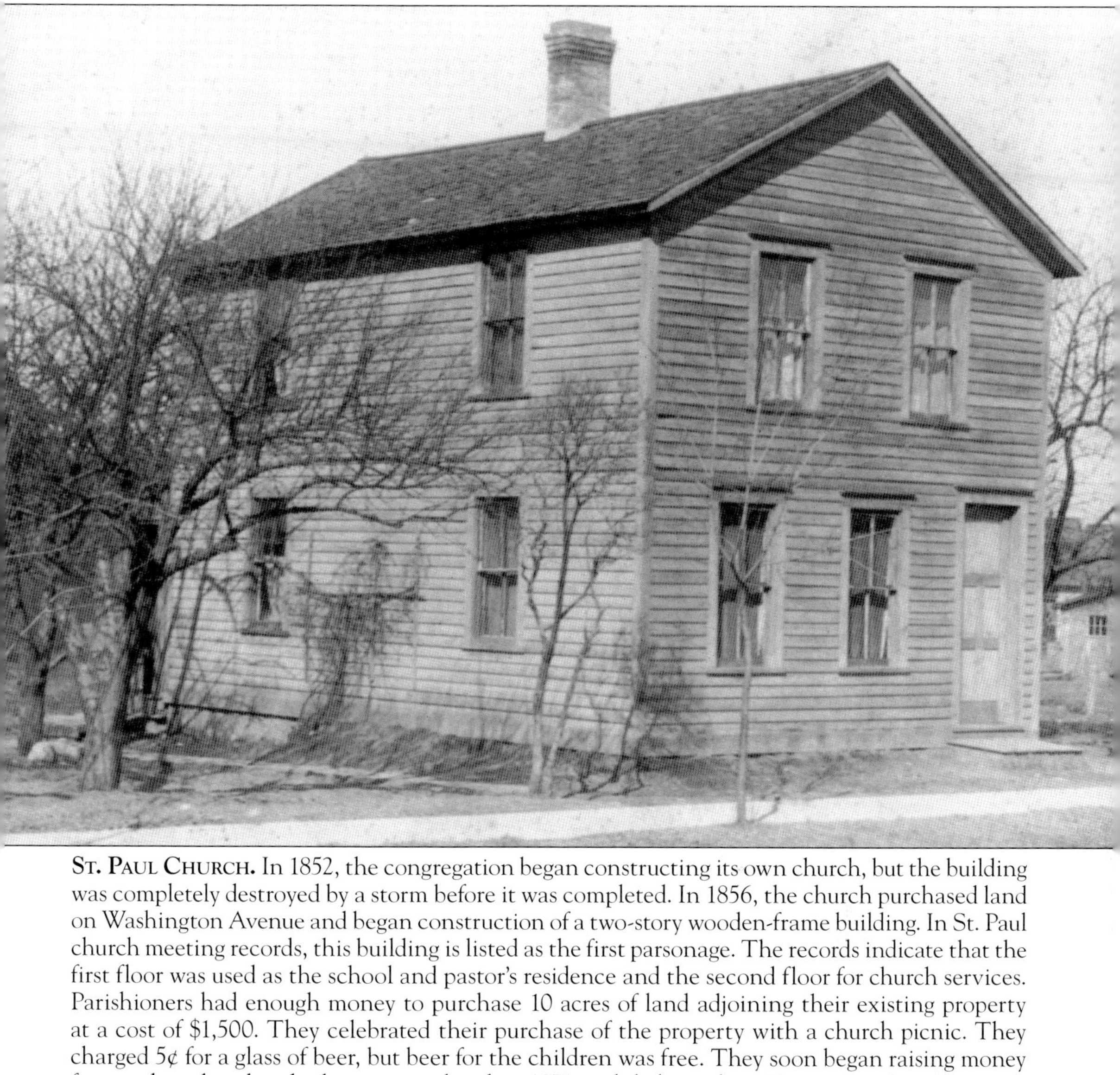

St. Paul Church. In 1852, the congregation began constructing its own church, but the building was completely destroyed by a storm before it was completed. In 1856, the church purchased land on Washington Avenue and began construction of a two-story wooden-frame building. In St. Paul church meeting records, this building is listed as the first parsonage. The records indicate that the first floor was used as the school and pastor's residence and the second floor for church services. Parishioners had enough money to purchase 10 acres of land adjoining their existing property at a cost of $1,500. They celebrated their purchase of the property with a church picnic. They charged 5¢ for a glass of beer, but beer for the children was free. They soon began raising money for another church, which was completed in 1871 and dedicated on Trinity Sunday. (Courtesy of St. Paul Lutheran Church.)

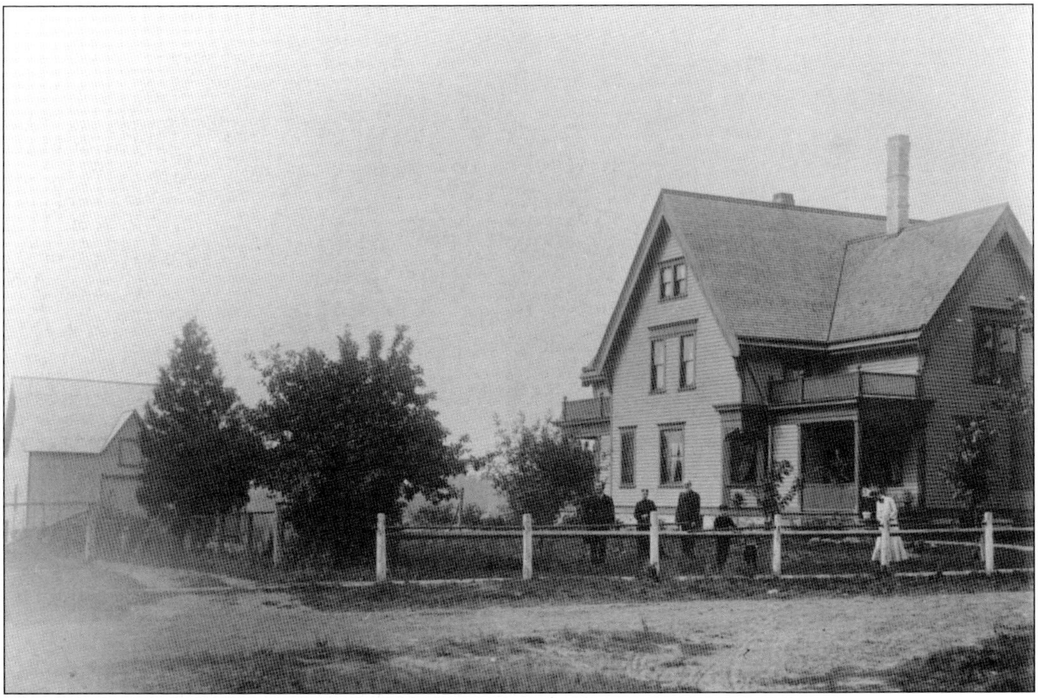

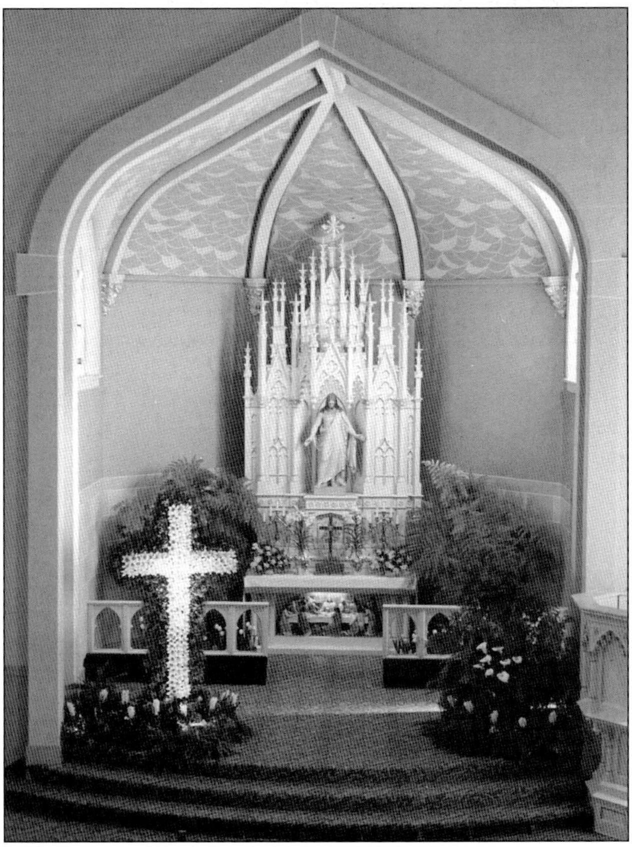

ST. PAUL PARSONAGE. Five people stand outside the St. Paul Lutheran Church parsonage. Pastor Schroeder is on the left, and his wife, Bertha, is on the right. The location of the parsonage was directly west of the old church, built in 1871. Note the unpaved road in front of the parsonage. (Courtesy of St. Paul Lutheran Church.)

ST. PAUL CHURCH INTERIOR. This is the interior of the old St. Paul church decorated for Easter. Built in 1871, it was demolished 100 years later, in the summer of 1971. In 1891, the congregation became debt-free and decided that the 20-year-old building needed bells in the steeple. The existing steeple could not accommodate bells, so the members decided to build a new one. They purchased three large bronze bells and rang them proudly. (Courtesy of St. Paul Lutheran Church.)

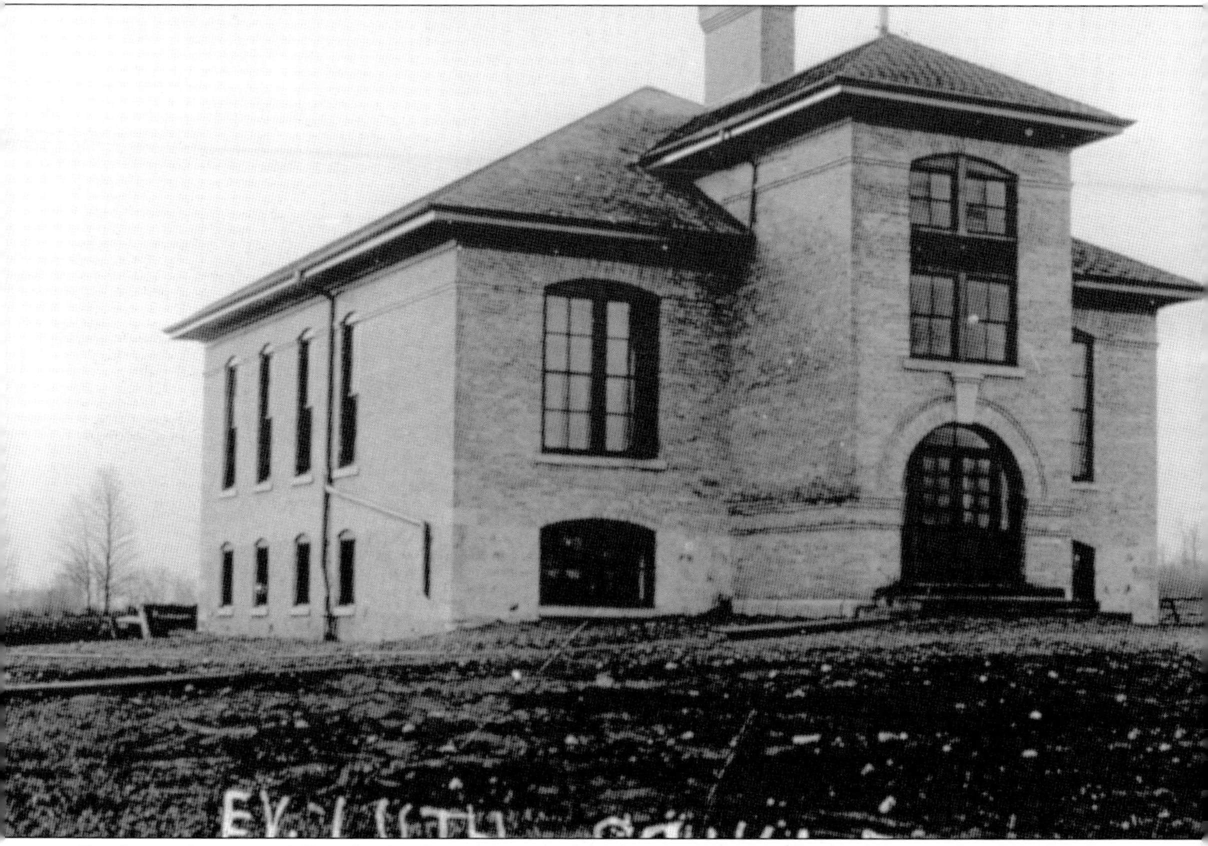

St. Paul School. The St. Paul Lutheran Church congregation built this new brick school a short distance west of the original school on Washington Street. The new school was a one-story building with two classrooms on the main floor and a fellowship hall and furnace room in the basement. It was completed in the fall of 1908 at a cost of $5,500 and dedicated on November 22. By 1950, enrollment had increased so much that a temporary classroom had to be set up in the church basement. Construction was begun on an expansion on the north side of the building, and the new addition was dedicated in 1951. Another expansion was needed only four years later, when the north half of the present south wing of the school was added. In 1959, the south half of the south wing was added, providing more classrooms and a gymnasium. Although the original school is surrounded on all sides by newer construction, the east classroom is still being used as a classroom. (Courtesy of St. Paul Lutheran Church.)

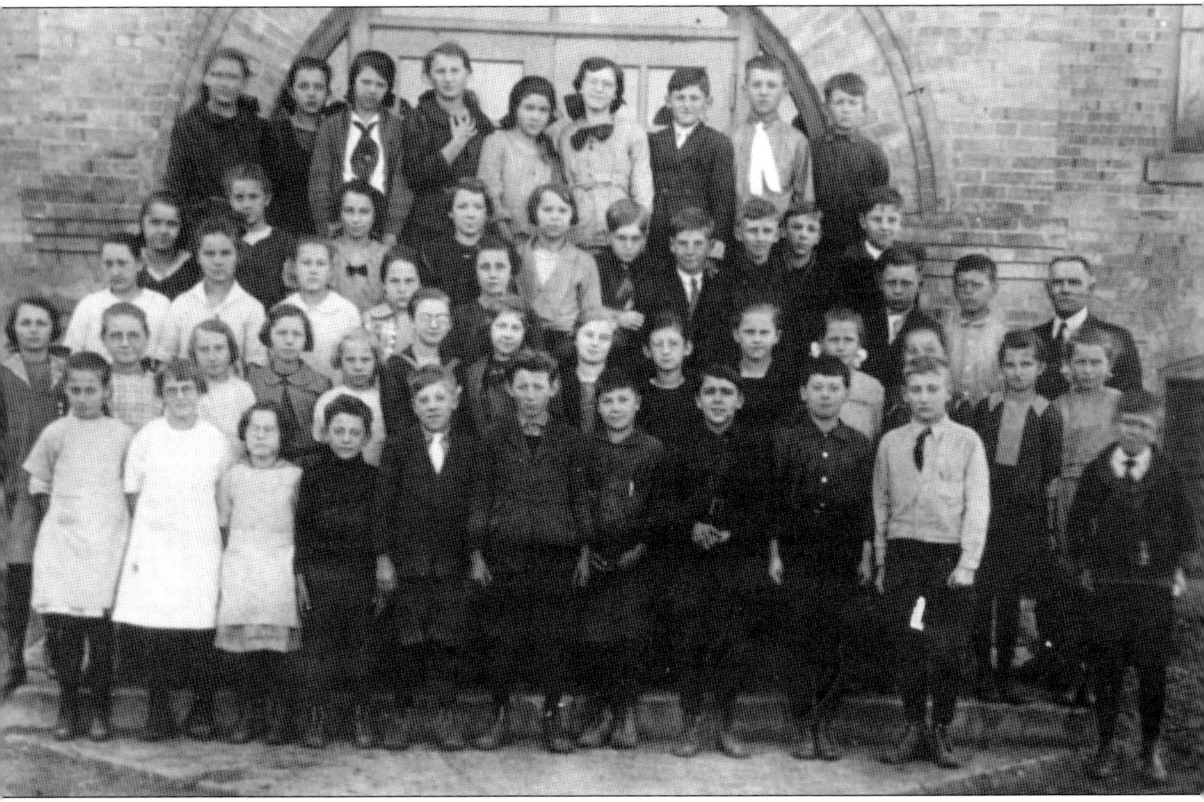

St. Paul Student Body. The students of St. Paul Lutheran School are shown here in the early 1900s. From left to right are (first row) Sophia Diener, Sybella Hornig, Molly Diener, John Diener, Edwin Musbach, George Mintzlaff, Robert Wegner, Alvin Kirst, Edward Uttech, Theofil Laubenstein, and Arnold Suelflow; (second row) Adeline Bruss, Hazel Lamp, Loretta Grisar, Mary Ann Hornig, Theodora Tiegs, Bill Krause, Lester Behrens, Arthur Nierode, Reinhold Kirst, and Harold Behrens; (third row) Louise Neimitz, Ilona Rathke, Rose Schroeder, Ruth Bothe, Elvira Behrens, Walter Kohlwey, and Luther Rathke; (fourth row) Evelyn Stock, Emilie Fromm, Sophia Mueller, Henrietta Stuebner, Edna Musbach, Eleanor Krause, Gertrude Mentzel, Ilona Miller, and Adela Schroeder; (fifth row) Adele Stauske, Georgiana Kohlwey, Irma Schlegel, Hilda Stauske, Myra Rose, Irma Miller, Herman Bielefeld, and Christ Fromm. The teacher was P.C. Meyer, shown at far right in the third row. (Courtesy of St. Paul Lutheran Church.)

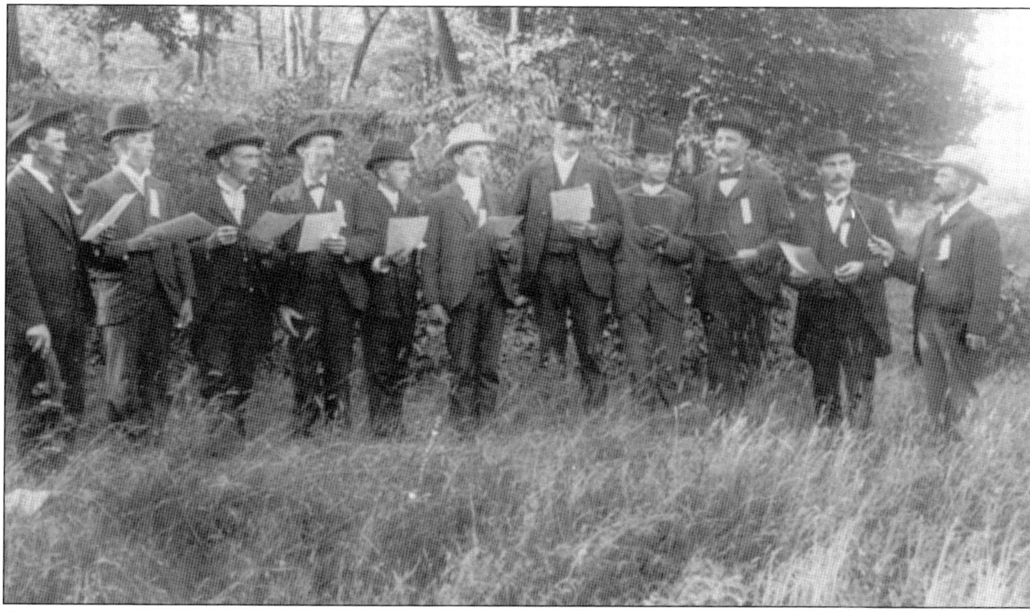

St. Paul Church Choir. These 10 men enjoying outdoor choral practice are part of the St. Paul Lutheran Male Choir. Conductor Mercken Slager is at far right. This scene was captured in 1910. Note the formal dress, including hats. (Courtesy of St. Paul Lutheran Church.)

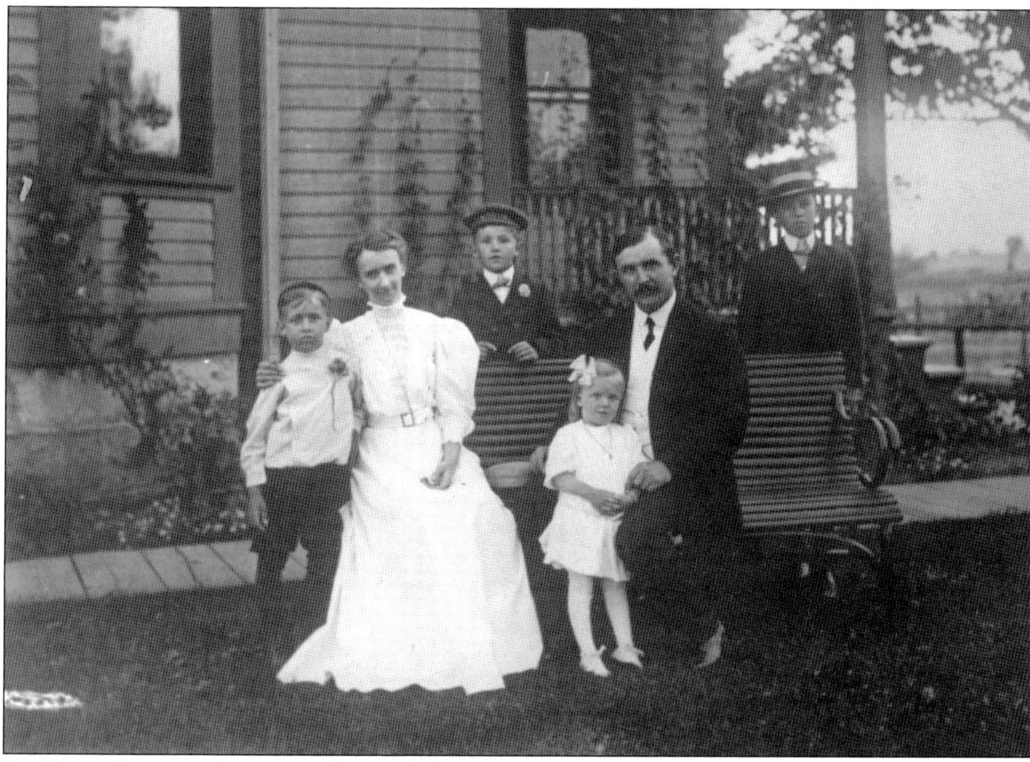

St. Paul Pastor. Sitting in front of the St. Paul Lutheran Church parsonage is Pastor John Schroeder with his wife, Bertha, and four of their children. The family eventually grew to eight. Pastor Schroeder served the church from 1903 until 1948. (Courtesy of St. Paul Lutheran Church.)

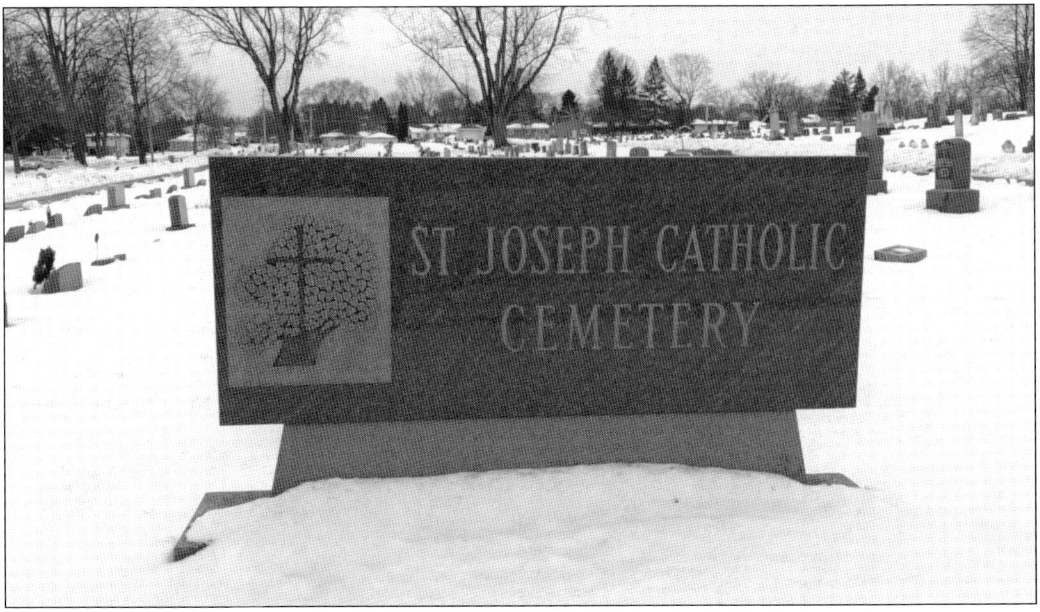

ST. JOSEPH CEMETERY. St. Joseph Catholic Cemetery was established in 1855. Among those buried in the cemetery are brewmaster John Steinmetz (1825–1872), hotel keepers John Simon (1818–1884) and John B. Simon (1855–1896), tavern keepers Joseph Lorenz (1862–1948) and Martin Barth (1862–1908), and pioneer resident and farmer Theodore Woltring (1812–1893). (Courtesy of the Grafton Historical Society.)

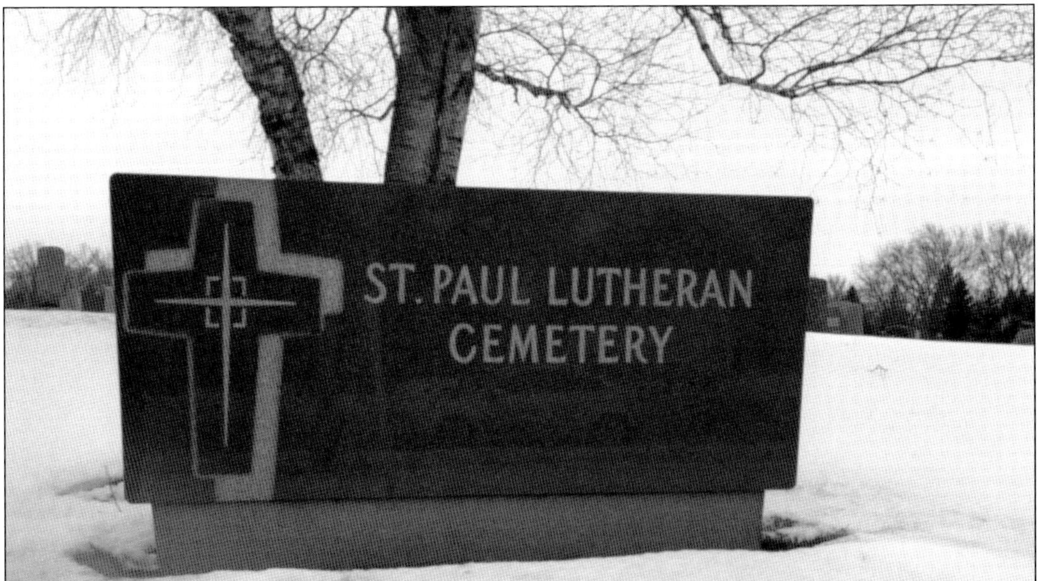

ST. PAUL CEMETERY. St. Paul Lutheran Cemetery was dedicated in 1876 and was established on land purchased for $325. The original cemetery occupied the northern portion of the present cemetery. Buried in the cemetery are stonemason Michael Port (1816–1893), blacksmiths Henry Kohlwey Sr. (1821–1896) and Albert Kath (1842–1917), farmers Herman Ahlers (1821–1884) and John Ahlers (1824–1896), and harness maker August Ploeger (1853–1907). (Courtesy of the Grafton Historical Society.)

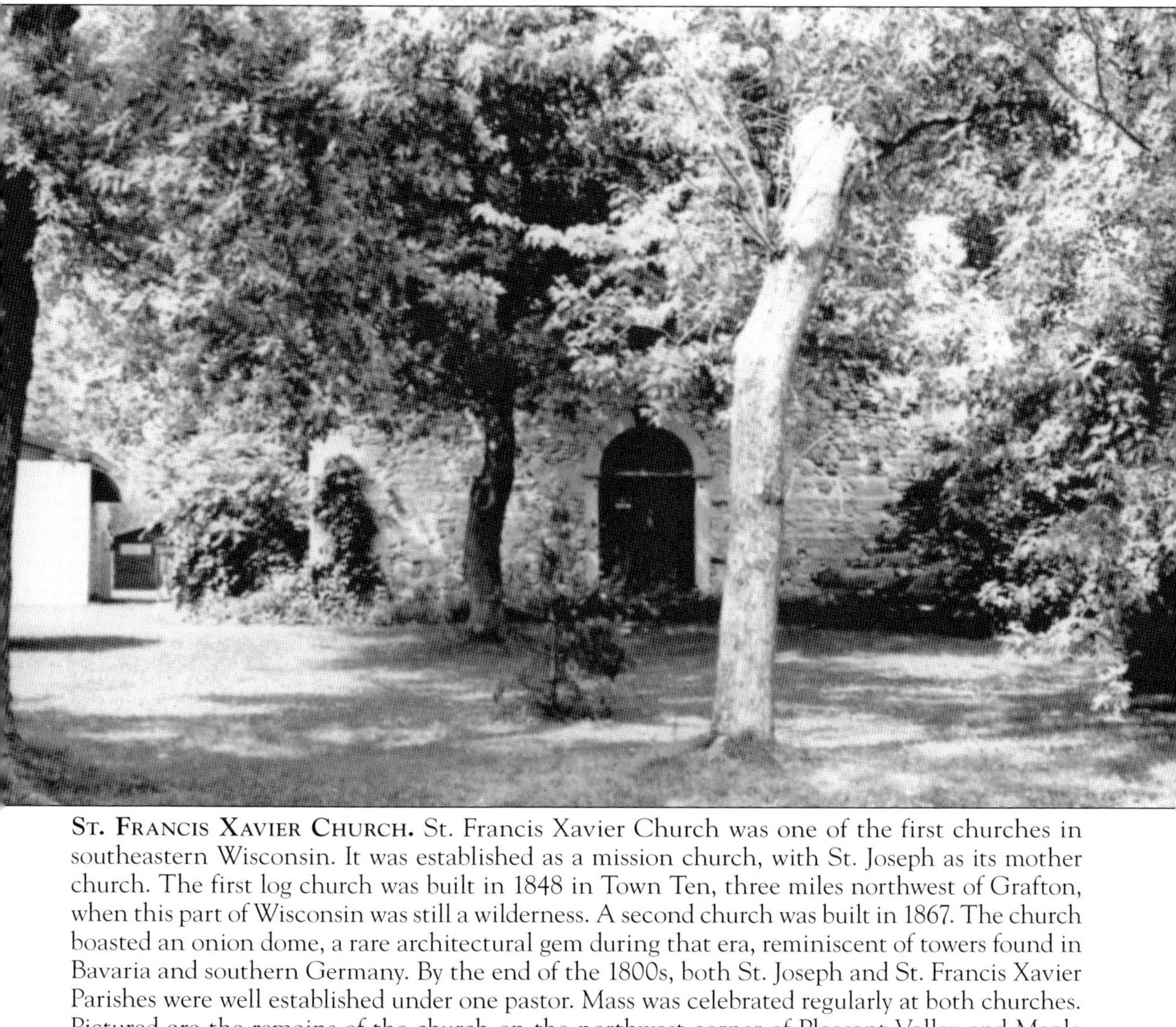

St. Francis Xavier Church. St. Francis Xavier Church was one of the first churches in southeastern Wisconsin. It was established as a mission church, with St. Joseph as its mother church. The first log church was built in 1848 in Town Ten, three miles northwest of Grafton, when this part of Wisconsin was still a wilderness. A second church was built in 1867. The church boasted an onion dome, a rare architectural gem during that era, reminiscent of towers found in Bavaria and southern Germany. By the end of the 1800s, both St. Joseph and St. Francis Xavier Parishes were well established under one pastor. Mass was celebrated regularly at both churches. Pictured are the remains of the church on the northwest corner of Pleasant Valley and Maple Roads. (Courtesy of St. Joseph Catholic Church.)

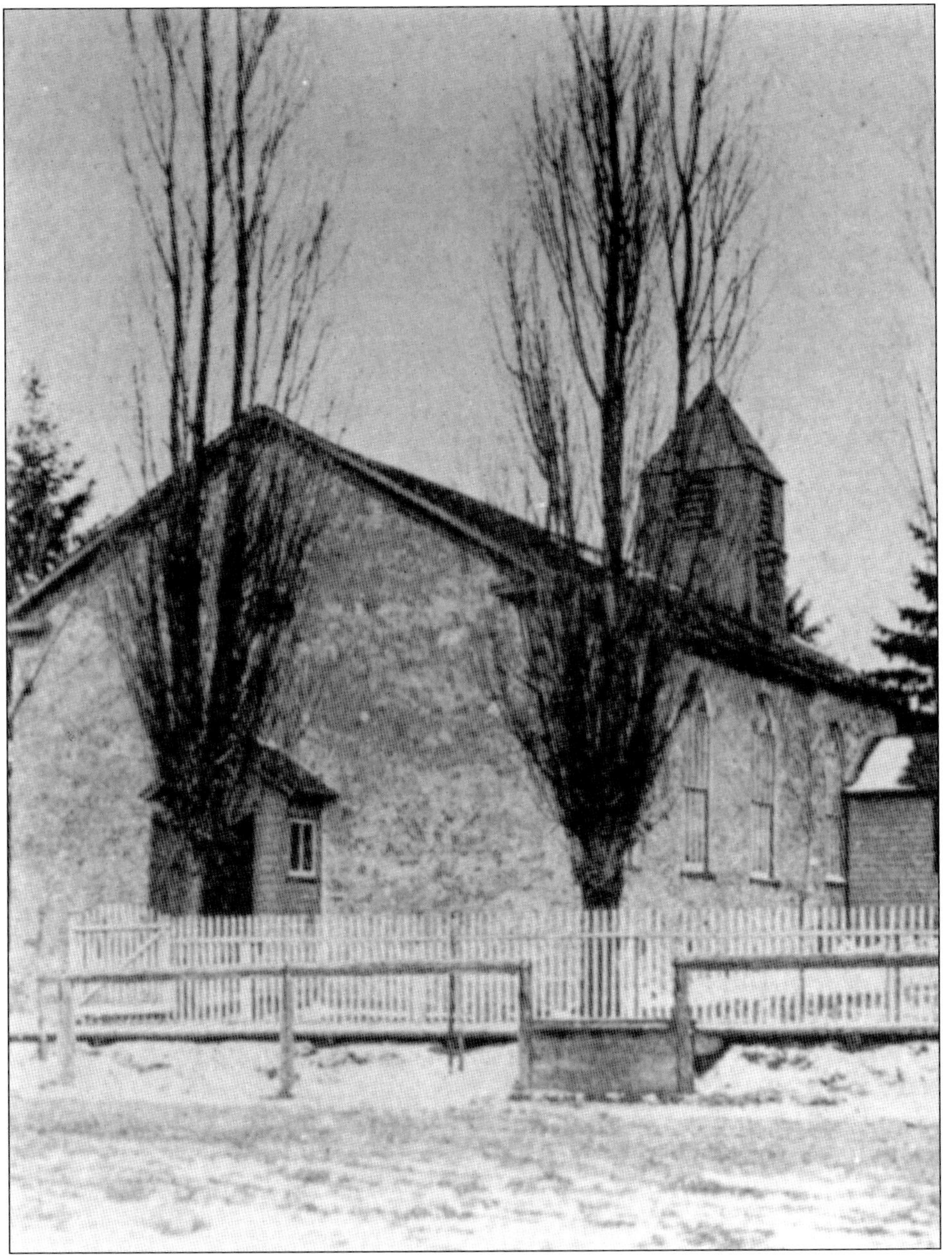

Early St. Joseph Church. The first Catholic services in Grafton were provided by circuit riders from St. John Cathedral in Milwaukee. The first missionaries were Bishop Henni, Fr. Michael Heiss, Fr. Martin Kundig, and Fr. Joseph Salzmann. In 1847–1848, a cholera epidemic hit the area, and Bishop Henni turned to Franciscan sisters newly arrived from Germany to help the settlers. St. Joseph Church was formally organized in 1849, with 24 charter families. From 1849 to 1860, church services were held at the courthouse. In 1860, the stone church was built. A single aisle went through the middle of the church, with pews on each side. Lightning and a resulting fire in 1864 burned most of the church furnishings, but they were replaced with money received from the Ludwig Mission Society in Europe. By 1897, the parish had grown significantly, and it was decided that a new church was needed. (Courtesy of St. Joseph Catholic Church.)

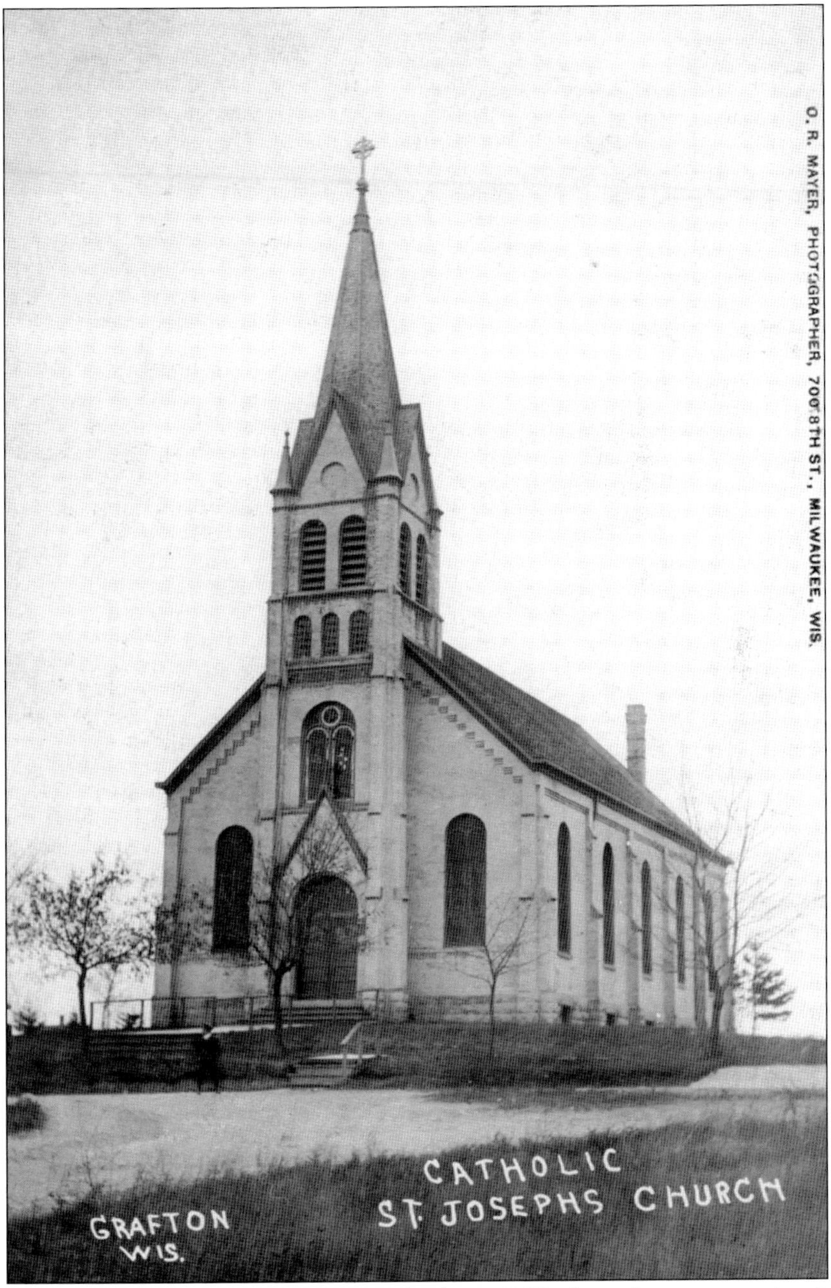

St. Joseph Church, 1897. This church was built in 1897 when the congregation had grown to 60 families. The church faced Sixteenth Avenue, south of Washington Avenue, where the only remaining reminder is the stairway from the sidewalk to the parking lot just south of the school. The church had a seating capacity of 260 and a pseudo-Gothic style similar to what the parishioners remembered from their homes in Europe. The stained-glass windows told a story in pictures and helped to subdue the intense heat of summer. In 1909, a system of pew rent was adopted. Each person was assigned a certain seat, and there were group discounts, with rates set at $9 for one, $12 for two, and $16 for three seats. This church was used until the current parish building was completed in 1968. It was then demolished. (Courtesy of St. Joseph Catholic Church.)

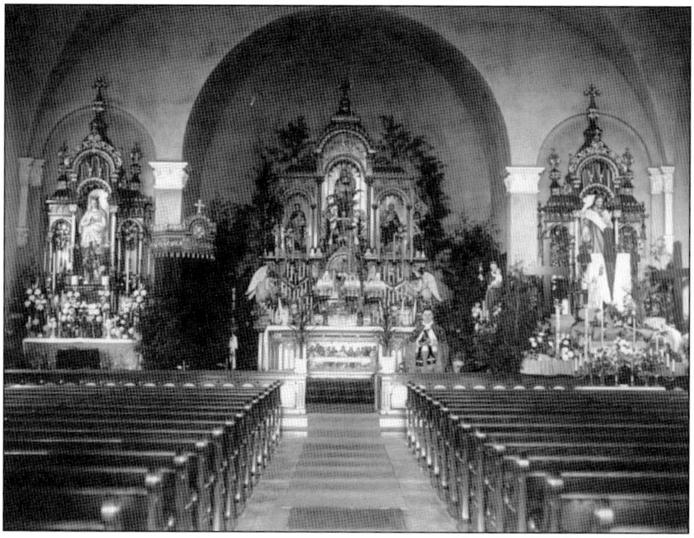

St. Joseph Church Interior. These very elaborate main and side altars at St. Joseph Church date from 1897. The interior of the church took on an even more festive look at the holidays. Natural materials such as boughs, live holiday plants, and candles were used as decorations. (Courtesy of St. Joseph Catholic Church.)

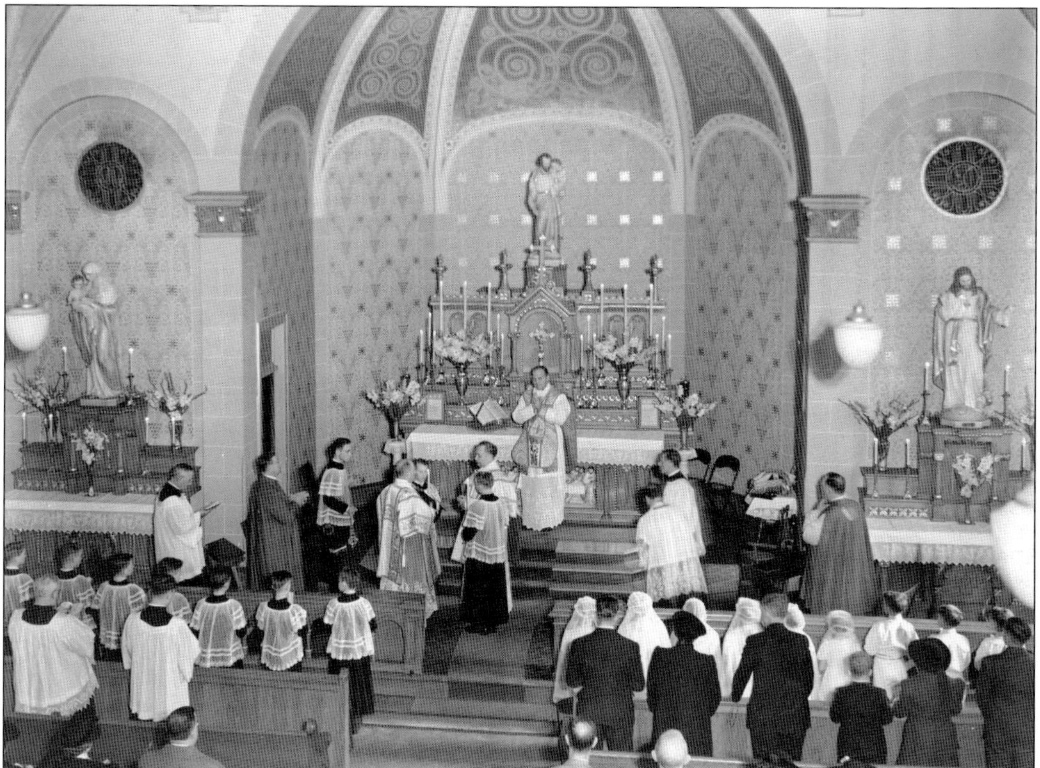

Fr. Joseph Brasky. Father Brasky celebrated the silver jubilee of his ordination on May 3, 1940, with a solemn high Mass at St. Joseph Church. The church's first communicants (first row) formed a guard of honor for the occasion. Later, Father Brasky achieved a different kind of recognition when a circular metal blade mysteriously landed on the front lawn of the church. He was featured in newspapers around the nation, and in one account, he is quoted as saying that although he would not claim it was a flying saucer, "It may or may not be one of those flying discs that have been reported all over the country." (Courtesy of St. Joseph Catholic Church.)

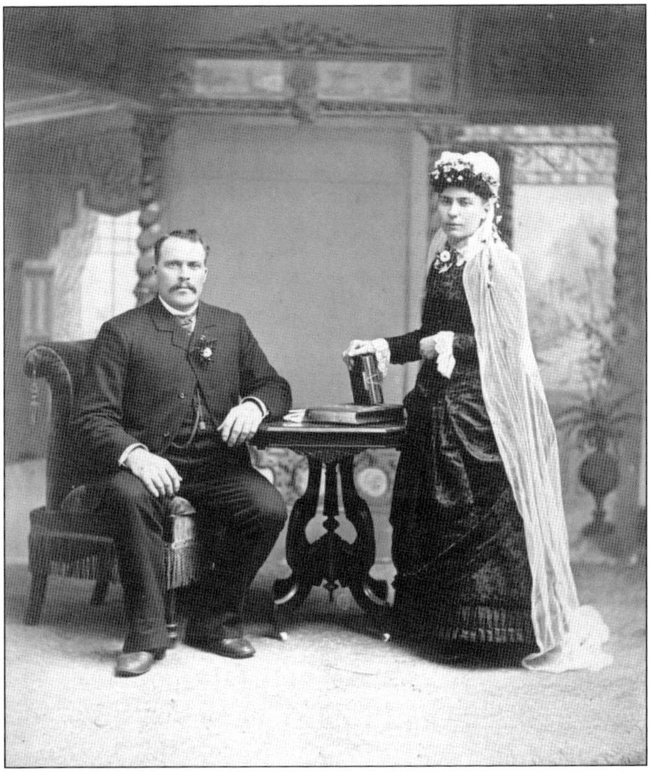

Doppel Wedding Portrait. Andrew Doppel Jr. and Barbara Bienlein were married on February 4, 1885, at St. Joseph Church. After the wedding, the newlyweds moved to Clinton, Iowa. Around 1890, they moved back to Grafton and settled on a five-acre farm on Seventh Avenue across from St. Paul Church. (Courtesy of Bill Malone.)

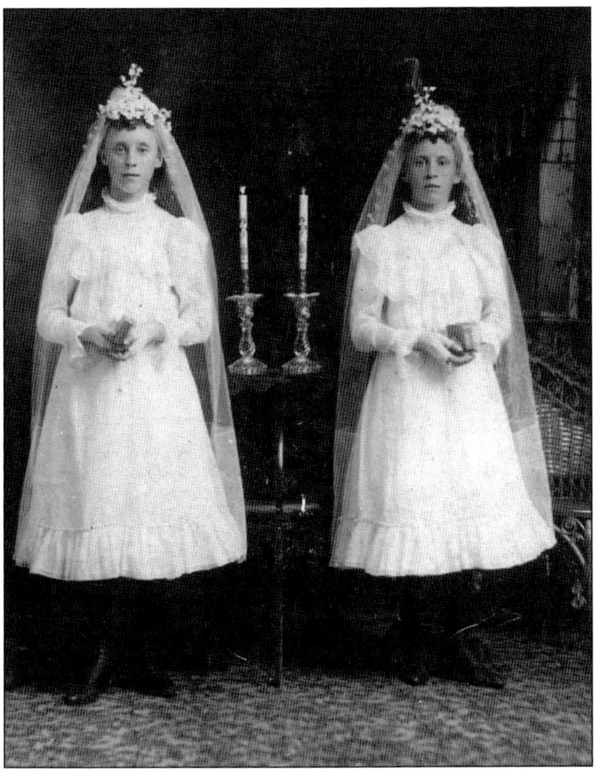

Doppel First Communion. Shown here in their identical first communion finery are the Doppel twins Margaret (left) and Ann. They were born in 1887 and had their first communion at St. Joseph Church at the turn of the 20th century. Ann later married Matt Becker, and Margaret married Joe Lorenz. This photograph was likely taken at the studio in Grafton. (Courtesy of Bill Malone.)

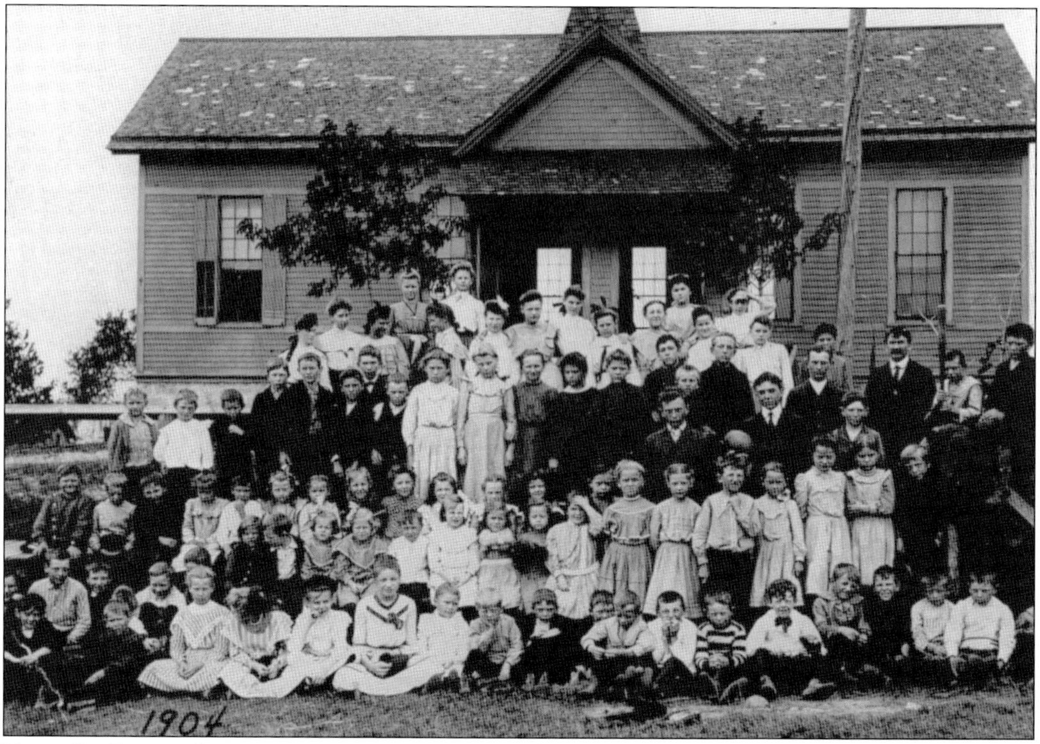

FIRST ST. JOSEPH SCHOOL. In 1890, a one-room schoolhouse became the first St. Joseph School. It had an enrollment of 35 students taught by a lay teacher. In 1908, the school was remodeled, and the parishioners arranged to have the School Sisters of Assisi come and teach. In those early years, it was a requirement that all education in parochial schools be conducted in English and German. Latin, the universal language of the Catholic Church, was also taught. This wooden structure was replaced by a new brick school in 1921. Below is a scene in front of the St. Joseph rectory. (Both, courtesy of St. Joseph Catholic Church.)

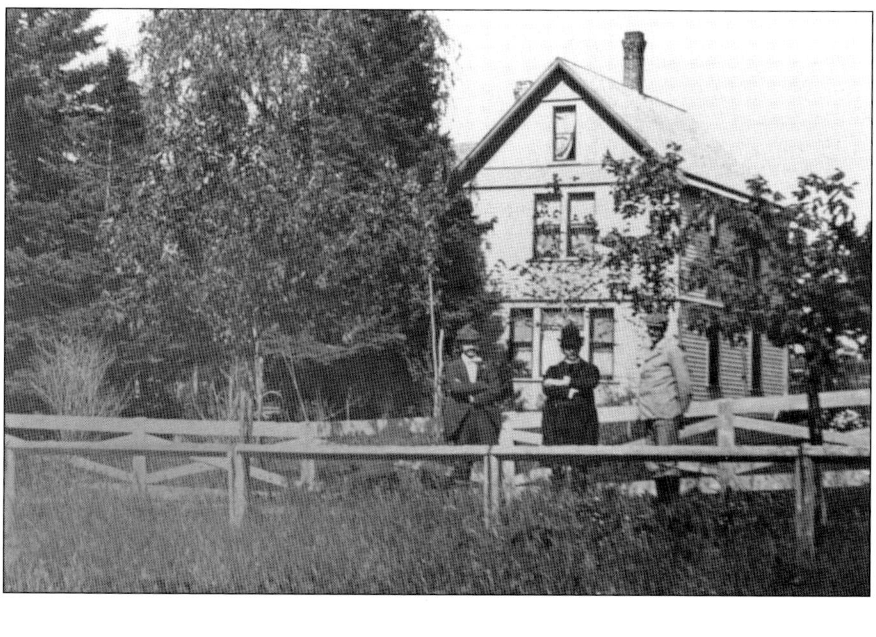

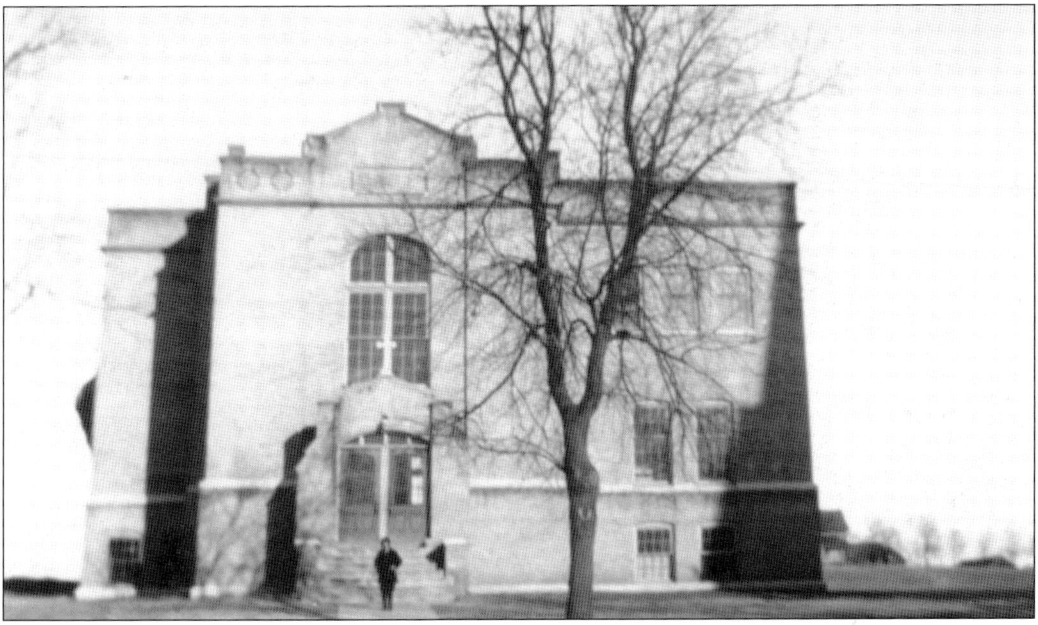

St. Joseph's School, 1922. A fundraising campaign by the parish raised $8,765 to begin construction of this new St. Joseph Parish School, which opened in 1922. There was no graduating class that year, but in 1923, all the seventh and eighth graders graduated together because Richard Berger, county supervisor of schools, decided that since they had all studied the same subjects, they should all graduate. At the time, all parochial school students were required to take a county exam to receive their diplomas. The school operated until it was taken down and a new school was built in 1958. (Both, courtesy of St. Joseph Catholic Church.)

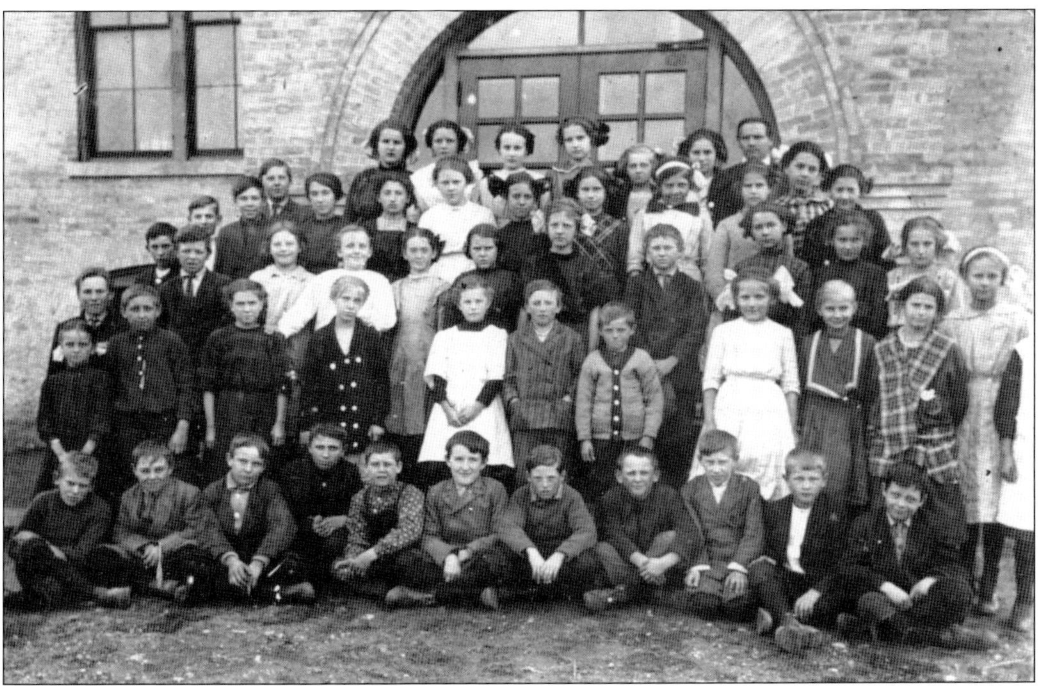

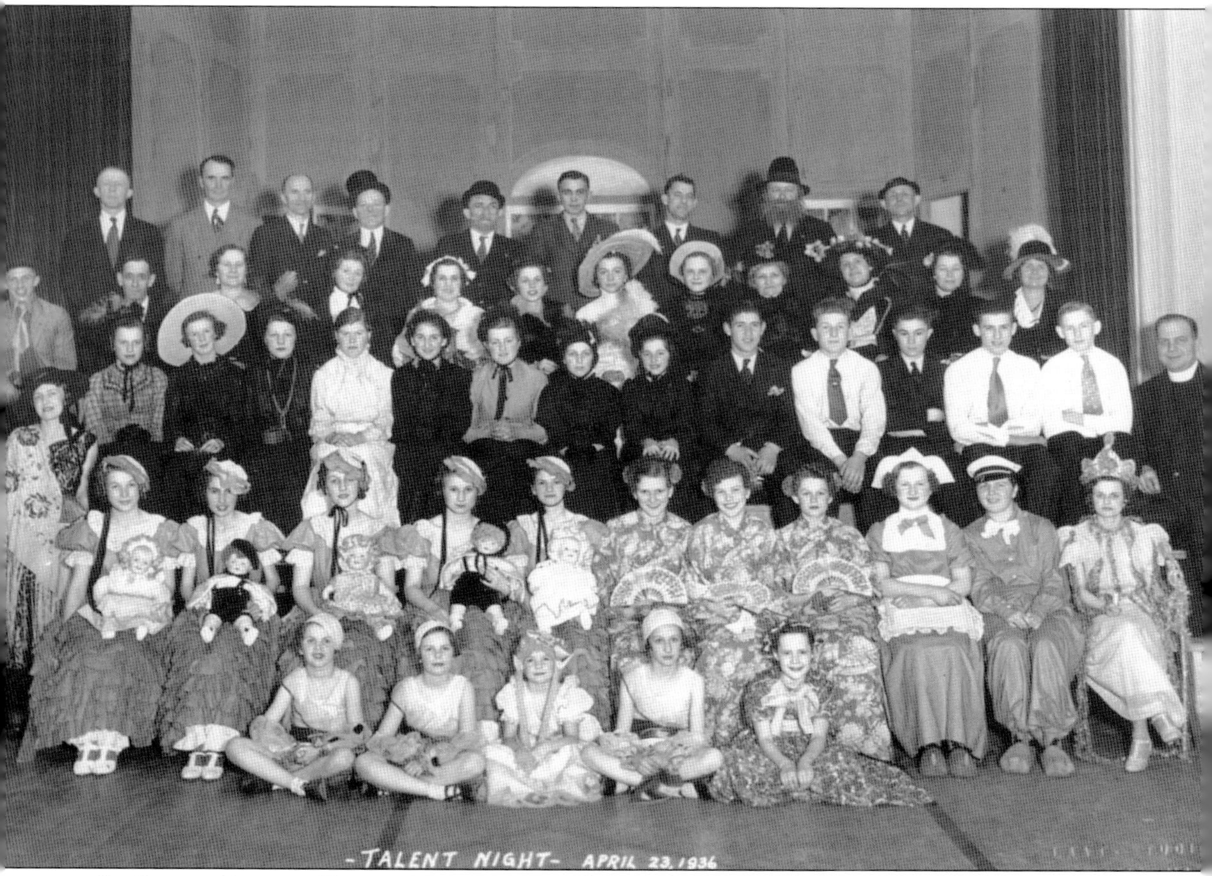

St. Joseph Church Talent Night. It was talent night at the Grafton High School auditorium on Thursday, April 23, 1936, to benefit St. Joseph Church. The five-act show featured singing, dancing, pantomime, comedy, and instrumental numbers and also Milwaukee guest entertainers the Festival Quartet. Among those pictured here are Bernice Schanen, Ed Thelen, Joseph Welzien, Anton Wollner, Wilmer Klotz, Joseph Meunier, William Vey, Helen Roob, Isabelle Hollrith, Rosalie Roob, Joseph Niesen, Margaret Jungers, Edna Jungers, Theresa Wollner, Margaret Beschta, Ardell Greiten, Rose Welzien, Melba Klotz, Helen Dickmann, Theresa Vey, Henry Kassens, Alice Stern, Lucille Dickmann, Ethel Niesen, Ruth Senger, Marceline Hilgart, Anna Freitag, John Long, Antoinette Wollner, Leone and Marie Buchholz, Virginia Bienlein, Martha Dichmann, Fred Blommer, Germaine Lucas, Barney Inkmann, Barbara Ann Rolfs, Mary Rose Rolfs, Donna Jean Schowalter, Gertrude Reichardt, Harriet Clapham, Loraine Dickmann, Margaret Meunier, Betty Riebe, Frank Buchholz, and Dorothy Schumacher. (Courtesy of Nic Schanen.)

Moving the Rectory. The rectory of St. Joseph Church had to be moved approximately 200 feet to make room for the new St. Joseph School. The house, which weighed about 90 tons, was moved from Sixteenth Avenue, where it faced west, to its new location on Washington Street, where it faced north. In preparation for moving the building, the porch and garage had to be taken off. (Courtesy of St. Joseph Catholic Church.)

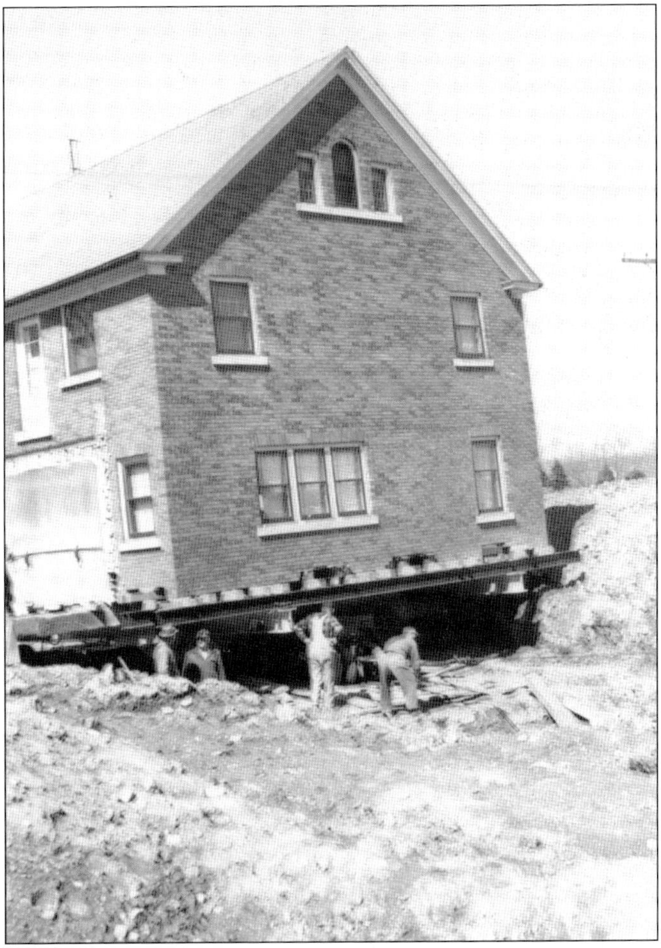

St. Joseph School, 1958. Following World War II, St. Joseph Church outgrew its old school, so a new one was built and dedicated in May 1958. The school was built at a cost of $300,000 with an initial enrollment of 282, which was to grow considerably over the next decade. The school had a bookstore, office, teachers' lounge, and auditorium-gymnasium. It still operates today. (Courtesy of St. Joseph Catholic Church.)

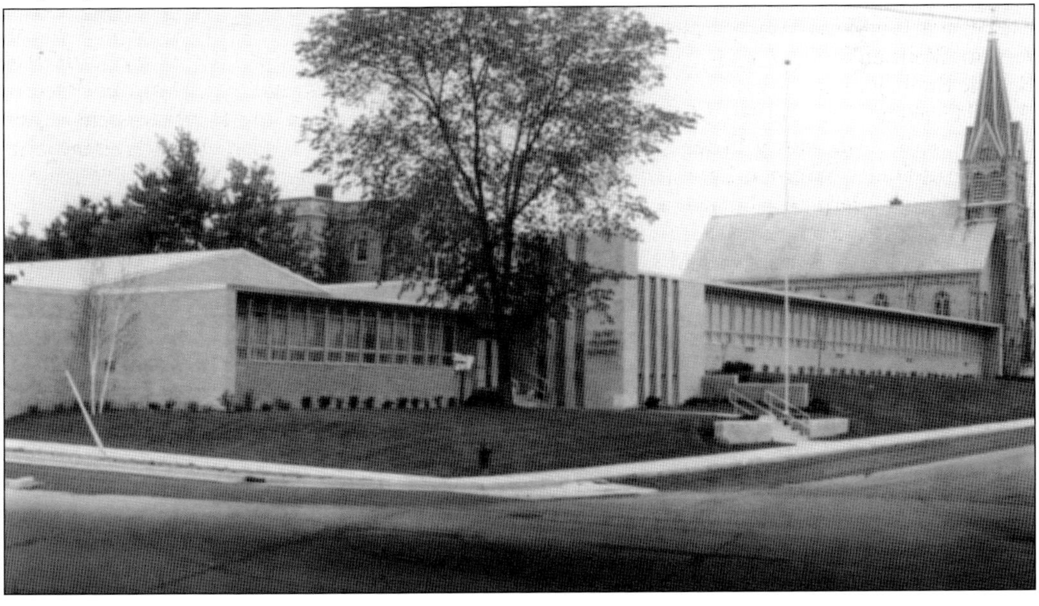

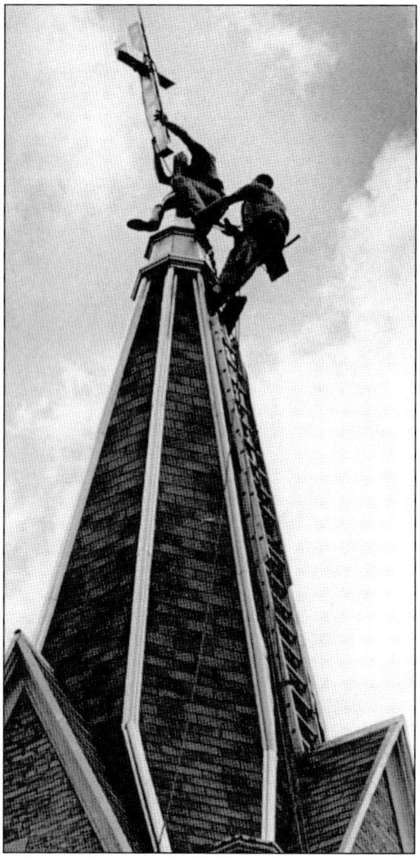

Steeplejacks. Before the 1897 church was razed in the summer of 1967, steeplejacks were hired to take down the cross at the top of the church spire. Workers were hired from McNitt Steeplejack Service of Sheboygan, Wisconsin. Shown at left taking down the cross are Tim McNitt and Don Kettle of Whitewater. In early 1968, ground was broken for a new church, which was officially dedicated on May 4, 1969. The new church was built at a cost of $460,000 and provided seating for 1,000 churchgoers. The first mass in the new church was celebrated on Christmas Eve of that year. (Both, courtesy of St. Joseph Catholic Church.)

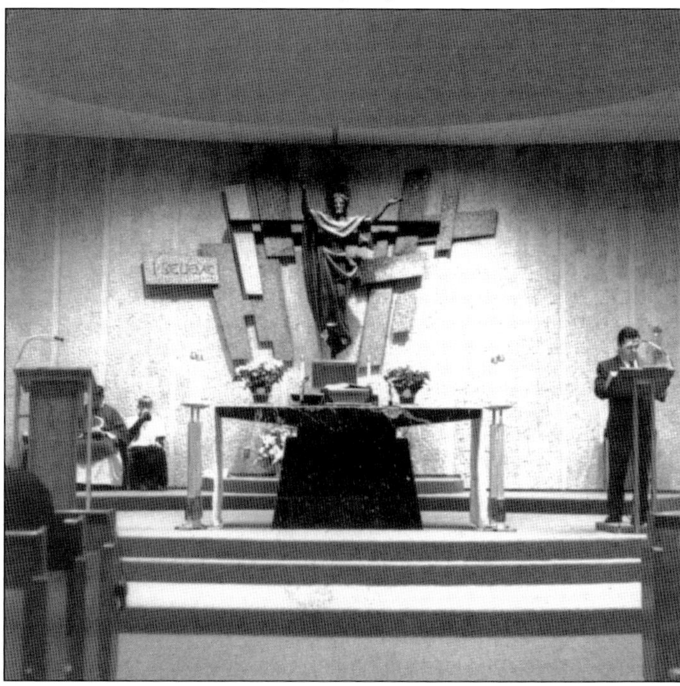

Five

TRANSPORTATION

From its earliest times, Grafton was a center of transportation for the area. It was a stop on the old Green Bay Road, one of the first roads in Wisconsin. The Green Bay Road was a military road from Chicago to Green Bay, following an ancient Native American trail that began in Florida and made its way to Hudson Bay. In 1825, a different kind of traveler came through the area when 99 cattle were driven through Grafton from southern Illinois to Green Bay by William Steven Hamilton, the son of Alexander Hamilton. Most of the early settlers traveled by ship from Chicago to Milwaukee and then rode horseback or walked to Grafton. By the mid-1800s, horses provided the main means of transportation, soon followed by rail, an electric interurban, and then automobiles. The Wisconsin Central Railway came to Grafton in 1871, providing transportation for the products of Grafton's mills and bringing new people to work in them. The Green Bay Road and Highway 60, the first turnpike from east to west in Ozaukee County, made Grafton a hub of transportation. The new and exciting electric interurban service provided by the Milwaukee Northern Railway Company arrived in 1906. Now people could easily travel from Grafton to Milwaukee or Sheboygan. It was not long, however, before the automobile took center stage. In 1910, cars were listed in property tax assessments in Grafton for the first time. There were four automobiles, valued at a total of $1,300, and 76 wagons, carriages, and sleighs, valued at a total of $2,070. In the 1940s, the interurban shut down, a casualty of the automobile and new highways. That highway system would, in part, be responsible for greatly increasing the population of Grafton. Between 1950 and 1980, the village population increased five times over, from 1,489 to 8,381. The construction of Interstate 43 in the mid-1960s also helped connect Grafton to other communities.

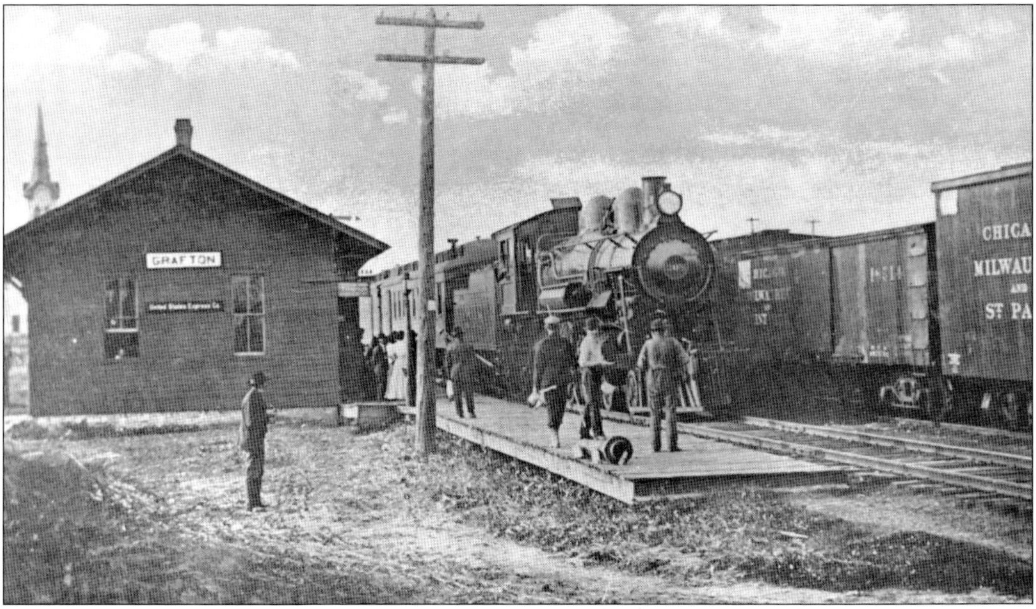

CHICAGO & NORTHWESTERN. A Chicago & Northwestern train is pictured here heading south. The St. Paul church steeple is in the background. In 1873, the Milwaukee, Lakeshore & Western Railroad arrived in Grafton in what was a very significant development for the village. It followed the valley of the Milwaukee River north to Green Bay. The name was later changed to the Chicago & Northwestern. (Courtesy of the Grafton Chamber of Commerce.)

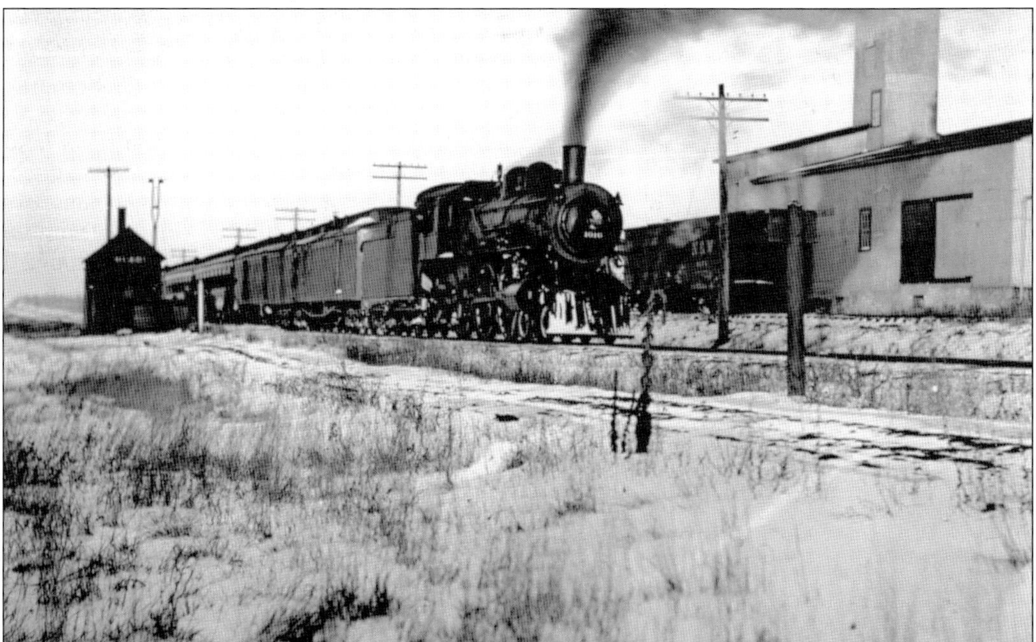

ULAO PASSENGER STOP. The Chicago & Northwestern passenger train had a stop at the Ulao feed, coal and grain elevator. A grain elevator, like the one shown here, had several compartments. The grain was held there by the farmer until he wanted to sell it. This was also a stop for passengers heading south. (Courtesy of Arnold Kaul Sr.)

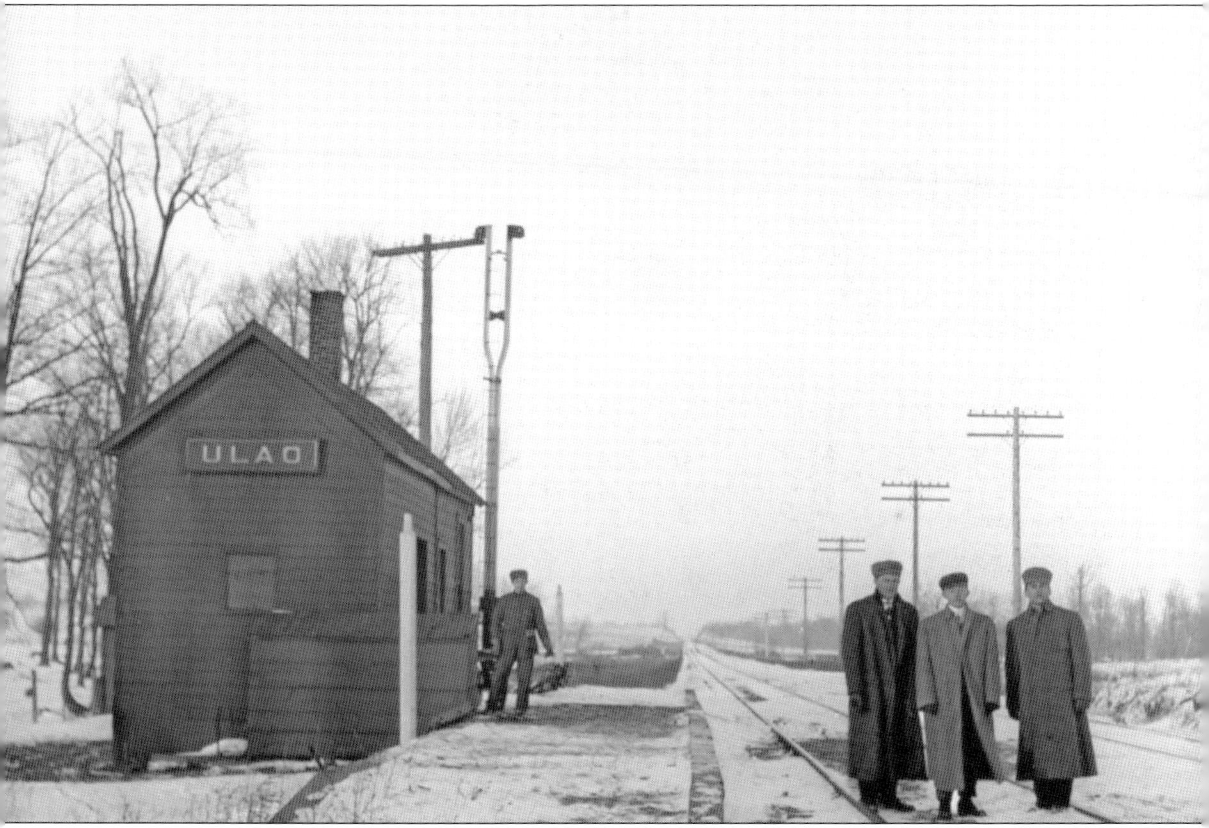

ULAO STATION. Pictured here is a view of Ulao station looking north from Highway 60. Standing on the tracks are Fred Helms (left) and Art Tess (center). Port Ulao was founded in 1847 by James T. Gifford of Elgin, Illinois, who sought to take advantage of the lake and the clearing of land taking place in the area. Gifford built a 1,000-foot wooden pier into the lake for steamers to dock. He then constructed a chute down the 150-foot bluff to the decks of the wood-burning steamships. The pier was also notable because during the Civil War, several companies of Milwaukee militia disembarked there to deal with a draft riot in Port Washington. The village of Ulao succumbed to the transition from wood to coal fuel for steamboats. (Courtesy of Arnold Kaul Sr.)

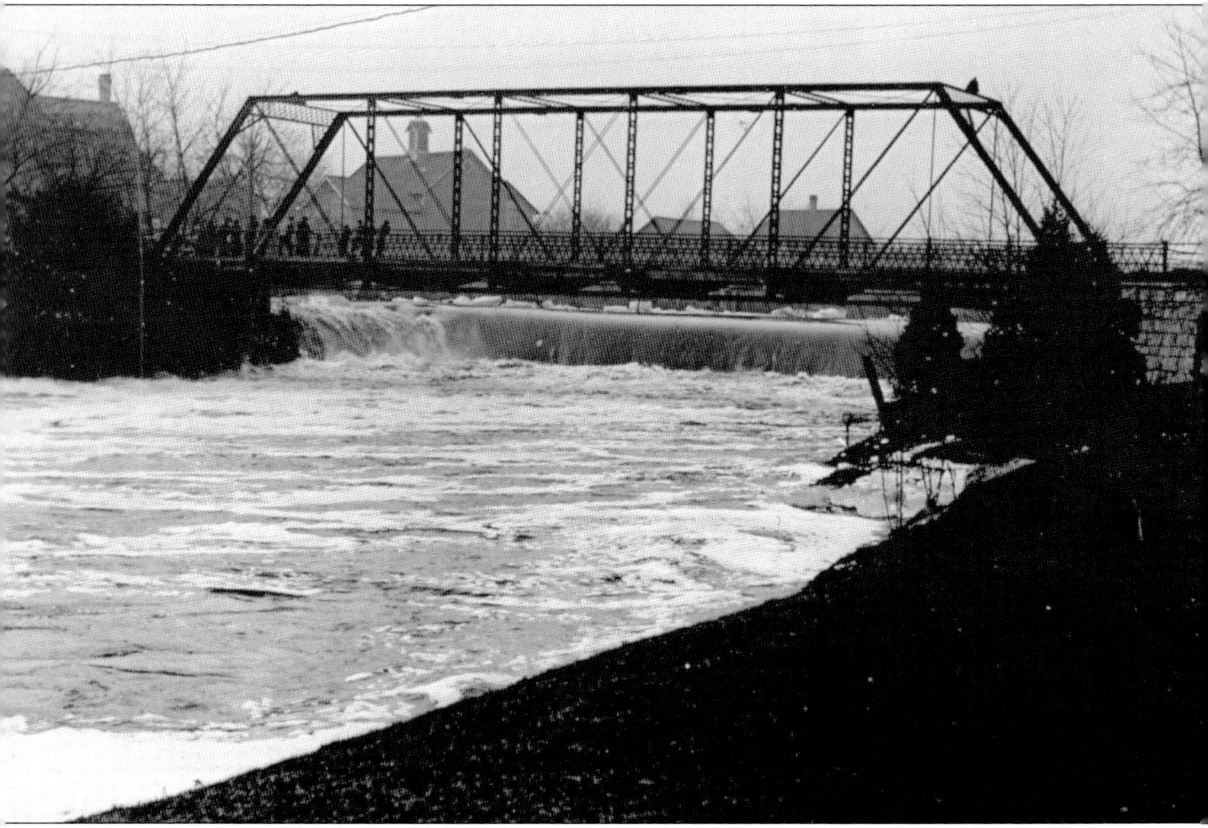

IRON BRIDGE. The first iron bridge in Grafton was built in 1888 by the Wisconsin Bridge and Iron Company of Wauwatosa to replace a previous wooden one. It was found that wooden bridges sagged under the constant weight of traffic, and so their span was limited. They were also subject to fire and rot; iron bridges solved those problems. This riveted iron bridge was the only way across the Milwaukee River in the village of Grafton until 1928, when a new concrete bridge was built on Washington Street to handle increased car and truck traffic. In 1996, the iron bridge was set to be demolished and replaced by another concrete bridge. Many people in the village asked that it be saved, so it was moved to Lime Kiln Park, where it is preserved today. Note the people on the bridge. (Courtesy of Arnold Kaul Sr.)

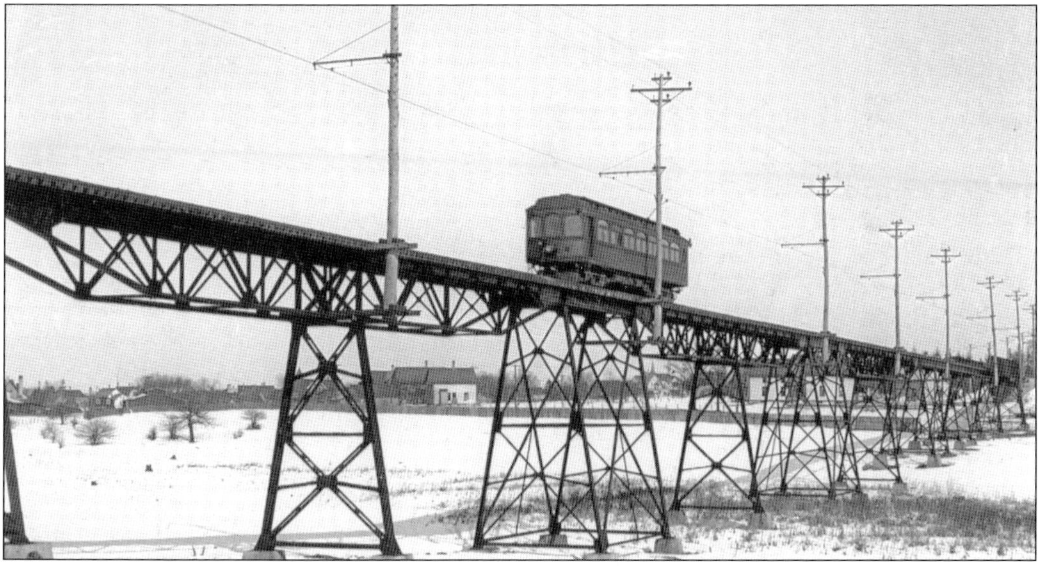

Interurban. The electric interurban line was built from Milwaukee to Port Washington in 1906 and extended to Sheboygan in 1908. It provided a safe, economical, and reliable way to travel across the county and to Milwaukee. The tracks were laid on a limestone bed, and power came from overhead wires. The iron trestle shown above was built in 1907 by the Milwaukee Northern Railway Company as part of its railway line. Trains ran seven days a week, on the hour. Blues recording artists used the interurban to travel to Grafton to record at the studio inside the Grafton Chair Factory. (Above, courtesy of Arnold Kaul Sr.; below, courtesy of Richard Scheer.)

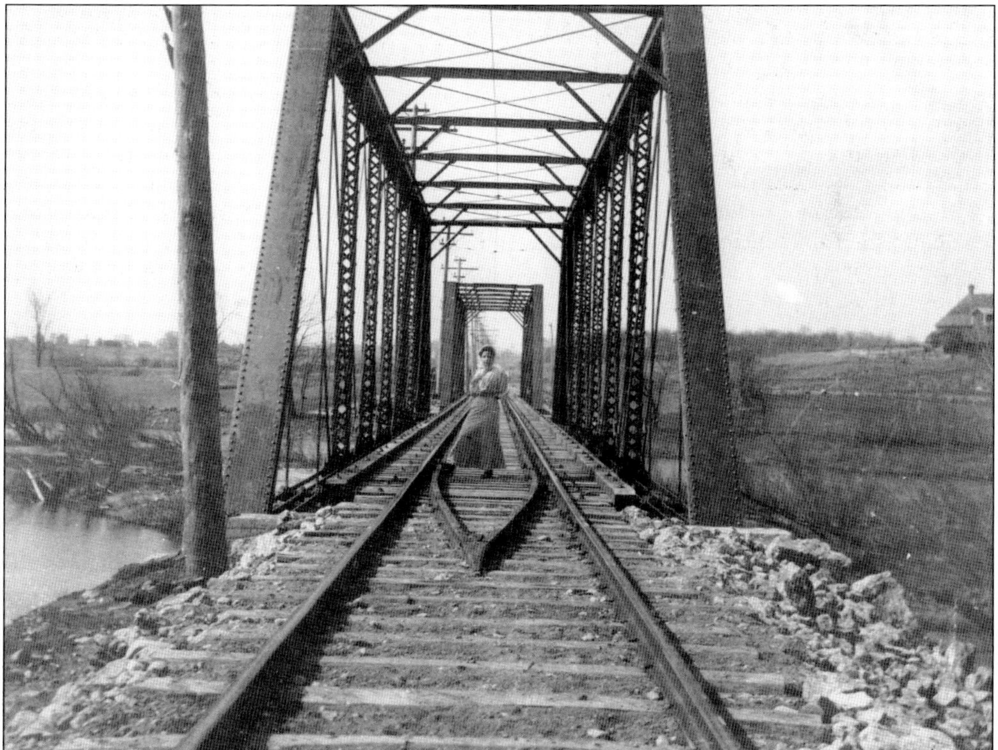

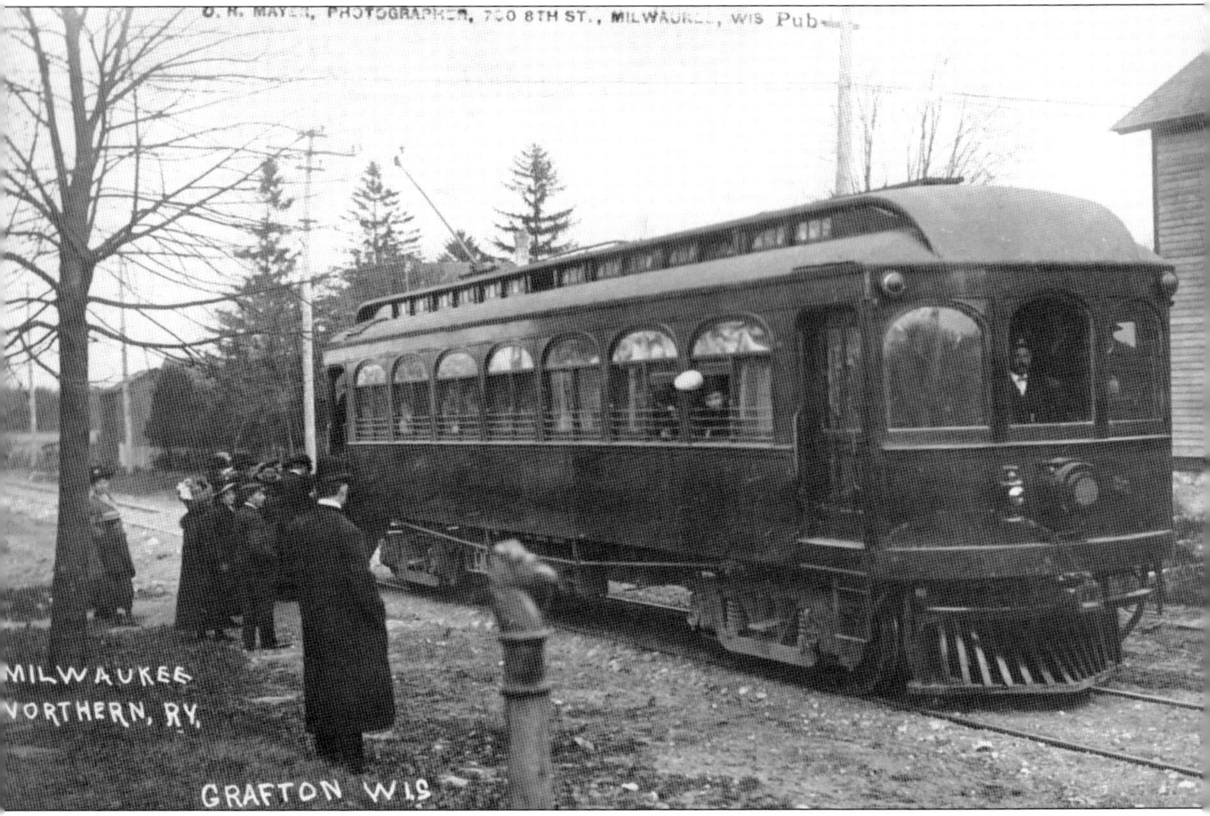

Passengers Board Interurban. Passengers wait to board the interurban in this scene from the early 1900s. The company was so intent on timeliness that motormen had to take their pocket watches every week to a jewelry store to have them inspected and regulated for accuracy. There was also an "Owl Car" in the evening for people who wanted to go to Milwaukee to see a show. The last train left Milwaukee at about midnight. The fare from Port Washington to Grafton was 10¢. The fare from Grafton to Milwaukee was 40¢. Interurban business peaked around 1915 and then decreased as more people could afford cars and more roads were paved. Service on the interurban ended in 1948. Notice the horse-head hitching post in the foreground and the elaborate traveling outfits of the waiting passengers. (Courtesy of Arnold Kaul Sr.)

SLEIGH POSTMAN. The postman's horse is tied up and waiting for his route to begin in this scene on Twelfth Avenue in Grafton. The post office is not visible, but is to the left. The sleigh was for winter mail delivery. The postman would ride inside the sleigh and put the horse's reins through the window in front. (Courtesy of Arnold Kaul Sr.)

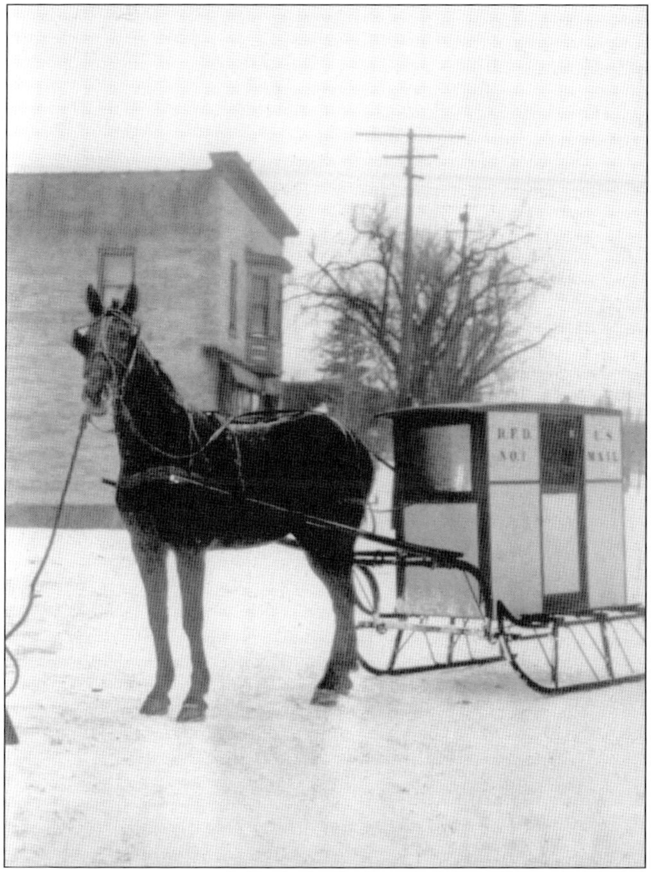

GRAFTON MAIL. In the early years of the village, Grafton mail was delivered through the Port Washington Post Office. Shown here is the Port Washington mail carriage at the Kaul farm just east of Port Washington Road on Arrowhead Road. Eventually, mail was delivered through the Grafton Post Office to farms in the area. (Courtesy of Arnold Kaul Sr.)

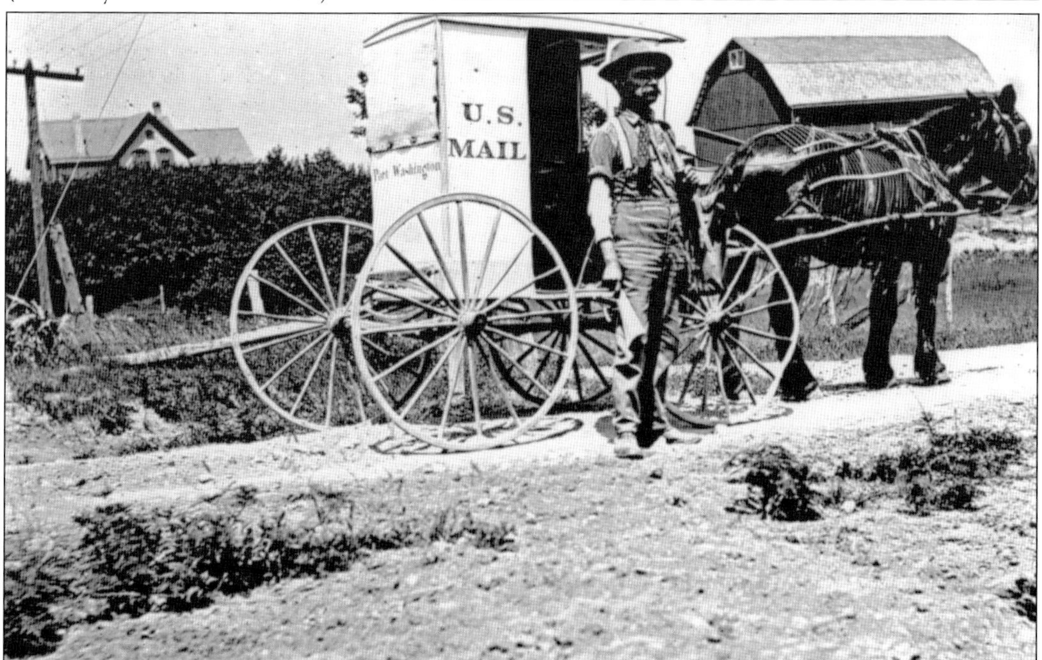

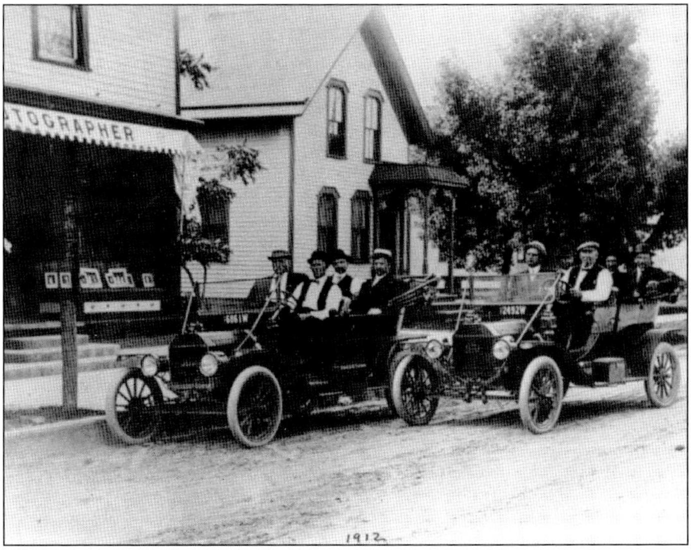

Model Ts. A group of early automobile drivers pose proudly in their Ford Model Ts facing south in front of Grafton's photography studio before beginning their drive. Also known as a "Tin Lizzie," "Leaping Lena," jitney, or flivver, the Model T was produced from 1908 to 1927. Note the wooden spokes on the wheels and the toolboxes mounted on the sides of the cars. (Courtesy of the Ed Rappold Photograph Collection at the Cedarburg Cultural Center.)

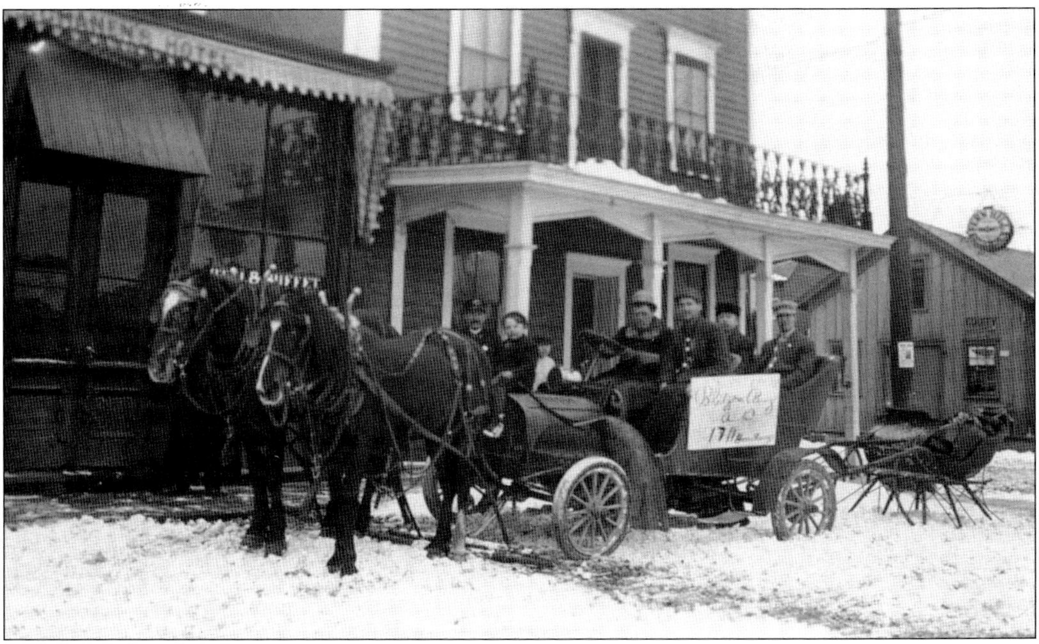

Auto, Horse, and Sleigh. A team of horses pulling a car, pulling a sleigh, is an unusual sight in front of Schanen's Hotel in this 1910 scene. The horses appear undisturbed at pulling a car rather than a buggy. The car has the steering wheel on the right. Before the Model T, virtually every car in the United States placed the steering wheel on the right. Ford made the change to make it easier for people entering on the passenger side to avoid oncoming traffic. There are also no headlights on the car. It had an acetylene light, which was not to provide light for the driver, but to make sure people saw the car coming. Note the sign on the side of the car. In those times, many people would put a sign on their car indicating their destination. (Courtesy of Nic Schanen.)

Six

Recreation

Hard work was a hallmark of life both in the village and on the farm in early Grafton, but as the 1800s turned into the 20th century, things began to slowly change for workers. While in 1860 the average workweek was about 70 hours, by 1890, it was reduced to 62 and decreased again to 55 hours per week in 1910. A fortunate result of this was that by the early 1900s, there was substantially more time for leisure and recreational activities. Photography became a popular hobby. Team sports, such as baseball, basketball, and football, were organized and attracted more and more spectators. People became interested in tennis, archery, bowling, and biking. There was also the Milwaukee River that had, for nearly a century, provided both necessities and recreational activities. It was a sanctuary for birds and a mecca for fishermen. A local fisherman's account described a spot just north of Veteran's (then Mill Pond) Park that provided excellent fishing with a likely catch of bullhead, bass, red horse, and occasionally, northern pike. The river was also an ideal place to canoe, swim, and in the winter months, ice skate. Entertainment was also provided by the hotels and taverns in town. Dominating the square was the Hotel Grafton, known as the finest hostelry in the area. With its distinctive turret and central location, it was a popular place for community gatherings. The hotel advertised "good rooms, excellent food and first rate drinks." The nearby Schanen Hotel also provided a beer garden and Saturday-night entertainment. Local "Saturday Night" bands sprang up and performed in the band shell on the square. In today's Grafton, recreation is still important. The village's recreation department offers more than 30 programs. There are 17 parks totaling 120 acres, a pair of baseball fields, a soccer practice field, a family aquatic center, and an interurban trail for hiking and biking.

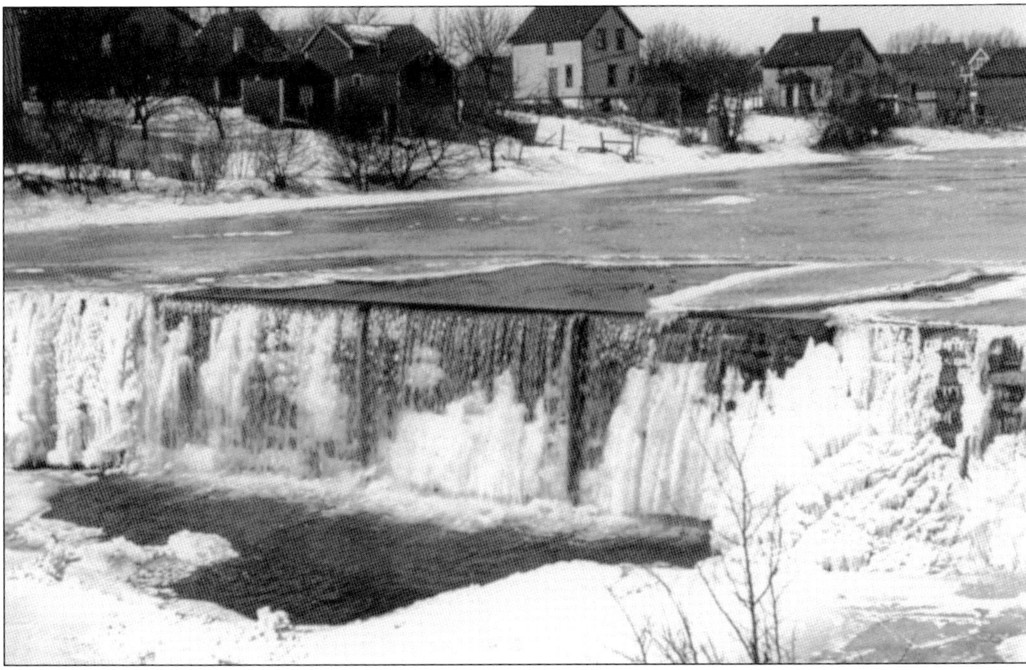

MILWAUKEE RIVER. The Milwaukee River in Grafton was a popular destination for canoeing and rafting and also a sanctuary for birds and a gathering place for fishermen. Large fish were caught there. (Courtesy of Arnold Kaul Sr.)

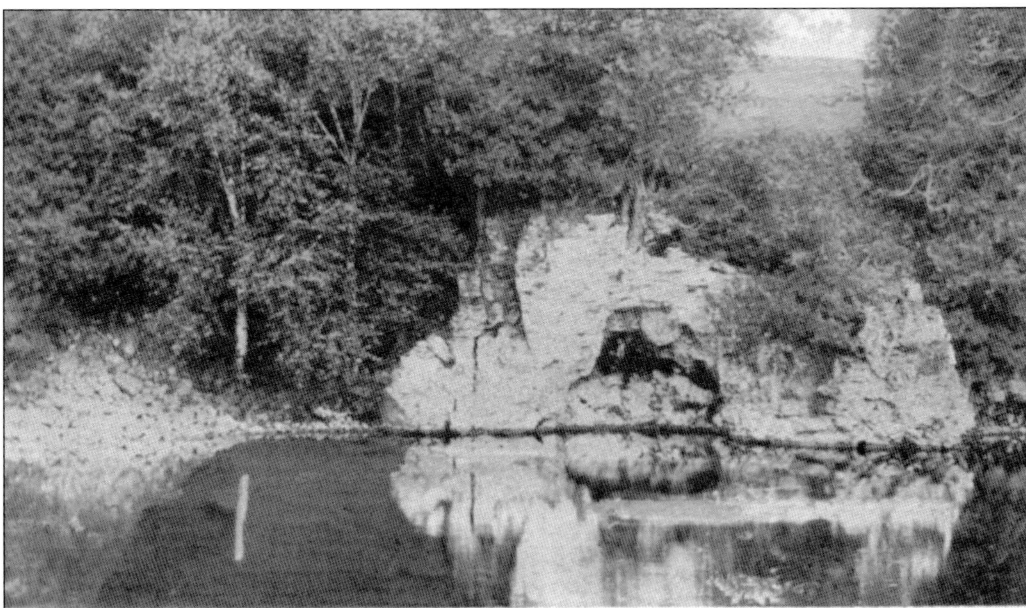

Rock Cave, Milwaukee River, Grafton, Wis.

ROCK CAVE. Rock Cave, shown here, is near Falls Road. Many of the formations in the area are sandstone, which wears away over time. Notice the man in the cave. (Courtesy of Vivian Scherf Laabs.)

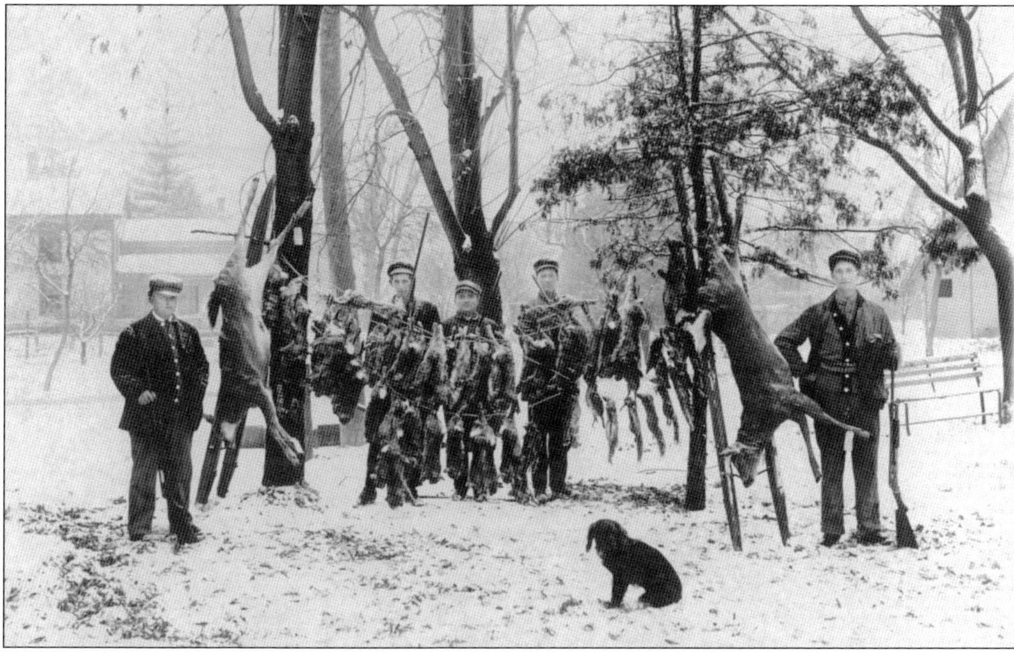

THE HUNT, 1918. These hunters proudly pose after a successful hunt. They would board the interurban with their guns and dogs, and it would take them to where they wanted to hunt and then bring them back again with their game. Pictured from left to right are Carlie Melcars, ? Hackbardt, Charlie Rilling, Jim Wegner, and Gust Wegner. (Courtesy of Nola Wegner.)

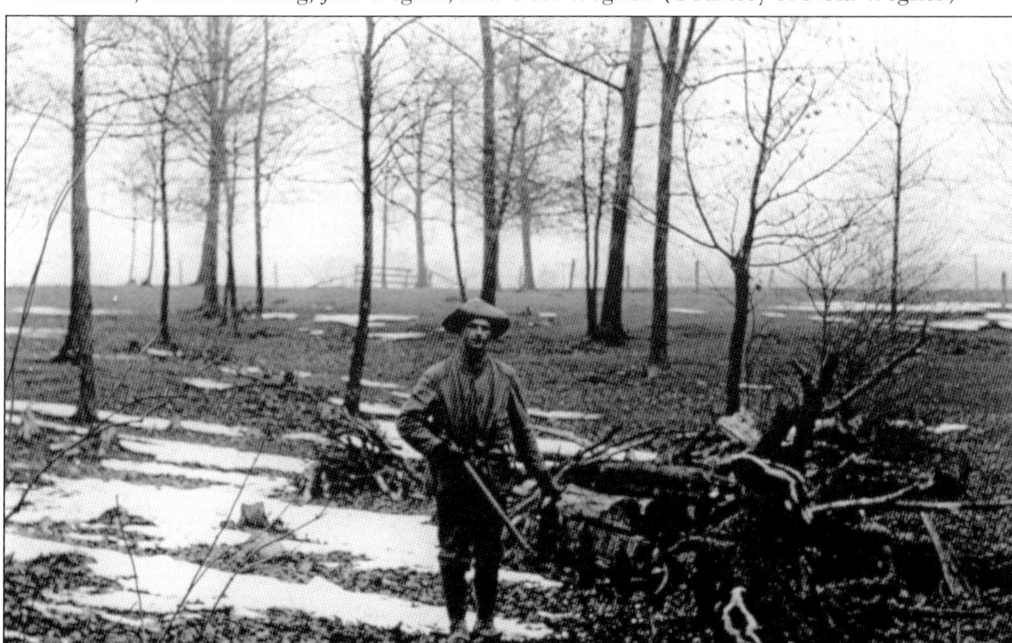

SKUNK TRAPPER. Another kind of hunting involved clearing skunks from farmers' lands. Shown here is Fred Prowatzke, a skunk trapper, with his catch. Early entrepreneurs would use skunk oil to produce a chest ointment that was thought to be good for whooping cough or croup. (Courtesy of Arnold Kaul Sr.)

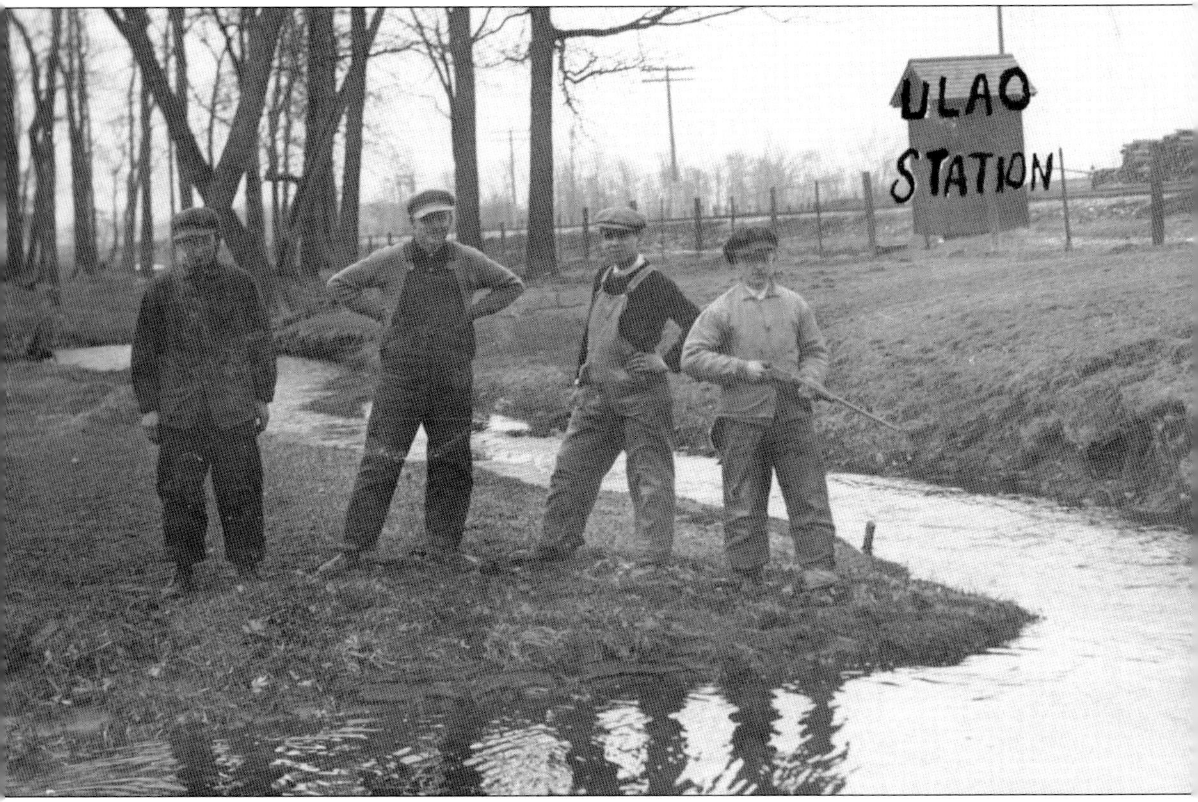

ULAO CREEK. Local residents found good hunting along Ulao Creek, a 9.2-mile tributary of the Milwaukee River that begins in a swampy area south of Port Washington in Grafton and flows south through Ulao. The Ulao railroad stop is in the background. Ulao gained some notoriety in the late 1880s for being the one-time home of presidential assassin Charles Guiteau, a disappointed patronage seeker who shot Pres. James Garfield on July 2, 1881, in Washington, DC. Hopes were high that Garfield could survive his wounds, but he died two and a half months later in September 1881. As a child, Guiteau spent time in Ulao, in the township of Grafton. His family moved to Ulao from Grafton in 1850. Accounts differ, but it appears he lived there from two to five years before returning to Illinois. (Courtesy of Allen Buchholz.)

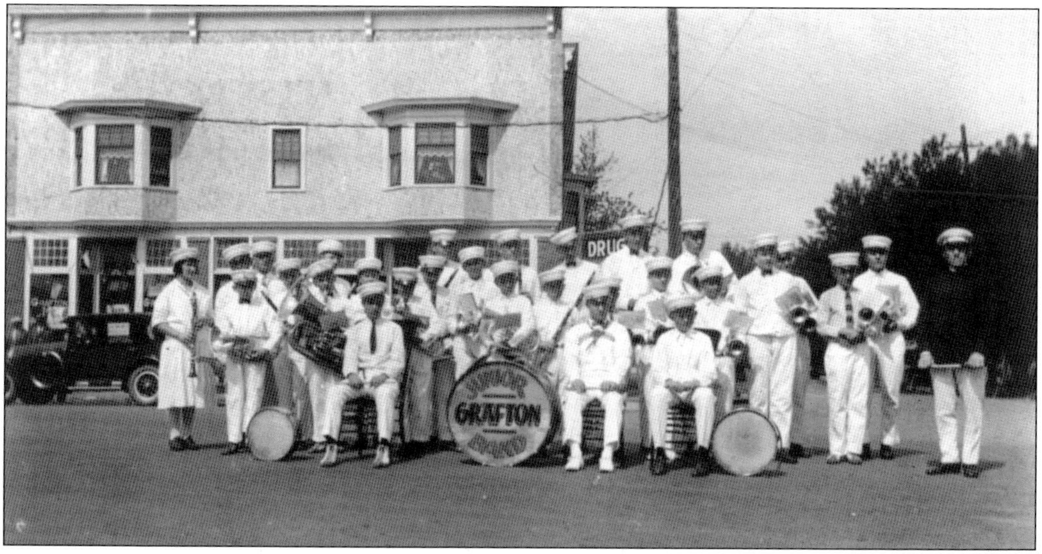

GRAFTON JUNIOR BAND. The Grafton Junior Band was one of the "Saturday Night" bands that provided music in Grafton. The band director shown here is Louis Krenke. The band welcomed male and female musicians. (Courtesy of Allen Buchholz.)

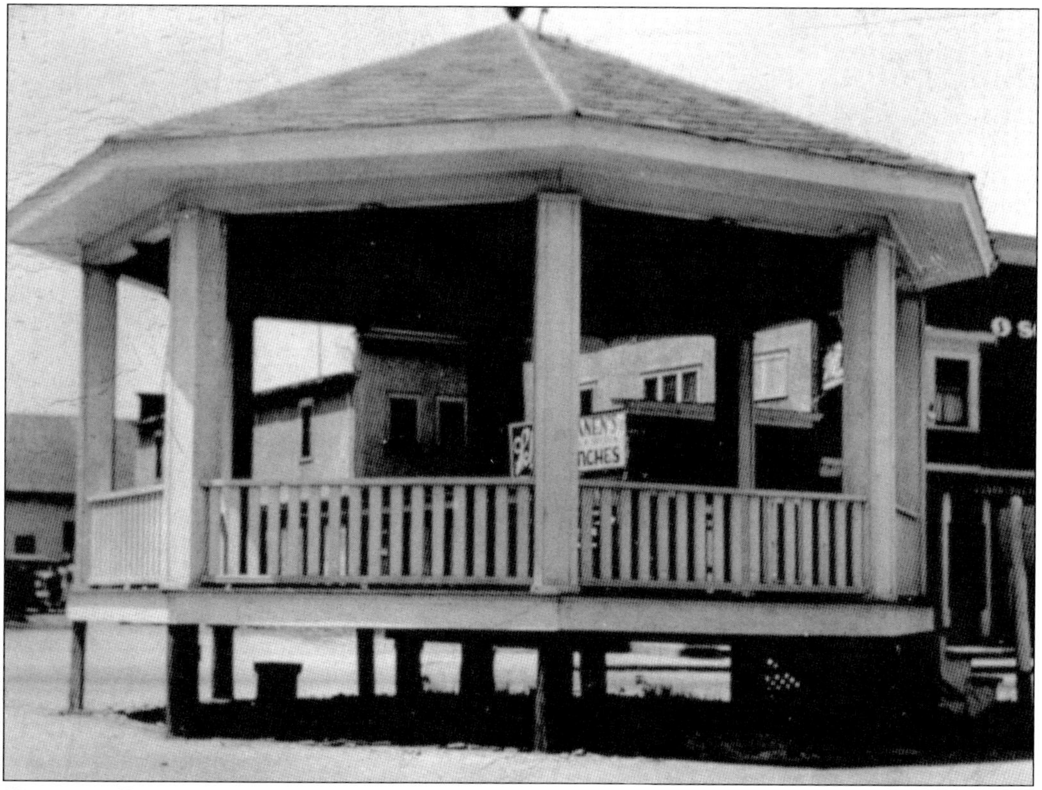

GRAFTON BANDSTAND. For many years, Grafton residents gathered at this bandstand every Saturday night in July and August to hear band concerts. The concerts were popular, and people would begin to gather as early as 5:00 p.m. The bandstand was next to the Hotel Grafton. The Schanen Hotel is visible in the background. (Courtesy of the Grafton Chamber of Commerce.)

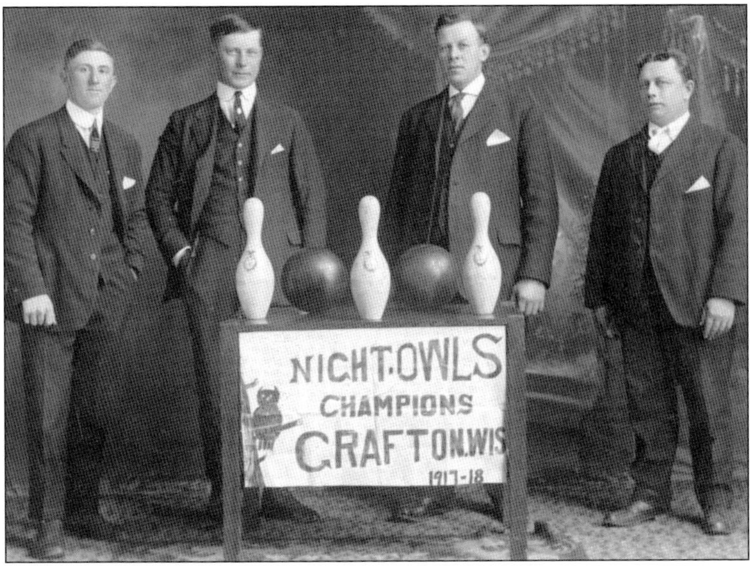

Championship Bowling Team. The Grafton championship bowling team for 1917–1918 is shown here in a formal portrait. Fred Tillmann is on the left, and Nic Schanen is on the right. Tillmann was an ardent supporter of bowling when it was considered slightly disreputable and in a class with pool rooms. He was also the first to advocate for special shoes for bowling. (Courtesy of the Tillmann family.)

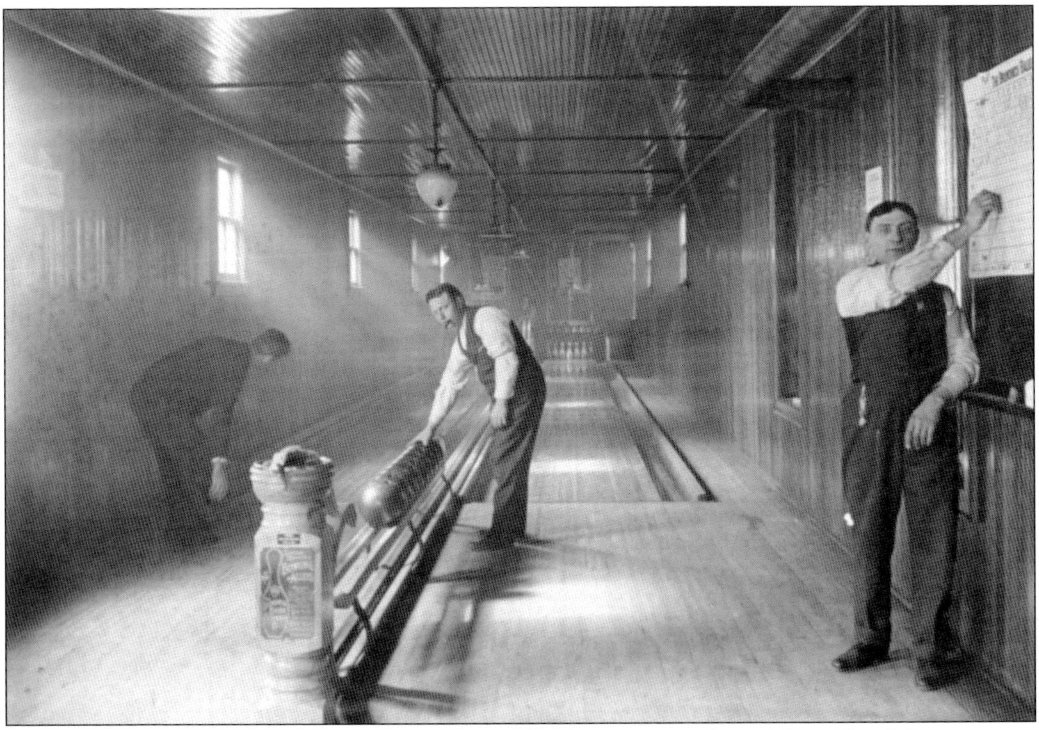

Schanen's Bowling Alley. In this scene from Schanen's Bowling Alley, Nic Schanen is in the center getting ready to bowl while William Hilgart Sr. is keeping score. The early bowling balls shown here were made of wood. In the early 1900s, bowling was a very popular sport in Grafton and around the country with estimates of 50 million bowlers nationwide. (Courtesy of the Gramoll family.)

RIEBE'S SUPER SIXES. The Super Sixes were a popular Grafton basketball team in 1929, sponsored by Riebe's auto dealership. Albert Riebe is at far right in the second row. During the 1920s, basketball was very popular around the United States. When World War II began, however, the leagues fell apart. (Courtesy of Bill Riebe.)

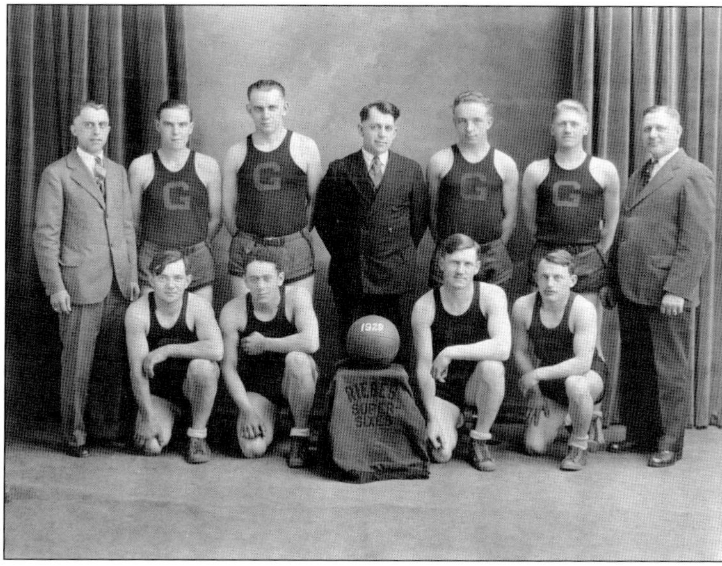

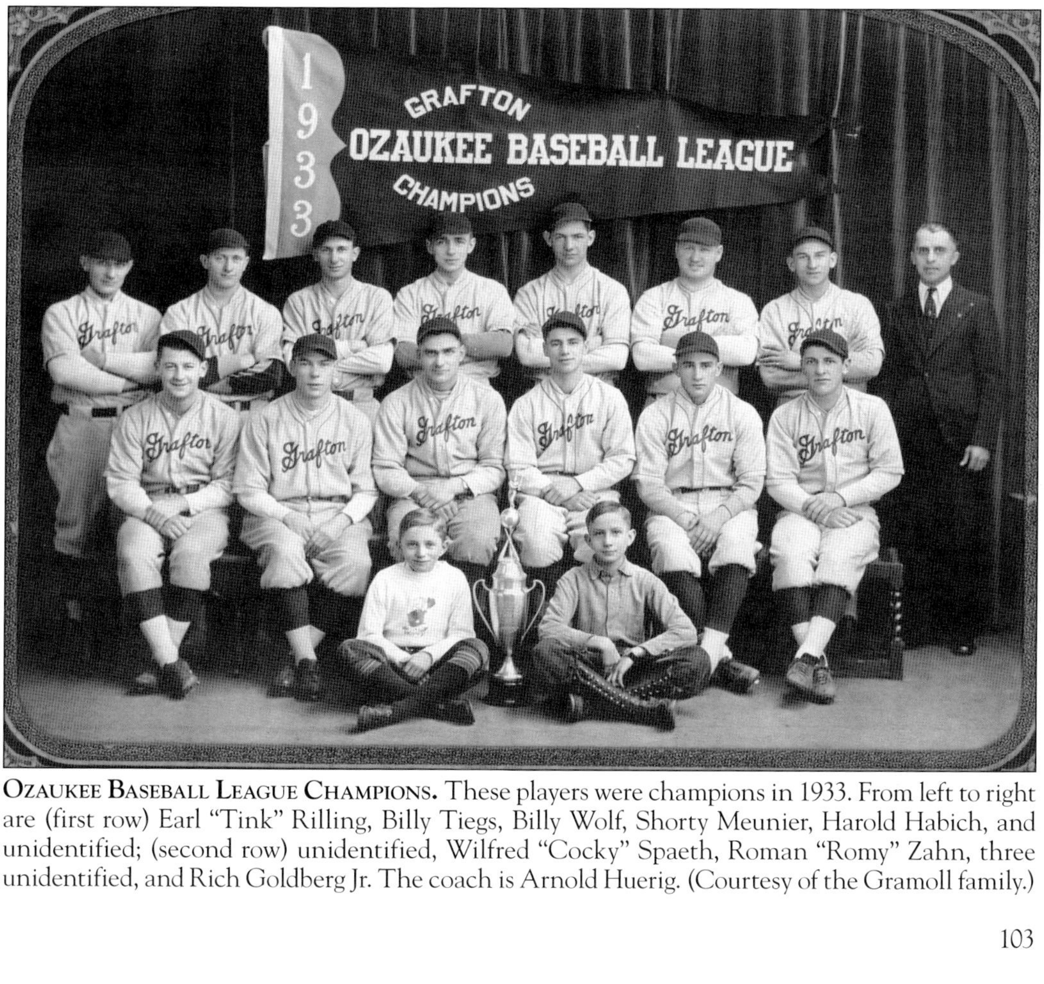

OZAUKEE BASEBALL LEAGUE CHAMPIONS. These players were champions in 1933. From left to right are (first row) Earl "Tink" Rilling, Billy Tiegs, Billy Wolf, Shorty Meunier, Harold Habich, and unidentified; (second row) unidentified, Wilfred "Cocky" Spaeth, Roman "Romy" Zahn, three unidentified, and Rich Goldberg Jr. The coach is Arnold Huerig. (Courtesy of the Gramoll family.)

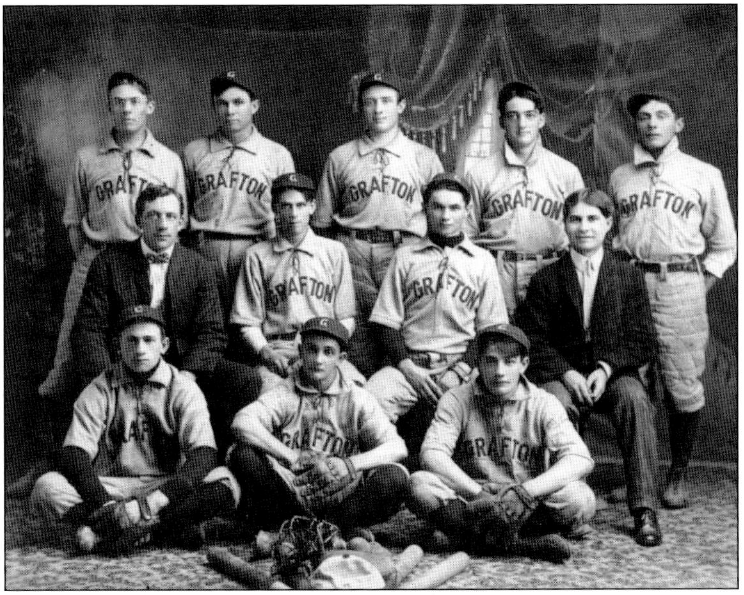

Grafton Baseball Team. These Grafton players pose for a formal team photograph in the early 1900s. Those identified are Doc Habich (first row, far left), Kelly Heuer (second row, second from right), Louie Heuer (second row, far right), and Charlie Niesen (third row, second from right). (Courtesy of the Gramoll family.)

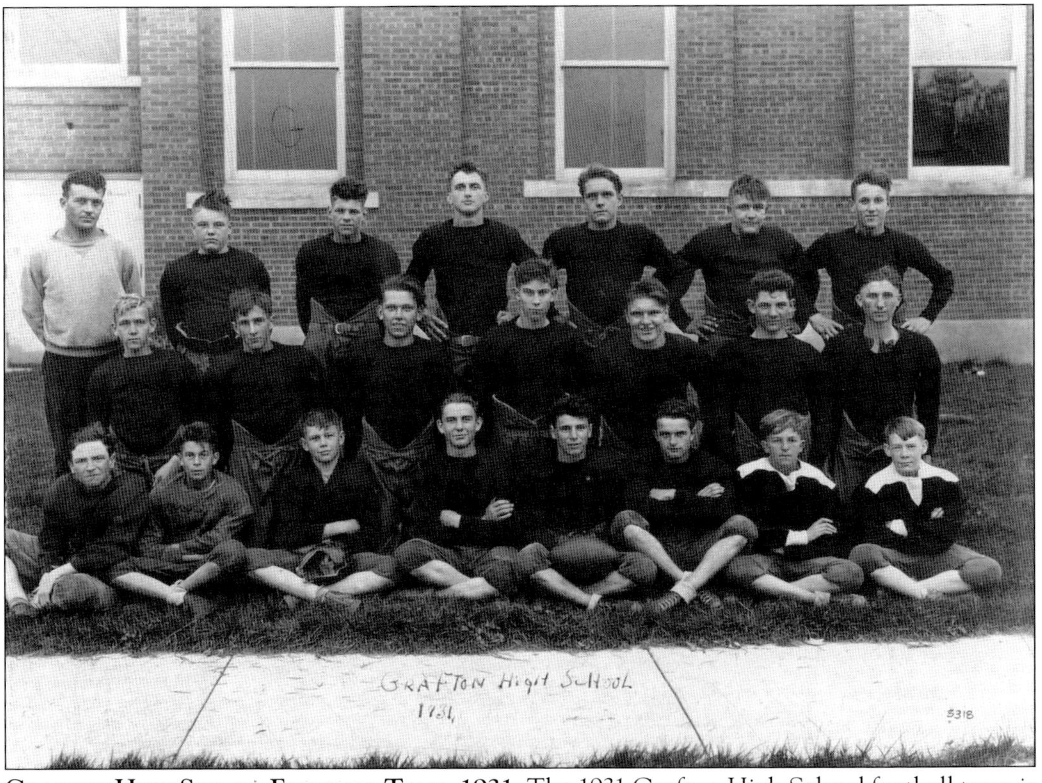

Grafton High School Football Team, 1931. The 1931 Grafton High School football team is shown here in front of the school. From left to right are (first row) Ambrose Driscoe, Mel Dickman, Roy Harms, Wendal Walters, Shorty Meunier, Ray Schanen, Al Plesic, and Chad Long; (second row) George Habich, Carl Sohns, John Schmitz, Clyde Horn, Herb Robel, and Elroy Woltring; (third row) coach Oliver Maechtle, Roland Clausing, George Clausing, William Janke, Epps Heuser, Harry Sohns, and Chip Ferry. (Courtesy of the Gramoll family.)

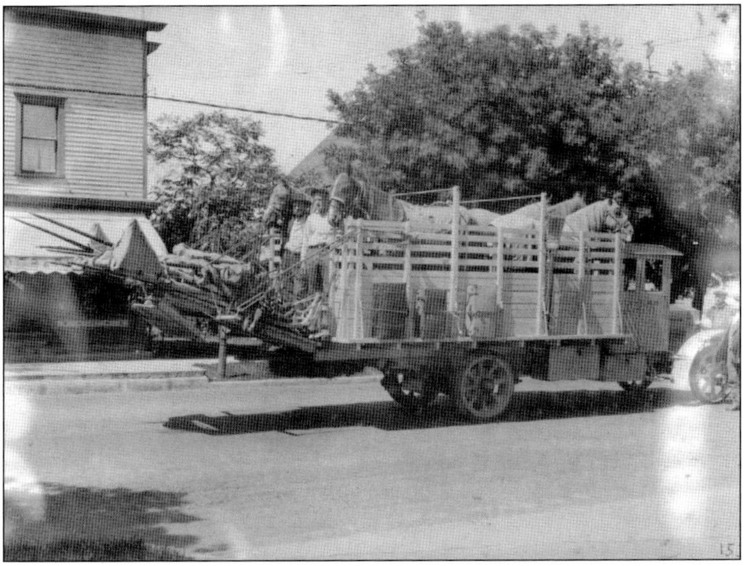

Race Horse Transport. Race horses are being transported to the Cedarburg race track in this scene from the 1920s. The racing surrey is packed in the back of the truck, and the race driver is Clem Tillmann. The truck is in front of Grafton's photography studio. (Courtesy of the Tillmann family.)

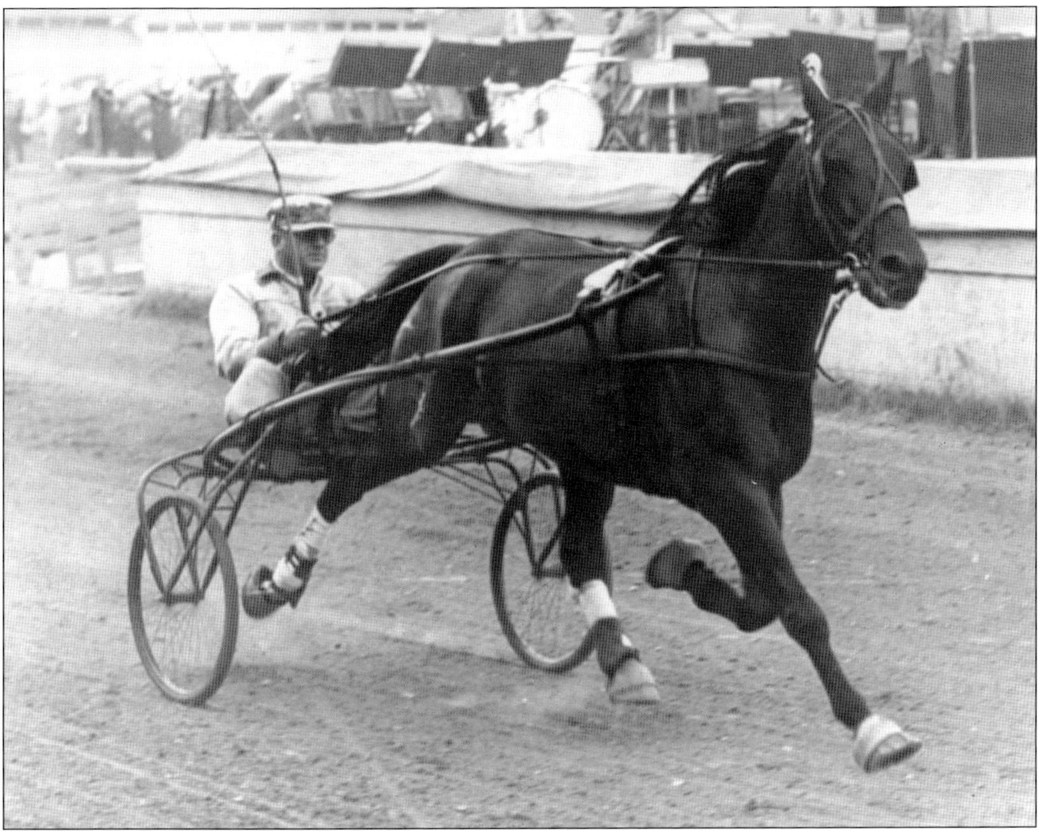

Clem Tillmann Racing. Clem Tillmann is shown here racing at the Cedarburg track in the 1920s. With the war over, people had more leisure time, and horse racing became one of the most popular sports of the time. It was the decade of the "wonder horse" because of their incredible racing speed. Besides racing, Tillmann owned an implement dealership in Grafton. (Courtesy of the Tillmann family.)

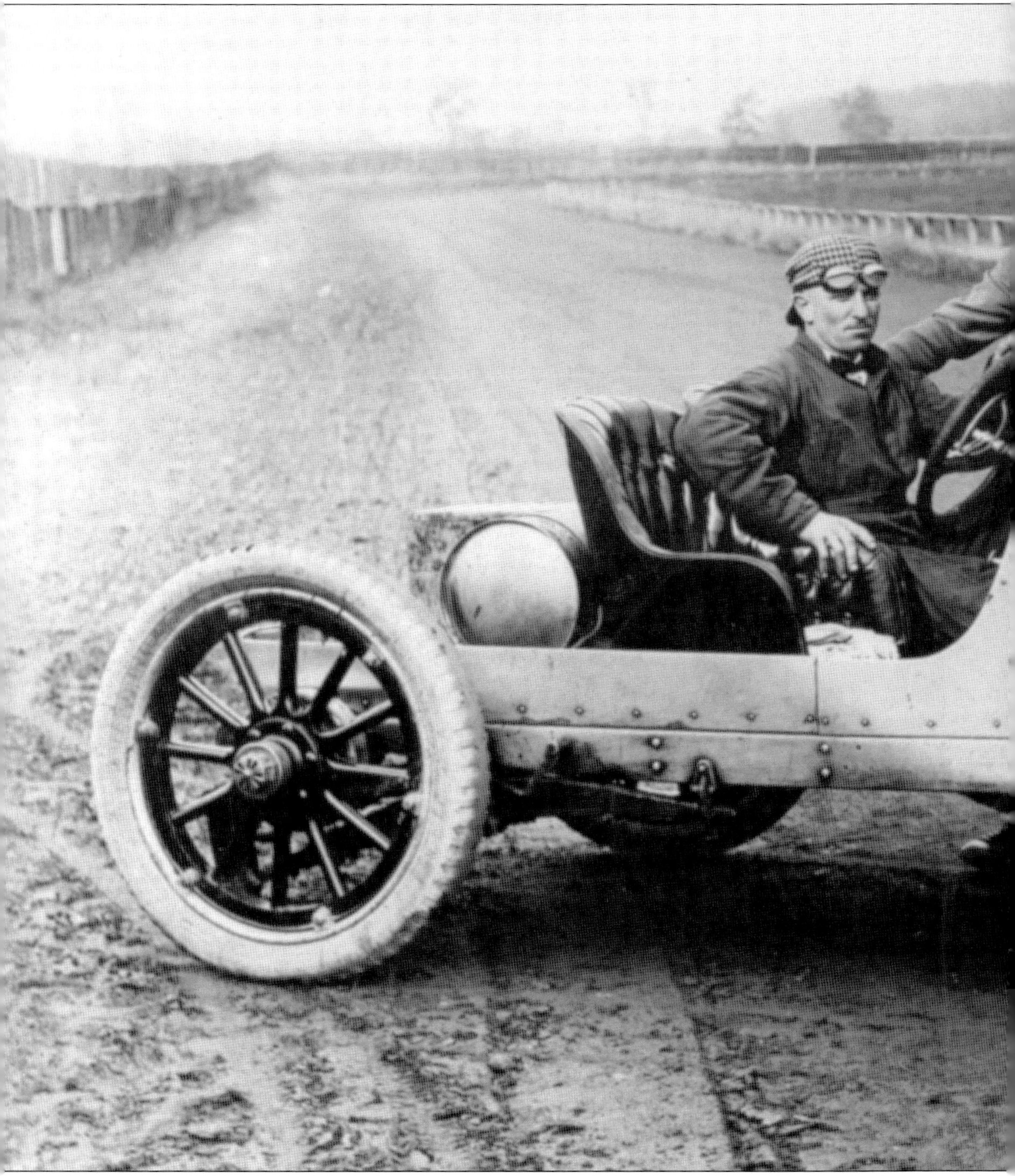

FRED TILLMANN'S BRISCOE. Fred Tillmann is shown here in his light-colored No. 2 Briscoe racing car. A Cedarburg news story from the time describes the 1916 race at the Cedarburg Fairgrounds that Fred won: "1,500 persons paid a total of $501 at the gate to see Fred Tillmann in his Briscoe display amazing speed on the straightaway as he captured first place." Tillmann recalled that the wooden spoke wheels on the car would crack under strain. He won first place at the Oshkosh

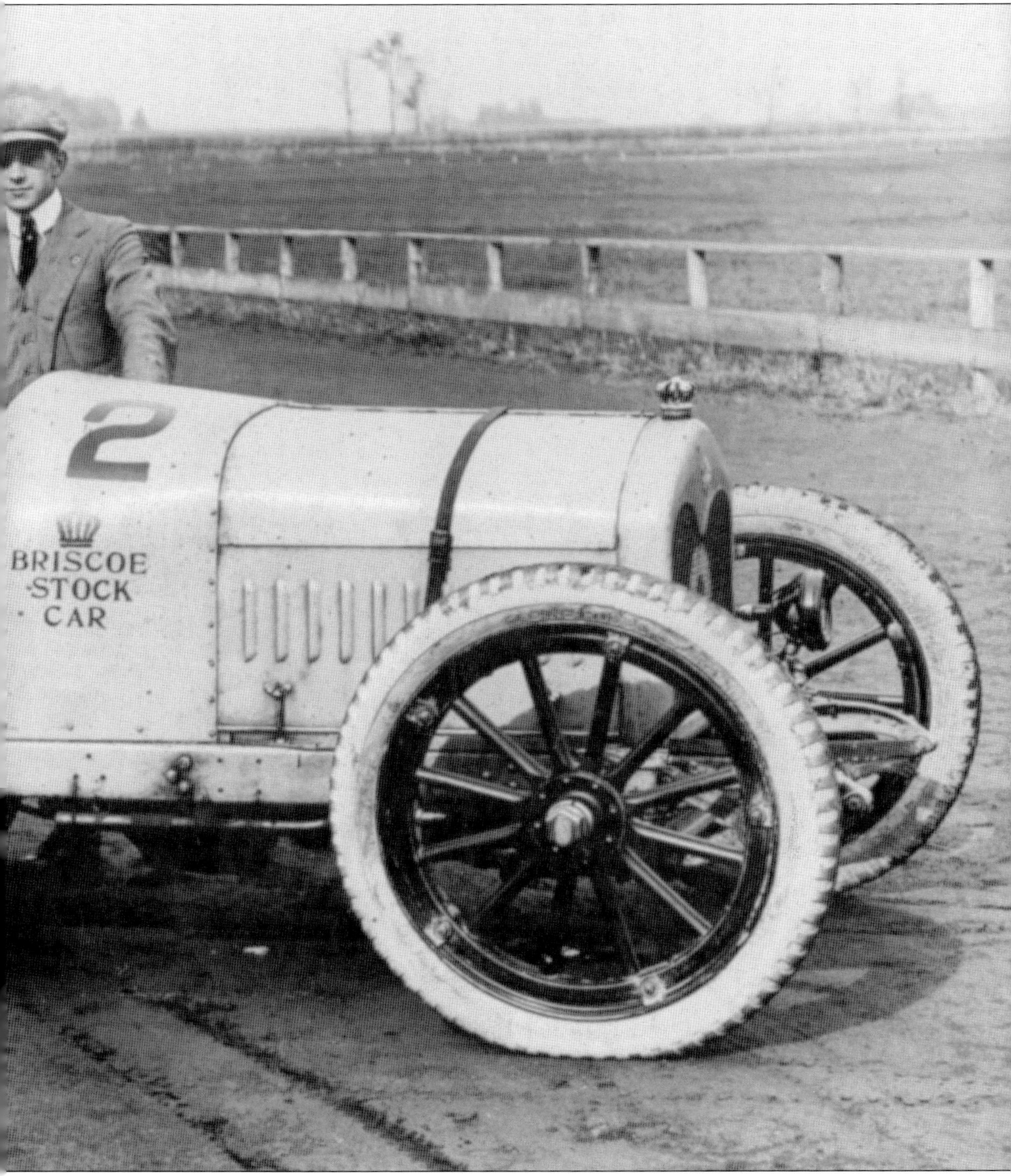

race in 1916 driving the same car. In 1919, Tillmann won the first state championship at the age of 27 when he drove around a one-mile dirt track in a time of one minute, twelve seconds. The Briscoe was gasoline powered, but some of the cars racing at that time were steam or electric powered. (Courtesy of the Tillmann family.)

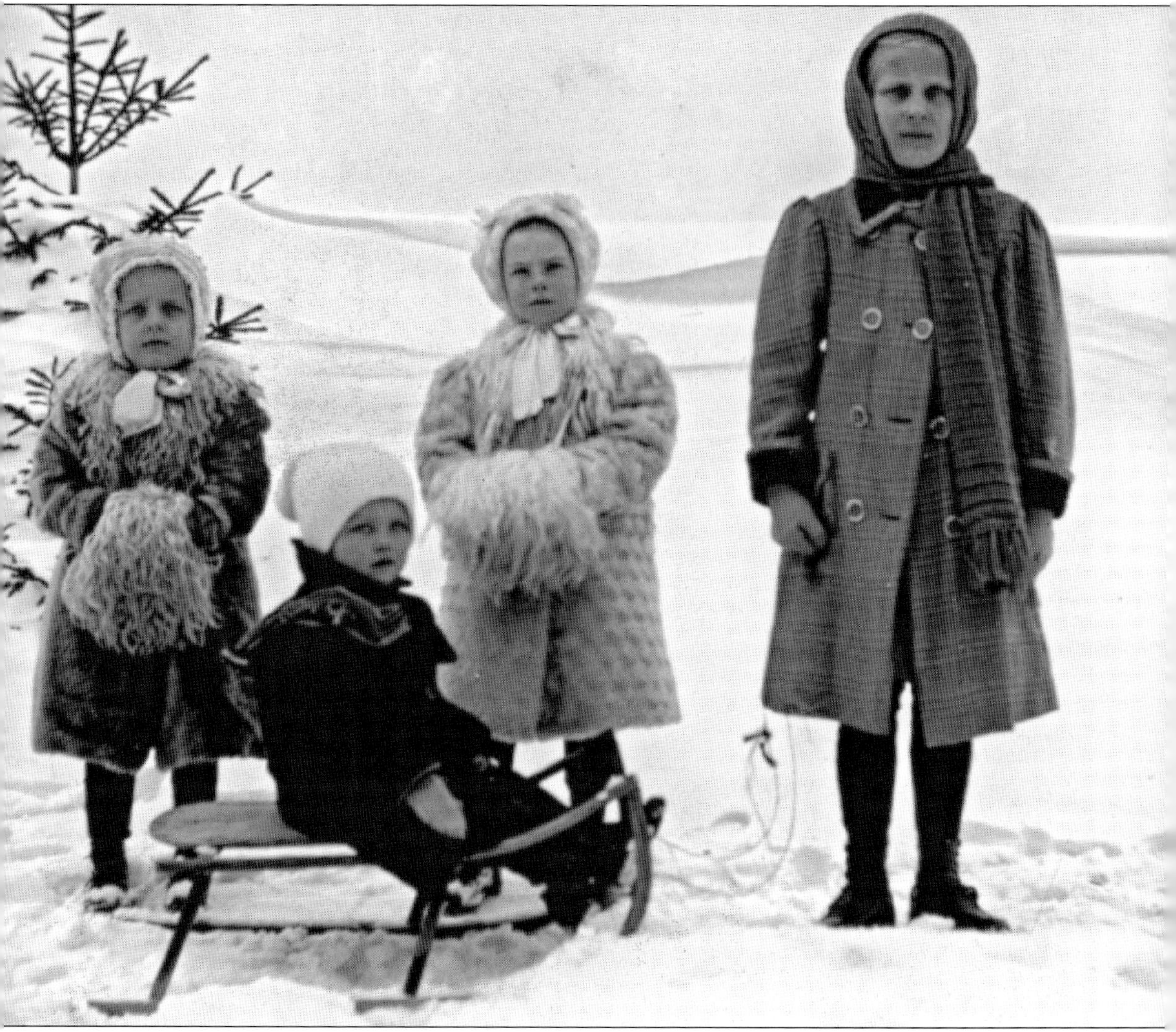

WINTER SLEDDING. Winter was a fun-filled time for children in the early 1900s in Grafton. Sledding was popular, as was building snowmen and skating on Ulao Creek and the Milwaukee River. The children in this scene are getting ready to sled on the hill behind the barn on the Kaul farm. Lore Kaul is at center. The sled they are using most likely came from the Sears catalog. When it was too cold to play outside, children liked to play indoor games like checkers and chess. Card games were also beginning to become popular at the time. Note how warmly these children are dressed for the winter weather, with fur and wool coats and fur hats. The beautiful muffs the girls are sporting add a fashionable touch. (Courtesy of Arnold Kaul Sr.)

Bienlein Family. Bienlein family members pictured here are, from left to right, (seated) Henry and Theodore; (standing) Andrew, George, and John. The Bienleins were well known in Grafton for Beinlein Park, a popular riverside gathering place for company picnics and events, such as Independence Day picnics. (Courtesy of Bill Malone.)

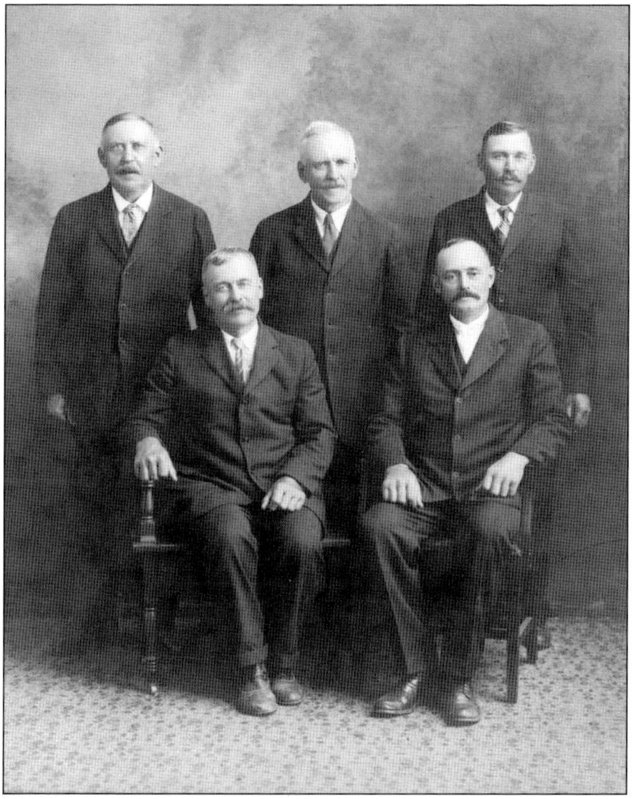

Fourth of July at Bienlein Park. Grafton residents gather for a Fourth of July celebration at Bienlein Park in 1909. Even though the revelers in this scene are dressed in their holiday finery, the Fourth of July in the early 1900s could be a hazardous activity. Fireworks, Roman candles, dynamite, and other strong explosives were often part of the celebration. (Courtesy of Allen Buchholz.)

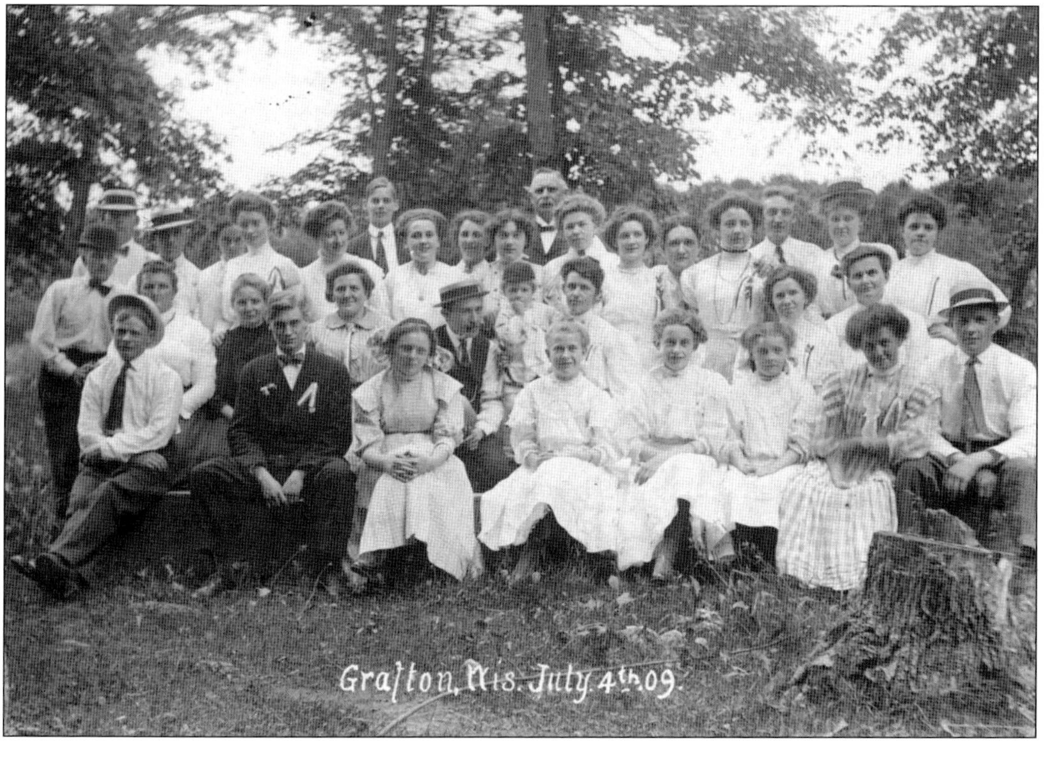

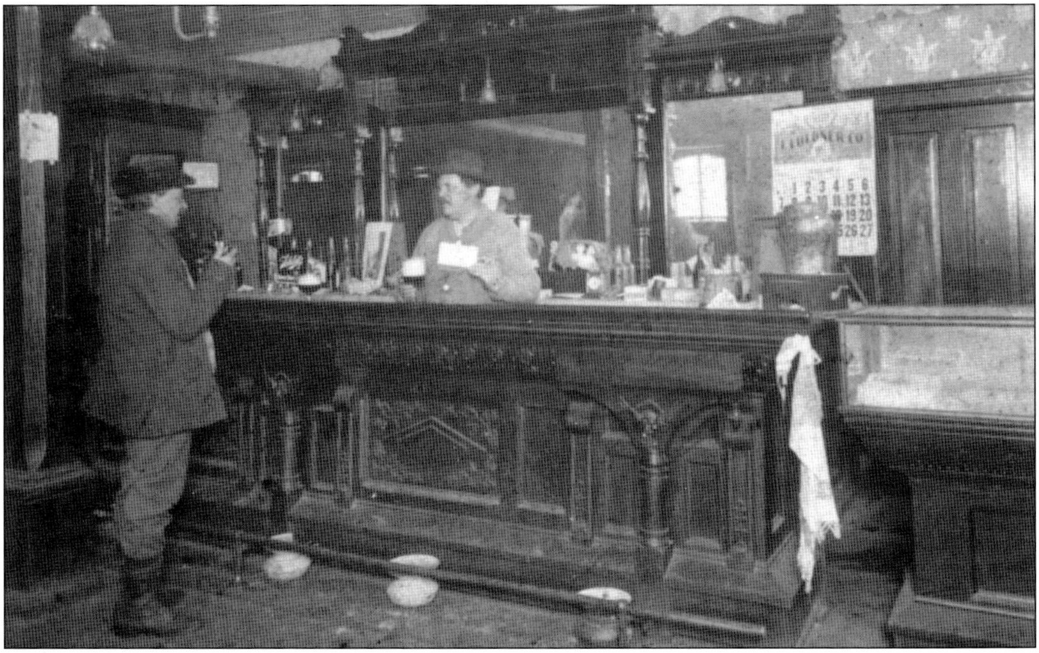

Marv's Tap. This tavern was on Twelfth Avenue. After the original owner, it was run by Marvin and Evelyn Tonn and was called Marv's Tap. It was also called Walker's. The building is no longer standing. Note the spittoons and the intricately carved bar in this scene from 1912. (Courtesy of Karen Schmidt.)

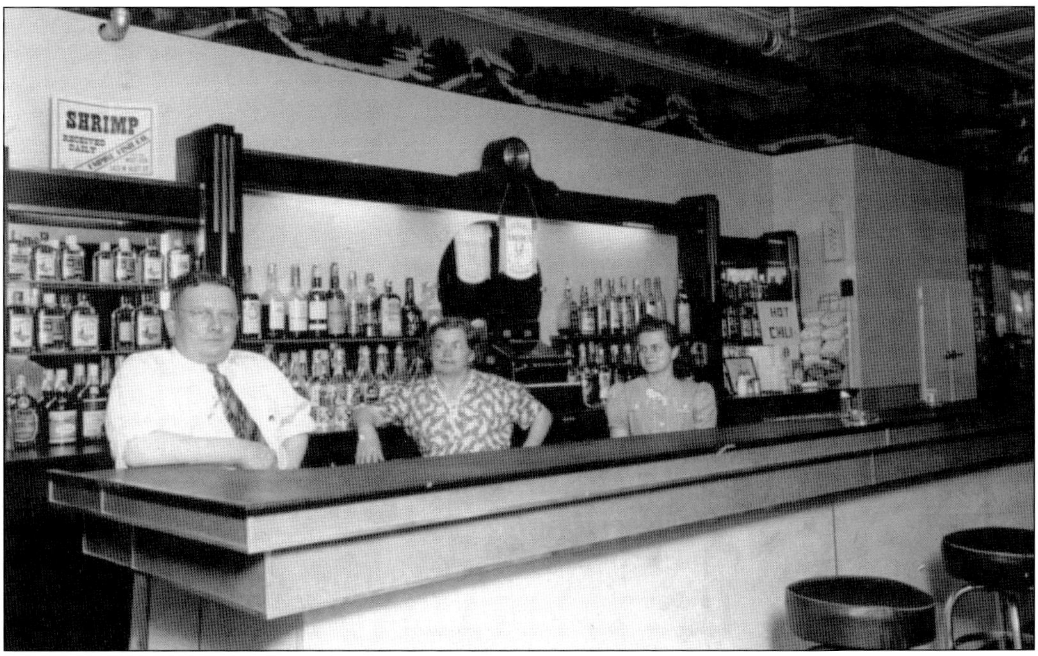

Bar at Schanen Hotel. Posing at the bar of the Schanen Hotel are, from left to right, Nic, Maggie, and Bernice Schanen. Once during Prohibition, Bernice forgot to replace the floorboards that covered the hiding place of the hotel's liquor supply, and it was lost to federal agents when they raided the establishment. (Courtesy of Nic Schanen.)

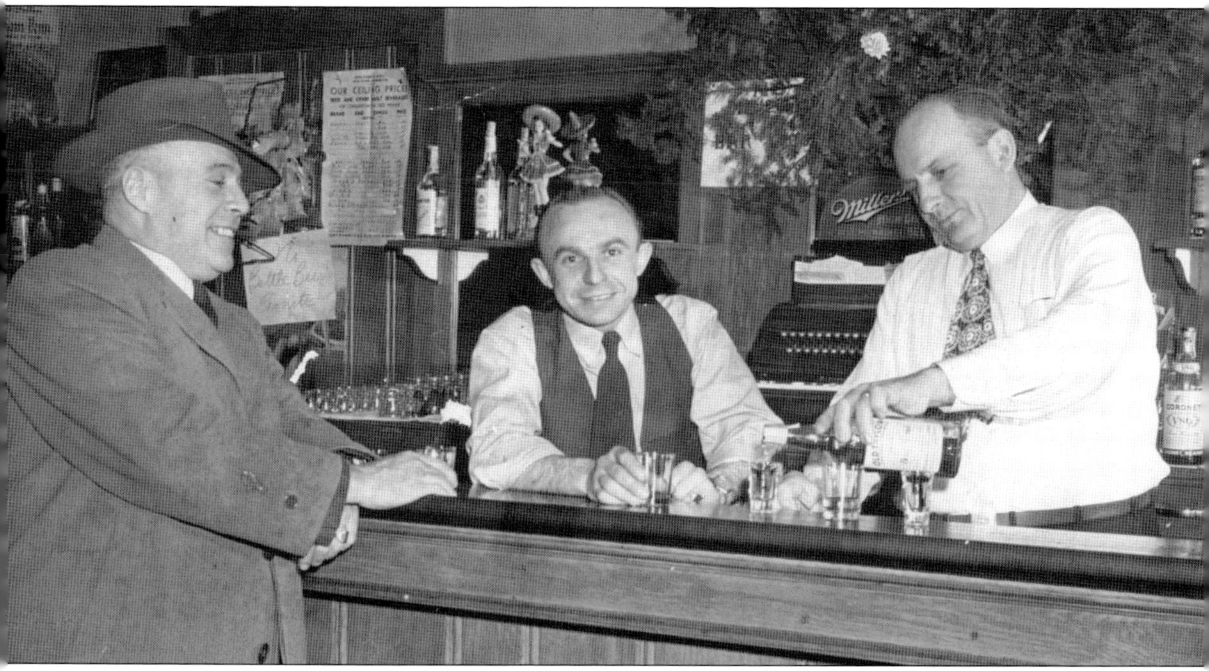

MICHAEL J. SCHMIT AT SCHMIT PAVILION. Pouring a drink in the tavern at the Schmit Pavilion is Michael J. Schmit. Besides putting in his time behind the bar, Schmit was also an auctioneer, real estate broker, and developer of dance halls. The Schmit Pavilion ballroom was built in 1926, and the tavern was added after that. Later, the name was changed to Schmit's Ballroom, and its motto was "The Best Dam Floor in the World." The ballroom served food and had dances every Saturday night, often featuring two eight-piece orchestras. Schmit was born in 1894 and died in 1969 at the age of 75. (Courtesy of the Schmit family.)

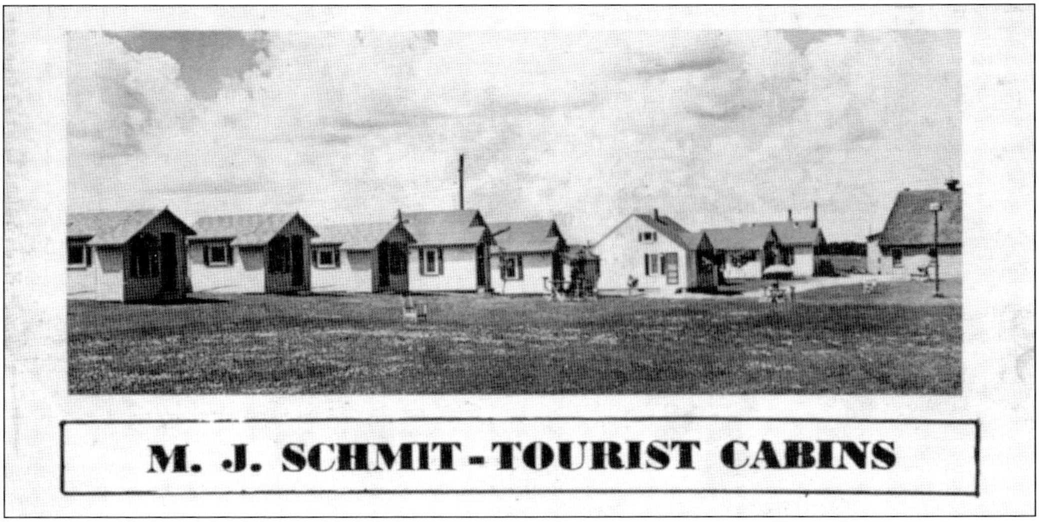

MICHAEL J. SCHMIT VACATION CABINS. The Schmit vacation cabins were opened in the late 1940s and operated until the 1960s. They were a popular destination, as they were located approximately halfway between Milwaukee and Green Bay. An early advertisement described them as "the most modern tourist cabins with all modern conveniences around Milwaukee. We invite you to make your headquarters here while visiting in Wisconsin. Inner spring mattress, hot and cold water and Lake Michigan accommodations. Modernistic barroom where you can enjoy your favorite drink and dancing every Saturday." They also offered lunch and dinner to their guests. (Both, courtesy of the Schmit family.)

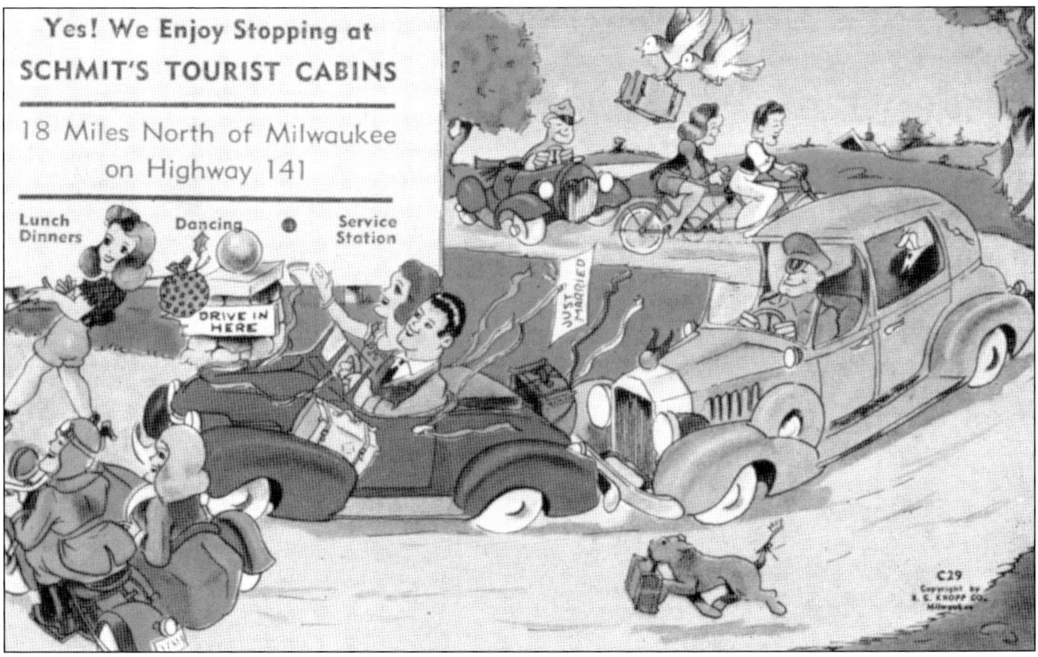

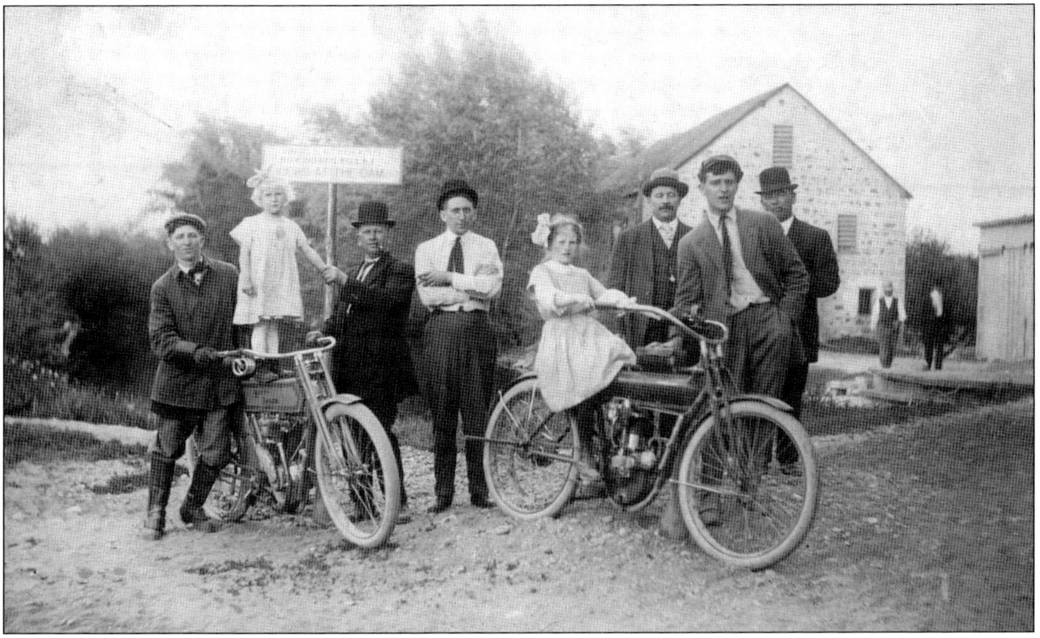

Grafton Motorcycle Enthusiasts. Motorcycles were a popular means of transportation and recreation in the early 1900s. Shown below in 1913 are, from left to right, Frank Scheer with a one-cylinder Harley Davidson costing $110, Nic Dickmann wearing high boots and posing with a one-cylinder Flying Merkel, Ferry Sailor with a two-cylinder Pope, Joe Demeron with a two-cylinder Flying Merkel with the gas tank on top of the handlebars, and Sailor's brother straddling a bicycle. Merkel was based in Milwaukee and later relocated later to Middletown, Ohio. The motorcycle was produced from 1911 to 1915. Pope began manufacturing motorized bicycles in 1902 and continued with motorcycles until 1918. These early riders often had to deal with deeply-rutted roads. (Above, courtesy of the Tillmann family; below, courtesy of Richard Scheer.)

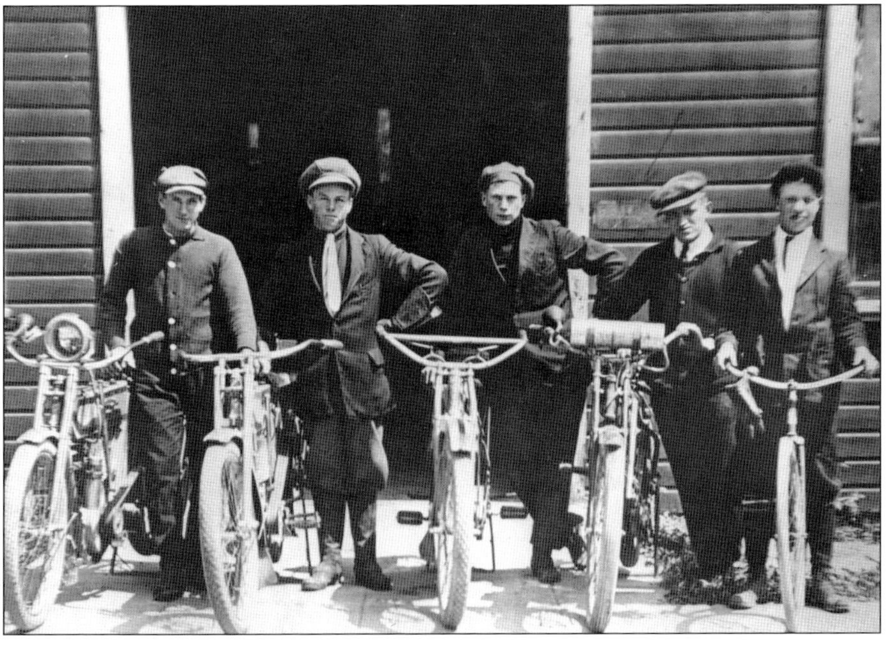

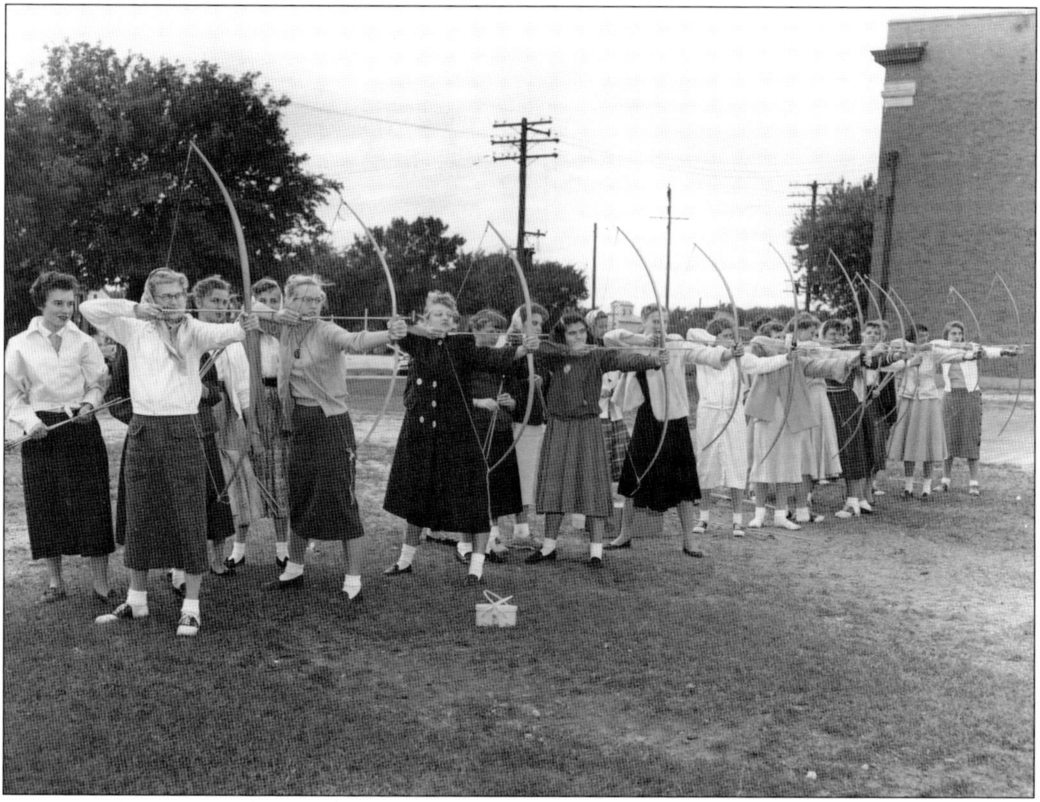

WOMEN'S ARCHERY. Young women practice their archery skills during a class at Grafton High School in 1957. Women helped to popularize target archery in the 1940s, 1950s, and 1960s. Fourteen of 72 inductees into the Archery Hall of Fame and Museum during this time were women. (Courtesy of the Vern Arendt Photograph Collection at the Luxembourg American Cultural Center.)

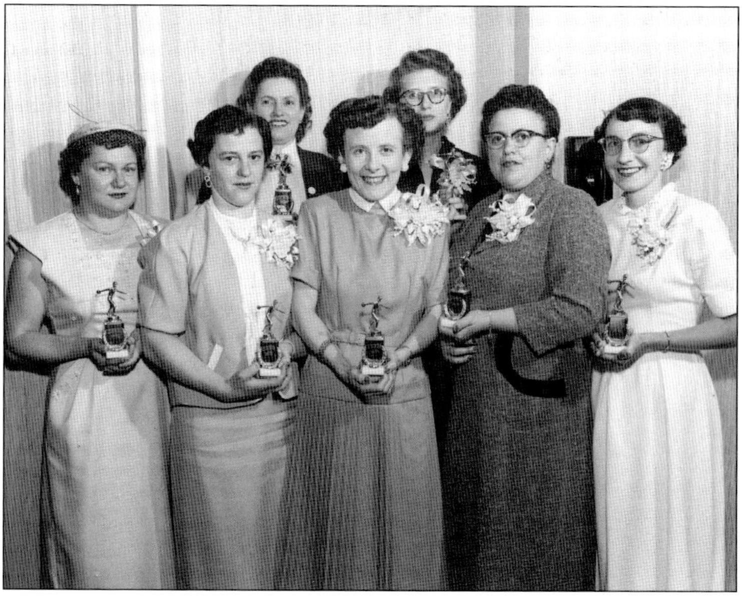

WOMEN'S BOWLING. The Grafton women's bowling champions pose in 1955. Today, women's bowling is still popular, with the US Bowling Congress women's championships being the largest women's sporting event in the world. The bowlers here are not identified. (Courtesy of the Vern Arendt Photograph Collection at the Luxembourg American Cultural Center.)

Seven

Civic Pride

Grafton's civic and service life has been a strong thread through the community since its beginnings. On June 26, 1896, just a few months after Grafton was incorporated as a village, a group of citizens met to draft bylaws and a constitution for a volunteer fire department. That department came into being on July 1, 1896, with 64 members. The department today has 50 volunteers and a full-time chief to answer the approximately 1,200 fire calls each year. They have state-of-the-art firefighting equipment and fully trained EMS personnel.

Grafton citizens also have a proud history of service to their country. When the call came for recruits for the Civil War, 71 men from Grafton registered for service. In World War I, 47 men served from Grafton. One of them was Fred Rose, whose name was chosen for the American Legion Post No. 355 that was formed in 1934. In 1946, members voted to change the name to the Rose-Harms Post in honor of Roy Coulson Harms, the first World War II casualty from Grafton. In 1945, the auxiliary was formed, and in 1951, the legion had a new home on Thirteenth Avenue.

In 1955, a group of young mothers, with the help of the Grafton Women's Club, the Grafton Lions Club, and other community groups, began planning for a library for Grafton. It opened in April 1956 and was first housed in the old theater building on Bridge Street. The library outgrew that space, and in 1989 was replaced with a new building on Eleventh Avenue. In 1995, the library was computerized, and the downstairs youth library was added. In 2019, the library circulated 197,009 items, including 24,492 digital items. The library offered 324 programs attended by 4,631 people.

Today, there are 17 service and civic groups actively contributing to the safety and wellbeing of those who make Grafton their home.

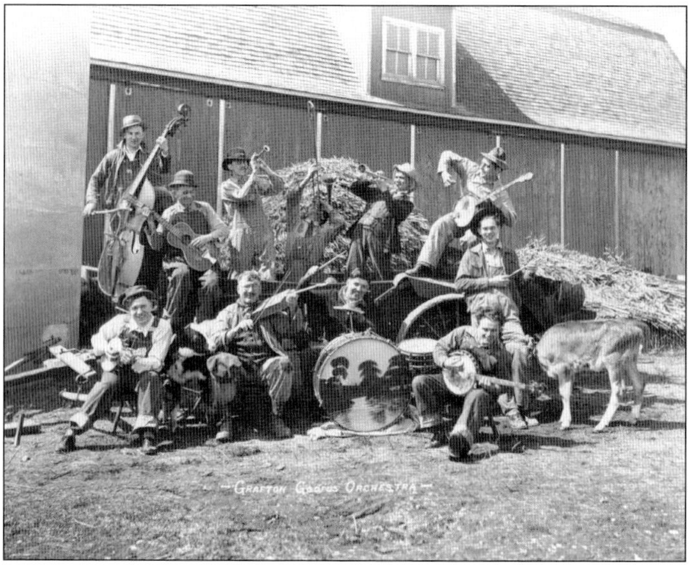

Grafton Goofus Orchestra. The Grafton Goofus Orchestra was a highlight of the 1930s, performing comedy and musical skits for charity. The orchestra was begun and directed by Art Hill (first row, far left). The other members are, from left to right, (first row) Dominic Thill, Gordon Roth, Ray Schanen, and Al Thill; (second row), Chet Goldberg, Harry Mulholland, Gene Thill, Ambrose Thill, and Mickey Mulholland. (Courtesy of Rich Scheer.)

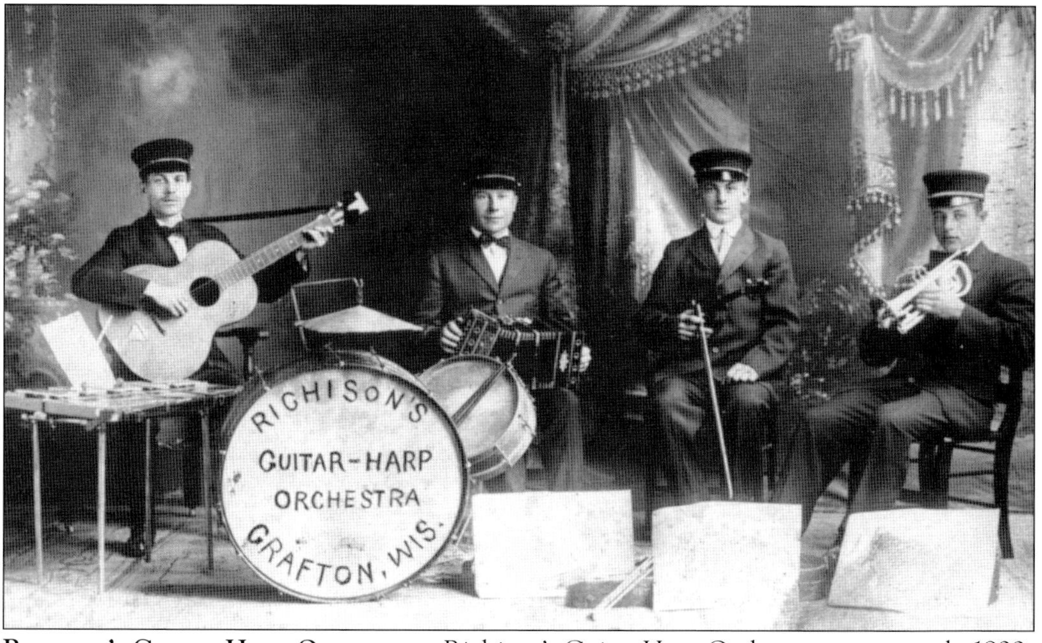

Richison's Guitar-Harp Orchestra. Richison's Guitar-Harp Orchestra was an early 1900s orchestra in Grafton under the leadership of local barber Harry Richardson, who had his barbershop in the Hotel Grafton. The orchestra played at local dances for donations rather than a set fee. (Courtesy of St. Joseph Catholic Church.)

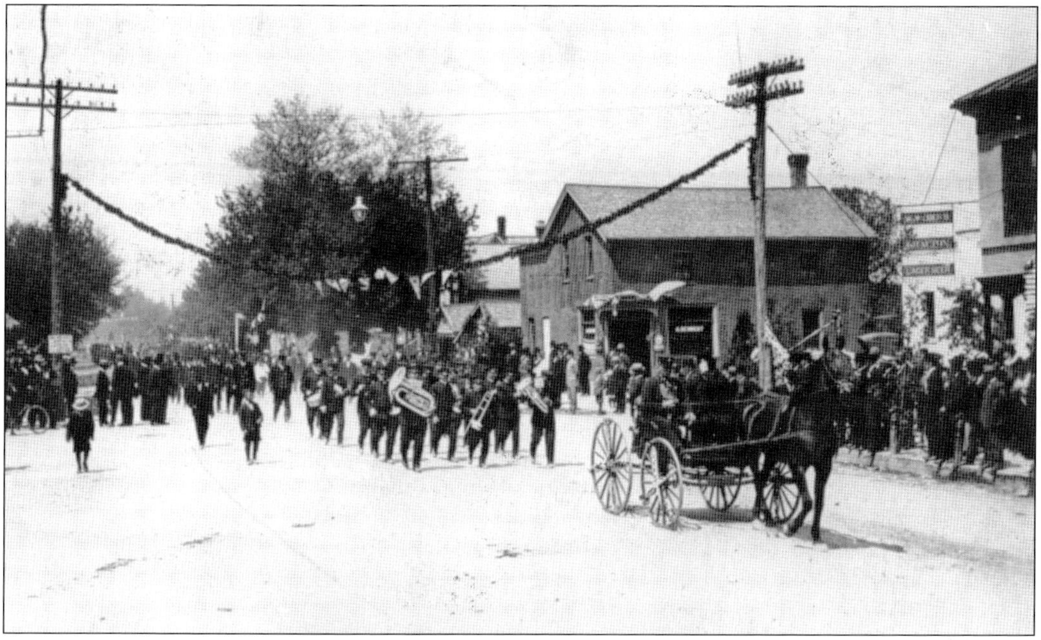

GRAFTON FIRE DEPARTMENT PARADE. This parade leads off the festivities for the June 1913 Grafton Volunteer Fire Department Tournament. The chief and his lieutenants rode in the buggy. The tournament was a combination of civic duty and entertainment for the community and surrounding areas. (Courtesy of the Ed Rappold Photograph Collection at the Cedarburg Cultural Center.)

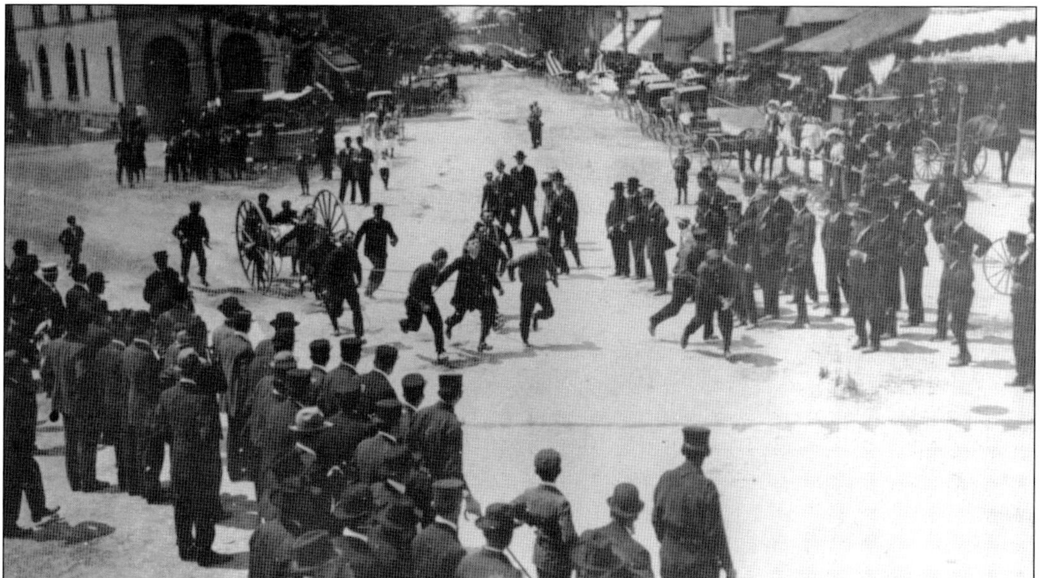

GRAFTON FIRE DEPARTMENT TOURNAMENT. Shown here is the firemen's tournament held on June 12, 1910. The tournaments were usually preceded by a parade. These were real community events, with everyone in town attending to support the fire department. It was an annual event held with neighboring communities and showcased firefighting skills. Popular events included ladder climbing and the bucket brigade. (Courtesy of the Grafton Fire Department.)

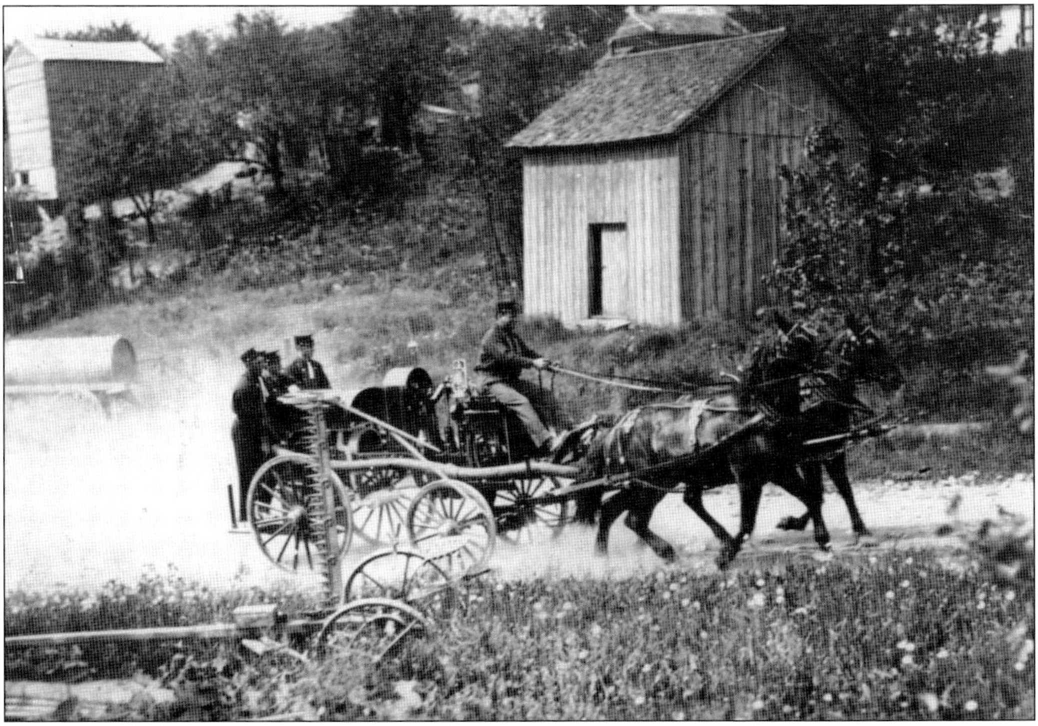

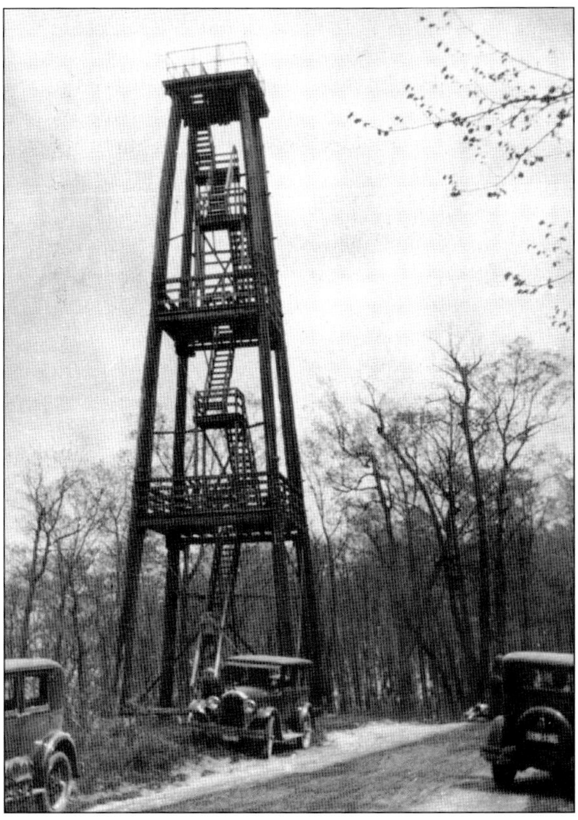

Grafton Fire Department Picnic. The first firemen's picnic and tournament was held in Grafton in 1899. As the village grew, so did the fire department. In 1899, a hook-and-ladder wagon and team of horses were purchased for $4. In 1905, total expenditures for the fire department were $38.05. The original firehouse was south of the parking lot of the Hotel Grafton. (Courtesy of the Grafton Fire Department.)

Grafton Fire Department Training Tower. This is an early firefighter's training tower. As firefighters faced the challenges of growing urban areas with multi-story buildings and automobiles, the need for better training was recognized. Departments began to formalize their training using planned drills. The current training tower is at Tenth Avenue and Mole Drive. (Courtesy of the Grafton Chamber of Commerce.)

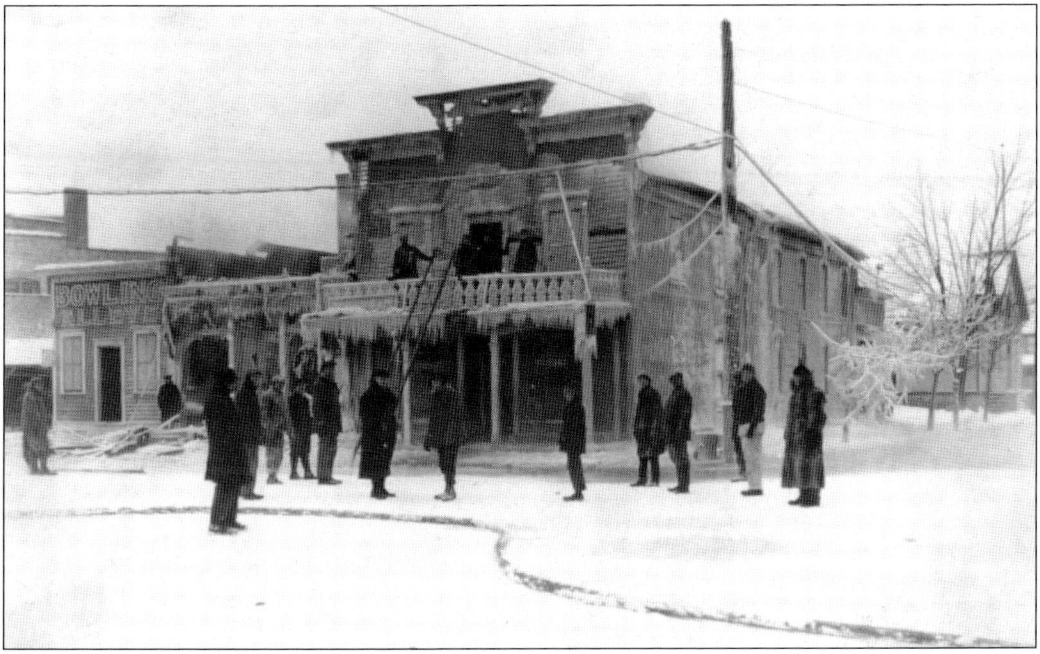

SCHANEN HOTEL FIRE. The Schanen Hotel fire occurred in January 1924. Since the hotel was established, it was a focal point for meetings and social events. The building dates from 1866 and was located across the street from the Hotel Grafton. The cause of the fire is unknown. Because of the quick response of the Grafton Fire Department, the roof burned, but the structure was saved. The hotel was rebuilt but without the distinctive notch in the roofline and without the balcony. At this time, before the introduction of telephones, fire calls were by word of mouth. Villagers would ring the fire bell at the Schanen Hotel to summon the fire department. The original bell has since been restored and is on display at the Grafton Fire Department. (Both, courtesy of Nic Schanen.)

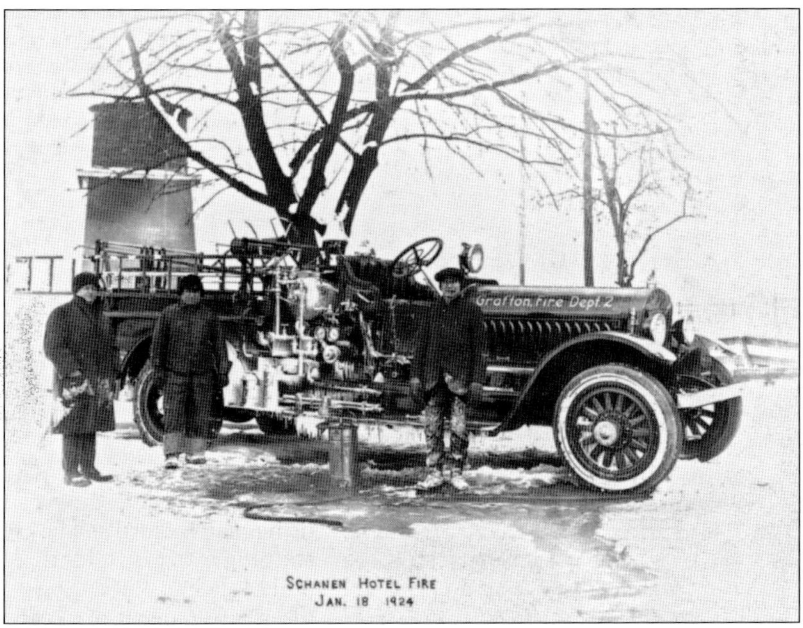

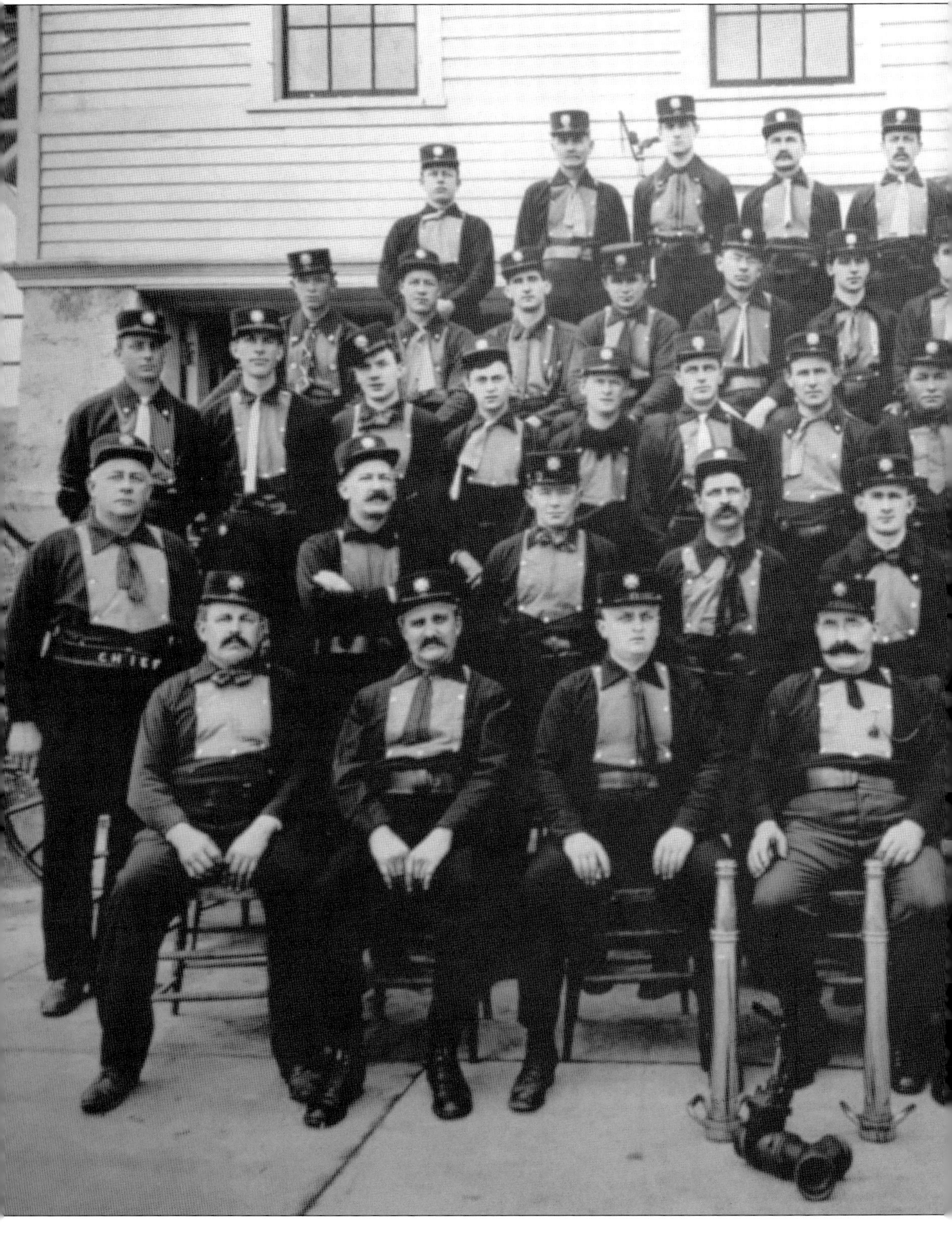
CHIEF

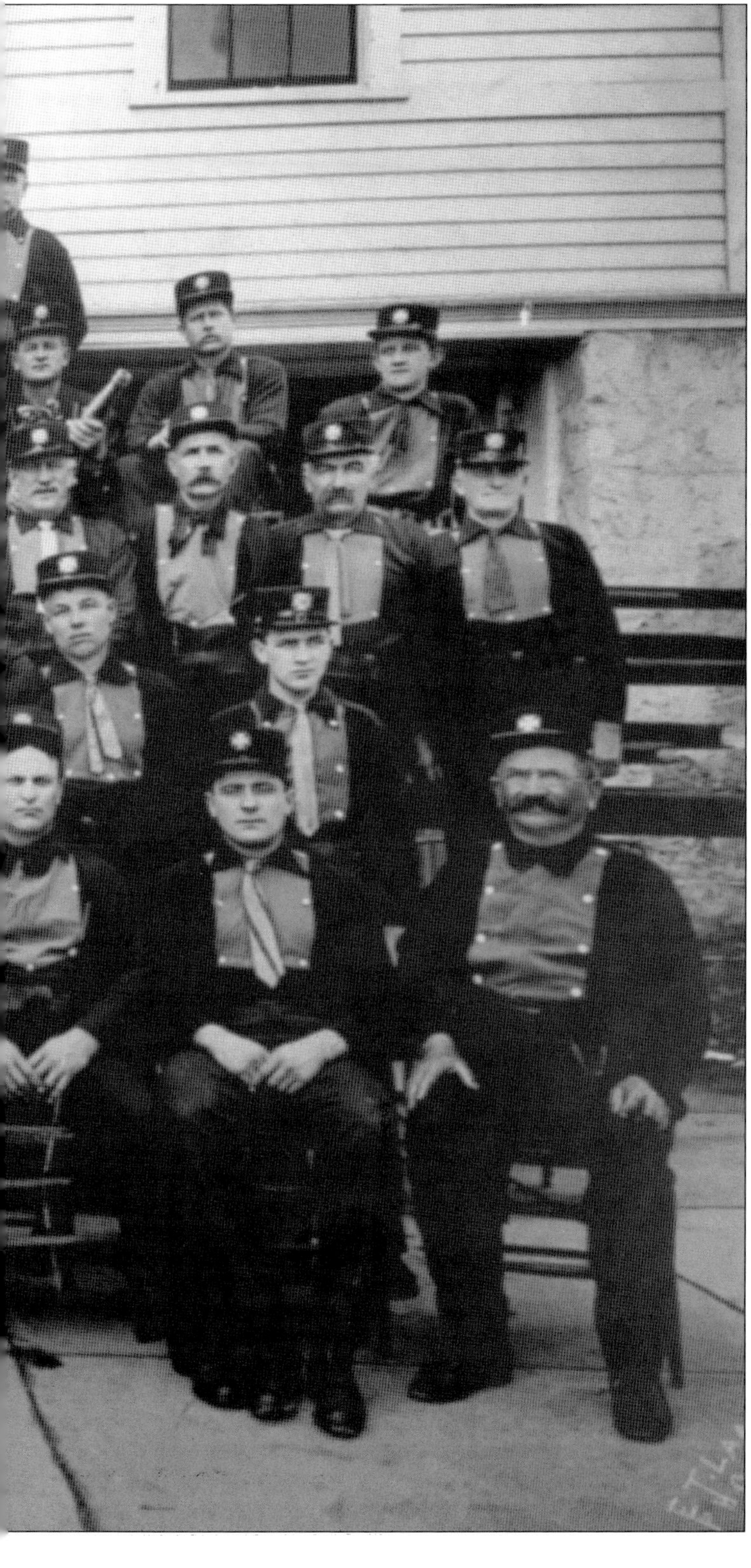

Grafton Fire Department Portrait, 1911. This famous portrait of the 1911 Grafton Fire Department includes 42 of its members. The volunteers pictured here are, from left to right, (first row) Nick Hollrith, Martin Blank, Charlie Melkers, ? Spehn, ? Tiegs, Charlie Rilling, and ? Vey. (second row) William Weber, Joe Niesen, Clem Tillmann, August Wachter, George Habich Sr., Gus Klausing, and Bill Vey. (third row) Henry Wegner, Herman "Shorty" Wegner, Albert Schletz, Bill Hilgart, Andrew Habich, Adolph Ploeger, Otto Freianmuth, Oscar Spehn, ? Schletz, Valentine Hartman, Robert Schnabel, and Ed Mueller; (fourth row) Charles Tillmann, Charles "Jim" Wegner, John Woltring, Kelly Heuer, Louis Neuhaus, Robert Zaun, Bill Aberwald, Otto Just, Lambert Van Langen, and Bill Roebken Sr; (fifth row) Nic Schanen, Charles Thiermann, Bill Hinz, Herman Mintzlaff, Matt Hollrith, and Ernst Klausing. (Courtesy of the Grafton Fire Department.)

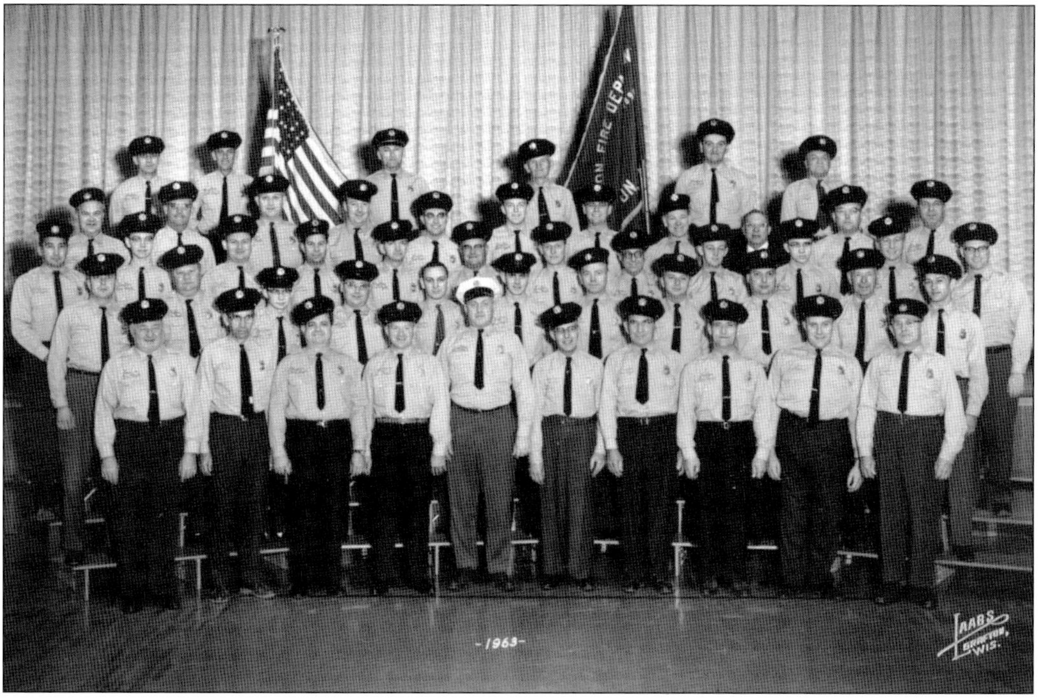

GRAFTON VOLUNTEER FIRE DEPARTMENT, 1963. Pictured above are the 1963 Grafton Volunteer Fire Department members. Chief Carl Wegner is in the middle of the first row, wearing the white hat. Identified are (first row) Al Wegner (far left), ? Bulgrin (second from left), and Carl Arentz (second from right); (second row) Ed Wegner (second from left) and Joe Bienlein (second from right); (third row) Harold Habich (far left) and Erv Stern (far right); (fourth row) Bob Wegner (far left); (fifth row) Howard Wegner (second from left), Elroy Hintz (third from left), and Joe Woltring (fourth from left). Below, Ed Wegner (center) is presented with a cake to celebrate successfully completing his firemanship course in 1959. Pictured with him are Elmer Kruetzer (left) and Chief Carl Wegner. (Both, courtesy of Marty Wegner.)

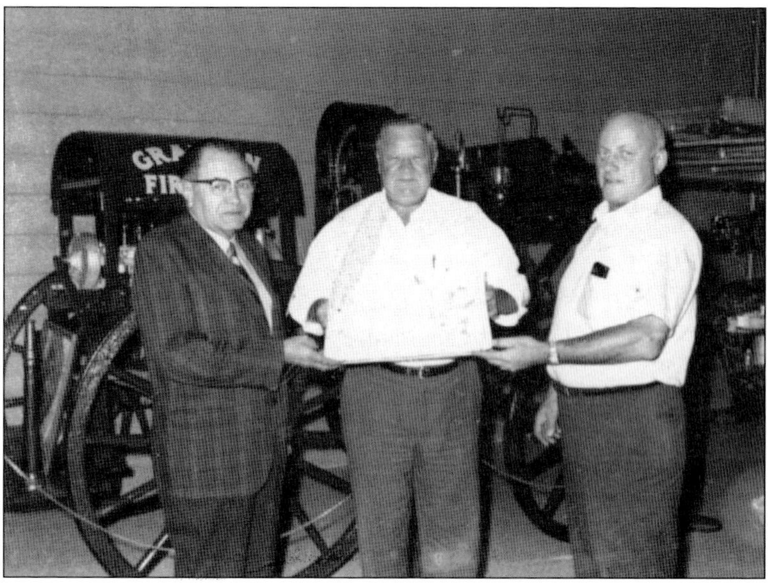

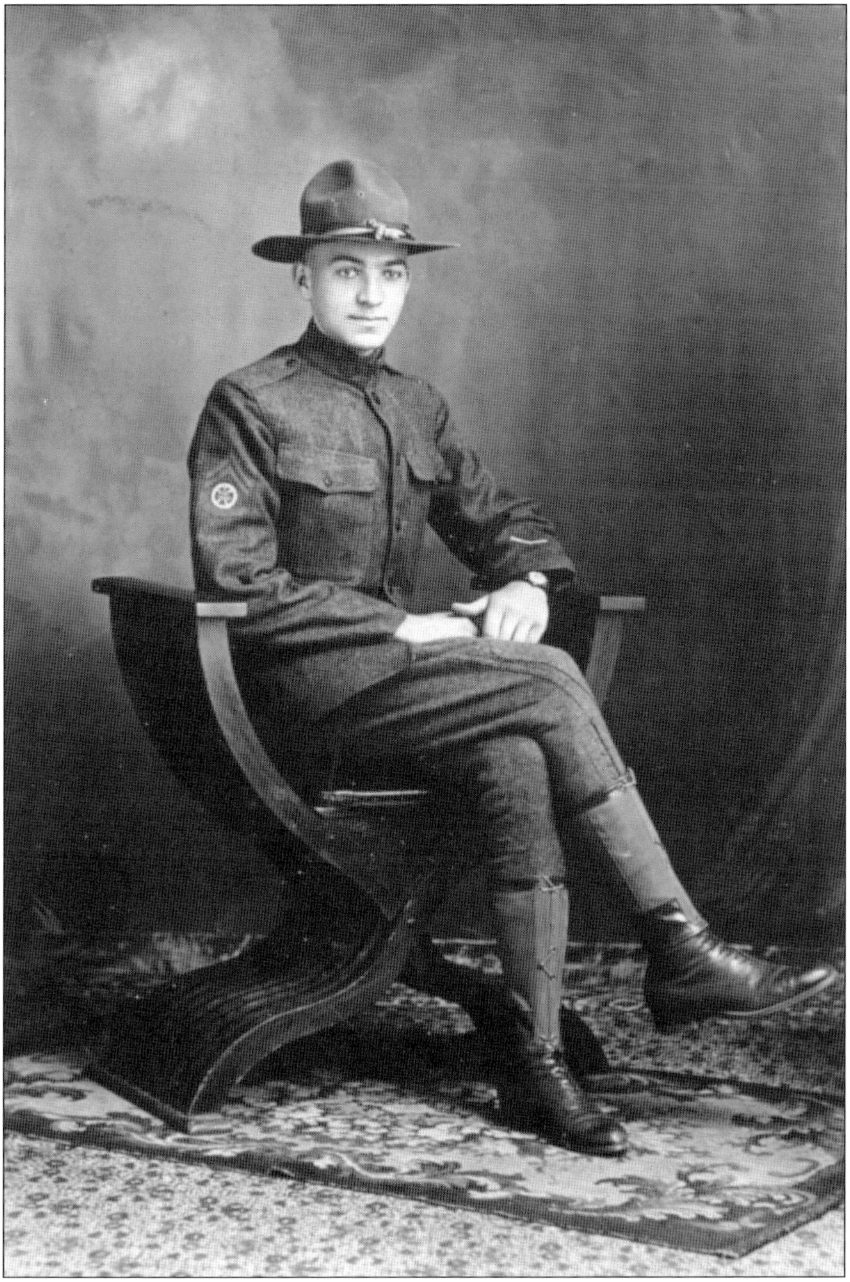

ALFRED PORT. Alfred Port, shown in this formal portrait, was one of 47 men from Grafton to join the armed forces in World War I. Port was born in the town of Grafton in 1897, the son of Christ and Bertha (Oberheu) Port. He entered the service on October 23, 1918, in Milwaukee and was honorably discharged from Camp Shelby, Mississippi, in May 1919. He was a member of the Motor Corps. While Port returned safely from the war, 27 Ozaukee County men were casualties. The United States officially entered World War I on April 6, 1917. The war ended on November 11, 1918. The war years were a time of high tension in Wisconsin because of the large German American population and dominance of the Progressive Party, which opposed entry into the war. (Courtesy of the Grafton Historical Society.)

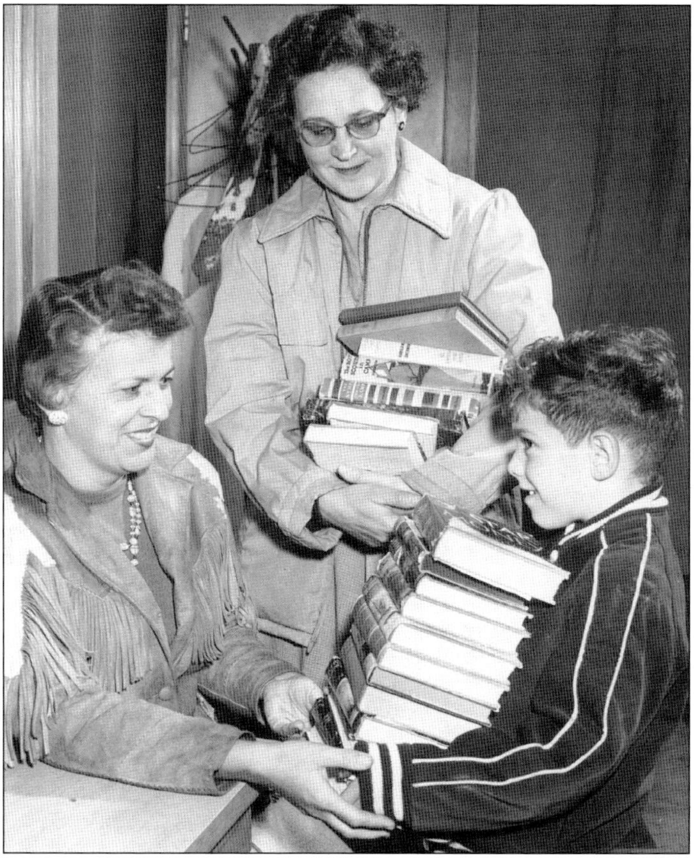

Grafton Public Library. Grafton's first library, located on Bridge Street, opened in April 1956, with 2,500 volumes netted from a book drive. The idea originated with the Grafton Parent-Teacher group in 1954. The library grew from one office to 2,500 square feet by 1971. In July 1989, thanks to fundraising efforts by Grafton citizens, the library opened a new building at 1620 Eleventh Avenue with 12,500 square feet for books and library services. The library serves both the village and town of Grafton. Shown below is the construction of the new library. (Left, courtesy of the Vern Arendt Photograph Collection at the Luxembourg American Cultural Center; below, courtesy of the USS Liberty Memorial Library.)

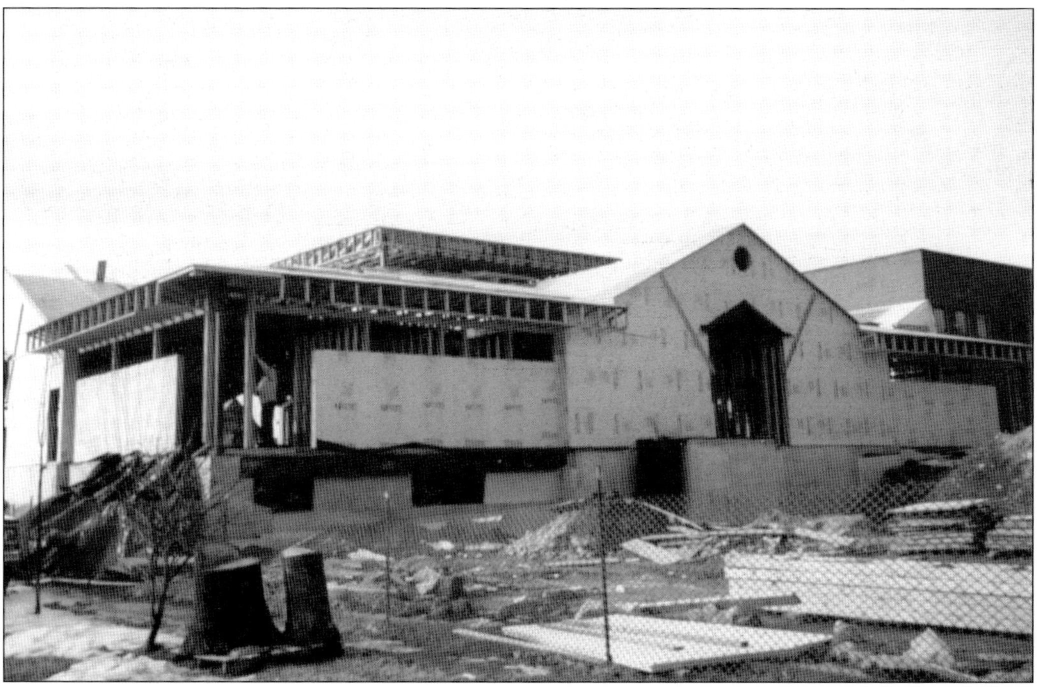

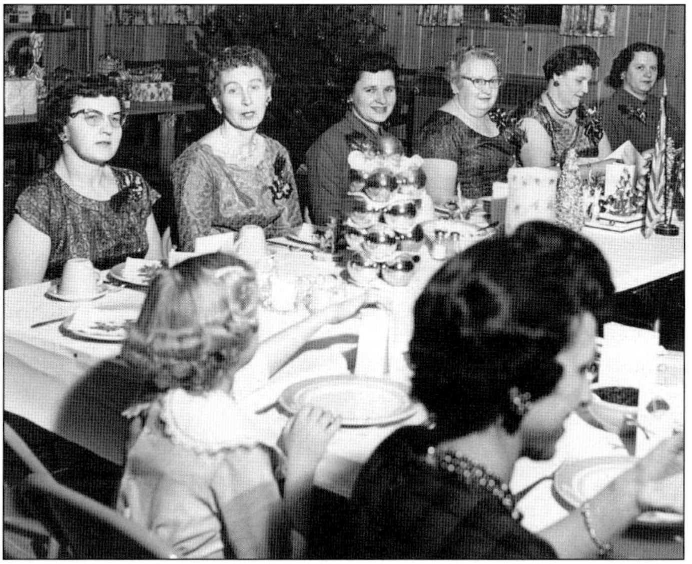

Women's Auxiliary. American Legion Women's Auxiliary officers attend a dinner in the 1950s at the Rose-Harms Post No. 355 in Grafton. The officers are, from left to right, Leone Buchholz, Gertrude Gramoll, unidentified, ? Eidenberger, and two unidentified. The Women's Auxiliary was formed in 1945 and continues to serve veterans and the local community. (Courtesy of the Vern Arendt Photograph Collection at the Luxembourg American Cultural Center.)

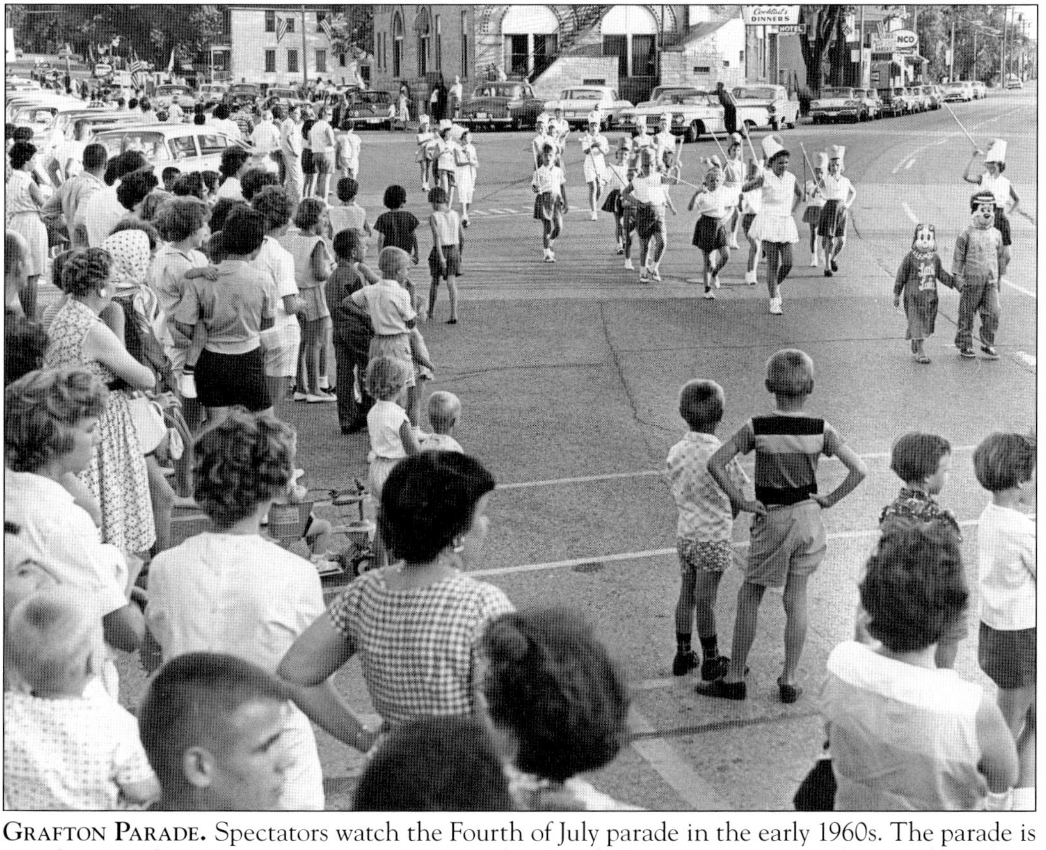

Grafton Parade. Spectators watch the Fourth of July parade in the early 1960s. The parade is traveling north on Wisconsin Avenue. Note the Woods Restaurant sign on the Hotel Grafton. For the past 40 years, Grafton has also hosted one of the largest Christmas parades in the state. (Courtesy of the Vern Arendt Photograph Collection, Luxembourg American Cultural Center.)

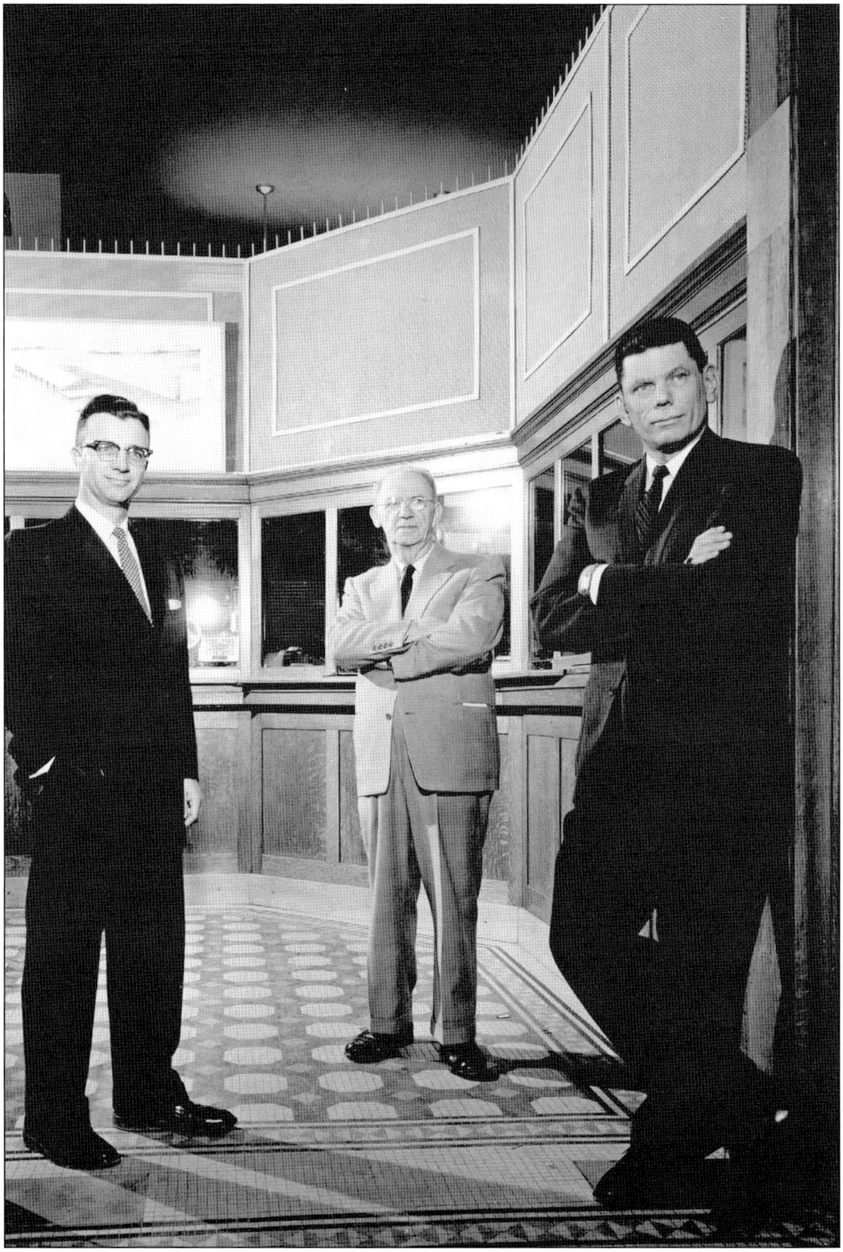

Ralph Zaun. Ralph Zaun was an early chronicler of Grafton history. He co-authored a book on Grafton history and gave many presentations to local groups. He was also a noted philanthropist and volunteer. He spearheaded efforts to save the historic lime kilns and is credited with saving the iron bridge and moving it to its current site in Lime Kiln Park. In that same park, he initiated the building of Zaun Pavilion, a community facility funded largely by a foundation established in his father's memory. Zaun was born in Grafton and graduated from Grafton High School and the University of Wisconsin. He served during World War II and graduated from Harvard Business School. Zaun worked in the banking and insurance industry in Grafton and also served in the Wisconsin Assembly from 1947 to 1951. Pictured from left to right are Robert Monnot, Robert Zaun, and Ralph Zaun. (Courtesy of the Cedarburg Landmark Preservation Society.)

Bibliography

Apps, Jerry. *Wisconsin Agriculture: A History*. Madison, WI: Wisconsin Historical Press, 2011.

Arendt, Laurie and the Ozaukee County Historical Society. *Ozaukee County Wisconsin: A Photographic Journey into the Past*. Cedarburg, WI: Ozaukee County Historical Society, 2004.

Early History of Ozaukee County, Wisconsin. Wisconsin: 1965.

Early Ozaukee County Historical Sketches. Cedarburg, WI: Ozaukee County Historical Society, 1967.

Henning, Donald S. and Ralph L. Zaun. *Grafton, Wisconsin: A History of the Place and People*. Grafton, WI: Zaun Memorial Foundation Ltd., 2005.

Horton, Virginia Harms. *Lest We Forget: A History of a Family in Grafton, Wisconsin Since Early Pioneer Days*. WI: self-published, 1976.

News Graphic. Centennial souvenir issue. Cedarburg, WI: Lakeshore Newspapers Inc., 1996.

Noltze, Kathy. *Ulao: Footsteps on the Bluff*. Arizona: Property Purveyor, 2011.

"Salute to Grafton-Centennial." *Ozaukee Press*. Port Washington, WI: Port Publications Inc., 1996.

"Tour of Historic Grafton, Wisconsin." Grafton Junior Woman's Club Inc., 1982.

Van der Tuuk, Alex. *Paramount's Rise and Fall: A History of the Wisconsin Chair Company and its Recording Activities*. Denver, CO: Mainspring Press, 2003.

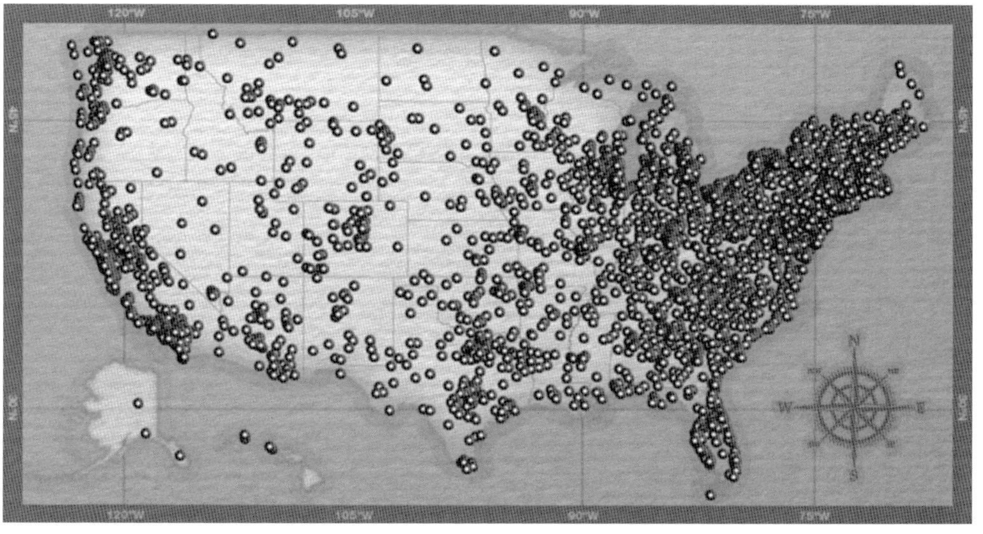